Hotel Management and Operations
Third Edition

Hotel Management and Operations
Third Edition

Edited by
Denney G. Rutherford, Ph.D.
Ivar Haglund Distinguished Professor
Hotel and Restaurant Administration
Washington State University

JOHN WILEY & SONS, INC.

Copyright © 2002 by John Wiley & Sons, Inc., New York.

This publication is designed to provide accurate and authoritative information
in regard to the subject matter covered. It is sold with the understanding that
the publisher is not engaged in rendering professional services. If professional
advice or other expert assistance is required, the services of a competent
professional person should be sought.

Library of Congress Cataloging-in-Publication Data:

Hotel management and operations / edited by Denney G. Rutherford.—3rd ed.
    p. cm.
  Includes bibliographical references and index.
  ISBN 0-471-37052-5 (paper : alk. paper)
    1. Hotel management.   I. Rutherford, Denney G., 1942– .

TX911.3.M27 H663 2001
647.94'068—dc21

                                              2001024023

Printed in the United States of America.

10 9 8 7 6 5 4

The third edition of *Hotel Management and Operations* is hereby dedicated on behalf of all contributors to this book to our late friend, Eddystone C. Nebel, III. Eddy's influence and presence in this book go beyond his writings included herein. He was the teacher, mentor, fellow researcher, friend, sports angler, and inspiration to many of the other authors included in this and previous editions. Through those authors and Eddy's contributions to the hotel management literature, he has also profoundly influenced generations of students. We will all miss his wise counsel, research prowess, and great sense of humor, but most of all, we'll just miss Eddy, because he was fun to be around.

D.G.R. 2001

Contents

Contributors

Je'anna Abbott, University of Houston

Robert O. Balmer, General Manager, Doubletree Hotel, Bakersfield, California

James A. Bardi, Penn State Berks-Lehigh Valley College

Cherylynn Becker, Associate Professor, Washington State University, Swiss Center Campus

Rich Benninger, CMP, Executive Director of Catering Sales, MGM Grand Hotel and Casino, Las Vegas, Nevada

Matt Berge, Director of Operations, The Westin Galleria, Starwood Hotels and Resorts, Dallas, Texas

Robert H. Bosselman, Dedman Chair of Hospitality Administration, Florida State University, Dedman Department of Hospitality Administration

Rick Bruns, *Lodging Magazine*, Akron, Ohio

Peter Cass, President and Chief Executive Officer, Preferred Hotels, and Resorts Worldwide, Inc., Chicago, Illinois

Paul Chappelle, Brand Revenue Manager, Red Lion Hotel and Inns, Vancouver, Washington

Mark Conklin, Vice President, Market Management, Marriott Hotels, Resorts, and Suites, San Antonio, Texas

Melissa Dallas, Florida Atlantic University, College of Business

Agnes Lee DeFranco, University of Houston, Conrad N. Hilton College

Chekitan S. Dev, Cornell University, School of Hotel Administration

John Dew, President, Inn Ventures, Inc., Bellevue, Washington

Garry Dickover, Director of Suites, Venetian Hotel and Resort, Las Vegas, Nevada

Michael J. Draeger, Controller, Cal-Neva Resort, Crystal Bay, Nevada

Tom Dupar, President and CEO, Dupar Associates, Bellevue, Washington

Kurt Englund, Director of Rooms, Regent Beverly Wilshire, Los Angeles

Cathy A. Enz, Cornell University

C. Lee Evans, Vice President Program Development, Level Source, Inc., Las Vegas, Nevada

Emilio Fabico, General Manager, Rosen Centre Hotel, Orlando, Florida

William P. Fisher, President and CEO, American Hotel and Lodging Association, Washington, D.C.

Gil Fried, University of Houston

Gene Fritz, Washington State University, Hotel and Restaurant Administration Program

Ajay Ghei, Cornell University School of Hotel Administration

Robert K. Griffin, University of Massachusetts, Amherst

Bianca Grohmann, Doctoral Candidate, Washington State University

Thomas Jones, University of Nevada, Las Vegas

John Lagazo, General Manager, Embassy Suites, Chicago, Illinois

Melenie J. Lankau, University of Georgia, Terry College of Business

Stephen M. Lebruto, University of Central Florida

John D. Lesure, Research Director, Smith Travel Research, Altamonte Springs, Florida

Valentino Luciani, Instructor, University of Nevada, Las Vegas

Jon P. McConnell, Washington State University

Rhonda J. Montgomery, University of Nevada, Las Vegas

Susan V. Morris, Vice President, HQ Global Workplaces, Dallas, Texas

Suzanne K. Murrmann, Virginia Polytechnic Institute and State University, Department of Hospitality and Tourism Management

Eddystone C. Nebel, III, Purdue University

Michael D. Olsen, Virginia Polytechnic Institute and State University

Eric B. Orkin, Founder and President, Eric B. Orkin Associates

David V. Pavesic, Georgia State University

M. Chris Paxson, Washington State University, College of Business and Economics

Bob Peckenpaugh, Hotel Manager, Rancho Bernardo Inn, San Diego, California

Dominic Provenzano, Rennaissance Madison Hotel, Seattle, Washington

William J. Quain, Florida International University, School of Hospitality Management

Clinton L. Rappole, University of Houston, Conrad N. Hilton College

Louis B. Richmond, President, Richmond Public Relations

Carl D. Riegel, Florida Atlantic University, Graduate School of Business

Denney G. Rutherford, Washington State University

Jeffrey D. Schaffer, University of New Orleans

Raymond S. Schmidgall, Michigan State University, School of Hospitality Business

Michael Sciarni, Michigan State University, School of Hospitality Business

Margaret Shaw, University of Guelph

Susan B. Sheridan, Owner, Taughannock Farms Inn, Trumansburg, New York

Patti J. Shock, University of Nevada, Las Vegas

Judy A. Siguaw, Cornell University, School of Hotel Administration

Randell A. Smith, CEO, Smith Travel Research, Hendersonville, Tennessee

Eric R. Spangenberg, Associate Professor, Washington State University

John M. Stefanelli, University of Nevada, Las Vegas

Robert W. Strate, National Aeronautics and Space Administration

Nancy Swanger, Washington State University

W. Terry Umbreit, Washington State University

Fletch Waller, Principal, FCW Consulting, Seattle, Washington

Glenn Witham, Executive Editor, *The Cornell Hotel and Restaurant Administration Quarterly*

Robert H. Woods, University of Nevada, Las Vegas

Cheri A. Young, University of Nevada, Las Vegas

Foreword

The lodging industry in the United States, indeed throughout the world, has experienced unprecedented growth in the past several years. In transition from a profile of independent operators, the industry is now characterized by publicly held global operators, franchises, management companies, and multimarket segmentation. These range from luxury metropolitan hotels, to resorts, convention properties, midscale properties, all-suite properties, long-term-stay facilities, economy lodging properties (some with food and beverage operations, some without), budget properties, condominiums, vacation ownership, and timeshare units, to mention just a few.

The good news is that projected growth for the industry is highly favorable. The challenging news is that human resources are in short supply, and the industry has the daunting task of finding people to support its growth.

Moreover, the training of employees becomes paramount if hotels are to offer and execute world-class service to satisfy their guests. This is where Denney Rutherford's book *Hotel Management and Operations* makes a significant contribution to the literature theory and practice of running a hotel. Not only is the editor a renowned hospitality industry educator and author in his own right, he has included the thoughts, sentiments, experiences, know-how, and advice from well-regarded actual practitioners who "tell it like it is" in their areas of expertise. Accordingly, the book serves not only as a text, but also as a diary about people in their roles as developers, general managers, food and beverage managers, financial experts, human resource directors, et al.

The book makes for informative and exciting reading, and will be a valuable addition to a student's book portfolio and an operator's business library.

William P. Fisher, Ph.D.
President and Chief Executive Officer
American Hotel and Lodging Association

Preface: Notes to Readers, Teachers, and Students

The first edition of this textbook project was originally born out of a range of frustrations. While there are many outstanding textbooks in the hotel management field that deal with significant portions of operations, particularly housekeeping, front office, and food and beverage, there are very few that try to treat in a balanced and in-depth way each department in the hotel. One frustration was that some texts that dealt with these departments spent an inordinate amount of time focused on one aspect of the hotel operations—usually either front of the house, food and beverage, or marketing. Other departments for better or worse were treated as minor players. Consequently, students and readers of such texts were given only a cursory introduction to the intricacies of these "minor" departments, their management, their people, and their interactive functions in the overall hotel organization.

Another frustration I encountered was using currently available material to promote the idea of critical thinking among students of hotel administration. By critical thinking I refer to that process whereby the student is exposed to a number of different viewpoints within a theoretical structure. From an analysis of those viewpoints, students become better able to synthesize a viewpoint about hotel operations that enables an intelligent approach to whatever practical situations they may find themselves confronted with in the "real world."

There is a conventional wisdom that goes, "something may be okay in theory but it doesn't work in practice." Like economist Milton Friedman I reject that statement. If theory doesn't work in practice, it is lousy theory. What professors need to guide students in understanding is that theory (in the words of Friedman) explains, predicts, or controls and does this in different ways given different variables in different organizations. This is another issue or frustration that subsequent editions have been designed to further address.

By helping the reader gain an appreciation for what a *variety* of observers, thinkers, researchers, and commentators think about a topic—in this case, a hotel department—a student or hotel professional can feel better prepared to find ways to apply theory in a practical setting or situation.

As I went about planning and designing the third edition of *Hotel Management and*

Operations (I have come to refer to it as *HMO III*), I felt the need to continue to remind myself of the lessons of the frustrations listed above. I wanted to make sure the original idea behind this book did not get lost. Fortunately, I remembered something that happened at a meeting of hospitality educators (the International Council on Hotel, Restaurant, and Institutional Education—CHRIE).

Bob Woods, Ray Schmidgall, Mike Olsen (all contributors to this book), and I were in an elevator at the Stouffer Esmerelda Resort in Palm Desert, California. The elevator stopped to board another passenger, and a young professor got on, took a look at our name tags, and said "My gosh . . . I feel like I'm looking at my bibliography," meaning that she had used a lot of our collective research in her own work. It then dawned on us that we had somehow, magically, become "senior establishment members" or some such. I remembered how I, as a young assistant professor, had had much the same reaction to the old-timers I held in such awe at my first few CHRIE meetings. What I came to learn is that none of us knows everything there is to know about any subject; we all need an inventory of ideas to advance our knowledge.

The reason this anecdote was helpful in the design of *HMO III* is that it reinforced to me the value of never thinking I (or the collective authors) know it all. So, for *HMO III*, I worked to achieve a blend of senior researchers and industry members (who really do have well-established points of view). Additionally, you will find the observations and experiences of a great many young managers who have shared "Days in Their Lives" or told it "As They See It." This helped keep me focused on providing the reader—whether you are a student or practitioner—an interesting and broadly diverse reading inventory. In the final analysis, it is up to you to make the best use of *HMO III*, because like I said above, none of us knows it all. Good luck; it is my pleasure to do this work for you.

BOOK ORGANIZATION

The book is divided into nine parts, each part dealing with a specific department or hotel organizational activity. At the outset of the book is an introduction and overview with editorial comments, followed by some basic organizational theory, and then a part on general managers. General managers are included as a brief separate part in order that students may gain some insights into that job, which is at the apex of every hotel organization.

Each succeeding part deals with a separate hotel department or logical grouping of organizational activities. The part on financial control and information management, for instance, includes financial leadership and purchasing, in addition to several insights into the hotel controller's job. It also adds readings on the management and storage of information—a topic that is changing as rapidly as these pages can be turned.

The readings relative to these hotel departments are chosen to illustrate the mission of the department, the personnel of the department, issues of management in the department, and (in some cases) interdepartmental relations and issues.

Each part is preceded by introductory and bridging material written by me as the editor. These segments are meant to be separate readings. They represent a synthesis and overview of my observations, study, and research about hotel organizations. In some cases the reader will find my editorial comments to be controversial; that is exactly what is intended. In some cases the reader will find areas with which he or she may disagree. It is also intended. This is a dynamic and rapidly changing industry. In many ways hotel organizations are adapting to meet new market and operational realities. To do this effectively and successfully, hotels are going to be experimenting with a lot of new ideas. My purpose in these introductory comments, in addition to providing overview, is to float some "trial balloons" of potential new ideas, or, frankly, give the reader my "take" on things.

PEDAGOGICAL IDEAS: HOW TO USE THIS BOOK IF YOU ARE A PROFESSOR

The instructor should choose readings from these sections in such a manner that would best present the material according to his or her course plan. In most cases not all of the readings will be valuable or pertinent to every instructor's course outline. Additionally, at the end of each section are suggested readings that serve to enhance either in breadth or depth, and in some cases both, a student's knowledge and understanding about the material in that section. For instance, I will typically assign some of the suggested readings for the single purpose of getting students into the library and looking through industry-related research, trade journals, and books.

Another specific technique in this regard is to add readings of the professor's own choosing, especially topical, popular, or business literature. These can be stories that compare or contrast with how "theory" plays out in the real world. It also gives the instructor the opportunity to "customize" these sections to his or her specific course design requirements.

CASES

The reader will note that most parts include a short, fairly straightforward case. This is intended for a couple of reasons. First, typical students at this level are not fully versed in the "case method," and this is a course and a book that does not necessarily lend itself to the form of in-depth case analysis as practiced in upper-division and graduate school classes with multiple-page cases. The other reason is that because most issues that face any given department manager in a hotel organization are significantly interrelated to other departments, to be useful in the context this course is normally taught, cases should be designed to be analyzed in a short time frame.

The cases presented here are designed to be most successfully attacked in a multidimensional way. The student who does the best job of analyzing these cases will be the one who critically thinks about the central issues involved. That includes not only how the issues relate to the primary character in the case, but how that central character may have to utilize the other resources and departments of the hotel to address his or her problem.

A simple analytical framework for cases such as these follows the model that normally goes:

- What are the problems?
- What are the facts?
- Who are the important players?
- What are the potential solutions?
- Based on analysis of the above, take a stand from among the list of potential solutions and defend it.

Using this model, there is no "right" answer. The instructor is free to judge the quality of the students' work based on variables such as analytic ability, use of resources, demonstration of understanding of departmental and managerial roles, and so forth.

GUEST SPEAKERS

I generally use two to three guest speakers per term in this class. I have some tried-and-true "designated hitters" who will always respond, and I know from experience that they are outstanding presenters who bring an excitement and affection for the industry to class that is truly inspiring to students. I then also have sought out and used on a random basis people with very narrowly defined roles who serve to illustrate one emerging topic or issue.

The cautions here are to avoid overloading the class with guest speakers, because in the final analysis, most of these people are not pedagogically trained in instructional processes. As a result, they can sometimes find themselves in difficulty getting their points across. I should add, however, that at no time in my experience in the classroom has a guest speaker ever significantly contradicted what I have been asking the students to learn in the classroom. It has just simply never been an issue. One hotel may run a front office a little bit differently than another hotel, but from the standpoint of adhering to a "theoretical structure," there has never been a problem.

One technique that we have used with success is to encourage the students (as part of what may be an extra-credit process) to assemble a panel of managers from among their friends or employers. These people will be charged with addressing one specific issue of interest to the entire class. This gives the students some experience in, first of all, talking with managers; second, coordinating, defining, and producing a specific event; and third, leading a discussion toward some agreed-upon goal. This has been a very popular event in our educational term, and every year we can look forward to those times when the students can effectively take over a class period and actively participate and contribute to the learning process.

LECTURE AND PRESENTATION IDEAS

The use of a resource book such as this lends itself to creating a classroom environment built around a very simple outline that uses a "semi-Socratic" framework based on generating insights to the following questions:

- Mission of the department: How does this department fit in the big picture of the hotel's organization? What is its role?
- People: Who are the personnel? What are the jobs? How do these jobs fulfill the de-

partmental role? What are the opportunities? What are the good and bad points of work in this department? What are the practical realities in this department?
- Interactions: In what ways does this department connect to other departments in the hotel? With which departments does it work most closely? With which departments is it most interdependent? Which departments does it not interact with on a regular basis?
- Management: Who are the managers of this department? What is the career track for these people? Where do they go from here? What are the major issues they face in managing this department?

Utilizing a book of readings as a resource for a classroom structure such as this allows the instructor to ask a lot of "compare and contrast" questions and explore an issue in some depth. An example would be talking about policies of overbooking in the front office or reservations departments. There may be a number of critical issues that are involved here in playing off the various authors' and researchers' ideas. Involving the students in this sort of dialogue allows them to debate the issue in a way that enhances the learning process rather than simply memorizing a list of facts and figures and regurgitating it back on an objective exam.

This sort of material also lends itself to essay-test-type questions. However, those who prefer objective examinations can construct numerous test items from each reading assigned.

PRESENTATION FORMATS

This material lends itself to use with a presentation program using either PowerPoint or Astound. Highlights of the articles, illustrated by photographs, make for interesting lectures, depending upon how much time is spent designing them. Instructors are encouraged to experiment.

FILM CLIPS

I have had great success using short film clips from commercial movies and television to illustrate and dramatize specific points. Care should be taken to use only those very short scenes that serve to cement a single concept in students' minds. Generally speaking, such use is legal under the "fair use" provisions of federal copyright laws, but it would be a good idea to check with your state's attorney general representative for specific guidance.

By way of example, here is a short list of film scenes I have used to illustrate one specific concept:

- *Pretty Woman*: The scene where the Julia Roberts character returns from the unsuccessful shopping trip to Rodeo Drive and is confronted by Hector Elizando about her presence. This illustrates the hotel's right to question suspicious characters and is useful in discussing security.
- *Ace Ventura, Pet Detective*: The opening credits where the Jim Carrey character portrays a package deliveryman and destroys the package on the way. This scene is useful for illustrating the importance of carefully managing the mail/message/delivery function for hotel guests. In this day of instant messaging and overnight delivery, guests expect the function to be managed as well by the hotel as it is by their own organizations.
- *Beauty and the Beast*: The scene where Lumiere leads the kitchen utensils and equipment in "Be Our Guest." I use this to suggest the renewed importance of the hotel's food and beverage (F&B) department. The words of the song speak volumes, and students are urged to consider them in the F&B context.

There are many more. I encourage instructors to seek these out and share with the author. I have successfully made this an extra-credit assignment for our students; they are remarkably resourceful and creative in using their knowledge of movies and television.

PROJECTS, TEAM AND OTHERWISE

Analysis of Hotel Department Management—A Team Exercise

Students are assigned to teams of four to five and asked to study a specific hotel department of their choice. The team assignment is to analyze the relationship between theory from the text and other resources and practice in that department.

To accomplish this assignment, the team must, among other things, have a meeting, pick a department they are interested in or where one of the members has a contact, and arrange an interview with the manager of that department. The questions that they formulate for this interview *should be generated as a result of their reading of the literature and class discussion* and basically formulated around the following six major categories that are important to understanding the department's functions and roles.

They must generate questions along these lines from class and readings.

1. *Mission of the Department*: How does this department fit in the big picture of the hotel's organization?
2. *People*: Who are the personnel, what are the jobs, what are the opportunities? What are the good points and challenges about work in this department? What are the practical realities of work in this department?
3. *Interactions*: How does this department connect to other departments in the hotel? With which departments does it work most closely? Which departments does it not interact with on a regular basis?
4. *Management*: Who are the managers of this department? What is a typical career track for these people? Where do they go from here?

5. *Issues:* What are the major issues that the managers and staff of this department face on a regular basis? How are these issues resolved? Are these issues common to all hotels, or are they unique to this hotel or this type of hotel?
6. *Budget*: What are the major budget variables? How do they vary? What sort of authority does the manager have over the budget?

Basic requirements of the paper:

- Introduction: Describe the location, size, type of property, and major market segments.
- Chain of command for the hotel property including all the major departments: A hotel organization chart would be helpful here but be sure to describe verbally the key chain-of-command relationships.
- Identify the department as either a cost or profit center. Describe the major expense or revenue components.
- Describe the functional relationships and tasks of the department under study. (What do they do?)
- Describe the department's contribution to the hotel's marketing strategies. Be sure to include aspects of both internal and external marketing activities.
- Conclusion and in-depth discussion of what principles and theories you have learned

from the textbook and class that were specific to the department you analyzed. How does theory work in practice?

Other:

- The interview should be with a property outside of the university or college area.
- Include as an appendix the interview questions (and their sources) and a copy of the thank-you letter and the addressed and stamped envelope written to the manager.
- Must be word-processed and double-spaced—maximum 12-point type. Paper should be a *maximum* of 15 pages (*not* including cover sheet, table of contents, and appendixes).

CONCLUSION

This book has been designed to provide a broad range of thinking, research, and commentary about contemporary issues in the management of modern hotels and their associated departments. It is also intended to provide maximum flexibility to the professor, students, and readers in the hotel professions. If the reader has suggestions that may improve future editions of this book, please feel free to contact the author directly at denneyford@wsu.edu.

Acknowledgments

There is no way I could have done this alone, so I would very much like to acknowledge and thank those who have assisted, advised, contributed, and consulted with me on this book. While it has been a team effort, all of its flaws, and there probably are some, are solely my responsibilities.

First of all, the authors of the various pieces included here who knowingly or unknowingly have contributed their thoughts, research, ideas, opinions, and expertise to this exercise in critical thinking about hotel departmental operations deserve recognition. Without the rich mixture of interest and talent extant in the hospitality profession and its educational establishment today, this collection of readings would not have been possible. It is my great good fortune that my friends, colleagues, and former students could devote the time they did to contribute to this project. My badgering, cajoling, begging, and bribing aside, I think we're all still friends.

I want to particularly salute those who crafted "custom" pieces for this edition and those professionals who contributed "Day in the Life" and "As I See It" pieces. They have made this edition a richer and more user-friendly book. They also add a view of the real world that has been missing. I would also like to thank Phillip Hayward, executive editor, *Lodging* magazine, for his generous assistance with articles published in that professional industry resource.

The support and encouragement of my colleagues at Washington State University was critical. HRA Program Director Terry Umbreit and a whole bunch of students all contributed to the success of this project with advice, counsel, and suggestions.

My good friend, colleague, and sometime production assistant Lillian Sugahara helped me tremendously. Her "magic" with the computer literally saved this project by translating many files done on Page Maker for Macintosh to something I could edit in Word. Because she kept accurate files of the manuscript for the second edition, we were able to overcome the problems attendant to the transfer of the project from VNR to Wiley. Lillian, you are the greatest.

JoAnna Turtletaub, my editor at Wiley, provided needed support regarding previously published material by Wiley, and discussions of some of my "off the wall" ideas have truly made this a better project. Thanks, JoAnna.

My wife and best friend, Sandy Sweeney, continues to provide the encouragement, support, and understanding she always does on big writing projects. Her understanding is particularly important when I disappear to work on "the book" when we could be doing other, more fun things. She does understand the rhythms of an author's life and endures losing me to "the book" with style and grace. The last time I did this we were moving—and surprise—it is happening again. We are moving to Spokane, so I will be the family commuter. I love you, Sandy.

Without the assistance of my friends and colleagues listed above, this edition would probably still be in the "talking" stage. I sincerely hope that anyone who attempts similar projects has the great good fortune to be supported as I have.

Denney G. Rutherford
Pullman/Spokane, Washington
2001

I

Overview

1.1 Introduction

INTRODUCTION

The vast majority of research articles and essays in this book deal with one or more aspects of what has been called the art and science of modern hotel management. It should be noted that the word *modern* can signal an expression that is loaded with the potential of much misunderstanding. Hotels are changing and will continue to change. As a result, the techniques of management of modern hotels have to adapt to changing circumstances. Subsequent sections of this book are designed and intended to help the student and practitioner discover information, methods, and techniques to deal with these changing circumstances.

INFLUENCES

Like many other American businesses, hotels have been affected by shifts in emphasis among the country's *living patterns.* People and industry have moved from the so-called rust belt to the sun belt. There has been a concentration of hotel activities in reborn and reconstructed central cities. The explosion of technology and information-based companies have concentrated human endeavor in "technological corridors" in California, Massachusetts, Washington, Texas, and North Carolina, to name a few. It can be safely said that where the jobs are, and major concentrations of economic activity occur, hotels will follow.

Among other current and ongoing "influencers" of hotel design, construction, marketing, and operation are the following (this list is neither exhaustive nor exclusive):

Demographics play a major role in this regard and will continue to influence the foreseeable future. As the "baby boom" generation and its children mature, the population of the country will for many years be older, healthier, and more well educated than previous generations. These facts will present new challenges and opportunities to all business managers.

Technology in the form of computers and labor-saving mechanical equipment has had and will have a major effect on the way in which hotels are managed and operated. The speed with which information is accumulated, stored, manipulated, and transferred is such that today most travelers expect that the hotel rooms they rent will allow them to be as productive as they are in the office or at home. Increasingly, with portable computing, personal data assistants (PDAs), wireless communication, and virtually everything somehow connected to the Internet, hotels have to provide services and access that allow guests seamless transition from the business, travel, or home environment to that of the hotel.

The concept of *market segmentation*, ever increasingly finely tuned market definitions, will dictate hotel structures and organizations, and management tactics that are designed to pay particular attention to those market segments has become even more important to the management of hospitality service businesses. With the increased power in the information and data manipulation realm, hotels have available to them ever-expanding databases about guests and are creating new products to attract those markets.

One of the effects of the aging demographic is the emergence of vacation resorts—a modern incarnation of the time-share properties of several decades ago. Because these are being developed and operated by "name" hotel companies and are marketed to that affluent, healthy, well-educated population segment, resort managers have had to learn some new managerial realities.

The well-documented change in the complexion of the *national economy* from one that emphasizes goods to one that emphasizes services has kindled a number of new ideas about the way in which we manage the design and delivery of these services. Hotels, restaurants, and travel services are now seen as unique entities that dictate special kinds of managerial techniques and strategies. The national economic expansion since the preparation of the last edition of this book has increased the personal wealth of large numbers of the population and provided an unprecedented number of new jobs to the economy. This, in turn, has spurred a new boom in hotel development.

Changes in people's *travel patterns* have also altered the way in which we manage our hotel properties. Deregulation of the airlines has driven a change in the way millions of people travel each year with the hub/spoke design of airline services. Many hotel companies are now locating major hotel properties adjacent to hub air transport facilities, taking advantage of the fact that business travelers may not need to travel to a central business district (CBD) to accomplish their purposes in a given area. Meetings and conferences can now be scheduled within a five-minute limousine ride from the air terminal, and the business traveler can be back on the plane for his or her next destination before the day is over without having to stay overnight in a CBD hotel.

New *patterns of investment* in hotel facilities have emerged in the last two decades, and more attention is now paid to achieving optimum *return on investment*. Because people from outside the hotel industry are now participating in the financial structuring of the hotel industry, hotel operations are no longer dependent on the vision of a single entrepreneur. Managers now have to design tactics and strategies to achieve heretofore unanticipated financial goals. This has also altered the complexion of management and organization of the modern hotel. This is especially true of publicly owned hotel firms, where Wall Street stock analysts heavily influence stock prices through expectations of quarterly revenues and profits. This puts pressure on hotel companies and their operations managers to perform, on a quarterly basis, in a way that is contrary to many managers' instincts.

Most of the foregoing issues and influences still operate (to a greater or lesser extent) on the organizational structures and strategies of the modern hotel. Since the last edition of this book, however, other phenomena of an economic, cultural, and social nature have come to the fore, further complicating our view of hotel management. This furthers the argument that the hotel industry is a part of the greater economy and at the mercy of elements often totally and completely out of its control.

The cyclical natures of the American and international economies have recently impacted significantly hotels' ability to respond to changing circumstances. In early 1993, for instance, employment growth was stagnant; corporate profits were low; the expansion of the gross national product was only a marginal percentage above previous years; and travel among most segments was down due to corporate restructuring, downsizing, or reorganizing. Vast layoffs in the hundreds of thousands had been announced every month. While fuel prices continued to be relatively stable, consumer-spending patterns and high employment growth had not materialized, particularly in light of corporate layoffs and an ongoing nervousness among consumers over whether their financial wherewithal was safe.

Now consider late 2000—as this is being written. Unemployment is at an all-time low; the Dow Jones Industrial Average is between 10,000 and 11,000; hotel occupancies have stabilized nationally in excess of 70 percent; and the federal government is running a surplus for the first time in the memory of most.

One of the influences mentioned in the second edition, foreign investment and ownership of hotel firms, appears to be undergoing somewhat of a change, and it is not clear as of yet what it will mean for the long-term operations of hotels in the United States. However, according to a study by Greenberg (1993, pp. 15–23), foreign investors will continue to account for a relatively constant share of hotel investment, but of a generally smaller available market. Greenberg goes on to say (p. 23) that, "Japan is likely to remain the single largest player, but the recent decline in its relative importance suggests a smaller future role." Other trends documented in this article suggest that the buyers are shifting more toward real hotel operating companies as opposed to real estate and/or construction and development companies who dominated these transactions in the 1980s.

The point of the above is that no matter who an international investor may be, that company will bring a changed or different set of values to the management and operation of hotels. This is neither necessarily good nor bad but needs to be recognized as an influence that may significantly impact the way in which future careers in the hotel industry are developed.

Among the predictions I made in the last edition of this book was that cultural diversity will play a role in the management and organizational structure of the modern hotel in the United States. As surely as living patterns, economic cycles, and market segmentation have influenced the hotel industry, so will the change in ethnicity of the workforce. The cultural backgrounds that an increasingly diversified workforce will bring to hotel operation may be seen as a problem and/or challenge. To most operators, it will be seen as an opportunity to demonstrate to an increasingly diverse *clientele* that hotel companies are committed to hiring and training a workforce structure that mirrors society.

As discussed in a number of essays and articles in the first two editions of this book, legal and government regulation can play a significant role in not only the day-to-day, but the strategic management of any hotel property. Examples abound, but those that affect the entire industry such as the Americans with Disabilities Act that was signed into law and became effective in 1992 have for the most part been, at least in the near term, beneficial to hotels. Many operators have found those small investments in "accessible" rooms and public areas have paid financial benefits by opening the hotel to guests that in the past simply did not travel much. Indeed, hotels that have embraced the provisions of the act have found themselves to be pleasantly surprised with additional business from a heretofore ignored market segment. Additionally, some hotels that do a lot of business with state, local, and federal government agencies have found themselves to be singled out as the preferred designated hotel because of their ease of access.

The legal and regulatory environments are increasingly important to all business managers, and hotel operators are no exception. Increasingly, operators have to be aware of and alert to realms of risk that can engender lawsuits against them. Several articles and essays in this edition highlight these threats to hotels and their guests. It should also be noted that between the U.S. Congress and fifty state legislatures, on an annual basis there are numerous opportunities for lawmakers to (whatever their intentions) significantly affect the way in which hotels are operated. Awareness of the risk environment and the regulatory realm are also factors that affect your ability to compete in the early part of the twenty-first century.

INTRODUCTORY READINGS

I have attempted in this edition to present some new and (sometimes) different takes on the hotel business. Rather than focus exclusively on the operations of the major chains, the readings here are from the perspectives of operators, leaders, and experts such as regional operators, major industry consultants, and independent branded hotels.

Smith and Lesure (1999) provide a comprehensive overview as of 1999 that contemplates the state of the industry at the turn of the last century. The reader should remember though, as Bob Woods points out in his article in Part 9 (p. 459), predicting is difficult and we will never know all the variables that will have an effect on our ability to manage hotels. The baseline provided by Smith and Lesure, though, provides the reader with a departure point from which to consider other, complementary or contrasting readings in the book.

John Dew, president of Inn Ventures—a regional hotel management and development company that has built and operated many Marriott products, in addition to a proprietary hotel product—provides an insider's view of the steps to bring a hotel from conception to construction and operation. This is a unique view of hotel operations for this edition and connects the concept of hotel development with the realities of day-to-day operation. This should help aspiring managers understand how the intricacies of the development process may influence the marketing and management of the hotel.

With some 110 hotels, Preferred Hotels and Resorts Worldwide represents the "nonchain" aspect of the hotel hospitality business. These independent hotels, widely considered among the best and most luxurious in the world, have associated themselves in an organization that allows them to compete individually and as a group with the international chains. As president and chief executive officer (CEO) of Preferred Hotels and Resorts Worldwide, Peter Cass offers the reader insights into these independent brands heretofore unavailable in books of this nature. Cass makes the case that the future success of independent hotels is linked to their ability to find ways to maintain their independence while sustaining competitive advantage in the luxury segment.

With all the activity in the hotel industry in the last ten years, with a lot of consolidation, buying and selling, and new construction, a little-known activity has come to play a very important role in the process of industry change. When a hotel company acquires a hotel or is contracted with to manage a hotel previously operated by a different company, someone has to oversee the process of "rebranding" the property. This is a complicated process and must be accomplished within critical time frames to coincide with marketing, financial, and operational variables. Tom Dupar is a seasoned veteran at this fascinating and important activity and has participated in rebranding operations around the world. His essay on the intricacies of this process represents another aspect of the hotel operations and management process that has not been treated elsewhere.

Perhaps proving the axiom that "everything old is new again," the concept of time-share resort ownership has reemerged in the hotel industry in a big way. Having burnished up a previously tarnished image, the time-share vacation market has been given new and vigorous life by many of the major hotel brands. In his article "Back by Popular Demand," Rick Bruns illustrates the current state of this segment of the lodging industry.

At the end of this section are a number of suggested readings for the reader who would like to gain more in-depth knowledge about the hospitality industry in general and specific historical antecedents. In particular, the books by Hilton and Jarman look closely at some of the intermachinations of the establishment by two early pioneers of the industry, one of whom, Conrad Hilton, lives on in an international, publicly traded company operated by one of his sons. E. M. Statler's contributions to the modern hotel business are legendary in that he is generally credited with founding and operating the first commercial hotel concept that recognized the realities of the early business traveler at the turn of the century. The suggested articles are drawn from recently published historic overviews of the hotel side of the hospitality industry in the United States. They also highlight some of the other major forces in the development of the modern hotel business.

1.2   The U.S. Lodging Industry Today

Randell A. Smith and John D. Lesure

The U.S. Lodging Industry Census database maintained by Smith Travel Research (STR) consists of approximately 35,000 U.S. hotels containing over 3.6 million rooms in 173 markets. From that database, we calculate each month the number of rooms available for each market and segment within the industry. Using our sample, which represents over 60 percent of the total rooms in the United States, and a sophisticated system of weighting, we obtain an estimate of the rooms sold and room revenue for each market and segment for our published statistical reports. We do not include revenues from gaming, and the census database includes only properties with 20 or more rooms—but we are confident that the published performance measures represent the industry and the associated segments as accurately as possible.

HUMPTY DUMPTY'S GLOSSARY

Just like the Lewis Carroll character, when we use a word it means just what we choose it to mean—no more nor less. We have defined the segments of the lodging industry precisely so that there can be no misunderstanding when one reads the various STR reports. Following are definitions of most of the terms we use here.

U.S. Lodging Census: The STR database of nearly 35,000 lodging establishments having 20 rooms or more. The census is updated continuously to reflect changes in room supply, published room rates, and hotel affiliation.

Supply: The number of rooms available for sale at any time.

Demand: The number of rooms sold during a defined period.

Revenue: Room sales.

RevPAR: Room revenue per available room per day.

Market: A geographic area of a Metropolitan Statistical Area (MSA; e.g., Atlanta), a group of MSAs (e.g., south central Pennsylvania), or a group of counties (e.g., Texas north). A market must contain a sufficient number of participating hotels to permit subdivision into geographic tracts and price segments. There are currently 173 U.S. STR markets.

Market tract: A geographic area that is a subset of an STR market; tract boundaries may be defined by counties or zip codes.

Market price segments: The five hotel categories of a metro STR market defined by actual or estimated average room rate:

- *Luxury*: Top 15 percent of average room rates.
- *Upscale*: Next 15 percent of average room rates.
- *Midprice*: Middle 30 percent of average room rates.
- *Economy*: Next 20 percent of average room rates.
- *Budget*: Lowest 20 percent of average room rates.

In rural or nonmetro STR markets where there is no luxury category, the top 30 percent of average room rates are classified as upscale, and the other price brackets remain the same.

Location segment: Classifications dictated by the physical location of the hotel, as follows:

- *Urban*: Hotels located in the central business district (CBD), usually the downtown area of large metropolitan markets (e.g., Atlanta, Boston, Denver).
- *Suburban*: Hotels located in the suburban areas of metropolitan markets (e.g., College Park or Marietta, near Atlanta).
- *Highway*: Hotels located on an interstate or other major road or in a small town or city (e.g., Evergreen, Alabama, or Colorado City, Texas).
- *Airport*: Hotels located within five miles (usually) of a major municipal airport.
- *Resort*: Hotels located within a market that attracts mostly leisure travelers, such as Orlando or Lake Tahoe.

Chain scale: Segments based primarily on the actual, systemwide average room rates of the major chains (independent hotels are included in a separate category):

- Upper upscale chains.
- Upscale chains.
- Midscale chains with F&B.
- Midscale chains without F&B.
- Economy chains.

STRONG, BUT FADING

As this is being written, about halfway through the fourth quarter of 1998, a quick view of the lodging industry revealed the following:

- The rate of change in demand for rooms had leveled off at about 2.3 percent annually.
- There was a declining trend in the percentage change in RevPAR.
- The change in the number of vacant rooms was expected to continue to climb, although not at the pace of the period 1996–1998. A few major chain operators had announced some curtailment of expansion plans, but hotels already under construction in 1998 will be opened in the next two years.

The trends in demand, RevPAR, and vacant rooms from January 1, 1993, to December 31, 1998, are illustrated in Figure 1.1. The year 1993 was selected as being the point at which the industry began to recover from the effects of the uncontrolled construction boom of the late 1980s and the economic recession of the early 1990s. The vital statistics of the lodging industry for the 12 months ended December 31, 1998 (estimated), the 12 months ended December 31, 1992, and the percentage change are shown in Table 1.1.

In the past five years, the percentage change in the number of guest rooms has risen less than the change in the number of hotels because of a drop in the average size of the properties that have been added. Since 1992 over 4,200 properties with almost 400,000 rooms have been opened in the small-size categories (under 75 rooms and 75 to 149 rooms), while the other size groups grew by fewer than 200 hotels and 81,000 rooms.

To identify those segments of the industry that either benefited or were adversely affected by the changes in supply, demand, and revenue, we analyzed the changes in market

FIGURE 1.1
Total U.S. lodging industry, 1993–1999 (estimated)

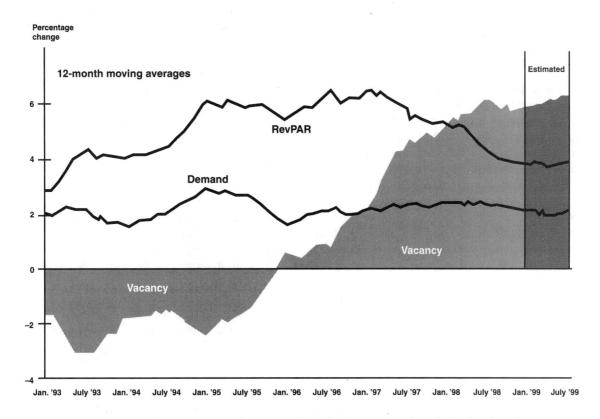

The change in the 12-month moving average for vacancy, demand, and RevPAR are shown by the three lines above. Figures for 1999 are estimated.

TABLE 1.1
Six years of industry expansion, 1992–1998

Industry statistic	Period ending 12-31-98	Period ending 12-31-92	Percentage change
Hotels	34,964	30,509	14.6%
Guest rooms	3,658,049	3,247,518	12.6%
Room revenue (US$billions)	$67.2	$44.3	51.7%
Room occupancy	63.9%	62.7%	1.9%
RevPAR	$50.37	$37.40	34.7%

share of the various classifications in our database over the past five years. The text that follows and the accompanying charts portray the results of that analysis.

PERFORMANCE

Comparative performance in the lodging industry can be measured by the changes in five benchmarks: room occupancy, average room rate, rooms available (supply), rooms sold (demand), and room revenue per available room (RevPAR). That last item is generally considered to be the most informative quick measure of relative performance. In Figure 1.2 we show the average annual changes in the performance ratios of the total industry and four major segments in the past six years. Some highlights of the analysis are:

- In the past five years there have been major shifts in development from independently owned and operated properties to chain-affiliated hotels, and from full-service properties (with food and beverage) to limited-service hotels (without food and beverage).
- Although there has been significant annual growth in the number of rooms available in chain-affiliated hotels for all scales in the past six years, the number of rooms sold (demand) slightly more than kept pace and occupancy increased.
- In spite of an annual rise of 4.6 percent in average room rates in the limited-service group, rooms sold (demand) did not increase at the same rate as rooms available (supply) and the change in RevPAR was lowest of the segments.

A DEFINITION OF MARKET SHARE

In any given year, the market for the goods and services of the lodging industry consists of the number of persons who travel and spend

the night in hotels, as against those who stay with friends and relatives (although some of the latter may dine out at a hotel and thus be hotel patrons). This ever-changing number, which we call demand (rooms sold), can be affected by such diverse factors as the economy, the availability of relatively cheap fossil fuels, the weather (El Niño), and, apparently, the activity of the stock markets.

Performance evaluation cannot be measured by demand alone, however. We must know how the changes in that measure are related to changes in supply (available rooms) and also the degree to which the property operators were able to receive a fair price for their services. We measure market-share performance, by using all three criteria—share of rooms available, share of rooms sold, and share of room revenue.

The comparison of the changes between 1992 (the base year) and 1998 in market share of supply, demand, and revenue for major sections of the country, for chain-affiliated hotels versus independents, and for those properties considered full- or limited-service are shown in Figure 1.3. A balanced market exists when the three ratios are the same or similar. The chain-affiliated group approaches that status. The annual increase in demand, however, was less than the gain in supply, and the room rate did not rise fast enough to retain the same share of revenue the group had in 1992. Put another way, if the market-share ratios for chain-affiliated hotels in 1998 had been the same as in 1992, the group would have had 210,000 fewer available rooms daily, and 129,000 fewer rooms would have been sold each day. That is the equivalent of over $8.6 million in daily room revenue. Other highlights of the analysis are:

- A lack of supply growth in the North Atlantic states lowered the share of total supply, but hotels in the New England and Middle Atlantic regions received only a slightly lower share of total demand and a bigger portion of room revenue.

FIGURE 1.2
Change in performing ratios by segment, 1992–1998

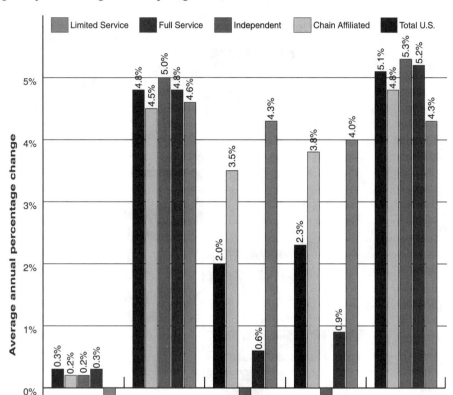

Source: Smith Travel Research. Figures are for the average annual change in performance ratios from 1992 through 1998, which is estimated.

- Hotels in the South Atlantic region had a slightly smaller supply share, but the drops in demand and revenue were excessive.
- Operators in the Central states failed to reach the shares of demand and revenue indicated by the increased share of total supply.
- Only in the Mountain region did the increased share of revenue exceed the growth in supply. However, demand did not rise proportionately.

- The sharp growth in the supply of limited-service hotels over the five-year period, beyond the increases in demand and revenue, is shown quite clearly.

ANALYSIS BY SEGMENT

In the past five years there was an increase of over 70 percent in the supply of rooms in midscale chain hotels without F&B service.

FIGURE 1.3
Industry statistics by region and segment, 1992–1998

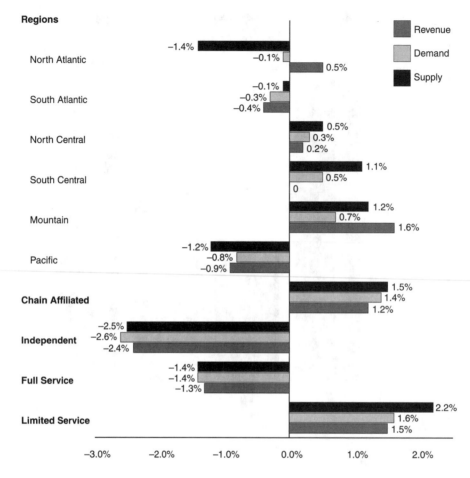

Source: © 1999, Smith Travel Research. Figures are for the average annual change for the 12-month period ending in December 1992 compared to the estimates for the 12-month period ending in December 1998.

However, the market share of demand for that group did not keep pace with the growth. Comparisons of the total changes in market share of supply, demand, and revenue between 1992 and 1998 (estimated) for the total industry, by segment, are given in Table 1.2.

Hotel guests are apparently not trading down the price spectrum, but instead are seeking newer and higher-price accommodations than formerly. The market shift by consumers from low-price properties to midprice and above is illustrated by the price-level analysis. There were not only increases in supply share in the upscale and midprice segments, but operators in those categories also saw improved demand and revenue shares. At the same time, the economy and price groups experienced declines in share of all three measures. Worse, the demand and revenue decreases were greater than the decline in supply share.

Few hotels were added in urban locations in the past five years, and the share of supply for that group dropped by nearly 5 percent. In spite of that, however, market share of demand for those accommodations did not change, and revenue share increased by more than 1 percent per year. That was a commendable performance by urban-hotel operators! At highway locations the changes were unfavorable. The share of supply decreased slightly each year, but demand share dropped nearly 5 percent, and the share of room revenue fell more than 6 percent.

We have commented on the shift in the size of the hotels added to inventory in the past five years; most have fewer than 150 rooms. The growth in market share of demand and revenue in the under-75-rooms group failed to keep up with the increase in supply, and in the 75-to-149-rooms segment the shares of

both demand and revenue were only about one-half of the increase in the market share of supply. In hotels with between 150 and 500 rooms the declines in demand and revenue shares were less than the drop in supply share. In large hotels (over 500 rooms) growth in market share of both demand and revenue exceeded the slight increase in supply by a significant amount.

OPERATING RESULTS

The decisive measure of performance is, of course, the so-called bottom line, in this case, pretax income. Since 1992, when our estimate of that measure was too small to register (in essence, zero or "break-even"), pretax income

TABLE 1.2
Change in market share by segment, 1992–1998 (estimated)

Segment	Supply	Demand	Revenue
Price level			
Luxury	−0.7%	2.8%	7.4%
Upscale	6.4%	6.3%	4.3%
Midprice	5.4%	5.0%	2.5%
Economy	−2.5%	−5.8%	−10.9%
Budget	−9.8%	−9.9%	−17.1%
Location			
Urban	−4.7%	0	5.1%
Suburban	5.9%	6.8%	5.3%
Airport	−5.5%	−4.8%	−1.2%
Highway	0.9%	−4.0%	−6.1%
Resort	−4.5%	−4.7%	−6.6%
Chain scale			
Upper upscale	−11.3%	−6.1%	−0.7%
Upscale	9.8%	13.0%	15.6%
Midscale with F&B	−19.4%	−20.5%	−22.3%
Midscale without F&B	70.4%	65.5%	71.5%
Economy	4.6%	−0.3%	−6.0%
Size			
Under 75 rooms	8.3%	7.6%	4.1%
75 to 149 rooms	4.4%	2.3%	2.2%
150 to 299 rooms	−8.7%	−7.8%	−5.2%
300 to 500 rooms	−9.2%	−6.2%	−2.2%
Over 500 rooms	0.6%	3.3%	2.7%

Note: Figures from Smith Travel Research. Percentages are relative changes in market share among the segments over the six-year period.

has increased to an estimate of over $20 billion (U.S.) in 1998. Total revenue from all sources has risen by more than $30 billion, and gross operating profit (GOP) has gone up over $20 billion. Those are surprising results for an industry supposedly flat on its back less than ten years ago. Our estimates are based on an ongoing analysis of the extensive databases developed from the annual Hotel Operating Statistics (HOST) reports since 1990 and our historical TREND reports. By means of standard forecasting and regression-analysis techniques, we extrapolate the reported operating results of full-service, limited-service, chain-affiliated, and independent hotels to cover the entire industry.

There are conflicting projections for the economy in the United States in 1999. A few months ago when the stock market was fluctuating widely (mostly downward), some economists were predicting an imminent recession (if not a depression). Lately consumer confidence appears to be rising, inflation is under control, and the outlook for 1999 is for continued solid growth.

We do not care to take sides in that question, but if the more optimistic views prevail, we expect lodging-industry revenues and income to continue to grow in 1999, albeit at a slightly more modest pace than in the previous years. More precisely, we estimate that the ranges for the key operating amounts and ratios in 1999 will be as shown in Table 1.3.

OUTLOOK FOR 1999

For 1999 lodging-industry performance is expected to include declining occupancy and only modest increases in average room rate and RevPAR. Some other predictions for the future are:

- The number of properties that will carry a chain-company logo will continue to rise substantially, mostly from the opening of hotels already under construction, but also by conversions from independent operation to chain affiliation.
- With a few significant exceptions, the changes in market share of supply, demand, and revenue in 1998 in the major segments of the industry will extend the five-year trends.
- The market share of revenue in the Northeast region is expected to increase by 4 percent over 1998, versus a past pattern of 0.5 percent annually, while that of the Mountain region is anticipated to drop by 2.5 percent from 1997 after rising by 2 percent each year since 1993.
- The annual decline in market share of supply in the independent group (2.4 percent) is expected to reach 5.5 percent, and what has been a 1.3 percent increase in revenue share in the properties without F&B is likely to become a 2.5 percent drop.

TABLE 1.3
Projections for 1999 hotel industry operating ratios

	1999 Range (projected)	1998 Estimate*
Room occupancy	62.8% – 63.0%	63.9%
Average room rate	$81.92 – $83.77	$78.83
Total revenue (US$billions)	$94.9 – $98.1	$91.2
GOP ratio to revenue	41.1% – 43.0%	42.0%
Pretax income (US$billions)	$21.9 – $25.1	$20.6

*The 1998 estimate is based on several months of data and is relatively firm at this writing.

WHAT'S NEXT

We can expect continued consolidation in the industry as the companies maneuver to increase market share and cover all of the accommodation choices. Wall Street has lost enthusiasm for its "buy" recommendations for shares in hotel companies, and analysts are taking a cautious "no growth needed" approach, at least publicly. One could argue that much of the blame for unrestrained development without corresponding increases in demand has been due to the pressures to increase stock values in publicly held companies. No one seems to bother to ask where the customers are going to come from when adding space indiscriminately.

In the past ten years the adult population of the United States (persons aged 18 and over) has risen at a compound annual rate of 1 percent while the number of rooms in hotels has gone up at 2.2 percent each year. If we add the number of foreign visitors to potential domestic demand (even though international arrivals have fallen off due to economic problems in other countries) while at the same time subtracting the number of persons in what the Census Bureau refers to as "group quarters" (i.e., nursing homes, hospitals, and prisons), we arrive at a base potential demand of about 250 million guests. To obtain the number of potential room-nights, that number must be reduced by a factor for those who travel but stay with friends and relatives (about half),

PRICEWATERHOUSE COOPERS:
U.S. HOTEL ROOM RATES SLOW THEIR ADVANCE

As occupancy at U.S. hotels dips further below the 25-year average in 1999, the lodging industry will experience ADR growth at the slowest pace in five years. Even so, rates will creep up, with upper-upscale and New England hotel rates leading the pack, fueling a third consecutive year of record profits for the lodging industry. So reports the Lodging Research Network, maintained by Pricewaterhouse Coopers.

The growth in ADR, which had been robust since 1994, will slow to 3.9 percent in 1999—from 4.5 percent in 1998 and 6.2 percent in 1997, said Bjorn Hanson, global partner for hospitality and leisure in the Pricewaterhouse Coopers Financial Advisory Services (FAS) practice. "In part, this is a reflection of the U.S. lodging industry's lower occupancy rate, which will fall further below the long-term average of 65.0 percent to 63.0 percent in 1999 from 63.9 percent in 1998," Hanson stated. Historical data are from Smith Travel Research.

With a year-to-year change of 3.9 percent, however, the prospective 1999 ADR rise is nearly twice the U.S. Consumer Price Index (inflation) rate, which

is forecast to be 2.1 percent this year, Hanson observed. "The revenue that comes from room rates higher than inflation will certainly sweep in the U.S. lodging industry to another year of record profits at approximately $20.5 billion in 1999, up from $18.9 billion in 1998."

At the Top
By segment, upper-upscale U.S. hotels will see the greatest rise in average daily rates—at 5.0 percent, according to the Lodging Research Network. Next are midprice hotels without F&B, at 4.5 percent; upscale hotels, at 4.4 percent; economy hotels, at 3.5 percent; and midprice hotels with F&B, at 3.4 percent.

New England hotels will lead the nation in ADR growth, at 4.6 percent in 1999, followed by the South Atlantic region, at 4.1 percent; and the Pacific and Middle Atlantic regions at 4.0 percent each. The East South Central region will struggle only to a 1.5 percent increase over 1998, and the once-hot Mountain region will rack up a year-to-year increase of only 0.9 percent.

and by a double-occupancy factor (about 40 percent).

The important point remains, however: if the potential demand is increasing at 1 percent annually, how much longer is it going to be economically feasible to add rooms at 4 percent, which is the rate projected for 1999? For the industry to have achieved a 70 percent occupancy in 1998 (with a double occupancy of 40 percent), we estimate that each potential traveler would have had to spend more than six nights in a hotel. That does not seem realistic, especially when we know that at least half of the travelers will stay with friends and relatives.

Barring a change in trends, the outcome is obvious: as supply outstrips demand, operators will begin to discount room rates to take customers away from their competitors. Past experience has shown that discounting can be a losing proposition (Makens, 1987; Hanks et al., 1992). In today's highly competitive, efficient operating climate, only a small portion of a room's expense is fixed, while each additional room occupied adds variable expenses. Studies have shown, for example, that to make up financially for a discount of 10 percent off the average room rate, a hotel with an existing occupancy of 65 percent would have to raise that occupancy to nearly 71 percent.

The industry is in generally good financial shape and can certainly absorb a few years of reduced profit margins. Let's hope we do not reach the point where excessive supply growth, at least partially forced by unreasonable investor anticipation, leads to that bane of the late 1980s—rate cutting!

1.3　The Hotel Development Process

John Dew

INTRODUCTION

The bulldozers are working and a construction crane is being erected on that vacant lot you pass each day going to and from home. The sign on the fence states that a new hotel is being built with a planned opening date of spring 20XX. If you have ever wondered just how that hotel was created, you may have wondered about some or all of the following questions:

- How did someone select that particular vacant lot?
- Who is it that actually develops a hotel?
- Who owns it?
- Where did they get the money to build it?
- How long does the process take from idea to grand opening day?
- Who selects the architect, the engineers, and the interior designer?

- Who will manage the hotel once it's open and the myriad of other details that go into the creation of a new hotel?

We hope to address these and other questions you may have in this chapter where we explore the hotel development process.

THE DEVELOPMENT COMPANY

The developer is the entrepreneur, the risk taker, who originates the idea for the hotel. The developer networks with commercial real estate agents on the lookout for a suitable hotel site. Depending on the type of hotel to be developed, a 2-to-4-acre (or more) site is required (for comparison, an acre is roughly the size of a football field). This property must be zoned by the city for a hotel, have visibility from a freeway or major street arterial, and have city approval for such construction activities as curb cuts, left-hand turn lanes, delivery truck access, and other criteria. Commercial realtors will offer sites for the developer's consideration that include maps, aerial photos, and proof of hotel zoning.

Sometimes the developer will view potential sites by driving the neighborhood within 5 miles of the site or touring multiple sites by helicopter noting where the potential guests live and work, and where potential competing hotels are located.

The price per square foot of the land is also considered. The higher the cost of land, the more the hotel will need to charge in their rates. Is the price too high for the average daily rate (ADR) in this particular market? Is it too low? Or is it acceptable? This is determined when the hotel financial "pro forma" document is created.

THE FEASIBILITY STUDY

When the developer selects a site, a feasibility study is often commissioned to obtain an analysis of the site by an objective third party. There are companies that offer hotel feasibility studies for a fee and are experts in a particular market, or developers may use the services of the consulting groups of the "Big 5" public accounting firms.

The company retained to do the feasibility study can spend up to several months gathering detailed data to see if, in their opinion, it makes economic sense to build the hotel. Their conclusion offers an objective third-party opinion as to whether the project is feasible or not, hence the name *feasibility study*. Generally, a feasibility study will consider, evaluate, and make recommendations about the project based on the following variables:

- The Site
  - For proper zoning.
  - Size in square feet/acres.
  - Visibility from arterials/freeways.

- Traffic counts/patterns.
- Accessibility.
- Proximity to where potential guests live, travel, or work.
- Barriers to competition coming into the market, if any.
- How adjacent property and businesses are being utilized.
- Master area development plans.
- Local permitting process and the degree of difficulty for that particular city.
- Impact fees charged by the city.
- The Economy of the Area
  - Major employers, government agencies.
  - Business trends for each employer/agency.
  - Hotel needs and demand for each.
  - Leisure travel demand in the area.
  - Tourist attractions.
  - Visitor counts.
  - Conventions, trade shows, and meetings history.
- The Hotel Market
  - The competitors, both existing and planned.
  - Historical occupancy of hotels in area.
  - Average rate.
  - Smith Travel Research: propriety data on area travel.
- Identification of Hotel Market Segment to Serve
  - Full service.
  - Limited service.
  - Extended stay.
  - Luxury.
  - Midprice.
  - Economy.
  - Budget.
- Selection of Appropriate Hotel Design
  - High rise.
  - Midrise.
  - Garden apartment style.
  - Hybrid design.
- Selection of Appropriate Hotel Brand
  - Franchised (Marriott, Sheraton, Hyatt, etc.).

- Licensed (Best Western, Guest Suites, etc.).
- Independent.
- Independent with strategic market affiliation (Luxury Hotels of America, Historic Hotels of America, etc.).
- Ten-Year Projection
  - Occupancy projection by year.
  - ADR by year.
  - Estimated cash generated for debt.
  - Estimated cash generated for distribution to investors.
  - Estimated "cash on cash" return (after-tax income divided by equity invested).
  - Overall projected yield.
  - Projected internal rate of return.
  - New present value of the project over ten years.

Once the feasibility study is completed, the developer is now prepared to move forward with the project. Often, at this stage of the process, the developer will purchase an option on the land to tie it up until the remaining development steps can be completed—and, coincidentally, keep it off the market from the competition.

CREATION OF THE OWNERSHIP ENTITY

An ownership entity (note that this is different and separate from the development company) needs to be created to hold title to the land and the hotel once it's built. Considering such things as limitation of liability to the investors, tax consequences, estate implications for the investors, and potential requirements of the mortgage lender, a business structure is selected, normally in one of the following forms:

- Limited liability company.
- Limited partnership.
- S corporation.
- C corporation.

THE DEVELOPMENT AGREEMENT

The newly formed entity now enters into a development contract with the development company to take the project to completion. The development company charges a fee, approximating up to 3 percent of the total project cost, for this service. The agreement will generally cover such variables as:

- Selection of architect/engineers.
- Selection and supervision of a general contractor.
- Processing all building and occupancy permits.
- Raising all the equity money from investors.
- Securing a construction mortgage loan.
- Selecting a franchise company.
- Securing the franchise.
- Selecting an interior designer that meets franchise company requirements.
- Purchasing all opening furniture, fixtures, equipment.
- Selecting a management company to operate the hotel.
- Liability for cost overruns.

SELECTING A FRANCHISE

Depending upon the type of hotel to be built based on the feasibility study, the developer recommends a franchise company to the hotel owner. A major consideration is what the best franchise brand may be for the market segment to be served. Each franchise company has different franchise fees, royalty fees, and marketing/miscellaneous fees as part of its agreement structure with the operating company. Consideration must also be given as to which brands are already represented in the target market and which may be available for franchise. The franchise company is approached, and a franchise is requested offering the feasibility study as backup for the request.

The next step in the process is for the franchise company to conduct an impact study of the market. They consider such things as any possible negative impact on existing hotels that carry the franchiser's flag. If the impact is judged to be insignificant, a franchise is usually granted to the ownership entity for a one-time fee of about $400 per room, depending on the franchise selected.

SELECTING AN ARCHITECT

Since the final product of this process is a building the operator has to run as a hotel, such things as the architect's experience in designing hotels, their experience with the prototypical drawings of the franchise selected, their fee, and their on-time record must be considered. Architect fees can run up to 5 percent of the cost of the project, but often are negotiated down from the 5 percent, if the project is big enough. The firm's experience and record on similar projects is critical, though, for the architects do not have to operate a hotel, but the developer wants them to design one that will be architecturally easy to run.

SELECTING A GENERAL CONTRACTOR

The major consideration is the quality/reliability record of the general contractor and that firm's use and relationships with the many subcontractors needed for a project as complex as a hotel. And again, experience in building the type of hotel is important. It is hoped that the general contractor has learned from any mistakes made in building other similar hotels. The general contractor and architect will often team up to bid the project; this helps the developer to determine the final cost. A "contingency cost" that allows for unforeseen circumstances is also built into the bidding process for the project.

FINANCING THE PROJECT

The important variables to determine to qualify for financing include:

- The cost of the land.
- Design and construction of the building.
- The cost of furniture, fixtures, equipment, supplies.
- Preopening marketing and labor.
- A six-month operating capital reserve.

The totals of these potential costs comprise the total cost of the project for purposes of securing financing.

With this information, the ten-year operating "pro forma" is updated to reflect actual costs. It's now time to go to the money market for construction financing. The terms and conditions of a construction loan can vary widely depending upon the individual lender. Some of the important terms, which can affect the cost of the loan, are:

- Personal guarantees by developers and equity partners/investors.
- Loan origination fees.
- Interest rate.
- Required loan to value ratio.
- Terms of repayment.
- Interest held in reserve requirement.
- Required debt service coverage ratios.
- Length of construction loan; length and costs of extensions.

These are only a few of the considerations that must be analyzed when selecting a lender. The developer on behalf of the owning entity then approaches a number of lending institutions. The lending institutions analyze the deal and offer a proposed term sheet that answers all of the borrowers' questions. This allows the borrowers to select the lending institution with which they wish to work. The lender then commissions an appraisal of the project by an independent appraisal company such as Hospitality Valuation Services (HVS) or other such companies. Based upon the appraisal, the lender will issue a loan commitment for the project that usually offers to loan up to 75 percent of the project cost. The balance must be raised as equity from investors.

RAISING THE EQUITY INVESTMENTS FUNDS

With the bank committed to about 75 percent of the cost, the remaining 25 percent must be raised in equity commitments by investors. As part of this process, the developer prepares an offering solicitation document that meets current securities and exchange law. This document is different depending on the type of business entity that was formed. For limited partnerships or limited liability companies, a private placement offering circular and project description is prepared. For S or C corporations, stock offerings are prepared for sale consistent with applicable federal and state securities law.

The developer now commences contacting money sources that have risk capital available to invest. These can include:

- Individual investors.
- Private asset managers.
- Opportunity fund managers.
- Venture capital funds.

These potential investment sources are offered the opportunity to invest in the hotel and, based on their study and evaluation of the reports, documents, and studies detailed above, decide whether or not to offer funding to the developer.

Once the loan has been secured, the equity raised, and the building permit issued by the city, the land is purchased and the 12–16 month construction process begins. If the architect's plans will work, if the general contractor has no problems with subcontractors, unions, or permits, if all the furnishings, fixtures, and equipment arrive on time, if the

weather cooperates, and if the employment market is such that you have sufficient human resources to open a hotel, then congratulate yourself, the hotel will open on time.

SELECTING THE MANAGEMENT COMPANY

While all the construction activity is happening, or often before, on behalf of the owning entity, the developer selects the appropriate management company to manage the preopening, marketing, selection and training of the opening staff, preparation of the operating budget, and day-to-day operations once the hotel is opened. Management companies charge 3–5 percent of revenue for this service. In recent years, management companies have charged 3–4 percent of revenue and 2–3 percent of gross operating profit so they can be measured and evaluated on both sales and profitability.

Often the franchise company offers to provide management services to their franchisees. Marriott International, Inc., as an example, manages about 50 percent of all hotels that carry the Marriott flag under 20-year contracts. Other independent management companies manage the remaining hotels under a long-term management contract of up to ten years duration, often with several five-year renewal options.

CONCLUSION

This has been a largely linear explanation of the complicated process that a developer goes through in order to create a hotel. It has been described in a step-by-step process, but in reality, many of the steps described are carried on concurrently to save time (and money). Nevertheless, the hotel development process takes about three years from original conception to welcoming your first guest. It is important to remember that during the initial stages of the process, the developer can have as much as $1 million (U.S.) or more at risk in the process before a final "go/no-go" decision is reached. It is only after the project is approved and all financing is in place that the developer can start to recover its up-front costs and start to collect a development fee. Believe me, this is the exciting part.

Hotel development with its component parts of hotel feasibility studies, hotel appraisal, hotel real estate finance, and hotel management are all among the career opportunities available to hotel and restaurant administration graduates like you.

1.4   The Emergence of the Branded Distribution Company

Peter Cass

The past 50 years have brought major changes to the hotel industry. Ownership and operating structures have evolved, the use of technology has expanded and enabled more sophisticated and effective marketing, chain hotel brands have become widely recognized, and consumers' expectations for quality, service, and facilities have increased dramatically. These changes arguably have the greatest impact on the independent hotel owner who, in the face of increasing pressure from larger, well-funded chains, has struggled to maintain independence and to compete on the basis of distinctive hospitality and character.

Over the course of this 50-year period, several organizations were established to provide independent hotels and resorts with reservations and sales services. As competition evolved and changed, some of these organizations have modified their structures and enhanced their services to meet the changing needs of independent hotels and competitive market dynamics. Today independent hotels may choose from among more than 20 such organizations that deliver varying degrees of competitive advantage and ownership independence.

A NEW MARKET PARADIGM

As we enter the new millennium, the face of the global hospitality market continues to change at a rate never before seen. There are four factors contributing to this rapidly changing environment. They are:

- The broadening and diversification of the global consumer market. Both the demographic and psychographic characteristics of the global consumer market are growing and changing radically.
- The rapid advancement and availability of technology. This includes internal hotel operating systems, revenue management, direct-to-consumer communications and booking technology (Internet), marketing technology (customer databases), and telecommunications and automated sales systems that enable central sales offices to become revenue producers.
- The growth and importance of global brands. Recognized brand names and brand attributes are important in reaching diverse customer segments and in creating customer loyalty.
- Consolidation of multiple brands under a single global management. The management and leveraging of multiple brands using similar technology platforms and shared sales and marketing infrastructures in a way to consolidate and direct consumer demand.

Some of the established ways of doing business—long-term, high-fee management contracts and franchises, a focus on traditional distribution channels, and traditional hospitality industry marketing techniques—are no longer effective in the new consumer-focused market. More and more hospitality marketing budgets are being directed toward technology-enabled customer booking and communication. The facts are overwhelming: current forecasts from Forrester Research project e-commerce travel revenues by the end of the year 2000 will range from a low of $11.7 billion (U.S.) to a high of $26 billion (U.S.). Inherent in this realignment is the need to further segment the consumer market to meet unique customer requirements. This shift from traditional hospitality marketing techniques will evolve over several years and cost millions in telecommunication, e-commerce, data warehousing, and one-to-one marketing investments. The independent hotel or resort and many small branded management companies will not be able to fund this requirement.

This shift will not affect all independent hotels and resorts simultaneously. The first wave of change will impact the global business and city hotel market, primarily because of brand competition and the fact that the business travel distribution network is more structured and driven by multinational corporations desiring lower and more predictable costs. The second wave will impact the leisure market, but the changes could follow closely the impact on the business market and city hotels if leisure travel content, including packaging on the Internet, increases rapidly or the presently fragmented leisure travel distribution network becomes more unified and efficient through consolidation.

The emergence of e-commerce models in the hospitality industry are not eliminating the intermediary and empowering the individual property but, rather, are creating new, more powerful intermediaries. Some of these intermediaries will evolve from the hospitality industry while others will be opportunistic e-commerce companies.

WINDS OF CHANGE

Prior to 1960, the most typical hotel was an independently owned and operated, full-service property catering to the out-of-town business traveler and, particularly in food and beverage, to the local community. Resort hotels offered a greater range of services and were, for the most part, seasonal in operation.

Some early efforts at chain organization were made in North America by Statler and Hilton who gained a competitive advantage through their ability to refer business within a group, or chain, of hotels as well as provide guests with a consistent level of service and facilities. The new owners needed to generate money to pay for their expansion, so newly devised analytical operating techniques and central purchasing became these chains' operating model. The chains were also able to market more effectively than the independent hotel owner by taking advantage of economies of scale in operations, marketing, and sales. The result was that they usually became more profitable than their more traditional independent competitors.

At the same time, independently owned and managed hotels in North America and Europe began attempts to counter the chain competition by forming their own referral groups as a way of achieving critical mass in marketing and sales. For example, in the late 1950s, Robert F. Warner started Distinguished Hotels and Resorts, which provided referral and reservation services for independent properties.

MANAGEMENT COMPANIES AND FRANCHISES

In the 1970s, hotel chains continued to evolve as the need for capital to invest in additional properties restricted growth opportunities. This pressure bolstered the proliferation of the "management contract" whereby the chain offered the hotel owner the rights to use its brand name, established facility and service standards, as well as trained operations management, reservation, and marketing services for a significant fee, usually a percentage of sales. During this period the general practice was a fee of 3 percent of gross revenue or 15 percent of gross operating profit, whichever was greater. This was referred to commonly as 3-15-30 with the "30" representing the number of years in the contract. On top of this fee was a marketing fee of between 1.5 percent to 2 percent of gross operating revenue. Occasionally these contracts also included an additional incentive based upon the achievement of an operating profit goal. This structure enabled management companies to focus on growth strategies, operations, and marketing, leaving the owner with the obligation of meeting the debt services and the expectations of any equity investors. The management contract also guaranteed a steady, and potentially risk-free, stream of revenue to the management company and were heavily weighted in management companies' favor.

The pressure to grow also fostered the development of the franchise concept and franchise system in North America. The franchise differed from the management contract in that the owner had responsibility for operations, including meeting the franchise standards.

These new business structures continued to threaten the traditional independent owner by accelerating the growth of chains' share of the lodging market. In response, the marketing/referral organizations formed in the 1960s began to offer a wider range of services. For example, Preferred Hotels® started to provide reservations and sales/marketing services in the early 1980s. While these additional offerings leveraged linkages to the global distribution systems and developed strong relationships with travel agents, the consumer was largely ignored and the organizations did very little to generate consumer brand awareness.

BRAND DEVELOPMENT

By the mid-1990s the hospitality market was focused on brand marketing, but without a true commitment to brand integrity. This proliferation of more than two hundred brands was further confused by franchise and management companies spreading their brand over several subsegments thereby weakening their overall brand identity. In addition, mergers, acquisitions, and ownership and/or management changes in the parent hospitality companies resulted in a change of standards or focus within a brand or across brands and further confused the customer.

As the consumer market became more diverse, and the hospitality product more segmented, branding became increasingly important. By the late 1990s if an owner/developer did not have a recognized brand affiliation or a close relationship with the lending community, it was very difficult to get permanent financing on a new hotel or resort. Lenders, feeling that an established brand provided greater economies of scale and established infrastructure, opted for the lower-risk alternative. In this brand-driven environment the independent hotels' distinctive style and character became a competitive advantage, but only if the hotels were able to meet recognized standards. As a result, the need for independent hotels to be associated with a clearly defined, well-trusted brand became more critical than ever before.

In the late 1990s, independent hotels, particularly those in Europe, began to face the daunting costs of upgrading their technological infrastructure and facilities to accommodate changing consumer needs. Such upgrades as new property management systems, high-speed Internet access, two-line phones, in-room faxes, spas, health clubs, and more sumptuous bathrooms became critical to maintaining competitiveness. When coupled with the ever-increasing costs of consumer marketing, these costs put unprecedented strains on an independent hotels' finances. As a result, independent hotels became increasingly focused on getting greater returns from their reservation affiliation.

RESERVATION AFFILIATIONS— A CHALLENGE TO THEIR EFFECTIVENESS

The relationship of independent hotels and resorts to reservation affiliations has been long and generally successful. These relationships operated best in a market environment that was stable, somewhat homogeneous in terms of demographic market segmentation, and where travel influencers played a dominant role in transient business, group, and leisure travel. These reservation affiliations were most effective in regional hospitality markets that did not have multiple brand competition and when the goals and objectives of the reservation organization were in alignment with the goals of the independent hotel owners. A contributing element to the attractiveness of reservation affiliations has always been the networking and camaraderie opportunities for the professional management at independent hotels.

Reservation affiliations focus on traditional channels of distribution. Access to the global distribution systems (GDS) is no longer a competitive advantage; the GDS is a universal pipeline. The new competitive playing field is proprietary distribution channels leveraged by consumer segmentation, e-commerce technology and partners, and innovative customer management programs.

In the new technology-driven and consumer-empowered global market, the strength and effectiveness of reservation affiliations is challenged by new market and operating imperatives. The cost to compete against chains will grow exponentially. As competition intensifies, it is probable that local and regional market share at independent hotels and resorts will be drawn off by local and regional licensees of strong global brands. Independent hotels therefore need to draw more national and international business to fill occupancy gaps. This requirement runs counter to the established business model and capabilities of reservation affiliations. The average room-night contribution of reservations companies to affiliated independent hotels is less than 5 percent of available rooms.

There are at least four emerging factors that challenge the effectiveness of traditional reservation organizations.

- The growing demographic and psychographic complexity of the global consumer market requires significant new expertise and resources in the area of segmentation and analysis. The independent hotel must have access to market expertise that includes consumer segmentation and a customer record identification and capture process.

- The emergence of consumer direct-booking Internet technology requires new and ongoing large investments, including a technology-supported process to create and maintain a relationship with each customer. This includes not only external communications with the customer but capturing individual customer preference at each hotel.

- The new marketplace requires innovative global brand management, and the resources to establish and maintain a brand in the face of intense competition. This expertise includes the establishment and maintenance of consistent brand standards as well as consultative services in the areas of hotel design, training, and recruitment for developer/owners. To be competitive a brand has to attract new development, and to do this the brand has to be strong enough to convince lenders to commit to permanent financing. Brand management also includes loyalty program management and the development of regional and global partners to strengthen and extend the effectiveness of the brand.

- The corporate objectives and governance policies of traditional reservation organizations are influenced by the need to grow and meet shareholder profit requirements. These goals for growth can be at odds with the goals and expectations of independent hotel and resort members. As an example, a reservation brand can be primarily motivated to add additional independent hotels and resorts rather than optimizing the revenue production and relationship with each individual member hotel or resort. This mandate for growth can also undermine the consistency of the brand. The independent hotel becomes a client and has little or no influence in the direction of the business relationship.

The traditional reservation affiliations must change not only their focus but also their structure if they want to succeed in this new competitive world.

The traditional reservation organization must be prepared to respond to competitive challenges by increasing their resources and skills necessary to increase its average room-night contribution to affiliated independent hotels to 15 percent—an average growth per member hotel of at least 200 percent over present performance levels.

In response to this competitive environment and the need for a more cooperative and focused business relationship, a new hospitality business structure has evolved. This new structure provides independently owned and managed hotels and resorts with the marketing expertise, multiple technologies, strong global brand awareness, and a focused commitment on performance. This new structure is called the branded distribution company.

CHARACTERISTICS OF A BRANDED DISTRIBUTION COMPANY

The ideal branded distribution organization is a conventional stock corporation with ownership shared by the individual hotel owners who have direct input into the corporation through an elected board of directors. This ownership structure creates a true "operating partnership" and a sharing of energies toward the common goal of creating value by increased brand awareness and room sales. Corporate profits must be adequate to maintain technical and managerial leadership and to support the shareholders' investment.

Unlike reservations and representation companies, a branded distribution corporation owns and builds a branded distribution network asset. *Distribution* means consumer segmentation—the use of technology to capture customer accounts, customer identities, and preferences—and then communicating that information back to a customer or a set of consumers in a way that converts the customer or the consumer segment into a predictable revenue stream. The network includes multiple technologies, customer data and relationships, distribution and marketing partners, and management expertise. The sole focus is performance for the affiliated independent hotels and resorts.

A branded distribution corporation provides multiple technologies as well as other, more familiar services such as loyalty programs, partnership marketing, centralized purchasing and insurance, training, quality assurance, design consultation, and recruitment. Joining such an organization is highly appropriate for independently owned and managed hotels and resorts that want to keep owner control, but require effective and low-cost distribution, global consumer brand awareness, and group purchasing benefits without the encumbrances and costs of a traditional hotel chain franchise or management contract. Above all, it promises the independent hotel awareness of, and access to, their target consumer and rapidly emerging technology through cooperative ownership.

THE BENEFITS OF THE BRANDED DISTRIBUTION COMPANY

This new business structure is efficient in a number of ways. From an owner's or developer's standpoint, it requires less up-

TABLE 1.4
Hospitality Structures and Corresponding Brands

Types of Business Structure	Representation Firms (Group Meetings Only)	Reservation Services Only	Reservation/ Sales Affiliations	Branded Distribution Companies	Flagged & Franchise Management Companies
General Attributes	• Primarily Trade-Focused • Primary Reservation Technology • Disparate range of abilities in: — Management Expertise and Depth — Marketing, Sales, and Reservation Support			• Consumer- & Trade-Focused • Performance Focused • Brand Management • Quality Standards and Assurance • Multiple Technologies • Integrated Marketing and Technology Solutions • Customer Recognition & Loyalty Programs • Full-Service Provider — Purchasing, Technology — Recruitment, Training — Consultative & Design Services • Management Expertise and Depth	
Examples of Organizations, Brands, and Management Companies	ALHI David Green Helms Briscoe Hinton/Grusich Krisam	Flag Int'l Lexington Pegasus/ Rezsolutions Supranational TRUST	Concorde Golden Tulip Historic Hotels Leading Hotels Relais & Chateaux Small Luxury Hotels Sterling Summit SRS World Hotels	Preferred Hotels & Resorts Worldwide	Accor brands Bass brands Cendant brands Choice brands Four Seasons Hilton brands Hyatt Mandarin Marriott brands Starwood brands
Relationship of Hotel Owner to Structure	**Client**	**Client**	**Member & Some Owners**	**Member & Owner**	**Licensee**
Owner Control	**High**	**High**	**High**	**High**	**Low**
Room-Night Production	**Low**	**Low**	**Low – Medium**	**High**	**High**
Consumer Focus	**Low**	**Low**	**Low**	**High**	**High**
Overall Fees	**Low**	**Low**	**Low**	**Low**	**High**

front cash, carries a shorter contract term, is easier to negotiate, and allows for substantial owner control over the operation, style, and character of the hotel. Unlike management contracts that create inherent conflicts between owner and the management company because they remove a great deal of control from an owner and often require very lengthy negotiations, the branded distribution contract preserves the independence of the owner and is often negotiated and signed in as few as 45 days. In addition, expenses, in terms of fees and reservation commissions, are significantly lower than with either a pure franchise or management agreement. For instance, a franchise fee of 9 or 10 percent that can equal 50 percent of gross profits is not uncommon.

The branded distribution company can free hotel management from the daunting and increasingly expensive task of acquiring profitable new customers and allows them to focus their attention and operating skills on the delivery of an exceptional hospitality experience. What solidifies the relationship between the owner and the branded distribution company, however, is that both enter into the agreement with the same primary objective—revenue. After all, the branded distribution company receives no revenue if it doesn't produce for the hotel or resort. This shared goal strengthens and energizes the relationship between the two partners.

From a branded distribution corporation's standpoint, this structure allows the brand to expand faster because capital is not used to subsidize additional construction or support an older business. Instead, funds are used to build and maintain an up-to-date global distribution network and infrastructure composed of telecommunications, e-commerce functions, reservations software, data warehousing capability, and sales and marketing. The efficiency of the operation is insured by a focus that is almost entirely on the most important part of this business relationship—the generation of brand awareness and measurable room-night revenue for each affiliated hotel or resort.

Unlike hard flags that focus primarily on hotel operations and asset management, and reservation affiliations that focus on professional camaraderie and traditional distribution channels, the branded distribution company is primarily market-focused; its full attention is on customer and travel influencer communication, relationship technology, and revenue streams.

In contrast, asset management, profitability, and operating efficiency are the major concerns of management companies that are usually a public company with stockholder expectations that must be met. It is often the case that strategic asset management concerns will conflict with tactical operating needs. This is evident in Marriott's recent move to separate its ownership and operating divisions to the benefit of both.

This same conflict can arise between the independent owners of a hotel property, focused on real estate concerns, and the management company they have hired. Such misunderstandings can sour what should be a mutually supportive relationship. The fact that management contract fees are charged and collected, even when the cash flow is negative, does not create owner confidence in the "partner." A franchise relationship can cause a similar conflict and put a financial and operating burden on an owner.

In contrast, participation of an independent owner/operator as a shareholder in a branded distribution corporation, while not eliminating the real estate/operational conflict, enables the owner/operator to move beyond these concerns and focus on their operation and the consumer—the source of their revenue and the basis of their success.

For a graphic illustration of the differences between a branded distribution company and other types of hospitality business structures, see Table 1.4.

Preferred Hotels and Resorts Worldwide, Inc. is an example of a traditional referral/reservation organization that has evolved into a shareholder-owned branded distribution company. Focused entirely on the high end of the market, Preferred has the most stringent quality assurance program in the industry, a brand that stands for distinctiveness and excellence, recognized industry expertise in distribution and marketing, and a very attractive return on investment for shareholder independent hotels and resorts.

ENSURING COMPETITIVE ADVANTAGE

Independent hotels face significant risk in today's marketplace. Given the advances in technology and the profitability pressures put upon chain hotels by shareholders, competition for customers will increase to a level never before seen. While the independent owner can choose from among several types of affiliations and representation firms to gain access to traditional distribution channels, keeping in step with competitive chain hotels will present a significant challenge due to the cost and management of technology.

A branded distribution corporation has an inherent advantage going into this new competitive arena; its sole focus is on customer acquisition and management and the development of new technologies to accomplish this task. This competitive advantage also extends to the independent hotel aligned with a branded distribution company. By providing the independent owner with a global brand and the technology and expertise to acquire profitable new customers, the branded distribution company enables the hotel management to focus its attention on the delivery of exceptional service and profits to the owners. This separation of skills, expertise, resources, and operating cultures in a cooperative business relationship provides a model and formula for success.

Independent hotels and resorts that align themselves with a branded distribution company will not only continue to operate profitably in the new global marketplace, they will flourish.

1.5   "Meet Me at the Westin, er, Make that the Hilton": Life on the Front Lines in Rebranding a Hotel

Tom Dupar

WHY DO HOTELS CHANGE NAMES?

Hotel management and franchise companies protect their brand names. This is referred to as *brand integrity*. The brand's quality assurance standards dictate the services and products that their customers expect. When you check into a Four Seasons, you expect multiple in-house dining options. When staying at one of Marriott's many brands, you expect the Marriott frequent-customer program benefits.

There are many reasons and scenarios for changing a hotel's brand identity. Consider that there are up to three entities involved in a hotel's operation: the owner, the manage-

ment company, and a brand affiliation agreement.

With these entities variously involved, the following are among the reasons brands change:

- Change in ownership (Sheraton sells a hotel to Hilton).
- Owner wants to reposition a hotel for a better return on investment (brand X has a higher profit return than brand Y).
- Owner is dissatisfied with current brand affiliation or management company. This occurs when the management or franchise agreement is terminated. This can happen when the contract expires or is terminated

for nonperformance of the contract. Nonperformance can occur on the owner side or franchise/operator side. Both parties must meet certain benchmarks. These benchmarks include financial goals (i.e., bottom-line results by the operator or capital infusion by the owners).

- Mergers of hotel management companies consolidating the brand name (Doubletree merges with Red Lion).
- A management company purchases a portfolio of hotels with one of the new hotels operating within the restrictive covenant of an existing management contract. A common clause in a brand agreement specifies that the brand will not place another same-brand hotel within a certain geographical area for a certain period of time. If brand X operates a hotel with a noncompete clause within zip code 98101 and then purchases a portfolio of properties that includes property Y within that geographical area, that brand cannot operate that property as brand X unless the owners of property Y agree.
- Hotel does not meet brand standards and owner is unwilling or unable to upgrade the property. My uncles were the franchisee a local Holiday Inn. Holiday Inn dictated that they renovate the property to meet the current brand quality assurance standards. My uncles did not want to invest the required funds and the contract was mutually terminated. The property was then operated as an independent.

BUDGETED STEPS IN CHANGING A HOTEL'S IDENTITY

Once a decision is made to reflag a hotel, the first step is to prepare a detailed conversion budget. The costs associated to change a flag include the following four categories and their associated subcategories. Examples have been included, but this list is neither exhaustive nor exclusive.

1. Signage and Identification

This classification includes items that have the existing brand's name or logo on existing items, which must be replaced on the day of the name change. This also includes items that are required by the incoming brand's standards to have their logo imprinted. The following subcategories and pertinent examples are listed in order from highest to lowest cost.

- *Exterior:* Building signs, vehicle signs, highway signs, flags, and glass decals.
- *Marketing:* All brochures (rack, wedding sales, catering menus, rate cards, sales videos), new photography, promotional items, employee reception.
- *Guest rooms:* Laundry bags, keys, guest services directories, stationery, Do Not Disturb signs, matchbook covers, information tents, and anything with the previous logo.
- *Lobby:* Guest folios, registration cards, safe-deposit access cards, countertop signage, and directional signage.
- *Food and Beverage (F&B):* Menus, menu jackets, coat check tickets, sugar packets, podium plaques, and all staff uniforms and linens with logo.
- *Housekeeping:* Ash-sand urn imprinters, existing logoed equipment such as floor polishers and vacuums.
- *General:* Uniforms (if logoed), name tags, administration stationery, in-house advertisements, and all business cards.

2. Minimum Brand Standards

This classification includes items that are required by the incoming brand's standards, but do not currently meet the new standards. As you can see, this may mean a significant expense; consider, for instance, buying irons and ironing boards for a 1200-room property.

- *Standard guest rooms:* All amenities, irons and ironing boards, in-room coffee service, mini bars, properly sized televisions, coat hangers, luggage racks, bed and bath linens, and bed sets and other furniture.

- *Upgraded or business guest rooms:* Fax machine, two-line speaker telephone with data port, office supplies, bathrobe, ergonomic desk chair, and adequately sized desk.
- *Suites*: Stereos, wet bars, oversized televisions, and other luxury amenities.
- *F&B:* Wares (china, glass, flat, and hollow), linens, banquet equipment (tables, chairs, riser, podiums), and even carpeting.
- *Special brand programs:* Special children's clubs or guest services programs, such as Sheraton's Rapid Response or Westin's Service Express.
- *General:* Guest fitness center equipment and training programs, for example.

3. Human Resources

This classification includes all costs associated with hiring and relocation.

- *Hiring costs:* Head hunters, advertisements, out-of-pocket costs for employment candidates, and other special recruiting costs.
- *Relocation:* Temporary housing, household goods moving, meals, travel, new home allowances, and even costs such as mortgage fees and title searches.

4. Computer Information Systems

This classification includes all costs for hardware, software, cabling installation, and training associated with converting to the new brand's information systems requirements.

Reconfiguring computer systems can cause a domino effect of problems for the reflagging manager. The brand agreement usually dictates that the operator use the brand's proprietary reservation system. This is one of the major considerations that the owner decides upon: how can this brand put more "heads in beds" than other brands? The brand's reservation system also includes their frequent-guest program database. This database must be fully integrated into the reservation system to ease the transition of making reservations, program awards, and guest preferences for room accommodations (for example, John Doe always requests a nonsmoking king room on a lower floor).

From an operational standpoint, the reservation system is the most important consideration. Therefore, this system must be fully integrated to the front office system. Most proprietary reservations systems interface with only one or two off-the-shelf front office systems. If the systems do not interface, then all reservation transactions (bookings, cancellations, changes, early checkouts, no-shows, etc.) must be *manually* transferred between the two systems. This can add expensive labor costs to a profit and loss statement.

Then, the domino effect begins to take effect. The reservation system now dictates the front office system. The front office system now dictates the voice mail software, back office system, and the point-of-sale system.

These various systems can include some or all of the following:

- *Reservations system:* The brand's proprietary guest reservation and frequent-guest program software.
- *Front office system:* The basic system to check in guests, interfacing with the brand's proprietary reservation system.
- *Back office system:* Finance division, including receivables, payables, purchasing, and general ledger.
- *Point of sale:* For all food and beverage outlets, spas, fitness centers, gift shops, etc.
- *Sales and catering automation:* Group sales leads, tentative and definite contracts, and catering event scheduling and forecasting.
- *Office automation:* Hardware and off-the-shelf software for administration staff.
- *Guest history:* Frequent-stay programs.

- *Time and attendance:* Basic payroll package.
- *Engineering maintenance tracking:* Work orders, preventative maintenance, and inventory tracking.
- *Networks:* The necessary routers and hubs required so that all systems interface with each other.
- *Telecommunications:* Telephone switch equipment, guest-room handsets, PABX consoles, operational guest-name display handsets, cabling, voice mail, interfaces, installation, and staff training.

As you can see, fully integrating and coordinating these facets can grow exponentially into a major headache.

The foregoing discussion and examples of major budget categories is but a glimpse into the intricacies of preparing a hotel to carry a new brand, or flag as we call it in the industry. Buying all that stuff is one part, but the real challenge (to me, at least) involves integration and coordination of the physical and human assets of the newly named hotel.

OPERATIONAL CHALLENGES OF A CONVERSION

From a planning standpoint, the ideal lead time for a conversion is six weeks. This allows adequate time to plan all of the necessary tasks, order the required supplies, and give vendors time to fill the various custom orders. This is critical to properly reidentify the hotel.

Regarding sales and marketing, the shorter the time frame the better. When the "rumor on the street" targets a hotel for a name change, group sales clients do not book their events for fear that the new management company will not honor their contract. The less time the hotel is under the suspicion that a name change is imminent, the less leery potential clients are.

The two major challenges of converting a hotel are the timing of the physical change-out and human resource issues. The severity of these two issues is vastly compounded when the outgoing management company has lost the management contract and the conversion, or takeover, becomes hostile. In a friendly takeover, the outgoing management company welcomes the incoming management company. This enables the new brand to talk to the hotel staff prior to the conversion.

On the day of the name change, the former name must be completely and totally removed; this is the physical change-out mentioned above, and why all that stuff was budgeted for and purchased. This is required for two reasons: contractual legal requirements and the new brand's awareness impact.

From a legal standpoint, you cannot use a former flag's registration card to check in guests at the new brand's hotel. This is a legal contract. The requirements apply to credit card imprints, purchase orders, sales contracts, and virtually everything else, from banquet event orders to valet claim checks.

From the standpoint of the new brand's legal liability, some other items must also be changed immediately. These include such emergency advisories as evacuation plaques, safe-deposit box access cards, liability notices (pool code-of-conduct signage, self-park claim tickets, and innkeepers code) if previously logoed or identified with the outgoing brand. These are just some of the items that must be changed out by the early morning hours on the conversion day.

In terms of (new) *brand awareness*, the goal is to have guest go to sleep under brand X and wake up under brand Z. Gradual changes lead to gradual brand awareness. Overnight total change to the new brand results in instant brand awareness for the in-house guests and the local business community. I always get a kick out of watching early departing guests on the conversion day. They literally do a double take and tell the front office clerk that they thought they checked into brand X when they are handed their bill with the new brand's logo.

Human resources provide the most sensitive challenge, for when a property's owners are investigating a flag change, the staff rumor mill kicks into high gear. All of the staff, from dishwasher to general manager, are asking the what-if questions:

- Will I lose my job?
- How will my pay be affected?
- Will my insurance coverage change?
- What new systems do I have to learn?
- Who do I have to prove myself to this time?

These are just a few of the questions anybody would have under similar conditions of uncertainty.

Another human resources problem that occurs when a management contract change is under consideration—sometimes for many months—is that the process of hiring *management* for the existing company comes to a halt. Job candidates, whether transfers from inside the company or new hires, are justifiably leery of accepting a position with a company that may soon leave the hotel. Meanwhile, the existing management company is transferring their star performers to other properties. The nonstar performers realize this, and they begin looking elsewhere for job opportunities. This places the incoming management company in the awkward position of trying to fill the vacant positions quickly. I have been involved with some conversions where the number of vacant positions tops 30 slots.

The incoming management company will want to replace some, if not all, of the key executives. The key positions are the general manager, operations manager, sales and marketing director, controller, and front office manager. The human resources manager is usually asked to stay because he or she knows the local job market and has a comfortable relationship with the remaining staff. If changes are to be made in the executive suite, they need to be made immediately. This shortens the change process and gives the staff a feeling of a new beginning.

Hourly staffs are not replaced. Although the staff fears this as a distinct possibility, the incoming management team does not have a team waiting in the wings to take over their jobs.

The incoming management team will send in a team from other hotels and their corporate offices to assist with the transition. This team will include most disciplines: sales and marketing, human resources, rooms, food and beverage, and finance. The purpose of this team is to assist for a short period of time, usually one to four weeks depending on the discipline. The task force usually arrives a few days prior to the conversion. Some task force members return to the property for multiple visits. Financial team members will return and assist with one or two month-end financial closing cycles.

Task force duties will include training staff on new programs including the new computer systems and enrolling all staff to the new benefit programs (health, dental, life, and disability insurance plans and new W-2 forms). The rebranding manager will also direct task force efforts to provide sales and marketing support, set up new national contract purchasing programs, and establish new financial reporting requirements. Their goal is to assist with the transition and to not overwhelm the staff, thus alienating them.

During this staff anxiety, I have found one task that instantly puts most of their fears to rest. I make sure that on the day of conversion all employees have new name tags and all managers have new business cards. In the staff's mind, this shows a new bond with the incoming management company.

CONVERSION DAY MINUS ONE

The activity on-site at the rebranded property really jerks into high gear the day prior to the official conversion.

Typically, all physical items required for the change-out have been ordered in the weeks prior to the conversion day by the incoming management company. The question is, where do you have them shipped? The outgoing brand does not want the responsibility of overseeing the receiving and storage of these goods. Therefore the simplest method is to contract with a moving and storage facility. The storage facility will receive the goods, prepare daily receiving reports, and deliver the goods when it is required by the incoming brand.

This method allows the new brand to track shipments and, more importantly, follow up on the items that have not been delivered. The new brand then dictates the exact timing of the delivery of all the goods to the site by the moving and storage company. This is very helpful when the transition occurs on a weekend or holiday.

Typically the goods are delivered in the late afternoon on the day prior to the flag change. All task force members on-site assist with the receiving and distribution of goods. This allows the team to install the goods on the swing and midnight shifts. The goal is to have as much of the items replaced prior to the opening shift arriving on the conversion day.

The incoming brand works with the outgoing brand to set aside blocks of vacant rooms for the team to convert the night before the conversion. This enables early arrivals on the conversion day to check into the new brand's product. These rooms are then used as training rooms for the housekeeping staff on opening day.

The day prior is also the desired day for the exterior sign company to arrive on-site. If the outgoing brand agrees, the old signs are removed. If they do not agree, the sign company usually begins the staging process. This process involves the receiving of the new sign units, raising the workers platforms onto the roof, and blocking off parking lot areas for access to each sign location. The sign installation contractor will begin the tasks around midnight and will work 16-hour days until the job is complete. Sign installations can take up to three days for an extensive project.

CONCLUSION

Being involved with reflagging is a demanding, draining, and stressful process that is exhilarating and extremely rewarding. When done properly, the staff and the owners are reenergized and embrace the brand and their team.

1.6   Back by Popular Demand

Rick Bruns

Cleaned up and moving upmarket, time-share properties have renewed appeal to baby boomers and hoteliers.

At destination resorts from Orlando to Oahu, a building boom is in full force. In Colorado ski country, on the New Jersey shore, and in Las Vegas, the units are being opened for sale by the thousands. They are time-share properties, mostly purpose-built to answer the surging demand for a once-shunned product.

"This is my twenty-third year in the business, and it's very interesting to see," says Bob Miller, president of Marriott Leisure and chairman of the time-share industry trade group, the American Resort Development Association (ARDA). "Our product is such a positive for consumers, the market is judging us favorably." Miller, a time-share entrepreneur whose first resort became the foundation of the hospitality giant's growing time-share empire, is a prime mover in the effort to build public and regulatory acceptance of a tamed industry.

And, please, call it *vacation ownership*. The term emphasizes what the consumer really gets—the experience and the title. Once state-level regulation of the industry sent unscrupulous operators packing, several market forces began to power its resurgence. Those drivers are the baby boomers, major brands, and greater flexibility.

Having driven surges of demand for everything from Dr. Spock to minivans since their infancy, baby boomers are ready to invest in a consistent, quality vacation experience. According to ARDA research, the average time-share buyer is 49 (actually, they are mostly couples), and another boomer turns 50 every 7.5 seconds. More than 75 million Americans will hit the "big 5-0" over the next 20 years.

Other industry data indicate the median household income of the recent first-unit time-share buyer is just above $70,000 and rising faster than the U.S. median. These college-educated, higher-earning customers are attracted by new and better products being brought to the market by trusted name brands like Disney, Four Seasons, Hyatt, Marriott, and Sheraton.

Rising demand for a growing volume of time-share units at steadily rising average prices has yielded year-over-year sales growth of 14 percent to 17 percent, stretching back for a decade. ARDA estimates total U.S. sales of units, or their equivalent in points, will be about $4 billion this year.

BRINGING BRANDING TO BEAR

The second factor energizing vacation ownership is the arrival of the major brands to the industry. Where they are not creating their own vacation ownership divisions, the big hospitality players are buying or partnering with leading independents.

Starwood Hotels and Resorts Worldwide acquired Orlando-based developer and operator Vistana last October and kept its pair of top managers in place. "They believed time-share was a missing product in their arsenal of brands and products," says Raymond Gallein, chairman/co-CEO with Jeffrey Adler, president/co-CEO. "The appeal of the product from the hospitality perspective is as a brand extension. The customer satisfaction rate is higher than the rate for most hotel brands; the occupancy levels are higher; and the spending patterns are higher. Having a relationship with this customer is what business is all about today."

The Starwood alliance has brought Vistana access to a world of sales prospects and prime resort locations for future growth. "Westin and Sheraton guests are almost perfect vacation ownership buyers for us," Gallein says.

Taking a different approach, the Carlson travel empire has partnered with Island One Resorts, a developer and operator based in Orlando. Rather than acquiring Island One, the Carlson Vacation Ownership unit will provide marketing support as Island One expands. Island One will build new properties (with some under Carlson brand flags), including a new Radisson Vacation Villas property in Orlando.

"This allows us to keep control of our own destiny, but have the benefits of Carlson as a marketing company," says Deborah Linden, founder/CEO of Island One.

Linden, a leader in the campaign to stabilize the industry, brought in Robert Webb, a veteran vacation ownership lawyer, as president of Island One in January. "The time-share product was looked at by the hotel industry as cannibalistic," Webb says, "but it has dawned on them that it's complementary."

The key differences are visible in the floor plan of a resort hotel's room compared to a vacation ownership unit at the same resort. The hotel room may be one bedroom or a suite with one bath. The ownership unit will have two or three bedrooms, at least two baths, and some kind of kitchen. The better designs can lock off one bedroom/bath portion of the unit to increase flexibility of use.

The hotel and vacation ownership units share several attributes that make them highly compatible under one brand. Guests and time-share owners need many of the same hospitality services and maintenance; they can share some facilities on the property, though often they have their own swimming pool, for example.

Most importantly, the customers for each are cut from the same cloth, meaning that management works to meet or exceed just one level of expectations.

When management succeeds, the hotel guests become prime vacation ownership prospects themselves and can be rewarded for referring their friends to visit and hear the marketing presentation.

FLEXIBLE FLYERS AND BUYERS

The most significant customer expectation that vacation ownership operators must meet is choice. What began as ownership of a bit of a resort and the right to stay one week per year in one place has expanded in every dimension. Now, time-share owners enjoy their choice of any week within a season, part-weeks, part-units, different locations, and different resort owners. They can move up or down in the market and trade for other services.

As the major brands have entered the market, they have created clubs for their owner-members, offering their own portfolio of locations. Marriott Vacation Club International, for example, has built itself from the Monarch Resort on Hilton Head Island, South Carolina, to 46 resorts in 23 locations from Vail, Colorado, to Marbella, Spain.

Beyond their bartering, the time-share owner can now convert a week into points and redeem them for air travel, car rentals, and cruises.

When Island One allied with Carlson, the time-share company could offer members of its own Club Navigo a link to Carlson's Gold

TABLE 1.5
Measuring Time-Shares

Worldwide number of time-share owners **1985:** 805,000 **2000:** 6,078,000	**BUYER PROFILE:** **Age:** 49	**Median members of household:** 2 **Single:** 9%
U.S. share of all owners: 44%	**Annual household income:** 88% earn $50,000 or more	**Own more than one week:** 40% **Own a computer at home and/or use at work:** 88%
U.S. share of all time-share resorts: 33.2%	**Education:** 64.2% have a college degree or above	**Purchase travel-related services or products via the Internet:** 31.5%
U.S. weighted average price of time-share unit-week, 1997: $10,537		
Average size of new projects by the 35 largest time-share developers worldwide, 1998: 91.5 units	*A survey of U.S. time-share owners affiliated with Interval International in 1999 found these demographics:* **Married:** 81.6%	**Average nights spent away from home per year:** 34.8 **Of these, at time-share:** 12.4

These statistics were developed from research gathered for the American Resort Development Association using data from 1985 to 1998 and estimating figures for 1999 and 2000.

Points Rewards loyalty program. Now, they can redeem points at countless locations, such as T.G.I. Friday's restaurants.

The Disney Vacation Club takes a different approach to providing flexibility and rewarding loyalty. First, the owner gets a real estate deed and an annual allotment of vacation points.

The real estate ownership of present Disney properties, like those in many non-U.S. timeshares, expires after a certain date (specifically, January 31, 2042) and reverts to Disney.

The points, meanwhile, are applicable not only at the four present vacation ownership locations (two more are in development) but also at other Disney hotels, its cruise line, and through an affiliation program with hotels and resorts around the world. To move upmarket, or to stay longer, a member can bank two years of points and spend them on one vacation.

These programs coexist but also compete with the exchange companies, Resort Condominiums International (RCI) and Interval International. The vacation ownership developer affiliates the property with one or the other (the two represent nearly all vacation ownership properties), and the unit owners pay fees to exchange their units for others in a huge worldwide inventory. Last year, RCI, the larger of the two and a Cendant subsidiary, executed more than two million exchanges.

Craig Nash is a 22-year industry veteran and a lawyer who was a leader in establishing the regulatory environment that now protects the vacation ownership industry from abusive sales tactics and underfunded players. Chairman/CEO of Interval International, Nash welcomes the arrival of the name brands.

"As the brands enhance quality in general, we are able to provide higher quality," he says. "The market is broadened with their transient guests, and sales are enhanced with more members and more opportunities. It's already happening."

To help developers, Interval provides program design and support services and is allied with the HVS international consulting firm, which provides feasibility studies and research.

Though the hotel and vacation ownership businesses can be synergistic, there are differences that can break an unsophisticated new entrant, Nash warns. "One mistake is to neglect the marketing and operating costs, which are a lot greater," he says. That means negative cash flow for years before the units fill up to that glittering occupancy rate.

THE NEXT GENERATION

For those with the expertise to put the right development in the right place, the future looks very bright.

The wave of baby boomers should lift all boats that can float, and Nash is looking beyond them, too.

"The generation X and younger segment have more disposable income than the baby boomers did at the same time, and they have a greater propensity to acquire," he says. "The industry was not tarred and feathered when they were growing up, so they have a neutral view."

Another powerful factor is the rapid growth of Internet usage at all age levels. Sophisticated database and network technologies are beginning to be used to present the vast array of time-share choices and to conduct reservations and exchange transactions.

The Internet expands the audience exponentially, but may also intensify competitive pressures. "The buyers will be able to shop with near-perfect information," Vistana's Gallein says.

Vacation ownership developers and marketers still are limited, however, by state regulations on the content of their message. ARDA is lobbying to develop a national standard for full disclosure and other criteria, so that a given property under a major brand flag, or an independent, can be sold everywhere in the world with one message.

With globalization will come efficiencies of scale, and many developers likely will align themselves with a brand, both to take advantage and to survive. Recalling her own beginnings, Island One's Linden predicts, "You won't see many father-daughter companies like ours was."

"It's going to be tougher and tougher for the small entrepreneur to compete," Gallein says. "It's very clear the brands are going to rule."

References

Greenberg, Carol. 1993. "Coopers and Lybrand's 12-Quarter Lodging Forecast and Foreign Hotel Investment Shows Some Signs of Revival after Declining 73% in 1991, as Operators Assume a Greater Role." *Hospitality Directions* 3(1):4–10, 15–26.

Hanks, Richard D., Robert G. Cross, and R. Paul Noland. 1992. "Discounting in the Hotel Industry: A New Approach." *Cornell Hotel and Restaurant Administration Quarterly* February: 33(1):15–23.

PLAYING THE NICHES

Some 20 years ago, Bob Miller was the chief financial officer (CFO) of a petroleum distribution company in Florida, married, with three kids. "The youngest was six months old," he recalls. "I was looking around for something entrepreneurial to do." A friend sought his advice on a troubled time-share investment, and Miller saw an opportunity. "If you could do it right, this industry had a great future," he believed then.

That was a big *if* in those days, but Miller told his wife, Diana, he wanted to quit his job and become a vacation resort developer. "She had great confidence in me," he says, "but she thought I must have hit my head on something."

The advice-seeking friend became Miller's partner in American Resorts, which chose as its first location Hilton Head Island, South Carolina. They built the Monarch Resort on the beach and planted landscaping that won a national award, presented at the White House by first lady Nancy Reagan. "We went upscale," says Miller, pricing the unit-weeks from $6,000–$12,000 in 1982.

A premium property in a prime location got the attention of Marriott in 1984. The hospitality giant made an offer not just for Monarch but for Miller and company, too. "They recognized that time-share is a very different business from hotels," Miller says.

Miller was in charge of growing the Marriott time-share portfolio, which he did for 13 years. Today, Marriott Vacation Club International claims to be the largest time-share company in the world, measured in annual sales, with 46 resorts in 23 destinations.

In 1997, Miller turned over the reins to Stephen Weisz and pursued his passion, creating new products within the category and developing strategy. He has introduced a Ritz-Carlton luxury time-share product in Aspen, Colorado, and St. Thomas, Virgin Islands, selling now at about $30,000 a unit-week. Closer to earth is his Horizons by Marriott concept at $12,000.

Miller is a niche player in his spare time, too. He likes to fish in the saltwater shallows of eastern Florida, and he and his wife enjoy rounds of golf. Their oldest son, David, a lawyer, was just married, and his parents gave the newlyweds—what else?—a time-share at the Grand Ocean resort on Hilton Head. Meanwhile, those units back at the Monarch, Miller notes, "are selling today in the mid-20s."

James C. Makens. 1987. "Business at Any Price." *Cornell Hotel and Restaurant Administration Quarterly* August: 28(2):13–15.

Suggested Readings

Books

Gomes, Albert J. 1985. *Hospitality in Transition.* New York: AH&MA.

Hilton, Conrad. 1957. *Be My Guest.* Englewood Cliffs, NJ: Prentice Hall, Inc.

Jarman, Rufus. 1952. *A Bed for the Night: The Story of the Wheeling Bell Boy, E. M. Statler, and His Remarkable Hotels.* New York: Harper and Row.

Rushmore, Stephen, Dana Michael Ciraldo, and John Tarras. 2000. *Hotel Investments Handbook.* Boston, MA: Warren, Gorham, and Lamont.

Articles

Brown, Terrence E., and Michael M. Lefever. 1990. "A 50-Year Renaissance: The Hotel Industry from 1939 to 1989." *Cornell Hotel and Restaurant Administration Quarterly* 31(1):18–38.

Greger, Kenneth R., and Glenn Withiam. 1991. "The View from the Helm: Hotel Execs Examine the Industry." *Cornell Hotel and Restaurant Administration Quarterly* 32(3):18–35.

Lee, Daniel R. 1985. "How They Started: The Growth of Four Hotel Giants." *Cornell Hotel and Restaurant Administration Quarterly* May:22-32.

Page, Gary S. 1984. "Pioneers and Leaders of the Hospitality Industry." In *Introduction to Hotel and Restaurant Management,* 4th ed., Robert A. Brymer (ed.), Dubuque, Iowa: Kendall/Hunt, pp. 21–29.

Staff article. 1985. "The Evolution of the Hospitality Industry." *Cornell Hotel and Restaurant Administration Quarterly* May: 36–86.

Source Notes

Chapter 1.2, "The U.S. Lodging Industry Today," by Randell A. Smith and John D. Lesure, is reprinted from the February 1999 issue of *The Cornell Hotel and Restaurant Administration Quarterly.* © Cornell University. Used by permission. All rights reserved.

Chapter 1.3, "The Hotel Development Process," by John Dew.

Chapter 1.4, "The Emergence of the Branded Distribution Company," by Peter Cass, excerpted with permission of the author from *Ensuring the Long-Term Viability of the Independent Hotel and Resort.*

Chapter 1.5, "'Meet Me at the Westin, er, Make that the Hilton': Life on the Front Lines in Rebranding a Hotel," by Tom Dupar.

Chapter 1.6, "Back by Popular Demand," by Rick Bruns, is reprinted with permission from the July 2000 issue of *Lodging Magazine,* Philip Hayward, editor.

2

Organization

2.1 Introduction

CLASSIC ORGANIZATION

In the organization of hotels in the United States at the turn of the twentieth century, the classic "European" hotel organization model was predominant. This structure was built around two major hotel managerial personalities: the chef and the maître d'hôtel. The chef was the chief or "king" of the kitchen. In many ways he represented a feudal lord on his estate who held sway over everything that had to do with selection and preparation of food in the hotel. This structure recognized the importance of the role that food and its preparation played in the hotels of the time.

Similarly, the maître d'hôtel was the "master" of all service in the hotel. It was his responsibility to make sure that the interaction of the hotel's staff organization and the guest was managed in a way to assure that the guest was always served promptly, properly, and in line with the hotel's policy. Even the titles *chef* and *maître d'hôtel,* translated from the French as *chief* and *master of the hotel,* suggest a strong European influence. That these terms are still in use today attests to a continuing

influence, but the roles have changed and evolved. In several places in this book, we will have the opportunity to consider the ways in which people, times, organizations, and jobs have changed in the hotel industry.

For many of the same reasons cited in the introduction to Part I as to why management of hotels has changed, hotel organization structures also changed. As our knowledge of our guests and the markets they represented enlarged and became more precise, specialization within the hotel organizational structure grew to help most effectively the organization manage and deliver its services.

Hotel organization structures are not immune from the influences of the economy and business cycles, so the difficulties that befall business in general during economic downturns also affect hotel organizations. *"Downsizing"* or *"reengineering"* are also terms used to describe the changes hotel companies have undergone.

In the early 1990s, some hotels eliminated entire levels of management or combined managerial responsibilities so that the organization became flatter. In the typical functional chart such as depicted in Figure 2.1, the executive assistant manager was often eliminated, making division heads directly responsible to the general manager (GM). Some hotels have eliminated separate managers at the division level, with all department managers reporting directly to the GM.

However this restructuring has occurred, organizations are still formed around principles such as those outlined by Stoner and Wankel (1986). They said that the organizing process involves balancing a company's need for both stability and change. They go on to comment upon "organizing" as a multistep process based on that proposed by Dale (1967).

- Organizing details all of the work that must be done to attain the organization's goals.
- Organization provides for dividing the total work performed into a group of activities that can be performed by one person or a group of people.
- Organizing combines the work of an organization's members in some logical and efficient manner.
- Organizing sets up a mechanism to coordinate the work of the organization members into a unified, harmonious whole.
- Organizing sets up a mechanism to monitor the effectiveness of how well the organization is achieving its goals.

FIGURE 2.1
Typical hotel organization chart

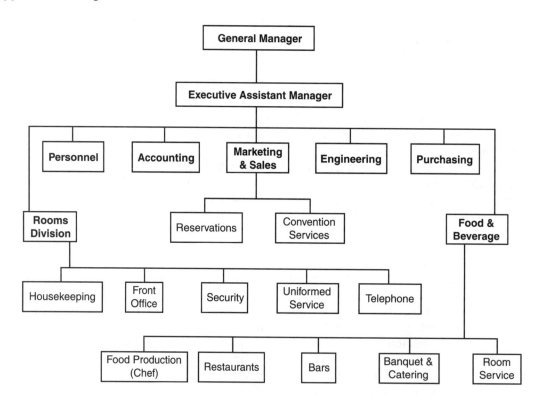

In the modern hotel organization, even a reengineered one, a linear line and staff structure has emerged to reflect this theoretical organizing process.

Figure 2.1 depicts a typical hotel organization chart for a large hotel. Note that with the exception of top managers, function rather than title identify the other departments. This is to indicate that in most modern hotel organizations we find job titles and their inherent duties varying from company to company and, as noted, may be combined or eliminated to reflect current conditions. Looking at an organizational chart by function rather than by job title allows us to look at the organization from an industrywide perspective, for the services a hotel delivers have to remain the same even through financial emergencies.

Note also that in this chart the two major operating divisions have been identified as *Rooms Division* and *Food and Beverage Division*. Again, on a company-by-company basis individual functions may find homes in various divisions, but basically hotel organizations are set up to deliver these two basic services to their guests, either through the sales of rooms and/or food and beverage.

What may differ in a given hotel company's organization are the placements of the other departments. The departments on this organization chart should only be considered typical and illustrative of a generic hotel organization chart.

For purposes of illustration, the aforementioned "line" and "staff" functions are defined as follows.

Line Functions

The line function employees are hotel employees in organizational components who have regular or semiregular contact with the organization's guests. The line operations in a hotel organization are the rooms division and food and beverage division. Obviously, some departmental functions within each line division will have more or less guest contact than others, depending on the nature of their jobs. The underlying commonality in these cases is that most of these employees are "hands-on" participants in the assembly and delivery of the hotel's services.

For instance, under most circumstances members of the hotel's security staff will not have much regular guest contact; housekeeping staff may have somewhat more guest contact and are obviously major participants in the production of the hotel's services. However, in the rooms division, the front office staff will have the vast majority of highly visible face-to-face contact with the guest.

Similarly, in the food and beverage division—another line division—the employees of the restaurants, bars, room service, and banquet departments will have a tremendous amount of face-to-face guest interaction. Like the housekeeping staff, however, only under special circumstances will the food production staff under the hotel chef interact on anything but an irregular basis with the guests. Because of their importance in the service production process, they still clearly fall under the line rubric.

Staff Functions

The staff functions are generally those "behind-the-scenes" activities that support the line functions and under most circumstances have little or no guest contact, although major components of their jobs are to influence the quality of a guest's stay.

In this chart, for instance, engineering has been included as a staff function for those reasons. The success of the engineering function heavily influences the quality of the guest's stay and at the same time the other functions of the engineering department support the activities of almost every other department in the hotel.

For instance, the engineering department maintains and repairs equipment that is crucial to all of the hotel's line functions from the food production equipment in the kitchen. They can be called upon to repair the tables and chairs in the dining room, the furniture in the lobby, and the carts that the bellhops use to transport guest luggage. Viewed from those perspectives, the engineering department can be considered a true staff department that serves and supports at any given time any or all of the other departments in the hotel.

Other typical hotel organization charts will place the engineering department in the rooms division. This may be because that is where engineering works best in the hotel's organization, or may be only tradition.

This situation may also be true for other departments that in the past have been traditionally thought of as "rooms division" functions. Security is one example. In some organizations housekeeping has been changed to a staff function rather than strictly rooms, for housekeeping by definition "keeps" the entire house.

ORGANIZATIONS FOR THE MODERN ERA

Organizations, of course, are more than just boxes and charts. The most modern business organization structures have not changed much in form since the Roman Catholic Church first designed the pyramidal structure as a visual depiction of organizational relationships with which we are so familiar today. If you think about it, the military, government, school systems, and nearly all businesses follow the same model.

What does affect organizations, not so much in their pictorial view, but in the way in which the organization responds to external and internal stimuli, can be seen by analyzing several of the readings included here and those that are suggested at the end for further study.

At the time of his untimely death, Professor Eddystone C. Nebel, III, was the C. B. Smith Professor of Hotel Management at Purdue University. He had recently spent a sabbatical leave researching and observing ten outstanding general managers and 53 total key subordinates. During this research Nebel gained some critical insights into how hotel organizations function. Abstracted from several chapters of his book, *Managing Hotels Effectively: Lessons from Outstanding General Managers* (1991), Nebel weaves together the insights gained from the GMs with organizational theory, and then couples this with the increasingly important role that committees can play in the successful organization.

Another view of the peculiar dynamics of hotel organizations is provided in this edition by Mark Conklin in his essay on how he "sees" how the leadership can influence a hotel's effective organization. In his position as vice president–market management for Marriott Hotels and Resorts he is positioned to comment knowledgeably. In this instance, he proposes a radical new view—one neither the Catholic Church nor the military might be comfortable with. It does, however, appear to be well suited to hospitality.

When Jeff Shaffer and I agreed to collaborate with Eddy Nebel on the general topic of reengineering the hotel organization, we had no idea it would be among the last of his research projects. The project was interesting and fun, due in no small part to Eddy's talents, humor, and intellectual acuity. It was also challenging, because when product businesses "reengineer," they typically lay off hordes of people, but the production process can usually go on. In the hotel industry, like many service businesses, because the intensity of the service encounter by definition involves a lot of people-to-people contact, this becomes trickier. Our article, included here, examines the theory behind this and other aspects of the reengineering process.

While there is no lack of literature and commentary on hotel organizations, the research and opinions presented here serve to highlight some of the current thought about the relationship between organizational structure, interdepartmental relationships, and the organization's people. Additional insights can be gained from parts of suggested readings.

2.2 Organizational Design

Eddystone C. Nebel, III

This chapter will review some of the general management principles of organizational design, including the important but often neglected topic of a hotel's committee and meetings structure.

THE ELEMENTS OF ORGANIZATIONAL STRUCTURE

If the efforts of people in organizations are to be channeled toward productive ends, structure must be given to their activities. Aldag and Stearns (1987) list five ways by which managers give structure to organizations: (1) work specialization, (2) departmentalization, (3) patterns of authority, (4) spans of control, and (5) methods of coordination. Whenever a manager decides to make an organizational change, he or she will usually have to take these five elements into account.

Specialization

If there is more than one way to accomplish something, management must make a conscious decision about how to divide tasks among workers. At one extreme is the case of little or no specialization, where an individual worker is responsible for all of the tasks required to complete a job. An example is the chef in a small country restaurant who single-handedly prepares an entire meal for twenty guests. It's rewarding to have total control over a project and motivating to see the results of one's efforts. The problem, however, is that as the demand for products or services increases, it becomes more and more difficult for individuals or small groups to increase their output without changing the way they are organized.

One of management's tasks is to determine the extent to which work and jobs should be specialized. As a general rule, specialization holds out the possibility of greater worker productivity and managerial control over tasks. On the other hand, dividing complete jobs into smaller subunits tends to increase the need for coordinating the activities of numerous workers, each involved in separate, specialized tasks. Also, overspecialization can result in jobs so narrow that workers lose interest, motivation drops, error rates increase, and quality suffers.

Departmentalization

As organizations grow in size, managers are faced with the need to group certain jobs together in order to ensure efficient coordination and control of activities. Most restaurants have chosen to departmentalize with food preparation and food service as separate functional departments. This is a very logical and practical solution. There are distinctly different kinds of work performed in preparing and serving food: both the process and the function of the two activities are different. Forming departments along *functional lines* is the most common method of organizing a business.

Authority

Every time managers restructure a job or group working together into different departments, they are faced with the question of how much decision-making authority to grant individual workers, managers, or departments. Organizations are never totally centralized or decentralized with regard to decision making. Rather, they tend toward one direction or the other. A number of factors must be taken into account when deciding the pattern of authority that is best for an organization. Managers must take into consideration the experience and personality of subordinates, the environment in which they work (is it stable or rapidly changing?), the business strategy to be followed, and the management style with which they feel most comfortable.

Line executives are those who have responsibility over business units that provide products or services to customers and account for the revenues of the business. It's the rooms and food and beverage departments that account for most of a hotel's revenue. On the other hand, staff departments are set up because the principles of work specialization and departmentalization suggest efficiencies from such an organizational design. The personnel and engineering departments of a hotel are examples of staff units. Once set up, however, staff departments sometimes cause organizational problems.

The basic issue is how much authority should functional staff executives have over line executives? At one extreme, line executives could be given total authority. At the other extreme, staff executives, in their specialty areas, could be granted authority over line executives. Two examples between these extremes would be (1) line executives would be required to only consult with staff specialists before making a decision, and (2) line and staff executives would be required to make joint decisions. Whatever the situation, a top executive, such as the hotel general manager (GM), must arbitrate line-staff disputes when they develop.

Span of Control

Span of control relates to the number of subordinates reporting to a supervisor. In the past, some management scholars advocated an "ideal" span of control of exactly seven subordinates. That simplistic view is no longer held. The ideal span of control is dependent on:

- *Task similarity*: The more similar the tasks of subordinates, the wider the span of control can be.
- *Training and professionalism*: The more trained and skilled a subordinate, the less supervision required and the greater the span of control can be.
- *Task certainty*: The more routine and predictable work tasks are, the greater the span of control can be.
- *Frequency of interaction*: If relationships require frequent interaction, the span of control must be narrow.
- *Task integration*: The more a supervisor must integrate and coordinate the tasks of subordinates, the narrower the span of control must be.
- *Physical dispersion*: The more widely dispersed subordinates are, the fewer a manager can properly supervise.

Some of these factors may work in opposite directions. For example, fast-food restaurants are operationally quite similar to each other, suggesting a broad span of control. However, their physical dispersion works in the (opposite) direction of limiting span of control.

Coordination of Activities

Problems arise when organizations do not properly coordinate their activities. In simple organizations of only a few people, coordination is usually not a major concern. Problems develop, however, as organizations grow in complexity. As previously discussed, work specialization and departmentalization are organizational responses to a business's growth. As duties are subdivided, it becomes increasingly important to coordinate the activities of individuals and groups toward common goals. The kind of coordination required depends on how various tasks and activities are linked together. These linkages result in a variety of different kinds of interdependence between individuals and groups.

Pooled interdependence refers to activities that can be performed with little interaction between individuals or groups. Suppose a hotel has three telephone operators. Each can usually perform the required duties independently (that is, without any interaction with the other), as can room maids and cashiers at food outlets. Because these workers need not interact among themselves, coordination of their activities is best accomplished by prescribing standardized rules and procedures for each to follow, by intensive individual training, and by direct supervision. The role of coordination is to ensure that each independently performed task is carried out at the same level of efficiency and quality.

Sequential interdependence occurs when one task's output becomes a second task's input. This is typical of production line operations where products are progressively assembled. A hotel example is the guest check-in process. The "output" of a front desk becomes an "input" to the accounting department in the form of a guest billing record, or folio. A well-planned system linking the rooms department and the accounting department is needed for this activity to go smoothly. Proper coordination is ensured through detailed planning, scheduling, and standardization. Coordination also requires identification of the linkages that exist between activities.

Still greater coordination is required in cases where the output of Unit A is input for Unit B, and the output of Unit B is input for Unit A. Whenever there is a high level of interaction between work units they are said to exhibit reciprocal interdependence. One example is the coordination needed to host a major convention. Rooming decisions made by the front desk must be coordinated with accounting, sales, housekeeping, and reservations; function-room usage requires interaction between convention services, engineering, food and beverage, and accounting. Because any one department's output and activity affect numerous other departments, mutual adjustments among each are required. Close coordination is possible only through *direct communication* and joint decision making between the units involved. While standardized plans and procedures are helpful, they cannot possibly solve all of the problems resulting from such a high degree of departmental interaction. Direct communication and group meetings become a necessity to ensure proper coordination when activities involve reciprocal interdependence.

STATIC PRINCIPLES OF ORGANIZATIONAL DESIGN

Experience has accumulated for centuries about how to organize institutions such as government bureaucracies, the military, religions, large commercial trading companies, and since the industrial revolution, large manufacturing concerns. A number of principles regarding how to structure organizations have been developed. While these principles do not hold in all circumstances, they are important and should be understood and applied where appropriate.

Chain of Command

The chain-of-command principle holds that everyone in an organization should have a superior to whom he or she is responsible. A hotel's organizational chart depicts the chain of command. It should be possible for any employee to trace his or her way up the organization chart's chain of command all the way to the GM. The typical pyramid shape of an organization chart is a consequence of the chain of command and the span of control concept discussed previously. Chain of command is a very powerful concept. It provides structure in an organization by setting forth a system of subordinate-superior accountability for everyone.

The chain of command affects communication within organizations for both subordinates and superiors. If a GM wants to make a change in housekeeping, chain of command considerations would have the GM communicate through the rooms department manager, who in turn will speak to the director of housekeeping. The traditional chain-of-command structure in a hotel would have the baker responsible to the chef and the chef responsible to the food and beverage director. Accordingly the baker should communicate with the chef and not directly with the food and beverage director.

While it is important to be aware of possible chain-of-command problems, too strict an adherence to this principle can take away the spontaneity in an organization. Experienced hotel GMs often break this principle, but in a way that is not harmful to the hotel. The immediacy of some problems in hotels sometimes requires hotel executives to issue orders directly to subordinates two or more levels down in the organization. GMs may also want to maintain personal control over some project or aspect of the hotel and choose to bypass immediate subordinates in order to do so. This does little harm as long as everyone knows what is happening and the organizational climate is otherwise healthy and trusting.

Unity of Command

The unity-of-command principle states that each employee is responsible to one and only one superior. That is, each person has only one boss. Unity of command is violated quite regularly in most organizations. A safety officer who reports to the personnel director might correct a food server, whose boss is the restaurant manager, for a safety violation. The server feels as if she has two bosses, and in effect, she does. This common problem occurs as organizations grow in size and task specialization takes place. Specialists in safety (or accounting, personnel, data processing, and so on) often do have authority, in their specialty area, over workers who do not report directly to them through the chain of command. Problems can develop because of conflicting orders from more than one boss. The solution is not necessarily to eliminate specialization and staff positions but rather to ensure, by closely coordinating activities, that order rather than confusion reigns. The GM plays a key role in affecting coordination throughout the hotel.

Delegation

Young managers often find delegation a difficult task to master. A subordinate's ability to successfully carry out an assignment depends in part on the clarity of his or her superior's delegation instructions. Delegation can range from assigning a minor task to a subordinate to granting complete responsibility for a major undertaking. It's important for both superior and subordinate to understand and agree on the level of responsibility, the freedom of action, and the amount of authority that accompanies a delegated task.

There are various levels of delegation, each of which is useful in different circumstances. Here are some examples of orders that result in different degrees of delegation: (1) gather information for my decision; (2) set out two or three alternatives; I'll then choose; (3) make a recommendation for my approval; (4) make a decision, but inform me of it before proceeding; (5) take action, but inform me of it before proceeding; and (6) take action on your own; it's not necessary to communicate with me regarding this matter. The extent to which authority is delegated depends in part on the experience of the subordinate. Young, inexperienced subordinates can expect only limited delegation until they have proven themselves. The amount of authority delegated will usually increase as trust between superior and subordinate is built.

It's been said that when a person becomes a manager he or she gives up earning an hon-est living. Hotel managers don't usually make beds, cook food, or provide service directly to guests. Rather, their job is to see to it that the organization they manage provides proper guest services.

THE HOTEL FUNCTIONAL ORGANIZATIONAL DESIGN

Individual hotels are usually organized along functional lines with departments grouped according to the particular work activity in which they are engaged. Figure 2.2 depicts a typical organization chart for a 500-room ho-

FIGURE 2.2
Typical hotel organization chart

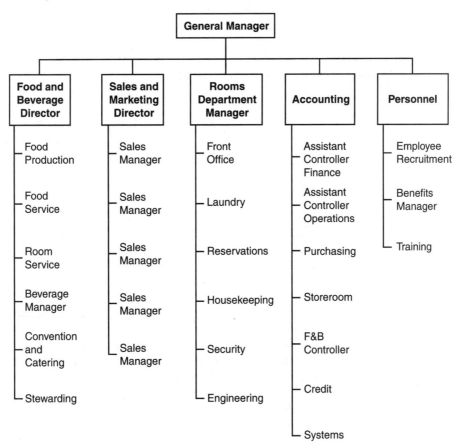

tel. The hotel is divided along functional lines into five separate administrative departments: rooms, food and beverage, accounting, sales, and personnel. The five department heads report directly to the GM. As Figure 2.2 shows, each department is further subdivided into smaller organizational units. These subdivisions represent additional refinements of the work performed and the knowledge and skills of the people in each subunit.

The Rooms Department

The rooms department performs the lodging function of a hotel. Reservations must be accepted, guests must be hospitably received and assigned clean rooms, the status of available and occupied rooms must be kept current, guests must receive mail and phone messages promptly, security must be maintained, public spaces such as lobbies must be kept clean, and guest questions must be answered. These are some of the important functions of the rooms department. The rooms department is divided into a number of subunits, each of which performs rather specialized tasks. In many instances, these subunits are also referred to as departments. For example, the laundry department, which in a 500-room hotel is quite large, is responsible for cleaning and pressing all the hotel's linens and employee uniforms as well as guest laundry. Its function is extremely specialized. Little of the knowledge and skills required to manage a laundry operation are transferable to other areas of hotel operations.

The front office is where guests are greeted when they arrive at the hotel, where they're registered, and where they're assigned to a room. Telephone operators and other guest communications functions usually fall under the front office department. The hotel's bell staff is also part of this department. Reservations takes and keeps track of a hotel's future bookings. The housekeeping department is responsible for cleaning guest rooms and public spaces. Security is responsible for guest safety. Finally, the engineering department is responsible for the operation and maintenance of the hotel's entire physical plant, including electrical, mechanical, heating, air-conditioning and ventilation, structure, and plumbing. It also performs minor repairs and renovations.

A great deal of interdependence exists within the rooms department, thus calling for close coordination of activities between subunits. Linkages exist between the front office and the reservations department. Reservations must inform the front office of the number of presold rooms each day to ensure that a current inventory of rentable rooms is always available. Conversely, the front office must let reservations know whenever walk-in guests (those without reservations) are registered. Linkages also exist between the front office and housekeeping. Information regarding room status must flow both ways: when a guest checks out, the front office must inform housekeeping so the room may be cleaned. Once it is cleaned, housekeeping must inform the front office so that the room may be sold. These are both examples of reciprocal interdependence in which individual units provide each other with inputs. Other linkages within the rooms department are illustrative of sequential interdependence, which occurs when the output of one unit becomes the input of another. An example is housekeeping's inability to properly provision a guest room if the laundry does not supply enough clean towels or bed sheets. Another less obvious example deals with the output of information from one department to another. For example, engineering cannot replace a defective light switch in a guest room if housekeeping does not report the problem. These examples illustrate the reciprocal and sequential interdependence that exist between individual units within the rooms department. Effective management under these conditions calls for standardized plans, procedures, schedules, and deadlines. Coordination between units also requires frequent direct communications between executives.

The Food and Beverage Department

The primary function of the food and beverage department is, of course, to provide food and drink to a hotel's guests. In earlier times, when an inn had only one dining room, this was a much simpler task. Today, however, providing food and drink is much more complicated. The 500-room hotel in this discussion might well have a coffee shop, a gourmet restaurant, a poolside snack bar, room service, two banquet halls, and ten separate function rooms where food and beverage may be served. It might also have a piano bar and lounge, a nightclub, and a lobby bar. This adds up to nineteen separate food and beverage outlets, excluding room service! On a busy day (or night) it's likely that each of these outlets will have functions. Often, more than one function will take place in an outlet during a twenty-four-hour period.

There is great diversity in the kinds of activities performed by a food and beverage department and considerable variety in the skills required within the department. So within the food and beverage department there are a number of functional subunits where tasks are further specialized. To begin with there is the food production, or kitchen, department. In a 500-room hotel this unit is headed by the executive chef, a person of great stature and authority in a first-class hotel. Under the executive chef are a variety of culinary specialists responsible for different aspects of food preparation. The service of food in a hotel's restaurants is usually the responsibility of a separate department, which in a large hotel is headed by an assistant food and beverage director. The food service department is responsible for service in the hotel's restaurants and food outlets. It contains the individual restaurant and outlet managers, maître d's, waiters, waitresses, and bus help. Because of the special problems associated with room service, many large hotels have a separate subunit responsible only for room service. The high value and profit margins associated with alcoholic beverages causes hotels to form a separate department with responsibility over the bars, lounges, service bars, and other alcoholic beverage outlets. Most full-service hotels do considerable convention and catering business. A convention uses small function rooms for separate meetings, larger rooms for general sessions, and even larger facilities for banquets. Catered events include local parties, wedding receptions, business meetings, and other functions held by local groups. To provide for the unique needs of these customers, hotels often organize separate catering and convention departments that specialize in this kind of business. Finally, the job of cleaning the spaces of the food and beverage department, dish and ware washing, and general food and beverage expediting is often assigned to a separate subunit known as the stewarding department.

Sales and Marketing

This department is quite small, thus making intradepartmental coordination much easier. Also, the department is removed from most day-to-day operational problems faced by other departments. Still, there is a division of work among sales managers based usually on the type of customers a hotel is attempting to attract. Individual sales managers often specialize in corporate accounts, conventions, or tour and travel markets. Also, sales managers are sometimes further subdivided along geographical lines such as regional or national accounts. Still, the sales staff, even for a 1000-room hotel, usually does not exceed a dozen or so. Sales managers work more or less independently in their particular market segments. Thus, problems of intradepartmental interdependence are usually not severe (Pelletier, 1988).

Personnel

A hotel's personnel department is a staff organization set up to handle a specialized function. It serves no customer, books no business, and prepares no meals, yet it plays a vital role in a hotel's efficient operation. In Figure 2.2, the personnel department is subdivided into three subfunctions: employee recruitment, benefits administration, and training. The personnel director is expected to be an expert on labor law and to advise managers in other departments. While these three subfunctions are related to each other, there are not many problems of interdependence. Instead, the personnel department's major challenge occurs as it attempts to interact with other hotel departments. Personnel may recruit, interview, and screen prospective employees, but final hiring authority resides in the line departments. The same is true of promotion and disciplinary decisions, where the personnel department's input is only advisory. As a staff department, personnel's effectiveness is largely dependent on its manager's ability to form effective working relationships with other departments.

Accounting

The accounting department often combines both staff and line functions. Its traditional role is recording financial transactions, preparing and interpreting financial statements, and providing management with timely reports of operating results. Responsibilities also include payroll preparation, accounts receivable, and accounts payable. These functions are the responsibility of the assistant controller for finance. There is, however, another dimension to the accounting department that deals with various aspects of hotel operations, cost accounting, and cost control throughout the hotel. This aspect often results in the department being called the controllers department rather than the accounting department. The two areas that are the central concern of accounting control include rooms, and food and beverage. The accounting department's front office cashier keeps track of all charges to guest accounts. The night auditor must reconcile all guest bills with the charges from the various hotel departments. Although these employees work at the front desk and sometimes have direct guest contact, they are members of the accounting department and report to the assistant controller for operations.

The food and beverage controller, and the food and beverage cashiers, working in the accounting department, keep track of the revenues and expenses of the food and beverage department. Food and beverage cashiers report to the assistant controller for operations, and the food and beverage controller reports directly to the hotel controller. The food and beverage department may be responsible for food preparation and service, but the accounting department is responsible for collecting revenues! The food and beverage controller verifies the accuracy and reasonableness of all food and beverage revenues. The accounting department is responsible for keeping track of and preparing daily reports on the costs of the food and beverage used in the hotel. In many cases, the accounting department is also responsible for purchasing and storeroom operations. Finally, the director of systems is responsible for designing the accounting and management information systems used throughout the hotel. This discussion demonstrates the accounting department's direct involvement in a number of day-to-day operational aspects of the hotel.

Two final points about the accounting department: accounting is responsible for collecting and reporting most of a hotel's operational and financial statistics. It therefore plays an important hotelwide staff role as data provider for decision making and budget preparation. Secondly, the accounting department head has a dual responsibility not only to the hotel's GM but also to the hotel chain's financial vice president or to the hotel's owner. The reason for this dual reporting relationship is to provide the hotel corporation an independent (from the GM) verification of the accuracy of the financial and operating results of the hotel. Thus, unity of command is routinely violated in the case of hotel controllers.

STRENGTHS AND WEAKNESSES OF A FUNCTIONAL ORGANIZATION

The reason for organizing a business along functional lines is to group together employees who perform similar tasks or have similar skills. The strength of a hotel's functional organizational design is the resulting efficiency within individual departments or subunits. Performance of common tasks allows for work specialization, which increases overall productivity. Since functional departments perform similar tasks, workers will rapidly develop specialized skills and knowledge. Training is easier because of task similarity and the many opportunities for inexperienced workers to learn from experienced workers. This helps new employees quickly learn the skills and behavioral patterns that lead to success.

A functional organization is a logical way to organize work because it fosters efficiency, teamwork, and coordination within departments. However, the functional design's most important strength is also the source of its greatest shortcoming. The success of a hotel is measured by its overall performance, not the performance of one department. A functional department's strength lies in its ability to focus on its own tasks and activities. Although this is surely important for departmental efficiency, it does not necessarily ensure the overall effectiveness of a hotel. Because they are specialized, it is sometimes difficult for functional departments to fully appreciate the relationship between their performance and the overall performance and goals of the hotel. All departments must keep hotelwide goals of customer service and profitability in mind rather than focus narrowly on their own concerns. A method must be found to coordinate the activities of individual departments and to set hotelwide strategies and goals. Left to them, it is unlikely that individual depart-

ments would be capable of doing this. Specialization at the department and subdepartment levels results in the need for leadership at the top of an organization. Someone above the departments must set the overall strategic course of the hotel, set hotelwide goals, coordinate activities between departments, and arbitrate interdepartmental disputes. A hotel's functional organization demands strong leadership at the top.

While functional departments produce specialists within a narrow skill category they do not develop executives with broad hotel exposure. Consider the heads of a hotel's marketing and food and beverage departments. These two executives might have only superficial knowledge of the other's specialty. Their education and work experience will likely be so different that either would be at a loss if placed in the other's department. The director of sales might have a marketing or general business degree and might have spent a career in sales-related work. The food and beverage director, on the other hand, could have a culinary diploma and a hospitality degree, extensive food production and service experience, and little or no sales experience. One often finds accountants running the controller's office, engineers in charge of engineering and maintenance, individuals with degrees in personnel administration heading the personnel department, and a variety of educational backgrounds among rooms managers.

Managers educated in hotel administration are capable of filling most department head slots. The longer managers stay in one department the more narrowly specialized they become. While a manager may perform well within one department, he or she may be unprepared when it comes to problems that require a hotelwide knowledge and perspective. Narrow specialization can result in bias, mistrust, and friction between departments unless upper management takes steps to counter this. Individual departments may pursue their own narrow interests rather than broader overall goals and objectives (Dann and

Hornsey, 1986). This is a particular problem for hotels because of the need for close interdepartmental cooperation in providing guest services.

HOW MEETINGS HELP COORDINATE THE ACTIVITIES OF A HOTEL

There are numerous possibilities for service breakdowns in hotels. A well-thought-out set of standard operating procedures and systems can decrease the chances of many routine mistakes. Still, because of the amount of reciprocal interdependence that exists between departments, close cooperation is a must. Nowhere is this more important than at the department-head level where differences in functional specialties are most extreme (Dann and Hornsey, 1986). The vehicle often used to foster cooperation between functionally specialized departments is the executive operating committee (EOC).

The Executive Operating Committee

The EOC is made up of the GM and other hotel senior executives. There's no magic formula as to who should be on the EOC, but usually it's those executives who report directly to the GM. Thus, the EOC consists of the most senior members of a hotel's management staff: the heads of the functional departments who report directly to the GM and are responsible for the hotel's major budgetary units. A subgroup of these executives—the GM, rooms manager, sales and marketing director, food and beverage director, and controller—usually produce the hotel's occupancy, revenue, and profit forecasts for each year. This forecast forms the basis for the hotel's overall annual budget, and meeting annual budget goals determines executive bonuses.

The exact duties of an EOC vary from hotel to hotel. The duties and responsibilities of groups can be spelled out in detail or left ambiguous. A hotel's EOC could be loosely structured or highly structured. An important question GMs need to answer is the amount of authority they wish to delegate to the EOC. Depending on the circumstances, one EOC might be structured to make certain group decisions, a second to play a strong though consultative role to the GM, and a third to have a weak or nonexistent decision-making role.

Quite apart from decision making, EOCs play an important communications role within hotels. This occurs by virtue of the fact that EOC members meet regularly to discuss hotel business. Anytime meetings are held, communications take place.

Scott and Mitchell (1976) identify four functions of communications:

1. To provide information that helps executives in their decision making.
2. To be motivational by fostering a commitment to organizational objectives.
3. To act as a control device by resolving ambiguities regarding the role, responsibilities, and duties of executives.
4. To afford individuals the opportunity to express their feelings and emotions.

It is important to note that all four of these functions of communication may take place during meetings. Meeting frequency, agenda, and the amount of decision making delegated to an EOC will depend on a variety of factors. The more participative the GM's management style, the more likely the EOC will be engaged in joint decision making. Authoritarian GMs will find little need to foster a strong EOC. The greater the need for change within a hotel, the more likely it is that frequent EOC meetings will take place. The less experienced the hotel's department heads, the more helpful frequent EOC meetings will be because they can serve as a learning and training vehicle for inexperienced managers.

Under the influence of a skilled GM, the EOC can play an important role. Some of the ways it may be useful are:

- To foster group problem solving and decision making.
- To build a feeling of joint responsibility for overall hotel performance.
- To help instill common attitudes and beliefs among top executives.
- To foster top-down, bottom-up, and horizontal communication.
- To assign duties, assess progress, and control activities.
- To build interdepartmental cooperation.
- To teach, coach, and build a responsive senior executive team.
- To ensure acceptance of priorities and decisions by senior management.

Other Hotel Committees and Meetings

Well-managed hotels address the need for coordination of activities through an elaborate structure of committees and meetings. Just like a hotel's organization chart, these committees and meetings constitute a formal part of a hotel's organizational structure. The GM usually proscribes a hotel's committee and meeting structure. Each group's responsibilities are spelled out (sometimes in great detail), regular meeting schedules are promulgated, and minutes are often taken and distributed to participants, and to higher-level executives including the GM. The committee and meeting structure of a hotel should be a well-thought-out part of a hotel's formal organizational structure.

The purpose of the committees and meetings in a hotel is as varied as the hotel. They address a variety of concerns, including daily operations; intradepartmental and interdepartmental issues; hotelwide concerns; and financial, personnel, and marketing issues. Table 2.1 lists the regularly scheduled meetings for a typical large hotel. While not the meeting schedule for an actual hotel, it could be. It will pay dividends to review this list carefully. The meetings a hotel holds provide clues about what it takes to manage it.

One of the first things to note is the sheer number and diversity of meetings. Surely, one might say that if a hotel were to hold all of these meetings there would be little time left over to do any work! In fact, the effective management of hotels requires frequent meetings. They *are* part of the work of the hotel. Table 2.1 shows an average of 249 scheduled meetings each year dealing with interdepartmental issues. Also, the GM attends 295 regularly scheduled meetings each year. In many hotels this is literally the case.

There is no denying that meetings are time-consuming and sometimes unproductive. Still, there doesn't seem to be a better alternative to effectively manage a hotel (Conlin, 1989). One often finds frustrated, dissatisfied executives in hotels where there are too few meetings. These executives complain about not being kept informed of what is going on. As elementary as it may seem, it is very easy for a hotel to fail to keep its managers and employees adequately informed. This shortcoming can have disastrous consequences with regard to the attitudes and morale of a hotel's staff. A second complaint relates to service breakdowns that occur as a consequence of too few meetings. Hotels are subject to frequent, usually daily, changes. Meetings must be scheduled frequently in such an environment or their effectiveness will be lost. Having too few meetings results in confusion over a hotel's goals and objectives. People need to know what is important to the hotel. What does it value most? What does it stand for? What constitutes good performance? Since hotels provide many intangible services, a constant effort must be made, at all levels, to provide answers to these questions. Meetings are an effective means of accomplishing this vital management function (Hosansky, 1989).

Hotels are businesses that require an extraordinary degree of interdepartmental cooperation in order to provide quality guest service. The functional organizational design used in most hotels fosters efficiencies within each department of a hotel but is weak when it comes to coordination between departments. One of the organizing strategies employed to overcome this problem is a formal meeting structure designed to foster interdepartmental communication and cooperation. Thus, an important part of management's organizing function is to design an effective meeting structure that compensates for and complements a hotel's functionally departmentalized organization.

TABLE 2.1

Typical meetings structure for a major hotel

Meeting	Attendance	Frequency	Purpose	Meeting Length
Operations	GM, department heads, front office, manager on duty, housekeeping, security, engineering, executive chef	1 to 5 times per week	Review upcoming day's activities and previous day's results	15 to 30 minutes
Staff	GM, department heads, all subdepartment managers reporting to department heads	Weekly	Review last week's performance, this week's activities, next week's plans and special projects; present performance awards	1 to 2 hours
Executive Committee	GM, department heads	1 to 4 times per month	Performance review, policy, strategy formulation	1 to 2 hours
Sales Forecast and Marketing	GM, resident manager, front office, sales, reservations	1 to 4 times per month	Review room demand for upcoming 90 days, devise strategies to increase room-nights, average rates, or both	1 to 2 hours
Department	GM as needed, department head, and all subdepartment heads, managers, and supervisors	1 to 2 times per month	Review departmental issues	1 hour
Subdepartment	Department head as needed, subdepartment head, all members, management, and staff	Monthly	Subdepartment, department issues	1 hour
Credit	GM, controller, sales, front office, reservations, catering and credit manager	Monthly	Review accounts receivable	1 hour
Safety	Personnel, food and beverage, housekeeping, and engineering	Monthly	Review safety program and safety record	1 hour
Energy Conservation	Chief engineer, resident manager, food and beverage, personnel, rooms, and housekeeping	Monthly	Control of energy costs	1 hour
Supervisory Staff Meeting	All management and supervisory personnel	Biannually	Review hotel performance, present awards, start new programs	1 hour
Annual Meeting	All hotel management and employees	Annually	Year-end review of performance and awards	1 hour
Employee Meetings	GM and selected employees from throughout the hotel	Monthly	Informal communication and discussion	1 hour
Supervisor/ Junior Manager	GM and selected first-line supervisors and junior managers	Monthly	Informal communication and discussion	1 hour

2.3   As I See It: Hotel Organization Structure

Mark Conklin

One way to represent the environment in our hotel is a chart that I use at our new-hire orientation class (see Figure 2.3). I call this a reverse organizational chart; it is also referred to as an organizational pyramid, and as you can see, the GM is on the bottom of the hierarchy.

At the top is the customer. They are the reason we are here. This focus on our guests creates alignment throughout the hotel. Our mission is to ensure that every guest leaves satisfied and wanting to return, thus ensuring customer loyalty. One of Marriott's fundamental beliefs is "if you take good care of your employees, the employees will take good care of your customer." This belief is at the core of who we are and what we believe in as a company.

I say that we have two types of customers—external customers, which are our guests, and internal customers, which are the hotel's associates. I don't use the term *employee* but have replaced it with the word *associate*. The difference is that employees work *for* you and associates work *with* you. *Associate* implies partnership and working together, which is a subtle but very powerful message. *Employee* suggests a class structure wherein someone is always organizationally *inferior* to someone else.

It is my belief that the front line associate is the most important person in the hotel since they serve the customer. The job of the supervisors, managers, and the leadership team is to

- Support the front line and remove the barriers to doing good work.
- Lead and help people do their jobs better.

This means managers support the front line by

FIGURE 2.3
Reverse organizational chart

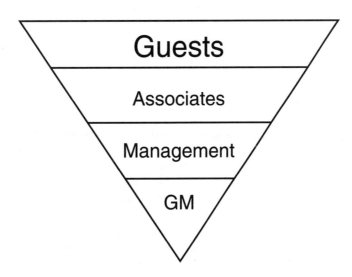

- Demonstrating concern for associates (and it must be sincere).
- Solving their problems quickly and fairly.
- Above all, treating them with dignity, kindness, and respect.

To accomplish this, leaders must develop working relationships with associates that are based on mutual trust. Quite simply, it is my fundamental belief that our associates will not treat our customers any better than we treat them. This is the cornerstone of our culture, and the challenge is to keep this legacy alive as the company grows. As leaders, it is our job then to establish the direction and to create the environment where people focus on our customers. We set the tone for outstanding service, which requires a lot of coaching and leadership.

With the GM on the bottom of the pyramid, it denotes that as the leader, you actually work for the people who work with you. I view my role as doing whatever it takes to gain and keep customers. To create this environment, I've tried to capture the following key operating principles.

Select the Right People

We work very hard at selecting the right people, using predictive screening tools. We look for people whose talents predispose them to provide great service and who have the highest potential to fit in with our culture.

Also, our hourly associates are involved in the selection process; after all, they have to work with the new associate. Therefore, line associates and managers take collective responsibility for the success of a newly hired associate.

Invest in Training

Our emphasis on training is a reflection of Marriott's corporate culture. We invest in building the skills and knowledge of associates to give them the tools to succeed. We also provide them with an operational framework (standard operating procedures) that represents the foundation for our training.

Create Empowered Associates

The foregoing combination of training and standards creates empowered associates who have the authority, accountability, and confidence to do their jobs. Years ago we were challenged to operate our hotels with less managers. To accomplish this and improve customer service, we had to have trained, empowered, and involved associates running the business.

It is these systems, standards, and attention to detail that help deliver a consistent product and reliable service, which gives customers confidence and trust in our brand name.

Recognize and Promote

Recognition in our organization takes place in many forms to create a positive environment. One of the greatest ways to show appreciation is by promotion. More than 50 percent of our managers started as hourly associates.

Our associates like us, they trust us, and they act in our best interests. Recent companywide associate opinion surveys indicate that 95 percent of our associates rated Marriott as an average or above average place to work. This is 15 points above the service industry norm.

Finally, it is my strong opinion that our managers should be "hands-on." The hands-on manager is one who stays close to the customer and close to the associate . . . and hands-on managers never forget who is making them successful.

2.4   Reengineering the Hotel Organization

Eddystone C. Nebel, III, Denney G. Rutherford, and Jeffrey D. Schaffer

Three important, and we believe permanent, trends call for a reexamination of hotels' organizational structures. The first trend is the increasingly competitive environment of the hotel industry in all market segments and all geographic regions. While some temporary aberrations may result in less competition, the forces that are shaping the hotel industry dictate that intense competition in all market segments will be the rule and not the exception.

The second trend is the increasing demands guests are placing on hotels. This is part of a worldwide trend of consumers demanding more value for the goods and services they purchase. More-demanding customers require that hotels meet or exceed guest expectations to earn repeat business. Such customers coupled with intense competition means that successful hotels have to do what was once viewed as impossible: provide better service at lower prices.

It may not be possible to lower costs, provide better service at those lower prices, and become more efficient by relying on traditional methods, such as exhortations for harder work, traditional across-the-board cost cutting, and so-called downsizing. New ways of doing business may be the only answer to the challenge of providing more for less.

A third, promising trend is the tremendous increase in the sophistication, variety, and affordability of information technology available to hotels. Information technology is already helping hotels solve some of their operating problems. It also makes possible organizational changes that previously may have been unmanageable or impossible.

According to one industry analyst, businesses are facing a "permanent white-water world" where disruption will be the natural order (Wilson, 1994). In that competitive world, the companies that succeed will be the "game changers" who do things differently as a result of looking for novel solutions to problems, and who overcome the rigidities inherent in mature organizations.

Hotels and other hospitality organizations are not immune to the new business climate. Examples include the elimination of regional staffs; the elimination of front office managers; cutbacks in housekeeping, with housekeeping directors reporting directly to top management; the elimination of divisional managers; the consolidation of sales-manager responsibilities; and the consolidation of all guest-contact activities under a redesigned division called "operations."

At this time it is unclear whether those changes are traditional, albeit aggressive, attempts to contain overhead costs or the first glimmerings of a new organizational design. Given industrywide occupancy figures wallowing in the low sixties for the past few years, we suspect it is more the former than the latter. Nonetheless the effect is to illustrate at least some of the characteristics of a new organizational design.

TRADITIONAL "FUNCTIONAL ORGANIZATION"

Most small- and medium-size businesses, including hotels, have been organized in the same way for years. This common form is the functional organization. People who perform similar tasks or have similar skills are grouped together into one department. This way of organizing is based on the notion that greater productivity—that is, output per unit of labor input—can be achieved when workers specialize in just a few tasks or activities. The division of labor, where workers are assigned only one or a few specialized tasks and are provided with specialized tools or machines to help them perform those tasks, can result in greater output per worker than could be achieved by the same number of workers each working alone. According to Aldag and Stearns (1987) functional organizations share similar strengths and weaknesses.

FUNCTIONAL ORGANIZATION IN HOTELS

In a functional organizational design, each hotel department is organized narrowly around the particular function it is intended to perform. A detailed analysis of the organization, duties, and requisite skills of the members of each department would demonstrate a high degree of consistency of purpose, a logical hierarchy of positions, and a somewhat common body of skills. The narrow focus within each department fosters departmental efficiencies and clarity of departmental goals and career paths. However, owing to the narrow focus, many of the skills learned in one department are not easily transferable to other departments. Moreover, the narrow focus of departments also makes it difficult for members of one department to fully understand or appreciate the contributions of other departments.

Functional hotel departments can be depicted as watertight cylinders. Each department is designed to perform certain functions and has become efficient in channeling information and work both upward and downward within its cylinder.

The flow of information or the coordination of activities among cylinders tends to be difficult, however. Career paths are strictly within single departments, and as each becomes absorbed with its own activities, tasks, and goals, departmental viewpoints become more myopic and the opportunity for interdepartmental dispersion of ideas and cooperation becomes more difficult.

How well can this type of organization meet the operational needs of hotels? Before we can answer that question, we must first discuss the operating challenges hotels typically encounter.

The common characteristics and operating challenges of hotels include:

- The perishability of their product.
- The broad scope of the services provided to guests, and the wide variety of hotel staff, drawn from many different departments, needed to provide those services.
- The unpredictability of many of the problems hotels face.
- The need for quick action to resolve service breakdowns.
- The intangible nature of many hotel services.
- The need for service consistency.
- The fluctuations in occupancy and the consequent fluctuations in hotel activity levels.
- The fact that most service and customer contact takes place between guests and hourly employees.
- The relative inexperience and transience of hotel staff.

Hotels need to be flexible organizations capable of quickly responding to a wide variety of customer demands by calling on an array of human resources and service assets. Flexibility is key since hotels have to expect the unexpected, and coordinated action is important since customer demands are many and varied.

PROBLEMS OF FUNCTIONAL ORGANIZATION

The attributes of functional organization (see Figure 2.4) can actually make the efficient operation of hotels difficult, for the following reasons, among others.

FIGURE 2.4
Strengths and weaknesses attributed to functional organization

WEAKNESSES
- Central, slow decision making
- Unwieldy cross-function coordination
- Unclear responsibility for overall performance
- The need to coordinate cross-functional activities from the top
- Limited opportunity for training of general managers
- Stifled innovation

STRENGTHS
- Efficient resource use
- In-depth skill development
- Straightforward career paths
- Better coordination within departments

Central Decision Making

Authorization for purchases often must be signed by GMs, slowing down the response time for special needs (e.g., special equipment for upcoming banquets, replacement or repair of kitchen equipment). Because authorization to set room rates usually rests at the top, all negotiations generally must go through the GM. With sales and marketing having little authority to set rates, the result can be constant delays in the negotiation process.

Difficulty of Cross-Functional Coordination

The coordination of activities requiring the cooperation of more than one department represents a major organizational challenge for hotels. Property managers can cite a list of operating problems that seem never to be solved:

- The difficulty of coordinating the numerous services required of hotels by convention and meeting groups.
- Conflicts between the room-service and housekeeping departments as to whose responsibility it is to remove dishware from guest rooms and corridors.

- Guest-service problems with restaurant cashiers who report to the controller's office, and not to the food and beverage department.
- Kitchen equipment maintenance, which is the responsibility of the engineering department instead of being under the authority of the executive chef.
- Confusion (and differences) in goals set by the reservations department and the sales and marketing department.
- Differences between what catering sales promises and what the food and beverage department can deliver.
- Differences between what the sales department sells and what convention services can deliver.

The above examples illustrate that attempts to meet the overall goals of the hotel are often frustrated because more than one department is involved in the provision of a service or the accomplishment of a task.

Unclear Responsibility for Overall Performance

The specialization of sales effort by function leads to difficulty in determining overall responsibility and commissions. Consider room sales in a large hotel: The sales and marketing department may be organized around group sales (e.g., national associations, corporate meetings, incentive travel) and nongroup sales (e.g., tour and travel, business, pleasure), with different sales managers responsible for each specific market segment. In addition, the reservations department and the front desk also play an important role in room sales.

The Need to Coordinate Cross-Functional Activities from the Top

Because people work within the limits of their own departments, their knowledge of the functions and problems of other departments is limited. Managers in convention and banquet sales, lacking knowledge of culinary and service skills, might promise customers service that cannot be delivered.

Limited Opportunities for General-Management Training

Empirical evidence shows that hotel general managers in the United States follow career paths mostly within one department during their rise to GM (Nebel et al., 1995). Because of a lack of cross training within hotels, young managers have a thorough knowledge only of the major department in which they have worked and thus lack an overall perspective of the hotel. Consequently, many people do not learn what they need to know until after they have been promoted to general manager.

Stifled Innovation

Central decision making and coordination often results in a bureaucracy that focuses power in the hands of one or only a few people at the top of the organization. Suggestions by subordinates are often viewed as encum-

brances. Consider, for example, the time it has taken for hotels to adopt comprehensive management-information systems, and the delay in taking advantage of various energy-saving technologies. While airlines have developed sophisticated reservation systems that include seat reservations, special meals, and confirmed preboarding passes, guests at most hotels must still stand in line to check in even if they hold a reservation.

When the tendencies of a functional organization are compared with the operating challenges hotels face, many inconsistencies and misalignments become apparent. For example, hotels are continually confronted with unpredictable problems requiring rapid response, but they are organized in such a way as to foster slow, central decision making. The broad scope of a hotel's services requires the coordinated actions of many people; however, hotels are organized in such a way that coordinating the activities of functionally separated departments is difficult. And because many hotel services are intangible yet must be consistently high quality, a clear understanding of who is responsible for overall performance is important. Instead, traditional hotel organization leaves responsibility for overall performance unclear.

TRADITIONAL RESPONSES TO ORGANIZATION WEAKNESSES

How can hotels overcome the weakness of a functional organizational design? One obvious way is to select strong and effective general managers who are capable of monitoring and coordinating interdepartmental activities and arbitrating disputes. Thus the search for the "super general manager" is always going on. Of course, as hotels become larger and more complex, demands increase on general managers and may outstrip their ability to cope.

Another strategy to overcome functional organizations' weaknesses is to develop interdepartmental committees to help coordinate the activities of different departments that must work together. Properly designed interdepartmental committees improve communication among departments that serve each others' customers and provide a forum for averting problems. Committees foster direct communication among members of different departments, but they are also time-consuming and add an additional element of complexity to an already complex organization. In addition, while providing the opportunity for coordination and cooperation, they do not ensure it.

REENGINEERING THE ORGANIZATION

We now introduce a new way of viewing hotel organizations that holds the promise of overcoming many of the inherent weaknesses of a functional organization and, at the same time, is more in tune with the operational imperatives of the hospitality business. Our approach challenges the principle of division of labor. The fundamental premise of this reengineering is that hotels currently organized by departments around tasks should reunify those tasks into coherent business processes. Furthermore, arranging work into business processes will dictate what the organization will look like. Thus, to understand how the hotel of the future might be organized, it is necessary to approach the task indirectly by first understanding the concept of business processes and reengineering.

Reengineering Defined

Reengineering has been defined as "the *fundamental rethinking and radical redesign of business processes* to achieve *dramatic improvements* [emphasis added] in critical, contemporary measures of performance, such as cost, quality, service, and speed" (Hammer and Champy, 1993, p. 32).

   To understand reengineering, let's take a close look at its components.

1. *Fundamental rethinking* means asking questions concerning what a business does and how it does it, and questioning basic assumptions regarding the *why* and the *how* of a business.
2. *Radical redesign* means starting over, not fixing or improving what is already there. Existing job descriptions, organizational structures, procedures, and rewards may all be changed.
3. *Business processes* identified by reengineering are fundamentally different from the traditional departments of a business. Processes, simply stated, are what a business does for its customers. They are a logical collection of work that creates the business's product. The work that takes place in business processes (e.g., customer communication, product development, problem resolution) often requires input from people performing different tasks who, in traditional organizations, are located in different functional departments.
4. *Dramatic improvements* rather than marginal or incremental gains are characteristic of reengineering. A 12 percent decrease in guest checkout time is an incremental gain. Instant check-in/checkout procedures (or the elimination of check-in/checkout altogether) represent the kind of dramatic improvement reengineering seeks.

Naming Processes

It helps to understand the concept of business processes by giving them names that suggest their beginning and their end. For example, what might be named the employee recruitment and development process in a hotel would include the selection, indoctrination, initial training, placement, development, and evaluation of new workers. Those steps describe an understandable process that goes on constantly in hotels, although it may often be unnamed or invisible in the organization. More important, the process may also be unmanaged and unaccounted for in terms of setting goals and assigning responsibility.

Once the basic processes of a hotel are described it is possible to construct a *process map* that depicts how work flows within that hotel. As we pointed out earlier, typical organization charts depict formal reporting relationships and groupings of people according to the similarity of the tasks they perform. A process map, however, depicts logical groupings of the work an organization performs. The end result of this work could be products, services, or both. Similar to an industrial-engineering flow diagram, a process map describes, in terms of the work to be performed, what the hotel is trying to accomplish for its customers. For example, see Figure 2.5, which illustrates a process map for seeing to the arrival of a motor-coach tour group. Each box in Figure 2.5 identifies in basic terms the work and activities that need to be performed. Below each box are listed the traditional hotel functional departments from which staff would be drawn to perform the work activities.

In actual practice, much greater detail would be used to describe each activity and to make staff assignments. In addition, performance standards would be established to verify the successful completion of each activity. Nevertheless, even in the simplified form of Figure 2.5, it's possible to see how organizing staff functions around the arrival *process* will help to focus staff activities on customer-driven objectives.

Once hotel executives begin to think in terms of processes versus isolated functions, they may begin to discuss such issues as those presented in Figure 2.6, the principles of reengineering.

When reengineering takes place, the work of the people who are involved in business processes is altered, often radically. Part and parcel of reengineering business processes is deciding on the groupings of people into process teams, the unit around which the reengineered business is organized. Whereas traditional organizations grouped workers performing similar tasks, reengineered organizations group a variety of workers into process teams.

FIGURE 2.5
Group-business process map

Example illustrated: Bus-tour group
The traditional hotel functional departments noted below each activity must cooperate and communicate with each other to accomplish the tasks at hand.

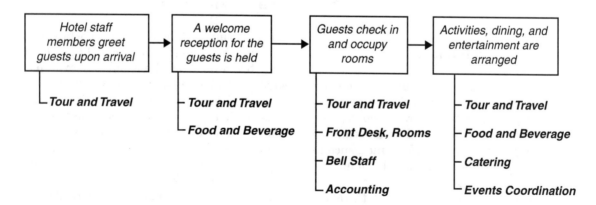

FIGURE 2.6
Principles of reengineering

- Work is best organized around desired outcomes, not around tasks.
- People with different skills and responsibilities should be grouped into process teams that are capable of achieving desired outcomes.
- Information should flow directly to where it is needed, unfiltered by a managerial hierarchy.
- There should be as few people as possible working in a business process, so several jobs may be combined into one.
- The steps in a business process must be completed in their natural order and performed where they make the most sense.
- Decisions should be made by workers knowledgeable about the process.
- Processes may have multiple versions depending on customers' needs.
- The checking and controlling of processes should be minimized, but not the accountability.
- Eliminating the causes of customer complaints, rather than simply improving reconciliation, is the goal.
- A "case manager" can be used as a single point of contact with the customer.
- The process should be kept simple, while allowing the jobs within the process to become complex.

STEPS TO REENGINEERING

The following steps are instrumental to reengineering hotel operations (Furey, 1993):

1. Identify process objectives from customers' perspective.
2. Understand existing process.
3. Benchmark.
4. Reengineer the process.
5. Implement the new process.

Step 1: Identify process objectives from customers' perspective.   Work is always performed for a customer, either internal or external to the business. Examples of customer-driven objectives are low prices, quick service, and a variety of service options. Traditional systems concentrate on currently existing processes, with the goal of improving what is already there. This gives little thought to the underlying assumptions regarding what the customer really wants. For example, are guests interested in checking out of (or checking into) hotels faster, or would they really like to dispense completely with the need to do either? Hammer and Champy (1993, pp. 130–132) suggest asking questions to better understand customer needs:

- What are their real as opposed to superficial needs?
- Do they really want what they say they want?
- How do they use your output and what processes do they perform on that output?
- What are their underlying goals?

One does not usually get creative or novel answers to those questions from customers themselves. When they are asked for suggestions for improvements, customers usually respond in terms of current processes and current assumptions, leading to incremental improvements of existing service.

Once customer needs are fully understood, it's time to look at how a hotel's existing processes meet those needs. Some hotel guests, for example, may be happy to bypass the front desk if they are frequent travelers or have no special requests regarding their room or credit status. Airport-limousine drivers or bell staff could be trained to handle simple check-ins, assign rooms, code keys, and update room inventories using laptop computers. Airlines have been using skycaps in this way for years.

Step 2: Understand existing process. Since reengineering will result in radically different processes, it is not necessary to study existing process in great detail. Instead the goal is to understand the reasons for the process (Hammer and Champy, p. 130). Observing and performing the existing process is the best way to really understand it. One way to better understand an existing process is to engage in "benchmarking."

Step 3: Benchmark.   Benchmarking entails learning from the best practices of successful firms without regard to whether those businesses are hospitality related. To make order-of-magnitude improvements, companies should benchmark from the best in the world, not just the best in their industry. For example, hotels might benchmark American Airlines for the best practices in yield management, IBM for customer-complaint processes, and W. L. Gore and Associates for examples of employee empowerment.

Step 4: Reengineer the process.   A good place to begin reengineering is by restating the problems that led to the decision to reengineer a process in the first place. After a brief review of the current process, including its cost, cycle time, results, and how it is or is not meeting customer needs, reengineering may proceed by:

- Identifying and destroying erroneous assumptions.
- Applying one or more of the principles of reengineering.
- Creatively using technology, including information technology, whenever possible.

Widely held assumptions in an organization are often vestiges that have lost their validity. Process teams need to make explicit the assumptions that drive current business practices and then challenge them. It wasn't many years ago, for example, that everyone assumed an attendant was needed to pump gas into motorists' cars.

Step 5: Implement the new process. Reengineered processes cause fundamental changes in organizational relationships and goals. Reward systems, job descriptions, management tasks, criteria for promotions, and other important human-resources aspects can be expected to change with reengineering. As a result, stress, uncertainty, and fear can accompany the reorganization. For this reason, although a business process can be reengineered in about six months, its implementation may take much longer.

REENGINEERING HOTEL PROCESSES

The following is an example of how one hotel-business process might be developed and how, as a result, a hotel's organization can begin to change. Many hotels attract a sufficient number of conventions and large-group meetings to suggest that those properties might consider reorganizing around the actual work that must be done to host those kinds of guests successfully, rather than around traditional functional departments.

To get the new approach off the ground, a hotel reengineering team would spend time developing a detailed large-group-business process map. The result will be clear evidence that virtually every hotel department is involved with group business in one way or another. Next the reengineering team evaluates the hotel's known performance shortcomings with regard to large-group business that may result in inconsistent group (customer) satisfaction.

Next, before specific-process teams can be implemented, the reengineering team should start revising job descriptions throughout the hotel, reevaluating procedures and reward programs, and learning how to apply information technology creatively. The ultimate goal of all this prep work is to eliminate the difficulties of coordinating large events that are created by staff members who may have divided departmental loyalties and allegiances, or who are receiving different instructions from different sources.

The approach to group business that the hotel is heading for is to consider each piece of large-group business as an individual "project," one that requires a team of people to be drawn together for a period of time to complete the project cooperatively. Such teams are common in the construction, advertising, and motion-picture industries.

Individuals from the hotel's various departments are organized into a large-group-business process team and are given complete responsibility for the success of specific clients' large-group business and events. Working toward its clearly stated process-specific goals, the team is self-contained and possesses the resources and authority to get the job done well.

When all of the process teams of a hotel are specified for the various projects and challenges that any hotel faces, there will likely be some workers and managers who are members of more than one team (e.g., kitchen and wait staff). In addition, certain support groups (e.g., engineering and computer-systems sup-

port) may be needed that do not fit the strict definition of a process team.

REENGINEERING AND CHANGE

Successfully reengineered organizations will change along the lines given in Figure 2.7 and can expect to reap the benefits listed in Figure 2.8. As reengineering causes business processes to become the dominant concern of a hotel, jobs change, organizations are structured by process teams, management systems and performance measures become customer-driven, and basic values and beliefs are altered or trashed, and new ones are created. Most importantly, firms that engage in reengineering report dramatic improvements in employee performance and customer satisfaction.

The principles of reengineering we discussed here are already influencing organizational redesign in other industries and are being experimented with by a number of major hotel companies, including Ritz-Carlton, ITT Sheraton, and Radisson. The environmental conditions faced by hotels present serious economic challenges that suggest the need for bold new approaches to doing business in the hospitality industry, too.

FIGURE 2.7
How organizations change when reengineered

- Fundamental work units change from functional, task-driven departments to process teams.
- Organizational structures change from hierarchical (pyramids) to flat.
- Jobs within process teams become multidimensional.
- Workers become empowered to make decisions.
- Job preparation shifts from training to education.
- Performance is measured by results that are customer-based rather than task-oriented.
- Executives change from checkers and arbitrators to leaders and facilitators.
- Advancement is based on ability rather than on past performance.
- Employees and departments become less protective of their turf and more productive.

FIGURE 2.8
Benefits of Reengineering

- Employees are organized into teams where the work focuses exclusively on customer-driven outcomes.
- Team performance is measured by customer-based criteria.
- Teams are able to coordinate their activities without the need for outside intervention.
- Decisions are made where the work is being performed.
- Executives become facilitators and leaders rather than checkers and arbitrators.
- Dramatic improvements in output measures are possible, whereas traditional approaches offer, at best, incremental gains.

2.5 Case Study: Organization

THE WICKMAN HOTEL

Gene Larkin, managing director and 60 percent owner—his family trust owns the remaining 40 percent—was contemplating the future of the Wickman Hotel.

The Wickman is a 450-room property in downtown St. Louis, Missouri. It has been remodeled in the last two years and was recently awarded a fourth Mobil star recognizing the quality of its furniture, fixtures, and equipment (FF&E); its food service; its facilities; and its management sensitivity to providing the correct "ambience" to its target clientele, the frequent business traveler. While the Wickman does feature a ballroom and meeting space, it has never specifically targeted the meetings and conventions market, preferring to focus on corporate guests who are generally more individually valuable in terms of average transient rate (ATR) and food and beverage (F&B) expenditures.

Throughout the early 1990s the Wickman has enjoyed good financial success. Its average annual occupancy percentage has been in the low seventies for the last three years, and revenue-producing department profit margins have generally been around acceptable figures.

With all this good news, Larkin wonders why he has some nagging worries about the Wickman's future. Among these worries is a tendency of each hotel department to increase staff—especially non-guest-contact staff—and with this, a corollary increase in overhead costs.

These increases in overhead have not been particularly burdensome but have been a steady trend of three to four points above inflation for the last five years. To this point, Larkin and his management staff have produced more revenue through additional sales and careful price increases to maintain profit levels. Because of new properties in the St.

Louis area, though, the market will be more competitive in the immediate future, and until markets can be expanded and demand grown, the Wickman faces a potential squeeze on profits.

Larkin, who has been with the hotel since his teenage years, does not want to do anything as drastic as laying staff off but recognizes the growth in overhead and non-guest-contact staff needs to be either stopped or reversed. He is also loathe to make all of these sorts of decisions by himself, preferring to seek input from the department-level operating managers who will have to manage whatever changes are decided upon.

As he contemplates the makeup of the ad hoc committee he will form to chart a new organizational path for the Wickman, Larkin decides the committee should be driven by three fundamental criteria:

- There will be no diminution of service to the Wickman's guests.
- The Wickman will do nothing to jeopardize its four-star rating.
- Hotel employees will not be terminated, except as a last resort, and only then on the basis of merit and productivity.

Case One

Determine for Mr. Larkin who should be on the ad hoc committee to study the problem. Included should be a complete rationale for each manager's inclusion, explaining what expertise and knowledge his or her departmental role can contribute to the committee's tasks.

Case Two

Explain and discuss a number of alternative solutions you think the ad hoc committee would propose. In doing this, remain true to any assumptions you made in case one *and* the three fundamental criteria set forth by Larkin.

Choose one of these alternatives and elaborate on its potential positive and negative effects on the Wickman, its employees, and its guests.

References

Aldag, Ramon J., and Timothy M. Stearns. 1987. *Management*. Cincinnati: South-Western Publishing Co.

Conlin, Joseph. 1989. "Management Strategy: Get Control!" *Successful Meetings* 38(7):37–42.

Dale, Ernest. 1967. *Organization*. New York: American Management Association, p. 9.

Dann, D., and Timothy Hornsey. 1986. "Towards a Theory of Interdepartmental Conflict in Hotels." *International Journal of Hospitality Management* 5:23.

Furey, Timothy R. 1993. "A Six-Step Guide to Process Reengineering." *Planning Review*, March–April, pp. 20–23.

Hammer, Michael, and James Champy. 1993. *Reengineering the Corporation*. New York: HarperBusiness.

Hosansky, Mel. 1989. "Meetings Give You a Leg up the Corporate Ladder." *Successful Meetings* 38(5):51–52.

Nebel, Eddystone C., III; Lee Ju-Soon; and Brani Vidakovic. 1995. "Hotel General Manager Career Paths in the United States." *International Journal of Hospitality Management* 14(3–4):245–260.

Pelletier, Ray. 1988. "Overnight Success Takes Some Time." *HSMAI Marketing Review* 7(1):16–20.

Scott, W. G., and T. R. Mitchell. 1976. *Organization Theory: A Structural and Behavioral Analysis*. Homewood, IL: Richard D. Irwin., Inc.

Stoner, James A., and Charles Wankel. 1986. *Management*. Englewood Cliffs, NJ: Prentice-Hall, pp. 233-234.

Wilson, Larry. 1994. "Changing the Game," presentation to the International Association of Conference Centers, March 19, 1994, Williamsburg, VA.

Suggested Readings

Books

Nebel, Eddystone C., III. 1991. *Managing Hotels Effectively: Lessons from Outstanding General Managers*. New York: Van Nostrand Reinhold.

Articles

Pondy, L.R. 1967. "Organizational Conflict: Concepts and Models." *Administrative Science Quarterly* 12:296–320.

Schaffer, Jeffrey D. 1984. "Strategy, Organization Structure, and Success in the Lodging Industry." *International Journal of Hospitality Management* 3(4):159–165.

Schaffer, Jeffrey D. 1985. "A Dynamic Model of Organizational Performance in the Lodging Industry: The Role of Competitive Strategy and Organization Structure." *Proceedings*. CHRIE Conference, Seattle, WA, pp. 168–173.

Source Notes

Chapter 2.2, "Organizational Design," by Eddystone C. Nebel, III.

Chapter 2.3, "As I See It: Hotel Organization Structure," by Mark Conklin.

Chapter 2.4, "Reengineering the Hotel Organization," by Eddystone C. Nebel, III, Denney G. Rutherford, and Jeffrey D. Schaffer, is reprinted from the October 1994 issue of *The Cornell Hotel and Restaurant Administration Quarterly*. © Cornell University. Used by permission. All rights reserved.

3

General Managers: A View at the Top

3.1   Introduction

In most companies someone who has attained the title of general manager or something similar heads the organization. It is generally considered the acme of one's career for most of us in the hotel field. In many hotel companies the job of general manager (GM) is one that serves as the springboard to corporate jobs for some, and larger and more prestigious properties for others.

In this part of the second edition of this book, I said it was surprising how very little has been written about hotel general managers. Little structured attention had been paid to specifically how these managers' career have developed and to what sorts of skills and strengths they bring to their jobs. Strangely, this is still the case.

In a 1981 article by Arnaldo, a statistical profile of hotel general managers was presented. Arnaldo drew a demographic picture of his sample of 194 and went on to comment that although the GMs changed jobs frequently, they reported a high degree of job satisfaction. He also provided an analytical framework for reporting how these GMs allocated time and importance to a number of classic managerial roles. The most important of these managerial roles ranked by the GMs were (in descending importance): leader, entrepreneur, monitor, and disseminator, with six others (figurehead, liaison, spokesman, disturbance handler, resource allocator, and negotiator) assuming less importance (see also Mintzberg, 1973).

If Arnaldo's article is read (see references at the end of this part), the reader may be struck by some of the similarities that echo through Nebel and Ghei's contribution to this part (see below). Another useful comparison can be made by reading Arnaldo's work with that of David Ley (1980, see suggested readings). This work, based on a small sample of seven GMs in comparable properties in one hotel company, recorded how much time the GMs allocated to the same managerial work roles (Mintzberg, 1973). The difference here was that Ley asked for a corporate-office rating of each GM's effectiveness. The effectiveness ratings (*highly effective, effective*, and *less effective*) were then compared to the observed time allocations of the GMs to leadership and entrepreneurial activities. Ley concluded that in this small group, the more highly effective managers spent more time on *entrepreneurial* activities than *leadership* activities. Contrasting Arnaldo's much larger group, who devoted much more time to leadership roles than entrepreneurial, should pose for the reader some interesting questions about what sorts of activities might best prepare future GMs for that role.

This makes the Nebel and Ghei piece all the more interesting, for while still a small group, these GMs were studied intensely, and the authors propose a structural framework from which to view the job of GM.

A central aspect of career development among GMs is explored in the suggested reading article by Rutherford and Wiegenstein (1985), which looked for the first time at the role of mentoring as it could be measured to affect the success and satisfaction of a modern hotel GM's career.

Although the demographic, salary, and operational data in that article are out of date, the focus of that research can still be useful to those who aspire to this top job in a hotel organization. Also, because the literature on hotel GMs is so sparse, the insights gained from the managers studied in this case add some "flesh and tone" to the work of the other authors included in this section. In the mentoring research, Rutherford and Wiegenstein conclude that there is ample evidence that seeking out and developing mentoring relationships can have positive impacts on several aspects of a GM's career; see also the contribution by Melenie Lankau on mentoring in the human resources section (Part IX) of this edition.

Another view of career and personal aspects of the GM's job is discussed in the suggested reading by Pavesic and Brymer (1990). In a

number of studies in recent years, they have looked at the roles job satisfaction and stress play on managerial careers. In a review of this technical research, the authors provide interpretations about the behavioral dimensions of the GM's career, work values, and personal challenges. Hotel careers are challenging, but as these researchers point out, they do not have to be arduous.

In the research reported by Woods, Schmidgall, Sciarini, and me we sought answers to questions regarding the importance of various operational measures, and at the same time asked about what suggestions the GMs would have as to the structure of a hotel-related education. Students reading this article will find solid suggestions from successful GMs, as the sample for the study was drawn from mostly upscale and luxury hotels with more than 500 rooms.

Speaking of success, the two GMs who contribute their thoughts on the job of GM have attained that level in separate areas of the country and for two different organizations.

Emilio Fabico is the GM of the Rosen Centre Hotel in Orlando, Florida. At 1300 rooms, the Rosen is a large, very busy convention hotel in one of the most popular destinations in the world. Speaking through his writing like he was a guest in your class, Mr. Fabico shares his insights about this fascinating job.

In its own way Las Vegas is also a wildly successful resort and convention destination. Rob Balmer's hotel, a Doubletree Club Hotel, is part of the Hilton family of hotel products. On a daily basis, he leads his hotel in dealing with all of the challenges implicit in the GM's job, but overlaid with the atmosphere of the largest gambling (they call it *gaming*) resort complex in the world. His view of this job in this area is fascinating.

From an academic standpoint, the Nebel and Ghei contribution can be considered the overarching theory guiding the hotel GM's job. Woods et al. apply that theory to determine how it works in practice. Fabico and Balmer in their contributions provide us with the insights of insiders and some clear evidence that the "theory" actually works. This is my goal for this edition of this book: to provide the reader with the opportunity to see that there should be a connection between the "book learning" from the classroom and what happens in the "real world."

Someone who exemplifies that goal is Matt Berge, the director of operations at the Westin Galleria Hotel in Dallas. Mr. Berge is completing probably the most important step in his career progression to hotel GM. In his essay, you will see being played out many of the "theories" that have been presented earlier in this section and elsewhere in this book. When he expresses his affection for this industry, you can draw direct lines to the knowledge, experience, and training he has accumulated over his professional life. Berge is another, like Emilio Fabico and Rob Balmer, who are living the theory of hotel general managers.

3.2   A Conceptual Framework of the Hotel General Manager's Job

Eddystone C. Nebel, III, and Ajay Ghei

Major hotels of today are diverse, multifaceted, and fast-paced businesses, engaged in a wide variety of operational activities. Their organizational and operational complexity increases with size. A hotel, irrespective of whether it is an independent or part of a chain, can be managed as a separate, independent business entity. Thus each individual hotel can, in effect, be treated as a unique profit center. While it takes more than one person to effectively manage a hotel, the executive with overall operational responsibility for this business is the general manager (GM) of the hotel. "The general manager is the key implementer of the business strategy for the property and the behavioral role model for the entire management team" (Eder and Umbreit, 1989, p. 333). It can thus be argued that the GM is the central management figure in the hotel business. The demands and challenges of managing hotels are reflected in the complexities of the GM's job.

This chapter takes a close look at the context in which GMs of major hotels work and how this context affects the nature of their job. It is based on the research of one of the authors (Nebel, 1991) into the managerial effectiveness of hotel GMs. The purpose of the research was, in part, to better understand the nature of the GM's job, and through this understanding develop a conceptual framework of it. As Dann (1990) has stated, "... there is now a need to ... develop a conceptual framework for the better understanding of the actual nature of managerial work in the hospitality industry."

Ten extremely successful GMs of some of America's finest hotels agreed to participate in the study. Each of the GMs studied was an experienced, top-rated hotel executive with an average of ten years' experience in the position. One research goal was to study hotels that exhibited the fullest range of operational and managerial complexity. Thus, the smallest participating hotel was an internationally renowned luxury property of about 400 rooms, and the largest was a great convention hotel of nearly 2000 rooms. The author stayed as a guest at each hotel; observing each GM for three days, as he proceeded through his normal workday, and recording his every activity. The research methodology followed closely

FIGURE 3.1
Influences that shape the general manager's job

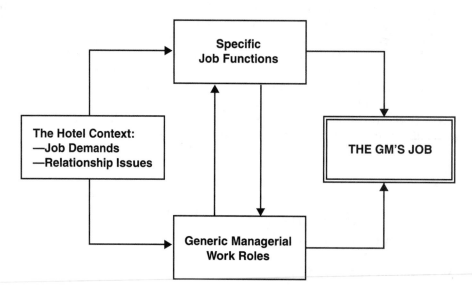

that employed by Kotter (1982). It employed a combination of participant observation of GMs at work, extensive personal interviews with both the GMs and 53 of their key division heads, background surveys, and analysis of organizational and operational information from each hotel. The personal interviews extended over a number of days and took between four and six hours with each GM, and about one hour with each of their division heads. In addition, informal interviews were conducted with at least 100 other executives and employees of the ten hotels. The field research was conducted while on sabbatical leave and resulted in over 700 pages of field notes, which were subjected to extensive qualitative data analysis.

From this analysis and from an exhaustive review of the literature on managerial work in hotels (Guerrier, 1987; Guerrier and Lockwood, 1991; Koepper, 1988; Ley, 1978; Shortt, 1989; Umbreit, 1986) there has emerged a view of the hotel GM's job that is given in Figure 3.1, which presents a model of the influences that shape the GM's job. The

model in Figure 3.1 incorporates ideas found in the research of Kotter (1982) and Mintzberg (1973). Kotter (1982, pp. 10–33) showed how job demands and relationship demands affect executive behavior. Mintzberg (1973, pp. 55–99) described ten separate work roles that managers perform. Figure 3.1 reflects how the hotel context influences the various job functions and managerial work roles GMs must perform in order to be effective.

The two major contextual elements of the GM's job that affect the specific job functions and the generic managerial work roles are job demands and relationship issues. These job demands and relationship issues, depending on whether they relate to the short-run, the intermediate-run, or the long-run time frame, give rise to certain specific job functions. They also suggest in general the various managerial work roles GMs are required to perform. It is the symbiosis between these specific GM job functions and the generic managerial work roles that actually defines the GM's job. We now proceed to discuss each of the elements described in Figure 3.1.

JOB DEMANDS AND RELATIONSHIP ISSUES

Table 3.1 lists key GM job demands and relationship issues according to whether they relate to a hotel's short-run, intermediate-run, or long-run time frame. The structure for this table has been adapted from Kotter's study of managerial behavior (Kotter, 1982, pp. 10–33).

The Short Run

The short-run demands on hotel GMs revolve around the daily, ongoing, operational issues of providing quality guest service, controlling costs, and maximizing revenues. Hotel GMs bear direct responsibility for their properties and thus, like operational managers in charge of profit centers anywhere, are under tremendous pressure to produce short-run results.

They must therefore devote a substantial amount of their time and efforts toward exercising effective operational control. An important functional characteristic of hotels is that many of their day-to-day business problems have extremely short lead times. That is to say, most service-centered problems in hotels must be solved quickly or not at all. Moreover, major hotels are both organizationally and operationally complex businesses in which numerous, highly diverse activities take place constantly as well as concomitantly.

To stay on top of this complicated short lead-time business is unquestionably the single most challenging and demanding aspect of the GM's job. To be able to do so effectively and in a proactive manner so as to retain the ability to influence events, GMs must engage in intense, verbal communication and interact frequently with subordinates. In discharging these responsibilities, a hotel GM can be said

TABLE 3.1
Key job demands and relationship issues of hotel GMs

Time Frame	Key Job Demands	Key Relationship Issues
Short Run	Day-to-day operational control of service, costs, and revenues. Intense pressure to earn profits and render quality service.	Intense and frequent downward, internal, verbal communication and interaction with hotel subordinates.
Intermediate Run	Train and develop subordinates. Fine-tune hotel's service strategy to changing external environment. Develop and refine the organization structure.	Downward internal communication. Lateral communication with the external environment. Upward communication with corporate superiors and staff specialists, or owners.
Long Run	Capital expenditure decisions in line with hotel's strategic service vision. Develop and sustain organizational stability and vitality.	Downward internal communication to further stability and vitality. Lateral communication with the external environment. Intense upward communication with corporate office or owners.

to be performing the job function of operational controller. However, the heavy workload of short-run operational demands must not take up all the time of GMs as they need to also concentrate on intermediate-run and long-run demands and issues.

The Intermediate Run

In addition to their involvement in daily operational issues, effective GMs must train and develop subordinates as well as formulate plans and programs that systematically improve their operational control over the hotel. As changes take place in the external environment, GMs must adapt and fine-tune the hotel's service strategy and organizational structure on an ongoing basis to keep abreast of these changes. These initiatives represent a proactive response to the operational demands of the business; they take time to implement, and comprise the bulk of intermediate-run demands faced by a hotel GM. These intermediate-run demands, then, are concerned with putting into place a hotel's organizational structure, systems, and people that are capable of quick and effective response to external stimuli and that can simultaneously help the hotel meet its demanding daily operational commitments. Thus, in effect, the GM is fine-tuning the hotel's service strategy and refining and realigning its operating systems in order to ensure a smoothly functioning business.

All these efforts require intense, downward, internal communication and a high degree of interaction with subordinates. In addition, intermediate-run job demands require the GM to develop communication channels and to nurture relationships that extend beyond the specific domain of the hotel. These relationships include, first, a wide-ranging network of hospitality industry and community contacts the GM needs in order to better understand the hotel's external environment, and, second, the GM's corporate superiors and staff

specialists whose cooperation is needed to enable the successful implementation of the formulated specific plans and programs for the hotel. In carrying out these responsibilities, the job function of a hotel GM can be referred to as that of organizational developer.

The Long Run

Two important long-run demands of a GM's job relate to seeing to the capital needs and the organizational stability of the hotel. Capital expenditure decisions are required in order to ensure the long-run viability of the hotel and therefore must be consistent with the hotel's strategic service vision. The other important long-run demand of GMs is the need to develop a degree of organizational stability and vitality that is also in tune with the hotel's carefully planned and clearly defined strategic service vision.

The key relationship issues for long-run capital expenditure decisions are communications upward with corporate executives or owners and laterally with an assortment of industry and community contacts as sources for intelligence concerning the hotel's competitive operating environment. Developing organizational stability depends on an ongoing program of human resources training and development, and sequential career progression. Many of the human resource programs that foster intermediate-run goals will ultimately benefit long-run organizational stability and vitality.

Organizational stability enables a hotel to consistently deliver quality service and effectively control day-to-day operations. Organizational stability and vitality also give the hotel the maturity and experience that is required to allow it to rethink its basic marketing and service strategies in the event of altered market or environmental conditions. Finally, it permits the hotel to make any required transition with minimal disruption to its regular operational practices. Key relationship issues associated with organizational stability include continual monitoring of the external environment, and intensive, downward, internal communication within the hotel. In fulfilling these responsibilities, the GM's job function can be described as that of business maintainer.

ROLES PLAYED BY A GM

This section is organized around Mintzberg's study (1973), in which he suggested ten generic work roles for managers. Mintzberg grouped these ten work roles under three broad categories: interpersonal, informational,

and decisional. Interpersonal work roles included those of figurehead, leader, and liaison; informational work roles covered those of monitor, disseminator, and spokesman; and the decisional work roles were those of disturbance handler, entrepreneur, resource allocator, and negotiator. A brief description of these ten generic managerial work roles is given in Table 3.2.

The influence of Mintzberg's work is reflected in the studies of hotel GMs by Arnaldo (1981) and Ley (1978), and that of restaurant managers by Ferguson and Berger (1984). The previous section explained how job demands and relationship issues had an impact on the

TABLE 3.2
Generic managerial work roles

Work Role	Description
Interpersonal	
Figurehead	Symbolic head of the organization. Required to perform certain legal activities and attend to social activities.
Leader	Responsible for staffing, training, direction, and motivation of subordinates.
Liaison	Develops a network outside the organization to gather information.
Informational	
Monitor	Seeks and analyzes a wide variety of outside information (from liaison role) and inside information (from leader role).
Disseminator	Transmits information received both from outside and inside the organization to other members of the organization.
Spokesperson	Transmits information about the organization to outsiders.
Decisional	
Disturbance Handler	Takes corrective action whenever organization faces unexpected, nonroutine disturbances.
Entrepreneur	Looks for ways to change the organization for the better. Seeks information externally and internally for improvement ideas. Initiates and supervises improvement projects.
Resource Allocator	Responsible for allocating all important resources of the organization, both financial and human, including how the manager schedules own time, programs work, and authorizes actions.
Negotiator	Responsible for the organization's major outside negotiations.

job functions of GMs. It was from that discussion that we proposed the three specific GM job functions of operational controller, organizational developer, and business maintainer. Each of these three job functions requires GMs to perform various managerial work roles in order to be successful. Combining the various *managerial work roles* with the specific *job functions* helps provide a clearer understanding of the GM's job. These relationships are shown in Table 3.3.

Although the GMs studied were observed performing each of Mintzberg's ten managerial work roles, the Interpersonal roles of Leader and Liaison; the Informational roles of Monitor and Disseminator; and the Decisional roles of Disturbance Handler, Entrepreneur, and Resource Allocator were found to be of particular significance. These roles were performed regularly as GMs carried out their various job functions. We now proceed to describe the managerial work roles most often performed by GMs while discharging their three primary job functions.

Managerial Work Roles as Operational Controller

The GM's work as operational controller is characterized by a high degree of involvement in the daily operations of the hotel. Because the activities of a hotel are both numerous and diverse, GMs must be constantly *monitoring* and *disseminating* detailed information pertaining to daily operational matters. Time and again throughout the course of the working day GMs will interact with a variety of subordinates to stay on top of the numerous operational problems that occur. GMs must also be available to effectively and quickly *handle disturbances* that are either not covered by a hotel's routine procedures, or those that subordinates perceive as being beyond their scope

TABLE 3.3
Combining managerial work roles and job functions in defining the GM's job

Time Horizon	GM Job Function	GM Managerial Roles
Short Run	Operational Controller	• Monitor and Disseminator (of internal information) • Disturbance Handler • Resource Allocator (of own time) • Leader
Intermediate Run	Organizational Developer	• Liaison • Monitor and Disseminator (of both external and internal information) • Entrepreneur • Resource Allocator (of own time, programs, and funds) • Leader
Long Run	Business Maintainer	• Liaison • Monitor and Disseminator (of external and internal information) • Resource Allocator (of programs and funds) • Entrepreneur • Leader

of authority or experience. In order to effectively play this managerial work role of disturbance handler, GMs must have rapid access to reliable internal information and, in turn, be able to quickly process and disseminate this information downward in the organization. While functioning as operational controller the GM's work role as *resource allocator* revolves mostly around the allocation of his or her own time to the numerous short-run demands of the job. GMs can, of course, allocate a proportion of their hotel's financial and human resources to help solve short-run operational problems; but it is the manner in which they allocate their own scarce time that is of paramount importance when referring to the short-run operational problems of the job.

GMs perform the *leader* role through every contact with subordinates. Every action of a GM will be analyzed and interpreted by subordinates; thus every interaction with subordinates provides GMs with an opportunity to exercise leadership (Hales and Nightingale 1986). That is why outstanding GMs realize they are constantly in the limelight all through the duration of the working day. GMs also exercise leadership by deciding the operational issues on which to concentrate. Subordinates automatically look for clues regarding what GMs deem important; thus by deciding which operational issues to focus on, GMs send an unequivocal message downward in the organization regarding what they consider important.

Managerial Work Roles as Organizational Developer

As organizational developer, the managerial work roles of GMs extend beyond the immediate confines of the hotel. GMs need to *monitor* information about both the community and the competitive environment; this requires them to become a *liaison* between the hotel and the outside world. Further, the informa-

tion GMs gather from the external environment needs to be analyzed and *disseminated* to subordinates within the hotel. Both externally and internally obtained information must be processed by GMs in order to effectively play the work role of *entrepreneur,* the importance of which has been stressed by Ley (1978). As entrepreneurs, GMs are the developer of specific plans and programs geared to improve the operating efficiency and service strategy of the hotel. Any new plan or program imposes additional time obligations on both the GM and on subordinates. Furthermore, new plans and programs often involve the allocation of financial and human resources, as well. Therefore in the course of developing and implementing these specific plans and programs for the hotel, GMs play the decisional work role of *resource allocator.*

Finally, the GM continues in the *leader* work role by virtue of, first, continuing relationships with subordinates as an integral component of the job and, second, by choosing which specific plans and programs to implement. As leader, the GM must contend with the challenge of ensuring that subordinates fully accept the plans and programs outlined for the hotel and are committed to work toward their successful implementation. This requires that the GM pay careful attention to the work roles of monitor and disseminator of information.

Managerial Work Roles as Business Maintainer

The final job function of business maintainer requires the GM to see to the long-run capital requirements, and organizational stability and vitality of the hotel. In seeking capital and planning a strategy for organizational stability and vitality, the GM's work roles of *liaison, monitor,* and *disseminator* of external and internal information upward to corporate executives or owners are critical, as is the work role of *resource allocator* of scarce financial resources. The resource allocator role, more often than not, requires detailed presentation of formal budget proposals that include careful financial justification. This is especially true if the GM is proposing a major directional shift in the service strategy of the hotel. As maintainer of organizational stability, the GM also plays the work role of disseminator of important information downward to subordinates. The GM must act as *entrepreneur* as regards important human resource development plans and programs and, as with all activities, continue as *leader* in the ongoing role of nurturing and developing managerial talent.

While GMs perform three different job functions with different time horizons, it is not necessarily the case that these job functions are performed independently of each other. That is to say, it is altogether possible for GMs to perform two or even all three job functions simultaneously. It is clear from Table 3.3 that many of the "Mintzbergian" managerial work roles are common to more than one job function. In fact, the work roles of monitor, disseminator, resource allocator, and leader are common to all three, while those of liaison and entrepreneur are common to two of the job functions. Thus, when GMs are engaged with short-run operational concerns they often do so in the context of longer-run considerations. For example, while responding to a short-run operational problem of slow guest check-ins (that is, functioning as operational controller), a GM may simultaneously be monitoring and evaluating the effectiveness of a front-desk clerk training program (that is, functioning as organizational developer). The GM may also be formulating a long-run plan to purchase an advanced front-office computer system (that is, functioning as business maintainer). The actual manner in which effective GMs perform this delicate balancing act is not covered here but will be the topic of another chapter.

CONCLUSION

A hotel GM's job can be better understood by examining the contextual variables that influence and help shape it. A hotel's context presents GMs with a series of job demands and relationship issues that they must deal with effectively in order to be successful. As seen, these job demands and relationship issues differ depending upon the time frame under consideration. These considerations give rise to specific job functions that GMs perform through a variety of work roles.

In the short run, the GM job function was described as that of operational controller. Here, GMs are involved with the day-to-day internal operational control of their businesses, requiring intense and frequent downward verbal communication within the hotel. They must be adept at the managerial work roles of monitoring and disseminating a wide variety of internal information, handling nonroutine disturbances, and allocating their own scarce time to important operational issues.

In the intermediate run, the GM job function was described as that of organizational developer. Here, GMs are faced with the challenges of developing subordinates, formulating specific plans and programs to improve their operational control of the hotel, and fine-tuning the hotel's service strategy in the context of external environmental conditions. In addition to internal downward communication, these challenges require intense lateral communication with both the hotel industry and local community sources. This helps the GM to stay abreast of market and environmental trends. The GM also maintains upward communication with corporate superiors and staff specialists to ensure their cooperation in the successful implementation of operational plans and programs. Here, the GM's work roles require them to monitor and disseminate external as well as internal information, thereby acting as liaison between the hotel and the outside world.

They also may initiate, as entrepreneurs would, the various plans and programs designed to improve the hotel's operational and organizational efficiency. This requires the allocation of their own time, as well as the financial and human resources of the hotel, to these plans and programs.

In the long run, the GM's job function was described as that of business maintainer. Here, GMs must ensure the long-term viability of the hotel through capital expenditure decisions that are consistent with the hotel's strategic service vision, and by developing a degree of organizational stability that allows the hotel to carry out its strategic plan. Intense upward communication to corporate superiors, staff specialists, and owners, as well as lateral communication with a wide variety of industry and community contacts highlight the relationship issues of this job function. GMs are required to play the work role of liaison between the hotel and corporate office or owners, as well as industry and community sources. This involves monitoring the widest variety of external and internal information and disseminating it laterally, downward, and upward. In addition, GMs play both the work role of resource allocator of capital funds as well as that of entrepreneur when seeing to the organizational stability of the business. All three job functions require GMs to be leaders, a work role they play through every contact with subordinates. Finally, these job functions need not and often are not performed independently of each other.

Three important conclusions about the GM's job can be drawn from this analysis:

1. By their very nature, major hotels of today provide GMs with a variety of challenges that require careful attention be paid to short-run, intermediate-run, and long-run time-frame issues. Thus, GMs must be able to successfully carry out three separate and different job functions. They must be effec-tive as operational controllers, organizational developers, and business maintainers if they are to enjoy long-term success as effective GMs.

2. To be effective at all three job functions requires that GMs perform a large variety of managerial work roles. While GMs perform all ten of Mintzberg's managerial work roles, they must be particularly effective at seven of them to be successful operational controllers, organizational developers, and business maintainers. They must develop the wide variety of skills necessary to play the work roles of leader, liaison, monitor, disseminator, disturbance handler, entrepreneur, and resource allocator.

3. The importance of communications in the hotel GM's job becomes apparent from this analysis. Every job function and every managerial work role carries with it a communications requirement. GMs must be adept at gathering, analyzing, and disseminating external and internal information, and they must be able to effectively communicate laterally, downward, and upward. Without good communication skills, GMs cannot possibly be effective in any of their three job functions (Worsfold, 1989).

Today's major hotels are complex businesses engaged in a wide variety of activities. The demands of managing these businesses are reflected in the complexities of the GM's job. To be effective at their job, hotel GMs must understand the key job demands and relationship issues hotels thrust upon them. They must perform three separate job functions that relate to different time frames. To do this they must become adept at a number of different managerial work roles, depending on the job function they are performing. Finally, hotel GMs must become accomplished communicators if they are to effectively meet the variety of challenges they face.

3.3   As I See It: The Hotel GM

Emilio Fabico

As I see it, my notion of what it's like to be a hotel general manager has gone through an evolution of sorts, and continues to do so. It all started in college. I can remember it very clearly. After classes, my classmates and I would retire to one of our favorite social watering holes and share our theories with one another on what the hospitality industry would be like in the future. What it would take to be successful? What our futures would hold? As graduation approached we were so hungry for it, we could taste it. Soon, we would be the men and women in the suits, in the elegant hotels. We knew what was in our future. Within a few short years, we were going to be general managers. Or so we thought.

As I worked my way through the servitude of entry-level management, I found myself looking at my GMs as the hotel patriarch— older, highly respected gentlemen that lived in their offices and had no first names. They were always Mr. Dolan or Mr. Franklin. They seemed so much older and wiser than I could ever be. And I began to find out from others, because one never really spoke to the GM, that it took them a fraction more than a few years to attain their positions. The goal that was palpable in college seemed quite a bit more distant now.

As the years passed, I temporarily lost sight of that GM target. I was focusing on the various management positions I held. Trying to survive the personal and professional twists and turns one encounters throughout one's life. Learning to deal with so many different people and situations. Being faced with unfamiliar challenges that often were slightly over my head. Being stressed to the point of often thinking that a career change was the only thing that the hotel business had in store for me. What I didn't realize then was that what I was experiencing was later going to be the most professionally valuable period of my ca-

reer. Through experience and observation, I was learning how to be a leader.

What I later discovered was that all of those experiences were a necessary part of my education and growth. By this I mean education and growth that never stop. Both good and bad experiences continue to provide me with lessons, as long as I look hard enough. I've found that managing a large hotel is like managing a small city, therefore I have found that being a general manager requires me to utilize every last one of those lessons I have learned and all the skills that I have been able acquire throughout the years. My job calls on me to be multidimensional. I interact with so many different people on so many different levels, I often have to be all things to all people.

To the owner, who in my case is a single individual, I must be a trusted steward of his investment. I must ensure that all of his assets—the hotel, his money, his employees, and his guests—are all well looked after and cared for. I must manage as if each of these assets were my own. I must cultivate new business, so that his investment will continue to grow. I must be a member of the community that favorably and accurately represents both our owner and his company. To the managers who report to me, I must provide the proper amount of timely support and leadership. I must be able to identify each of their needs and work to assist them in filling those needs. Not too unlike Oz—the man behind the curtain, who really doesn't impart anything that wasn't already there, rather helps others to recognize and apply their talents.

To our associates, I must lead by example. I must manage fairly and respectfully. I must always be prepared to assist my co-workers, whether it be to bus a table, to assist with a work-related problem, or just to be a good listener. I must be their advocate and be relentless in providing them with the tools and support to do the jobs that they were hired to do. I must remember every day that they are the lifeblood of the hotel, and treat them as such.

To our guests, I must ensure that our staff always works to meet or exceed their expectations. I must be the bottom line, the guest advocate, when it comes to their needs. After all, they are the ones that pay our salaries.

Now that I've fully pumped myself up, I have to say that what we do is not brain surgery. Quite frankly, the majority of it is common sense. In fact, my experience has led me to the conclusion that the key to success or failure can be summed up in two words. People skills. Sometimes in all the details, it's easy to lose sight of the reason that most of us originally became enamoured with our industry. People. The favorable interaction of which is critical to our success.

While people skills have always been important, I believe that in today's work setting, lack of strength in this area can be professionally fatal. With guest-service expectations greater than ever, one poor service experience can quickly deliver your guests into the hands of a waiting competitor, of which there are a growing number. With record-low unemployment, an associate that does not feel valued or treated with respect has no reason to tolerate such an environment. They can easily seek out and quickly find an organization that insists on a respectful and caring atmosphere. The potentially fragile relationships with these two entities, which completely make up our business, can be strengthened only through personal interaction. An effective leader must exemplify these skills and make it known that respectful treatment of people is a principle to embrace and be successful by. He or she must be intolerant of an environment or leadership that does not embrace this value. The successful leader is not an office person. That's not where the people are. He or she is out and about the property, interacting with those that he or she serves. I have sadly seen numerous successful "old school" managers lose their jobs because of their inability to grasp the importance of this value.

A few weeks ago, I was driving home from work when some people trying to change a flat tire flagged me down. The wrench they were using had broken, so they asked to borrow mine. While we worked on changing the tire, we chatted and I found out that three of the individuals were college interns working in a local hotel. They were walking home and saw a lady with a flat tire and decided to help. We had some great conversation while we completed our work. In the end, the woman that owned the car was extremely grateful to us and relieved that strangers would offer her assistance. As I drove home, I felt a sort of high—a sense of accomplishment that a group of us worked together to help someone. We had provided someone with such a great experience that she went home very happy. I thought to myself, "This feels great. How can I get more of this feeling? Maybe I should stop and help people more often." Then the bell went off. I was a little embarrassed that I didn't see it sooner. If I'm doing my job properly, isn't that what I do for a living? Another lesson learned.

3.4 Hotel General Managers: Focused on the Core Business

Robert H. Woods, Denney G. Rutherford, Raymond S. Schmidgall, and Michael Sciarini

Hotel general managers may occupy the single most-studied position in United States hotels. Researchers' focus on GMs is not without good reason, for no other single position has greater effect on the success of a hotel property. Stud- ies on GMs stretch back nearly 20 years, but looking only at studies published in the last ten years, we found research on demographic and career data, studies documenting GMs' heavy work schedule, studies of the GM's role in hotels, studies of essential personality traits, and studies of requisite job skills. (See examples in the references section.) Indeed, the hotel general manager is the topic of one entire book (Nebel, 1991).

The author of that book was Eddystone C. Nebel, III, who was also the principal author of a 1992 study about hotel GMs (Nebel et al., 1995). That article reported on the career paths of 114 general managers working in midrange, upscale, and luxury hotels in the United States. Much has happened in the industry since Nebel et al. collected their data over five years ago. While we sought to provide updated information on GMs, we focused on managers of large hotels, sending our mailing only to GMs who managed properties with at least 500 rooms.

OUR METHODS

Specifically, we sent survey forms to 460 GMs at hotels with 500 or more rooms. We picked participants randomly from the American Hotel and Motel Association (AH&MA) member database and asked each respondent to complete a five-page questionnaire and to return it in the envelope provided. We advised our respondents that the Michigan State University Committee on Human Subjects had approved our study and that responses would be kept anonymous.

The 460 surveys yielded a total of 77 responses, or 16.7 percent. As the demographic information in Table 3.4 indicates, the respondents managed hotels with an average of 759 rooms. Just two of the respondents were women.

EDUCATIONAL INFLUENCES

One objective of our study was to identify which courses of study the GMs believed were most useful. Participating general managers rated several subjects using a six-point scale,

with the results shown in Table 3.5. Participants were also given the opportunity to add subjects not on our list.

The top five subject areas are found in all business and most hospitality-management curricula. This clearly suggests that the GMs considered a strongly "business-focused" curriculum to be most valuable. On the other hand, our study appears to indicate that programs that emphasize food and beverage and production are not the most effective for persons who aspire to a position as large-hotel GM. This would not apply to graduates entering the restaurant industry, and it may not even be true for those interested in managing small hotels.

We should also note that the Nebel group's 1992 study had different results when it came to food and beverage operations (Nebel et al., 1995, pp. 252–256). In that study, approximately 45 percent of responding GMs had most of their experience in F&B, 26 percent had their second-most experience in F&B, and more GMs under 43 years of age (half of the sample) had more experience in F&B than in any other department. In addition, compared to our study, more GMs in their study listed F&B as the most important departmental experience an aspiring GM could receive. This shows, among other things, how the differences in samples between the Nebel study and ours can affect the findings. Our emphasis on large hotels has apparently influenced our results.

We also asked our participants to identify one change they would make in what colleges and universities teach (see Table 3.6). While few respondents answered this question, one suggestion that topped the list wasn't a subject area at all. The respondents wanted to see graduates with more hands-on experience. "People management" was the subject area that our respondents most wanted to see added to hospitality-education programs, followed by marketing.

The curriculum changes suggested by our respondents reflect changes in the lodging in-

TABLE 3.4
Demographic profile of the sample (N = 77)

Age (mean = 46)		Mean salary	$118,378*
30 to 35	4	**Salary range**	$27,500 to just over $300,000
36 to 40	13		
41 to 45	20	**Annual salary ($000s)**	
46 to 50	19	Less than $76	10
51 to 55	16	$76 to $100	21
56 to 60	4	$101 to $125	20
61 and older	1	$126 to $150	12
		$151 to $175	8
College degrees		$176 to $200	3
Associate	14	More than $200	3
Bachelor's	64		
Master's	8	**Compensation from bonuses**	
M.B.A.	10	Number receiving an annual bonus	75
Other	6	Bonus based on...	
Note: Participants identified all		...performance	3
degrees held.		...bottom line	24
		...GOP	36
		...Employee or guest satisfaction	5
Professional certifications		...Other	7
CHA	30		
Other	5 (CPA or CFBE, for example)	**Bonus as a percentage of salary**	
		Less than 10%	1
Management history		11 to 15%	10
Years in lodging industry before		16 to 20%	14
first management job	3.14	21 to 25%	17
Years from first management job		26 to 30%	15
to general manager	9.27	31 to 40%	10
Years as general manager	11.58	41 to 50%	5
Years in current GM position	5.77	More than 50%	3

(Handwritten annotations: CHA "— Certified Hospitality Administrator"; CFBE "Certified Food and beverage Executive"; GOP "income before management fees")

*Compare to a 1992 study by Robert W. Dingman Co., based on 50 respondents, that found the average manager of a 4- or 5-star U.S. hotel earned an average annual salary of $138,000, inclusive of bonuses, with a range of $45,000 to $200,000. See: Glenn Withiam, "The Measure of a Manager," *Cornell Hotel and Restaurant Administration Quarterly*, Vol. 33, No. 3 (June 1992), p. 8.

dustry. One change is what appears to be shrinkage in the number of traditional management positions that one could use as stepping-stones to the GM job. Three-fifths of our respondents indicated that those jobs are being eliminated. A few years ago, for instance, food and beverage production was near the top in importance (based on the Nebel studies) and was in many companies considered the road to success. By contrast, one-fifth of our respondents identified the F&B manager position as becoming less relevant as a departmental position in their properties. This was, by far, the most-mentioned such position. In second place was the resident-manager position, but that was mentioned by only five of the respondents.

Another way to look at what prospective GMs will need to know in the future is to examine the specific skill areas GMs need right now. Based on a pretest, we offered respondents a list of specific skill areas that GMs might need. Our participants rated the importance of those skills for managers who wish to attain GM status (see Table 3.7).

We found a dichotomy of sorts when investigating these issues. While our participants believe future GMs must master certain skill

TABLE 3.5
Importance of hospitality-management-education subjects

Subject Area	Very important (6)	More important (5)	Some importance (4)	Slight importance (3)	Little importance (2)	No importance (1)	Average (scale of 1–6)
Marketing	65.8%	18.4%	13.2%	2.6%	0	0	5.5
Management	63.2	23.5	11.8	1.3	0	0	5.5
Human resources	46.8	29.9	18.2	5.2	0	0	5.2
Finance	41.3	33.3	16.0	9.3	0	0	5.1
Accounting	31.5	28.8	24.7	13.7	1.4%	0	4.8
MIS	9.6	27.4	32.9	27.4	1.4	1.4%	4.1
Law	8.5	14.1	39.4	28.2	9.9	0	3.8
Statistics	6.9	16.7	31.9	27.8	13.9	2.8	3.7
Food service	2.7	33.8	33.8	20.3	9.5	0	4.0
Economics	1.4	22.2	34.7	30.6	8.3	2.8	3.7
Food production	1.4	13.9	44.4	30.6	9.7	0	3.7

Other subject areas listed (in order of respondent ranking, each with more than one mention):	Each of the following tied (with one mention each):
Communications	Behavioral science
Engineering and maintenance	Common sense
Cultural diversity	Languages
Project management	Leadership
	Negotiation skills
	Owner relations
	Public relations

Note: Rating with highest percentage frequency is shown in boldface.

TABLE 3.6
One change you believe that hospitality-management programs should make

Require more on-the-job training and internships	13
Teach more human-resources and people-management skills (including leadership skills)	13
More emphasis on sales and marketing	6
More real-life case projects	6
Clear examples of the realities of the business	4
Oral and written communication skills	4

TABLE 3.7
Skill areas needed to attain GM status

Subject Area	Very important	More important	Some importance	Slight importance	Little importance	Average (scale 1–5)
Increasing GOP	63.6%	29.9%	5.2%	1.3%	.0	4.6
Team building	59.7	32.5	5.2	2.6	.0	4.5
Community involvement	53.2	28.6	13.0	2.6	2.6%	4.3
Empowerment	46.7	36.4	16.9	.0	.0	4.3
Total quality management	37.7	42.8	16.9	1.3	1.3	4.1
Benchmarking	19.2	43.8	24.7	9.6	2.7	3.7
Restructure management contracts	13.3	31.8	28.3	13.3	13.3	3.2
Owner's involvement	10.8	28.4	31.1	21.6	8.1	3.1

areas, they do not necessarily agree that what sounds useful in theory is in all cases effective in practice. More than half found the first six skills (or concepts) either "very important" or "more important." Only management contracts and owner's involvement drew low ratings. When asked about the effectiveness (Table 3.8) of applying these same concepts, however, the GMs dropped the much-discussed concept of total quality management (TQM) to the bottom of the list (along with owner's involvement and management contracts). We think that the respondents downgraded TQM because ensuring a TQM program's success extends beyond the GM's sphere of influence and requires a companywide commitment for success.

The dichotomy can be seen more clearly in a comparison of the mean scores of importance and effectiveness for each of the eight concepts (using t-tests), as shown in Table 3.9. We found a statistically significant difference between how important the managers felt the concepts were and their judgment of those concepts' effectiveness in every case except owner's involvement.

We consider the following an important finding: These GMs consider all but one of the managerial concepts in question to be more important than effective. While we hesitate to generalize to all GMs, given the sample size, this finding is nonetheless a signpost that these GMs, although they buy into the potential importance of these much-discussed managerial theories, still seem to view them with some suspicion when it comes to how well they work in their hotels. We suggest further research regarding whether the bloom is off the TQM rose, along with its common components of benchmarking, team building, and empowerment.

Our participants also offered some advice to others interested in becoming general managers in terms of what types of financial outcomes and cost measures are the most valued or important. The list in Table 3.10 depicts the general managers' opinions about these issues.

The first three profit indicators all appear on one of the principal financial statements prepared by hotels, and the other three are comparisons of net profit to various indices, such as total investment, total assets, and

TABLE 3.8
Effective management tools

Subject Area	Very effective	More effective	Some effect	Slight effect	Little effect	Average (scale 1–5)
GM involved with community	42.8%	27.3%	22.1%	3.9%	3.9%	4.0
Increasing GOP	40.3	45.4	11.7	2.6	.0	4.2
Team building	40.3	40.2	14.3	5.2	.0	4.2
Empowerment	25.0	30.3	32.9	11.8	.0	3.7
Benchmarking	16.2	36.5	27.0	13.5	6.8	3.4
Owner's involvement	12.0	22.7	29.3	21.3	14.7	3.0
Total quality management	11.7	36.4	41.6	3.9	6.5	3.4
Restructure management contracts	6.5	22.6	35.4	16.1	19.4	2.8

TABLE 3.9
Differences between importance and effectiveness ratings

Subject	Importance mean	Effectiveness mean	t-score
GM communication	4.27	4.01	3.368*
Increase GOP	4.56	4.23	4.090**
Team building	4.49	4.16	3.759**
Empowerment	4.30	3.68	7.210**
Benchmarking	3.67	3.42	3.288*
Owner's involvement	3.12	2.99	1.055
Restructuring management contracts	3.20	2.90	3.038*
Total quality management	4.14	3.43	7.456**

*$p = > 0.01$ (ranging from $p < 0.002$ to $p < 0.004$ range)
**$p = > 0.000$

number of shares outstanding. According to these results, GMs in our study seem to be principally focused on net profit—hardly a surprise. Cash flow is considered very important, second overall with an average score of 5.35. Our respondents' focus on the top three revenue items in Table 3.10 indicates the concern GMs have with operations, as compared to the financial indices that investors might want to consider (i.e., ROI, ROA, EPS). This result is consistent with our finding on how general managers spend their time (discussed later and shown in Table 3.11).

Regarding cost measures, our responding GMs gave the greatest attention to the most costly items and those over which they had the greatest control. For instance, direct labor cost, at approximately 33 percent of revenue, is considered the most important measure. Other direct costs (e.g., rooms) controlled by GMs and by department heads also get plenty of attention, as do overhead costs (e.g., A&G, marketing). However, Table 3.10 also shows that factors generally falling under the supervision of owners or corporate boards (e.g., management fees, fixed costs) receive less attention from GMs.

EPS = (Net Income − Dividends on Preferred Stock) / Average Outstanding Shares

TABLE 3.10
Importance of financial indices

	Very important	More important	Some importance	Slight importance	Little importance	No importance	Not applicable	Average (scale of 1–6)
Measures of profit or return on investment								
Net profit	60.0%	29.3%	6.7%	1.3%	0	0	2.7%	5.5
GOP	54.5	24.7	15.6	2.6	1.3%	0	1.3	5.3
Cash flow	53.2	26.0	14.3	2.6	0	0	3.9	5.4
ROI	39.4	30.3	13.2	7.9	1.3	0	7.9	5.1
Return on assets	19.7	27.7	18.4	10.5	10.5	0	13.2	4.4
Earnings per share	12.0	12.0	5.3	9.3	6.7	9.3%	45.4	3.6
Cost measures								
Direct labor costs	64.9	26.0	5.2	1.3	0	0	2.6	5.6
Direct costs	45.4	32.5	11.7	6.5	0	1.3	2.6	5.2
Operating overhead	37.7	48.0	9.1	1.3	1.3	0	2.6	5.2
Management fees	24.6	16.9	23.4	10.4	5.2	2.6	16.9	4.5
Fixed charges	9.1	27.2	23.4	19.5	10.4	3.9	6.5	3.9

Note: Relative importance of each measure is based on the percentage of the sample rating each item on a scale of 1 through 6.

TABLE 3.11
GMs' workweek

Less than 40 hours	1.3%
41 to 50 hours	9.2%
51 to 55 hours	26.3%
56 to 60 hours	36.9%
61 to 65 hours	15.8%
66 to 70 hours	6.6%
More than 70 hours	3.9%

HOW GMS SPEND THEIR TIME

Our study confirmed the general perception that hotel managers work a great many hours each week. More than one-quarter of our participants indicated that they worked over 60 hours each week, and nearly two-thirds of the sample worked more than 55 hours per week. The median was 56.6 hours. Since few managers enjoy a five-day workweek, we judge that the average time these GMs spend in-house was nine to ten hours daily.

Finally, we asked managers about how long they worked in the industry before attaining GM status, even though we recognize that future paths to the GM position will almost certainly be different from past paths. The results, shown in Table 3.12, indicate that a recent graduate who does well could expect to be promoted to a department-head position by age 24 or 25 and to a GM position by age 34 or 35,

if all goes well with her career and the industry is prospering. Those are big ifs, however.

TOP MANAGERIAL POSITIONS IN HOTELS

We asked our participants to identify the top-three managerial positions in their hotels, excluding their own, and to tell us which positions constitute the hotel executive committee. Table 3.13 depicts their responses.

We consider those results to be in conflict with earlier results. For instance, if the food and beverage director is among the top three positions in large hotels, why would general managers indicate that F&B experience was becoming less important as precursor to the GM's position? We can only guess that F&B director is a position that will soon fade from its current top-three rating. Perhaps a few years ago F&B managers would have been rated more highly.

Another way to determine which are the most powerful or prestigious positions within a hotel is to examine who the general manager includes on the executive committee. Our respondents provided the listing found in Table 3.14.

Comparing the responses in Tables 3.13 and 3.14 offers some apparently contradictory indications. Among the interesting issues between the "top-three positions" and "who's on

TABLE 3.12
Managerial experience

	0 to 5 years	6 to 10 years	11 to 15 years	16 to 20 years	21 or more years	mean
Years before first management job (mean 3.14)	67	8	2	0	0	3.7
Years from first management job to GM (mean 9.27)	17	33	18	8	1	
Years as GM (mean 11.58)	18	20	21	9	8	
Years in current GM position (mean 5.77)	45	24	3	2	3	

TABLE 3.13
Top-three hotel-management positions

Position	Number of mentions
Director of sales and marketing	49
Finance or controller	46
F&B director	33
Resident manager	17
Director of human resources	13
Operations manager	10
Assistant general manager	9
Rooms-division manager	9
Hotel manager	8
Front-office manager	5

Under 5 mentions:

Executive housekeeper

Chief engineer

Director of convention services

Director of total-quality management

Note: Repondents could mention one, two, or three top positions.

TABLE 3.14
Members of the hotel executive committee

Position	Number of mentions
Director of sales and marketing	65
Director of human resources	62
VP of finance or controller	62
F&B director	55
Chief engineer	38
Rooms-division manager	22
Resident manager	19
Assistant general manager	15
Executive chef	12
Executive housekeeper	11
Operations manager	11
Director of convention services	11

Under 10 mentions:

Director of MIS

Front-office manager

Director of total-quality management

Director of security

Reservations manager

Director of guest services

Note: Respondents could mention multiple positions.

the executive committee" is the strange case of the human-resources (HR) directors. While HR directors are included on the executive committee of all but 13 of the hotels we surveyed, the GMs in our study indicated that HR managers are rarely considered one of the top-three management positions in the hotel (only 13 respondents so named them). Another dichotomy is found with chief engineers (on the executive committee of half the hotels, but considered one of top-three management by only three respondents). These findings lead in one of two directions: either the executive committee comprises members who are not really essential, or the GMs have a distorted view of human resources and engineering. The executive committees of the hotels we surveyed were not especially large. The median size was six members, and most hotels fell into a range of five-to-seven members—not much room for unessential members.

THE ROAD TO GM

One reason we conducted this study was to gain some insight into the importance the GMs themselves place on aspects of training and preparation for the demanding job that they hold. Contrary to the findings of studies in the recent past, this sample of GMs places high value on the core business disciplines of marketing, management, human resources, finance, and accounting. When asked to suggest additions to the university curricula in hospitality, they stressed more practical experience, on-the-job training, and internships. They also stressed more human-resources and people-management—for example, leadership—skills.

It would seem wise for students and those in the industry who want to become GMs to concentrate their training, education, and certification activities in those areas. The GMs are suggesting a blend of business theory and practical career experience.

Another reason we undertook this study was to see what effects reengineering, mergers, and acquisitions have had on the managerial structure of the large hotel. Most of our responding GMs run their hotel with an executive committee of about six people. Executive-committee membership was relatively consistent, including director of sales and marketing, director of human resources, controller, and F&B director. With the addition of resident manager, those positions also constituted these GMs' opinion of the hotel's top managerial positions, although we must conclude that the F&B post is no longer a well-worn path to the top.

The minor importance accorded such positions as front office manager, executive housekeeper, director of convention services, and director of TQM suggests how flat the organization of the modern hotel has become. What remains to be seen is the effect the flatter structure will have on managerial careers, many of which in the past included a stop as front office manager as part of building managerial experience and career depth on the rooms side of the hotel. We are not sure whether the changes mean the career track to the GM job will be necessarily longer (fewer stops, longer periods in bigger jobs, and more lateral movement) or shorter (fewer stops, but more directly to the top). What is certain is that career progressions will be less predictable and probably more sensitive to inappropriate career decisions.

Our study may raise more questions than it answers. At a minimum, the findings suggest that the hotel general manager's position has changed in the course of just a few years. Compared to earlier studies, the GM of today's large hotel focuses on core business factors; manages a flatter, more agile organization; and is still not completely convinced of the effectiveness of currently popular management theory.

3.5   A Day in the Life: General Manager of a Las Vegas Hotel
Robert O. Balmer, CHA

I have always described the experience of a general manager in a hotel as being similar to that of a city mayor. You wear several hats, juggle daily schedules and priorities, and deal with all walks of life while keeping a smile on your face at all times.

My day typically begins between 6:45 A.M. and 7 A.M. Upon arriving at the hotel I stop at the front desk to check on the previous night's occupancy and receive a briefing from the night audit staff. I am informed of the number of rooms occupied, ADR, and any guest

issues that might have occurred. We were running 103 percent last night. Did we walk anyone? The answer is "No, we had a clean fill!"

I then check on the daily banquet events and look in on the restaurant. Next I review the BEO (banquet event order) for the day's upcoming meetings, looking for attention to detail and ensuring that our guests' expectations are not only met, but exceeded! Meet and greet morning food and beverage staff and look for smiles and attitudes!

A large cup of coffee is next on the priority

list. While I consume a much-needed dose of caffeine, I like to scan the *USA Today* as well as the local paper looking for local news and global issues. It is amazing to me how reading the newspaper can affect the hotel. I look for economic trends, office relocations, closures, or expansions, labor disputes, hotel and travel news.

In addition to being a great tool for finding new sales leads, the newspaper can assist in guest interactions. Numerous are the times I have been able to use small bits of information, gleaned from my morning reading session, while conversing with a guest in the lobby. Perhaps the most memorable of these events concerned a small blurb announcing a new printing of the Bible illuminated with paintings from the Vatican. A one-paragraph article in *USA Today* and a throwaway remark in the lobby turned into a lively conversation between a guest and myself and a colleague of mine. The result, a well-satisfied guest who felt he had experienced more for his money than just a place to sleep for the night.

After I finish the newspapers, it is time to head to my office and check voice mail, e-mail, and the company mailbox for any correspondence. Then I make my way to housekeeping for morning roll call.

I have always been of the opinion that housekeeping is one of the hardest jobs in the hotel and view staff motivation in this department as essential. Each day the director of housekeeping conducts a short preshift meeting focusing on morale-building activities. She also takes the opportunity to brief her staff and assign special tasks for the day (e.g., baseboards are next on the deep-cleaning list, or a reminder that linen inventory is taking place this evening). I make a point of attending roll call each day, which gives me the opportunity to greet the room attendants and provide motivation. On the way back up from housekeeping I walk the hotel and say good morning to staff and department managers.

Sales are the lifeblood of the hotel. I coordinate the daily activities of the sales office and participate in the morning's revenue management meeting. Attending this meeting are the revenue manager, assistant general manager, the sales staff, and myself. We review the month's booking pace and sales leads and coordinate the sales managers' daily itinerary. The revenue manager briefs everyone on the upcoming occupancy status of the hotel and announces sold-out dates and group ceiling closeouts. With the kind of high occupancy rates our hotel is currently running, this can sometimes mean that the firector of sales urges everyone to new heights of booking enthusiasm. The sales staff is off and running to book those guest rooms.

By midmorning my e-mail box is usually 15–20 messages full. After weeding through them there are usually two or three from my area vice president, or someone at Hilton Worldwide Headquarters in Beverly Hills, California, that require immediate attention. After the ever-present e-mail is prioritized, onward moves the day.

Lunchtime always comes quickly. Lunch can consist of a quick bite grabbed on property or a business lunch with a client or another local general manager. It is a great idea to build relationships with other general managers in the area. Due to the Sherman Anti-Trust Act, of course, we cannot legally discuss room rates but it helps us stay abreast on all local issues and trends. A wonderful way to network.

After lunch I like to visit with the director of human resources to remain current on any hotel staff challenges and opportunities. We usually discuss coaching and counseling sessions, terminations of employment, hiring needs, and any other topics that impact our wonderfully dedicated and talented team members.

A majority of my day consists of hotel forecasting, EBITDA (earnings before interest, taxes, depreciation, and amortization) leverage, monthly reports, quarterly reports, variance reports, and labor reports. Sometimes I feel like I should have changed my major to finance!

Throughout my day everything is interrupted with phone calls, pages, faxes. Just today; Las Vegas police arrived with a warrant for a guest's arrest, the wind blew the garbage Dumpsters out of the garbage bin area and straight into a team member's minivan, the dryer in laundry broke down, a satisfied eld-

erly guest was made comfortable after we found her dentures in the soiled linen at the bottom of the linen chute, the hotel is sold out, and we are overbooked twelve rooms.

Just another "Day in the Life"... I wouldn't change it for the world!

3.6   Director of Operations: GM in Waiting

Matt Berge

People always give me a surprised look when I tell them that I knew that I wanted to major in hotel and restaurant management back in my early high school years. I guess I knew early on that I wanted a career where I could work with people and actually have fun doing it.

I'm now 13 years into my career and am one position/promotion away from reaching the goal I set back in college. My job as director of operations at the Westin Galleria, Dallas, is preparing me for the position of general manager. That day will come, but in the meantime I savor each opportunity that gives me the ability to learn more. I will always believe that to be successful, one must be a part of a successful team. My so-called daily routine centers on this philosophy, because as you will see, it is anything but "routine."

The Westin Galleria, Dallas, is a 432-room, four-star, business hotel located about 15 minutes from downtown. Our guests are very successful business people who are paying a premium for upscale accommodations. My responsibility is to make sure we deliver what they expect. Pressure? Not really, as long as I have a successful team with a quality product.

The department heads of the front office, housekeeping, Service Express (PABX, bell staff, and room service), guest services, security, culinary, stewarding, purchasing, ban-

quets, engineering, and the retail outlets all report to me. I report to the general manager. I am one of five on the executive committee that in our hotel includes the director of human resources, director of sales and marketing, controller, director of operations, and general manager. As a team we make the major decisions that affect the direction of the hotel.

What do I do each day? I'll start off by saying that it has become clear to me that no one in this industry has a "typical" day. That is why I enjoy it so much. You don't get bored doing this stuff! I average around 50–55 hours a week. Not too bad, anymore, but I must admit that there have been some positions that I have clocked up to 65–70-hour workweeks.

My day usually starts in the office around 7:30 A.M. each morning. The first hour is my most productive office time, and my managers know never to disturb me during this window. I think they know that it takes the first hour for the coffee to really kick in. Planning my day, going through e-mail, mail, etc., keep me occupied for that critical first hour. At 8:30 A.M. I attend the daily sales briefing with the sales and catering managers. This consists of 30 minutes of listening and discussing the various pieces of business that we are seeking. Since our hotel's location is very desirable and enjoys a quality reputation, we are fortunate that we can pick and choose what group and catering business we want to take. The variables we bat around are the room rate, number of rooms, F&B revenue, amount of meeting space, and day of the week. Each of these plays a part in making the right decision on each potential prospect.

My favorite and most effective meeting of the day is the one that takes place next, usually about 9:00 A.M. It's the operations meeting that includes all of the operations department heads. We discuss all of the previous day's incidents and financial results, as well as the present day's forecast and other activities throughout each department. While I know the managers are all busy, this important meeting gives me an opportunity to see them together, personally, on a regular basis, for perhaps 20 to 30 minutes each morning. It is a time to praise, guide, plan, and briefly discuss issues among the team members.

From then on, after our typical 9:30 A.M. adjournment, comes the unpredictable. The unpredictable takes on many forms and can include meeting with customers, vendors, the hotel's executive committee, and other various committees. On a fairly regular basis, I also meet with individual department heads, participate in completing guest room and public area inspections. Sandwiched in with all of this, I return phone calls and e-mail and work on corporate and capital projects, plus forecasting. As you can see, you don't get bored doing this stuff! As a matter of fact, the days fly by.

The time I spend with individual department managers is very important to me. As I mentioned earlier, I focus on developing a successful team, so in addition to the morning operations meeting, I spend time with each manager, every day. I do my best to mentor each one, in reviewing their progress on projects, guiding them on particular decisions, or just showing my support. It's not easy being a manager. They need someone they can count on, and I have to be that person.

As mentioned above, part of my day is spent managing capital projects and purchases. These are improvements to the asset that are directly funded by the owner. In other words, they are not reflected as an operational expense. Guest room, public area, and outlet renovations are some examples of capital projects. Other recent examples are new boilers, chillers, sewage pumps, telephone switch, software and hardware upgrades. A major part of the fun and enjoyment of my job is that I get to spend about $2 million a year on these types of projects.

Development and progression of yourself as a manager is also important. It is my view that a manager who has been doing the same thing year in, year out, for too long in the same place is usually no longer effective. A personal career goal has been to learn as much from each job assignment and try for the next rung up the operations ladder after two years. It is important to avoid being labeled a one-dimensional "specialist" when you are seeking the broad inventory of skills it takes to lead a modern hotel organization.

I found early on that it is important to take advantage of all the various paths that a hotel has to offer. This is the best way to fill out your résumé by demonstrating breadth in your career preparation. Although I have worked only for Westin Hotels and Resorts in my career, since Westin has experienced four different ownership changes, believe me, it has given me the experience of having worked for four different companies!

My most personal satisfaction comes from working with new managers and helping them learn how to become solid members of the team. I enjoy the candidate that comes along that has the eagerness that I had when I was in their shoes. The can-do, will-do attitude that partners with the will to learn helps them focus on being the best they can be.

They say it gets in your blood . . . this hotel business. I agree, and cannot see myself doing anything else.

3.7   Mini Case: Sunset Hotels and Suites

Shortly before the end of 2001, Mr. André Johnson, president of Sunset Hotels and Suites, Inc., heard through the informal company "grapevine" that several department and operational managers at the company's hotels in northern California were unhappy with their promotion prospects. Unwilling to risk losing these young managers, Johnson was contemplating how to mentor these men and women in how to best manage their careers, but at the same time make staying with Sunset attractive and challenging.

Sunset Hotels and Suites is a growing West Coast chain with nine properties in southern California; six in the San Francisco Bay Area (northern California), and five in the Seattle-Portland region. The hotels in the Bay Area were the most recent acquisitions and, although fewer in number than the southern California region, boasted 20 percent more rooms and were more recently built. They also included the youngest management staffs, many of whom were retained from the staffs of the acquired hotels. Sunset is a privately owned company, operated as an S corporation, with all of the corporate officers and hotel GMs holding shares of the company's stock.

Several of the unhappy managers had talked with their GMs and human resource officers about their frustrations. These included:

- Many of the GMs were also very young, in their 30s and 40s, successful, and tending to not move very often.
- There are no regional managers, as Johnson prefers to run a fairly flat corporate organization.
- Several of them feel that they have been locked into fairly narrow specialties (convention services, catering sales, housekeeping management, and front office) without any clear prospects for additional cross training to add breadth to their careers.

- They are not particularly unhappy with salaries and the usual benefits, but some have grumbled about the valuable stock options the GMs get, largely based on the performance of the operating managers' departments.

Johnson calls a meeting of the Bay Area managers at the Mark Hopkins Hotel in San Francisco (*not* a Sunset property) and invites all department managers from Sunset to be his guests for a two-day conference. Similar meetings are announced and planned in the Pacific Northwest and southern California.

References

Arnaldo, M. J. 1981. "Hotel General Managers: A Profile." *Cornell Hotel and Restaurant Administration Quarterly* 22(3):53–56.

*Bentivegna, Angelo N., and Leroy Sluder, III. 1989. "Hotel GMs Bring Diverse Backgrounds to the Job." *Lodging* June:61–62.

Brownell, Judi. 1994. "Women in Hospitality Management: General Managers' Perceptions of Factors Related to Career Development." *International Journal of Hospitality Management* 13(2):101–117.

Dann, D. 1990. "The Nature of Managerial Work in the Hospitality Industry." *International Journal of Hospitality Management* 9(4):319–334.

Dingman, H. Bruce. 1993. "The Right Fit: Executive Search by Retained Recruiters." *Cornell Hotel and Restaurant Administration Quarterly* 34(4):26–31.

Eder, R. W., and W. T. Umbreit. 1989. "Measures of Managerial Effectiveness in the Hotel Industry." *Hospitality Education and Research Journal* 13(3):333–341.

El Nasser, Haya. 1997. "Overworked, Overstressed: Who Has Time to Volunteer?" *USA Today* April 28, 1997: pp. A1, A3.

Ferguson, D. H., and F. Berger. May 1984. "Restaurant Managers: What Do They Actually Do?" *Cornell Hotel and Restaurant Administration Quarterly* 25(1):27–37.

Guerrier, Y. 1987. "Hotel Managers' Careers and Their Impact on Hotels in Britain." *International Journal of Hospitality Management* 6(3):121–130.

Guerrier, Y., and A. Lockwood. 1991. "Managers in Hospitality: A Review of Current Research." In *Progress in Tourism, Recreation, and Hospitality Management*, C. P. Cooper (ed.), London: Bellhaven Press, ch. 2, pp. 151–167.

Hales, C., and M. Nightingale. 1986. "What Are Unit Managers Supposed to Do? A Contingent Methodology for Investigating Managerial Role Requirements." *International Journal of Hospitality Management* 5(1):3–11.

Koepper, K. 1988. "Management Effectiveness: A Hotel Industry Appraisal." *Lodging* December: 14(4):53–57.

Kotter, J. P. 1982. *The General Managers.* New York: The Free Press.

Leonard, Saul. 1993. "The GM's Role in Maximizing Value." *Hotels* 27(11):80–81

Ley, D. A. 1978. "An Empirical Examination of Selected Work Activity Correlates of Managerial Effectiveness in the Hotel Industry using a Structured Observation Approach." Unpublished Ph.D. dissertation, Michigan State University, East Lansing, Michigan.

Mintzberg, H. 1973. *The Nature of Managerial Work.* New York: Harper and Row.

*Morey, Richard C., and David A. Dittman. 1995. "Evaluating a Hotel GM's Performance: A Case Study in Benchmarking." *Cornell Hotel and Restaurant Administration Quarterly* 36(5):30–35.

Nebel, Eddystone C., III. 1991. *Managing Hotels Effectively: Lessons from Outstanding General Managers.* New York: Van Nostrand Reinhold.

Nebel, Eddystone C., III, Lee Ju-Soon, and Brani Vidakovic. 1995. "Hotel General Manager Career Paths in the United States." *International Journal of Hospitality Management* 14(3–4):245–260.

Rutherford, Denney G., and Jane Wiegenstein. 1985. "The Mentoring Process in Hotel General Managers Careers." *Cornell Hotel and Restaurant Administration Quarterly* February: 25(4):16–23.

Shortt, G. 1989. "Work Activities of Hotel Managers in Northern Ireland: A Mintzbergian Analysis." *International Journal of Hospitality Management* 8(2):121–130.

Sparrowe, Raymond T., and Pamela A. Popielarz. 1995. "Getting Ahead in the Hospitality Industry: An Event Analysis of Promotions among Hotel and Restaurant Employees." *Hospitality Research Journal* 19(3):99–117.

Umbreit, W. T. 1986. "Developing Behaviorally Anchored Scales for Evaluating Job Performance of Hotel Managers." *International Journal of Hospitality Management* 5(2):55–61.

Willimann, Hans R. 1992. "One Day in the Life of Hans Willimann." *Hotels* 26(8):63–66.

Worsfold, P. 1989. "A Personality Profile of the Hotel Manager." *International Journal of Hospitality Management* 8(1):51–62.

Suggested Readings

Books

Powers, Thomas F. 1999. *Introduction to Management in the Hospitality Industry*, 6th ed. New York: John Wiley and Sons, Inc.

Woods, Robert H., and Judy Z. King. 1996. *Quality Leadership and Management in the Hospitality Industry.* East Lansing, MI: Educational Institute of the American Hotel and Motel Association.

Articles

Ley, David. 1980. "The Effective GM: Leader or Entrepreneur?" *The Cornell Hotel and Restaurant Administration Quarterly* 22(3):53-56.

Pavesic, David V., and Robert A. Brymer. 1990. "Why Young Managers are Quitting," *Cornell Hotel and Restaurant Administration Quarterly* 30:4, 90–96.

Source Notes

Chapter 3.2, "A Conceptual Framework of the Hotel General Manager's Job," by Eddystone C. Nebel, III, and Ajay Ghei.

Chapter 3.3, "As I See It: The Hotel GM," by Emilio Fabico.

Chapter 3.4, "Hotel General Managers: Focused on the Core Business," by Robert H. Woods, Denney G. Rutherford, Raymond S. Schmidgall, and Michael Sciarini, is reprinted from the December 1998 issue of *The Cornell Hotel and Restaurant Administration Quarterly*. © Cornell University. Used by permission. All rights reserved.

Chapter 3.5, "A Day in the Life: General Manager of a Las Vegas Hotel," by Robert O. Balmer, CHA.

Chapter 3.6, "Director of Operations: GM in Waiting," by Matt Berge.

4

Operations: Rooms

4.1 Introduction

Among other things, the student of hotel administration will find the front office referred to as the "hub," the "nerve center," the "brain," or some other name suggesting centrality in the modern hotel. As H. V. Heldenbrand stated in his now classic 1944 book, *Front Office Psychology*, ". . . To the guest, the manager is largely represented by the front office, and the unseen head will be judged favorably or otherwise by the guest treatment there" (Introduction). The observations, opinions, and research presented in this section are chosen to illustrate the centrality of the front office in the modern hotel.

A theme that recurs throughout many of the readings included in this section is that of communications. In an increasingly communications-oriented society and world, information, its storage, retrieval, dissemination, and evaluation can represent a competitive edge and, to a certain extent, power. Technology has given us the Internet, cellular phones, electronic mail (e-mail), telephone- and computer-transmitted facsimiles (faxes), overnight delivery of letters and packages, and personal data assistants (PDAs). These all

combine to generate an expectation of clear and nearly instantaneous communication and, by logical extension, fast and efficient services based on communications. This in turn has increased the complexity of the hotel's front office and at the same time given them increased opportunities to better serve the hotel's guests and has, therefore, significantly impacted the role of the front office and the front office manager from that described by Heldenbrand.

In 1985, the editor (Rutherford, 1985) studied a national sample of front office managers (FOMs) and concluded that communication emerged as a central issue. This centrality was linked not only to the predictable role of department manager but also as a facilitator and broker of communication in its various forms between and among the other hotel departments, the front office, and the hotel guests. The model that emerged from this analysis carries with it the powerful message that the FOM's job clearly revolves around communications in its various forms. A major conclusion of this study was that hotel firms should consider communication skills to be an important criterion in considering candidates for the position of FOM.

When this is coupled with the aforementioned complexity and guest expectations of instant communications service it is easy to see why the front office and its staff can be found to operate under considerable stress. Being the hub or nerve center of a modern hotel has as one of its positive aspects the fact that front office staff can be keenly aware of what is happening at virtually every level of the hotel's organizational structure. One of the negative aspects is that the front office also serves as a lightning rod for guest complaints. This can be one of the most difficult things for the front office staff to learn to deal with, especially the frequency and sometimes the intensity of guest complaints.

These are included in the central theme of the research and commentary presented in this section by Cheri Young. As part of a larger research project, Young worked as a front desk agent at a luxury New York hotel. She documents the causes and indicators causing stress at the front desk and analyzes the components of managing under these circumstances.

Successful FOMs will ideally possess the demonstrated competencies in both oral and written communications to competently deal with these complexities and challenges. The FOM, therefore, not only becomes a manager and a communicator among and between the front office staff, the hotel departments, and the guests, but the FOM also emerges as a communicator in yet another way—that of teacher and trainer.

This contextual theme of communications is carried forward in the essay contributed by James Bardi. Bardi further discusses the job of FOM, providing insights about the complexities of this job relative to not only communication, but elements of an FOM job analysis, intrahotel relations, and the emerging and popular concept of employee empowerment.

To see how this all fits together, walk a few miles in the shoes of FOM Garry Dickover. At the time this was written, Dickover was the FOM of two hotels: Marriott's River Center and Riverwalk Hotels in San Antonio, Texas. Currently director of suites for the Venetian Hotel Resort and Casino in Las Vegas, Dickover invites you to see the "inside" of the FOM's job and see how he practices the theory of managing the front office.

Glenn Witham, executive editor of *The Cornell Hotel and Restaurant Administration Quarterly,* contributes to this edition an essay that updates his 1983 article on concierges (Witham, 1983), broadened to include an expanded realm of concierge services, their management, and personnel. This essay looks at how guest services are evolving as a significant and more truly integrated function of hotel service delivery than the recent past. Previously, the combination of bell staffs, concierges, garage attendants, door people, and so forth were something other than a seamless part of the organization with a unifying service delivery theme. Witham looks at the concept of a professionalism paradigm for concierges in the modern era and provides the reader with additional insights as to how these jobs enhance the transition of the guests to the hotel and serve the guests throughout their stay.

The theme of active communications carries forth through the piece contributed by Bill Quain and Steve LeBruto. If hotels are going to actively find the best pieces of business, then there must be good communications channels between and among all the organizational components that guide the guest to a purchase decision. Whether this is at the front desk, through the reservations system, or through a travel agent, it is important to recognize what are the most attractive pieces of business and what potential bookings may be logically refused. Yes, refusing business is a central component of successful yield management, but not always. In their words: "Yield management is usually thought of in the context of turning away undesirable business during excess demand periods. However, the real art of yield management is in learning how to turn undesirable booking requests into desirable ones." Their article helps the reader, in an interesting and entertaining way, learn to make these management decisions.

Yield and revenue management are also treated in Part VII, the marketing section of this book, with other, in some ways, contrasting views by Orkin and Chappelle. The reader who wants additional insights into these concepts is directed to the contributions by those authors.

Another operations manager, Bob Peckenpaugh, provides additional insights into the direction of activities of a rooms division in a major resort hotel; in this instance the Westin Innisbrook Resort near Tampa, Florida. Peckenpaugh focuses on the need for attention to detail by the operations manager, but also the need to develop personal leadership skills and foster them in your staff.

The articles and essays presented here for your consideration represent only a suggestion of the potential range of issues attendant to any modern hotel front office. The duties, obligations, and responsibilities of front office personnel will change from hotel company to hotel company based on such variables as market segmentation, organizational structure, corporate philosophy, and individual leadership. There exists a large amount of management literature not specific to the front office, but that nonetheless pertains to the various issues and challenges that face FOMs. The articles chosen for inclusion in this section are as specific as possible to functional aspects of front office management. Other pertinent managerial insights may be applied from other contexts once the reader has a good functional grasp of the realm of front office activities. Included in the suggested readings are a number of specific textbooks that treat in great depth the functional and technical aspects of front office operations. What has been attempted here is an overview of pervasive managerial issues typical of those currently facing FOMs.

4.2   Raw Nerves at the Nerve Center: An Insider's View of Life at the Front Desk

Cheri A. Young

An area that needs special attention is the effect that the [front desk] agent has on the guest's perception of the hotel and the amount of satisfaction the guest will derive from his or her stay. The effect of a pleasant, friendly, helpful agent, as opposed to one that is rude, aloof, and uncaring, can easily be seen.

DeVeau et al., 1996, p. 35

Although many hotel managers may not understand the emotions of their employees, many are concerned about the effects of such emotions, particularly negative, on customer satisfaction. Emotional responses to stress must be coped with by front desk agents since they are generally not allowed to express negative emotions because of potentially detrimental effects on customers' perception of quality service (Schneider and Bowen, 1995). Despite experiencing stress, front desk agents are expected to "act pleasant and courteous continuously even if they are actually miserable or dealing with a particularly nasty or ungrateful customer" (Schneider and Bowen, 1995, p. 110–111). As such, front desk agents must carefully monitor the manner in which they display emotions. Yet, how these employees keep themselves from displaying negative emotions to customers is a poorly understood phenomenon.

In order to understand how front desk agents cope with negative emotions generally not condoned in servicing guests, I conducted a study at the front desk of a large, urban hotel to identify the stressful events faced, the negative emotions experienced, and the coping strategies employed by these high customer-contact employees. Stressful events are situations appraised as harmful, threatening, or challenging. They are considered objective or subjective threats to well-being in that the person assesses a situation as either "beyond his or her current capabilities or taxing those capabilities" (Thoits, 1984, p. 228). Research has demonstrated that workplace stressful events can result in negative emotional reactions (Kahn and Byosiere, 1992). Whether mild or intense, "these negative [emotional] reactions are likely to be experienced as subjectively unpleasant" (Thoits, 1984, p. 228) and are believed to motivate emotion management or what is called coping. _Coping_ is defined as attempts to manage (i.e., to master, tolerate, reduce, and minimize) negative emotions and/or the stressful events that caused them (Bhagat et al., 1991). I was particularly interested in how front desk agents coped with negative emotions they are forbidden from displaying in the presence of guests and that are generated by stressful events.

In the remainder of this chapter, after I review the stress of front desk work in general and how the study was conducted, I describe the types of stressful events I found that front desk agents faced. Next, I present the forms of coping responses exhibited by the front desk personnel in response to the onset of stressful events and/or negative emotions. Finally, I summarize and discuss implications for hotel managers.

THE FRONT DESK AT THE REGAL HOTEL

In a city of world-class hotels, only one is Regal. Embracing the architecture of two centuries, the gated grand courtyard and majestic arches are but a prelude to its inner elegance, ambiance and AAA Five Diamond Award excellence.

Marketing brochure from the Regal Hotel

I chose to study the front desk area of a 900+-room New York City luxury hotel known as the Regal Hotel,[*] due to the nature of the work, which included:

- A high degree of guest contact.
- Strict rules regarding the display of negative emotions.
- High guest expectations in terms of the service provided.

At the time of the study, room rates at the Regal ranged from $400 to $10,000 per night and 85 percent of the guests were business travelers. Business travelers are well-informed consumers and if paying $400 per night for a guest room, they expect exceptional, seamless service.

The front desk at the Regal was the nerve center of the hotel (DeVeau et al., 1996). According to Kasavana (1981, p. 20), "Regardless of how the hotel is constructed or organized, the front office is always an essential focal point." The front desk monitored the guest cycle and coordinated all guest services, from the guests' first contact (check-in) to their last (checkout). Front desk work is generally considered stressful; "because of the guests' familiarity with the desk, it tends to serve as . . . a sounding board for guest complaints" (Kasavana, 1981, p. 20). In fact, 47 percent of

---

[*]The name of the hotel has been disguised.

leisure travelers complain to the front desk about dissatisfaction with hotel service, while 26 percent contact a manager (*USA Today*, 1998). Thus, "tolerance is required when [front desk agents are] dealing with guest complaints and answering the same types of questions for different guests all day" (DeVeau et al., 1996, p. 36).

To understand how front desk agents coped with negative emotions generated by stressful work events, I worked for 301 hours over a three-month period at the Regal Hotel as a front desk agent, or as designated by the Regal a guest services agent (GSA). I did this without payment. In addition, I conducted in-depth interviews with 15 of the 17 GSAs regarding negative emotions they experienced at work resulting from stressful events. I looked for "cognition and behaviors, adopted by the individual following the recognition of a stressful encounter, that [were] in some way designed to deal with that encounter or its consequences" (Dewe et al., 1993, p. 7).

STRESSFUL WORK EVENTS

It is important to also consider the work setting when trying to interpret how and why the Regal GSAs cope. Not doing so would produce an incomplete and restricted view of coping. The stressful work events GSAs of the Regal Hotel coped with included interactions with people and things. The type of work performed and the interpersonal relationships involved makes certain stressful events more or less likely to occur, as well as influences the coping response and its outcome. As such, we will consider and account for the context of coping in the next section. Although by far the most frequently experienced stressful events for GSAs involved people (both guests and managers), the types of tasks and pace of the work also caused stress for the GSAs.

Work Pace and Tasks

The pace at the front desk was characterized by GSAs according to whether it was slow, busy, "crazy busy," or "bad busy" and whether the day was "smooth" or not. Slow days were a welcome change of pace after crazy busy days, but a steady diet of slow days was not a preferred mode of operating because of the distaste for boredom.

Busy days differed from crazy busy by the degree of smoothness. Smoothness referred to everything going well, with no problems. A busy, smooth day was the ideal for GSAs and led to much positive emotion. Time passed quickly and GSAs had clean, vacant rooms to play with and were able to satisfy guests' needs and requests. On crazy busy days, GSAs commented that "nothing's going right and nothing will go right. . . . Like every single guest there's something wrong." High demand ("people would just keep coming") and few available resources marked these days. Flexibility or slack in the system was limited ("no rooms to play with" to try to satisfy guests' needs and/or requests). The number of clean and vacant rooms and the types of available rooms defined resource availability.

The work pace influenced the degree of interaction between the guest and the GSA. The faster the work pace, the shorter the interaction. Although the number of guests waiting in line might be minimal, if only a few GSAs were working, the work pace was increased. At times like this, GSAs commented that "you really don't get a chance to talk anymore [with the guests]" and "you can't service the customer correctly." As a result, the GSAs coped by rushing to clear the line of guests. On crazy busy nights the hotel became like a "room factory," and GSAs questioned whether the hotel was truly servicing guests: "you're not full to the point where your guests are happy . . . it's like you're full and they're all bitching and complaining . . . so are you really helping yourself?"

Having to start a shift during a very busy or crazy busy day was another dreaded moment for a GSA. Said one GSA, "I hate to come when it's like jamming.... Like when you come in the midst of it 'cause it's like you don't have time to like put your bag down." GSAs would often "jump right in" to help their co-workers without getting fully prepared. Most favored an easier transition from nonwork to work and had daily routines they executed before getting down to work. These routines provided a transition and helped the GSA prepare mentally for the workday. When these routines were interrupted or thwarted because of guests' demands, GSAs experienced negative emotions that had to be coped with.

Once at the front desk, GSAs' work lives consisted mainly of checking in and out guests. The entire procedure for checking in guests took between two and three minutes if the requested type of room was clean and available, the guest's credit card authorized without a hitch, and the printer did not need a refill on paper. However, problems could happen at any step along the way. A common stressful event was the unavailability of the requested room type and finding an acceptable replacement.

In terms of checkout, the procedure took between one and two minutes as long as the GSA was not faced with having to separate charges on the guest's bill. Some guests' companies paid certain charges (room and taxes), but not others (telephone calls, food and beverage, videos, laundry, etc.). These guests wanted the charges put on separate bills. Other guests did not want their wives seeing the charges for phone calls made (the phone number was printed) or videos watched (typically pornographic). Also, other guests wanted charges separated on the bill between two guests sharing the room. Sometimes communication between the GSA and the guest was confusing, and GSAs experienced difficulties trying to figure out what charges guests wanted on one bill and not another. Although a common stressful event faced by all GSAs,

it nonetheless caused frustration and/or irritation the GSAs were forced to cope with since these emotion could not be displayed toward the guest.

Once the workday was nearing an end, GSAs were required to "bank out" approximately one half hour before their shifts ended. This meant printing a cash-out report summarizing all of the GSA's transactions for the shift, including the amount of cash collected and distributed, credit card charges, and allowances for guests' disputed charges. The GSA was then required to get his or her bank to balance.

Getting one's bank to balance was a frustration dealt with by all GSAs at some point in their careers. Every GSA was responsible for maintaining his or her own bank of $3000 for handling guests' transactions. Often GSAs had either a little more or less cash than they were supposed to have in their banks. If the bank was over or under, the GSA was punished with either a verbal or written warning, suspension, or termination depending on the severity of the discrepancy and whether this was a first, second, or third offense. Because they did not like the outcome of these events, GSAs devised methods for coping with these situations that avoided the negative outcome and the negative emotions (see the "Coping Responses" section below).

Stressful Events Involving Managers and Guests

In this next section, status, authority, and power differences between GSAs and managers and between GSAs and guests will be highlighted as they relate to the prompting of stressful work events, negative emotions, and coping. These differences in status, authority, and power acted out on the front desk stage of the Regal Hotel give rise to certain events occurring and influence the coping processes considered feasible and actually used by GSAs. Managers at the front desk were the source of many stressful events and negative emotions for the GSAs. Perceived status differences, beliefs that managers did not understand or care about the GSAs, discriminatory treatment, and poor communication about organizational changes triggered negative emotions. Guests of the hotel, too, were the source of many stressful work events. I will spend more time describing these two sets of organizational members, guests and managers, because of their influence on GSAs, than I will other organizational members (such as co-workers).

Interactions with Managers

The GSAs' perceptions were that managers did not understand the work or pressures of the GSA because the managers' jobs were of higher status. One GSA referred to feeling lowly in comparison to the managers and the rewards they received.

> We are the grunts here at the front desk. We are the front lines. We are the ones that they send out there to deal one-on-one with the guest. They are the generals. They are the officers that sit in the back, take all the glory, and make all the money.

A battle line existed between the managers sitting in the back and the GSAs standing out front at the desk, face-to-face with the guests. GSAs did not believe managers understood that "sometimes we have it hard because we have the guest in front of us . . . and sometimes [managers] don't get it." The lack of perceived understanding on the part of the managers was due to the fact that most managers did not know the work of the GSA because they (with the exception of one) had not worked as a full-time GSA. Thus they did not care about the workload or pressures of a GSA. This caused frustration, hurt, and other negative emotions for GSAs that had to be coped with on a daily basis. In addition, managers were conceived of as more powerful because they gave rather than received orders. These feelings about management were not related to

specific events necessarily, but were about the perceived status difference between GSAs and managers, and the lack of caring and empathy from the managers toward the GSAs.

Many GSAs believed their managers cared about something only if it affected the guest or the bottom line. "They wouldn't care, they, they wouldn't care [if] it's not affecting guests," commented one GSA. The perception was that managers did not care about nor recognize the hard work of the GSAs. One GSA said that "[The director] doesn't, doesn't praise people" and that he did not know that positive reinforcement was important. Another GSA said,

> I feel like, you know, the managers [are] like, "Well, pfff. Forget [the GSAs], you know. They're, they're working anyway. They'll work whether we pat 'em on the back or not." You know. I mean, it would be nice to have a little bit of recognition for the hard work that we do. And we work hard. And, um . . . I just feel like the [managers] don't care sometimes.

He believed that managers felt that GSAs were like machines that worked no matter whether a manager showed appreciation or not. This GSA indicated he believed that because managers did not care about him that "it makes [him] not care about the hotel." Bowen and Lawler (1992) support this relationship between management concern and caring for employees and employees' reciprocal caring behavior for the organization. Based on the results of customer service research performed at branch banks, they say that when employees believe management looks after their needs, they in return took better care of the customer. The GSA at the Regal believed that if he did care about the hotel more, he would be

> more enthusiastic with the guest [and] be more proud to work [at the Regal]. . . . [But] because I don't feel like . . . the managers care about me, it makes me not really care if the guests have, enjoy their stays, or . . . about the hotel in general.

Besides the lack of caring from managers, four GSAs complained about discrimination. An Asian GSA believed managers failed to notice how hard she and another Asian GSA, Bonnie, worked because they did not sit in the back office "ass-kissing" the managers like other GSAs.

We don't, Bonnie and I, we not kissing anybody's ass. We don't know how, and we won't, and we don't have time. . . . But [some GSAs] go in the back . . . some people left Bonnie and I working. And because we foreigners, maybe we speak with accent, and we not really, you know, foreigner usually not complain, you know. And then we not young, too, so, you know, we not going anywhere. So anyway, you will see that we always, like our feet is, is, is glued on the floor. Some people are like always in the back. Just talking. It's not about guests. It's, they just talking. And I blame managers. I blame the manager that cannot, cannot pick it out that some people work their best and some go in the back talking, having fun. . . . [And it's] unfair. Unfair. Yeah, but you know, we complain, nothing to win. You know, but, but, you know, we not going to win, you know, because we not Americans, so. What the hell. Why should? Just do work, go home. . . . You know, we foreigners. Yeah, when we work hard, you know, the [managers] don't care. You know, because we don't kiss their ass.

An African American GSA felt she was being discriminated against at the front desk because she was asked to put her hair up and none of the Caucasian GSAs were asked to. She was also told to remove her nail polish because it was not an approved color. This perceived discriminatory treatment caused her much anger, but she managed her emotions.

I try to let things slide because I don't want to make, I don't want to get too involved and really be upset. And I find that when I'm here, my feelings are very much mostly upset.

This GSA coped by trying to let "things slide." By not thinking about these potentially negative-emotion-inducing events, she may have reduced the likelihood of experiencing negative emotions that would have to be coped with. She was not reappraising the situation as having no effect on her well-being; she was aware that managers' actions toward her were different from how managers treated other employees. However, she attempted to break the connection between appraising these situations as harmful, threatening, or challenging and experiencing negative emotions. If she took action about this treatment (getting involved), she feared that more negative emotions would ensue. She appears to have coped by attempting to ignore the situation (let things slide) (see "Coping Responses" section below).

In addition to the perceived discriminatory treatment, some GSAs believed that management staff had a habit of not communicating changes to them. While I was at the hotel collecting data, the property management system (computer system) was updated, the GSAs' safes where their banks were kept were moved from behind the mail desk to downstairs near the locker room, and a new fax server that had been installed months ago was turned on. All these changes were made without notifying the front desk staff.

When the [fax] system was, you know, implemented, nobody in the hotel knew. . . . I even talked to [the director of front office operations]. He's like, "Oh yeah. It was turned on." But none of us were told.

The GSA referred to those early days with the new fax system as the "ugly days," and that guests "were frustrated," causing her frustration that had to be coped with.

Another incident occurred near the end of my time at the hotel. The director of front office operations had not communicated with all of the GSAs that he intended to move the safes downstairs in the basement near the locker rooms. Some GSAs who happened to be working during the day the move occurred knew about it. Others did not. One GSA got changed into her uniform downstairs as usual and proceeded upstairs to get her safe. She went into the safe room and the safes were not there.

The managers did not tell her about the new safe procedures. "They don't tell you. . . . " She said, "I'm used to it," meaning not being told about changes. However, she admitted, "I'm angry sometimes, mad" and that "it's, that's annoying." She said when the managers change things without informing her that it puts her "in a bad mood."

This perception of managers not considering the effects of their actions on GSAs was evident in them implementing new procedures and making other changes without considering the impact on GSAs. The perception was that management did not care about, understand, or appreciate the GSAs and the difficulty of their work, and this caused negative emotional reactions for the GSAs to cope with.

By far, most contact with management led to stressful events that produced negative emotions for the GSAs to cope with. However, GSAs spent more of their workdays servicing and interacting with guests than they did interacting with management. In the next section, I describe the stressful events and negative emotions produced from GSAs' contact with guests.

Interactions with Guests

Although interactions between guests and GSAs was sometimes a source of positive emotions for the GSAs, the interactions often resulted in GSAs experiencing stressful events and negative emotions. In the following, I describe GSAs' perceptions of guests and the influencing factors behind negative experiences between GSAs and guests.

GSAs described guests as "nasty," "rude," "stupid," and "not very friendly." Some GSAs believed that guests vented their frustrations from having a bad experience during the day on the GSAs, and that they yelled and

screamed or got an attitude when they did not get what they wanted. Some guests were described as "drunk executives," "assholes," or having "a massive chip on their shoulder." These descriptions of guests were often accompanied by descriptions of negative-emotion-producing events. It was not just that some guests were "nasty," it was that this nasty attitude translated into work events that caused negative emotions.

Many GSAs felt little control over their work environment. Yet some organizational behavior theorists argue that individuals want a sense of personal control over their environment (e.g., Bandura, 1982; DeCharms, 1968). Although GSAs could not control the work pace per se, they attempted to gain control by refraining from making eye contact with guests or pretending not to hear them. However, once the guest had gotten a GSA's attention, the GSA was required to satisfy the guest.

GSAs believed that guests were free to yell at employees when in a "bad mood" and "many guests attack[ed]" them. GSAs perceived it was their job to accept the guests' yelling and attitude.

> If a guest wants to stand there and scream at us, just let him scream at you, you know. That's why, a lot, in a lot of ways like I've become used to maybe dealing with people that are always angry. You know, you just, you're like, ah, ah, one of these dolls that they're supposed to like punch in these like psychiatric sessions. Like, oh, just punch him! You're angry! Punch him, you know. And like we're the innocent bystanders!

This GSA continued to comment on how guests' negative emotional reactions affect her. "There's like no privacy whatsoever. It's, you're exposed. You're completely exposed. You know, to any outbursts. So it's just so nerve-wracking, you know. You can't imagine how nerve-wracking it is." She believed that as part of her job she had to accept whatever behavior guests directed at her, whether it was pleasant or not. She had to learn to cope with such negative emotional outbursts on the part of the guests, and she admitted to having "become used to maybe dealing with people that are always angry." Although angry guests may not be a surprising occurrence, their angry outbursts or the anticipation of an angry outburst left this GSA feeling anxious, exposed, and frazzled.

One GSA said he believed the guest was always right, so he never said anything to angry guests when they did not get what they wanted. When guests did not receive the service they expected or desired, GSAs commented that the guests would "start screaming and making a big fuss," "get mad," "start yelling," or "throw things" at the GSA like credit cards, bags, faxes, or envelopes. Sometimes guests would go up the hierarchy and demand to see a manager; guests tended to believe the manager more than GSAs. One GSA said when a guest demanded to see a manager it made her feel like the guest had no respect for her, and that it "made [her] look dumb, like [she] didn't know what [she's] doing." Such negative feelings had to be managed by the GSAs, so that even if a guest was rude, insulting, or angry, the GSA was able to cope with his or her negative emotional reaction and refrain from expressing his or her feelings to the guest.

Whenever a guest made a demand, he or she typically did so because what had been promised or expected was not delivered. These guests' demands almost always produced negative emotions for the GSAs, particularly because the GSAs were not able to satisfy those demands. This negative emotional outcome was not surprising given that perceptions of control are central to one's sense of well-being (Thompson, 1981). Yet GSAs did not control or have the authority necessary to satisfy these types of guests' demands and, as such, faced a stressful situation capable of producing negative emotions for both the guest and the GSA.

Typically, when a guest asked or demanded to see a manager, the guest was satisfied with the outcome because all but one of the managers was known to "give in" to guests. This accommodating of the guest, however, had the effect of undercutting the GSA.

> I feel like . . . I'll do everything I can, um, to calm the guest down and . . . to negotiate something different with them [when we do not have the type of room they requested]. . . . I'll tell them there's nothing that I can do about it. . . . [But] sometimes they'll start screaming and making a big fuss, and demanding to see a manager. . . . I'll have to go and get the manager. . . . I'll explain to the manager what the situation is, and tell them what I've told the guest. But sometimes they'll just go and do it anyway. . . . The manager will come out and say, "Oh yeah, sure. We can do that" [because] maybe they don't want to deal with it. Maybe they don't want the conflict. . . . [But] it will make me look like a liar. And, um, I don't like that at all. . . . It makes me feel useless, like why am I here?

The manager's actions, while satisfying the guest, had the effect of making the GSA feel useless and like a liar. Besides having to cope with the guest's requests and being constrained by limited resources and a lack of authority to make adjustments that might satisfy the guest, the GSA also had to cope with the negative self-concept implied by the manager's actions. The manager, in effect, treated the GSA as incompetent and invalidated him. The GSA then coped with this manager by avoiding him.

Besides requesting or demanding to see a manager, guests sometimes complained about the service or problems with their rooms. These complaints were often lodged at the front desk. Although they empathized with the guests, GSAs often experienced frustration because they had no control over the situation. Although they received complaints related to many different departments, GSAs had no authority to fix problems not directly associated with the front desk.

Front desk . . . we get complaints. When someone's mad about their toilet, and they're at the desk, they're gonna tell us. . . . And it's gonna be on us. Not on engineering because maybe engineering didn't take care of the toilet properly or plumbing or whatever. And we're gonna get the blame for it. 'Cause we're the face-to-face contact with these people. . . . It's stressful. It's very stressful. . . . [The stress affects me by], it makes me, one, it makes me not want to listen to [the guests'] complaints. It makes me not want to. I know if I call engineering and tell 'em about the room. . . . They'll probably never go up there and fix it. Um, and then if the next [guest] comes up, I'm not as nice or happy or enthusiastic as I should be with the next person because I'm like, this [other guest] just chewed me out over something I had nothing, no control over.

The stress in this situation was caused not simply because the GSA received a complaint, but because she had no control over the situation. She also was frustrated because when the compliant was lodged; it reminded her that other departments were not doing their jobs the way she thought they should. This produced negative emotions for the GSA that had to be dealt with and not displayed to the guest. These frustrations and other negative emotions that resurfaced when a guest complained reduced this GSA's ability to service the next guest. The effect of negative emotions appears to have carried forward and reduced the serving ability of the GSA, and is a clear example of emotion-driven behavior.

In addition, when the GSA attempted to cope by calling engineering, she felt frustrated because from prior experience she knew she had no authority or control over engineering to make sure they fixed the problem. Another GSA commented on a similar situation. Guests also experienced frustration when problems were not fixed, and sometimes would "vent" their feelings to the GSAs. Although the GSA could empathize with the guests, she, too, felt frustrated because she knew that sometimes the problems did not get resolved.

The [guests] had to like vent their frustration. Usually, yeah, they, sometimes they get angry. Like, "I have to leave" and if they see me at the desk, like sometimes, there's a, there's a line at the front desk, they get angry. They just go ahead to [the mail] desk. And, yeah, they just get, they say what they have to say to vent their frustration and then they go. . . . What do I look like, a punching bag? Yeah, sometimes I feel like a punching bag. It's like, ugh! Yeah! It's like a punching bag, yeah.

This feeling of being "punching bags" for guests' frustration led to the GSA's own frustration that she then had to cope with. When the guests complained, she tried to get the problem fixed, but oftentimes she felt "frustrated because some [guests] do have a point. And some things have not been fixed." Lack of control over getting the problem fixed created more negative emotions that then had to be coped with. Perhaps she could have coped with being a "punching bag" for a frustrated guest if trying to fix the problem had not created more negative emotions. Certain means of coping are not always feasible since issues of authority and control placed constraints on GSAs attempting to cope.

EVENT-FOCUSED COPING RESPONSES

According to Thoits (1991), when individuals face stressful events that produce negative emotions, they must cope with the event and/or the emotions. Researchers (Lazarus and Folkman, 1984; Thoits, 1991) have identified two basic methods for coping with the event and/or the emotion: behaviorally or cognitively. When a person behaviorally copes, he or she directs action at the target of the coping: the event and/or the emotion. When a person cognitively copes, he or she attempts to think differently about the target of coping (the event and/or the emotion).

Thoits' work (1984, 1991) on coping with negative emotions indicated that emotions can be coped with by focusing not only on the stressful event that caused them, but also by manipulating components of emotions: physiological changes and/or expressive gestures. By manipulating these components either behaviorally or cognitively, the person is able to change his or her negative feelings to feelings that are less negative or more positive (see Table 4.1).

Behavioral, Stressful-Event-Focused Coping

The most obvious way of coping with one's emotions is by changing the event that provoked the negative emotional reaction in the first place. This type of coping involves acting upon or confronting the stressful situation, seeking advice, information, or assistance from someone else to deal with the problem, or withdrawing or leaving the situation. Guest services agents (GSAs) at the front desk of the Regal Hotel coped in this manner by using:

1. *Confrontation*: Attempting to directly change the stressful event.
2. *Escape*: Leaving the stressful event.
3. *Removal*: Limiting the duration of the stressful event.

4. *Avoidance*: Dodging interaction with the stressful event.
5. *Prevention*: Keeping a stressful event from happening.

Confrontation

Examples of confrontation coping responses from my study indicate that some GSAs confronted or discussed the problem with the person(s) involved or responsible for the situation. For instance, when faced with a room shortage, GSAs negotiated with the guest to resolve the problem. The following is an example of how a GSA offered different alternatives to a guest who wanted a west-side-view room on a high floor when none was available.

> I'll try to find the best room on the east side with a high, a higher floor. . . . If it's a high floor, the view is usually okay. . . . Or if, if for example, if they want a nonsmoking west view, usually we have a lot of smoking west views because people just don't want that, and I try to tell them that we can, you can go up to this room and if it smells like smoke, we'll change it, we'll deal with it and get something else. Um, usually they'll do that and they're fine.

This example clearly demonstrates behavioral, stressful-event-focused coping. This GSA

TABLE 4.1
Model of Coping

| Target | METHOD | |
	Behavioral	Cognitive
Stressful Event	Confrontation Escape Removal Avoidance Prevention	Reinterpretation Distraction Mental imagery Acceptance Wishful thinking
Physiological Changes	Relaxation techniques	Emotional distancing
Expressive Gestures	Emotional release Emotional regulation	Fantasy release

Modified from Thoits, 1991.

is not likely to be able to prevent this type of situation from happening in the future and, as a result, has learned from experience what strategies work when faced with this sort of situation. Other GSAs attempted to behaviorally manipulate the situation by seeking assistance from others in the form of information, advice, and/or practical aid. For example, "When [the guests] are rude and I can't deal with [them], I call a manager," said one GSA.

Escape

GSAs at the Regal Hotel had subtle ways of escaping a stressful situation, even on an extremely temporary basis (e.g., a few fleeting seconds on the phone with a significant other or a few stolen minutes in the safe room).

> "I go in the back. Sometimes I have, I have to go in the back in the safe room. . . . There's nobody around . . . and you can collect your thoughts."

> "I'm escaped for one second onto the phone with my boyfriend, escaped from work."

In many of these escape-coping responses, a GSA was able to return to work successfully after a temporary reprieve. Certainly sneaking into the safe room to collect one's thoughts is not a coping response for dealing with larger stressful events, but it does appear effective for coping with a temporary "stress-overload" and for restoring, even temporarily, equilibrium enough so that one can face coping with more stressful events. Folkman and Lazarus (1991, p. 215) state, however, that many escape-avoidance coping responses are not likely "to produce a beneficial effect, especially beyond the moment." Yet for the GSAs, a moment may be all they need or have time for, given the pace of their work.

Removal

Coping responses of this type involved more than trying to change the event; removal-type coping involved trying to get rid of the event so the individual does not have to deal with it. In the case of the Regal Hotel, removal of

stressful events equated to removal of stressful guests. Some GSAs behaved in ways to shorten the interaction time with the guest because they wanted the "stressful" guest to leave. For example, when one GSA was feeling stressed, she tried to get the guests "outta [her] face" as quickly as possible. To achieve this, the GSA limited her conversation with the guests to shorten the check-in or checkout process.

> If I'm stressed and I'm upset . . . I won't even mention certain things to [the guests], and it's not because I don't feel they deserve it. . . . I just want to check 'em in and check them out and get 'em going. And I, I mean that's bad to say but, that's honest. I really want to check them in, give a smile, blah, blah, blah, blah, and get them outta my face.

Using this type of coping response, the GSA is actually trying to eliminate the stressful situation, not by solving the problem necessarily but by actively attempting to remove the stressful event from the immediate environment.

Avoidance

Another type of behavioral, stressful-event-focused coping response that emerged from my research study involved avoidance. This type of coping involves avoiding stressful situations that, from prior experience, are known to trigger negative emotions.

> "I can't talk to [my co-worker] though. . . . I feel awkward. . . . So I'm at work trying to avoid him, you know, like always avoiding."

> [The director] seems to have an attitude, like, like he's too important, to deal with anything, with any of us. . . . He kind of looks down at, looks down his nose at people and . . . it makes me not like him. And it makes me avoid him.

Prevention

Prevention-type coping emerged as another type of coping engaged in by the GSAs at the

Regal Hotel. Being able to prevent a stressful event from occurring, however, requires previous experience with or anticipation of an event that is likely to produce negative emotions. GSAs actively attempted to manage their environments in ways that lessened the likelihood of negative events occurring. For example, to keep guests from getting angry because they were not given the upgrade they requested, one GSA used humor to prevent a negative emotional reaction from guests. She said, "I try to add a little humor and stuff, just to make it, like, the letdown a little bit easier." By doing so, she was usually able to prevent the guest from getting upset.

Another GSA warded off potential problems with guests who had requested a nonsmoking room when none were available. Rather than confirming the guest's room preference, the GSA simply sent the guest to a smoking room. "Sometimes, like when it's really busy, unless a guest specifically asks for [a nonsmoking room] . . . we'll just give a smoking room. And nine times out of ten they won't know, they won't know the difference." This GSA's coping response was successful. He did not have to cope with an upset, disappointed, and/or complaining guest, and his strategy typically caused no repercussions—the guest did not return to the desk.

One GSA was accused of being $100 short in her drop (the amount of money the computer system says a GSA collected during the day minus money returned to guests who made cash deposits on their rooms and spent less than they anticipated and were owed money back). The cashier (who counted the money in the GSAs' drops, confirmed the drops were correct, and deposited the money) had already distributed the GSAs' money from their drops and was not able to show this GSA her drop. Because she was given no proof the mistake was hers, she did not trust the cashier. However, the "cashier rules," she said, and she had to replace the $100 because she was "liable for the money in [her] bank." All GSAs sign an agreement when they start working

at the Regal indicating they accept liability for the $3000 in their banks. However, as a result of this situation, and her anger over the situation, the GSA vowed this would never happen again.

> I have my drop signed now. I have someone, a manager count it. I don't, I'm not trusting anymore. And I'm not saying that, I don't put anything past anybody. Never. So I'm just cautious now. Since $100 came out of my paycheck, my pocket, I'm cautious. I'll never get . . . it'll never happen again, ever.

In fact, she questioned who was at fault, and because she was given no proof, no longer trusted the cashier. Having been burned once, the GSA was extra careful to prevent this negative-emotion-producing event from happening again. Her precautions, however, were not to keep herself from bringing on the situation. Her strategies were to prevent the cashier from making a mistake and blaming it on her. The GSA protected herself from future blame and having to experience anger and frustration.

Cognitive, Stressful-Event-Focused Coping

Whenever behavioral manipulation of an event is not possible, cognitive manipulation is. Because manipulation of stressful situations "is most often limited to persons with power or resources (such as authority or money) . . . most people are likely to use other techniques to manipulate their reactions" (Thoits, 1984, p. 226). Guest services agents (GSAs) at the front desk of the Regal Hotel coped in this manner by using:

1. *Reappraisal*: Reinterpreting an event so it appears less threatening to well-being and thus produces a less severe negative emotional reaction.

2. *Distraction*: Attempting to distract oneself from thinking about the situation by keeping busy doing something.
3. *Mental imagery*: Cognitively attempting to keep oneself from thinking about a stressful situation. Rather than engaging in a new activity to halt focusing on a stressful event (like in distraction), this "thought-stopping" coping entails purely cognitive efforts.
4. *Acceptance*: Accepting the stressful event because it appears beyond one's control.
5. *Wishful thinking*: Fantasizing about a magical solution to, or escape from, the stressful situation.

Reappraisal

Much of the reappraisal type of coping used by the GSAs at the Regal Hotel involved dealing with stressful guests and evoking empathy for them.

> I understand when like [the guests] want what they requested when they make the reservation, 'cause if it me I'd probably flip out as well you know. You can't blame 'em.

By separating themselves from the focus of the guests' comments, and seeing the situation from the guests' perspectives, the GSAs appeared less likely to experience anger or frustration. The guests' comments were not interpreted as an attack, but rather as a venting of emotions regarding the situation. Having empathy for a guest was a coping mechanism reinforced by the hotel. GSAs were asked to anticipate and fulfill the needs of the guests, and this involved trying to understand the guests' perspective.

Distraction

Besides coping with a stressful situation using reappraisal, an individual may attempt to distract him- or herself from thinking about the situation by keeping busy doing something else. The following examples of this form of coping were found at the Regal Hotel.

> . . . I went [to the employee holiday party]. . . . And you know [my managers] knew that I was upset, so they made me get up and dance. And it helped me. . . . It helped me.

> [My frustration doesn't last long] 'cause then somebody else will come up and then another problem arises so you forget about the first one.

The distraction, as evidenced by the last quotation, does not necessarily have to be pleasant. A busy night at the front desk was apt to help this GSA forget about a stressful situation because a new situation presented itself.

Mental Imagery

Coping of this form involves cognitive attempts, rather than involvement in a new activity, to keep oneself from thinking about a stressful event. One GSA said about a stressful event he recently faced, "I just pretty much deal with it. . . . I just blow it off. . . . I try to put it out of my mind." Another GSA stated, "So you gotta go home and forget it—you gotta just forget about it." Coping of this form may entail simple instructions to oneself to stop thinking about the situation, or may involve attempts to think positively about a situation.

Acceptance

Accepting the situation sometimes is the only alternative available for individuals coping with stressful situations beyond their control. This type of cognitive, stressful-event-focused coping response was not uncommon the GSAs, since sometimes the only alternative for them was to resign themselves to the situation.

> We have to laugh because there's nothing else we can do.

> . . . For me I don't care. I say, okay, I don't care, you know, because I cannot change my looks, right?

Some of these passive attempts to simply tolerate or accept a situation the GSA believed he or she had no control over were combined with elements of reappraisal. When the GSA states she cannot change her looks (she was foreign and felt her manager discriminated against her), and then adds, "I don't care," she may be actively trying to convince herself she does not care. When one does not care about a situation, it is less likely to affect one's well-being.

Wishful Thinking

Wishful thinking is another example of cognitive, stressful-event-focused coping used by the GSAs at the Regal Hotel. For example, two GSAs were coping with an ongoing strain, that is, going to work. One said, "I really don't like coming to work. . . . I wish I could just go home sometimes." The other commented, "I wish I could win the lottery today. I don't want to go [to work] anymore." Their statements of desired outcomes appear to be triggered by their desperation, and simply fantasizing about a better place (being home or winning the lottery) may provide a needed, temporary, even fleeting, respite. When a situation feels like it is not under one's control, wishful thinking may provide temporary hope or something to look forward to.

EMOTION-FOCUSED COPING RESPONSES

Aside from coping with the stressful event, one may cope with the emotion. Either behaviorally or cognitively, an individual can alter a negative emotion, either eliminating it or replacing it with more positive emotions. As stated earlier, emotions may be coped with by targeting, in addition to stressful events already discussed, physiological sensations and expressive gestures.

Physiological Sensations

Less frequently observed or reported coping techniques involve manipulating physiological sensations either cognitively or behaviorally. Behaviorally, a person can use stimulants or depressants (e.g., caffeine, drugs), physical exercise, or relaxation techniques in order to "generate the physiological changes associated with a desired emotional state" (Thoits, 1984, p. 226). At the Regal Hotel, GSAs were not allowed to drink coffee at the front desk and could not easily leave the front desk to go smoke. If a guest was upset, a GSA could not tell the guest to wait while he or she smoked a cigarette or popped a pill. Obviously, this type of coping technique may not be applicable to discrete stressful work incidents.

Individuals may attempt to quiet a racing heart and/or rapid breathing in order to get control of themselves and their emotions. Note the coping responses that emerged from my data. Some responses, such as counting to ten, are useful for coping with discrete events while other responses, such as going home and having a drink, may be useful for coping with larger, or ongoing, strains.

. . . I usually try to calm myself down, be like one, two, three, count to ten.

You just hold back. You just let it, you gotta just like take a deep breath.

Or I go in the back. Sometimes I have, I have to go in the back in the safe room. . . . Just cool off . . . to take a, a deep breath.

My data clearly identified self-controlling coping through physiological means as a common method among the GSAs at the Regal Hotel. Certainly many of these behavioral, physiological coping responses such as counting and taking deep breaths are so temporary in nature and fleetingly employed that when asking respondents to identify how they coped with a stressful situation a week ago or a month ago, they would not be apt to remember, or perhaps might not even consider such responses as coping.

Altering physiological sensations cognitively is more difficult then altering other emotion components like situational cues or expressive gestures, and requires using techniques like biofeedback or progressive desensitization. Use of this coping technique is not likely to be found in an actual work setting. However, I found another type of "desensitization" via cognitive efforts that I labeled *emotional distancing*. This type of coping appears to reflect cognitive efforts on the part of the GSAs not to experience emotions, to detach himself or herself emotionally from a stressful discrete event or ongoing strain. Although one might argue that emotional distancing is an example of behaviorally manipulating one's expression of emotion, I argue that these coping responses go beyond the gesture; the individual is attempting not to have the feelings in the first place. The individual is numb, "zoned out," or "turned off" from feeling negative emotions.

> I prepare myself. . . . I pretty much become numb. . . . I don't have as much expression in the end [when interacting with difficult guests]. . . . I'm not smiling as much.

> I do this every, every day and I don't know, I don't feel anything.

> Nothing's relaxed. . . . That's why [the GSAs that have worked here a long time] zone everybody out. . . . The old-timers just stand there. . . . Like Melenie. . . . [A guest] could stand in front of her for five minutes and she won't look up until she's good and ready.

> I try not to let it affect the way I feel. And I try to just turn off when I come to work because, I mean, if I took everything too personally, and if I let all this stuff affect me, I'd be a basket case.

Most of these emotional-distancing coping responses are a reaction to an ongoing strain: work. In order to get through their days at work, some GSAs have learned to not feel any-

thing, become numb, or turn off—all ways of coping. Others who hypothesized about the impact of emotional labor demands may have recognized this coping response. Albrecht and Zemke (1985) warned that excessive contact with customers may cause employees to become "detached." Van Maanen and Kunda (1989) described amusement park ride operators who coped with rules regarding not expressing any negative emotions by going on "automatic pilot" or into a "trance" and experienced only "emotional numbness." Perhaps what these researchers were describing as the consequences of customer contact work was really just the display of coping responses to work-related stresses.

Expressive Gestures

Another emotion-focused coping strategy involves manipulating observable expressive gestures to elicit desired emotions. My research study at the Regal Hotel revealed clear examples of GSAs using this coping response to deal with negative emotions. Behaviorally, informants expressed emotion, a domain I labeled *emotional release*, and tried to hide, repress, or control feelings, a domain I called *emotion regulation*. Informants cognitively manipulated expressive gestures by fantasizing about expressing negative emotions, a type of coping called *fantasy release*.

Emotional Release

Although display rules at the Regal Hotel dictated repression of the display of negative emotions toward guests, GSAs did express emotions as a way of coping with stressful events. "Venting" was a popular coping response among the GSAs, and was the pressure-release valve to discharge built-up negative emotions.

> Usually you talk to your, your peers. . . . Like if you, sometimes we all go in the safe room. . . . We just talk about it in the back.

Once [the guest] leaves, [I] just . . . start cursing him out kinda under my breath.

We mumble amongst each other. I guess it's just like . . . we just express our frustration.

I vent with Mike all the time on the train ride home . . . so he just has to listen.

Sometimes I slam the phone. Like, like if a guest is really rude on the phone, I just slam the phone. I shouldn't but . . . [it] makes you feel better.

Clearly, even with organizational display rules dictating the types of emotions that can be displayed to guests, GSAs devised other ways to release their emotions. Supportive co-workers were the sponges for much of the emotional expression, although some GSAs did express emotion in private or through other means (cursing under one's breath or slamming the phone). However, most emotional expression was in the form of venting to supportive others.

Emotional Regulation

GSAs attempted to manage their expression of negative emotions either by hiding, repressing, or controlling their emotions. For example, one GSA spoke to herself, in essence to keep herself from crying, during a meeting between her and a co-worker with whom she was fighting over a desired morning schedule.

I was like trying not to cry. I was like, "I'm not going to burst here into tears, you know. I'm not going to do it." I kept telling myself. So I was too busy telling myself, "Don't cry, don't cry."

When it came to serving guests, GSAs were aware of the display rules. Guests were never to be the recipients of GSAs' negative emotions. One GSA described how she attempted to control her negative feelings triggered by a guest, repressing them so they did not influence her when serving other guests. Others simply kept their feelings to themselves—held

them in.

I just held it in and then I went, and I went back to work.

Sometimes it's like you have less . . . patience for other [guests] who might come by. And usually I try not to take it out on people 'cause you know, they have nothing to do with it, but you gotta repress it, so that it doesn't come through to other people, you know.

Self-control of emotional expression was a coping method employed by the GSAs for adhering to organizational display rules, but was also employed voluntarily by them.

Fantasy Release

Fantasy release is a type of coping involving fantasized expression of negative emotions on the part of the individual experiencing the emotions. At the Regal Hotel, GSAs were constrained from expressing any negative emotions toward guests (display rules), and also GSAs avoided expressing negative emotions toward each other (voluntary emotion work). Perhaps due to these constraints, and because other emotional expression outlets were not available (such as going into the safe room and venting to co-workers), GSAs resorted to cognitively manipulating expressive gestures, that is, fantasizing about expressing negative emotions to the individual who triggered them.

For example, the following GSA had been dealing with a guest and his problem regarding settling his account up to that point in his stay. The GSA was trying to explain the situation to the guest, but his frustration was becoming obvious and his patience wearing thin.

I wanted to say [to the guest], "You idiot! Why don't you understand what I'm telling you?" . . . I'd love to have like smacked him around! . . . You know, don't get irritable with me, you know. Don't get snippy with me or any of that, you know.

She did not say this to the guest because, she said, ". . . I don't outwardly come out to people that way. . . . But it doesn't mean I don't think those things. Those thoughts go through your head." Perhaps "pretending" to express her negative emotions brings enough release so that she can continue serving the guest without having her negative emotions "slip" out to the guest.

Another GSA desired expressing her negative feelings for her manager to her manager. Once while serving a guest, her manager attempted to interrupt her transaction with the guest by waving a paper in front of her. This interruption created negative emotions for the GSA, who fantasized about showing them. "I just want to take the thing and rip it," she said. Doing so would have allowed her to release her negative emotions in a symbolically angry gesture toward her boss. However, she was able to manage her negative emotions and did not rip the paper. Perhaps just wishing she could was enough release to allow her to continue with her work.

By releasing their emotions in their minds, the GSAs may have been better prepared to control their emotional displays. Controlling emotions is a necessary job task in face-to-face customer contact positions like front desk agents.

CONCLUSION

By uncovering the process of how front desk agents cope with the negative emotions generated from stressful work events, managers may better understand the coping methods these employees use to get through their days. Successful engagement of appropriate coping strategies can make the difference between an employee reasonably handling a customer service situation and an employee who lashes out at a customer, expressing inappropriate behaviors and signs of stress to the customer. An employee's ability to manage his or her behaviors, to cope with emotional reactions result-

ing from stressful transactions, has important ramifications on customers' perception of quality service (Schneider and Bowen, 1995).

This study has shown, however, that although coping strategies may be functional for the individual, they may actually interrupt, degrade, or enhance an employee's work performance. For example, when employees use avoidance or prevention coping responses, they may unintentionally negatively affect the quality of customer service provided. A case in point is the GSA at the Regal Hotel who, regardless of whether or not the guest had requested a nonsmoking room at the time the reservation was made, simply sent the guest to a smoking room if that was all he had at the time. Certainly, this is not an example of superior customer service. Simply because most guests did not return to the front desk to complain about being sent to a smoking room does not mean the guest was pleased about it either.

Another coping response that has direct implications for customer service is emotional distancing. This desensitization of the individual as a means of coping with work is apt to have negative consequences in terms of an employee's ability to provide caring customer service. By going numb and not feeling, an employee is less likely to be sympathetic to customers' needs. GSAs who go numb or "zone out" perhaps experience less negative emotional reactions to potentially stressful events, but also may deliver less attentive customer service.

Aside from understanding the many ways coping responses of service personnel may affect customer service, managers of service employees, by having a better understanding of coping, may be able to help new employees cope with the demands of their jobs. Having more senior employees with good customer service skills share with more junior employees effective ways of coping may reduce the stress experienced by these newcomers and at the same time help them deliver excellent customer service. For example, when the GSAs at the Regal Hotel used empathy to cope with stressful guests, they delivered better service because they understood the needs of the guests. In addition, other coping responses such as emotional release, when directed at a supportive other, may prevent the GSAs from expressing their negative emotions to the guests. This indirect expression of emotion may have provided enough relief that the GSA was able to tolerate another stressful event without expressing organizationally undesirable emotions. What might appear to be idle chatter among employees may actually be an effective coping response.

At the Regal Hotel, more stressful work events appeared to involve others at work than they did physical elements of the work environment. These types of "people events" may have been less amenable to change and thus prompted the types of coping responses found in this study. The most common coping responses of the GSAs at the Regal Hotel appear to provide temporary relief from stressful events. These types of temporary, stopgap measures may be the only feasible coping responses given the context in which the GSAs work. The pace at the front desk is quick, and certain time periods during the day are marked by heavy guest arrivals and departures. During these times, GSAs are essentially "glued" to the desk and have little time to think about how to solve a problem. Taking a deep breath to gain control of one's emotions, attempting to suppress negative emotions, or simply attempting to not think about a stressful event one cannot control may be the most logical and effective coping responses given the context and the constraints the context imposes on coping responses.

4.3   The Electrifying Job of the Front Office Manager

James A. Bardi

The exciting atmosphere of a hotel lobby often intrigues students of hotel management. People from all walks of life and corners of the world cross paths to discuss and share ideas, greet family and friends to celebrate special occasions, attend conferences to debate issues, or discuss business deals. Questions concerning arrivals, meeting times, rates, food and beverage services, directions, transportation services, or whereabouts of the management staff and guests create a commotion, which seems overwhelming at times. Is there someone in charge here? The preprofessional who sets a career objective of becoming the general manager of a hotel and hopes the required tenure as a front office manager (FOM) proceeds with haste will find the role challenging. If you begin your career in hotel management as a front desk clerk, bellperson, or cashier, you have a vast opportunity to explore just who is in charge.

In a 1985 study, Rutherford discussed the important dimensions of the FOM's job. Selected job functions reported in the research findings included communications—with guests and employees; facilitation—medical emergencies, selling up, power-failure procedures, walking guests due to overbooking, and design of the computer system for the front office; organizational interface—with the director of marketing, controller, food and beverage manager, and catering manager; and technical minutia. These job skills and interactions require a person to prioritize and to resolve many issues, to make quick decisions based upon sound corporate management concepts, to empower employees, and to refine communication techniques that are exemplary.

Bardi (1990, pp. 345–349) stated, "The front office manager must take an active role in gathering information of interest to guests and in developing procedures for the front office to use in disbursing this information." This information is also needed by various departments to assist in delivering and organizing hospitality. This is a tall order for the FOM to accomplish, especially considering the total realm of potential information guests may require and from what departments. Those hotel departmental areas and their sources of guest information are included in Table 4.2.

Thus the FOM must embrace the charge of becoming a proactive communicator and facilitator. This hotel executive must analyze and seek out what pieces of information the guest will probably need and which departments will need to interact to fulfill these needs.

Further inquiry into the role of the FOM can be accomplished by reviewing the elements of a job analysis of this position. Bardi (1990, pp. 49–50) presents a job analysis of an FOM's duties on a typical day.

- Reviews night audit report.
- Reviews incoming reservations for the day.
- Communicates information to employees on all shifts concerning reservations, room assignments, and room inventory.
- Communicates information to other departments—housekeeping, marketing and sales, banquets, food and beverage, plant engineering, and security.
- Resolves guest billing discrepancies and other complaints.
- Prepares budget with general manager and controller.
- Prepares forecasting sheet.
- Conducts business meetings to promote room sales.
- Assists in check-in, checkout, reservation confirmations, updating reservation system.
- Interviews potential front office employees.
- Communicates with night auditor.
- Maintains front office equipment.

TABLE 4.2
Interdepartmental communication

Department	Information Needed from Front Office
Marketing and Sales	Guest history, reservations, first impressions, relaying messages, and guest function information.
Housekeeping	Room status, potential house count, security concerns, and requests for amenities and supplies.
Food and Beverage	Relaying messages, accurate voucher information, posting of charges to guest accounts, predicted house counts, and paid-outs.
Banquet	Information on scheduled events, process of payment of guest charges for scheduled events, preparation of daily function board and marquee, and a public communication post.
Controller	Daily summary of financial transactions, financial data for billing, and credit card ledgers.
Maintenance	Room status and guest requests for maintenance service.
Security	Fire safety, emergency communication information, and investigation of guest security concerns.
Human Resources	Initial point of contact and screening for potential employees.

Scheduling

Although this list represents only a few of the many duties performed in any one day in the life of an FOM, it provides the aspiring hospitality professional with an idea of the range of managerial activities. The FOM must stay in control of all activities that affect the delivery of hospitality to the guest—a major function of a hotel's financial success.

If delivering hospitality to the guest is a major responsibility of the FOM, what are the components of this subsystem of the hotel operation? How does the front office and subsequently the FOM fit in? An answer to this question can be derived from reviewing the "guest service cycle" in a hotel (adapted from Albrecht and Zemke, 1985). If the FOM analyzes the various guest-departmental contacts, it is possible to gain insights toward understanding how the front office fits into the efficient delivery of the hotel's hospitality services. The potential departmental contacts in the cycle are:

- *Marketing*: Preparing and administering customer surveys with concern for guest satisfaction, advertising methods, and incentive promotions.
- *Reservations*: Developing and monitoring a reservation system with regard to ease of access to toll-free numbers, fax, and national reservation system, and to telephone manner of personnel with regard to reservations, cancellations, accommodation availability, complimentary services and products, and general information.
- *Registration*: Developing and monitoring a registration system with regard to concern for managing a guest transportation shuttle system; insuring a first-contact greeting; providing assistance with luggage; organizing an efficient check-in procedure; maintaining a room status system; processing credit cards; operating a guest information system that centralizes all communication between the guest and the hotel with regard to housekeeping, food and beverage, maintenance, and other hotel departments.

- *Guest stay*: Coordinating guest communications with all departments in the hotel to ensure guest satisfaction in restaurants, lounges, room service, gift shops, housekeeping services, security, wake-up calls, telephone system, and guest folio availability.
- *Checkout*: Developing and providing an efficient checkout system with regard to coordinating flexible checkout times, providing assistance with luggage, maintaining in-room video checkout option, monitoring guest wait-time in line, and providing folio accuracy and printout.

This listing of components in a guest service cycle suggests the vast array of duties the FOM will encounter in managing the delivery of hospitality services. However, there is one piece of "electrifying magic" that is still required to make front office hospitality relevant to modern service delivery realities: employee empowerment.

Sternberg (1992) discusses the concept of empowerment as a granting of authority to employees to make everyday decisions within guidelines. For example, many guests of a hotel feel they are in the middle of a bureaucracy when they want to have a charge adjusted on their account folio. "Step aside and I'll call my supervisor" is too often the response to a guest's inquiry of a charge adjustment. After all, the cashier is doing only what he or she was trained to do. However, the guest doesn't care what the training was; he just knows the system isn't "user friendly." As Sternberg emphasizes, if guidelines are established and communicated, the cashier should know what to do. Here is the manager's chance to provide that first electrifying "jolt" of empowerment.

Charges within a specified dollar amount that are debated can be credited or adjusted without the supervisor's approval. A corresponding control system can be implemented that will reveal the extent of the credit granted per cashier.

Another example of providing empowerment opportunities for front office staff is provided by Allin and Halpine (1988) in describing quality assurance training at the Waldorf-Astoria.

While there can be many reasons to combine the positions of registration clerk and cashier, and many aspects were considered at the Waldorf-Astoria, the decision was driven by a desire to improve guest service where its impact is most obvious—at the front desk. Cross-trained employees speed the check-in and checkout process by performing both functions, as the traffic at the desk dictates. Registration clerks can cash checks and cashiers can issue duplicate room keys, in many cases eliminating the necessity of having the guest wait in two lines.

Other opportunities to provide employee empowerment can be identified through careful analysis by the FOM of the progress of the guest through the "guest service cycle."

The potential opportunities to serve or misserve the guest can be appreciated when viewed in the context of guests times service contacts. If 12 million guests pass through a hotel company's entire system in a year and each has an average of 12 contacts with hotel staff—guest service staff, housekeepers, front office clerks, and others—that's 144 million chances for the chain to give a good or bad impression (Bardi, 1990, p. 233). As the gatekeeper of many, if not most of these potential contacts, the FOM is in a unique position to help his or her staffs enhance the guest experience. Empowerment is another powerful tool in the FOM's managerial arsenal.

The role of the FOM is one that demands a mastery of communication, operational details, and increasingly, empowerment. The challenging and attractive nature of this role allows the new hospitality professional to try various ways to apply interpersonal skills that will provide a profit for the hotel. It is a challenge, which will last a lifetime.

4.4 A Day in the Life of the Front Office Manager

Garry Dickover

It's 6:00 A.M. on a Saturday morning. The alarm clock is blaring its normal *beep, beep, beep, beep*. The sun is peering through the window. Time to start another day as front office manager. It's going to be a busy day: 800 arrivals, 750 departures. Plus, the hotel is 50 rooms oversold. It is going to be a fun one.

It's 7:00 A.M. The drive to work is an easy one this Saturday morning. It gives me a chance to think about what is on tap for today. There is a 9 A.M. preonvention meeting for the group that is arriving today. There is the regular morning prehift meeting. Today I also have to review hospitality standards with the front desk staff. You would think that it would be easy to have people smile and greet

the guest, use a guest's name, add a value statement about the hotel or city, and thank the guest for their business. I don't ask for much, but to train people to do those four things can be a challenge.

Preshift meetings are a very important start to the day, but it can be a hassle getting everyone together. There are a lot of reasons why an associate can't make a preshift meeting but that meeting is very important to the success of my department. It is the time that I have everyone together, let them know what is going on for the day, and get a chance to share with them the standards that we have set and how they can apply it to the customers. At 1:00 P.M. today I have a safety meeting, and at 4:00 I have my weekly rap session with the telephone department. Yeah, I think to myself, it is going to be a full day.

As I arrive to work, I can see that the checkouts have already started. It is nice to see the bellmen taking care of our guests. As I scan the grounds, I make sure that there is no trash on the ground, the bell carts are clean, and the valet parking staff is hustling to retrieve guest cars. I look at the windows of the entryway to the hotel to check for cleanliness. The front drive is the first and last thing a guest sees, so it has to be looking good. Today, all looks good. It is better for me to spot-check the area before the general manager comes by and sees any problems. As the FOM, I learned the GM's route when he arrived to work, so I make sure that the area is clean. (This is something that they did not teach me in college, along with how to repair printers and copy machines—some things you gotta learn by doing.) This morning, things look good.

It's 7:50 A.M., and I make my way to the back of the front office. My desk managers are busy getting information ready for the preshift meeting. As I walk through the area, I always make it a point to greet people and wish them a good morning. I know how important it is to give each and every associate a cheerful good morning. It sets the stage for the day. And you know, it really does make people feel good. A good department head recognizes his or her associates. The first words that come out of your mouth should be pleasant. The front office team takes the brunt of all the complaints. They don't need me to harp on them.

The preshift meeting goes smoothly. The desk managers prep the team for the day, I review the hospitality standards, and we are set. As we are about to finish, I notice some tension on the staff's faces. They know that they are in for a tough day (remember, 50 rooms oversold), so it is important that I don't let the team see on my face any stress I may feel. The team knows how important it is to sell out the hotel. They know that once a room has been empty overnight, you never get a chance to sell that room again. They also know

you have to oversell the hotel. This is the time that I can reassure them that the revenue department has calculated all of the slip percentages for the big group checking in. A *slip percentage* is the expected variation from stated arrival and room "pickup" percentages the group's meeting planner promised. It is very important for me to develop a good relationship with the revenue department. The FOM has to be active in the forecast meetings to ensure that you are not "sold up the river," meaning overcommitted by the sales staff.

Relationship building is also a very important job for the FOM. It is where trust is established—trust between you and the other departments. It is not "me versus them," it's *us*, trying to maximize revenue and occupancy and continue to build loyalty. This is the time to reassure the team that if we do our jobs as we have been trained, all will be fine. We do a little cheer, and out to the desk they go! Now, for a cup of coffee.

I review the plans with the desk managers for the sold-out night. This is also the time I check availability at other hotels, check the stay-over requests and no-show percentages, and check for duplicated reservations. It looks like they have it under control. I double-check the staffing during the peak periods and remind the managers to get everyone to lunch. (As simple as this sounds, sometimes we forget.) I check my watch, 30 minutes to the precon. Better pull out the group résumé, which is our profile of the group that includes, among many other things, a historical profile of the group's room pickups, occupancies, food and beverage revenues, etc.

At 8:45 A.M., I'm off to the precon. I head by the desk to wave to the staff, stop by the PBX, bell stand, and the concierge desk. All seems to be going smooth. At the precon, we all do our formal introductions, meet the group's representatives, usually including the meeting planner and members of the group's leadership. We each discuss our individual departments and what relationships we will have with the group. This is our time to "sell them" on how well we will do for their group. It is a successful precon; all of the parties seem to be happy. I spend just a couple of minutes with the group convention manager giving her an update on the oversold situation. If we have to walk guests, it is important to let the group convention manager know about the situation. Today I said we might, but we should be in good shape. She thanks me for the update.

As I make my way back to the front office, I end up walking with the resident manager (RM). He asks me how things went last night and how our hotel is for tonight. As an FOM, it is important to know what your boss is going to ask you. Each boss is different, but they always seem to ask the same questions. It is important to review the daily sales and occupancy report from the previous day so you know what is going on and can share this information with the RM. I gave the resident manager the information he wanted, always emphasizing the positives.

When I get back to my office, I have a couple of associates wanting to talk to me. They are bothered by the new schedule. They wanted some specific days off and, because of the business, they did not get them. This is a very delicate situation. You want to be fair to the team, but you also have to respect why your managers did what they did. The best thing to do is to listen to what your associates say and then review the situation. I have found that 80 percent of the time, there is an alternative. You want to create win-win solutions. By spending time with your associates, you demonstrate to them that you care about their situation; this helps build loyalty. *Remember that they don't care how much you know until they know how much you care.* Another situation solved.

The next couple of hours are spent reviewing the previous day's information and getting caught up on e-mail, memos, and other communications. Generally, this is the time that I get a couple of phone calls from upset guests. This could be for a variety of reasons. Before checkout, some people always want the let the "manager" know how things went. It is important to listen to your customers when they complain. It is a great way to find out what

type of deficiencies you may have in the hotel's service processes. Most complaints are caused because there was a breakdown in the process. Sometimes people can get upset over the smallest of things. Sometimes, they have a right to be upset. One example from past experience was the room being so cold that when the guest lifted the toilet seat, the water had a small sheet of ice on it. Ensuring customer satisfaction is the large part of the FOM's job. You have to own hospitality. Your team sets the stage for a guest's entire stay. It had better be good!

By now it is 12:15 P.M. and time for lunch. I grab the information I need for the 1:00 P.M. safety meeting. I will go directly to that meeting after lunch. As I make my way, I check on the desk and the house count. We are now only 29 oversold. We have had some cancelled reservations, and we also had 18 early departures. Things are looking good.

At 1:00 P.M. I walk into the safety meeting. This is never a very exciting meeting, but it is always a very important meeting. Accidents are very costly to the hotel. It is important to keep accident prevention at the "top of mind" for all associates. Today we talk about the most current accidents, how they could have been prevented, and what our next steps are. We also discuss the implications of safety and security interests for our guests. This is important to avoid lawsuits and provide guests with a safe and secure environment. The meeting wraps up at 2:30 P.M. Back to the front office.

As I come down the escalator, I see that the check-ins are starting to arrive. I head to the bell stand to check with the bell captain to see if he is caught up. All is well. Since there are some lines forming at the desk, I make my way back behind the front desk to handle a few check-ins. I always like this part of the job. It also gets a smile from the desk clerks. Before you know it, you have helped move the line. Since the desk is staying busy, it is time for me to move out to the lobby and "manage from the lobby." This is a great way to watch what is happening. You can view your whole front office team by being in the lobby. (You can also ensure the cleanliness of the area. This helps our friends in housekeeping.) A big part of the job in the lobby is just answering questions and giving directions. Every guest I help means that one guest did not have to go to the front desk and one more guest did not have to stand in line. This is the fun part of the job!

At 3:50 P.M. my pager goes off. It is a reminder about my 4:00 rap sessions. I can't believe 90 minutes passed while I was in the lobby. It is a good day.

Meeting with associates provides me an opportunity to get a pulse of what is going on. I do it in small groups or as a one-on-one rap. It helps build a relationship within the team and also helps identify challenges that you may not be aware of in your area. I ask some leading questions. I do this so the session does not become a "bitch session." This helps me control the meeting. During this meeting, some comments are made about some equipment that is needed and that we need another par (an addition to inventory) of uniforms for the team. It would be great to buy them all new uniforms, but we have to manage it within our budget. Sometimes that is hard to do. I take notes on their comments and will pass them on to the other managers. It is important for all of the managers to be in the loop. I always keep the raps to about an hour.

By now it is 5 P.M., our peak check-in time. I go back out to the lobby to see how things are going. On a busy day like today, I will typically spend the next couple of hours helping out in the lobby. At 5:30 P.M., the night man-

ager on duty (MOD) comes out to meet with me. We usually work the lobby together while I give him some updates from the day. He also shares with me any things that happened from the previous night. Of course, the first thing he shows me is the house count: 24 rooms oversold and 352 arrivals expected. We are in good shape. It is important to track the number of no-shows you have. This helps you make better decisions to maximize your revenue. The MOD is a little nervous, so I tell him not to worry, we will be fine. We review the "sold-out night" so we don't miss anything. He tells me that he already has the "walk letters" (expressing our regret and outlining our promises to a guest who is "walked" to another hotel) out on the desk. This brings a good laugh. We have done this plenty of times so I trust that the hotel is in good hands.

It's 7 P.M. and things seem to be in good shape. Time to go home. I make one more trip around to the different departments in the front office to see how they are doing and wish them a good evening. Another good day!

The day listed above is a typical day as a front office manager. Some days have different meetings, some days have more upset guests, some days have more upset associates, and some days are just better than others are. The thing that I have learned over the years is that the job of the FOM is the same. Take care of the associates, who will take care of the customer, who will take care of the business. It's the same job, just different players, and I love it.

4.5   Yield Management: Choosing the Most Profitable Reservations

[handwritten: get the right price for the right room at the right time.]

William J. Quain and Stephen M. LeBruto

INTRODUCTION

Yield management as a term is not very exciting. However, the *results* of a well-run yield

management program are certainly exciting! Properly implemented it means that a business can make more money. The keys are to sell more and sell more profitable items.

The first step in a yield management program is to determine who is the best customer. The best customer is the one who can spend the most money at your property purchasing profitable items. The products and services you provide are the best fit for their needs. The best customers for the property are the ones who receive the greatest benefit from your services. They are willing to pay more, buy more frequently, and remain more loyal because you are satisfying their needs.

Many operations do not know who the best customers are. However, the answer is in a property's data collection system. Guest histories, food and beverage checks, cash register receipts, and the records of strategically allied business partners contain most of the information any property needs to determine the ideal customer base. In order to properly implement a yield management project, the property must be viewed as a collection of profit centers. A profit center is a place where value is created and exchanged.

One of the attributes of yield management is to "let the guest in on the secrets" of the establishment. Give him or her all the information necessary to truly enjoy the experience. As part of the yield management plan, management must be willing to make experts of the guests by sharing information on how the guest can utilize all of the profit centers.

An important part of analyzing the potential of each profit center is to identify all the possible sources of revenue. This means analyzing both the revenue-producing outlets and the people who spend the money. In every establishment, there are a wide variety of revenue outlets. They can range from the sale of rooms to valet service. Flowers can be delivered for special occasions; specialty drinks, cigars, creative take-out or delivery services are possible.

Strategic alliances with car rental agencies, cooperative advertising, couponing, and packaging of all sorts will vastly change the number of channels that the guest can use to spend money in the profit centers of the enterprise.

Restaurants can increase revenues by serving take-out food, catering private parties off-premise, adjusting the menu mix, and developing unique reward systems for servers. Especially during hours of peak demand, restaurants can design product/price combinations that offer incentives to customers to change their demand patterns. Why accept *any reservation at any time?* Instead, select the most profitable reservations and use incentives to move the other reservations to nonpeak or shoulder times.

Profits are the only true measure of business success. The following groups all benefit from enhanced profits:

1. *Guests*: They are one of the primary beneficiaries of increased revenues and profits. If revenues are on the rise, it can mean only one thing: You are serving the guest better. They are happier, more loyal, and eager to tell others about the great experience they had.
2. *Employees*: In order to achieve long-term success, employees *must* be involved in the profit making *and* the profit taking. Let them earn as much money as they possibly can by making more money for the property.
3. *Management*: Structured reward systems are necessary for management. These systems reflect their need for income and achievement, and further the profit making of the property.
4. *Shareholders and investors*: Return on investment, dependable growth, share prices, etc., are all outcomes of increased revenue. Money attracts money, and the investors will relish the long-term growth potential of their investments.

There are six major obstacles that face management in their efforts to implement a yield management system. These impediments are:

1. *Lack of creativity*: Does your company do things the way they have always been done?

There is a need for standardization in recipes and operating procedures; however, this sometimes spills over into other areas. Training sessions in most organizations do not stress the creative side of customer satisfaction.

2. *Lack of attention*: It is difficult to stay in focus all the time. The minute you stop paying attention, things go wrong.

3. *Monitoring the wrong signals*: We tend to monitor the easy things to measure such as food cost and inventory. We should be looking for opportunities, not statistics.

4. *Conflict between sales and service*: When profits depend on a mutual delivery of both the sale and the service, conflict can arise. Front-of-the-house and back-of-the-house employees must work together for the common cause of serving and satisfying the guest.

5. *Targeting the wrong customers*: The right customers are the ones who will purchase the most of your products and services. Look for the customers with the money to spend to give you a reasonable profit. Use the marketing mix variables of product price, promotions, and distribution to attract and hold the right customers.

6. *Rewarding the wrong behavior*: Many sales management policies are designed to encourage occupancy and average daily rate. Restaurants, by allowing customers to reward the wait staff, may encourage promotion of higher-priced items. In either case, the sale may not reflect the best interests of the property. Yield management is designed to increase profit, not just gross sales.

BASIC CONCEPTS OF YIELD MANAGEMENT

Yield management requires knowledge of guests' expected behavior, plus an understanding of which business is most beneficial to a hotel—but it does not necessarily require high-power computers. There are three main revenue-management concepts that allow hotels to pick up relatively easy money, or "low-hanging fruit." This is accomplished by: simplifying the yield management system to make it manageable; examining the rate controls to make certain that they allow acceptance of the business that yields the strongest revenue return; and using length-of-stay controls to shift demand from sold-out periods to slack periods.

There is the special case of group business as it relates to the above three points. The change needed, if any, is to think in terms of which business is best for the property on a given date. By implementing the concepts discussed here, the property should see revenue gains in the next several months.

AN OLD PROFESSION

One may think of yield management as a relatively recent practice, but the lodging industry has applied yield-management principles for many years. In one early instance, Marriott Corporation used yield-management principles long before it installed its current sophisticated system. Back when young J. W. "Bill" Marriott was working at the family's first hotel, the Twin Bridges in Washington, D.C., the property sold rooms from a drive-up window. As Bill tells the story, the property had a flat single rate and made an extra charge for each additional person staying in the room. When availability for rooms got tight on some nights, Bill recalls leaning out the drive-up window to assess the cars waiting in line. If some of the cars were filled with passengers, Bill would turn away the vehicles with just a single passenger to sell his last rooms to those farther back in line who would be paying the charges for additional guests. That technique demonstrates the core concept of yield management.

From that simple start, yield-management mechanisms have become complicated—so complicated that some managers whom we have met seem to think that they cannot improve revenue unless they have access to the most sophisticated tools. Worse, the hotel manager may have created an overly complex system of discounts and packages. If the manager then insists on managing every different rate or package individually, the result is that the manager believes the property has too many programs to track and control, and it probably does. For this reason, the first suggestion for a straightforward approach to yield management is to cluster rates into a few groupings of similar programs, and then work on controlling these clusters or rate categories.

The goal of yield management is to select which business to accept and which business to turn away (when demand exceeds supply), based on the relative value of each booking. Most properties do not need more than four to six different "rate buckets" for their transient bookings. As an example, the following gives transient-rate categories that combine programs of similar value:

- *Level 1*: Rack (no discount).
- *Level 2*: 10 to 20 percent discount.
- *Level 3*: 25 to 35 percent discount.
- *Level 4*: 40 to 50 percent discount.
- *Level 5*: greater than a 50 percent discount.

Each level or bucket in the above hypothetical structure might comprise several different room rates. Given a structure like the above, a manager will not be agonizing over whether to restrict rooms offered at a rate of $150 in hopes of getting a rate of $155. While it is given that those $5 bills would pile up, the complexity is not worth it, especially when one might be working so hard on the $5 difference that one overlooks the opportunity to earn, say, $50 more by selling at rack rate.

If a given set of discounts isn't working, the hotel should change the categories. For instance, if a hotel's business fell entirely in level one and level two, with virtually no business in level three, a manager should rearrange the rate buckets. The three rate buckets could be

discounts from rack rate of 10 to 15 percent, 20 to 40 percent, and greater than 40 percent—or any other arrangement that makes a meaningful division among rate categories.

The following principles apply to setting up categories to manage rates at a hotel.

1. Segment programs based on clusters of discounts representing similar values. Yield management requires risk and reward management. Rate categories are designed to enable turning down one booking request in favor of a higher-value booking projected to come later. However, risking $150 in certain revenue in hopes of achieving a $155 booking seems to make little sense if the latter is not a sure thing.

2. In deciding whether to accept a particular customer's business, take into account both the cost of opening rooms and the offsetting ancillary spending that occurs when a room is sold. To take an extreme example, the most valuable guest for a casino hotel (the high-stakes gambler) might be paying the lowest room rate.

3. Limit the total number of transient rate categories to no more than six or so, particularly if there is not an automated yield-management system. The chief reason for that limitation is that yield management requires you to forecast demand for each rate category. Not only is it time-consuming to forecast numerous categories (with diminishing returns as the number of categories *increases)*, but the more categories created, the less accurate the forecasts will be for each category.

4. Each rate category should have a reasonable volume of activity to allow monitoring of traffic in that category. If it is found that one of the categories is rarely used, consider redistributing the rate hierarchy.

5. Group business should have a separate hierarchy of buckets to allow the operator to track pickups of room blocks. In addition, mixing group activity with individual booking activity will cloud the historical

information as your trend data by rate categories are collected.

RATE-CATEGORY CONTROLS

The point of yield management is to use demand forecasts to determine how much to charge for rooms on a given day. When the hotel sells out, the ability to determine which reservations to be accepted or denied is lost, because all requests for the sold-out date (including those for multiple-night stays that involve the sold-out date) must be rejected. A property's yield-management objective should be to sell out the hotel as close to the arrival date as possible, because the further in advance the hotel is sold out with discounted (or short-stay) business, the greater is the likelihood that high-value bookings will be turned away. This forecasting regime requires a continual process of comparing remaining demand for high-rate stays (and multiple-night stays) against remaining available inventory. Rate-category controls help ensure that there is available inventory to accommodate the projected high-rate demand.

Table 4.3 demonstrates how rate categories are controlled to increase total room revenue. The table assumes a 500-room hotel (or a hotel with 500 rooms remaining to be sold). The objective is to hold rooms open for high-rate demand without leaving a large number of rooms unsold. In this example, although the

hotel would prefer to sell all 500 rooms at rack rate, the hotel's managers project that they can sell 380 (or more) rooms at rack rate. Their inventory plan is set up to maintain room availability for this forecasted high-rate demand. The managers would like to sell the remaining 120 rooms in the next rate category down (Bucket 1), but their demand forecast projects they will not be able to sell all 120 in that rate category. Based on current trends, however, even though they have a total of 500 rooms to sell, they won't be selling any rooms in the deep-discount category because there is sufficient demand at higher rates.

When evaluating how well a property is managing its inventory, there are two basic indicators: (1) On dates the property is selling out, it should be observed how far in advance that sellout occurs; and (2) if the property is not selling out, it must be determined whether the property ever turned away business as a result of discount controls or because the property had committed too many rooms to groups. That is, if a group does not pick up its room block, did the hotel as a result refuse reservations from transient guests?

Full-occupancy dates frequently receive less attention from property managers than one might expect, given the revenue potential of a sellout. One reason for this is that some properties are too slow in closing out discounts to restrict room availability to expected high-rate business. Hotels do close the discounts, but not always soon enough. A common practice is to

TABLE 4.3
Hypothetical Room-Rate Structure

Rate Buckets	Discount off Rack Rate	Available Rooms (estimated)	Demand Forecast
Rack (General)	None	500	380
Bucket 1	10%–20%	120	63
Bucket 2	25%–35%	57	75
Bucket 3	40%–50%	0	140

set threshold levels at which discounts are closed at a predetermined level (90 percent occupancy, for example). While such an approach is well meant, all it succeeds in doing is to preserve the last 10 percent of the hotel's inventory for high-value guests—when a proactive approach might shut down discounts earlier and gain the hotel even more high-paying guests (and revenue).

Another reason that hotels often don't focus on sold-out dates is that the persons responsible for managing the hotel's inventory are also usually responsible for high-profile tasks, including forecasting daily occupancy. Thus, a revenue manager may end up spending more time determining whether a particular date will run an occupancy of 65 percent or 75 percent than in determining how to make the most out of excess demand on a projected 100 percent occupancy date. The process of forecasting a date's occupancy is important, but so is determining how to gain the most revenue from a sold-out date.

For all the time spent in month-end analysis of occupancy levels, average rates, and market comparisons, rarely is conclusive evidence found that properties perform as well as they could. Moreover, the more often those two questions are asked (i.e., did we fill too early? and did we turn away business on days we didn't fill?), the more employees work to give the desired revenue results. As occurs in many cases, you get what you inspect, not what you expect.

LENGTH-OF-STAY CONTROLS

Implementing length-of-stay controls takes the rate-management decision a step further. The essence of rate-category control is having one room left to sell and deciding whether to sell it to one guest for $100 today or to wait and sell it to another guest for $150. The essence of length-of-stay controls, on the other hand, is having one room left to sell at $150 and deciding whether to sell it for one night

or to wait, with the prospect of selling it to another guest for four nights. In the rate-category decision, the hotel can net an additional $50, while the stay-length decision can generate as much as $450 in additional revenue.

Managing stay lengths is complex, but mastering length-of-stay patterns may be the most rewarding of yield-management functions. The most sophisticated inventory management would control requests down to granular levels of detail: by program or rate category, by length of stay, or by day. This level of control really requires an automated system. As is the case with managing rate discounts, however, measurable revenue improvements connected to length of stay can be achieved without sophisticated automated systems, as long as the application of controls is kept fairly simple.

Just as setting rate-control categories requires an understanding of demand by rate category, length-of-stay management requires an understanding of demand by various length-of-stay intervals. To make the call in the above example, the manager would need to know the level of demand for four-night stays before he or she turns away (or accepts) the request for a one-night stay.

The most common length-of-stay statistic used in the hospitality industry is average length of stay, which describes the average duration of a guest's hotel stay over a range of dates. One needs more effective statistics than simple average length of stay to manage stay patterns. What the revenue manager needs to know is the total number of arrivals on a given date for one night, two nights, three nights, four nights, five nights, and so forth. To illustrate the difference between those two statistics, imagine that a manager was determining whether to apply minimum-stay restrictions on a peak night. Either the manager could know that the average length of stay is 3.6 nights, or the manager could have specific length-of-stay information (e.g., 10 percent of the arrivals on a given date are for one-night stays, 25 percent are for two-night stays, and so on). Naturally, the manager would want to know how much of the demand is going to be affected if the manager were to reject all one-, two-, and three-night stays with the expectation that the hotel can be filled with people staying four or more nights. Table 4.4 shows an example of a chart with this type of information.

Most central reservation and property management systems developed in the last few years facilitate stay pattern controls, although in varying levels of sophistication. The ideal system would enable a property's managers to set controls for each arrival date by discrete lengths of stay. Such a system would enable the property to close availability to one-, four-, five-, and eight-night stays, for instance, but allow stays of two, three, six, seven, or nine nights (or longer). Most new systems at least allow minimum stay controls by rate category.

As a word of caution, one aspect of yield-management systems' stay controls can become overused. Most systems allow managers to place a "closed to arrival" restriction on selected dates. This restriction enables a property to sell through stays arriving before the given date (that is, multiple-night stays for which the closed date is a second or subsequent night), but rejects all requests to arrive on that date. The problem hotels create for themselves by using this approach is that they end up saving space for two- and three-night "stay throughs," while rejecting multiple-night stays by guests proposing to arrive on the closed night.

Obviously, the hotel does not want to lose revenue from stay-through guests to those staying for just the closed night, but having the system forbid a multiple night stay that begins on the peak night may actually be worse than having no controls at all. In such a case, some form of minimum or other discrete length-of-stay controls would be appropriate. Any property still using a flat closed-to-arrival restriction should reconsider in light of this problem.

GROUPS: RATES, DATES, AND SPACE

Yield management is usually thought of in the context of turning away undesirable business during excess demand periods. However, the real art of yield management is in learning how to turn undesirable booking requests into desirable ones. Thus, an important element of yield management is teaching all employees the art of saying yes.

The art of saying yes is particularly important in the negotiation process for group business, which generally involves decisions about rates, dates, and space. Rates are how much the group is going to pay; dates are when the group is going to be staying; and space is how

TABLE 4.4
Hypothetical Stay-Length Forecast

Day	Occupancy	Arrivals	Arrivals per Day Length of Stay (Days)				
			1	2	3	4	5+
Wednesday	76%	117	7	9	21	41	39
Thursday	82%	103	8	17	21	24	33
Friday	90%	118	10	24	12	26	46
Saturday	100%	138	28	23	22	28	37
Sunday	83%	111	19	13	16	22	41
Monday	78%	86	12	13	18	21	22

many rooms the group will use. Turning an undesirable proposal into a desirable contract involves varying these components until both the hotel's sales associate and the meeting planner have what they consider to be a worthwhile package. Too often hoteliers either deny a group's request outright or focus on adjusting the group's proposed room rate to make the request appealing to the hotel. At times the better response is to give the group the rate it requests but to change the dates of the proposed business to a time when the hotel's forecast is for empty rooms. Even less obvious is the option to ask the group to change the number of rooms it proposes to block. Committing to more rooms (and thus more overall revenue) or fewer rooms (reducing displacement) leaves you the opportunity to sell to a second group interested in your property.

Applying revenue management principles to group business involves more than changing a group's proposal from undesirable to acceptable. Perhaps even more important is the ability to take the initiative to make a proposal that is merely acceptable into a contract that represents a great piece of business. Assuming that one is working within a hotel's normal acceptable boundaries, one thing that typically makes a proposed piece of business undesirable is when a hotel can sell that space to others at a better profit margin. That's why the most common response to an unacceptable proposal is to ask for a higher price.

Turning a mediocre proposal into an excellent piece of business might work as in the following example. Say that one group requests 200 rooms at a 350-room hotel for $80 per room, which is a $16,000 piece of business that was really not expected. The forecast shows that the total revenue without the group for that date would have been $29,000 with 290 rooms booked at an average rate of $100. The group's business will bring the hotel to 100 percent occupancy and generate a total of $31,000 in revenue (having displaced some of the forecasted transient arrivals). The revenue on the 60 extra rooms gives the hotel more

than enough incentive to accept this group, with a $2,000 increase in total revenue. (Assume per-room ancillary spending offsets the variable costs on the extra rooms.)

Any good sales director is going to feel good about the $16,000 in business he or she helped bring to the hotel. Even if someone points out that the business really brought only $2,000 in additional revenue to the hotel, it's still reason to feel good about this arrangement. Another way to look at this group, however, is that it represents $16,000 in unanticipated room revenue from which the hotel is extracting only an additional $2,000 in revenue because the group has displaced other, higher-rate business. By manipulating the other variables and, in this case, moving this group to a date that will displace little other business, the hotel can extract maximum value from this group. Even if the hotel needed to reduce the room rate to $60 to entice the group to move to other dates, the added value would be $12,000 instead of $2,000, because the group would be displacing less (anticipated) higher-rate business. Note that the calculations for this example are for only one night, but a group would typically stay for multiple nights, thus amplifying the benefit of moving the group and the "penalty" for accepting the proposal as offered.

The hotel could also propose that the group's room block be smaller, for example, in a situation where the group is attending a convention for which the dates are already fixed. This proposal is less effective from both the hotel's point of view and that of the group, but it still increases the value of the group. Since the forecast is that the group would displace 140 rooms that would have sold to transients at $100 each, the hotel gains back $20 in displaced revenue for every room the hotel sells to transients instead of to the group. Cutting the group's room block in half, for instance, actually nets the hotel another $2,000 in revenue. While the group has little incentive to reduce its request for rooms (unless the market is otherwise sold out), the hotel could have insisted that the group block fewer rooms if the group's original offer did not make up for revenues that the hotel would have obtained from transients.

CONCLUSION

Whether a hotel is just getting started or is ready to take the next logical step toward more sophisticated inventory controls, there are systems available to support the hotel's efforts.

One point to note is the concept of volume discount does not always apply in an environment where the supply is limited, as in the case of a hotel that is near to selling out. Sometimes less is more. This is a particularly important message for those meeting planners who inflate their numbers, assuming that this will make their business more appealing to the hotel.

Unfortunately, there are forces that may work against taking the types of revenue-enhancing actions discussed here. One is the tendency to accept the first option that clears the hotel's minimum standards, or to accept the business but maybe try to negotiate on the rate. Current sales-incentive plans are possibly another hindrance to these types of opportunities. Even the more progressive incentive plans that reward sales activities based on revenues rather than just room-nights can discourage behavior that benefits the hotel. This is done by encouraging the salesperson to book business that may not develop the highest revenue for the hotel, as in the example of the group that proposed to book 200 rooms.

CASE STUDY: THE POWER OF INFORMATION

This case study will explain how Disney uses simple information about hotel guests' stay patterns to increase revenues at their Orlando resort hotels (Quain et al., 1998). One of the highest-demand weeks of the entire year in central Florida is the holiday week between Christmas and New Year's Day. Ironically, this strong week is followed by one of the lowest-occupancy weeks of the entire year, the first week of January. Disney's Orlando resorts typically sell out the Christmas–to–New Year's dates by the end of September, if not sooner. But the first week in January has been a challenge for Walt Disney World's marketers, who have developed programs and events to fill the void caused by the exit of the holiday crowd. Although Florida residents can be tempted with deep discounts to boost the occupancy for the month of January, the resorts cannot develop enough demand to fill their rooms one week following one of the biggest holidays of the year.

Disney took many creative measures to boost the resorts' occupancy on that week. For example, the Walt Disney World Marathon, which was originally held during the three-day Martin Luther King, Jr., holiday weekend to help ensure the race's success, was moved to the first weekend of January. The move was a win for both the race and the hotels. The Martin Luther King holiday weekend maintained its strong occupancy levels without the marathon, and the end of the first week of January received a much-needed occupancy boost from the marathoners and their families. The good news for racers, moreover, was that more of them could find a room at the Walt Disney World resorts because they no longer had to compete with vacationers for limited rooms over the Dr. King holiday weekend. Despite the marathon's success, Walt Disney World's marketers knew this was not the complete answer, and they continued to look for ways to increase hotel occupancy immediately following the holidays.

As part of the effort to increase occupancy during the first week of January, the revenue management department at Disney began studying ways to use minimum-stay controls in conjunction with New Year's Eve to preserve rooms for guests who wanted to stay beyond New Year's Day. This was in the early days of yield management, when length-of-stay controls were relatively uncommon, and a new corporate culture needed to be developed. Such a seemingly extreme concept drew skepticism and concern within the company. Senior managers needed to be reassured that this new form of controlling inventory would not end up causing them to carry empty rooms during their busy season.

In another demonstration of how knowledge is power, the revenue management department had recently developed a report that summarized arrivals by length of stay (a concept further discussed by Cross, 1997). This report demonstrated two things: first, they did indeed have demand for guests arriving late in the holiday week and staying through several days into January; second, over 35 percent of arrivals during the holidays were guests staying only three or fewer nights. Disney's estimates of unconstrained demand over the holidays indicated it could easily afford to accept only stays of four nights or longer and still sell out its peak nights. (For a further discussion of unconstrained demand, see the article by Eric Orkin in Part VII, the marketing section of this book.)

Taking a deep breath, Disney's revenue managers set a minimum-stay restriction for arrivals during the holiday week that first season. Disney accepted only reservations for four nights or longer. This calculated decision was intended to improve revenue during the first week of January while at the same time presenting minimal risk to the normal, strong revenues during the preceding holiday week. The experiment attracted attention throughout the company. When late September came and the resorts were not sold out, some people were concerned that the holiday might not fill. However, the forecast predicted that the resorts would not be sold out by the usual late September date under the four-night mini-

mum-stay restraint. Because of the limitation, Disney was turning away shorter-stay requests that in previous years would have been accepted (and sold out the holiday week by September), with the forecasted expectation that the resorts could book longer stays to guests calling in October, November, and even early December. Trend reports helped to affirm the resorts were still on a pace that would sell out the hotels, which eased some minds in the revenue-management department. (It is worth noting that guests desiring a short stay could be offered almost their pick of rooms the week after New Year's Day.)

The final results were well worth the effort and nail biting. The hotels filled to capacity over the holidays, having sold out in late October. The first week of January's occupancy rose ten percentage points, almost entirely driven by guests arriving prior to New Year's Day and staying the minimum four nights. The room revenue contribution alone was worth over $1.5 million.

Disney's success in this example highlights a simple principle that many hotels miss. Disney was not paralyzed by the fact that it did not have perfect information or that it was not in a position to maximize revenue with "optimal" inventory controls. Instead, Disney's revenue managers made use of the information available to them to achieve a measured improvement in revenue while minimizing their risk.

THE REVENUE MANAGEMENT GAME

The following game, developed by Dennis Quinn, is an exercise that has been used by guest speakers at Cornell University's School of Hospitality Administration that can be used to initiate discussions on the objectives of yield management. It is not an exercise in identifying who is proficient at yield-management decisions. Rather, it is intended to demonstrate how capacity controls can affect a hotel's revenues and to develop an appreciation for the process throughout the organization.

The Game

Objective
Maximize room revenue for a five-room hotel.

Rules
As each reservation request from Table 4.5 is announced, participants decide whether they wish to accept the request at the time it is made. Accepted reservations are to be recorded on the booking grid in Table 4.6, with the room rate written in each date block. Once a day of week is sold out, any subsequent requests that include that day must be rejected. At the end of the game, participants add up the total revenue they generated for that week.

Hints
- Participants cannot go back and add a prior reservation once the next call is announced. The prior guest has hung up and booked with your competitor.
- No, you cannot overbook the hotel.
- The host should fill in a booking grid, as well, on a first-come, first-served basis, denying requests only when days are sold out. This will serve as the "no-control" method.
- You can let the audience know they will receive a maximum of 18 calls, if you want to help out.
- Remember, this is not a game of skill. It is a game for demonstration and discussion. The hotel's next revenue manager will not be selected based on the results of this game!

TABLE 4.5
Reservation requests

Call Number	Room Rate	Arrival Day	Stay Length	Comments
1	$ 80	Thurs	3	
2	$ 80	Tues	2	
3	$120	Fri	2	
4	$ 40	Mon	1	$40 is below your average rate goal for the week. Should you take it anyway if Monday is going to run vacant? We've seen incremental groups turned away because management warned sales to meet the monthly average rate goal. Be careful of what you ask for.
5	$120	Tues	1	
6	$ 60	Thurs	3	First, tell audience this is AAA discount (instead of telling them the rate). Point out the value of tracking rates versus source of business when managing inventory.
7	$120	Sat	1	
8	$ 60	Tues	5	
9	$ 60	Thurs	3	This is a package that includes dinner shows, meals, and recreation, which adds $110 in value to the hotel each night. Discussion: room revenue goals versus total profitability. Assign programs to rate buckets based on total value, not just room rate.
10	$ 40	Tues	5	
11	$ 80	Tues	5	
12	$120	Sat	1	
13	$100	Mon	2	
14	$ 60	Fri	2	
15	$100	Fri	2	
16	$100	Sun	7	What does it cost for you to lose this business?
17	$ 40	Sun	3	
18	$ 60	Sun	4	

TABLE 4.6
Booking grid for five-room hotel

Fill in the room rate for each accepted reservation for the appropriate number of days.

	Sun.	Mon.	Tues.	Wed.	Thurs.	Fri.	Sat.	Total
Room 1								
Room 2								
Room 3								
Room 4								
Room 5								
Total								

Game Discussion Points

Each participant should compare the difference between optimal revenue and the actual revenue they achieved. (Optimal revenue in the above game is $2360) Divide the difference by the actual revenue to show the percentage of potential improvement. For example, if one earned $2000, the potential for improvement is 18 percent; that is, (2360 − 2000) ÷ 2000 = 0.18 = 18 percent.

How much is that percentage improvement in annual room revenue worth to the hotel?

How about half that improvement? How much revenue might management be leaving on the table at the hotel? For example, what would be the hotel's annual room revenue multiplied by 118 percent? How about by 109 percent?

What is the percentage occupancy of the hotel in the no-control environment? How does that make participants feel about low-occupancy months?

Did anyone score below the no-control level? What does this tell you about the need to make responsible decisions when accepting reservations?

4.6　American Concierges Set Service Standards

Glenn Withiam

The assistance of Marjorie Silverman, chief concierge of the Hotel Inter-Continental Chicago, in developing this article is acknowledged.

Two things seem apparent regarding the concierge in American hotels. First, concierge service has become part of the definition of the hotel product for upscale properties. Second, guest-oriented service standards set by concierges have transcended the hotel industry to be embraced by other businesses. In 1983, I conducted a journalistic investigation of what was then a relatively new, expanding phenomenon—the rise of the concierge in American hotels (Withiam, 1983). Ten years later, the concierge is no longer new to hotel operators and guests, and the concierges themselves have taken continual steps to professionalize their field. In this article, I will discuss the status of the American concierge in the mid-1990s.

In the heart of Fort Worth, where business investors and city officials are busily redeveloping 28 blocks of mixed-use real estate, sits the 500-room, contemporary-style Worthington Hotel. In 1993, the hotel's management was shocked by the loss of one of its four Mobil stars, a loss that resulted from the need for a property renovation. Integral to the hotel's strategy for regaining that star is "rethinking service," as general manager Robert Jameson termed it. An important piece of that service is a concierge desk.

As Jameson sees it, guests are going to ask the kind of questions that concierges routinely answer, regardless of whether the hotel has a concierge desk. "When they need help, the guests are going to ask someone. Having the concierge desk in the lobby provides a specific location for guests to bring those questions. It also makes things easier for the bell staff, although that staff also needs to be versed in the basics." When he travels, Jameson said he always relies on the concierges in the hotels where he stays.

"To me, the concierge is an integral part of our operation," Jameson said. "So many people are not familiar with the community, and they need to be oriented. I just can't imagine not doing it."

Most four- and five-star hotels likewise no longer imagine being without their concierges. Although it was once a trendy innovation at the highest levels, concierge service has become an essential function in many hotels at all levels. "The concierge has become part of the definition of the hotel at a certain level.

Hotel inspectors look for concierge service," said John Neary, chief concierge at New York's Carlyle and president of the American branch of Les Clefs d'Or, the association of professional concierges.[*] Marjorie Silverman, concierge at the Hotel Inter-Continental Chicago, concurred: "Ten years ago, every third or fourth guest wanted to know what a concierge was. Today, guests come in looking for the concierge."

The fact that guests appreciate the service undoubtedly helped American concierges weather the recent decline in the hotel industry's fortunes. "Most hotels at the four- and five-star level would not be without a concierge at this point," Silverman observed. "The economic situation has created cutbacks that have been reflected in some concierge departments, notably by thinning out the staff. Some hotels have downgraded their service or combined the concierge desk with the front office manager's function." Ironically, Silverman said, European concierges are especially feeling the retrenchment because that is not something that has occurred before.

Holly Stiel, a former concierge who is now a concierge trainer and consultant, agreed that some American concierge desks have been eliminated due to the downturn. Retrenchment is evidently a problem that many concierges face, as one of the topics of the 1993 American concierge conference was how to manage when the concierge job is combined with another or lost altogether.

EXPANDING CONCEPT

At the same time, the philosophy of the concierge has been adopted as the guiding principle of service for entire hotel operations. "Every mission statement for every major hotel chain contains the words or idea of exceeding

---

[*]Les Clefs d'Or is so named for the traditional symbol of the concierge, crossed golden keys. Clefs d'Or members wear the crossed-keys pin as a badge of honor.

guests' expectations," Silverman said. Not only that, but the concept of the concierge has expanded beyond the hotel industry. Stiel pointed out that other businesses are installing the concept of the concierge into their own operations. Such enterprises as retirement communities, office buildings, and department stores now have persons designated as concierges. "Each one has its own twist, but the basic concept is to put service up front and make it noticeable. It's a point of difference and it's so visible," Stiel said. Such firms as Nordstrom and the Trump Shuttle consulted her when they installed their concierge desks.

PepsiCo has developed an unusual adaptation of the concierge in its Purchase, New York, offices. Noting that employees were frustrated by not being able to take care of personal errands (or that they were taking work time for personal matters), the company developed a concierge service that has been wildly popular with employees—so popular that it will eventually be marketed to other corporations (under the name XTra Ours) (Lopez, 1993). Corporate concierge Andy King is probably the first concierge with that title.

"We think time will be the benefit of the future," Margaret Regan, a principal of personnel consultants Towers Perrin, explained to the *Wall Street Journal*. Towers Perrin assisted PepsiCo with initiating the concierge service, which handles just about anything for company employees—from arranging for home repairs to scheduling automobile oil changes (at a mobile unit in the company parking lot).

THE MANAGEMENT CONNECTION

While a franchise corporate concierge is noteworthy, it may not serve to advance the cause or position of hotel concierges. Their status depends largely on the hotel's management, and not all management teams understand the full ramifications of concierge service. "We still haven't succeeded in gaining general understanding on the part of management of what we do and how we do it so they have more trust in us," said the Inter-Continental's Silverman. "Staffing has to be sufficient. Those nice words about exceeding customer expectations have to have meat behind them. Management must create the environment to make exceeding expectations possible."

The kind of resources a concierge needs actually involves having the hotel hire a team of concierges, as Stiel sees it. "The concierge is not a person. It's a staff. No one can do this all alone—and who would want to?" she said. In her view, a minimum team would be at least four persons working in pairs who divide the day into two shifts. In addition, three other persons would run errands, and an additional concierge might be responsible for late-evening coverage. In all, Stiel believes, a full staff would be six or seven persons. Neary's Carlyle staff comprises four persons, plus messengers to run errands. His desk is covered from 7:00 A.M. to 11:00 P.M.

Having two persons together at the desk is essential to the provision of full concierge service. "We're busy. It's nonstop. The phone doesn't stop ringing," Neary explained.

"Some managers think it's an easy job, so some concierges are handed the club floor in addition to their regular duties," Stiel said. "But you can't be at the desk for 12 hours trying to fulfill impossible demands and perform perfectly with no assistance and no one to run errands." Silverman pointed to the diminished service resulting from understaffing "If you have four calls on hold and ten people in front of you, it's hard to exceed guest expectations," she said.

Some hotel managers do understand the concierge position, however. Neary feels substantial support from the Carlyle's managing director, for instance, and the Worthington provides a traditional, full-service lobby concierge in the traditional mold.

In the estimation of the full-service concierges, only a person who offers the traditional full service should carry the concierge title. Even after more than a decade, some hotel managers hand the concierge title to a person who may be little more than a beverage server. "You don't get a concierge just by pinning on a name tag and hanging up a sign," Stiel said. "In some cases, hotels are contracting with tour companies to take over the so-called concierge desk, even though those companies cannot do what a full-service concierge can do."

Silverman added, "Some managements have what you might call a 'lobby-glamour' syndrome. They hire charming people who are nice to look at. The issue is whether they have the contacts to get guests into sold-out restaurants. We are still arguing for professionalization of the position."

GOLDEN KEYS

The concierges have done more than argue for professionalization, however. Through their trade association, Les Clefs d'Or, they have created a professional certification program, which includes an examination among its requirements. Even to join Clefs d'Or requires a minimum of five years of hotel experience, including three years behind a hotel concierge desk. The organization retains its focus on the classic hotel concierge. Persons with the concierge title in other businesses, such as apartment buildings, are not considered for Clefs d'Or membership.

Even though the number of hotels with concierges has stabilized, membership in Clefs d'Or has expanded over the past decade from about 50 members in 1983 to over 200 in 1993. The organization's 1993 conference was attended by more than 250 persons, compared to perhaps 30 for its 1983 meeting.

Clefs d'Or has become a mechanism for improving concierges' effectiveness. Through the organization, concierges have built a formal relationship with such service companies as American Express and American Airlines. "American Airlines has special numbers and service agents for concierges only, because our clients are their first-class and business-class customers," Silverman explained. "We can arrange for VIP services around the world and have flyers met at curbside." American Express publishes an international newsletter in conjunction with concierge service, and Clefs d'Or is in discussions with American Express to enhance services to gold- and platinum-card holders. Also backed by AmEx, Clefs d'Or has joined in support of the Academy of Travel and Tourism, a private foundation that teaches tourism topics in public schools.

Finally, Clefs d'Or has moved beyond issues of professionalism, education, and business relationships to philanthropy. "We have started a foundation to support persons with life-threatening diseases," Stiel said.

STABILITY

At a time when turnover in hotels is at legendary proportions, concierges remain remarkably loyal. Before Stiel became a consultant and trainer, for instance, she was concierge at the San Francisco Grand Hyatt for 16 years. Silverman left her position at the Hotel Westin Chicago for the Inter-Continental only because it represented an opportunity to begin at a brand-new hotel. Neary has been at the Carlyle since 1978. The stringent membership requirements for Clefs d'Or and the need to build up a well of information and contacts tend to discourage movement, although some people do move from one hotel to another within the same city. Stiel observed, however, that if a person is resourceful, moving to a new city and learning about it would not be a problem. Occasionally, a hotel or resort will recruit another operation's top concierge.

RENT-A-CONCIERGE?

Silverman believes that the concierge offers more than just an island of stability in a sea of turnover. The concierge may be the one familiar face for repeat guests, in view of the tremendous turnover at the front desk due to promotion and departure. But Silverman offers a suggestion for hotels that cannot afford a full-time concierge or those that have a sharply seasonal business. "Hotels are now hiring many part-time workers. My idea is that Clefs d'Or should prepare for the 'temping of America' by training a group of people to be concierge temps, perhaps using the AH&MA as a clearinghouse. That would be particularly effective for resorts or other seasonal properties," she said.

Not all resorts want or need a person with the concierge title, however. For years, the bell captain at the traditional modified-American-plan resorts has taken care of guests in much the way that a concierge does. At the Homestead, in Hot Springs, Virginia, for instance, the bell stand in the lobby has virtually all the information guests need and the bell staff stands ready to take care of guests' wishes of any kind. "It's worked for them for years," Silverman acknowledges. "Some hotels have other titles that really provide the service—and they *do* provide service. The point is to have a place designated where information is organized. Old-line bell captains have the information and the organization, so they are able to do the job."

he has to be a bit of a detective, have the desire to do the job, and want to figure things out," she said. "One thing a concierge often says is 'I don't know,' but that is always followed by 'I'll find out.' The people who are best at this are in the 'giving' professions (e.g., nurse, teacher, social worker)."

Stiel has completed what is probably the first book on how to be a concierge, but the instruction in the book is all by example (Stiel, 1993). "The book is full of concierge anecdotes to show the kind of thinking required to do the job well," she said. "I want to inspire people about the concierge role." The collected anecdotes also make interesting reading. They are similar to the story Neary told of a case he recently handled. "Things that seem easy have a way of turning out to be difficult," he recalled. "One of our guests wanted the videotape of a program he had seen on television the night before, but the guest didn't know which channel or what program—only the topic. First we had to sort through the 50 channels of the New York cable system to figure out which channel it could have been distributed on. It turned out to be the public-access channel. Then we had to track down the producer, who was out of town. Eventually we located the producer, who had the only copy of the tape in existence, and we were able to make a copy for the guest."

CONCIERGE CONSULTANT

As the first concierge consultant, Holly Stiel has found the educational task to be twofold. "You can teach certain organizational skills to concierges and instruct them in professional attitudes and standards, but you also have to teach managers to understand the role," she said. "Without a good manager, you cannot have a good concierge."

The essence of the concierge, however, cannot be taught, according to Stiel. "The basic attitudes must be inherent in the person. She or

CONCIERGE-TECH

Many hotels are applying technology to reduce the labor intensity of guest service, for example, with computer-generated wake-up calls and voice-messaging systems. Far from being a threat, computer-based technology may amplify a concierge's ability to serve guests. For the past few years, individual concierges have used stand-alone desktop computers to maintain their records of information sources. That's a step beyond maintaining guest histories at the front desk, which is also a valuable guest service, but Stiel points out that the personal touch added by the concierge is important.

"We now have computerized concierge files directly connected with the hotel's property-management system, for example, a hotel information system," Silverman said. "Instead of separate databases, the concierge software is now part of the hotel computer system." Silverman expects additional enhancements of the concierge's technical abilities to "move the position into the twenty-first century."

The concierge, like the hotel industry itself, has not achieved the blend of technology and management finesse that is metaphorically referred to as being in the next century. Since that century has arrived, the concierges hope soon to complete their project of educating management to the full scope of their role in the hotel.

MARRIAGE

"Every industry is at a crossroads—entering an age of enormous technical potential. That's true of the hotel industry, as well, especially internationally," Stiel said. "We need to open a dialogue between concierges and their managers. The concierge is the eyes, ears, heart, and soul of the hotel. A properly functioning concierge desk is a 'marriage' between a manager and a chief concierge who has a staff of people who understand the job. So, that's the concept for the next few years: educating managers, especially in America," Stiel continued.

PROGRESS FOR WOMEN

Although the educational job seems large, concierges have made considerable progress in the relatively short time they've been found in American hotels. In addition to making the American branch of Clefs d'Or a vital organization and force for professionalization, one particular achievement is to demonstrate conclusively how effective women are as concierges. When American hotels originally hired women as concierges, there was some concern internationally that women could not do the job. Today, women have been accepted internationally as concierges. Silverman herself is third vice president of the international Clefs d'Or and the first woman on the international society's board of directors—positions she believes would not have been given to a woman even ten years ago.

In short, whether women or men, American concierges have clearly demonstrated the value of the enhanced service they offer guests. That value is shown in the expectations guests have when they stay at upscale hotels. It is shown in the fact that other businesses have adopted the concierge concept for their own. And it is shown even in the resistance many hoteliers have shown to cutting back on concierge service, when they at least strive to keep the title and the service in some form, rather than eliminating it entirely. In an era when service has become a watchword for so many organizations, the concierge remains the epitome of service.

4.7 A Day in the Operations Life

Bob Peckenpaugh

The many hats of a director of operations might best be conveyed, in many cases, as the director of any one or all of the following: training, energy, empathy, enthusiasm, emergencies, follow-up and follow-through, communications, vision, priority management, the simple tasks, the difficult resolves, forecasting, complete customer focus, employee satisfaction, details, details, details . . . and more details. Expect the unexpected, for as you enter this career you are choosing an interesting, exciting, and diverse path.

Operating a hotel or resort is like operating a small city. As director of operations you will oversee professionals such as engineers, food, beverage, and culinary experts, accountants, human resource gurus, and possibly even a golf or recreation manager. Many of these individuals may have worked in different fields or have the potential to do so. They are professionals whose disciplines span many industries. Your general knowledge can be groomed and greatly enhanced through the years as you work with these individuals. From your days at the university right through the senior leadership roles you may attain, there are multitudes of things you will eventually be expected to understand. Unless you plan on choosing a different focus, it is time to start absorbing what you can now! If you really think about it, that small-city mayor needs his or her team of experts like those noted above for his or her ultimate success. He or she may have a legal background and know little of the world of finance, but the basics need to be understood.

As you begin your journey learning to manage people and processes you should expect to learn the details of the management of processes, but you also need to be acutely aware of when and where management stops and leadership starts. There is truth to the old adage that a manager pushes results while a leader draws the team toward success. Is it easier to push the elephant into the cage or to draw him there?

In a typical day for me, there are contracts to sign, purchase orders to fill out, checkbooks to manage, vendors to work with, forecasting to accomplish, bills to pay, and that is just in the financial area. While working on these tasks the chief engineer may call you to discuss the effects on your guests since the chiller just went down, or maybe he or she needs some advice as to which project needs priority attention. Oops, the director of human resources just paged you, and one of your managers just overstepped his or her bounds with one of the

employees. As you are comparing notes from the individuals involved, your cell phone rings and the chef is informing you that there is a challenge with a banquet dinner that evening. The garde-manger (the cold food, or pantry, chef) did not show up for work, and you may need to help with plate-up to ensure the success of the team.

On the department level, it is your responsibility to develop, mentor, and motivate department heads (executive housekeepers, front office managers, guest service managers, etc.). There will be leaders within this group of managers who can assist with the development of the more junior managers, and this in itself can act as a training ground for these leaders. It is, though, up to you to provide leadership and vision to the process.

As this team of managers (as well as any team) is developed it is important to understand the dynamics. What background talents do the players bring to the table? How can they help each other? And sometimes more importantly, will their competitive nature feed the others into more success or will they be detrimental to the overall game plan? My advice is to surround yourself with the best talent possible and set the level of expectation high. Find pride in helping others progress as you have.

With regard to the product and/or physical plant, it is important to understand life expectancies of furniture, fixtures, and equipment (otherwise known as FF&E). As you progress through different positions you need to develop an understanding of how the physical side of the hotel works. You will be expected to put together plans for replacement.

In your capacity as an executive housekeeper, you will be expected to understand the effects of traffic patterns on carpet wear and tear. As a chief engineer, you will learn to price major projects in square feet. Telecommunications and computer technology is ever changing and you may be asked to research these tools and put together proposals for the best operational efficiencies. Remember you have been hired to maintain this asset, and if any of your FF&E is not properly maintained or cleaned, you may end up spending more money than you or the owner of the facility expected.

As a director of operations, I call this *learning to inspect what you expect*. The more I know about the physical and service landscape of my hotel, the better I will do my job, the better my team will be, and the better experience the guests will have.

4.8   Mini Case: The New FOM

After being transferred and promoted to front office manager of a 600-room resort hotel in Miami from a smaller property of the same chain, Jennifer Waters has spent the first five or six months familiarizing herself with the hotel's markets, the area, and the resort's facilities and amenities. She has also spent a significant amount of time learning the job of front office manager and has concluded that it is significantly different from that of assistant front office manager in a smaller property.

The front office staff are young, mostly students, who are in south Florida for the weather and social amenities of the Miami area. Many want to become actors and are active in dinner theaters and various small theater companies in the greater Miami area. For the most part, they are bright and attractive people, but lack the innate professionalism that comes from a solid core of knowledge and training. Among the things that have come to concern Jennifer as FOM are the following:

- Several members of a national association board of directors complained of rude treatment while checking out of the hotel.
- Several times a week, after guests have checked in, they are escorted to rooms that

are either out of order, not clean, or already occupied.
- Four times over the last six weeks, cruel and demeaning practical jokes have been played on the front office assistant manager and the manager on duty during the evening.
- Guest complaints, either in person or by letter, about the hotel, its services, and staff have more than doubled over previous years and are outpacing complimentary letters and comments by a ratio of two to one.

Jennifer believes her relations with her staff are pretty good. Her relationships, however, with other managers in the hotel have become strained, particularly with housekeeping and sales.

As Ms. Waters seeks to understand the complexities of these problems, she decides to compile a list of what *could* be their root causes. What sort of items might be on this list? What form could their potential solutions take?

Be sure to include rationales for the solutions and a plan that will allow her to demonstrate to top management that the analysis and solutions are likely to result in resolutions of these difficulties.

poor hiring

4.9   To Change or Not To Change: A Case Study at the Front Desk

Nancy Swanger

Morgan Black has been described by the corporate office as the "miracle worker" because of the troubled properties that were turned around under Morgan's leadership. It is hoped the story at the Coug Inn will have the same happy ending; however, the Coug Inn is in a remote location, hundreds of miles from any other corporate properties.

The Coug Inn is a 150-room full-service property with several medium-size conference rooms, catering mostly to business travelers and visitors affiliated with the local university. The bulk of the revenue is generated between August and May, with periods when classes are not in session being extremely slow. The only times the hotel is at full occupancy are during football weekends and commencement. Occupancy has been declining for the last year or so, with last month's RevPAR at a record low. Since arriving at the Coug Inn, Morgan has made several observations about the hotel's current situation. It seems, however, most of the problems involve the front desk. After analyzing several previous months' comment cards and informally chatting with guests at the hotel, Morgan has sensed real dissatisfaction with the check-in process. Several common themes have emerged: the process seems to take forever; the paperwork at check-in is perceived as lengthy and hard to fill out; the front desk clerks always appear to be running around "like chickens with their heads cut off"; and guests have been checked into rooms that were not clean.

After discussing the problems with the front desk manager, Morgan is in a quandary about how best to move toward a solution. The front desk manager complains the reservationists do not always submit the day's reservations to the front desk in a timely manner. Thus, guests arrive and the desk clerks have no idea what rate was quoted or the room preference of the guest. This results in the guest having to refurnish information that was previously given when making the reservation. Many times, clerks are forced to leave the guest at the counter while they attempt to retrieve missing information from the reservationists. Further, with over 65 percent of the housekeeping staff speaking a first language other than English, communication is difficult at best and room status is often mistaken. The front desk manager suggests that the hotel advertise its check-in time to be from "say around 1:00 P.M. or 2:00 P.M. to 7:00 P.M." to reduce the "crunch" time and allow front desk clerks more time to work with each guest's particular check-in needs. The front desk manager further states that the new hotel in town, the Suite to Sleep Inn, has an earlier check-in time and "it seems to work okay for them!" Morgan asks the front desk manager how the staff might respond to moving to a fully automated property-management system. The response was not favorable; the front desk manager mumbled something about "old dogs and new tricks" and that the corporate office had not put any money into the place in years. What would make Morgan think they would put out the cash now?

In an attempt to reach a compromise, Morgan considers changing the check-in time in exchange for the front desk manager's support of the conversion to an automated system.

1. What must Morgan take into consideration before final decisions are made to adjust check-in time and install a fully automated property-management system?

2. How should Morgan proceed in resolving the communication issue?
3. Who needs to be involved in the final decisions? Why?
4. How might Morgan present the case to the corporate office?

References

Albrecht, Karl, and Ron Zemke. 1985. *Service America! Doing Business in the New Economy.* Homewood, IL: Dow Jones-Irwin, pp. 37–38.

Allin, Nancy J., and Kelly Halpine. 1988. "From Clerk and Cashier to Guest Service Agent." *Florida International University Hospitality Review* 6(1):42.

Bandura, A. 1982. "Self-efficacy Mechanism in Human Agency." *American Psychologist* 37:122–147.

Bardi, James A. 1990. *Hotel Front Office Management.* New York: Van Nostrand Reinhold.

Bhagat, R. S., S. M. Allie, and D. L. Ford, Jr. 1991. "Organizational Stress, Personal Life Stress and Symptoms of Life Strains: An Inquiry into the Moderating Role of Styles of Coping." *Journal of Social Behavior and Personality* 6(7):163–184.

Bowen, David E., and Edward E. Lawler. 1992. "The Empowerment of Service Workers: What, Why, How, and When." *Sloan Management Review* 33(3):31–39.

Cross, Robert G. 1997. "Launching the Revenue Rocket: How Revenue Management Can Work for Your Business." *Cornell Hotel and Restaurant Administration Quarterly* April:38(2):32–43.

DeCharms, R. 1968. *Personal Causation: The Internal Affective Determinants of Behavior.* New York: Academic Press.

DeVeau, L. T., P. M. DeVeau, N. J. Portocarrero, and M. Escoffier. 1996. *Front Office Management and Operations.* Upper Saddle River, NJ: Prentice Hall.

Dewe, P. J., T. Cox, and E. Ferguson. 1993. "Individual Strategies for Coping with Stress at Work: A Review." *Work & Stress* 7:5–15.

Folkman, S., and R. S. Lazarus. 1991. "Coping and Emotion." In *Stress and Coping: An Anthology*, A. Monat and R. S. Lazarus (eds.). New York: Columbia University Press.

"Handling Bad Hotel Service." 1998. *USA Today* July 27:1D.

Kahn, R. L., and P. Byosiere. 1992. "Stress in Organizations." In *Handbook of Industrial and Organizational Psychology,* 2d ed., vol. 3, M. D. Dunnette and L. M. Hough (eds.), Palo Alto, CA: Consulting Psychologists Press, pp. 571–650.

Kasavana, M. L. 1981. *Effective Front Office Operations.* Boston: CBI Publishing Company.

Lazarus, R. S., and S. Folkman. 1984. *Stress, Appraisal, and Coping.* New York: Springer.

Lopez, Jolie Amparano. 1993. "PepsiCo's Concierge Service Gets 'Xtra Ours' out of Work Force." *Wall Street Journal* April 1:A1, A9.

Quain, William J., Michael Sansbury, and Stephen LeBruto. 1998. "Revenue Enhancement, Part 1: A Straightforward Approach for Making More Money." *Cornell Hotel and Restaurant Administration Quarterly* October:39(5):44–45.

Rutherford, Denney G. 1985. "The Front Office Manager: Key to Hotel Communications." *Florida International University Hospitality Review* 3(2):38–48.

Schneider, B., and D. E. Bowen. 1995. *Winning the Service Game.* Boston: Harvard School Press.

Sternberg, Lawrence E. 1992. "Empowerment: Trust vs. Control." *Cornell Hotel and Restaurant Administration Quarterly* 33(1):69–72.

Stiel, Holly, and Delta Collins. 1994. *Ultimate Service: The Complete Handbook to the World of the Concierge.* Englewood Cliffs, NJ: Prentice Hall.

Thoits, P. A. 1984. "Coping, Social Support, and Psychological Outcomes: The Central Role of Emotion." *Review of Personality and Social Psychology* 5:219–238.

Thoits, P. A. 1991. "Patterns in Coping with

Controllable and Uncontrollable Events." In *Life-Span Developmental Psychology: Perspectives on Stress and Coping*, E. M. Cummings, A. L. Greene, and K. H. Karraker (eds.), Hillsdale, NJ: Lawrence Erlbaum Associates, pp. 235–258.

Thompson, S. C. 1981. "Will It Hurt Less If I Can Control It? A Complex Answer to a Simple Question." *Psychological Bulletin* 90:89–101.

Van Maanen, J., and G. Kunda. 1989. "'Real feelings': Emotional Expression and Organizational Culture." In *Research in Organizational Behavior*, vol. 11, L. L. Cummings and B. M. Staw (eds.), Greenwich, CT: JAI Press, pp. 43–103.

Withiam, Glenn. 1983. "Keeper of the Keys: Concierges in American Hotels." *Cornell Hotel and Restaurant Administration Quarterly* 24(3):40–48.

Suggested Readings

Books

Bardi, James A. 1996. *Hotel Front Office Management*, 2d ed. New York: Van Nostrand Reinhold.

Bryson, McDowell, and Adele Ziminski. 1992. *The Concierge: Key to Hospitality*. New York: John Wiley and Sons, Inc.

DeVeau, Linsley T., Patricia M. DeVeau, Nestor de J. Portocarrero, and Marcel Escoffier. 1996. *Front Office Management and Operations*. Upper Saddle River, NJ: Prentice Hall, Inc.

Ford, Robert, and Cherrill P. Heaton. 2000. *Managing the Guest Experience in Hospitality*. Albany, NY: Delmar/Thomson Learning.

Heldenbrand, H. V. 1944. *Front Office Psychology*. Chicago, IL: The Hotel Monthly Press. Editor's note: This little volume is out-of-print but generally is carried in hotel school libraries and some "seasoned" faculty offices. Many of Heldenbrand's observations are as valid today as they were in 1944.

Vallen, Gary K., and Jerome J. Vallen. 1996. *Check-In Check-Out*, 5th ed. Chicago: Richard D. Irwin, Inc.

Articles

Barrington, Melvin N., and Michael D. Olsen. 1988. "An Evaluation of Service Complexity Measures of Front Office Employees in the Hotel/Motel Industry." *Hospitality Education and Research Journal* 12(2):149–62.

Brownell, Judi. 1990. "Grab Hold of the Grapevine." *Cornell Hotel and Restaurant Administration Quarterly* 31(2):78–83.

Brymer, Robert. 1991. "Employee Empowerment: A Guest-Driven Leadership Strategy." *Cornell Hotel and Restaurant Administration Quarterly* 32(1):58–68.

Cadotte, E.R., and Normand Turgeon. 1988. "Key Factors in Guest Satisfaction." *Cornell Hotel and Restaurant Administration Quarterly* 28(4):44–51.

Kasavana, Michael L. 1993. "Front Office Operations." In *VNR's Encyclopedia of Hospitality and Tourism*, Mahmood Kahn, Michael Olsen, and Turgut Var (eds.), New York: Van Nostrand Reinhold.

Lewis, Robert C. 1983. "When Guests Complain." *Cornell Hotel and Restaurant Administration Quarterly* 24(2):23–32.

Lieberman, Warren H. 1993. "Debunking the Myths of Yield Management." *Cornell Hotel and Restaurant Administration Quarterly* 34(1):34–41.

Murthy, Bvsan, and Chekitan S. Dev. 1993. "Average Daily Rate." In *VNR's Encyclopedia of Hospitality and Tourism*, Mahmood Kahn, Michael Olsen, and Turgut Var (eds.), New York: Van Nostrand Reinhold.

Parasuraman, A., Leonard L. Berry, and Valarie A. Zeithaml. 1991. "Understanding Customer Expectations of Service." *Sloan Management Review* 32(3):39–48.

Rutherford, Denney G. 1985. "The Front Office Manager: Key to Hotel Communications." *Florida International University Hospitality Review* 3(2):38–48.

Van Dyke, Tom. 1993. "Guest Registration." In *VNR's Encyclopedia of Hospitality and Tourism*, Mahmood Kahn, Michael Olsen, and Turgut Var (eds.), New York: Van Nostrand Reinhold.

Vallen, Gary K. 1993. "Organizational Climate and Burnout." *Cornell Hotel and Restaurant Administration Quarterly* 34(1):54–59.

Vallen, Gary K. 1993. "A Comparison of Hospitality Burnout with Other 'High Burnout' Industries." *Hospitality and Tourism Educator* 5(2):31–36.

Williams, Peter W., and Michael Hunter. 1992. "Supervisory Hotel Employee Perceptions of Management Careers and Professional Development Requirements." *International Journal of Hospitality Management* 11(4):347–358.

Source Notes

Chapter 4.2, "Raw Nerves at the Nerve Center: An Insider's View of Life at the Front Desk," by Cheri Young.

Chapter 4.3, "The Electrifying Job of the Front Office Manager," by James A. Bardi, adapted from *Hotel Front Office Management*, 2d ed., by James A. Bardi, Copyright © (year and owner). Adapted by permission of John Wiley and Sons, Inc.

Chapter 4.4, "A Day in the Life of the Front Office Manager," by Garry Dickover.

Chapter 4.5, "Yield Management: Choosing the Most Profitable Reservations," by William J. Quain and Stephen M. LeBruto is adapted from the following two articles:

Quain, B., M. Sansbury, and S. LeBruto. 1998. "Revenue Enhancement, Part I: A Straightforward Approach to Making More Money." *The Cornell Hotel and Restaurant Administration Quarterly* 39(5):42–48.

Quain, B., M. Sansbury, and D. Quinn. 1999. "Revenue Enhancement, Part 3: Picking Low-Hanging Fruit—A Simple Approach to Yield Management." *The Cornell Hotel and Restaurant Administration Quarterly* 40(2):76–83.

Chapter 4.6, "American Concierges Set Service Standards," by Glenn Withiam, is reprinted from the Vol. 34, No. 4, 1993 issue of *The Cornell Hotel and Restaurant Administration Quarterly*. © Cornell University. Used by permission. All rights reserved.

Chapter 4.7, "A Day in the Operations Life," by Bob Peckenpaugh.

5

Operations: Housekeeping, Engineering, and Security

5.1   Introduction

HOUSEKEEPING

A while back, I was talking with a large group of housekeeping directors representing most of the major metropolitan hotels in a large northeastern city. I asked the following question: How many of you as part of your career plan initially considered housekeeping as a managerial role that had any attraction to you? The answer, not surprisingly, was none!

This points up a major dilemma facing modern hotel management structures. One of the most important, labor-intensive, and largest cost-centers in the hotel is neither universally understood nor respected by the bulk of the hotel's department managers, their employees, and (to a large extent) the hotel's guests and clients. There are some encouraging signs that this is a situation that is in a state of change. Some hotel companies are experimenting with taking housekeeping out of the rooms division and making it a staff function with the director of housekeeping reporting directly

to the general manager. Others are combining housekeeping and other property management functions along with maintenance and engineering. In one firm, housekeeping directors are titled director of services and have responsibility for all nongolf recreation, in addition to traditional housekeeping.

Historically, however, information on housekeeping administration for hotels has been organized around models set forth in a number of textbooks that date back to the 1951 treatment of hospital housekeeping by LaBelle and Barton. Brigham (1955) focused her analysis of the structure of the housekeeping functions and responsibilities on the small hotel. Tucker and Schneider (1982), Schneider and Tucker (1989), and Martin and Jones (1992) have provided a comprehensive inventory of the theoretical constructs, responsibilities, relationships, and techniques important to the modern housekeeper in a range of operational situations. (See Jones's contribution elsewhere in this section.)

Generally speaking, these works present information in a structure similar to that used in Holiday Inn University's housekeeping curriculum, which says the housekeeper administrates "four major areas of responsibility" (Tucker and Schneider, 1982, p. 38).

1. Management of people, equipment, and supplies.
2. Preservation of building finishes, fabrics, and furnishings.
3. Controlling costs.
4. Keeping records.

In analyzing the differences between the "folklore and fact" of the manager's job, Mintzberg (1975) came to the conclusion that there were substantial differences between what the popular or academic notion of managers' jobs entailed and what managers actually did.

In the last study of its type, Rutherford and Schill (1984) studied housekeepers in a similar fashion: what is the relationship between what has been written about housekeeping and what housekeeping directors themselves deem important.

A survey was sent to a national sample of housekeeping executives asking them to rate on a scale of 1 to 5 the importance of 100 theoretical constructs common to the housekeeping literature. Statistical procedures (factor analysis) grouped the housekeepers' responses into eight groupings. While the traditional responsibilities of records, costs, supplies, and furnishings were still important, the issues central to the management of people were of overwhelming importance. Specifically highlighted were the following:

- Leadership.
- Communication.
- Strategic planning.
- Hotel organizational interactions.
- Departmental management.
- Training.

The authors concluded that new arrangements of traditional knowledge, constructs, and tactics such as those explored in their model may present future managers with windows of operational, educational, or marketing opportunity that improve competitive position or streamline the transfer of knowledge. The dissemination of this knowledge in the most efficient and effective manner is also important, for, as Mintzberg (1975) points out, "The manager is challenged to find systematic ways to share his privileged knowledge."

Since 1985, there has still been very little, if any, analytic empirical research done on operational aspects of housekeeping and other labor-intensive hotel departments. Until such a time as there is, there will be little forward movement in the "theory" of housekeeping. There is, though, no lack of inspirational practical experimentation on the part of housekeeping managers.

When he started his career in hotel management, Kurt Englund, like the housekeepers referenced at the start of this section, never considered housekeeping would be a major stop on his career journey. It was, however, and he feels the many tasks that are involved in "keeping the house" for a major asset like a Four Seasons property prepared him well to be the director of rooms for the luxury hotel Regent Beverly Wilshire. A day in his current life is related here, and it is important to note that housekeeping is still one of his responsibilities.

Professor Tom Jones of University of Nevada, Las Vegas, writes on how housekeeping departments are organized and staffed. He provides an overview and organizational perspective of the department with particular attention paid to what are the responsibilities of the various personnel within the modern housekeeping department. Professor Jones brings deep knowledge of executive housekeeping management to his writing and structures his description of the organization with a real-world, "tell it like it is" narrative.

Now rooms director of a hotel managed by Interstate Hotels in Chicago, John Lagazo relates some of the highlights from his vast experience in managing housekeeping departments around the country. Since much of this experience was in Mobil Four- and Five-Star properties and other luxury hotels, Lagazo has written his essay in an engaging and entertaining manner, using great examples of the potential inventory of experiences in a housekeeper's day.

In most cases, the management of the housekeeping function is no longer the province of the "lead maid" type. Increasingly, the expense of running the department coupled with the large numbers of employees on its staff mandates a person to head this department who is well versed in all managerial skills and is a sophisticated and creative leader.

ENGINEERING

In a way, housekeeping, engineering, and security could all be considered "guest services." In most hotels guest services (see Part IV) is a very visible component that can include concierge, uniformed service, garage, and specialized recreational and leisure activities. Housekeeping, security for the hotel and its guests, and the maintenance of the hotel's engineering systems are under the best of circumstances behind the scenes and not generally noticed or experienced by the guest in any but an abstract sense. They are nonetheless services that are critical to a safe, comfortable, and by extrapolation, successful guest stay at your hotel.

As stated in the first of the two articles included here on the engineering function, in the past the chief engineer and his department have been metaphorically relegated to roughly the same position in the hotel's organization that it physically occupies—usually in the basement or at the bottom and out of sight. As explored in these two articles, there are numerous indications that the importance of the engineering function can no longer be ignored nor treated with any less respect than any other functioning member of management.

It is important that the reader recognize that the first of these articles overviews the department, explores some of the influencing issues that affect hotel engineering, and outlines typical job functions. Part of the thrust of this article is that unlike the past, the chief engineer is responsible for major components of the asset and the physical comfort of the guest. This argues for consideration of the chief engineer as not different from any other hotel department head.

The DeFranco and Sheridan article on how chief engineers (CEs) use financial information illustrates that idea. As their research demonstrates, computer technology and the use of financial information in the engineering department are vital in maintaining an efficient operation. This was not widely the case even ten years ago. This research reporting on CEs contributes to the argument that, similar to the executive housekeeper, the position of CE in the modern hotel organization mandates a leader who is now more manager/leader than technician. At the same time, the CE still has to manage a diverse collection of talents and skills among the engineering staff. In a fashion, this raises the question as to what type of manager such a person is. Structured research is still pretty sparse on this topic.

The number of employees for which the CE is responsible is going to vary widely, mainly based on the size of the hotel. One study set the ratio for engineering staff at 3.9 for each one hundred rooms (Fisher, 1986), but a lot has changed since then. Other factors that can influence the diversity of human-related management for the engineering manager are market niche, sophistication of the building's design and equipment, and corporate philosophy. Therefore, if a 1000-room hotel has 40 or more people on the engineering staff, each of them presumably highly trained, qualified, and skilled technical people, the CE's job takes on aspects of management that strongly suggest a need for refined people-related skills.

When Wasmuth and Davis (1983, p. 68) studied the management of employee turnover, they found it to be relatively low in engineering departments in the majority of the hotels studied. They also found that quality of supervision was a key element in maintaining low turnover rates among these engineering departments. The supervisory style that was most successful had as a critical element the talent that "allowed and encouraged (the engineers) to work autonomously."

Allowing the engineering staff to work autonomously pays tribute to both the nature of the various jobs and concern for the human side with management. It also suggests that while some supervisory or management styles may be appropriate in engineering departments, others may not. Managerial style refers to the way that we manage, control, motivate, and otherwise direct our subordinates. It is through the use of the various managerial styles that employees may or may not be encouraged and allowed to work on their own. The extent to which such an atmosphere is fostered by the manager significantly affects the range with a manager's human-related challenges, of which turnover is a prime example.

An unpublished, proprietary study of 49 hotel CEs with one hotel company sought to determine their managerial styles. They were asked to take a standardized managerial-style inventory and fill out a short demographic questionnaire in order to determine what managerial style predominates among the self-described successful chief engineers in a major international hotel corporation.

This inventory instrument judges primary managerial style to be in one of six categories (see below) with a secondary or backup style to be one or a combination of the others (McBer, no date).

Managerial Styles

- *Coercive*: The "do it the way I tell you" manager who closely controls subordinates and motivates by threats and discipline.

- *Authoritative*: The "firm but fair" manager who gives subordinates clear direction and motivates by persuasion and feedback on task performance.
- *Affiliative*: The "people first, task second" manager who emphasizes good personal relationships among subordinates and motivates by trying to keep people happy with fringe benefits, security, and social activities.
- *Democratic*: The "participative" manager who encourages subordinate input in decision making and motivates by rewarding team effort.
- *Pacesetting*: The "do it myself" manager who performs many tasks personally, expects subordinates to follow his or her example, and motivates by setting high standards and letting subordinates work on their own.
- *Coaching*: The "developmental" manager who helps and encourages subordinates to improve their performance and motivates by providing opportunities for professional development.

A managerial style profile reflects both primary and backup styles. *Primary* is the managerial behavior one uses most often, is most comfortable with, and is the style to which one normally turns under stress. *Backup* refers to an alternative way of managing one uses when the primary style is ineffective. Some individuals have more than one primary style and some utilize multiple backups.

The comparisons showed that each group of CEs is primarily affiliative in style, a trait that flies in the face of their reputation as "crusty curmudgeons."

With affiliative as the primary style of this group of engineers, it was somewhat surprising that the backup style was democratic. Combining the democratic backup style with the predominant affiliative style would certainly produce an organizational atmosphere where the employees would feel encouraged to be independent and autonomous.

The data developed through application of this instrument to this sample of CEs tends to support the theory that successful CEs and their departments should favor management styles that put people first. At least at this juncture, it appears that the affiliative style works best in the milieu with people and tasks managed by the CE. This was, however, a small study of a single company and as such can only be suggestive. They do, though, provide us with a broader view of the facets of management of the modern hotel engineering function.

SECURITY

It is an unfortunate fact of modern hotel management that the days of simply providing guest comfort, quality food, beverage, and lodging services, and a "home away from home" atmosphere are severely affected by the inventory of problems presented by the predatory elements of modern society. At the same time, hotel security departments have the additional responsibility of protecting the hotel's assets from loss.

Hotels are usually fairly closemouthed about their security, its functions, duties, and personnel. On an individual basis, a good overview of security can be found in a publication of the Educational Institute of the American Hotel and Motel Association listed in the suggested readings (Ellis, 1986). Typically, however, the modern hotel security department will be organized as a staff function with the director of security reporting directly to top management. We have very little data or insights about the manager of the hotel security function, as very little of any research has been done on that individual. Anecdotally, from the editor's experience, most of the managers recently hired to fulfill this function have come from a security background in the military or law enforcement career with civil authorities.

Typically, the director of security will have a staff analogous to the nature and size of the threats to a particular hotel, the size of the hotel, its location, and its managerial strategy. A director of security will administer the functions of his or her department against two broad and general classifications of threats—external and internal.

External threats are generally those that present risk for the hotel and its guests due to the actions of outsiders. Internal security is a functional area that generally is concerned with reducing the threat of loss of assets, and in most cases, this refers to control of the highly attractive and popular consumer goods such as wine, expensive foodstuffs, furnishings, and, of course, the hotel's cash.

A general listing of the responsibilities of the security manager to contend with the above threats will involve the following:

- Physical security, which deals with the perimeter of the hotel.
- Adapting policies and procedures to the building design and location.
- Utilization of electronics, modern telecommunications devices, proximity alarms, motion detectors, and closed-circuit TV to enhance the hotel's ability to eliminate threats.

Security directors have to participate in certain levels of administrative and/or operational responsibilities that deal with policies, training, education, and human resources to avoid hiring what has become known as the "high-risk" employee. This is due primarily to the increasing risk hotels and other employers face from the concept of negligent hiring.

Having policies and procedures in place to deal with the management of emergencies is also a fundamental aspect of the hotel security director's job. These emergencies can take a number of forms, but in recent years have been known to include fires, hurricanes, floods, earthquakes, blackouts, robberies, bombs or bomb threats, medical and dental emergencies, and some forms of terrorism. It is a fact of modern life that the properly managed hotel from a security standpoint in this day and age has to have contingency plans in place and training programs for its employees to deal with these potential threats.

A further responsibility of the security director is liaison with civil authorities. Increasingly, as the article included here (5.7æDe Facto Security Standards: Operators at Risk) points out, hotels are being held accountable for what they "either knew or should have known" about the realm of potential threats. The best way to keep up on this is a good relationship with the local police.

Finally, the major responsibility of a modern hotel security director is to assist in policy development. Hotels must have policies that guide the implementation of procedures, training, and inspection to meet the inventory of potential risk. Hotels also need to gather data to make sure they are aware of all facets of the risk environment. The security function must also assist the hotel in formalizing a structure that links all pertinent parts of the hotel's organization to the concept of total security for the organization, its employees, and its guests.

The article included here by Rutherford and McConnell deals primarily with the inventory of potential threats to a hotel's guests generated by outsiders. The article was written to suggest to the hotel industry, its management, and employees that while the industry has no published standards for security relative to a hotel's guests, increasingly, the courts have been mandating such standards. Courts apply the test of what a hotel "knew or should have known" about potential threats and therefore what was "foreseeable." If the threat was foreseeable and a hotel had not put into place policies and procedures to deal with the threat, increasingly, courts are finding hotels liable for a lapse in the degree of care they owe their guests. The authors present a number of typical cases brought by injured parties against hospitality operations. These cases

were not chosen for their dramatic impact. They were, rather, chosen for their potential as precedents for the courts to use as standards by which to judge the behavior of all hospitality and hotel operators.

In the legal analysis contributed to this edition by Melissa Dallas, she outlines and discusses the major families of risk facing hotel managers. She also includes in her up-to-date analysis current examples of how the law affects the management of hotels in the modern era. This comprehensive and detailed article is presented in a conversational and engaging style, unusual in most legal treatises.

The article included here by Abbott and Fried, the authors explore in some depth one of the trickiest risk environments that (literally) surround many hospitality operations: the parking lot. Since parking lots can be remote, poorly lighted, or not patrolled, they are increasingly sources of risk. Since courts are increasingly finding that landlords have liability for third-party criminal activity, operators are advised to be aware of this potential liability.

CONCLUSION

Housekeeping, engineering, and security—while not typical high-profile obvious functions—are nonetheless critically important to the management of any hotel. All of them are and have been evolving for the past several years into professionally managed departments that are responding to internal and external stimuli that can critically affect their interactive relationships with other hotel departments and ultimately in the delivery of hotel guest services.

A number of books dealing in-depth with these departments are listed as suggested readings, and the reader who is in search of more in-depth information can find it in any of the books listed therein.

5.2   A Day in the Life of a Director of Rooms

Kurt Englund

A day in the life with Four Seasons Hotels and Resorts focuses on people, both guests and employees. One of the first things that I do in the morning is walk around the different departments that are my responsibility (front desk, concierge, communications, valet parking, door attendants, bell desk, health spa, housekeeping, laundry, and valet). It is important to be visible with the staff that we depend on to provide a superior level of service to all of our guests. Knowing who they are and what they are facing for the day makes a big difference in how they carry out their jobs.

Every morning, we have an operational meeting to review how we are going to take care of our guests, the other key component in hospitality. This meeting is attended by a wide range of managers: the general manager, hotel manager, all of the planning committee (including the director of human resources), housekeeping, conferences services, sales managers, and catering managers. The entire day is laid out, reviewing the expected arrivals for the day, from the VIPs, to return guests, guests with pets, guests with special dietary requirements or mattress firmness. We discuss these to ensure that the requirements are met in advance of their arrival. We also include in the discussion all catering functions and any other movement of individuals en masse.

In our effort to provide a quality experience, we also discuss any glitch or poor experience any of our guests may have experienced. Our concern is not whose fault the glitch was, but rather how can we make it better for our guest and prevent it from happening to any of our other guests. If the city decides to jackhammer at 8:30 in the morning on a Saturday, it may not be directly our fault, but it is certainly our guests who have been inconvenienced. We will do a follow-up with the guest to explain what we know, offer a new room if appropriate, and ascertain their overall happiness with their visit.

We have a number of other meetings to keep the communication going. Our weekly meetings include planning committee, group résumé, and rooms division meetings. Every other week we hold a department head meeting.

As mentioned, we hold the care of our employees to be as important as taking care of our guests. One of the ways we do this is being prepared to work alongside them when business levels suddenly peak. We do our best to staff at appropriate levels, but there will be the times that everything hits at once. We call these "crunches" and respond with an all page for assistance to the area in need. The management response is incredible, from our general manager on down. We get the assistance we need to help in all areas: valet parking, bell desk, front desk, room service, and so on. This is an excellent example of the teamwork at our hotel, making an impact on the morale of the staff.

Walking around the hotel, checking in with staff is an important communication tool. Employees have developed a comfort level of bringing up concerns they may have about their jobs. It is equivalent to bringing the open-door policy to the employee in their work area. Issues have been brought to my attention in this format, such as conflicts with co-workers, questions about their paychecks, suggestions to improve a work procedure, and requests for assistance in following up with maintenance concerns.

Hiring new staff is another crucial role in day-to-day activities. Our interviewing process involves a screening by human resources, an interview with the department head, an interview with the division head, and a final approval from a meeting with the hotel manager or general manager. We attempt to be as flexible as possible when it comes to making time to interview these candidates. If the right candidate comes through the door, we make every effort to free our schedules so

that we can keep the interview process moving.

Balancing the needs of our guests and employees requires flexibility. There is no typical day in our business, which is one of the reasons that I enjoy my job. There is always a new challenge every day.

5.3   Housekeeping Organizations: Their History, Purpose, Structures, and Personnel

Thomas Jones

ORIGINS OF HOSPITALITY AND HOUSEKEEPING

By definition, hospitality is the cordial and generous reception and entertainment of guests or strangers, either socially or commercially. From this definition we get the feeling of the open house and the host with open arms; of a place in which people can be cared for. Regardless of the reasons people go to a home away from home, there is the presumption that they will need to be cared for. They will need a clean and comfortable place to rest or sleep, food service, an area for socializing and meeting other people, access to stores and shops, and a secure surrounding.

Americans have often been described as a people on the move, a mobile society. Even as our country expanded we required bed and board. Travelers in the early 1700s found a hospitality similar to that in countries of their origin, even though these new accommodations might have been in roadhouses, missions, or private homes, and the housekeeping might have included no more than a bed of straw that was changed weekly.

Facilities in all parts of young America were commensurate with the demand of the traveling public, and early records indicate that a choice was usually available, based on where

you might find the best food, overnight protection, and clean facilities. Even though the inns were crude, they were gathering places where you could learn the news of the day, socialize, learn the business of the area, and rest.

The business of innkeeping has graduated to become the hotel industry of today, but the main tenets remain: a clean, comfortable room, access to food and entertainment facilities, and a courteous and concerned staff who mean it when they say, "May we be of service?"

Housekeeping departments play a vital role in today's lodging industry. People involved in housekeeping operations service guestrooms, maintain and service public and special areas, and in many instances, operate laundries, recreational, and health facilities. In addition, the people of housekeeping are also a part of the overall team of hosts and hostesses who add their own welcome to our hotel guests. They show concern and care when something goes wrong with the guest's visit, and they are quick to initiate action that will make things right again.

Major hotel companies have been quick to recognize the value of housekeeping and other service industry workers. Good hotel management does not see housekeeping-type work as demeaning or menial. To the contrary, all quality hotel operational management personnel have at one time or another performed house-keeping functions and as a result understand the worth and value of those people who perform such functions regularly.

Those who study the service industry should periodically remember the statement made proudly by one of America's most prestigious resorts; the Greenbrier of White Sulfur Springs, West Virginia. This statement appears on a sign that is visible as you enter the resort: "Ladies and Gentlemen Being Served by Ladies and Gentlemen."

THE ROOMS DEPARTMENT

Front Desk and Housekeeping

The rooms department of a lodging establishment is considered to be that department that is directly and solely involved with all aspects of the sale, occupancy, and servicing of guest rooms. A person usually called the resident manager manages the department. Although the title is somewhat misleading in that it presupposes the idea that the resident manager lives on the premise; most do not. Other titles synonymous with resident manager are rooms manager, rooms director, director of rooms operations, or simply, hotel manager (not to be confused with the general manager).

The rooms department is usually thought of as a combination of two principal operating departments: the front office and the housekeeping department. The manager in charge of the front office oversees several subdepartments: reservations, front desk, bell staff, PBX, transportation, possibly concierge, and any other form of guest reception function.

The manager in charge of all housekeeping functions is most commonly known as the executive housekeeper. Depending on the size of the hotel, and in some cases, corporate policy, the person in charge of housekeeping may have any one of a number of different titles all considered synonymous with executive housekeeper. A few such titles are:

- Housekeeper.
- Housekeeping manager.
- Director of services.
- Director of internal services.
- Director of housekeeping operations.

For the purposes of this article, all such responsibilities will be directed at the manager known as the executive housekeeper.

There was a time when most housekeepers worked under the direction of the front office manager. They were, in fact, not executives but people who had worked their way up from a maid's position, but had little or no training as a manager. Today, however, the size, cost, and complexity of housekeeping operations has put the executive housekeeper on an equal footing with other department managers. As a result, they are now seen to share equally in responsibility under the resident manager for the operation of rooms departments.

The hotel industry is a highly labor-intensive hospitality business. There may be more total employees involved in food and beverage operations than in any other department. Because of the diversity of such operations, however (restaurants, lounges, banquet services, and kitchen), there are usually more managers to control the total operation. In housekeeping, however, there is one department head (the executive housekeeper) who is responsible for the largest single staff, operating cost center, and physical area of the property.

Today's modern executive housekeeper must be a trained manager skilled in planning, organizing, staffing, directing, and controlling operations. He or she must also be skilled in employee and human relations, have a superior knowledge in cost controls, and have a strong technical background in purchasing, decorating, and renovation. Last but not least, the executive housekeeper must be an able delegator. Without a strong expertise and inclination to create or pass tasks to others, convey the necessary power to act, and finally, hold others accountable for their actions, the executive housekeeper must personally perform all working functions. And, this writer has never found the person yet who could make 3000 beds in one day.

ORGANIZATION

Housekeeping organizations are as varied as there are types and sizes of hotels. Except for the very small bed-and-breakfast operations, the trend today is away from the small 80-room mom-and-pop hotel. For the purpose of discussing housekeeping organizations it would therefore be appropriate to discuss a size of hotel that might be considered a model appropriate to the greatest variation. The organization to be discussed would fit any hotel of 200 or more rooms. In most cases there would be identical functions, but size would dictate that one person might perform several such functions in a small hotel. Obviously, the larger the facility, the greater the need for a larger staff with more individuals to fill each unique function. Consider then, the following hotel:

- A modern suburban corporate transient hotel.
- Three hundred fifty rooms.
- Two restaurants (one 24-hour and one dinner house).
- Banquet area with 15,000 square feet of meeting space.
- Room service.
- Kitchen to support all food services.
- Main lounge with nightly entertainment.
- Banquet beverage service, and service bar outlets for both restaurants and room service.
- Outdoor pool, and winter indoor pool with health club facilities, sauna, and steam room.
- Game room (video games, pool, and table tennis).
- In-house laundry for rooms department and banquet linen.

- Two company-owned gift shops.
- Front desk fully computerized with a property-management system.

Hotel Organization

Prior to investigating the housekeeping department organization it is appropriate to visualize an organization for the entire hotel. The organization diagram in Figure 5.1 could easily be appropriate for the model hotel just described.

Note the position of the executive housekeeper within the organization. Executive housekeepers may occupy greater or lesser positions in any organization. Some executive housekeepers might report directly to the general manager; others might even hold corporate executive positions. Others might even report to the chief of maintenance. In this case, however, our executive housekeeper occupies the position of a middle manager—a full department head, equal to that of the front office manager and other principal department heads within the staff. Two junior managers—the housekeeping manager and the laundry manager—will report to the executive housekeeper. Both the executive housekeeper and front office manager report to the resident manager, who is a member of the property executive committee. This committee is the top policy-making body for the property under the general manager.

The Housekeeping Organization

Figure 5.2 describes a reasonable housekeeping department organization for the model hotel. Note the utilization of the two principal assistants. The housekeeping manager is the first assistant to the executive housekeeper and has been placed in direct charge of all guest rooms in the hotel. This emphasizes the delegation that has taken place in that the housekeeping manager is not just an assis-

FIGURE 5.1
Hotel organization (through department head)

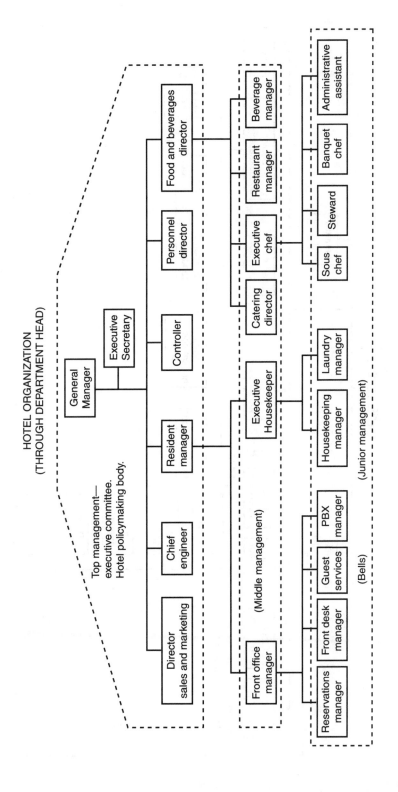

HOTEL ORGANIZATION
(THROUGH DEPARTMENT HEAD)

Top management—
executive committee.
Hotel policymaking body.

(Middle management)

(Junior management)

(Bells)

FIGURE 5.2
Housekeeping department organization

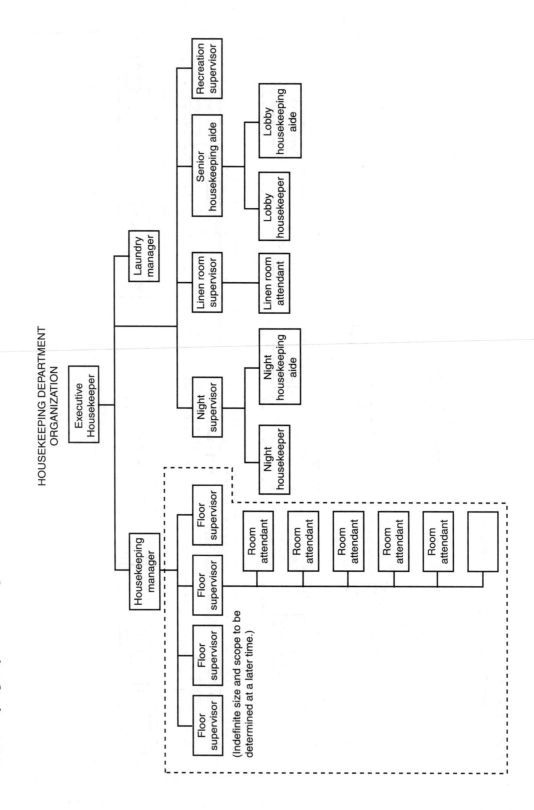

HOUSEKEEPING DEPARTMENT ORGANIZATION

tant to the executive housekeeper, but a junior manager with a functional responsibility. There are several ways in which this part of the organization can be managed. Each individual room attendant can be scheduled independently from one another, or they may be grouped into teams wherein they work as a team and are off together as a team. In this illustration, team staffing and scheduling will be presented because it provides for a more efficient technique of daily scheduling.

The laundry provides another specific function for the assignment of a junior manager. In this case, the technical expertise required is more specific. Such expertise would include knowledge of commercial laundry machinery and equipment, knowledge of piecework production, the utilization of chemicals, and their resultant effects on an expensive inventory of linen.

Both junior managers and the executive housekeeper have line supervisors that report directly to them. (Below the management level we recognize a structure for employees who are paid by the hour at a given wage rate as opposed to being on salary.) Each supervisor in turn would have one or more hourly workers who work for him or her to round out the department organization.

Note that the organization shown in Figure 5.2 under the housekeeping manager is incomplete. The number of floor supervisors or team leaders with their teams of room attendants and other team members is dependent upon the number of rooms each room attendant might be expected to clean in a given eight-hour period. The national standard for rooms cleaned by one room attendant in one eight-hour period varies from 13 to 20 rooms per day depending on the market mix of the hotel occupancy. Hotels occupied primarily by traveling or group business transient guests are more efficient to clean since occupancy is primarily single occupancy, and such guests are up and out of their rooms early each day. Also, they are inclined to leave their rooms in a lesser state of disarray. In such cases, room

attendants can clean from 18 to 20 rooms per day. When there is more double occupancy with families on vacation, access to rooms for cleaning is more difficult and will cut into the efficiency of staffing. In such cases room attendants will not be able to clean as many rooms in the same eight-hour period.

Staffing and Scheduling Concerns

In the case of our model hotel of 350 rooms, assume an 18-room workload per day. On any 100 percent occupancy day we would need approximately 20 room attendants to clean all guest rooms. Placing these room attendants in teams of five, working under one floor supervisor, creates a need for four such supervisors. Also assume that one section housekeeping aide will be assigned to each team to handle corridor cleaning, provide certain services to room attendants during the day, and to care for other public areas within the guest room portion of the hotel. Finally, assume that five laundry workers will be needed in the laundry regularly, and that persons hired to relieve room attendants on days off can also relieve in the laundry for the same purpose.

The complete organization should now come into focus, except for one remaining concern. Hourly personnel cannot work seven days a week but are usually confined to a five-work-day schedule. The following formula can serve to establish the entire rooms cleaning, laundry, and relief staff requirement; increasing the staff to allow for days off for regular room attendants, laundry workers, floor supervisors, and section housekeeping aides. (See staffing guide discussed later.)

At 100 percent occupancy on a continuous basis:

$$\text{regular staff} \times \text{seven days} = \text{total staff} \times \text{five-day maximum}$$

$$S_1 \times 7 = S_2 \times 5$$
$$S_2 = S_1 \times 7 \div 5$$

For the model, $S_2 = 25 \times 7 \div 5 = 35$ total working staff, all limited to a five-day work-week. The additional ten employees can be organized into two special teams identical in composition to the regular teams and the laundry workforce. These two teams are identified as *swing teams*, and they will "swing in" to relieve all regular and laundry personnel teams twice each week and have two days off themselves. This portion of the organization can now be scheduled to work by team units rather than as individual workers, which greatly simplifies personnel scheduling. (For further information on scheduling techniques, the reader is encouraged to read the basic text from which this article is drawn.)

The balance of the housekeeping organization is noted in the functions to be performed, and for purposes of illustration must be scheduled individually. Specifically, personnel required for the second shift, persons required to staff the linen room and housekeeping communications central, and personnel organized under the senior housekeeping aide for public area cleaning and maintenance round out the total department staff.

The entire housekeeping department staff might then take on the appearance provided in the staffing guide outlined in Table 5.1.

The staffing guide is created to accurately document the need for total personnel. Every position within the department is listed and can be used to fill vacancies when they occur. Note, teams are identified by color.

This identification system shows which teams are regular teams, which one works in the laundry, and which ones are considered swing teams. This particular staffing guide presumes that a 100 percent staff has been hired to support an occupancy averaging 85 percent or more for an extended period of time. Should occupancies be forecast as a lesser amount, a 100 percent staff need not be hired, and staff vacancies can be distributed over the entire team network. Fluxuations in daily occupancy should be dealt with by scheduling down within each team on a fair and equitable basis. This need to schedule down because of daily occupancy can be delegated to the floor supervisor, but controls must be in place that will guarantee fairness to all who must be cut out of a day's work due to low occupancy.

PERSONNEL AND JOBS IN THE HOUSEKEEPING DEPARTMENT

What follows is a listing of the various jobs one might find in a hotel housekeeping department. The basic function and scope of responsibility will be indicated for manager positions, and for hourly jobs, titles and responsibilities will be listed. Where several different names or titles apply to the same function in the hourly structure, each name will be noted.

The Executive Housekeeper

The executive housekeeper usually assumes complete direction, operational control, and supervision of the housekeeping, laundry, and recreation departments.

The scope of responsibility is normally broad to insure that the incumbent is given the freedom necessary to do the job. This position is now recognized as a career-enhancing step to future growth. The executive housekeeper is to operate the departments under his or her control in the most efficient manner possible through effective application and enforcement of company policies, the use of methods described in standard operating procedures, and the use of sound management principles. The incumbent is primarily responsible for the cleanliness of guest rooms and public areas assigned to the housekeeping department. The incumbent will accomplish tasks through proper training, motivation, and supervision of all personnel assigned to the housekeeping, laundry, and recreation departments.

TABLE 5.1
Department staffing guide

Position No.	Title	Name Assigned
	Management Team	
1	Executive housekeeper	_____
2	Housekeeping manager	_____
3	Laundry manager	_____
	Fixed Team	
4	Linen room supervisor	_____
5	Linen room attendant	_____
6	Senior housekeeping aide (public area supervisor)	_____
7	Public area housekeeper 1 (male)	_____
8	Public area housekeeper 2 (female)	_____
9	Public area housekeeper (relief)	_____
	Evening Team	
10	Night supervisor	_____
11	Night section housekeeper	_____
12	Night housekeeping	_____
13	Night (public area) housekeeper 1 (male)	_____
14	Night (public area) housekeeper 2 (female)	_____
15	Night (public area) housekeeper (relief)	_____
	Regular Rooms Cleaning Teams:	
	Red Team	
16	Senior housekeeper (supervisor)	_____
17	Section housekeeping aide	_____
18	Section housekeeper 1	_____
19	Section housekeeper 2	_____
20	Section housekeeper 3	_____
21	Section housekeeper 4	_____
22	Section housekeeper 5	_____
	Yellow Team	
23	Senior housekeeper (supervisor)	_____
24	Section housekeeping aide	_____
25	Section housekeeper 6	_____
26	Section housekeeper 7	_____
27	Section housekeeper 8	_____
28	Section housekeeper 9	_____
29	Section housekeeper 10	_____
	Brown Team	
30	Senior housekeeper (supervisor)	_____
31	Section housekeeping aide	_____
32	Section housekeeper 11	_____
33	Section housekeeper 12	_____
34	Section housekeeper 13	_____
35	Section housekeeper 14	_____
36	Section housekeeper 15	_____

(continued)

TABLE 5.1 (continued)

Position No.	Title	Name Assigned
	Green Team	
37	Senior housekeeper (supervisor)	
38	Section housekeeping aide	
39	Section housekeeper 16	
40	Section housekeeper 17	
41	Section housekeeper 18	
42	Section housekeeper 19	
43	Section housekeeper 20	
	Laundry	
44	Laundry supervisor (washman)	
45	Laundry helper/sorter	
46	Laundry attendant (ironer)	
47	Laundry Attendant (ironer)	
48	Laundry attendant (folder/stacker)	
49	Laundry attendant (folder/stacker)	
50	Laundry attendant (folder/stacker)	
	Swing Team 1	
51	Senior housekeeper (swing supervisor)	
52	Section housekeeping aide (ST-A)	
53	Section housekeeper A-1	
54	Section housekeeper A-2	
55	Section housekeeper A-3	
56	Section housekeeper A-4	
57	Section housekeeper A-5	
	Swing Team 2	
58	Senior housekeeper (swing supervisor)	
59	Section housekeeping aide (ST-B)	
60	Section housekeeper B-1	
61	Section housekeeper B-2	
62	Section housekeeper B-3	
63	Section housekeeper B-4	
64	Section housekeeper B-5	

The Housekeeping Manager

In the model organization the housekeeping manager assumes primary responsibility for guest room cleaning and servicing and acts as the primary assistant to the executive housekeeper.

Under the direction of the executive housekeeper, the incumbent is responsible for the efficient and orderly management of guest room cleaning, servicing, and the reporting of rooms status.

He or she represents those employees directly involved in rooms cleaning and should be directly involved in their work schedules. He or she must react to occupancy in scheduling in order that costs be kept under control.

The Laundry Manager

The laundry manager normally assumes primary responsibility for operation of the hotel's in-house commercial laundry. He or she will also act as second assistant to the executive housekeeper.

Under direction of the executive housekeeper, the incumbent is responsible for the efficient and orderly management and operation of the hotel laundry. Through the proper use of personnel assigned, the laundry manager will provide clean linen to the house and to the banquet department according to plans and budgets.

Hourly Employees

The Guest Room Attendant (also known as the GRA, maid, or section housekeeper)

The incumbent to this position is primarily responsible for guest room cleaning and servicing. He or she is usually assigned a section of rooms each day constituting a workload of a designated number of rooms to be cleaned. In general, the room attendant performs the same functions in each room assigned. The room attendant will also conduct certain room checks at set times to assist in determining the reporting condition of the house. Rooms occupied, rooms ready (vacant and ready to rent), and rooms on-change (vacant but not yet serviced, also known as checkouts).

The room attendant will also participate in general cleaning one or more rooms each day as it is serviced in order to keep quality standards high.

Most room attendants work in compliance with standard operating procedures (SOPs), which may specify as many as 60 items that must meet a given standard in each guest room. This is not as foreboding as it may sound, but the SOP system guarantees coverage where necessary.

Finally, the room attendant should reload his or her own linen cart at the end of each workday.

If so organized, the room attendant will be one of several members of a housekeeping team under a floor supervisor.

The Section Housekeeping Aide (previously section houseman)

The incumbent to this position works in the guest room portion of the hotel, attending to the regular and daily cleaning of corridors, elevator cabs and landings, stairwells, service areas, floor linen rooms, vending areas, and other special or unique public spaces in the vicinity of guest rooms. The section housekeeping aide also provides help to room attendants when associated with a general cleaning, if necessary. He or she will also remove soiled linen and rubbish from room attendants' carts on a regular schedule and will bring supplies from storerooms to floor linen rooms when needed. The section housekeeping aide works at the direction of the floor supervisor and, when so organized, also works as a member of a housekeeping team.

The Floor Supervisor (also sometimes known as senior housekeeper or inspectress)

Floor supervisors are team leaders, having several room attendants and a section housekeeping aide reporting to them. They are assigned to specific divisions of the rooms section of a property and are responsible for the quality of work performed in the sections to which their room attendants are assigned. They also are responsible for the public sectors that are assigned to their section housekeeping aides. They make inspections and reports and are in all respects supervisors of the persons assigned to their teams. They also assist in the personnel administration of the people assigned to them.

Floor supervisors are sometimes called inspectresses, which may be a misnomer. Many floor supervisors are inspectresses by virtue of the fact that they inspect rooms. Other inspectresses do nothing but inspect rooms and report directly to the manager on what they observe, but have no responsibility to correct discrepancies where found because no other staff is assigned to them for work purposes. (This writer is of the opinion that persons who do nothing but inspect guest rooms and have no employees or authority with which to take corrective action are a superfluous use of manpower.)

The Senior Housekeeping Aide (in the past known as head houseman)

The senior housekeeping aide is a major supervisor in the housekeeping department. He or she is usually placed in charge of all public areas not directly associated with guest rooms. Lobbies, major public corridors, public restrooms, offices, and other areas specifically negotiated as part of the overall housekeeping responsibility are the domain of the senior housekeeping aide. He or she is usually responsible for basic training of section housekeeping aides and supervision of utility housekeeping aides who might perform specific tasks such as shampooing carpets, washing windows, or performing project work. The senior housekeeping aide is usually responsible for the storage and accountability of cleaning and guest supply inventories. He or she normally works as a supervisory assistant to the executive housekeeper and performs such other tasks as the executive housekeeper might direct.

The Night Supervisor

The night supervisor presumes a second shift that has no management regularly assigned to it. This, of course, can vary depending on the size and complexity of night operations. Other than as intermittently visited by housekeeping management, the night supervisor assumes total control of the department after the major rooms and hotel cleaning evolution for each day has been concluded. Overseeing one or two night room attendants, a night section housekeeping aide, and several night lobby or public area personnel, the night supervisor is accountable for the balance of services to be performed by the housekeeping department for that day. The night supervisor insures that all rooms are left cleaned and ready to rent, that guest requests for service or equipment such as cribs, bedboards, extra linen, and the like are fulfilled. The night supervisor works closely with the hotel night manager, is usually on beeper, and is capable of making routine inspections throughout the hotel, until the department is secured each evening at the designated time. The night supervisor, like the senior housekeeping aide, is a major supervisor within the department.

The Linen Rooms Supervisor

Called the main linen room, this physical service area of the hotel is actually the hub of housekeeping communication and activity. As a result, it might be better described as housekeeping central. The linen room supervisor under the executive housekeeper is the supervisor in charge of the main linen room operations. Maintaining and operating the communication link to the front desk, engineering, and to each guest in need of housekeeping attention is the prime responsibility associated with the job of the linen room supervisor. In addition, the linen room supervisor is sometimes referred to as the chief status operator for housekeeping. Keeping up with, changing as necessary, and reporting the status of each guest room throughout the day is another major function of the linen room supervisor. He or she is the prime guest contact representative. Also, he or she would oversee the activities of one or more linen room attendants who perform supply and distribution functions for items such as bedspreads, blankets, bed pads, curtains, etc.. On the second shift, the night supervisor assumes the responsibilities of the linen room supervisor.

The Laundry Supervisor

Working as a principal assistant to the laundry manager, the laundry supervisor would supervise the activities of the laundry attendants. Normally the laundry supervisor would work as the head washperson and would be in charge of the use of all major wash equipment and chemicals. The incumbent to this position would also supervise the workload process and production. In our model hotel, when the laundry supervisor and team of laundry attendants is scheduled off, a swing team supervisor would assume the responsibilities of the laundry supervisor and would bring his or her swing team into the laundry. Since there are two swing teams, each swing team works in the laundry one day each week, providing the entire department with maximum flexibility and training.

The Recreation Supervisor

In our model hotel, the recreation supervisor under the direct supervision of the executive housekeeper would assume responsibility for all recreation areas of the hotel. All swimming pool attendants would work for the recreation supervisor and would be fully qualified as Red Cross or water safety instructors. (Swimming pools would be properly "signed" to indicate, "No lifeguard on duty. Swimmers do so at their own risk." This prevents the guest from abdicating responsibility for their own and their children's safety. However, all pool attendants would be fully qualified to save a life.) Pool attendants under direction of the recreation supervisor would also service the heath club, sauna, and game room for service to guests, cleanliness, and maintenance of order.

Other Employees

There are other employees that might be found in the department, and their title indicates their activity and who they might work for. All positions have titles appropriate to either male or female employees and are therefore nonsexist. Such positions are as follows:

- Utility housekeeping aide.
- Linen room attendant.
- Lobby housekeeping aide.
- Seamstress.
- Laundry attendant.
- Housekeeping trainer (a secondary job sometimes carried by a room attendant to insure standardization of training).

NEW HORIZONS IN HOUSEKEEPING

The National Executive Housekeeper's Association (NEHA) has long recognized the similarity in responsibilities of persons performing housekeeping functions in hospitals, hotels, and nursing homes. The association draws its membership not only from hotels, retirement centers, and contract cleaning establishments but also from hospitals and nursing homes. Also, the movement of management personnel between these fields is well documented. When asked how difficult it is for a manager to make the transition in either direction, a member in hospital service once remarked, "The main function of housekeeping in both areas is to clean rooms and public areas and to dispose of trash and rubbish. There is only one major difference, however, and that is in hospitals, we know exactly what we are walking into, and in hotels, you don't know what you may be dealing with." That was true—until the advent of the AIDS crisis.

On December 2, 1991, new rules issued by the federal Occupational Safety and Health Administration (OSHA) made it mandatory that employers provide certain information to all employees who might, as a result of their job classification, come in contact with human blood or other bodily fluids. This information, training, and compliance with federal precautions is designed to maintain a safe workplace with regard to bloodborne pathogens (microorganisms, especially HIV and HBV, that can cause disease in humans).

Specifically; department managers must establish control plans to combat the threat and provide access for employees to read and understand the OSHA compliance standard. Employees such as housekeeping and laundry personnel, who as a part of their regular daily assigned duties come in contact with bodily fluids such as blood, semen, sputum, vomit, or spent needles (sharps) that have been discarded in the trash by diabetics or drug users, must be advised of the potential dangers. Furthermore, they must be trained and tested in how to handle such risks when they occur, and they must be offered the opportunity to be inoculated against the hepatitis B virus (HBV) at company expense. Records must be kept of all training conducted and of all exposures that occur.

CONCLUSION

Being involved with housekeeping operations is no longer the exclusive territory of the female, nor is it considered menial or less important than any other function in the hospitality organization. Should anyone think to the contrary, they should try to imagine hotel operations without housekeeping and they might find general managers and presidents cleaning rooms.

Because of the large staffs involved, housekeeping operations provide junior managers outstanding opportunities to develop leadership potential and supervisory skills; an opportunity not always available in other departments.

This writer recalls a moment of truth several years ago when a general manager was overheard commenting to a utility houseman who at the time happened to be mopping a men's room at 1:00 A.M. in the morning. The general manager said, "You know, what you are doing is just as vital and necessary as what I do every day. We just do different things and work at different skill levels. When the company thinks they can do without either one of us, they'll abolish our jobs. I don't think they will, so until they do, don't forget, your job is just as important around here as mine is!"

5.4 "On Being an Executive Housekeeper"

John Lagazo

Ah yes, those were the days, sitting in our university classes, wondering where our education and futures would take us. I thought it would be quite easy—go through the management training program, become an assistant department head for a little while, move to department and then division head, then presto—general manager!

After going through the management training in my first company, I decided I wanted to stay in the rooms division—more specifically front office, so the path was laid out: Hotel assistant manager, then front office manager, brief exposure in either housekeeping and/or reservations; then so on and so on. Never did I think I would be the executive housekeeper in arguably what are some of the finest hotels and resorts not only in the United States, but even the world.

Why housekeeping? When my friends would ask what I do and I would say, "Executive housekeeper," the first question is "Oh, so you clean rooms?" Depending on who was asking, I either would agree or say it is "much, much more." Over the years I have had trainees or first-time assistant managers that would say that housekeeping was never their primary choice, but by the time they were done, they had a different appreciation for the department.

So what is housekeeping? Is managing housekeeping just making sure the maids (not a politically correct term anymore!) clean all the rooms every day? It is actually just a little more than that.

It is managing what usually is the greatest number of regular staff and the dollar amount to pay them. It is managing supplies—whatever is in the room for the guests to use, also what is used to clean anything and everything in the hotel—from the sidewalks, to the staff areas (i.e., locker rooms, cafeteria, offices), not only the rooms, but the meeting space and food and beverage outlets.

It is managing teamwork and the coordination between and among all other departments in the hotel—making sure the rooms are ready for the guests when they arrive. We need to make sure that all of the instructions/requests from sales are done. Accounting must be satisfied that we are making sure dollars are in control. I need to make sure that the food and beverage outlets are kept as clean as the guest rooms. We must make sure all of the human resource reporting requirements are met.

For the hotels that have a full-service laundry, it is managing that, too—and if the hotel utilizes an off-property service (laundry, overnight cleaning of the kitchens and public areas, uniform and guest clothes cleaning), the executive housekeeper must "manage" that operation! Even though the off-property services are their own business, they represent the hotel; if they do not clean the linens well or are not efficient, it will cost the hotel money.

It means you have to be very detail oriented and organized. Housekeeping is a "24/7" department, and if you don't have a handle on what is going on, it can get away from you very quickly. So you will get phone calls at 11 P.M. saying that your staff has not shown up, or that because the boilers are down, there is no steam for the laundry. The wildest calls I received (not too often, thank goodness) were when I worked in Hawaii. Because of the staffing challenges, I had room attendants and housepersons ferried over from a neighboring island. If the weather was bad or there was a mechanical problem with the boat, the phone would ring around 4 A.M. to tell me so. I then had to figure out "plan B" for cleaning rooms and the rest of the hotel that day.

Getting away from the technical side of things, being an executive housekeeper taught me a lot about managing people. I was "diversity managing" well before it became politically correct and one of the new management buzzwords. The staff is usually the most ethnically diverse, with an accompanying challenge being the level of English competency and overall education. This is the staff that is asked to work with various hazardous chemicals and a high "accident potential" environment (pushing and pulling heavy weights, exposure to bacteria, working with dangerous equipment such as sheet or towel folders and garbage and cardboard compactors).

These are the people who have one of the most detail-oriented jobs; a room checklist can have as many as 150 individual items that need to be completed to proper standard.

Contrary to popular belief, this staff should also have high guest contact skills. Just because the room attendant or other housekeeping staff does not interact with guests every time they perform their duties does not mean they should not be skilled in guest contact. One of my former room attendants would consistently tell me the travel plans of one of the regular CEOs that stayed with us. She would write his travel dates down and let us know if his wife would be with him. Since he was such a regular, typically there were no problems in accommodating him even if we were sold out, and he always had the same room with the same room attendant.

In many of the hotels, the challenge was to pull the different ethnic groups together to work as a team. Housekeeping gave me a great chance to learn about different cultures; I probably would still not know what a *quincinera* is (a sweet 15 birthday/debut in Latin American countries). I have eaten foods that I probably would not have otherwise and have picked up smatterings of many different languages (Spanish, Creole, Tongan, Polish, Cantonese, Filipino)—which, depending on the situation, could either get me in serious trouble or let me have a good laugh.

I learned about "management styles" and "group dynamics." I would advise all of you who read this to learn as much about these items as possible. I learned about identifying the informal leaders of groups and how to influence them. I learned about individual personality styles and how to manage and gel them together to get things done. With the different cultures I have worked with, I learned about the ones that avoided eye contact when you would speak with them, and I learned about the ones that had Old Country traditions—for instance, not respecting a female or young boss—and then how to turn them around.

Housekeeping taught me how to adapt—which, on the outside, should not have really been an issue because "I am the boss" and the staff should do as I say (traditional management). As we have seen, managing people continues to change and evolve. First, there was total quality management, then generation X management and whatever new theories that may be out there. To me, the bottom line is, to be a success, you need to manage not only yourself, but also groups of people. Manage and lead the environment (department), and you will be successful in your endeavors. Get exposure to different environments. Work in city and remote resort locations. Know and understand that everywhere you go, you will have a different guest and staff makeup. If you are adaptable, you will also be successful.

There are some other interesting things, too. When I shop for home cleaning items, I know way more than I need to. Don't bother listening to commercials; send me an e-mail or work in housekeeping and you will know why I will not buy "window cleaner with ammonia." Having managed laundry operations, I shop for clothes not only for style, but for materials used and construction of the item. For instance, if you buy items with lots of extra frills, beads, decoration, metallic buttons, and brought it to my dry cleaning store, don't be surprised if I charge you extra for what it takes to properly clean it. Or I may even turn you down and say I won't clean it unless you sign a damage waiver. I now know that the dry cleaning and laundry processes are murder on fabrics.

I have many great memories from housekeeping over the years:

- Using a bullhorn to conduct "morning meeting" with 70 room attendants.
- Being able to successfully prove a Mobil inspector wrong (I had been in their room during the incident in question).
- Being the executive housekeeper at the host hotel for the Mobil Five-Star winners award ceremony; imagine having every room checked with a magnifying glass and white gloves!
- Having a local TV station doing a *60 Minutes*–style report on hotel cleanliness; we passed with flying colors!
- Having my rooms director keep checking on me to make sure I did not get food poisoning because of some of the food my staff would give me; I was adventurous enough to eat whatever was placed on my desk, and, yes, the jellyfish does have an "interesting" texture.

There have definitely been some other situations, too. After a suicide in a hotel room, I could get only new staff members to go into the room because of the strong superstitious beliefs of some staff. I have managed through both strikes and decertifications in union hotels. The celebrity stories—that alone can take up a whole book, and perhaps make me rich from doing so?

I am glad my career path has taken me through housekeeping. At the end of the day, it really is the memories of the people I have met and the friends made over the years that have really made the difference. I think I would have learned the "technical" aspects one way or the other, but the people skills have been even more valuable. Yes, I did hold the positions of hotel assistant manager, front office assistant manager, and front office manager during various times in my career, in addition to spending time in all housekeeping management positions, including laundry/valet manager.

Where did I get all of these memories and experiences? Since leaving my alma mater in the mid-1980s, I have been at:

- Hyatt Hotels in California and Louisiana.
- A Wyndham Hotel in California.
- Ritz-Carlton Hotels/Resorts in California, Boston, Florida, Hawaii, and Puerto Rico (when I worked in these hotels, they were all Five-Star and/or Five-Diamond, except for Puerto Rico—it is still too new).

- Four Seasons Hotels in Boston and Chicago (both Five-Star, Five-Diamond properties).
- Short stints in St. Louis and Florida with Adams Mark and an independent Four-Star resort.

All of this prepared me for my present position, rooms director for an Interstate Hotels Corporation–managed property in Chicago. Can I say my housekeeping experience helped me? You bet! The varied experience with people, places, and management styles have prepared me for *anything* in this great hospitality business.

5.5   The Hotel Engineering Function: Organization, People, and Issues in the Modern Era

Denney G. Rutherford

INTRODUCTION TO THE ENGINEERING DEPARTMENT

History of the Department

Historically, the functions and duties of the chief engineer, his staff, and the engineering department have been relegated to the subconscious of hotel management and certainly to the hotel guests. Their place in the organization was roughly analogous to their place in the building structure: toward the bottom and basically out of sight. The only time the functions of the engineering department became noticeable was on those unhappy occasions when something went wrong with one of the building systems and guests and/or management were inconvenienced.

Consequently in the past, "out of sight, out of mind" treatment evolved for the engineering department, and as a result the relative importance of that department assumed a diminished role. Also, the personnel of the engineering department were craftspeople and semiskilled workers, usually managed by one of their number who through longevity and perseverance worked their way up through the ranks to supervisory status.

Evolutionary Stimuli

There is now clear evidence that this department is changing in many of the same ways that other departments of a modern hotel have had to change. The reasons for these evolutionary changes are many, but four can be highlighted here. Several of them, of course, are closely interconnected.

Competition

As more and more hotel organizations seek the business of ever more carefully segmented markets, many of the mechanisms of competition manifest themselves first in features of the physical plant. These can range from building design, landscaping, elevators, in-room amenities, and facilities, to the latest in traditional fixtures and building systems such as plumbing, kitchen equipment, elevators, heating, ventilating, and air-conditioning (HVAC), and the other behind-the-scenes paraphernalia that make up the domain of the chief engineer.

Sophistication

Many of these building systems in today's hotels are interconnected and managed in conjunction with other departmental systems and monitored by computerized facilities. This increased sophistication has mandated more sophisticated and knowledgeable management in all departments, but perhaps the most drastic and substantive changes will be (and are) occurring in engineering.

Return on Investment

Many modern hotel plants are the result of plans and investments by a wide range of participants, including (but not necessarily always) the management firm that operates the hotel. These investors have the expectation of a certain return on their investment and subsequently expect that the hotel company will not only keep the hotel filled with guests but keep the property in such a state that the guests will continue to want to come there. This also mandates new dimensions to the engineer's job. The combination of increased competition and sophisticated systems make for more than a traditional "repair and maintenance" approach to providing the engineering support in all areas of the hotel. To keep the hotel positively contributing to the investor's return on their money, the engineering staff has to be considered a major role player in the financial health of the organization.

Impact of OPEC Oil Embargo, 1973–1974

The cost, use, management, and conservation of energy have added a new and singular dimension to the job of the chief engineer—one that did not exist in pre-1973 operations,

simply because energy was so cheap. Buildings were not engineered or managed specifically to save energy.

Since the mid-1970s, most hotels and most modern hotel companies have come to recognize energy as one building expense in which significant savings can be made. If accomplished with care, engineering can provide delivery of hotel services without adverse or negative effects on the guest. We want to avoid, for instance, the extreme circumstances of requesting guests to take short showers while at the same time asking them to pay $180 a night for their room.

The residual effects of the embargo are twofold. Hotels that were build prior to 1973 were not constructed to be particularly energy efficient. Engineers that are managing their departments in those sorts of hotels have a more difficult job with respect to managing energy.

On the other hand, hotels that were designed and built after 1973–1974 have exhibited increasingly more sophisticated systems to manage and conserve energy without adverse effects to the guests.

The first instance represents a managerial problem of "making do" for the engineering manager; the second presents the dilemma of expanding one's knowledge in a rapidly changing technological environment.

In no business system as complex as a hotel is any mechanical or electronic system the only answer. A tremendous amount of attention must be given to training of personnel to overcome wasteful habits where energy is concerned. One of the classic examples is that of the kitchen employees who turn on every appliance in the kitchen at 6:00 A.M., when maybe only 20 percent of the appliances are used for the preparation of breakfast and most of the rest of them are not needed until close to lunch. These are representative of the sort of wasteful habits that are basically out of the control of the engineer but something that the engineer is obligated to point out to other department heads.

Those sorts of examples in and of themselves suggest further complications to the engineer's job—specifically that the engineer (as opposed to the role relegated to the bottom of the organization chart and the back of the house as earlier stated) now needs to have an active presence as a full member of the management staff and needs to become adept at interacting with other department managers.

PERSONNEL

Manager of Engineering Function

Variously referred to as the chief engineer, director of building operations, building superintendent, or some other combination of those terms, this is the individual who is responsible for the management of the building's systems, its maintenance, repair, and upkeep.

As stated earlier, in the past the chief engineers typically were people who worked their way up through the ranks from either one of the crafts or as an engineering employee specializing in one of the building systems. They may have been in hotels all of their professional careers, or may have come to a hotel company from engineering positions in organizations as diverse as shipping lines or manufacturing companies, or may have been building engineers in office buildings, university settings, or hospitals.

Research evidence, however, exists that suggests this trend may be changing (Rutherford, 1987). Chief engineers responding to this survey describe themselves collectively according to the data set forth in Table 5.2. Over 25 percent of those responding to this nationwide survey indicated they have a university degree. Of those, three-quarters were in some area of engineering. This suggests that the sophistication of modern hotel building operations may be mandating management by those whose formal education is more extensive than that required in the past.

In this study, the typical engineer was 44.5 years old and had been in the hospitality busi-

TABLE 5.2
Chief engineer demographics

		(Raw Number if Applicable)
Average Age	44.5	
Percent male	100.0%	
Percent Caucasian	92.9%	
Median salary	$35,000	
Percent university degree	27.0%	(20)
Percent of degrees in engineering	75.0%	(15)
Percent of degrees in hotel/business	25.0%	(5)
Average years in hospitality industry	10.9	
Average years at present hotel	6.3	
Average years in present position	6.15	

74 respondents

ness about 11 years. This suggests that this "typical engineer" has probably had significant on-the-job experience or training in his field in other industries and only recently came into the hospitality industry. After entering the hospitality industry, however, it appears that the chief engineers moved rapidly into management and have been fairly stable in their careers, as evidenced by the congruence of average years in their present position and average years at their present hotel.

Commenting on these data, one chief engineer said that in his experience more and more industry engineering managers in the larger or international hotel firms are being recruited from among those people who have had at least some college education, if not actually holding a college or university degree in engineering. He suggested that in his company this does not necessarily reflect a preference for academic training over practical experience; but recognizes the realities of doing business in today's competitive environment. It also suggests a requirement for understanding and being able to manage the sophisticated building systems that the company anticipates

installing and being developed for new hotels into the next century.

In that comment lies one key to understanding the future of the chief engineer's job. The most successful engineers of the future will very likely be those whose training and education prepares them to think strategically, to recognize trends, and to do his part to help the hotel and its owners meet and deal with the evolutionary issues discussed earlier.

Other Departmental Management Staff

Referring to Figure 5.3, depending, of course, on the size of the hotel and the extent and sophistication of the engineering functions in the hotel, the chief engineer may enjoy the services of a staff of administrative people, including assistant managers. These people help carry out the administrative details of operating an increasingly complicated hotel department. Included in these would be secretarial support, which may be combined with a clerical function.

FIGURE 5.3
Engineering department organization

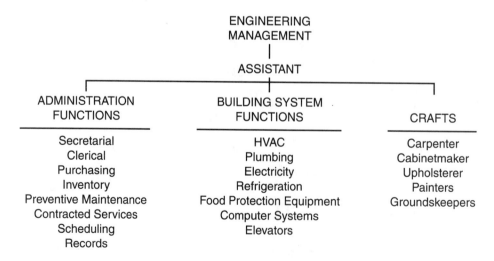

Among the most important administrative functions for the engineering department are:

- Helping other department heads make purchasing decisions.
- Keeping an inventory of spare parts and building equipment.
- Arranging for the performance of preventive maintenance on all building systems.
- Administering contract services such as pest control, window washing, landscaping, swimming pool maintenance, grounds-keeping, and various construction projects.

As the department grows in size and scope, a major administrative function involves scheduling of equipment and personnel to accomplish the tasks of the department. That is another major series of daily tasks that face administration of an engineering department. While scheduling may benefit greatly from technological advances such as the hotel's computer system, in a building whose systems are as complicated and interrelated as a hotel, part of the engineering function has to be prepared to react to nonscheduled events ranging from overflowing toilets to stuck elevators to gas leaks and so forth.

A final administrative function involves setting the groundwork for and maintaining the basis for managerial and administrative decisions that affect the long-term operation of the engineering department and by extrapolation the hotel itself. That function is to keep accurate and up-to-date records regarding the various building systems and installation of capital equipment for which the engineer is responsible.

These are the sorts of administrative details that complicate the job of any manager but may be particularly troubling to the engineer. One of the main reasons for this is that while the engineering department is responsible for the maintenance and repair of sophisticated and complicated building systems, under most circumstances these systems or component parts of these systems are often operated by (and perhaps misused by) a wide group of people ranging from employees to guests. Particularly in the case of guests we have little or no control over the way in which they treat guest room equipment and fixtures for which the engineer is responsible. Those engineers who have the luxury of a well-developed administrative staff find their job in managing the building and its systems and the attendant problems much easier if complete, accurate, and up-to-date records are available to formulate the basis for planning, purchasing, budgeting, and control.

Technical Specialists

Typical building functions that are the responsibility of the engineering department are listed in Figure 5.3. Each has its own place in providing for the comfort of the guest and participating in the delivery of the hotel's services to the guests. Each has attendant complications that provide challenges for the management and staff of the engineering department.

Heating, ventilating, and air-conditioning (collectively known as HVAC) is concerned with supplying the various production, public, and guest room areas of the hotel with a clean, controlled, and comfortable indoor environment. Modern building HVAC systems provide for heating or cooling the air; adding or deleting moisture from the air to adjust for optimum relative humidity; filtering or cleaning the air; and moving the air from place to place within the hotel providing for a number of complete changes of air in a room per hour dependent upon local codes and activities within that particular area of the hotel.

Among the complicating factors here that challenge the engineering department are that various areas of the hotel have various requirements for air. For instance, there is a different requirement in the guest room areas than there is in the kitchen area. There is a different requirement in public areas such as the lobby and areas such as bars, restaurants, or housekeeping laundry facilities. The engineers call this *providing the system with balance*, and it is a major function of the individuals who are in charge of the HVAC to deliver the optimum environment to each of those various areas of the hotel and adjust the HVAC system accordingly.

The plumbing system in a modern hotel has to perform a number of balancing functions, also. First and foremost in the minds of management, of course, is the delivery of quality water service to guest room areas. Guests want high-quality water that is free from visual defects such as dirt or rust, does not carry any odors, and tastes clean and fresh. Guests also want water that is hot enough to shave, bathe, and wash without the danger of scalding themselves, and they also want that water in generous supply. Nothing is more frustrating to a hotel guest who is paying over $200 a night for a room to find that the hotel has run out of hot water in the middle of a morning shave or shower. At the same time the engineering department is expected to deliver "production" hot and cold water to the kitchen areas, the housekeeping and laundry areas, and the various food service areas. Providing for the delivery of high-quality water service to the various user groups in the hotel is a major part of the engineering function; one that, of course, is noticed only when there is some obvious defect in the delivery of that particular service.

A similar case may be made for the delivery of electricity to the various areas within the hotel. As in providing high-quality plumbing services, the electrical systems of the hotel also have to be designed and maintained to serve various user groups. Again, like plumbing, there is no substitute for adequate electricity. The engineering staff must provide the hotel with electrical service designed to meet the needs of individual departments and the needs of guests.

Refrigeration, food production equipment, and computer systems are examples of other building system functions that may be the responsibility of the engineering department to repair, maintain, replace, and/or manage. While the maintenance of many of these systems may be contracted with outside agencies such as the supplier, the engineering department nonetheless is the first line of defense in keeping the systems operating efficiently.

In most modern hotels the installation and service of elevator systems are generally the province of the elevator manufacturer, and hotels will typically have extended maintenance agreements for the elevators. Most engineering departments will, however, closely monitor the operation of the elevator systems. In modern high-rise hotels with high-speed elevator service, the slightest problem with that service should be quickly and easily identified and reported to the contractors. It is generally the responsibility of the engineering department to monitor these services and their contracts closely and carefully.

The various crafts represented in Figure 5.3 are included to illustrate the sorts of specialized skills required in varying ways by most hotel engineering departments. Depending upon the size of the hotel and complexity of a hotel's services, an engineering department may employ on a full-time basis one or more carpenters and cabinetmakers to maintain, repair, and build fixtures and furniture for the hotel's guests and staff. Similarly, if not contracted out, hotels may employ an upholsterer whose major task is to maintain a high-quality appearance of the vast collection of furniture in a typical hotel.

Painting and upkeep of the hotel's grounds and landscaping also represent ongoing functions that require constant attention. These represent services that may be contracted to outside agencies or suppliers but are included here to suggest the range of functions for which the engineering department is responsible.

ISSUES

In the previously mentioned study (Rutherford, 1987), the engineers surveyed were asked to judge the relative importance of each of a list of 58 statements relating to the operation of a modern hotel engineering department. A statistical procedure was applied to rank order the statements in terms of their rated importance. The ten most important facets of an engineer's job derived from this list are reproduced in Table 5.3 and serve as the basis for suggesting the most pressing issues facing hotel engineering managers at this time.

Departmental Management

Items 4, 6, 7, and 8 in Table 5.3 suggest that the modern hotel engineers deem activities relating to management of their departments of high importance to success. Communicating with employees; providing for a safe environment; being able to organize the various tasks, activities, and personnel in the department; and providing leadership—all suggest that one of the foremost issues facing the chief engineer today encompasses those that refer to managerial skills rather than the traditional view that held the chief engineer to be

more concerned with the technical aspects of his job.

Energy

The fact that three energy-related items were rated in the top ten by all responding engineers suggests that the entire realm of issues relating to energy have not yet been addressed satisfactorily by the majority of these professionals. It also suggests that energy will continue to be an issue in the foreseeable future.

Relations with Top Management

Another major dimension of the engineer's job can be seen by the importance attached to this issue. Of the other departments that the engineers were asked to rank their relationships with, only two, housekeeping and purchasing, ranked within the top 50 percent of these 58 items. Many of the chief engineers contacted for comment agreed with this ranking with top management. They said on a regular basis it is becoming an increasingly important

TABLE 5.3
Importance of this item to operation of my department

Rank	Item	Mean	SD	N
1.	Knowledge of maintenance of equipment	4.760	.633	75
2.	Energy conservation	4.655	.804	74
3.	Energy management	4.589	.761	73
4.	Responsibility for communication with employees	4.587	.680	75
5.	Relations with top management	4.520	.811	73
6.	Responsibility for leadership	4.514	.726	74
7.	Responsibility for safety	4.486	.904	72
8.	Responsibilities of an effective organizational ability	4.453	.810	75
9.	Energy costs	4.444	.854	72
10.	Knowledge of the types of equipment	4.370	.791	73

Scale: 1 = not at all important
         5 = of vital importance

part of their job to not only report to top management but educate top management as to the importance of the engineering function.

Equipment

It should be noted that the more technical aspects of the chief engineer's job are not in any way totally ignored by the collective rankings assigned to these operational statements. That knowledge of maintenance of equipment ranked clearly first among the other statements and knowledge of types of equipment made it into the top ten, suggests that while the job of the chief engineer may in fact be evolving toward one of a more managerial nature, some of the tradition technical aspects of the job still play a major role in the daily discharge of an engineer's responsibility.

FUTURE AND CONCLUSION

Data from Empirical Research

Interpretation of the data gathered in the survey from a broad cross section of chief engineers and subsequent follow-up conversations with selected engineers suggests that the job of the chief engineer is in fact evolving as suggested at the outset of this chapter.

The engineers themselves describe many incidents of having to deal more with issues and problems related to people and departmental action and interaction than in the past when most of the issues and problems they had to face on a regular basis involved equipment and systems.

It also appears that in the future chief engineers are going to have to be more adept at inter- and intradepartmental organizational politics. To provide the hotel and its guests with high-quality services relative to the physical and environmental systems of the building, the chief engineer is going to have to compete with other department heads for scarce resources related to personnel, technology, and "operating elbow room."

Summing up, the engineering department, its management, and to a certain extent its staff and technical experts represent an organizational function of the modern hotel that is in the process of evolutionary change. As stated at the outset, this change is driven by a number of factors. The future of successful hotel organizations will hinge to a great extent on the ability of hotel managements to recognize the importance of the contributions of the engineering department to the delivery of guest services and maintaining a high order of return on investments for the owners of the property.

5.6 The Engineering Department and Financial Information

Agnes Lee DeFranco and Susan B. Sheridan

The engineering department is a vital part of a hotel. Energy cost alone runs anywhere from 4 to 6 percent of a property's total operation budget. Savings in energy cost can be accomplished by instituting simple steps such as modifying staff members' behavior (Dale and Kluga, 1992). How can financial data be used

to continuously improve the performance of the engineering department? To answer this question, a survey was performed to collect data from hotel engineers to determine their use of financial information. It is postulated that if financial information is analyzed correctly, the engineering department can serve its profit centers better, which in turn will assist these profit centers in reducing both their cycle time and errors.

A number of studies have been done on the use of financial information by managers in profit centers of hotels, but not many were performed specifically to collect information regarding the engineering department. Malk and Schmidgall (1995) discuss the use of financial statements and information in the food and beverage department of a hotel, particularly in an effort to contain costs and maintain a profit. Turkel (1993) also advocates the development of profit and loss statements and allocating costs properly to ascertain the profitability of a food and beverage department. Malk and Schmidgall (1994) also investigate the cost percentages in the rooms division to help rooms division managers with cost containment. Quain (1992) explores the use of profit analysis by customer segment in addition to yield management, and the topic of menu engineering to improve profits in food and beverage establishments has also been discussed (Bayou and Bennett, 1992: Dougan, 1994). However, few, if any, studies can be quoted for the engineering department.

THE SURVEY

The purpose of the study was to investigate the use of financial information by hotel engineers. Therefore, questions asked included the types of financial information used, the frequency at which this information was generated, the methods used to generate the data, and the type of hardware and software used in the department. Hotel engineers were also interviewed to see how their use of financial information could improve quality in their departments by reducing cycle time and eliminating errors.

The population for this study consisted of directors of engineering in American hotels that were listed in the *Hotel and Travel Index*, Spring 1994 edition. The sample was randomly selected from this index, and the selection criteria was based on the number of rooms in the property. The sample hotels all had 200 or more rooms. It was believed that hotels of this size would probably have an engineering department. The sample size was 400 hotels, and the sample hotels were located throughout the 50 states.

For the first mail-out, a cover letter and a questionnaire were sent to the general managers of each sample hotel. It was felt that if the surveys were addressed to the general managers by name, they would be more likely to read the surveys and pass them along to the directors of engineering. The initial response rate, however, was only 15 percent. In order to improve the response rate, three weeks after the initial mail-out, a second mail-out was sent. The second mail-out was addressed specifically to the director of engineering. Follow-up letters and questionnaires were sent to the entire sample. A total of 97 of the 400 questionnaires were eventually returned for a response rate of 24.25 percent.

THE TYPICAL CHIEF ENGINEER

Of the sample, 38 percent of the respondents reported that chief engineer was their official title, while 36 percent held the title of director of engineering and 7 percent were directors of property operations. The majority of the respondents (52 percent) had less than six years of experience with their present company, and less than three years with their specific property (51 percent). However, when asked their years of experience within the hospitality industry, most of them (56 percent) had 6 to 15 years of experience.

The respondents also reported having substantial experience in engineering and property operations and maintenance departments. The highest response category was 9 to 18 years (39 percent), followed by 18 to 27 years (22 percent), and then, 0 to 9 years (16 percent).

The majority of the respondents (60 percent) worked in hotels that had 200–400 rooms, and these hotels had an average daily rate of $95.60. The largest group of respondents (32 percent) employed seven to nine engineering employees. Overall, the work performed was primarily done in-house and by outside contractors. Table 5.4 provides a summary of the characteristics of the respondents.

TABLE 5.4
Profile of Respondents

	n	%
Job Title		
Chief engineer	33	38
Director of engineering	32	36
Director of property operations	6	7
Facilities Manager	3	3
Others: Eleven different titles	14	16
Number of Years with Company		
0–3	31	32
3.1–6	19	20
6.1–9	11	11
9.1–12	11	11
12.1–15	13	14
15 and over	12	12
Number of Years with Property		
0–3	49	51
3.1–6	17	18
6.1–9	10	10
9.1–12	12	12
12 and over	9	9
Number of Years in the Industry		
0–3	5	5
3.1–6	9	10
6.1–9	12	13
9.1–12	23	24
12.1–15	18	19
15 and over	28	29
Number of Years with Engineering Department		
0–9	15	16
10–18	37	39
19–27	31	32
28 and over	12	13
Number of Rooms in Property		
200–300	29	31
301–400	28	29
401–500	16	17
501 and over	22	23
Average Daily Rate		
Less than $50	2	2
$51–$100	48	56
$101–$150	26	31
$151 and over	9	11
Name of Employees in Department		
3–6	16	17
7–9	31	32
10–12	13	14
13–15	11	11
16 and over	25	26

HOW IMPORTANT IS FINANCIAL INFORMATION?

In order to assess how financial information can affect the performance of the engineering department, the respondents were asked to rate ten different criteria. A Likert rating scale of one to five was used with "1" being not important and "5" being very important. Table 5.5 ranks these ten criteria as perceived by the directors of engineers.

The one area that received the highest mean score of 4.70/5.00 was "control costs more effectively," with 80 percent of the respondents rating the criterion at a five and 14 percent at a four. This was followed very closely by "evaluate the performance of the department" and "plan ahead more effectively," both rated at 4.49. The criterion that received the lowest rating of 3.55 was "improving communications with the department staff." Therefore, the majority of these managers were aware that financial information was an essential and integral part of the operations of the department.

THE COMPILATION PROCESS

With such overwhelming agreement that financial information can enable managers of the engineering department to control costs more effectively, the respondents were then asked about the compilation process. They were asked to specify the types of financial reports that are generated, the frequency at which they were generated, the number of people involved in the process, and the methods used to compile these reports.

All respondents used budgets or cost tracking in their property. Variance analysis, comparing the budgeted and actual figures, was done by 95 percent of the respondents, and 60 percent stated that a departmental income statement was prepared.

The frequency at which these reports were generated was quite varied. The respondents were asked to indicate whether the above-mentioned statements were done on a daily, weekly, biweekly, monthly, or annual basis, and to check all that applied. For the departmental income statements, monthly reporting was the norm (51 percent). This was also true for the budgeted income statement (50 percent), cost tracking on individual accounts (40 percent), variance analysis (49 percent), and flexible budget (55 percent).

In addition to preparing these statements on a monthly basis, 22 percent of the respondents prepared daily department income statement and 31 percent did cost tracking on

TABLE 5.5
Usefulness of financial information

Criterion	Ranking	Mean Score	Standard Deviation
Control cost more effectively	1	4.70	0.09
Evaluate the performance of my department	2	4.49	0.14
Plan ahead more accurately	2	4.49	0.15
Be a better manager	4	4.47	0.16
Have information for evaluation purposes	5	4.33	0.16
Be more flexible financially	6	4.00	0.19
Be more innovative	7	3.99	0.19
Staff accordingly	8	3.93	0.22
Improve communication with my staff	9	3.63	0.22
Improve motivation of my staff	10	3.55	0.23

a daily basis. Although budgeted income statements and variance analysis were not done on a daily basis, they were compiled on a weekly basis.

The number of people involved in preparing these statements varied from one to ten. The responsibility, however, was generally shared between the engineering department itself and the accounting department. Half of the respondents reported that cost tracking was done by their own department and by the accounting department. Cost tracking was the analysis that the engineering department performed on their own more often than they did any of the other four analyses. The accounting department, on the average, performed 62 percent of the engineering department's financial work.

The majority of the respondents used computers to prepare these statements. Approximately 60 percent of the respondents used computers to compile all of the five statements. A combination of manual methods and computers was the second most commonly used method (40 percent), and no respondents reported that financial information was compiled only manually.

COMMENTS FROM THE FIELD

In addition to the surveys, a number of engineers in a large metropolitan area in the southwestern United States were interviewed in an effort to determine, in greater depth, how they used financial information. One of the engineers stated that he used financial information now more than he used to. His role as an engineer has changed over the years, and he is currently much more of a financial planner than he used to be. He reviews all of the financial statements that relate to his department with his supervisory employees in an effort to help contain costs. This process was found to help empower employees because they could see how their performance was directly linked to the results of these statements.

Budgets were critical to all of these engineers, and they generally felt that it was important to properly allocate their costs. This information was also useful because it showed if their costs (particularly repairs, maintenance, and utilities) were in line with their projections. One engineer was particularly adamant about properly accounting for his costs. In his hotel, bonuses were given on overall profitability of the hotel, and he wanted to make sure, as much as he could, that everyone received their bonuses. Another engineer stated that he used financial information to help conserve and cut down on waste. He also used his financial information to be proactive in dealing with costs. The engineers believed that financial information could help them in eliminating errors such as ordering their inventory, or to just make sure that their departments were operating as efficiently as possible, thereby reducing cycle time.

CONCLUSIONS AND IMPLICATIONS

It was apparent that managers of engineering departments recognized the importance of financial information. They also worked together with the accounting department to compile budgets, actual statements, and variance analyses, which were then used to evaluate the performance and success of the engineering department. Computer technology was also prevalent in their operations.

However, improvements can always be made to achieve zero defects, reduce cycle time, and enhance employee empowerment. As noted, "improve motivation of my staff" and "improve communication with my staff" were rated as the bottom two of the ten criteria given. In addition, two was the average number of people involved in the preparation of these reports. If it is not practical to have more employees share in the compilation process, the least that an engineering department can do is to have more employees participate in the analysis process. When more employees are involved, motivation and communication tend to increase. This positive attitude may be passed along to other employees and guests.

Asking employees to be involved does not mean that they must "do" the accounting work. Rather, those who compiled the information can share with other staff members the importance of cost control and how cost savings in the engineering area can affect the bottom line, which may ultimately affect their job performance and bonuses. These discussions can also be in the form of employee meetings where they may make suggestions for improvements. Since employees encounter day-to-day problems and situations that the managers may not be aware of, they may be able to offer comments and suggestions that address concerns such as staffing, costs control, and physical plant improvements. This process may help the entire department to become more innovative and further empower engineering employees, reduce cycle time, and possibly eliminate errors.

The majority of respondents (60 percent) used computers to compile financial information. The rest used a combination of computers and manual methods. Therefore, those engineering departments that do not use a computer in their own department may find that working with one may help improve their overall efficiency.

As this study has shown, computer technology and the use of financial information in the engineering department are vital in maintaining an efficient operation. According to the National Restaurant Association's 1994 Restaurant Industry Operations survey, utility expenses for restaurants increased 6.9 percent from 1992 to 1993 while repairs and maintenance increased 5.8 percent in the same period (Riehle, 1994). If not watched, these costs will probably continue to eat away the profits. Therefore, it is up to the engineering department of restaurant managers who deal with these areas to use their financial information to help contain these costs.

5.7   De Facto Security Standards: Operators at Risk

Denney G. Rutherford and Jon P. McConnell

Successful management involves being able to predict and control situations, people, or things. If something can be anticipated, managers must have in place policies or procedures with which to deal with the event. From time to time, however, despite all attempts to provide a safe and secure environment, something that was not anticipated may cause a guest to experience injury or loss.

Increasingly, courts are holding that those acts and events that harm a guest on a hotel's premises can be foreseen and are therefore preventable. As a result, the hotel industry is now operating at greater risk than in the past.

A Tradition

The duty of innkeepers and restaurateurs to provide safety and security to their guests has been recognized for centuries. English innkeepers, for instance, as early as the fifteenth century, had to accommodate any well-comported person who applied to the inn. The rationale for such a rule was that the English countryside was infested with robbers and brigands, and because life itself was chancy except within the confines of an inn. It was established that the innkeeper had an affirmative obligation to admit such guests as the inn could accommodate.

Moreover, first by default and then by decree, the inn and its caretakers became the insurers of the guests' property. To prevent innkeepers from entering into collusion with thieves to steal the property of guests, the innkeeper at common law was made responsible for the loss of a guest's property. (This rule has been modified by statute in virtually every state in the United States.)

Innkeepers and restaurateurs have never been held to be the insurers of the safety of guests. Rather, the standard of care has been that they owe the guest reasonably safe premises and that they must take reasonable steps to protect their guests from harm.

Foreseeability

The concept of foreseeability, then, becomes important in the context of prevention and reasonable care. If an establishment's manager *should* be able to foresee danger to any guest, the manager is required to take steps to deal with the danger. That brings into play our current concern with security.

As the following cases illustrate, courts have held and are continuing to hold that if criminal activity is foreseeable, reasonable steps must be taken for the protection of guests and diners. This has been the law for decades. Our concern is with the *increase* in criminal activity that necessitates increased measures of security for the safety of guests.

Stricter Standards

What courts have done in deciding for plaintiffs (guests) in hotel-security cases is to interpret common and statute law in ways that suggest de facto managerial security standards. Most of these legal interpretations involve instances where the court felt that had the hotel applied a stricter standard of care to a foreseeable event, the injury or loss would not have occurred. Generally, such security

"deficiencies" involve incidents related to three categories of security standards (see Table 5.6):

1. Physical or property related.
2. Personnel or training related.
3. Administrative or procedure related.

COURTS FIND DEFICIENCIES

What follows is an analysis of legal cases in which the courts have found deficiencies, and we argue that the remedies of those deficiencies have the potential to become security standards imposed upon hospitality operators by the courts. After a brief discussion of each case, we present data from our survey of hotel-company security executives that show those officers' reactions to such "new" standards and the extent to which hotel companies have actually paid attention to those standards.

Court-Mandated Security Standards

In each of the cases we discuss, courts found that inns or restaurants and their managements exhibited some deficiency of care. The courts held that those deficiencies resulted to some degree in a traumatic, injurious experience for the guest—certainly not what the guest expected upon checking in or entering the premises.

We believe that in deciding for the plaintiffs in these cases and pointing out specific deficiencies of care, the courts have established *court-mandated security standards* (CMSS) for hotels. Because the courts' findings may well be used as the basis for future decisions in cases involving similar circumstances, the decisions are tantamount to a mandate. Our analysis of *Banks v. Hyatt* (Rutherford and McConnell, 1987, pp. 58–63) suggests that hotels have to become proactive in predicting areas of risk vulnerability, then establish policies and procedures to eliminate the greatest foreseeable portion of that risk.

TABLE 5.6
Types of security standards and related court cases

Court-Mandated Security Standard	Pertinent Case Citation
Physical or Property Related	
Regularly inspected locking systems that work and provide more than minimum security.	*Garzilli v. Howard Johnson Motor Lodges* *Kveragas v. Scottish Inns, Inc.*
Adequate lighting in halls and other areas where guests are expected.	*Boles v. La Quinta Inns*
Remote monitoring by TV or other surveillance systems.	*Virginia D. v. Madesco Investment Co.* *Orlando Executive Park, Inc. v. P. D. R.* *Peters v. Holiday Inns*
Limit access to guest areas in order to exclude unauthorized persons.	*Virginia D. v. Madesco Investment Co.* *Nordmann v. National Hotel Co.* *Orlando Executive Park, Inc. v. P. D. R.* *Peters v. Holiday Inns*
Personnel Related	
Regularly employed security personnel who also patrol guest areas and other hotel premises.	*Virginia D. v. Madesco Investment Co.* *Nordmann v. National Hotel Co.* *Banks v. Hyatt Corporation* *Orlando Executive Park, Inc. v. P. D. R.* *Peters v. Holiday Inns*
Employ armed security guards in operations that have high rates of criminal activity in area.	*Taco Bell, Inc. v. Lannon*
Training and instruction for security personnel who are armed.	*Harris v. Pizza Hut of Louisiana, Inc.*
Train staff in procedures for reporting and dealing with criminal activity when discovered by hotel personnel.	*Nordmann v. National Hotel Co.* *Boles v. La Quinta Inns* *Harris v. Pizza Hut of Louisiana, Inc.*
Administrative or Procedure Related	
Monitor and be aware of criminal activity in area of operation.	*Banks v. Hyatt Corporation* *Taco Bell, Inc. v. Lannon* *Peters v. Holiday Inns*
System for advising guests of dangerous areas and/or criminal activity around the hotel.	*Banks v. Hyatt Corporation* *Orlando Executive Park, Inc. v. P. D. R.*

The cases presented here illustrate common deficiencies on the part of hotels and restaurants and the subsequent harm that may befall guests. This is neither an exhaustive inventory of such cases nor a group selected for dramatic effect. These cases fairly represent the field of potential liability and are, sadly, typical.

GARZILLI V. HOWARD JOHNSON MOTOR LODGES

In this case, it probably didn't help the defendants that the victim was a celebrity, namely, Connie Francis. Nevertheless, the facts of the case show that the hotel operators *could* have done a better job at providing security (*Garzilli v. Howard Johnson Motor Lodges*, 1976).

Guest's Complaint

Connie Francis was staying at the Westbury, New York, Howard Johnson motel. She was criminally assaulted by a man who entered her room through the room's sliding glass doors. From the inside the doors gave the appearance of being locked, but could be opened from the outside without much difficulty.

The Decision

On the basis of psychiatric testimony that her lucrative career as a singer was ruined because of the traumatic experience, Francis was awarded $2.5 million and her husband, $150,000. On appeal, the award to the singer was affirmed but that to her husband was reduced to $25,000.

Deficiencies

The inn violated elementary principles of security by providing sliding glass doors that could be opened from the outside. Howard Johnson's fault was a relatively slight oversight, but it led to a tragic incident that could have been prevented. Doors that seem to lock but in fact do not are an invitation to all kinds of trouble.

KVERAGAS V. SCOTTISH INNS

Even the simplest remedies can help mitigate the legal consequences of personal violence inflicted upon guests (*Kveragas v. Scottish Inns, Inc.*, 1984).

Guest's Complaint

Plaintiffs were occupying a room in the Scottish Inns motel in Knoxville, Tennessee. At about 10:10 P.M. three intruders broke down the door to their room and assaulted plaintiffs, stealing $3,000 in cash and shooting and severely wounding plaintiff Kveragas. The door that was kicked in was a hollow-core door that fit poorly into the door frame. The only lock was one inside the doorknob, described as a third-grade lock. A security chain that had been secured broke when the door was kicked in.

The Decision

The trial court issued a directed verdict for defendant, the plaintiffs appealed, and the circuit court reversed the trial court and ordered a new trial.

Deficiencies

In this day and age, adequate doors and locks are available, and even small motels run a great risk if they do not install such equipment. The evidence in this case showed that adequate locks that could have withstood the force used to break down the door were readily available.

VIRGINIA D. V. MADESCO INVESTMENT

Problems with trespassing and unauthorized access should be taken seriously and dealt with decisively. Act on the recommendations of your security force, and find ways to monitor those areas open to the public (*Virginia D. v. Madesco Investment Corporation*, 1983).

Guest's Complaint

Plaintiff was a guest at the restaurant within the defendant's hotel. While using the ladies' room designated by the restaurant for its female patrons, she was grabbed from behind and sexually assaulted.

The ladies' room was located in the lower lobby of the hotel, an area containing meeting and banquet rooms (those rooms were not in use at the time of the attack) and various hotel offices. Although it was past office hours (5:30 P.M.), four hotel employees were still in their offices. Access to the lower lobby could be gained from any floor of the hotel by an elevator or from the upper lobby by using a flight of stairs. The upper lobby was accessible through two sets of doors on the front of the hotel and through a rear entrance used by employees and vendors. No employee was stationed in the lower lobby on a regular basis. There was no television or video monitoring of the lower lobby.

Warning Signs

There was abundant evidence in the recent past of minor crime and trespassing in the area of the lower lobby of this hotel. Apparently, the entry of unauthorized persons was a concern of the hotel's security staff, but little was done about it. For a time the women's restroom had been kept locked after hours, but this caused objections from the restaurant and the practice was abandoned. There was one security guard whose duty was to patrol the entire hotel. He was not in the lower lobby at the time of the attack. The agency through which the guard was hired had recommended a second guard, but this suggestion was not implemented.

The Decision

A jury verdict at the trial court awarding plaintiff $100,000 was reinstated by the Supreme Court of the State of Missouri. A jury could easily find on the evidence that entry to the lower lobby was largely uncontrolled and that criminals might well enter into it, and yet no steps were taken for the protection of guests.

Deficiencies

Three major deficiencies existed: (1) unlimited access to an area where patrons of the hotel and restaurant would be expected to go; (2) lack of security personnel in that area; and (3) no television or other forms of monitoring to discourage criminals from lurking about the premises.

NORDMANN V. NATIONAL HOTEL

Hotel employees must have some common sense and be empowered to use it. Failure to respond to a guest's call for help can result in big problems (*Nordmann v. National Hotel Company*, 1970).

Guests' Complaint

Mr. and Mrs. Nordmann were guests at a ball in a 1200-room hotel in New Orleans. They left the ball and headed for their room in the hotel. As they prepared to enter their room they were accosted by a robber and forced at gunpoint into the room. The robber bound Mr. Nordmann and began harassing Mrs. Nordmann. A guest next door heard what was transpiring and called the hotel telephone operator, requesting that the operator call the police.

Instead of calling the police, the operator debated for a time whether that would be helpful. The operator eventually called the room clerk. The room clerk, too, delayed for some time despite the caller's urgent request and vivid description. The room clerk decided against calling the police and set out to find a security officer or house detective.

Evidence showed that 40 minutes elapsed before the police were called, yet when they were called it took them only four minutes to arrive at the hotel. By then the gunman, who had attempted to rape Mrs. Nordmann, had long since fled. The room clerk, when asked why he took so long to call the police, responded, "We were real busy at the time and we can't be calling the police for everybody that calls down here."

The Decision

The jury awarded $16,000 to Mrs. Nordmann and $5,000 to her husband. This was affirmed on appeal, at which time the award was characterized as "modest."

Deficiencies

By any standard, a hotel with 1200 rooms and a large function under way is not adequately staffed if it has just one security guard, a single room clerk on duty, and only one bellhop. In the case of this hotel, it appears there were no procedures in place as to what should be done in the event of the discovery of a possible crime in progress. Furthermore, this hotel's halls and elevators were not secure.

BOLES V. LA QUINTA INNS

Here's another example of how employees' actions—or lack thereof—can undermine a hotel's responsibility to its guests (*Boles v. La Quinta Inns,* 1982).

Guest's Complaint

When Boles opened her door at the La Quinta Motor Hotel, she was met by a prowler who pushed her into the room and raped her. The attacker bound and gagged Boles, threatened to return and kill her, and left her in the dark. She managed to kick the telephone receiver off the hook and to call the front desk, pleading for help.

The employees at the front desk seemed to take little interest in Boles's pleas. She talked to at least three different employees, none of whom showed any concern or sympathy with her plight. One informed her they would not be coming up to her room to help her, although they had called the police. Two assistant managers and the manager stationed themselves outside her room listening to her screams but none attempted to assist her.

Boles sued La Quinta, alleging that (1) the motel was negligent in failing to maintain a safe, well-lit corridor, and (2) the motel employees were negligent in the manner in which they responded to her call for help.

The Decision

The jury found that the hotel was negligent in not maintaining a well-lit corridor, but that this was not the cause of the rape, and no damages were awarded on this charge. However, the jury found that the dilatory conduct of the employees contributed to other physical and psychic injuries. Those injuries were divided into two categories: $35,000 for damages from the date of the attack to the time of the trial and $43,000 for future damages. Defendant appealed the award for future damages.

On appeal, the court reviewed the evidence and found abundant reason for believing that the employees' callous actions in permitting Boles to remain bound in the dark and in fear for her life for 20 to 25 minutes caused psychic injuries. A psychiatrist so testified. The trial court's judgment was affirmed.

Deficiencies

The major problem here was that the hotel's procedures for dealing with a guest during an emergency in his or her guest room were totally inadequate. Poor lighting in the corridor could easily have been cited as a contributing factor in this case, and it was merely good fortune on the defendant's part that such was not held to be a cause of the attack.

BANKS V. HYATT

It's not enough to be diligent within the confines of your property. The standard set by this case is that establishments have a high degree of responsibility for guest security even on public property *adjacent* to their facilities (*Banks v. Hyatt Corporation*, 1984).

Guest Fatality

Dr. Banks was returning from a dinner engagement to the Hyatt Hotel in New Orleans when he and his companion were accosted by two armed robbers. Dr. Banks was shot dead directly in front of the entrance to the hotel. When he fell, his head was 30 feet from the street curb and his feet were only four feet from the glass doors at the entryway of the hotel.

Banks's widow and children brought suit, charging the hotel with providing inadequate security and failing to warn of the danger of being assaulted at the entrance to the hotel.

The Decision

A jury found negligence on the part of the hotel and awarded plaintiffs $975,000. This was affirmed on appeal.

Deficiencies

The hotel's security procedures were found to be deficient in two ways: (1) the property, located in a high-crime neighborhood, had inadequate security patrols around the circumference of the hotel; and (2) the hotel staff failed to warn guests of the dangers inherent in that neighborhood and, therefore, around the hotel.

Comment

This case has generated controversy because the plaintiff was assaulted not within the ho-tel but, instead, before the hotel's entryway. In its opinion, the court devoted a good deal of discussion to the fact that a proprietor of a business can be held liable for injuries of persons entering or exiting even if they are not actually on the proprietor's property. Such appears to be the court-mandated standard.

ORLANDO EXECUTIVE PARK v. P. D. R.

It's imperative for guests' safety that safeguards and warnings be enacted if prior events have shown that a property is vulnerable to criminal activity (*Orlando Executive Park, Inc. v. P. D. R.*, 1981).

Guest's Complaint

The plaintiff was a registered guest at the Orlando, Florida, Howard Johnson Motor Lodge. Sometime after 9:30 P.M. she left her first-floor room and went to her car to get some papers. Upon returning to her building's interior hallway, she was sexually attacked by an intruder.

Plaintiff alleged that the motel was negligent in the following ways: (1) allowing the building to remain open and available to anyone who entered, despite previous attacks on guests; (2) failing to install television or video monitoring; and (3) failing to warn guests of previous attacks at that property.

The Decision

There was evidence by which the jury found the defendant did not meet reasonable standards for providing security. This was affirmed on appeal.

Deficiencies

This property was deficient in at least these four ways: (1) no regular security force, (2) no security devices (such as television monitors) in hallways or other common areas, (3) no policy for warning guests of previous criminal incidents, and (4) no procedures for excluding unauthorized personnel from the premises.

TACO BELL, INC. v. LANNON

Those who must conduct business in a high-crime area may be subject to standards that don't apply elsewhere (*Taco Bell, Inc. v. Lannon*, 1987).

Guest's Complaint

Lannon entered a Taco Bell restaurant, perceived there was a robbery in progress, and fled. A robber shot at Lannon, injuring him on the ring finger.

There had been ten armed robberies at that restaurant in the past three years, including one only two nights before the robbery involving Lannon. Although the restaurant was located in a high-crime area, no security guards of any kind had been hired by Taco Bell.

Lannon argued that the restaurant had a duty to take adequate security measures to protect him from the foreseeable criminal acts of third persons and that Taco Bell was negligent in failing to take such measures. The defendants argued that the customer, Lannon, was guilty of contributory negligence. In other words, it was his own fault for attempting to flee from the restaurant. The jury awarded plaintiff $40,000. Defendant appealed.

The Decision

The court of appeals affirmed that the restaurant had a duty to take "reasonable measures to prevent or deter reasonably foreseeable acts, and to alleviate known dangerous conditions . . . specifically, the risks associated with armed robberies."

On appeal to the Colorado State Supreme Court, almost the entire discussion involved the question of whether Taco Bell was responsible for providing reasonable measures for the safety of its customers. The court held that there was a duty on the part of the restaurant to protect customers from foreseeable harm and that, under the circumstances, injury by armed robbers was foreseeable. The court of appeals was affirmed, with three of nine judges dissenting.

Deficiencies

Despite the high court's decision, it's difficult to see what steps could have been taken toward preventing the harm that actually occurred. Because the restaurant is located in a high-crime area, hiring armed security personnel may be an acceptable option. It's also possible that television monitors and burglar alarms may help deter armed robberies of this sort.

HARRIS v. PIZZA HUT

Hiring security personnel is not, in and of itself, a surefire way to avoid being held responsible in the event any of your guests experience some harm. In the case of *Harris v. Pizza Hut*, special training and written procedures for its security staff may have helped (*Harris v. Pizza Hut of Louisiana, Inc.*, 1984).

Guest Fatality, Injury

Members of the Harris family were dining at the Port Street Pizza Hut in a high-crime area of New Orleans. At about 9:10 P.M., Maxie Walker, a police officer moonlighting as a security guard at the Pizza Hut, appeared on duty. He obtained some food and sat down to converse with a friend. Walker's view of the door and his presence by those entering through the door were obscured by a partition.

At about 10:00, a masked, armed robber entered the restaurant and went to the cash register. Walker drew his gun but another robber with a sawed-off shotgun got the drop on him. Walker moved to the right and the shotgun was discharged. The gun blast injured one of the Harris children and killed her mother.

The Decision

The court found Walker to be negligent in the following ways (and his negligence is imputed to be his employer's, the defendant): (1) Walker should have been stationed in a highly visible part of the restaurant (the main purpose of a security guard is to act as a deterrent, and the deterrent effect is maximized when the guard is highly visible); (2) the guard should not have been eating and conversing with a friend while on duty (it was noted that the defendant gave no specific instructions to Walker as to how to carry out his duties); and (3) when confronted with a firearm, Walker should have remained motionless rather than moving aside (his movement put at risk the lives of patrons in the restaurant).

Three judges dissented from the majority rule holding Pizza Hut liable. The dissent argued that Walker was being held to such a high standard of care that, in effect, if an establishment hires a security guard at all, the court is saying that the establishment is made the insurer of its guests' safety, rather than being held to the universally accepted standard of providing reasonably safe premises.

Deficiencies

Here there were but two deficiencies, both related to training. One involved the lack of instruction to security personnel as to what their duties were and what was expected of them. The other was inadequate procedures as to how to respond in an emergency.

Comment

This case and *Taco Bell, Inc. v. Lannon* present a difficult dilemma to inns and restaurants in high-crime areas. The Taco Bell case discussed earlier showed that a restaurant may be liable if it doesn't employ a security guard in a high-crime area. Now we see that even if the restaurant does hire a security guard, it may be liable if the guard does not use perfect judgment. The best answer to the dilemma is to be sure that, if you determine you should have guards on duty, the guards are clearly instructed as to what they should do in an emergency. Adequate procedures are often the best legal defense.

PETERS v. HOLIDAY INNS

In this example. a trial court's summary judgment in favor of the defendant was overruled and a new trial ordered. The appeals court held that a jury could find negligence based on the several deficiencies noted by the trial court (*Peters v. Holiday Inns*, 1979).

Guest's Complaint

Four men parked in front of the Holiday Inn West in Wauwatosa, Wisconsin, at 3:00 A.M. One of the men, a former employee of the motel, entered the lobby and asked about an employee who was not on the premises. The ex-employee proceeded to the kitchen where he stole a shirt used by room service personnel. After entering the guest room section of the motel, attired in the shirt he had found in the kitchen, he knocked on Peters's door. When Peters heard the knock, he peered through the peephole, saw a man in a room service uniform, and opened the door. Peters was assaulted and robbed, and forced to accompany his assailant to the waiting car.

Meanwhile, an alert policeman had spotted the car, become suspicious, radioed for backup, and traced the assailant's steps. Peters was rescued from the four men who were in the process of abducting him, and the four were arrested.

At this motel, guest rooms were equipped with a dead-bolt lock, a chain lock, and a one-way viewer (peephole). The hallway was well lit, but there were no security guards employed at this motel, as police patrolled the neighborhood and there had been few violent incidents.

The Decision

The trial court's decision was based on affidavits and additional facts introduced at trial. On appeal the court held that summary judgment should not have been granted, and a new trial was ordered, giving Peters the opportunity to present the various security inadequacies of which the motel was evidently guilty.

Deficiencies

The deficiencies cited by the appeals court included: (1) the building housing the plaintiff's room was not locked; neither was it monitored by closed-circuit television, by motel staff, or by security personnel; (2) this section of the motel was separate from the lobby, and it was not necessary to pass through the lobby to reach this building; and (3) there was no provision for monitoring areas of the motel away from the lobby.

TOP HOTEL COMPANIES RESPOND

To gauge the extent to which hotel companies have paid attention to these court-mandated security standards, we surveyed the top 50 U.S. hotel firms as to what importance is placed on these standards in establishing policies and procedures. These firms were selected based on their total number of rooms, as reported by

Martin (1987). Telephone canvassing yielded the correct names and titles for the chief legal, risk, or loss-prevention executive for each company, and the survey packages were addressed to those company officers. After three mailings, 24 usable surveys were returned (a 48 percent response rate).

While 24 returns may seem modest, it should be noted that the original sample represented (at the time) almost 1.6 million hotel rooms nationwide out of a potential total of 2.7 million. We are confident that the 24 returns we collected represent a good cross section of hotel-company types as well as a broad potential range of opinions and managerial practices. A copy of our survey instrument is available from us upon request.

What We Asked

We presented ten court-mandated security standards (CMSS) and asked the legal and risk officers in our sample to rate each one, individually, on a scale of 1 to 5. A rating of 1 would mean the CMSS was of little or no importance in formulating and establishing legal policies and procedures for their company, and a grade of 5 indicated that that standard played a role of utmost or vital importance in their company's policies and procedures. The mean importance of each, along with standard deviations and rank order, is displayed in Table 5.7.

According to our survey results, the hotel-company officers determined the following rank order of importance (most to least) for the ten standards we presented: staff training, lighting, securing (lock) systems, hiring security personnel, monitoring criminal activity in the area, controlling access to the property, training for armed security personnel, communicating risk to guests, remote electronic monitoring, and employing armed security personnel. When the ten standards presented in our survey are categorized according to the type of deficiency they seek to

TABLE 5.7
Corporate response to court-mandated security standards

Court-Mandated Security Standards	Mean Importance	Standard Deviation	Rank Order
Physical or Property Related			
Regularly inspected locking systems that work and provide more than minimum security.	4.417	0.654	3
Adequate lighting in halls and other areas where guests are expected.	4.542	0.588	2
Remote monitoring by TV or other surveillance systems.	2.958	1.122	9
Limit access to guest areas in order to exclude unauthorized persons	3.833	0.917	6
Personnel Related			
Regularly employed security personnel who also patrol guest areas and other hotel premises.	4.167	1.007	4
Employ armed security guards in operations that have high rates of criminal activity in area.	2.818	1.5	10
Training and instruction for security personnel who are armed.	3.762	1.729	7
Train staff in procedures for reporting and dealing with criminal activity when discovered by hotel personnel.	4.625	0.77	1
Administrative or Procedure Related			
Monitor and be aware of criminal activity in area of operation.	4.083	1.018	5
System for advising guests of dangerous areas and/or criminal activity around the hotel.	3.13	1.254	8

remedy (refer to Table 5.6), four of them can be seen to relate to physical or property functions; four are personnel related; and two involve administrative or procedural policies. When viewed according to these categories, personnel-related issues were highest ranked (training, rated as number one, and patrolling, number four), and property-related issues were ranked second (lighting is number two, and lock systems is number three). Monitor-

ing criminal activity in the area, an administrative function, was ranked fifth.

Of the ten proposed standards presented to our survey sample, the top five were collectively ranked with mean scores in excess of 4.0 (Table 5.7). Those five standards evidently play a vital role in helping hotel companies nationwide establish policies and procedures to avoid areas of legal risk and at the same time safeguard their clientele from the most common mishaps that occur on hotel and restaurant premises.

Bearing Arms

Of the lower-ranked standards, the two having to do with armed security personnel clearly generated the widest diversity of opinion. On the question of employing armed security guards, six respondents ranked this standard as the lowest (1) while the balance of the responses to this question were approximately evenly distributed along the rest of the scale (2 to 5). The standard growing out of *Harris v. Pizza Hut,* which was ranked number seven overall, further exemplifies the split opinion about armed guards: 15 respondents ranked it either a 4 or 5, and seven ranked it either a 1 or 2. The other respondents did not rate this item.

The issue of arming security guards is one that is loaded with potential problems, as can be seen from the dissension by several of the judges in the *Harris* case. Our respondents offered such comments as "never arm security guards" to "only arm security personnel if they are sworn police officers employed off-duty." Typically, employing off-duty police officers was the only circumstance under which an armed guard was considered appropriate. Furthermore, comments regarding training of those off-duty officers mentioned that insurance coverage would most likely be jeopardized if training was *not* made available.

Despite the court's activism in favor of armed guards as reflected in the *Harris* and *Taco Bell* cases, hotel companies as a group are still wary of the concept of employing armed personnel in security capacities. The standard deviation of the mean ranking (1.729) suggests that this is an issue that will take some time to work out. The nature of the hospitality business precludes significant emphasis on the presence of obviously armed personnel, and that factor makes the issue even tougher to resolve.

Training

The five top-rated standards in this study represent areas in which major hotel companies have always maintained at least an above-average level of activity. Staff training (ranked number one), while being among the easiest to accomplish, is not without its problems. The dedication of personnel to ongoing training programs, given the high state of turnover in hotel companies, requires a significant allocation of budget resources in order to achieve a level of vigilance acceptable to the courts.

Minimal training in the proper response to emergency procedures or criminal activities may obviate the vast majority of the problems typified by the *Nordmann* and *Boles* cases. While there are no published industrywide security standards, most hotel companies at least pay some attention to the sorts of training activities needed to instill in their employees the importance of the proper response to certain types of situations.

Lights and Locks

Providing adequate lighting and more than minimally secure door-locking systems can now be considered de facto industry standard, based on general industry knowledge of the potential for legal problems based on cases typified by *Boles, Garzilli,* and *Kveragas.* For example, it would appear that the respondents to our survey recognize the importance of the potential risk embodied in these standards and have implemented policies and procedures to insulate their companies from that risk. (It is surprising, then, given the wide dissemination of defects of care outlined in such cases, and the notoriety of the *Garzilli* case, to note the number of similar cases that continue to be brought based on such precedents.)

The low standard deviations of the mean rankings for staff training, adequate lighting, and locking systems clearly indicate that there is solid agreement among the respondents on the importance of these standards in the formulation of policies and procedures for their companies.

Guards: Visible or Not?

There is less agreement among respondents on the importance of regularly employed security personnel maintaining a visible presence on a property's premises. The ranking of this standard as number four, however, is nonetheless an indication that in the modern era of hospitality management, a security staff has probably also become an industrywide standard in all but the most special circumstances. Survey comments indicate that most hotel companies employ a security staff at least for certain hours of the day (usually late evening and early morning).

Also, special occasions such as dances, banquets, and other large-scale events in the hotel may require a special security presence. Among the examples of court cases we cited above, five referred to a deficiency of security personnel. In this regard, the courts take seriously the efforts of hotel companies on behalf of their guests. In *Nordmann,* the court went out of its way to chide the hotel company for failing to provide extra security during a fancy-dress ball that was widely reported by the local media and that might be expected to attract a criminal element.

THE COURTS' MESSAGE IS "DUE DILIGENCE"

It is encouraging to note that "being able to monitor and be aware of criminal activity in the hotel's area of operation" ranked among the top five standards. The action of the court in deciding the *Banks* case and in remanding *Peters* for retrial sent a clear message that courts expect hotels to understand the physical, social, and criminal environment within which they operate, and established that the hotel's responsibility for the safety of its guests

does not necessarily end at the hotel's property lines.

While the precedent established by the court in deciding the *Banks* case may have been, at first, a shock to the industry, the data from our survey seem to suggest that the court's message regarding due diligence was received loud and clear.

Neighborhood Watch

At the trial level in the *Banks* case, the judge said in his charge to the jury that an innkeeper "is liable for injuries to guests or patrons caused by intentionally harmful acts of third persons, if, by exercise of reasonable diligence, he could have discovered that such acts were being done or were about to be done and could have protected his guests or patrons by controlling the conduct of the [wrongdoer] or by giving adequate warning to enable the guest to avoid him." (Rutherford and McConnell, 1987, p. 60).

On appeal, since there were no disputes over the facts, the U.S. Court of Appeals, Fifth Circuit, reviewed the inferences of law to be drawn by the situation of Banks's murder outside the hotel's immediate presence. The court reviewed the trial judge's charge to the jury and found it adequate.

A New Standard of Care

The logical conclusion from the *Banks* case is that the court has, indeed, made a clear statement that any previously assumed standard of care has been expanded. Now hotels must be aware of criminal activity in their vicinities and be capable of analyzing these threats in order to respond adequately and appropriately to the potential for harm to the hotel's guests.

Candid Camera

The significance of remote monitoring by closed-circuit television or other surveillance systems and limiting access to guest areas appear to our respondents to be somewhat problematic and may account for the relatively low ranks assigned to these items.

Many felt that remote monitoring by television may send the wrong signal to guests, and that guests would be uncomfortable walking in hallways and other public areas where television cameras were panning back and forth.

Limiting access to guest areas is a difficult feat to achieve from a physical standpoint, given architectural peculiarities of most properties. Limiting access, in most cases, falls on the shoulders of hotel employees. This is accomplished either through those who are trained and regularly employed as security personnel, or by relying upon whatever training can be instilled among those employees who have continual access to a wide range of guest areas. In particular, the bell staff, housekeepers, and maintenance employees can be the "eyes and ears" of hotel security management if they are properly trained.

It also appears that in any property other than a high-rise building where the elevator banks are under the direct observation and control of hotel personnel, overseeing the coming and going of guests and nonguests is difficult at best. Short of a system of concierges or coded access locks, limiting access to nonguests generally means limiting access to guests.

To Tell or Not to Tell?

Among the security standards that seemed to make the hotel officers in our study most uncomfortable is the one that proposed a system for advising guests of dangerous areas and criminal activity around the hotel (as suggested in *Banks* and *Orlando Executive Park*). By tradition and training, hotels are extremely leery of actively suggesting to guests that there may be something inherently dangerous about the guest's choice to stay at a particular hotel. On the other hand, it can be argued that few,

if any, travelers who frequent urban hotels are ignorant of the potential for harm or loss.

So far as the courts are concerned, hotels will be serving their clientele if they provide guests with information about personal security. Realistically, such warnings can be carefully worded and couched in terms no more threatening than those used to advise patrons of fire-emergency procedures, the availability of safe-deposit boxes, and the importance of double-locking guest room doors when the room is occupied.

Because most travelers are aware that crime and violence are a reality in today's society, hotels that go out of the way to communicate specific dangers to their guests should not fear any loss of business. Consider that the airline industry has for years been warning travelers about the dangers of flying, without any loss of business. Metal detectors, safety lectures, and emergency procedure cards now are an accepted part of the flying experience. There's no reason to think hoteliers will scare away guests as a result of promoting personal safety.

DE FACTO CONSENSUS

The data developed through our survey indicate that hotels are making a real effort to comply with at least some of the court-mandated security standards presented by this study. Those issues dealing specifically with staff training, lighting, and locking systems appear to have, in fact, become industry standards *because* of the high level of agreement among hotel companies.

Because there is a lack of industry standards published by any hospitality-industry group, hotels can expect to find that such standards will be imposed upon them by courts as deficits of care are found in the courts' analyses of hotel policies (or lack thereof) that allow harm to befall guests. Hotel-industry standards, therefore, may be derived from a de facto consensus that comes from hotels being figuratively "beat over the head" by courts so that the hotel companies internalize court-mandated standards as policies and procedures designed to insulate hotels from further losses.

Clearly, this is the case with present-day standards for staff training, adequate lighting, and providing locking systems. We suggest that the regular employment of security personnel and the regular and accurate accumulation of criminal-activity data in a property's neighborhood are also emerging as industry standards.

A National Trend?

It is less clear how court-mandated standards will work their way into standard policies and procedures for hotels nationally. The use of armed guards, for example, creates a controversy that will probably be resolved only on a case-by-case basis. Given the commentary of respondents, if guards are desired, that will usually be accomplished through the use of off-duty police officers. Peace officers are presumably properly and specially trained, although the facts of *Harris* suggest that this is not always the case.

To protect themselves and their guests from harm and loss, hotel owners, managers, and operators have learned to pay more careful attention to what is being decided *for* them by precedent-setting cases moving through various court systems. With that in mind, we remind you that the ten cases described as part of this study are more typical than not of liability cases affecting the hospitality industry.

Formalizing Risk Management

A recent study involving six individual hotels representing different national chains reported that of those companies, five had designated some formal form of risk management or assessment (Saied, 1990). The roles and policy implementation activities of such functional units varied widely, according to that study, but each included some aspects of the suggestions and conclusions discussed here. The most closely related, recurring theme was that of training.

We feel strongly that attention to what the courts have said relating to security standards is an essential part of both a hotel manager's responsibilities and of a company's risk-management structure.

5.8   The Legal Environment of Lodging Operations

Melissa Dallas

Hotels, like other business entities, are subject to a large and continually changing body of law. However, because lodging facilities are complicated systems, the laws affecting them are more numerous and complex than those affecting most other types of businesses. Since not complying with laws can result in fines, lawsuits, and even imprisonment, it is important that managers be familiar with the many legal dangers to which hotels are subject. This

does not mean that they have to be lawyers, but managers should have enough legal knowledge to be aware of how to develop strategies to minimize the property's exposure to potential litigation and to train employees to minimize risks in their departments.

This chapter is a brief introduction to the legal environment in which hotels operate. We begin with a discussion of where our laws come from and how they are classified. This should give you a fundamental understanding of the legal content. Then we will take a look at the laws and regulations that are specific to typical hotel departments. You will notice that there are a significant number of detailed references and footnotes. These are included to provide further detail for specific discussion points and to provide a source for further reference.

HOW LAW WORKS

The following section will briefly introduce you to the law—where it comes from and how it is classified. This will help you when we turn our attention to the specifics of the law and how it applies to the lodging industry.

Sources of Law

Law comes from four different sources: (1) judge-made common law (also called *case law* and *stare decisis*); (2) the U.S. Constitution; (3) legislative statutes and ordinances; and (4) administrative agencies. Each of these will be discussed below.

Common law originated in England and although decisions issued by courts in the United States have added considerably to this body of law, some decisions made several hundreds of years ago still influence present-day judicial decisions. The primary purpose of common law is to provide stability and predictability as judges rule on cases. Judges use past decisions as a precedent for deciding current cases. This decision becomes binding for lower courts in that jurisdiction and can even be used as "persuasive authority" for courts in other jurisdictions faced with cases having a similar pattern of facts.

Constitutional law, of course, is derived from the U.S. Constitution, which protects individuals from government excesses. When the Supreme Court, made up of nine justices, grants a writ of certiorari, it agrees to hear the case and will then render a decision, which becomes

the "law of the land." On the other hand, if the Court refuses to issue a writ, the law stands as decided by a lower court.

Statutory law is made by local, state, or federal legislatures or other governing bodies. Federal and state laws are called statutes, and local laws are called ordinances. Legislatures can choose to modify or change common law by enacting statutes that codify, or spell out, a new law.

Finally, administrative law consists of regulations passed by agencies such as the Food and Drug Administration and the Occupational Safety and Health Administration. Congress approves the agencies, then authorizes them to make regulations that affect businesses as well as individuals.

Classifications of Law

Laws generally fall into one of three major classifications—civil, criminal, or international. Most complaints filed against hotels are civil suits in which an individual has been wronged by another individual or by a corporation (which, incidentally, is a "legal" individual). The injured party—the plaintiff—files a lawsuit that describes the facts of the situation and asks for damages. These damages may be compensatory or punitive or both. Compensatory damages are meant to restore people back to their original conditions and include monetary judgments for actual damages such as back and future wages, medical costs, pain and suffering, and breach of contract. Punitive damages, on the other hand, are awarded to punish the wrongdoer. Since punitive damages in civil suits are awarded only in the case of violence, malice, or fraud, they are relatively uncommon.

Most civil cases filed against hotels involve claims of negligence. In order for plaintiffs to be successful, they must prove four elements. First, they must prove that the hotel had a duty to them. Next, they must prove that the hotel breached that duty. Third, they must show that the breach was the reason for the incident occurring in the first place and that the hotel should have been able to foresee injuries. Finally, they must have been injured in some way so they can collect damages. The theory of negligence requires a hotel to act reasonably to prevent foreseeable injuries to guests and visitors. To illustrate this theory, assume that a front office employee did not require identification when issuing duplicate keys. A person was issued a room key by this employee, then used the key to enter a guest room and injured a guest. Here, the hotel would likely be found negligent because by not practicing proper key control, it breached its duty to keep guests safe. The intrusion and resulting injury would not have happened "but for" the employee issuing a duplicate key without requesting identification, and this omission resulted in injuries to the guest.

In order for someone to be criminally prosecuted, on the other hand, they must commit a wrong against society as a whole. Crimes require intent on the part of the defendant, and, if found guilty, the defendant may be charged a fine, imprisoned, or both. Crimes most often affecting hotel operations include theft, assault, and battery. Theft, of course, can relate to goods, services, or both. Assault is defined as the "imminent threat of bodily harm," and battery is the actual harmful physical contact. An example of an assault would be if a bouncer in a nightclub wrongfully threatened a patron and ran toward the patron with his arms raised. If the bouncer picked up the patron and wrongfully threw him down the steps and out the door of the club, battery has occurred.

Although the hotel industry is becoming increasingly global, international law that is actually enforceable against an individual or a hotel company is rare. Most international law is in the form of treaties, while others are customary laws followed by nations over time. The primary international laws that are applied to hotel companies are treaties that govern intellectual property such as trademarks and copyrights.

The Paris Convention of 1883 affords its signatories (meaning citizens of the countries that have signed the treaty) the right to file for trademark protection in any country that also signed the treaty. Suppose, for example, a hotel chain named Paradise Lodges opened in the United States. Under the Paris Convention, the owners of Paradise Lodges could file for trademark protection in other countries, thereby globally protecting the identity of Paradise Lodges.

The Berne Convention of 1886 gives its signatories the right to file for copyright protection of any original literary or artistic material. Here, suppose a hotel wanted to prevent other hotel chains from using its unique jingle or song that is integral to its marketing efforts. Under the Berne Convention, the hotel could safeguard its song and prevent others from using it in their advertising campaigns.

LAW AND THE LODGING INDUSTRY

Now that you have a basic understanding of how law works, we will get more hotel-specific. The only way to protect a hotel company from lawsuits is to practice preventive law. This requires management to know the common legal dangers for each department and to follow the law as closely as possible.

However, we must first review one other concept. *Respondeat superior* is a Latin term that literally means *let the master answer*. Under the theory of *respondeat superior*, employers are liable for acts of their employees if the employees are at fault and were doing work for the employer at the time of the accident or incident. The financial implication of *respondeat superior* for a hotel is obvious – the hotel pays!

Food and Beverage

Potential costly legal situations are present in all restaurants and bars. The most commonly litigated areas involve food safety and alcohol service.

Food Safety

Many laws governing food safety are administrative laws that are established by the Food and Drug Administration (FDA).[1] The FDA regulates everything from food processing[2] and labeling[3] to packaging.[4] Food and beverage sales are controlled by the Uniform Commercial Code (UCC), which lays out rules governing the sale of goods and, specifically, requires all food and beverages to be *merchantable*, or fit for human consumption.[5] This warranty is applies whenever and wherever food or beverages are sold.[6]

In order be protected from lawsuits, the food preparation area should be inspected regularly to ensure that no hazards exist. For example, employees should make certain that no light bulbs or food shields are broken since glass could easily get into the food. If a server breaks a glass in an ice bin, the bin must be emptied and carefully cleaned out before it is refilled with fresh ice.

Additionally, food must be properly handled to ensure its safety. E. coli, bacteria often present in undercooked hamburger, can be dangerous or even deadly.[7] This threat has prompted some restaurants to cook all their hamburgers to 160 degrees to kill the bacteria.

Salmonella, bacteria that can result in severe diarrhea, fever, and abdominal cramping, is most often found in undercooked eggs, beef, and poultry, but can also be found in milk and vegetables. Cooking meats until all juices run clear and training employees to practice good hand-washing techniques is imperative. Eggs pose a more difficult dilemma, however. In order to be perfectly safe, a restaurant would warn patrons about the possibility of salmonella before serving poached, over-easy, or over-medium eggs, hollandaise sauce, Caesar salad dressing, mayonnaise, and tiramisu. The practicality of this practice is doubtful, but perhaps a general warning on the menu would suffice.

Food and beverages need to be served at safe temperatures, as well. In an often discussed case involving McDonald's,[8] a seventy-nine-year-old woman, Stella Liebeck, was seriously burned when coffee spilled on her lap. After her grandson gave her the coffee he purchased from the drive-through window, he stopped so Liebeck could add cream and sugar to her drink. The entire contents of the styrofoam cup spilled on her lap, and she received third-degree burns on over 6 percent of her body. The temperature of the coffee was initially believed to have been between 180 and 190 degrees Fahrenheit. A McDonald's quality assurance manager testified that this was the standard serving temperature range for the company's coffee. For the sake of comparison, the temperature of most home-brewed

---

[1]Pure Food and Drug Act of 1906, 21 U.S.C. Sections 1–5, 7–15 as amended by the Federal Food, Drug, and Cosmetic Act of 1938, 21 U.S.C. Section 301.

[2]See Food Safety and Inspection Service, Department of Agriculture, 9 C.F.R. Chapter III establishing HACCP and other controls.

[3]Nutrition Labeling and Education Act of 1990, 21 U.S.C. Section 343.

[4]Fair Packaging and Labeling Act of 1966, 21 U.S.C. Sections 1451–1461.

[5]U.C.C. 2–314.

[6]See, for example, *Webster v. Blue Ship Tea Room*, 198 N.E.2d 309 (1964) in which the court held that the fish chowder was merchantable since bones were a natural part of fish and should be reasonably expected. See also *Evart v. Suli*, 211 Cal.App.3d 605, Cal.Rptr. 535 (1989) in which the court held that a jury could find that hamburger containing a large bone might not be merchantable. Finally, see *Kilpatrick v. Superior Court*, 8 Cal.App.4th. 1717, 11 Cal.Rtpr.2d 323 (1992) in which the court decided that bacteria in oysters were "foreign" to oysters and, thus, made the food unmerchantable.

---

[7]In 1993, more than 600 people in Washington got sick from eating Jack in the Box hamburgers contaminated with E. coli bacteria. Foodmaker, the parent company of Jack in the Box, set aside $100 million to cover lawsuit settlements. The largest single-case settlement was $15.6 million to the family of Brianne Kiner who lapsed into a coma for 42 days after eating a tainted burger. *The Seattle Times*, October 30, 1997.

coffee usually reaches between 135 to 140 degrees.

The jury initially awarded Liebeck $200,000 in compensatory damages, which was reduced to $160,000 since Liebeck was found to be 20 percent at fault, and $2.7 million in punitive damages. An investigation following this verdict revealed that the actual serving temperature of the coffee was 158 degrees Fahrenheit, so the court reduced the punitive award to $480,000 or three times compensatory damages. McDonald's and Liebeck then agreed to an undisclosed settlement to close the case.[9]

The point here is that hotels need to serve safe food and beverages, and serve food and beverages safely. At the very least, customers should be advised of any known risks so they can decide for themselves whether to eat the food or drink the beverage. Food and beverage does not need to taste good under the UCC, but it must be safe![10]

Alcohol Service

Establishments that serve alcohol are opening themselves up to a different type of legal danger. Dram shop laws are state statutes that permit an injured third party to sue the establishment that unlawfully served the alcohol. For example, let's say that a bartender at the XYZ Hotel overserved a patron. The patron then got into his car to drive home. On the way home, the intoxicated patron lost control of his car and severely injured a bicyclist. Dram shop laws would permit the injured cyclist to sue the XYZ Hotel for damages. Some of the states that have not enacted dram shop laws also permit third-party suits under their common law theories of negligence.

Increased attention to responsible alcohol service has caused an increasing number of states to require their managers, servers, and bartenders to be trained in responsible alcohol service.[11] Although training will not completely protect an establishment from alcohol-related suits, it could lower punitive damages.

Housekeeping and Maintenance

Inspection and Repair

The primary legal dangers in both housekeeping and maintenance are negligence related and involve lack of inspection and repair. Broken furniture, loose carpeting, slippery floor surfaces, potholes in parking lots, unmarked changes in elevation, snow- and ice-covered walkways, and faulty electrical cords can easily injure guests and visitors alike. In fact, injuries sustained from slips and falls are the most common type of lawsuit hotels encounter! Failure to regularly inspect rooms and public spaces for dangers could be grounds for a successful suit. Recovery for a plaintiff would be even more likely if the hotel knew about a danger and did not address it.

Probably the most tragic maintenance-related cases involve injuries or even death to children. The *attractive-nuisance doctrine* holds a property owner liable for any injuries resulting from "a potentially harmful object so inviting or interesting to a child that it would lure the child onto the property to in-

[8]*Liebeck v. McDonald's Restaurants, P.T.S., Inc.*, No. CV-93–02419, 1995 WL 360309 (N.M. Dist., 1994).

[9]Miller, Norman & Associates, Ltd. *Electronic Newsletter*, 1(1), April 3, 1996. Can be found at: http://rrnet.com/mna/newsltr1.html.

[10]The Educational Foundation of the National Restaurant Association offers both ServSafe and HACCP certification.

[11]The Educational Institute of the American Hotel and Motel Association offers Controlling Alcohol Risks Effectively (CARE) certification. The Educational Foundation of the National Restaurant Association offers Bar Code certification. Also widely used is Training for Intervention Procedures (TIPS) certification. For the current laws of individual states, go to: http://www.gettips.com/.

vestigate."[12] It recognizes that children, because of their age, cannot fully appreciate danger.

Lodging facilities with more than one level and those that have swimming pools must be extra diligent. Children should not be able to open windows more than a few inches, and all balconies must have railings that are close together to prevent accidental falls. Swimming pools must be maintained properly and should be able to be accessed only with a room key. Signage around the pool area should be large and clearly written and require adults to accompany children at all times. Children should be entirely banned from Jacuzzis and saunas.

The best way to prevent suits in these areas is to be attentive. Both housekeepers and maintenance workers should be required to follow a regular preventive maintenance schedule. Professionals can also be hired to complete periodic safety audits of hotels.

Lost and Stolen Guest Property

The housekeeping staff in hotels collects an amazing array of items left behind in guest rooms. Potential privacy problems arise if a hotel contacts guests to notify them of articles they left behind. The better way to handle this is to transfer the items to a secured area, then hold them until the guest contacts the hotel. Many states have laws that govern the finding of lost property. Generally, if the owner cannot be found in a certain period of time, the property may be sold in accordance with the state statute.

Stolen items pose an entirely different set of challenges. All hotels are required to provide safes for guest use. Many hotels now have in-room safes that must be programmed by the guest and are reset when the guest checks out. If guests choose not to use the safe and find some valuables missing from their room, the hotel is generally not liable.[13]

All states have enacted *limiting liability statues* that limit a hotel's liability for guests' property losses. These statutes vary from state to state, but in all cases, a hotel must strictly comply with the requirements to be protected.[14] Common requirements include posting the availability of the safe, as well as stating the maximum amount that the hotel is liable for in case of theft.

Front Office

Reservations and Overbooking

Every time someone phones a hotel for a reservation, they are forming a contract with the hotel for a room. What if the hotel overbooked or if a guest stayed over and a room was not available for a guest with a reservation? Technically, the hotel breached the contract. To avoid liability, front desk agents should check area hotels for availability if they know that overbooking is likely. In the case of a civil suit for breach of contract, the would-be guest could recover compensatory damages including payment for travel to a different hotel, the additional cost of lodging if any, and other costs associated with the inconvenience.[15]

---

[13]See, for example, *Gooden v. Day's Inn*, 395 S.E.2d 876 (Ga. App. 1990) in which an innkeeper was not liable for the theft of a bag of money from a guest's room. The court recognized that the hotel provided a safe for guests' valuables and the guest assumed the risk of theft by failing lock up the money.

[14]See, for example, *Searcy v. La Quinta Motor Inns, Inc.*, 676 So. 2d 1137 (La. App. 1996) in which the motel was liable for $4,938.95 for property stolen from a guest's room, despite a state statute limiting the motel's liability to $500. Although the motel posted notices of the statute in guest rooms, it failed to do so in the registration area as the statute required.

[15]See *Vern Wells et al. v. Holiday Inns*, 522 F.Supp. 1023 (Mo., 1981) in which Vernon Wells and Robert Hughes had reservations with a Holiday Inn in San Francisco. The hotel could not honor the reservations since it was overbooked. The plaintiffs paid less to stay at another hotel, but were awarded reimbursement for their cab fares to the other hotel.

---

[12]From 'Lectric Law Library at: http://www.lectlaw.com/def/a090.htm.

Due to the potential legal liability and the damage to their reputation and goodwill, some large hotel chains have completely eliminated the practice of intentional overbooking. Others continue to take that risk to ensure that their hotel is completely full.

Key Control

Poor key control practices are dangerous, potentially expensive, and mostly preventable. Too often, hotel guests have been injured or even killed when a stranger entered their room using a key given to him by a front office staff member. Jury awards have been staggering, especially if the guest was raped or killed due to employee negligence and if the hotel had been "put on warning" by a similar event that occurred in the past.

Good key control practices include:

- Requiring identification when issuing a replacement or additional key.
- Installing a key card system.
- Changing locks when a room key is missing (assuming the hotel does not have a key card system in place).
- Limiting the number of master keys that are issued to employees.
- Installing elevators that require a key to activate.
- Not having room numbers displayed anywhere on the key.
- Writing, not announcing, the assigned room number when a guest checks in.
- Not verbally confirming a name and room number by telephone within earshot of a nonemployee.
- Refusing to give out room information— period. The front desk agent should always phone guests to verify visitors or inquiries.
- Placing key drop boxes behind the counter on the front desk, not on top of the counter.
- Regularly inspecting room locks for damage and wear.

Although a hotel is not a complete insurer of guest safety, it must show diligence in its duty to provide a safe environment. Employee negligence is often the cause of some very violent crimes against guests, but proper training and reinforcement of acceptable key control practices can drastically reduce, if not eliminate, this type of lawsuit.

Sales

Writing sales contracts is a regular part of any salesperson's job. Contracts are written for catered events, wedding receptions, conventions, meetings, and many other purposes. In the case that one party does not honor the contract, the other party can sue for breach, so it is essential that all sales staff receive careful and thorough training.

Everything agreed upon between the hotel and the client should be written in the contract. This practice ensures that the contract will be enforceable in court and leaves no doubt as to the agreement. All the contract terms must be clear and unambiguous. It is important to note that contracts are always interpreted against the drafter, so in the case of a breach, the contract would be interpreted in favor of the client rather than the hotel.

A good rule of thumb for sales staffs to follow is the more complex the event, the more detailed the contract. No detail is too small to put in writing!

Human Resources

Wrongful discharge, discrimination, and Federal Labor Standards Act (FLSA) claims are becoming more and more commonplace. The human resource staff handles the resolution of these types of claims and many more.

Wrongful Discharge

Even in a state that follows an *employment at will* doctrine, which permits an employer to terminate an employee at any time, without cause or reason, wrongful discharge suits are relatively common. Wrongful discharge claims arise when an employee is fired for reasons that are not legitimate. These wrongful discharge cases are one of two types: traditional or constructive.

Traditional wrongful discharge claims would arise when an employee is unlawfully fired. An example of this would be firing an employee for filing a workers' compensation claim, assuming that the state had a statute making this discharge unlawful. Another example would be firing an employee for whistle-blowing (reporting a company's illegal activities to an official).[16]

Constructive discharge occurs when an employer's actions, such as continual or severe harassment, force an employee to quit. If the hotel company is found liable, the plaintiff can receive both compensatory and punitive damages.

The wisest strategy for hotels to follow is to develop a formal policy manual that details the possible reasons for discharge and disciplinary procedures. Employees should be thoroughly advised of these policies, and all supervisors and managers need to follow the policies as closely and systematically as possible. Finally, management should document, document, and document some more!

Discrimination

Discrimination in the workplace has not always been unlawful. In fact, it was not until 1964 that a federal statute was enacted that addressed discrimination. Since that time, other important federal statutes have been passed dealing with pregnancy, age, and disabilities. Sexual harassment suits have become commonplace recently, and they are, in effect, based on gender discrimination.

Title VII of the Civil Rights Act of 1964[17] made it illegal to discriminate against applicants or employees based on race, religion, color, national origin, and gender. It applies to employers with 20 or more employees, and created the Equal Employment Opportunity Commission as its enforcement arm.[18]

Only in the case of "business necessity" or "bona fide occupational qualification" (BFOQ) can a hotel legally discriminate.[19] Note that the courts interpret these exceptions quite strictly, often resulting in rulings for the plaintiffs.

The Pregnancy Discrimination Act of 1978[20] made it illegal to discriminate against pregnant women unless the discrimination is a "business necessity" or not being pregnant is a BFOQ for the job. For example, a hotel could probably refuse to hire a woman who is seven-months pregnant as a lifeguard since the pregnancy could affect her ability to save lives quickly.

The Age Discrimination Act of 1967 was amended in 1986[21] to make it illegal to discriminate against an applicant or an employee who is 40 years old or older. Although portraying a youthful and energetic image is important to many hotels, it is simply illegal to discriminate against an employee who is at least 40 year olds as long as that employee can perform the job as well as a younger employee.

The Americans with Disabilities Act of 1990[22] (the ADA) forbids discrimination against otherwise qualified individuals on the basis of a physical or mental disability. Title I of the ADA bans discrimination in employ-

---

[16]A number of states have enacted whistle-blowing statutes for both the public and private employment sectors: California, Connecticut, Florida, Hawaii, Illinois, Iowa, Louisiana, Maine, Michigan, Minnesota, New Hampshire, New Jersey, New York, North Carolina, North Dakota, Ohio, Rhode Island, and Tennessee.

[17]Title VII of the Civil Rights Act of 1964, as amended, 42 U.S.C.A. Sections 2000e–2000e-17.

[18]Title VII of the Civil Rights Act of 1964, as amended, 42 U.S.C.A. Sections 2000e et seq., Section 705.

[19]See *Wilson v. Southwest Airlines Company*, 517 F. Supp. 292 (N.D. Tex. Dallas Div. 1981) in which the court held that being female was not a BFOQ for flight attendants.

[20]42 U.S.C. 2000e(k).

[21]29 U.S.C. Sections 621–634.E

[22]42 U.S.C. Sections 12102–12118.

ment and applies to applicants or employees who are "otherwise qualified" for the positions. This means that the applicant or employee must be able to perform the essential elements of the job regardless of the disability. Title III bans discrimination in public accommodations (lodging facilities, for one) and commercial facilities. The ADA requires all accommodations to be "reasonable"[23] and to create "no undue burden"[24] for the business. The courts, on a case-by-case basis, determine what constitutes an undue burden.

Finally, the Civil Rights Act of 1991[25] gave plaintiffs claiming discrimination the right to a jury trial as well as possible punitive damages. The possibility of larger awards for plaintiffs has caused more employers to adopt stricter and clearer policies for selection, promotion, layoffs, and termination.

By now, most are familiar with the plethora of sexual harassment claims that have been filed in courts. The nature of the hotel industry leaves it vulnerable to more claims than in most industries—the late and long hours of work, the privacy of hotel rooms, and the alcohol service.

Courts recognize two types of sexual harassment. The first, *quid pro quo*, literally means *this for that*. Quid pro quo[26] claims occur when one person threatens action against another unless he or she agrees to perform a sexual act. *Hostile work environment*[27] claims are much more common. Here, the behavior must be sufficiently severe or pervasive, unwelcome, and not voluntary, and must affect a term, condition, or privilege of employment. Certain workplace behaviors found to create a hostile work environment are repeatedly sending sexually suggestive letters and notes,[28] sending risqué e-mails,[29] and prominently displaying nude pictures (when combined with other lewd behaviors).[30]

The best tactic for management to employ is to adopt a no-tolerance policy. This policy should be included in the handbook and posted conspicuously throughout the hotel. Also, employees need to feel free to speak with more than one person in the event of a sexual harassment complaint, since their supervisor might be the person who is doing the harassing.

It is important to note that states and localities can adopt even stricter laws than the federal statutes. For example, some areas prohibit discrimination based on sexual orientation.[31] Others disallow discrimination based on marital status.

---

[23]42 U.S.C. Section 12111(8). See, for example, *Martin v. PGA Tour, Inc.*, No. 9835309 (9th Cir. 2000) in which the court held that it was reasonable to permit professional golfer Casey Martin, who has a congenital disability, to drive a cart during golf competitions since doing so would not alter the nature of the sport.

[24]42 U.S.C. Section 12112(b)5(A). See, for example, *Rascon v. U.S. West* in which a U.S. West network technician suffered from posttraumatic stress disorder as a result of his service in Vietnam. The court required U.S. West to grant Rascon's leave for treatment since doing so would be a reasonable accommodation and would place no undue burden on U.S. West.

[25]42 U.S.C.A. Sections 2000e et seq. Section 105(b).

[26]The first case decided under the quid pro quo theory was *Barnes v. Costle* (D.C. Cir. 1977).

[27]The first sexual harassment case to reach the Supreme Court was *Meritor Savings Bank v. Vinson*, 477 U.S. 57 (1986) in which the Court defined a hostile workplace environment.

[28]*Ellison v. Brady*, 924 F.2d 872 (9th. Cir. 1991).

[29]See, e.g., *M. V. v. Gulf Ridge Council Boy Scouts of America, Inc.*, 1988 WL 85195 (Fla. D. Ct. App. 1988), which holds that an employer can be liable if the employer knew or should have known that a supervisor was harassing an employee and failed to take any action or even investigate the claim. More recently, in *Faragher v. City of Boca Raton*, 524 U.S. 775 (1998), a court tightened the standard and held that employers would be liable only if they knew that the harassing activities were occurring. The "should have known" was eliminated. Therefore, if employers know of harassing e-mails or jokes being sent to employees, they would likely still be held liable.

[30]*Andrews v. City of Philadelphia*, 895 F.2d 1469 (3d Cir. 1990).

[31]Currently, at least 14 states have executive orders, at least 71 cities or counties have civil rights ordinances, and at least 41 cities or counties have council or mayoral proclamations banning sexual orientation discrimination in public employment.

Federal Labor Standards Act

The Federal Labor Standards Act[32] (FLSA) mandates minimum wages, overtime pay, and equal pay for equal work, and restricts child labor.

The rate of minimum pay is established by Congress and applies to all virtually all employers with annual sales of $500,000 of more.[33] The FLSA, however, includes certain exceptions such as *training wages*[34] and *tip credits*.[35] Training wages at 85 percent of the minimum wage may be paid for the first 90 days to employees who are between the ages of 16 and 19 and entering the workforce for the first time. Tip credits permit employers to pay regularly tipped employees, such as servers, at a rate of pay equal to one-half of the current minimum wage. However, the combination of tips and actual wages must equal at least the current minimum wage rate. For example, if the minimum wage is $6 and a server receives tips averaging $3 per hour, the hotel would pay the employee at a rate of $3 per hour. If a server made only $2 per hour in tips, the hotel would be required to pay the server at a rate of $4 per hour to raise the hourly wages to the minimum $6 required by law. Some states or localities require a minimum wage rate higher than the federal mandate.

Overtime wages must be paid to *nonexempt* employees, meaning those who must be paid at least minimum wage, who work over 40 hours in one week. These wages are mandated at a rate equal to 1.5 times the regular hourly wage rate.[36] On the other hand, overtime rates need not be paid to *exempt* employees. The FLSA defines exempt employees as those who spend 40 percent or more of their time performing management functions or work for a seasonal amusement or recreational establishment.[37]

It is important to understand that the FLSA uses a weekly pay period to determine overtime. This is especially important to hotels who pay employees on a biweekly basis. For example, if an employee works 30 hours during the first week of the pay cycle, and 50 hours during the second, the hotel must pay 10 hours of overtime for the extra hours worked during the second week of the cycle, even though the total hours worked during the pay period equaled 80.

The equal pay for equal work requirement of the FLSA requires that employers pay employees at the same rate if they perform substantially similar work that requires equal skill, effort, and responsibility.[38] Human resources must identify the *core* or *essential elements* of each position since the courts look at these elements when comparing jobs.

Child labor laws affect many hotels since many of the employees are younger, especially during the summer season. The FLSA requires all employees to be at least 14 years old. Further, the act restricts the number of hours that teenagers under the age of 18 can work during a one-week period. During school days, 14- and 15-year-olds cannot work more than 18 hours per week and no more than three hours per day.[39] Some states have laws even stricter than the federal ones, further restricting work hours for teenagers.

Violations of the FLSA are reported to the U.S. or state Department of Labor and can be costly for hotels. If the violations were found to be intentional, employers may be fined up to $10,000 per offense. A second offense may result in imprisonment for up to six months.[40] Many states have even stricter penalties for noncompliance.

---

[32]Fair Labor Standards Act of 1938, as amended, 29 U.S.C. 201, et seq.

[33]29 U.S.C. 201, Section 3(s)(1)(A)(ii). 29 U.S.C. 201, Section 6(a)(1) sets the minimum wage.

[34]29 U.S.C. 201, Section 6(d)(2)(g) and Section 14(b)(1)(A).

[35]29 U.S.C. 201, Section 3(m)(1) and (2) and Section 3(t).

[36]29 U.S.C. 201, Section 7(a)(1) and Section 7(e).

[37]29 U.S.C. 201, Section 13(1) and (3).

[38]29 U.S.C. 201, Section 6(d)(1) and 29 U.S.C.A. Section 206(d).

[39]29 U.S.C. 201, Section 3(l).

[40]29 U.S.C. 201, Section 16(a).

Security

While larger hotels often hire their own security personnel, smaller properties usually either outsource this function or rely on local law enforcement officials in the case of a problem. Regardless, every employee is responsible for the security of the hotel's guests. Most jurisdictions require that lodging facilities exercise reasonable care to protect guests and patrons from reasonably foreseeable crime risks.

When deciding what preventive actions are reasonable, courts look at certain factors to determine if the hotel was "put on notice." Courts consider factors such as the frequency and severity of past crimes, a recent increase in the area crime rate, and security problems posed by the facility's design. Courts also look at training and personnel activities and design modifications the hotel has undertaken in an effort to keep its guests safe.

The most common areas in which crimes are committed against guests are in guest rooms and immediately outside of the property. While proper key control is imperative to guest room safety, so is the regular inspection of hotel room doors and locks. In a highly publicized case, singer Connie Francis was raped at gunpoint by a man who entered her room through a sliding glass door that could easily be unlocked from the outside. Francis recovered $2.5 million.[41]

Crimes can also occur in hotel parking lots. Low lighting levels support an ideal environment for crimes. If the hotel had been put on warning of criminal activity, meaning that it was aware of previous crimes that occurred on the property or in the immediate neighborhood, it should take further security precautions. These precautions might include hiring additional personnel, installing more lights, constructing a fence around the parking lot and adding a guarded gate, or adding more security monitors.

Again, all hotel employees are responsible for keeping the property as safe as possible. Employees need to report any suspicious activity or person to management. Guests, too, can do their part. Placards should be conspicuously placed in guest rooms that warn guests to keep their doors locked, not divulge their room numbers, and report any concerns to the front desk.

CONCLUSION

Many laws at the federal, state, and local levels affect hotel operations. It is the responsibility of management to be well informed of these laws and to take preventive measures to protect its employees, guests, and owners. Since laws often change and, in the case of a jury trial, damage awards can be quite high, it is important for management to keep abreast of the constantly evolving interpretation and application of all applicable laws. The best ways to keep current are to become active in professional associations, read trade journals on a regular basis, and utilize the resources of legal counsel.

---

[41]*Garzilli v. Howard Johnson Motor Lodges, Inc.* 419 F. Supp. 1210 (N.Y. 1976).

5.9   Asphalt Jungle

Je'anna Abbott and Gil Fried

Because criminal activity can occur near major public facilities, developing risk-management solutions for parking facilities is now a focus of concern. Due to courts' findings of landowner liability for third-party criminal acts, eliminating or at least reducing the risk of any criminal activities must be an important component of any property's risk-management plan. Ensuring public safety within the facility itself is, of course, essential. Parking lots and adjacent areas, however, are equally important and should not be overlooked. This article discusses the landowner's potential liability for the criminal acts of third parties and describes some crime-abatement actions that can be accomplished through facility design. Of course, landowners should seek their own counsel for specific remedies that might fit their particular circumstances. For the purposes of this article, the term *landowner* will include owners, managers, tenants, and lessors.

PARKING FACILITIES AND CRIME

Little in-depth analysis is available concerning criminal acts occurring in parking garages or parking lots. Crime statistics, however, clearly indicate that parking facilities are the location of much criminal behavior. A Crime Control Institute study in Minneapolis showed that many of police departments' chronic-call locations were businesses with parking lots (Berlonghi, A. 1990, p. 259). In 1993 over 6 million simple assaults were reported throughout the United States, and a large percentage of those incidents occurred in parking facilities (Maguire and Pastore, 1995, p.249). In 1994 parking lots and garages represented the second most frequent location for attempts to take property without injury and the most frequent location for motor-vehicle thefts (Maguire and Pastore, 1996, p. 230). Furthermore, the same report showed 8 percent of all violent crimes, 7 percent of all rapes and sexual assaults, and 7 percent of total assaults in 1994 occurred in parking lots or garages.

Despite the risks, however, parking lots and garages clearly are critical to the success of major public facilities. In terms of sports events, only 5 percent of fans attending games use public transportation, while a similar number arrive on leased buses (Baim, 1994, p. 200). Considering the large number of professional-sports venues (both indoor and out) as well as managed college stadiums and arenas, and adding to those the number of hotels, convention centers, and similar public-access facilities, one can easily imagine that there are several million parking spaces in use by major facilities in the United States.

Security Risk

Parking facilities generally cover large areas and are open to the public. While there is plenty of activity inside a shopping mall, office building, stadium, or convention center, there is relatively little or, at times, no activity at all in the parking lot. Additionally, to make the best use of space, cars are parked fairly close together resulting in tight, shadowy spaces between parked cars that generally are excellent hiding places for criminals. Moreover, due to the cost and availability of land, many venues rely on multilevel parking garages. Parking garages typically have poor sight lines and numerous dark corners and stairwells, making them a potential harbor for criminal activity. Patrons walking through a parking lot or a parking garage may be inattentive to such hiding places or to other individuals in the lot.

As we've just described, then, parking facilities present a significant opportunity for criminal activity. Hospitality-industry professionals, however, often rank parking lots and related facilities near the bottom of their list of risk-management concerns. For example, a 1991 survey of approximately 600 sports- and special-event professionals evaluated a variety of risk concerns (Berlonghi, 1996, 13). Few of those surveyed felt that parking lot security was a concern. Indeed, only one in ten felt that "no parking lot security" was a problem at all (when offered that choice among a list of security issues). In other words, parking lot security was rated lower by these events professionals than were other risk concerns such as weather conditions, insufficient budgets, one-of-a-kind or first-time events, and slippery surfaces. We wonder, however, whether those survey results indicate that parking-lot-related crimes are simply underreported. Outside security firms or police often handle those crimes and may not report specific events to facility managers. It's also possible that landowners misunderstand and underestimate the magnitude of potential problems, perceiving crimes perpetrated in parking areas to be low risk. On the other hand, when specifically asked about just parking lots, "lack of security" represented the highest-rated concern by those same survey respondents.

CIVIL LIABILITY

Victims of criminal misconduct are increasingly seeking compensation from the owner or manager of the property on which the criminal activity occurred (Gordon and Brill, 1996, pp. 1–6). Such claims fall under the rules of premises liability and, typically, Gordon and Brill point out, allege a problem with the property's security system. Premise liability is founded on negligence principles. In a negligence claim, a plaintiff must prove (1) the defendant owed the plaintiff a particular standard of care, (2) the defendant deviated from that standard, and (3) the deviation caused the plaintiff's injury.

In the case of a person's injury or loss while using a parking facility, the critical question is whether the landowner had a duty to protect that individual while she was using the parking facility. A landowner normally does not have a duty to protect individuals from the criminal acts of third parties unless the acts are foreseeable. Yet if crimes on the property are likely, then a landowner has some duty to warn customers, guests, and others who may seek access to the property. A landowner incurs varying degrees of duty toward three types of people: "business invitees," licensees, and trespassers. The scope of this article is limited to the first category of individuals.

The duty owed to someone who is on the premises for a business purpose or who is providing some benefit to the landowner (i.e., a business invitee) is a high duty. The court requires a landowner to protect this person from any hidden dangers the landowner knew about or should have known about. With respect to parking facilities, the fact that such areas may be remote does not alleviate a landowner's duty to warn a business invitee of all possible risks and, of course, to keep the facility well maintained and in good repair (see Ammon, 1993, and Maloy, 1993).

Burden of Proof

Premises liability can arise from such seemingly innocent activities as a drunk committing an unintentional battery. In one case, for example, a female spectator was walking across a parking lot after a college football game when an intoxicated man fell on her, breaking her leg (*Bearman v. University of Notre Dame*, 1983). The court in this case considered whether the university had notice of the potential harm and, once the university had notice, whether it had a duty to protect its patrons. The court concluded that the university not only had notice but also owed the spectator, a business invitee, a duty of safe ingress and egress from the facility.

Another pertinent case involving a parking lot and foreseeable conduct is *Bishop v. Fair Lanes Georgia Bowling* (1986). A group of bowlers complained to the bowling alley's management of harassing behavior by the bowlers on an adjacent lane. The management took no action and, moreover, continued to serve alcohol to the harassing group despite their obvious intoxication. At 2:30 A.M. the two parties were the last to leave the facility, at which opportunity the intoxicated group attacked the other bowlers in the alley's parking lot. The *Bishop* court concluded that a jury could reasonably find that the bowling alley's managers knew or should have known of the potential for a dangerous altercation between the patrons before the altercation occurred and would, therefore, be negligent for taking no action and failing to make its premises safe for invitees.

Thus, the key point of analysis is the existence of information that puts a landowner on notice that an assault or accident is foreseeable (Miller, 1993; Van der Smissen, 1990, p. 3). Attaching foreseeability to seemingly random accidents further expands the specter of liability should serious criminal acts occur. In other words, don't be in denial about potential liability.

The Premonition

Notice is the key requirement for proving foreseeability. For instance, in a suit stemming from a brawl during a 1980 AC/DC rock concert, the concert promoters claimed they did not have notice because "no unruly behavior had taken place in the arena, no fights had broken out, and no drinking had been observed" (McCarthy, 1995, p. 7). Even though the arena had no prior problems, the court nevertheless concluded that the promoter was on notice because a police officer had investigated prior AC/DC tour stops and had knowledge of various problems at other venues, which he reported to the concert promoters. The officer also knew that when the band appeared at the arena the previous year, the band had attracted a rowdy, drunk, drug-using crowd even though apparently no specific incidents of inappropriate behavior had officially been reported (*Comastro v. Village of Rosemont*, 1984). Other cases have also stressed the need for landowners to act assertively to deter criminal conduct when they have information that indicates the possibility of such conduct (see, for example, *McNeal*

v. Days Inn of America, Inc., 1998. and *Whataburger, Inc., v. Rockwell*, 1997).

Mean Streets

If a facility's location is in an area with a significant history of assaults, muggings, and robberies, landowners may be liable if they take no steps to protect patrons from known potential dangers. That is, foreseeability issues can extend even to criminal activity in surrounding neighborhoods (Clery, 1995, p. 5).

A classic example of such a case is *Banks vs. Hyatt Corporation* (1984). Hotel guest Dr. Robert Banks was robbed and shot to death as he approached the New Orleans Hyatt Hotel's front entrance. His widow and family brought a lawsuit against Hyatt, asserting that, although Banks was not actually on the hotel's property at the time of the robbery and shooting, reasonable precautions had not been taken by the hotel to protect him, and the hotel had a duty to do so. Hyatt argued that it had taken reasonable precautions to protect its guests and could not be expected to protect guests who were off the premises. Besides, the hotel contended, "Dr. Banks was guilty of contributory negligence or had at least assumed the risk by going out" (Rutherford and McConnell, 1987, p. 60).

The jury heard testimony from both sides, including evidence that Hyatt managers were aware of numerous robberies and shootings that had previously occurred in and around the same area where Banks lost his life. Further, Hyatt employees had logged incidents, many involving weapons, in other areas around the hotel. The jury looked at the evidence of prevalent crime in the area and determined that the security precautions provided by the hotel were simply not sufficient; that the hotel did have a duty to "take reasonable care for the safety of its guests, and that the duty [extended] to adjacent areas where guests [were] likely to go and where the hotel could effectively maintain control of safety"

(Rutherford and McConnell, 1987, p. 62). The jury awarded the Banks family $975,000.

Back to the Future

To a degree, the frequency of prior acts represents the probability that a certain risk or injury might occur (Nilson and Edington, 1982, pp. 34–37). Yet even in the absence of prior criminal activity, landowners must take precautions to prevent reasonably foreseeable crimes. Rather than examining just the frequency of prior acts, courts are examining all the circumstances that together indicate whether a landowner should have reasonably foreseen a harm. In making this determination, the court considers the following factors (Berlonghi, 1996, p. 13; Gordon and Brill, 1996, pp. 5–6).

1. The nature of the facility.
2. The facility's surrounding locale.
3. Whether the facility's records are adequately maintained.
4. The experience of the facility manager.
5. Whether the manager was aware of the criminal activity levels at the facility.
6. Security personnel's compliance with assigned patrols.
7. The lack of customary security precautions.

Therefore, it is vital for landowners to work on the implementation of a comprehensive crime-prevention program, addressing all reasonably foreseeable criminal actions. This means that landowners should include parking-area security as a critical concern in their risk-management plans (Ammon, 1993, p. 117; Berlonghi, 1990, pp. 10–11). While it is impossible to eliminate all potential suits, risk-management plans can help identify, document, and eliminate potential risks, and may reduce the prospect of being sued (Van der Smissen, 1990, p. 3).

To determine liability, courts determine whether a property's security precautions were sufficient to prevent the criminal activity and whether patrons were warned of impending risks (allowing for the impossibility of predicting all dangerous incidents or violent behavior). When reviewing specific precautionary measures, landowners should ask the following (Clery, 1995, p. 5):

1. Are statistics maintained on the frequency and type of criminal activity occurring at the parking facility and in the surrounding neighborhood (within a quarter mile)?
2. What is being done to prevent criminal behavior?
3. Do both security and nonsecurity personnel understand and use proper security measures?
4. Is there a program in place to inform patrons and employees about security concerns?
5. Have security policies been reviewed, revised, or updated, and implemented? Does such a review take place at least once a year?
6. Are there any long-range plans for enhancing security and crime-prevention initiatives?
7. What is the cost-benefit analysis of adding security measures in light of the possible harm or injury sustained by a guest, or in light of a potential jury award to a victimized patron or visitor?

Later in this paper we address common yet critical approaches to risk management (e.g., security patrols, alcohol management, crowd control). First, we discuss design factors that are often overlooked, yet that can substantially affect the safety and protection that a facility can offer its guests.

ENVIRONMENTAL DESIGN

Environmental design refers to the process of building or renovating facilities so that their physical characteristics serve aesthetic and practical functions, including crime abatement or prevention. The use of architectural details to enhance patrons' security is spreading throughout the world (Sheard, 1995, pp. 26–28). Litigants claiming negligent facility supervision are starting to argue that an approach such as Crime Prevention through Environmental Design (CPTED), first addressed by Jeffery (1971), could have reduced criminal activities or, had a CPTED-like system been used, it would have uncovered foreseeable hazards (Gordon and Brill, 1996, pp. 1–6).

CPTED Principles

CPTED is a relatively easy and economical way to augment security efforts if incorporated at the time of facility construction. It is possible although somewhat more complicated to implement CPTED after the fact. The general principles of CPTED include natural surveillance, access control, and controlling the environment, all of which can be used effectively to discourage violence in parking facilities.

CPTED involves carefully selecting building features, materials, and systems to meet established passive-security and active-security requirements. Passive security refers to the physical design, such as lighting, while active security refers to the human element, such as uniformed guards, intercoms, and closed-circuit cameras.

Even though CPTED has been around for almost 30 years, many parking facilities have been designed with little or no attention to security. There are several reasons for this oversight. For one thing, little time is devoted to parking-facility design in architecture curricula, and the principles of CPTED are thus not widely recognized by developers and architects. Further, since the parking lot's design is often looked at as basic if not routine, that task is generally left to the newest and least experienced person on the architectural team. Lack of planning, therefore, means that

active security methods are later needed to correct problems that could have been avoided if the architectural team had incorporated CPTED principles from the start.

CPTED Concepts

With respect to parking facilities, CPTED includes the following areas: lighting, natural surveillance, stair towers and elevator access controls, and restrooms.

The Light Ahead

Lighting is generally considered to be the most important security feature in parking facilities. It is a well-established fact that good lighting deters criminal activity and increases the public's perception that the facility is safe (which may increase patronage). Installing a parking lot lighting system reduces the need for active security and reduces or eliminates car break-ins.

The basic principles of lighting design include illumination, uniformity, and glare. Illumination is simply the intensity of light falling on a surface. Uniformity refers to the ability to achieve a consistent level of lighting throughout the parking facility. (Consistent lighting can allow both patrons and security personnel to see into the far edges of parking stalls, as compared to seeing only the driving lanes well.) Glare reduces the contrast of an object against its background, making it difficult for the eye to perceive depth accurately. This condition is especially dangerous for individuals with weak or impaired vision. Glare can be minimized by the careful selection and positioning of fixtures in the parking facility. (For example, many light manufacturers design lights with glare shields, and those lights can be located above the parked cars rather than in the driving lanes, to further reduce glare.)

One approach to achieving the desired quality of lighting is the level of service (LOS) approach developed by Mary S. Smith (1996, pp.

2–9). Each level is represented by a grade, and this approach should be as familiar to parking-facility owners, city officials, and architects as it is to traffic engineers. The highest grade is LOS A, which denotes superior design; LOS B is above average; LOS C is average; and LOS D is the Illuminating Engineering Society of North America's minimum standard.

In addition to meeting industry standards and providing glare-free lighting, lights must be reliable, easy to maintain, able to withstand the elements, and vandal proof.

Where good lighting is not available due to design or expense, concrete staining may be an alternative. Concrete staining is the process of dyeing walls, ceilings, and beam soffits white to increase brightness. This cost-effective method has been shown in some designs to increase the LOS by an entire grade. A top-quality concrete stain will last about ten years. A good white paint will have the same effect but requires constant maintenance. (One problem with white stain or paint, however, is that it may encourage graffiti. Fortunately, there are antigraffiti stains that accommodate easy cleanup.)

Vision Quest

The second most critical security-design issue is natural surveillance, or the ability of individuals to observe their surroundings. Natural surveillance is easiest to achieve in open parking facilities; however, it is not impossible to achieve in parking garages. The most difficult garages in which to use natural-surveillance concepts are those garages that have numerous sloped parking areas. So today's designers are shying away from extensive ramps. Moreover, because openness increases natural surveillance, high ceilings and open exterior facades are now preferred, as well. Clearly, an underground parking garage cannot allow for open facades. Yet there are underground-design schemes that incorporate natural light and ventilation, and that make it easy to hear a person in distress.

Natural surveillance also includes the manner in which employees direct people and vehicles within the parking facility. For example, it is best to direct pedestrians to designated areas where other people are likely to be walking (and criminals absent), rather than to let those guests wander through the parking facility. Likewise, concentrating entrances and exits makes supervision of those areas easier.

The Glass Tower

Since stairs, lobbies, and elevators are high-risk areas for personal injury, CPTED addresses such areas with an eye toward open design. One of the basic precepts of CPTED is to plan stairways and elevator lobbies as openly as the building codes will permit. The more visibility one has the better, including using exterior and open-air spaces. Where that option is not available due to weather or code constraints, glass may be a compromise, allowing both protection and visibility.

A Safe Place

If the facility is in a low-risk area, access control may seem unnecessary at first. Nevertheless, it is prudent to consider access control in the design stage, as the risk level may change with time. Screens and gates can be used to discourage unauthorized people from entering the parking area. If possible, the parking facility's design should guide vehicular traffic through gated pathways. Even if there is no charge for parking, an individual receiving a ticket and interacting with an attendant is given the impression of security. Moreover, measures such as those discourage criminal activity.

Location of security personnel is a critical CPTED component. Some landowners don't wish to "advertise" potential security concerns, and therefore locate their security personnel and parking-attendant booths to the rear of the facility. That thinking is backward; according to CPTED principles, landowners should locate security personnel or attendant booths at the front of the parking area, next to the primary entrance. Besides giving security employees a clear view of the property, it's a way for the owner to make a public statement about the importance of security and guests' safety.

The Hiding Place

Landowners should not include restrooms in parking-facility designs, especially in underground garages. Such restrooms present special security problems because they make excellent hiding spots for criminals. Many patrons recognize the potential danger and avoid using such facilities themselves, resulting in minimal traffic and thereby presenting a potentially dangerous condition for the patron who happens to use the restroom. Within the confines of the shopping mall, convention center, or office building is a much more appropriate place for public restrooms.

Secret Weapons

While CPTED generally encompasses passive design concepts, a few active ones are notable. Active design concepts include panic buttons, emergency phones, intercoms, sound surveillance, closed-circuit cameras, and trained guards. Parking facilities that failed to incorporate CPTED during the planning stage often find it necessary to use active techniques later. Although all of those features have obvious advantages, by themselves they are not an alternative to CPTED. Further, they tend to be expensive, and some are prone to abuse by pranksters and vandals.

OTHER RISK-MANAGEMENT STRATEGIES

In addition to CPTED methods, there are other critical aspects to risk management that are well known but sometimes overlooked. We address a few of those here.

Watch It

In a recent survey of municipal football stadiums, 86 percent of the respondents "always" had security personnel located in the parking lot before and after the game (Ammon, 1993, p. 117). According to that study, only 3 percent of the respondents did not offer any security protection in parking lots. In 63 percent of the stadiums, law-enforcement authorities provided protection. Private security firms, facility employees, or a blend of employees, private security, and law-enforcement agencies provided the remaining security. There is no consensus on the number of on-duty security personnel required for given situations or even about the best security measures. Risk-management professionals agree, however, that providing adequate security is an ongoing, evolutionary process that requires consistent and detailed monitoring (Ammon, 1993, pp. 117–120; Christiansen, 1986, pp. 46–52; Miller, 1989, pp. 419–437; Ross, 1985, pp. 22–29; Van der Smissen, 1990, p. 3).

One common measure is the use of roving security patrols. In many parking lots, such as those of malls, hotels, schools, and large stores, roving patrols can be effective and useful. Wal-Mart, for example, now employs uniformed security personnel on golf carts in some regions. Wal-Mart conducted a study on store crime and discovered that 80 percent of nonshoplifting crimes occurred outside the store. A Wal-Mart in Tampa, Florida, in particular, had been the scene of 226 car thefts, 25 purse snatchings, 32 burglaries, and 14 armed robberies prior to its implementing the golf-cart idea. Once the golf-cart program was in place, however, crime outside the Tampa store was reduced to zero (Lee, 1997, p. E1). Although a guard with a vehicle of some sort and the necessary security equipment (e.g., two-way radio, flashing lights) can cost about $45,000 a year, there is a strong possibility that such an investment can reduce actual risk and therefore help the store avoid costly lawsuits (or, at least, give the store's security efforts some credibility once in court). Wal-Mart, for example, was ordered to pay 75 percent of a $1.5 million award to a man shot in the head in a Wal-Mart parking lot (Lee, 1997, p. E1). With that in mind, $45,000 a year is a small price to pay to achieve better security and a reputation within the neighborhood and among customers as a safe place to shop.

The Crowd

Another risk-management technique used to protect patrons when entering and exiting a facility involves the use of crowd-management personnel (Ammon, 1995, pp. 16–19). Traditionally, those individuals were used to inspect patrons' belongings for alcoholic beverages at the entrance to events (e.g., a football game or a concert). Today, those same workers are as likely to assist individuals (e.g., the elderly or disabled) as required and to direct visibly intoxicated individuals to a secure waiting room. Crowd-management personnel are now used for all sorts of public events, whether it be a rock concert, an exposition at a conference center, or a farmers' market at a shopping mall. In all cases, some training for the job is desirable. The number of security staff needed can vary based on the following factors (Berlonghi, 1996, p. 13):

1. The type of facility or event.
2. The number of entrances and exits.
3. The number of limited- and restricted-access areas.
4. The number of parking levels (or areas) in the facility.
5. The facility's capacity.
6. The facility's history of unruly behavior or dangerous conditions.
7. The time and length of the event (and, in some cases, the expected weather).
8. The number of spectators.
9. The demographic profile of the expected crowd.
10. Whether admission was free or paid.
11. Whether alcohol consumption is allowed or expected (see sidebar "Alcohol Management").
12. The types of security personnel on duty (including municipal law-enforcement officers) and the level of supervisory expertise.
13. The presence and location of electronic protection devices.
14. Specific requirements imposed by insurance carriers.

ALCOHOL MANAGEMENT

For certain types of events, alcohol management is a key component of a risk-management plan. Arrests or evictions at sports events often revolve around alcohol abuse.[1] Alcohol-management policies can be enforced in several ways, including by preventing patrons from bringing their own alcoholic beverages into the facility. Also, in many venues, the sale of alcoholic beverages is eliminated after a certain period in the competition (e.g., after the seventh inning or at the end of the third quarter).

Additional risk-management strategies designed to reduce alcohol-related injuries and incidents include controlling tailgate parties and creating a designated-driver program.[2] Finally, designating certain areas within the stadium or facility as alcohol-free zones may make events more attractive to families and other users[3] and reduce the likelihood that under-the-influence fans will disrupt or interfere with sober patrons.

---

[1]B. Gilbert and L. Twyman, "Violence: Out of Hand in the Stands," *Sports Illustrated*, January 31, 1983, pp. 62–72.

[2]R. E. Ammon, Jr., "Alcohol and Event Management," *Crowd Management*, Vol. 1, No. 4 (1995), pp. 16–19.

[3]R. E. Ammon, Jr., "Risk and Game Management Practices in Selected Municipal Football Facilities," unpublished doctoral dissertation, University of Northern Colorado (Greeley, CO), 1993.

Sign of the Times

Signs are an important consideration in a risk-management and safety plan. In the parking facility itself, signs should assist patrons in moving quickly through the lot or garage to their destinations. Lost and confused guests—whether arriving or leaving—make easy targets for criminals. Landowners therefore should strive to provide clear, visible signs that are both understandable and memorable so those guests can safely move to and from their vehicles. Furthermore, signs can be used to deter criminals by announcing that regular security patrols and electronic-monitoring systems are in place.

Contract

Risk-management planning should, of course, reduce potential fiscal losses arising from the misconduct of others. Appropriate contractual provisions help to protect against such losses—in this case, when dealing with parking-security personnel retained from outside firms. Contracts with independent security vendors should contain a clause promising indemnity and setting forth what specific risk-management steps are to be taken to secure the parking areas. The contract should specify the number of security personnel to be deployed, when those workers will change shifts, what quality-control measures are to be used (e.g., spot inspections), how security personnel will handle intoxicated persons, what specific actions to take should a criminal act or personal-injury event occur, and what follow-up reporting procedures are appropriate after an injury or crime.

THE SECURITY AUDIT

The design of a parking facility and the level of security needed depend on many factors. Because there is no "one size fits all" solution, a security audit is a good way to determine exactly what security a particular facility needs.

The security audit is actually quite simple. A facility might exist that originally incorporated CPTED but that has undergone many physical changes over the years. For example, imagine a convention center that started out as a simple rectangular structure. Now, picture how various asymmetrical additions could be built into the parking lots over time. Such additions now make it impossible to view large sections of the parking lot at the same time from the same vantage point. A facility such as this should undergo a security audit to identify the security lapses caused by the building expansions. Additionally, if the facility has not changed its exterior lighting system, the older system will almost certainly be insufficient to meet the current needs of the reconfigured parking areas, including being unable to light some corners at all (Gordon and Brill, 1996, p. 6). A security audit will show what actions need to be taken to return the level of security to where it once was.

Witness for the Defense

One aspect of crime prevention is that the sight lines of potential witnesses (patrons, employees, security personnel, and passersby) not be obstructed or hindered. For example, there should always be a clear view into and out of any cashier's cubicle. If the windows of the cubicle are covered with posters, handbills, or other advertising or personal effects, a cashier would be unlikely to witness a nearby crime, should it occur. By the same token, the posters would also hinder a potential witness's view of an attack on the cashier (Gordon and Brill, 1996, p. 6).

HESITATE, THEN LITIGATE

Protecting facility visitors and lowering the risk of liability exposure is a primary concern of landowners. To avoid liability, many landowners are not waiting for criminal activity to occur, but are implementing risk-management plans, including for their parking-facility operations. Security patrols, crowd control, signs, alcohol management, and concise agreements with independent security providers are just some of the ways a landowner can make the parking facility safer. Using CPTED concepts is another effective method of reducing crime and liability. Today, with litigation so frequent, it seems absolutely mandatory for a landowner to take all precautions possible.

5.10 Case Study: Housekeeping, Engineering, and Security

INTERDISCIPLINARY SECURITY PLAN

As a regional manager for a hotel chain that operated three urban-core hotels in a large eastern city, Denise Tomes was becoming very concerned in 2001 that the hotels for which she was responsible were increasingly vulnerable to threats of physical harm and/or financial loss to guests from a variety of criminals. She knew through news and media reports that the streets of the city her hotels operate in were becoming increasingly unsafe due to a wide variety of aggressive panhandlers, street crime, muggings, physical and sexual assaults, and automobile-related felonies.

Because her hotels total in excess of 1500 rooms and cater mainly to convention, corporate, and free independent traveler (FIT) markets, Tomes knew that at any given time a large number of her guests were on the streets of the city and that additionally, due to the public nature of hotels in general, it was likely that criminals could enter the hotel properties seeking victims.

These hotels were built during the early 1980s, and although regularly redecorated and remodeled to continue to appeal to the upscale market, from the physical and operational standpoints, they still reflected the architectural and security consciousness of their era in operational terms. This means that guest room door locks were still of the standard keyed variety; elevators, fire stairs, outside hotel entrances and exits, and parking structures were relatively obscure and unmonitored; and housekeeping, engineering, and guest services staffs training had not, as yet, reflected the security concerns of the twenty-first century.

To help her in dealing with the potential problems presented by the current situation, Denise Tomes has called a meeting of the heads of security, housekeeping, and engineering. She challenges them to come up with a plan to increase security for the hotels and their guests without seeming to become armed fortresses. The task of the directors of security, housekeeping, and engineering is to set forth for Tomes an analysis of the potential risks. Then they must produce a range of alternative suggestions as to how those risks might be managed through the efforts of their departments and respective staffs, combined with specific recommendations for equipment and facility upgrades.

References

Ammon, R. E., Jr. 1993. "Risk and Game Management Practices in Selected Municipal Football Facilities." Unpublished doctoral dissertation, University of Northern Colorado, Greeley, CO.

Ammon, R. E., Jr. 1995. "Alcohol and Event Management." *Crowd Management* 1(4):16–19.

Baim, Dean V. 1994. *The Sports Stadium as a Municipal Investment.* Westport, CT: Greenwood Press, p. 200.

Banks v. Hyatt Corporation, 722 F. 2d 214 (5th Circuit, 1984).

Bayou, M. E., and L. B. Bennett. 1992. "Profitability Analysis for Table Service Restaurants." *Cornell Hotel and Restaurant Administration Quarterly* 33(3):49–55.

Bearman v. University of Notre Dame, 453 N.E.2d 1196 (1983).

Berlonghi, A. 1990. *Special Event Risk-Management Manual.* Dana Point, CA: Event Risk Management, p. 259.

Berlonghi, A. 1996. *Special-Event Security Management, Loss prevention and Emergency Services.* Dana Point, CA: Event Risk Management, p. 13.

Bishop v. Fair Lanes Georgia Bowling, 803 F.2d 1548 (1986).

Boles v. La Quinta Inns, 680 F. 2d 1077 (5th Circuit, 1982).

Brigham, G. H. 1955. *Housekeeping for Hotels, Motels, Hospitals, Clubs, Schools.* New York: Ahrens.

Comastro v. Village of Rosemont, 461 N.E. 2d 616 (1984).

Christiansen, M. L. 1986. "How to Avoid Negligence Suits: Reducing Hazards to Prevent Injuries." *Journal of Physical Education, Recreation, and Dance* 57(2):46–52.

Clery, B. 1995. "Commercial Insurance Carriers Write Disclaimer for Crime." *Campus Watch* 1(1):5.

Dale, J. C., and T. Kluga. 1992. "Energy Conservation: More than a Good Idea." *Cornell Hotel and Restaurant Administration Quarterly* 33(6):30–35.

Dougan, J. 1994. "Menu Engineering with Electronic Spreadsheets." *Bottomline* 8(6):15–17.

Ellis, Raymond C., Jr. 1986. *Security and Loss Prevention Management.* East Lansing, MI: Educational Institute of the American Hotel and Motel Association.

Fisher, Reed Allen. 1986. "A Documentation of Factors which Determine Staffing Levels for the Engineering Department of a Hotel Property." *MPS Monograph.* Ithaca, New York: Cornell University School of Hotel Administration.

Garzilli v. Howard Johnson Motor Lodges, 419 F. Supp. 1210 (E.D. New York, 1976).

Gordon, C. L., and W. Brill. 1996. "The Expanding Role of Crime Prevention through Environmental Design in Premises Liability," NCJ Publication No. 157309. *NIJ Research in Brief.* Washington, DC: U.S. Department of Justice, pp. 1–6.

Harris v. Pizza Hut of Louisiana, Inc., 455 So. 2d 1364 (Louisiana, 1984).

Jeffery, C. Ray. 1971. *Crime Prevention through Environmental Design.* Beverly Hills, CA: Sage Publications.

Kveragas v. Scottish Inns, Inc., 733 F. 2d 409 (6th Circuit, 1984).

La Belle, A. M., and J. Barton. 1951. *Administrative Housekeeping.* New York: G. P. Putnam's Sons.

Lee, L. 1997. "Parking Lots Open to Crime." *Houston Chronicle* April 27, p. E1.

Pastore, A. L., and K. Maguire (eds.). 1995. *Bureau of Justice Statistics: Sourcebook of Criminal Justice Statistics—1994.* Albany, NY: Hindelang Criminal Justice Research Center, p. 249.

Pastore, A. L., and K. Maguire (eds.). 1996. *Bureau of Justice Statistics: Sourcebook of Criminal Justice Statistics—1995.* Albany, NY: Hindelang Criminal Justice Research Center, p. 230.

Malk, M., and R. S. Schmidgall. 1994. "Financial Analysis of the Rooms Division." *Bottomline* 8(6):18–21.

Malk, M., and R. S. Schmidgall. 1995. "Analyzing Food Operations." *Bottomline* 10(3):23–27.

Maloy, B. P. 1993. "Legal Obligations Related to Facilities." *Journal of Physical Education, Recreation, and Dance* 64(2):28–30, 64.

Martin, Frances. 1987. "200 Leading Hotel Chains in 40 Countries Report 2.7 Million Rooms." *Hotels and Restaurants International* July:42–92.

Martin, Robert J., and Thomas J. A. Jones. 1992. *Professional Management of House-keeping Operations,* 2d ed. Copyright © 1992 by John Wiley and Sons.

McBer & Company, Managerial Style Questionnaire. No date.

McCarthy, P. 1995. "Lessons in the Law: To What Extent Must a Venue Owner Be Held Responsible for Injuries On-Site?" *Crowd Management* 1(4):7.

McNeal v. Days Inn of America, Inc., 498 S.E.2d 294 (Ga. 1998).

Miller, A. W. 1989. "Risk Management." In *Law For Physical Educators and Coaches,* 2d ed., G. Nygaard and T. Boone (eds.), Columbus, OH: Publishing Horizons, pp. 419–437.

Miller, L. K. 1993. "Crowd Control." *Journal of Physical Education, Recreation, and Dance* 64(2):1–32, 64–65.

Mintzberg, H. 1975. "The Manager's Job: Folklore and Fact." *Harvard Business Review* July–August:49–61.

Nordmann v. National Hotel Company, 425 F. 2d 1108 (5th Circuit, 1970).

Nilson, R. A., and C. R. Edington. 1982. "Risk Management: A Tool for Park and Recreation Administrators." *Park & Recreation* August:34–37.

Orlando Executive Park, Inc. v. P. D. R., 402 So. 2d 442 (Florida, 1981).

Peters v. Holiday Inns, 278 NW 2d 208 (Wisconsin, 1979).

Quain, W. J. 1992. "Analyzing sales-Mix Profitability." *Cornell Hotel and Restaurant Administration Quarterly* 33(2):57–62.

Riehle, H. 1994. "Table Service Restaurants Post Sales Gain in 1993." *Restaurants USA* 14(9):43–44.

Ross, C. 1985. "Managing Risk." *Athletic Business* June:22–29.

Rutherford, D. G. 1987. "The Evolution of the Hotel Engineer's Job." *Cornell Hotel and Restaurant Administration Quarterly* 27(4):72–78.

Rutherford, Denney G., and Jon P. McConnell. 1987. "Understanding and Managing Your Liability for Guest Safety." *Cornell Hotel and Restaurant Administration Quarterly* 27(4):58–63, 600.

Rutherford, D. G., and William J. Schill. 1984. "Theoretical Constructs in Practice: Managers Rate Their Importance." *International Journal of Hospitality Management* 3(3):101–106.

Saied, Jamelia. 1990. "Approaches to Risk Management." *Cornell Hotel and Restaurant Administration Quarterly* 31(2):45–55.

Schneider, Madelin, and Georgina Tucker. 1989. *The Professional Housekeeper,* 3d ed. New York: Van Nostrand Reinhold.

Sheard, R. 1995. "Architectural Influences in Crowd Management in the U.K." *Crowd Management* 2(2):4–7, 26–28.

Smith, M. S. 1996. "Crime Prevention through Environmental Design in Parking Facilities," NCJ Publication No. 157310. *NIJ Research in Brief.* Washington, DC: U.S. Department of Justice, pp. 2–9.

Taco Bell, Inc. v. Lannon, 744 P. 2d 43 (Colorado, 1987).

Tucker, G., and M. Schneider. 1982. *The Professional Housekeeper,* 2d ed. Boston: CBI.

Turkel, S. 1993. "Deflating F&B Results." *Bottomline* 8(2):8–10.

Van der Smissen, B. 1990. *Legal Liability and Risk Management for Public and Private Entities.* Cincinnati: Anderson Publishing Co., p. 3.

Virginia D. v. Madesco Investment Corporation, 648 S.W. 2d 881 (1983).

Whataburger, Inc., v. Rockwell, 706 So.2d 1226 (Ala. 1997).

Wasmuth, William J., and Stanley W. Davis. 1983. "Strategies for Managing Employee Turnover." *Cornell Hotel and Restaurant Administration Quarterly* 24(2):65–75.

Suggested Readings

Books

Cournoyer, Norman G., Anthony G. Marshall, and Karen L. Morris. 1999. *Hotel, Restaurant, and Travel Law: A Preventive Approach,* 5th ed. Albany, NY: Delmar Publishers, Inc.

Marshall, Anthony G. 1995. *Don't Lose Your Hotel by Accident*. Cleveland, OH: Advanstar Communications.

Martin, Robert J. 1998. *Professional Management of Housekeeping Operations,* 3d ed.. New York: John Wiley and Sons, Inc.

Newland, Loren E. 1997. *Hotel Protection Management: The Innkeeper's Guide to Guest Protection and Reasonable Care*. Scottsdale, AZ: TNZ Publishers, Inc.

Prestia, Kenneth Lane. 1993. *Chocolates for the Pillows, Nightmares for the Guests*. Silver Spring, MD: Bartleby Press.

Schneider, Madelin, Georgina Tucker, and Mary Scoviak. 1999. *The Professional Housekeeper,* 4th ed. New York: John Wiley and Sons, Inc.

Smith, Harry. 1993. *Hotel Security*. Springfield, IL: Charles C. Thomas.

Articles

Bean, Nelson R. 1992. "Planning for Catastrophe: The Fast Track to Recovery." *Cornell Hotel and Restaurant Administration Quarterly* 33(2):64–69.

Source Notes

Chapter 5.2, "A Day in the Life of a Director of Rooms," by Kurt Englund, Director of Rooms, Regent Beverly Wilshire.

Chapter 5.3, "Housekeeping Organizations: Their History, Purpose, Structures, and Personnel," by Thomas Jones, adapted from *Housekeeping Operations*, 2d ed., edited by Robert Martin, Copyright © 1992. Adapted by permission of John Wiley and Sons, Inc.

Chapter 5.4, "On Being an Executive Housekeeper," by John Lagazo.

Chapter 5.5, "The Hotel Engineering Function: Organization, People, and Issues in the Modern Era," by Denney G. Rutherford.

Chapter 5.6, "The Engineering Department and Financial Information," by Agnes Lee DeFranco and Susan B. Sheridan.

Chapter 5.7, "De Facto Security Standards: Operators at Risk," by Denney G. Rutherford and Jon P. McConnell, is reprinted from the February 1991 issue of *The Cornell Hotel and Restaurant Administration Quarterly*. © Cornell University. Used by permission. All rights reserved.

Chapter 5.8, "The Legal Environment of Lodging Operations," by Melissa Dallas.

Chapter 5.9, "Asphalt Jungle," by Je'anna Abbott and Gil Fried, is reprinted from the April 1999 issue of *The Cornell Hotel and Restaurant Administration Quarterly*. © Cornell University. Used by permission. All rights reserved.

6

Food and Beverage Division

6.1 Introduction

In discussing in a preceding section the ways that hotel organizations have changed, it was pointed out that in earlier times food played a significant role in the organizational structure and product/service mix of the hotels of that era. It has been speculated that the preeminent role played by hotel food service in society became significantly diminished with the onset of Prohibition and during the 1920s. People stopped going to food service establishments where they couldn't "get a drink." Prohibition gave rise to competition from street restaurants that operated sub rosa as speakeasies. These restaurants were not constricted by the very visible public nature of hotel dining rooms. This diminished role was compounded in many ways by the Depression years of the 1930s and the war years of the 1940s.

In general it was very difficult for most hotels' food service to recover from the effects of recognition lost during Prohibition. It also proved extremely difficult during the years of economic downturn during the Depression and the uncertainty and reordered national priorities during World War II.

At the conclusion of World War II, well-documented major shifts in population and economic emphases began to occur. Freestanding restaurants continued to compete very effectively with hotel food service. There was movement away from downtown or central business district hotels. Motels and motor hotels were built on highway and freeway interchanges to take advantage of the mobility of the American family. Fast-food restaurants, too, made a major impact on the away-from-home eating habits of the American family. Consequently, many hotel companies saw as too great the cost of providing high-quality competition in the face of these forces. The net effect of these factors led many hotel guests and operators to believe that hotel food service was little more than a "necessary evil." For many operations this became a self-fulfilling prophecy and hotel food service floundered for many years.

It should be noted that this appears to be a trend that has been reversed in recent years. Of the many factors mentioned earlier that mandated organizational change (market segmentation, return on investment, demographic shifts, and so forth), it would seem that return on investment has played a dominant role in this turnaround. The "double whammy" issues of construction cost and return on investment expectations by people from outside the hospitality world strongly suggest that space devoted to food service should contribute at least its share to the profit structure of the modern hotel service system.

As a result, hotels seem to be willing to try anything to capture additional revenue, prestige, and competitive advantage. Among the tactics addressed in several of the articles and essays included in this section are partnering with restaurant companies; outsourcing a hotel's food service; new catering and beverage management strategies; celebrity chefs; and rethinking the entire role of hotel food and beverage.

FOOD

Over 35 years ago, Allen Hubsch (1966) suggested a number of prescriptions to revitalize hotel food and beverage service that has proven to be eerily prescient. Among his suggestions then were:

- Hotel food and beverage facilities must become profit centers—no longer a necessary evil.
- New and increased professionalism of food and beverage management—less reliance on the old chef-maître d' model.
- Food and beverage outlets need to become amenities that produce room nights.
- Hotel food and beverage units need to adopt street-restaurant philosophies—merchandising, advertising, decor/ambience, menu, and service need to compete with local competition.
- Use food and beverage to fill marginally profitable space in rentals, storage, or production areas.
- New food and beverage outlets can leverage existing facilities like storage and kitchens by spreading fixed costs over a wider sales base.

Hubsch's article, now considered a classic, remains among the suggested readings for this section.

Looking ahead to the current and future state of hotel food and beverage operations, the article by Bob Bosselman provides an indepth analysis of the way the hotel food and beverage organization has changed over the last eight to ten years. They provide some tantalizing clues and examples that echo the prescriptions proposed by Hubsch. They also address the structure of the organization, interactions of food and beverage elements within the lodging operation, operating ratios, and potential trends in this major, and expensive, operational component.

Dominic Provenzano is assistant general manager of the Renaissance Madison Hotel in Seattle. From the perspective of his previous position as director of food and beverage, he provides "front lines" detail of how the theory of Bosselman plays out "as he sees it" for the position of food and beverage director.

In a major research effort that began in 1998, Laurette Dubé, Cathy Enz, Leo Renaghan, and Judy Siguaw of the Center for Hospitality Research at Cornell University studied the "best practices" of hotels in the U.S. lodging industry. In their words, "the goal of this research was to surface and summarize practices of use and value to the entire lodging industry" (Dubé et al., 1999, p. 7). Siguaw and Enz summarize several of the practices from that study that have been developed by hotels to achieve the "strategic charge of profitably meeting customer needs" (Dubé et al., 1999, p. 50). The authors describe how their top hotels integrate the ideas of restaurant design and conceptualization with all of the variables that affect the quality of the food and experience for the guest.

When the concept of outsourcing was mentioned earlier, it was in the context of how some hotel companies are rethinking the role of hotel food and beverage, and how to best maximize investments in facilities, furnishings, and equipment for food service outlets. According to Strate and Rappole (1997) since hotel restaurants have often been managed as a secondary function of the hotels, owners and operators are questioning the conventional wisdom about how hotel food and beverage is conceived and managed. They state that this new focus on hotel food service results in innovative concepts and strategic alliances with well-known restaurant brands. In their article, they analyze this trend outlining historic antecedents of the practice and use a Texas hotel firm, Bristol Hotel Company, as a case study.

Most would agree that should a hotel choose to do its own food service, a first-class executive chef should be the norm to allow a hotel organization to compete effectively for food and beverage business in today's market. It is, however, fairly clear that the chef does not today have the dominant role that chefs had at the turn of the century. Given the importance of the food and beverage function established by the foregoing articles, the chef then becomes an integral part of the competitive strategy and a full-fledged department leader. He or she is no longer purely a technician. This individual needs to have developed a significant range of managerial skills to complement the technical and artistic training that we have come to expect from an executive chef. The appearance of ultra-high-profile "celebrity chefs" adds another interesting variable to the mix of challenges to the food and beverage director. If a hotel commits much of its food and beverage strategy to the talents of one famous person, they can enjoy a significant competitive advantage, but also become hostage to one person's whims and personalities.

Chef Gene Fritz explores the domain of the modern chef and the emerging influence of the celebrity chef. His analytical structure focuses partially on the historical antecedents and theoretical aspects of the chef's job, but also explores and develops the idea of the role of the celebrity chef in today's hotel kitchen.

When David Pavesic states in his essay on menu marketing that "the menu should communicate a restaurant's personality to the public. I believe that the menu is the primary communication link between a restaurant and the customer," he links the process of restaurant conceptualization and food preparation through the organizational structure to the customer or hotel guest.

Patti Shock and colleague John Stefanelli highlight the importance of the banquet and catering functions of hotel food and beverage. With the increased national attention and focus on the importance of conferences, conventions, and meetings of all kinds, these food service professionals who make it their specialty to plan and serve meals and beverages to large groups of people become increasingly important. The authors say that "although on-premise catering is generally the second largest source of revenue for most hotels, following sleeping rooms," and "often the highest visibility the hotel has on a local level," banquets and catering are still too often ignored by hotel school curricula. In this article, we attempt to partially address this lack.

It is these catered affairs that represent a significant contribution to the profit picture of hotel food and beverage service. The efficacy of a hotel's efforts in selling and servicing the group business market may very well be the difference between profitability of the food and beverage function and some less desirable outcome. Their article explores the organization, personnel, and processes of the catering department and provides the reader with some in-depth looks at catering executives and their banquet organizations. This article also includes Internet addresses for additional information.

It is the revenue and visibility importance of the catering function that makes the energetic essay by Rich Benninger so intriguing. From rising at 6:00 A.M. or so, thinking today is the day he will "get everything done" in the catering office of a 5000-room resort hotel casino in Las Vegas, to hitting the sack after midnight, Benninger provides the reader an insider's view of life in the fast lane of Vegas catering. Benninger, as executive director of catering sales at the MGM Grand Hotel and Casino is uniquely positioned to provide these insights.

BEVERAGE

In any hotel that has more than one formal bar, there is usually a separate function within the food and beverage department called bar or beverage management. Ideally, that office coordinates all matters that concern liquors, beers, and wines. The beverage manager will have responsibility for purchasing, receiving, storing, and issuing the liquor, wine, and beer inventory, and quite obviously have the managerial responsibility for controlling that inventory.

Additionally the beverage manager

- Hires, trains, schedules, and controls all beverage and bar personnel.
- Promotes the various beverage department services.
- Coordinates the requests of other departments that require beverage services, for instance, banquet and catering, room service, chefs, management.
- Assures that his or her department is in compliance with federal, state, and local laws and regulations.

The beverage manager administers or manages up to four different types of bars.

The *front* or *public bar* is that in which the guest can, if he or she so desires, interact with the bartender and other service personnel. There are provisions for guest seating at the bar itself, which may be part of a restaurant or a separate room or area. There may also be separate tables and stand-up areas available for beverage service. A front bar may or may not include provision for entertainment.

A *service bar* is a "hidden" bar that's designed to be used by the hotel's food and beverage service staff only. It may serve one or more food service areas and/or room service, and it is designed specifically for efficiency and economy of service. In most cases speed is considered to be the essential ingredient in service bars over decorative ambience. Service bars are typically centrally located in the back of the house out of guest view.

Portable bars are those that are designed for maximum flexibility and can be used in conjunction with beverage sales associated with guest activities anywhere in the hotel or on its grounds. This may be extended in resort areas to include recreational areas.

A new facility popular among many hotels is that of the *in-room bar, minibar,* or *honor bar*. While sometimes the responsibility for inventory of these bars rests with room service, the beverage manager in most cases is also deeply involved in their design, marketing, and control.

In many ways the beverage manager's job can be compared in terms of historical stereotype to that of the housekeeper. Often the beverage manager is one who has worked his or her way up through the ranks of beverage server and preparer and through experience, longevity, and interest become the beverage or bar manager. There is reason to believe that in many ways this may be changing. Like many other areas of management within the hotel, the beverage management function is now faced with a range of issues that are more sophisticated and complicated than those traditional beverage management problems of the past. It may very well be that the beverage managers of the future will have to be able to bring to their job a managerial, organizational, and administrative level of sophistication that heretofore has been unnecessary.

The issues, responsibilities, and structural management of the hotel's beverage function are analyzed and discussed in this section by Valentino Luciani, professor of beverage management at the University of Nevada, Las Vegas. Luciani's new essay for this edition draws upon his industry experience, research, and teaching in the various areas of beverage management and provides a view of how the modern beverage manager has evolved from his or her historical counterparts.

The planning, preparation, service, and management of food and beverage in modern hotels has changed significantly in the time since the first edition of this book was writ-ten. The essays, research, and commentary presented here are chosen to illustrate the breadth and depth of this process of change. The reader who is interested in hotel food and beverage should be able to synthesize a good vision of the practices and realities of this major operational division of modern hotels.

6.2   Hotel Food and Beverage Organization and Management

Robert H. Bosselman

Similar to the overall lodging industry in general, food service in the hotel market has improved in recent years. A general characteristic would be a market posting steady but not significant growth and, rather, an emphasis on cost containment. As lodging food service competes with the multitude of commercial food service operations for the consumer dollar, the focus of both operators and consumers will remain value. Recent research has identified food and beverage services as a primary creator of unique value to a customer's lodging experience (Dubé, Enz, Renaghan, and Siguaw, 1999).

In this introductory essay, the reader will find a discussion of the mission and goals of food and beverage departments in lodging operations, the organizational structure of such departments, interactions of food and beverage elements within the lodging operation, operating ratios, and potential trends in the area.

MISSION AND GOALS

"The goal of our food service operations is to provide the highest quality of food and service in a sophisticated, comfortable ambience, by friendly and professional staff, ensuring that every patron returns," cites the Four Sea-sons Hotel in Las Vegas. This statement, succinct and focused, exemplifies what lodging operations nationwide are seeking. Most lodging executives would identify food and beverage operations as one of the more difficult areas to manage in the entire lodging arena. Lodging food service not only involves the traditional difficulties associated with both producing and serving food and beverages, but the performance of these functions every day, often 24 hours a day. The resulting labor costs and operational expenses can prove burdensome for many lodging establishments. In order for these food and beverage operations to survive and thrive, they must draw not only guests of the lodging facility, but also consumers from the external market of the property. Hoteliers are analyzing their operations to identify ways of increasing the capture rate, the percentage of guests who stay to dine on-site (Ruggless, 1999).

In fact, the more profitable lodging food and beverage operations obtain more than 50 percent of their business from nonguests of the property. The hotel or motel guest is not a captive diner; today there exist too many other opportunities for dining. Yet, in order to have a profitable hotel property, a significant percentage of sales must be produced by the food and beverage operation. To accomplish this, lodging facilities must successfully compete with the numerous chains and independent restaurants that offer a variety of services. It becomes critical for lodging operators to examine how travelers want and need food, and how their specific operation can better serve the traveler (Ruggless, 1999). Many hoteliers are choosing not to compete in this environment. Instead, their strategy has been to eliminate food and beverage operations altogether, or to lease food and beverage operations to outside companies, either chain-operated or an independent. In particular, food and beverage sales in motels and motor-hotel restaurants are projected to decline, primarily as a result of an increasing number of lower-priced lodging operations offering free breakfast of some type and no other meal service (Restaurant Industry Forecast, 1999).

While the reader may start to think that hotel food services are not major players in the overall food service market, 1999 projected sales were estimated at $18.7 billion (Restaurant Industry Forecast, 1999). There are, according to information on hotel chains, five major chains whose food service sales per hotel average more than $2.6 million. At the top lies Hyatt, whose properties average well over $4.2 million in food service sales (Ruggless, 1999). Clearly food service professionals have as much, or more, opportunity for success as in other segments of the food service industry. With potential sales like those noted, lodging food services remain a critical partner of both the revenue and profit of the property. A smart, resourceful manager will make the food service operation unique, thus attracting additional patrons to the lodging establishment. Thus, food service can be looked on as a means of gaining competitive advantage over other lodging operations.

The field of lodging has had a long history of serving people during their travels. From the earliest days of the Roman Empire, when people traveled on foot, on animal, or in vehicles drawn by animals, to the modern age of air, rail, and car transportation, hotels and inns provided for their needs. In fact, these early hotels were the center of community activity and often the only place one could eat away from home. The glamour years of the late nineteenth and early twentieth centuries produced grander hotel properties, the so-designated palaces of the people, which solidified this perception of hotels as centers of public entertainment and as sources of food and drink for guests. This reputation continued well into this century as hotels became the logical place to meet for entertainment and business discussion. Food service operations independent of hotels were rare even in the larger urban centers. It was not until the post–World War II era that independent restaurants and restaurant chains grew in both number and influence over the customer. As we enter the twenty-first century, lodging food service accounts for approximately 5 percent of the total food service market. From total domination of the market to its role as a secondary player today, lodging food service has undergone dramatic change. As properties struggle with the decisions of food service or not, number of food service units, and the level of service offered, future managers need to recall what the goals and mission of the food service operation should be:

1. To provide the appropriate level and degree of food and beverage service to the property's guests.
2. To support the overall goal(s) of the property.
3. To assist the property in gaining a competitive advantage over other lodging establishments.
4. To function efficiently and effectively in order to produce a profit.

ORGANIZATIONAL CONSIDERATIONS

The organization of food service departments within lodging establishments varies depending on type of facility and, in the case of chain operations, corporate policies. Since this degree of variety exists, categorizing lodging properties can be difficult. For example, a property located in a resort environment may also have extensive convention space. A property known primarily as a convention hotel has room enough to accommodate large groups. Food service outlets will likely include restaurant(s), lounge(s), banquet facilities, and room service. A resort property provides all the amenities that focus on guest entertainment and relaxation. There will be a greater emphasis on specialty restaurant(s), as well as room service. Unique problems may face resort managers with respect to seasonality of operations, location, and layout. The latter points are important since the property itself, as well as individual food and beverage outlets, may be located in hard-to-access areas, thus impacting on operational expenses.

An example of a resort is the American Club in Kohler, Wisconsin. Jim Beley, director of lodging operations, is responsible for three full-service restaurants, as well as banquet and conference services. Jim notes that his facilities aim for an upscale perspective, highlighted by regional and contemporary menu influences and currently characterized by booming wine sales. He identifies the property clientele as wanting a more relaxed environment in food and beverage services. He and his staff provide a "white glove" atmosphere of service. (J. Beley, personal communication, October 1999).

Lloyd Wentzell, vice president of food and beverage, provides a slightly different view of food and beverage services for the Riviera Hotel and Casino in Las Vegas. "The food and beverage operation here is an amenity. The buffet and coffee shop are for our in-house guests, and the [three] gourmet rooms are for our guests including those who come to our shows [four entertainment venues]. The snack bar in Nickel Town is used to bring visitors from nearby properties. Room service is a necessary loss leader used to maintain our resort hotel status" (L. Wentzell, personal communication, September 1999).

Airport properties have grown with the increase in air travel. Quite often travelers will choose these properties based on the convenience factor. While occupancy rates are high during weekdays, weekend business tends to drag. There does not appear to be an emphasis on food and beverage operations in such facilities.

Economy properties are currently the segment of the lodging area with the most growth. It has been this segment that often rejects the role of food service operations in the property. Midscale brands such as Holiday Inn and Hampton Inn are noted for their aggressive growth in building new properties with little or no food services. Additionally, significant growth is expected in the lower-tier extended-stay market. However, there are some properties attempting to redefine the concept of value to the customers. One such example has been Courtyard by Marriott, which combines comfortable lodging with downsized food service operations. All-suite properties remain one of the hottest concepts in the lodging field. While some units contain kitchen facilities, many offer complimentary food and beverage services for the busy traveler.

Four Seasons Hotel in Boston demonstrated one example of how a hotel food and beverage operation can be organized. The food and beverage division has four departments: food preparation, catering sales, stewarding, and sales outlets. The latter has five operations: private bars, room service, a full-service lounge, a fine dining restaurant, and banquet facilities. Each department has line employees who report to assistant managers, who, in turn, report to department heads, who then report to a director of restaurants and bars, who, in turn, reports to the director of food and beverages. Regardless of the size of the lodging facility, food and beverages need to be produced and served. However, the increased size and complexity of some operations makes it critical that those managers communicate well with all levels of employees. A sample organizational chart from the Riviera Hotel and Casino in Las Vegas can be observed in Figure 6.1. There may be a trend toward flatter organizational structures, as well as to completely separating out certain functions of the food and beverage area.

FOOD SERVICE PERSONNEL

Who are the key people in the organization of lodging food service? Our attention here will focus on the operational players, those individuals most often responsible for the work of pleasing the guest and holding the line on costs.

In most kitchen operations, an executive chef will be responsible for management related to production activities. Depending on the size and complexity of the operation, the executive chef may actually perform little in the line of food production. In a small operation, the chef may also be a part owner and will perform most of the food-related functions. One of the exciting trends today is the use of big-name chefs in hotel food services, often allowing the chefs to create a signature room in the lodging property.

With the trend toward downsizing operations, it would be the rare organization in lodging food service that employed numerous back-of-the-house employees engaged in a single function. Some examples of the past might include *sous-chef*—the executive chef's assistant and often the staff supervisor; a *saucier*—a sauce cook; a *garde-manger*—cook in charge of all cold food preparation; a *chef pâtissier*—a pastry chef; and a banquet chef in charge of catering. There may be various assistants to each of these positions. In addition, there may be a steward, a purchasing manager, a storeroom clerk, and several janitorial staff.

Some other examples of how lodging food service organizes were recently observed in a study of industry best practices (Dubé et al., 1999). The Boulders, located in Arizona, created a food forager position to improve quality of products. Menus are designed around

foods located, thus saving time trying to find ingredients to fit the menu, while providing guests with a unique dining experience. The Greenbrier, located in West Virginia, designed a formal three-year culinary apprentice program. This has allowed the resort to attract a continuous supply of talented chefs, as well as create a cooking school for guests (thus adding value to the guest experience). The Pierre in New York City utilizes an independent consultant to manage purchasing. This frees the chef to focus more attention on food production and has led to reduced food and labor costs.

The dining room can have an equal degree of complexity, depending on the operation. There may or may not be a supervisor, often called a host/hostess, or maître d'. This individual greets guests and also supervises the wait staff. At the actual service level, we have the capacity for captains, servers, busers, and cashiers. If a lounge operation is present, we also include bartenders and cocktail servers. As one can readily ascertain, it becomes imperative to work as a team.

In today's cost-control environment, food and beverage operations are trimming payrolls and consolidating job responsibilities to cut operational expenses. This cross training of staff allows an individual to take on multiple responsibilities. The Breakers Hotel in Palm Beach, Florida, utilizes a cross-training program that allows the property to completely reorganize its staff annually. This facilitates upward mobility of staff as well as better service to guests (Dubé et al., 1999). In the past, it was not uncommon for the food and beverage operation to employ workers around the clock, as most items were made from scratch. With modern equipment and usage of more convenience food items, such as preportioned meats, it becomes rare to find such parts of the operation like the butcher shop or the pastry shop. Again, hotel operations are concentrating on quality, value, and cost. If the property can find a product rather than producing it, the trend then will be to purchase rather than make from scratch.

FIGURE 6.1
Sample Organization Chart

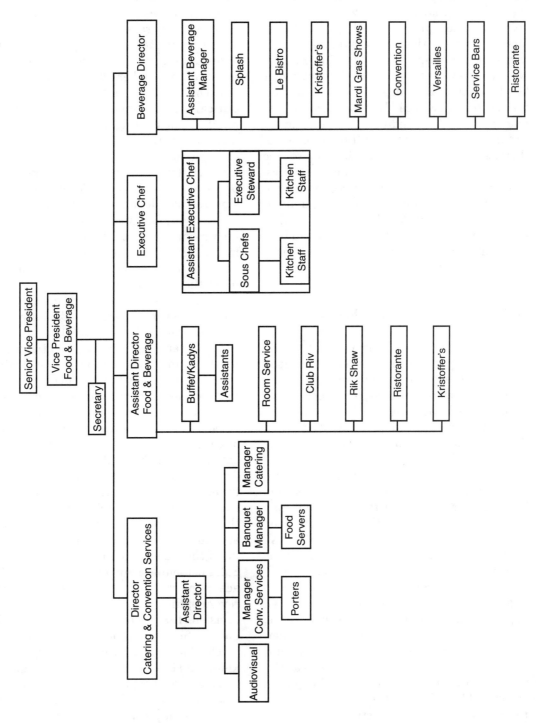

There has been increased attention on the education level of chefs in lodging operations. In recent years traditional culinary arts programs have expanded from two-year to four-year education programs, while traditional four-year institutions have expanded their curricula into culinary arts. The University of Nevada, Las Vegas, was the first four-year hotel administration degree program to offer a bachelor of science (BS) in culinary arts management. These individuals can command rewarding pay, but much will be expected of them, as well. They must be able to produce quality products utilizing minimal resources. They must also direct all activities in the back of the house, including the training and supervision of employees. Their responsibility becomes the means by which a food and beverage unit produces profit for its parent institution, the lodging facility.

OPERATIONAL INTERACTIONS

Hotels are complex institutions that are divided into separate operational areas, among them rooms, engineering, administrative, accounting, human resources, and sales, in addition to food and beverage. These divisions interact in every imaginable way 24 hours a day to produce a quality experience for the guests.

Perhaps the best way to describe this interaction would be to characterize food and beverage and other departments as mutually dependent. Direct interaction can be observed between food and beverage and the front desk with respect to specific guest service issues. Direct interaction can also be observed with the sales department, and the convention/banquet department. Indirect interaction between departments comes from areas such as rooms, in the form of overnight cleaning; engineering, in the form of maintenance and repair; and accounting, in the form of financial analysis. As Jim Beley of the American Club notes, "Food and beverage must communicate their reservation needs or restrictions to concierge and bell staffs. One example is announcing a new menu that has been initiated, or that a special activity will occur. This type of information is valued by guest services. Likewise, food and beverage depends on information submitted to them regarding occupancy, VIPs, or demanding guests" (J. Beley, personal communication, October 1999).

No matter the type of lodging property, it is critical for management and staff to meet regularly, discussing department interaction and better ways to service the guests. Another example to consider would be a casino resort hotel. Historically food and beverage has been perceived as an amenity for players. The casino and slot departments are continually in contact with food and beverage units, particularly room service, to request special arrangements for their clients. These requests might range from amenities being delivered and set up in the guest room, to supplying the gaming area with special foods and drinks (L. Marr and J. Thacker, Luxor Hotel Casino, personal communication, October 1999).

The revenue-generation potential of a lodging food and beverage operation is significantly impacted by the type of client sleeping in your guest rooms. Since a majority of your food and beverage customers may be hotel guests, it is important you book the right type of people in the hotel. Do you know the utilization rate of the food and beverage outlets for the various market segments? Do business travelers eat more or drink more than the leisure/pleasure market? Which convention uses the food and beverage outlets more than others? Your management and sales staff has to know the answers to these types of questions. Sales personnel cannot just be concerned with achieving room-night quotas or generating revenue; they must know the impact of their decisions throughout the rest of the hotel and how it affects the profitability of the hotel.

The food and beverage manager has to know who the customer is and how many patrons one may expect. Information about the hotel guest such as house counts, market mix reports, group commitment reports, and arrival/departure patterns assists the food and beverage team in making decisions on scheduling, food ordering, and whether or not to close a particular outlet.

Every hotel employee is a sales agent for the property's food and beverage outlets. The staff must be trained to always refer and recommend hotel services to the guest. It is clear that the quality of food and beverage operations can impact overall hotel operations and profitability. Quality would be particularly important for convention hotels and resort hotel properties. Guests have come to such properties for specific purposes. Therefore, a reputation as a quality food and beverage operation will serve to attract customers. These operations will generate word-of-mouth advertising from travel agents, corporate meeting planners, cab drivers, airline companies, and tourism offices. While this reputation can attract guests, it becomes the responsibility of management to plan effectively for client needs.

Consider if you run a hotel restaurant, operate room service, provide food and beverages for employees, and now in addition are catering several different types of meals/functions for different groups. Recall that the goal of the hotel property is to service its clientele. Therefore, each area of the hotel must complement the other in providing the service. Managers, particularly in food and beverage, must communicate effectively and train constantly in order to maximize the goals of the lodging operation.

OPERATING RATIOS

There are many operating ratios utilized by the food and beverage department. Controlling operational expenses is perhaps the biggest challenge facing food and beverage managers. Managers at every level must be controllers. Randy Morton and Tamir Shamel of Four Seasons Hotel in Las Vegas note that "... all ratios affect the productivity and prof-

itability of the operation" (R. Morton and T. Shamel, personal communication, October 1999). Jim Beley of the American Club reports that operating ratios are important to keep expenses in check, as well as monitor improvements or income contribution from one area of the property to another. He identifies food cost and labor cost percentages as most important (J. Beley, personal communication, October 1999). Lloyd Wentzell and Miguel Ferreira from the Riviera Hotel and Casino identify common operating ratios such as "cost per cover, percentage of sales, cost per employee, utilization rate (number of covers / number of guests), revenue per occupied room, sales per hotel guest, average check, sales per employee, table turnover, inventory turnover, revenue per square foot, revenue per seat, cost per square foot, return on investment, covers per employee, average covers per day, and average sales per day" (L. Wentzell and M. Ferreira, personal communication, September 1999). They note that ratios are only tools and it is more important to have a clear idea of what needs to be measured and the impact the variable has on the overall operation.

What we can observe is that food and beverage managers utilize ratios to determine whether they have been successful in generating revenues and minimizing expenses. Such ratios can then be compared with figures from prior accounting periods of that operation. Let us examine some of the more common ratios.

Food and Beverage Sales per Available Room

$$\frac{\text{Total Food and Beverage Sales}}{\text{Number of Available Rooms}} = \$$$

Food and Beverage Occupancy

$$\frac{\text{Number of Covers}}{\text{Number of Seats}} = \text{Turns}$$

Sales per Available Seats

$$\frac{\text{Food and Beverage Sales}}{\text{Number of Available Seats}} = \$$$

Average Check

$$\frac{\text{Food and Beverage Sales}}{\text{Number of Covers}} = \$$$

Ratio of Beverage Sales to Food Sales

$$\frac{\text{Beverage Sales}}{\text{Food Sales}} \times 100 = \%$$

Food Cost Percentage

$$\frac{\text{Food Cost}}{\text{Food Sales}} \times 100 = \%$$

Labor Cost Percentage

$$\frac{\text{Food and Beverage Labor Cost}}{\text{Food and Beverage Sales}} \times 100 = \%$$

Note that costs are usually stated as a percentage of sales. These percentages can then be compared with those of previous time frames. While the dollar values for costs are necessary to determine the percentages, it becomes difficult to compare dollars to dollars expended per time period. Measures of revenue often tell management how much effort food and beverage staff have expended for the benefit of the operation. Those ratios combining food and beverages can be broken down to each respective category. Note from the comments provided earlier that ratios utilized will vary depending on the operation. Your goal as manager will be to gain the best information available in order to assist you in making decisions.

Individual units, such as catering, room service, coffee shop, and sit-down restaurants will have different, as well as similar, factors. For example, average check would be common to all, while a measure of seat turnover would apply only to the coffee shop or the sit-down restaurant. The accumulation of information should be as easy as possible for management. The use of point-of-sale technology will enhance this process. Managers should not spend all their time determining what the ratios are or what they mean. Management should be able to quickly ascertain what has occurred in the operation and take any corrective action, if necessary.

TRENDS IN LODGING FOOD SERVICE

In presenting trends, we must exercise caution, as what works in one food and beverage operation may not in another. Recall that the goal of lodging food and beverage operations is to focus on meeting hotel guests' desires, with attention paid to price, value, quality, service, and atmosphere. Food and beverage managers would be wise to study other similar hotel operations, as well as restaurant operations. Guest surveys are also essential to determining customer desires. Your objective should be to discover what travelers want and need in terms of food and beverage products and delivery, and how your operation can better serve its guests (Ruggless, 1999).

The Breakers Hotel in Palm Beach, Florida, has replaced their existing formal dining and casual dining restaurants with single-theme outlets to give guests choice of cuisine rather than choice dictated by guest attire. This has led to stronger hotel restaurant identities and an increased capture rate (Dubé et al., 1999). Peacock Alley in New York's Waldorf-Astoria hotel has replaced appetizers and main courses with a variety of dishes of in-between portion sizes. The chef added more wines by the glass and half bottle to complement the expanded possibilities of the new menu. This version of a tasting menu was in response to diners, who kept substituting dishes from the regular menu (*Wall Street Journal*, October 25, 1999).

The concept of branding has also impacted hotel food and beverage operations. Country Inns and Suites has cobranded with established restaurant concepts (see also Chapter 6.5, by Strate and Rappole). The restaurants average approximately 20 percent of their business from hotel guests. This arrangement eliminates the capital cost of building a restaurant on-site (Dubé et al., 1999). Westin is teaming up with established steak house chain operators the Palm and Shula's Steak House in its properties. Doubletree is also developing steak houses, but with their own proprietary concept called Spencer's.

Another example of branding your own concept comes from the Riviera Hotel and Casino. They created Hound Doggies as an outlet that targets the walking traffic on Las Vegas Boulevard (the Strip). The location is only a few steps off the sidewalk and has proven successful in drawing nonstaying guests into the property. They implemented this concept only after studies identified walking traffic as a potential market. The goal for this outlet was quite basic: bring people in the door. Through the use of a 1950s theme, combined with quality food at very low prices, the Riviera has exceeded the expectation of nonstaying guests. As the unit was not created specifically as a revenue-generating center, success has been measured on the impact in other areas; such as increased slot play (L. Wentzell and M. Ferreira, personal communication, September 1999).

Some Four Seasons Hotels and Regent Hotels and Resorts are promoting the strategic use of a single food and beverage outlet coordinated with the concept of cuisine choices. This strategy has resulted in a more focused approach. In properties where implemented, the strategy has resulted in significant capture rates, as well as increasing local traffic (nonstaying guests) (Dubé et al., 1999).

Starwood is also focusing strategic attention on food and beverage operations, planning renovations where appropriate and conversion of some restaurants into more profitable banquet facilities (Ruggless, 1999).

One of the more exciting trends in lodging food service operations pertains to hotel beverage operations, specifically hotel bars. In many large-city properties, hotel operators have found such facilities to be considerable moneymakers—as much as 50 percent bar profit margin. These bar operations are clearly driven by the youth and vitality of the new Internet generation. The bars are seen as lively gathering places where business and personal time merge (Bounds and Higgins, 2000). Lodging chains are taking notice of such activity. Starwood recently purchased a stake in a company that initiated a popular bar chain. Even the names of the bar operations reflect the youthful vitality associated with the location—Whiskey Blue, Skybar, and Whiskey Rocks. One concern associated with these bar operations is the impact on traditional hotel guests. Many outsourced bar operations do not extend traditional amenities to lodging guests, such as billing to room, preferred seating, and even reservations. In fact, the clientele of the bar operation may be quite different from the hotel guest. As one hotel guest seeking a spot to conduct a business meeting with a client indicated upon entering one of these bars, "It was like Studio 54" (Bounds and Higgins, 2000).

In order for your lodging food and beverage operation to succeed, sound marketing and keen observation of what people want must accompany quality food and service. While consumers choose your hotel for specific reasons, such as price or service, they seek more creativity in a food and beverage operation. If you cannot attract the hotel guest, you will find that attracting clientele from the local area is also difficult. Quite likely, each hotel has its own character that suggests a variation of food and beverage operations in different markets. Management would be wise to remember that a food and beverage unit in a hotel serves the interests of the hotel as well as its own.

While some limited-service lodging operations have entered into cooperative relationships with food service companies, this concept holds significant potential for the appropriate market. One example would be where the hotel's food service operation was marginal at best. The lodging property can concentrate its resources on rooms and lease the food and beverage service to an identifiable brand. Hotels should be aware, though, that in certain situations, such a restaurant company might not be familiar with room service or catering. In an extreme case of moving away from food service, some lodging properties limit services to in-room minibars and microwaves, with limited food items available for sale in the gift shop. In some cases, the gift shop is being transformed into a convenience store.

We have observed that some properties sense a rebirth of simplicity in food and beverage operations. A good example of this would be a coffee shop. What has occurred over the last ten years has been the abandonment of this concept in favor of higher-priced dining. But in letting a coffee shop be a coffee shop, you tap into the consumer's consciousness of value as well as menu variety and fast service. While some find the concept boring, very often customers seek the comfort of knowing they can get a good meal at a good price day after day in your operation.

The area of room service is also seeing significant changes. In some properties, the concept of room service has been eliminated, while in others, room service has been revised. For example, menus have been limited to particular concepts, such as pizza or Asian food. Food items are packaged to appear as though they came from a freestanding restaurant. Some lodging properties even list the room service phone number under the name of the food item (for example, pizza). The key, again, is to know your clientele. But the move to simpler menus, accompanied by lower prices, could bring room service back as a major contributor to overall operations. Some larger hotel operations are focusing on a tighter menu and faster service through room service. For example, one property has converted a freight elevator into a mobile kitchen unit, thereby providing service within minutes of an order. While this option may not be possible for all hotels, it again points out knowing what to offer your specific clientele. Room service has seen resurgence in certain lodging properties, primarily as a result of guest lifestyle. With more adults working, and engaged in active lifestyles, convenience and accessibility become paramount. Room service fits the criteria of convenience and accessibility.

CONCLUSION

As can be seen from the foregoing discussion, it can be difficult to pinpoint which trends may be most important to any individual hotel. What we can say is some lodging properties, notably chain properties and large-size properties, seem to be differentiating themselves to provide excitement for their food and beverage clientele. These operations are essentially reinventing themselves in order to keep fresh and provide creative food and beverage opportunities for staff and guests. These operations view food service as integral to the overall success of the lodging operation.

On the other hand, we can also see a trend toward reduced or even no food service, primarily in smaller properties and the lower-end chain lodging properties. These operations view their business as strictly lodging and leave running food service to someone else, now often a well-known national brand.

It should be obvious from reading this overview that an emphasis on cost control will likely be a key strategy for lodging food services. With increased competition from other potential food service operations, hotels are finding it more difficult to generate revenues and increased customer counts. Attention to value and service will be of significant concern to consumers. Managers of lodging food service will need to utilize better control tools, such as sound forecasting techniques and menu analysis. Banquets, catering, and room service hold the most potential for profit generation in lodging food service. These functions allow management the best opportunity for accurate forecasting and staffing. Beverage areas, such as lounges, will continue to be profitable despite a trend toward less alcohol consumption by the population.

The probabilities of producing profit in hotel restaurants will depend on the type and size of restaurant. There is no reason why a hotel cannot do well, but attention to detail is often lacking in some operations. It is clear that lodging food service offers managers unique challenges in the ever dynamic world of food service management. Food and beverage operations may not be the major focus in a lodging property. However, food and beverage operations may have significant impact on the customer's perception of quality with respect to the property. Therefore, food and beverage operations in lodging properties can serve to differentiate top performers from the crowded lodging market and enhance guest loyalty for the specific property.

6.3   As I See It: Hotel Director of Food and Beverage

Dominic Provenzano

A food and beverage director in a major lodging property needs to be ready for a variety of tasks each and every day. In one sense, this position requires two different individuals to keep the operation moving forward. One is the leader, or strategic visionary, looking ahead to the future of the operation (that may be just one or three months, or it could be one full year out). The other is the day-to-day manager, constantly moving through the organization to be sure all events are performing according to plan and guests are treated beyond their expectations.

In this position I have the responsibility of overseeing several departments: culinary, banquets, room service, Maxwell's Restaurant, Prego Restaurant, and all private bars. While an ideal day would be spent on planning, more often than not I find myself in discussion with staff or guests. Some examples of regular meetings include the following:

- Daily
  - *Banquet Event Orders (BEO) Meeting*. Purpose: to go over BEO for the day.

- Weekly
  - *Food and Beverage Meeting*. Purpose: review operations with department managers.
  - *Executive Meeting*. Purpose: overview of operations with all executive committee members and the general manager of hotel.
  - *One-on-One Meetings*. Purpose: meet with individual food and beverage departmental managers to establish goals and cover issues specific to that department.
- Monthly
  - *Staff Meeting*. Purpose: review of operations by all department managers and general manager of hotel.
  - *Employee Recognition Meeting*. Purpose: attend luncheon at which employees of the month are honored.

To gain a better appreciation of the job of a director of food and beverage, we should look at an actual job description. Again, recognize that all job descriptions are written as an ideal, and there are day-to-day deviations from that ideal given the unique daily circumstances found in any dynamic lodging property.

DIRECTOR OF FOOD AND BEVERAGE JOB DESCRIPTION

Position: Director of Food and Beverage
Reports to: General Manager

Objectives

1. Meet and exceed guests' needs and expectations by ensuring proper service standards, providing quality food and beverages, and managing all aspects of operations resulting in an increasing guest satisfaction index (GSI) and decreasing guest complaints.
2. Provide all guests with the highest-quality food and beverage experience by working as a team with all food and beverage (F&B) outlets ensuring prompt, courteous, and professional services, resulting in increasing employee morale, decreasing employee turnover rates, and lowering employee service times.
3. Seek profitability in the F&B department by decreasing all costs, maximizing sales in all outlets, achieving budget and profit guidelines, creating promotions, and meeting and/or exceeding long- and short-range goals.

Specific Operations Functions

- Provide the highest quality in food, beverage, and service in all F&B outlets. Includes at least a daily walk-through of all F&B areas.
- Maintain existing programs and develope new programs ensuring the highest qual-

ity of food and service. Consists of daily talks with all staff and managers, reviewing plate-ups in different outlets.
- Maintain a high-quality hotel image through effective housekeeping and sanitation in the F&B operation.
- Maintain physical security of all F&B property and inventories.
- Maintain knowledge of local competition and current industry trends. Includes changing menus based on seasonality, product availability, and input from staff.

Specific Management Functions

- Direct and coordinate the activities of all assigned personnel and departmental responsibilities. Some examples are daily contacts with staff and conducting performance reviews.
- Maximize sales potential through aggressive marketing of each F&B unit. Includes ongoing monitoring of business levels and review of daily performance.
- Achieve budgeted sales and maximum profitability.
- Maintain an appropriate level of community public affairs involvement.
- Maintain fair wage and salary administration in the department in accordance with division policy.

Guest Relations

A major part of my job involves maintaining warm, hospitable guest relations in all guest contact and positive employee relations in a supportive environment. I also try to increase guest satisfaction index scores (our feedback mechanism) and lower guest complaints by ensuring prompt, courteous, and proper service and surveying guest comment cards to correct situations immediately.

It is also important to ensure that my division is operating in compliance with all local, state, and federal laws and government regulations. To assure that our guests will have a quality stay, I am also responsible for communicating effectively within and between departments, ensuring good safety practices of employees, and performing special projects as requested.

In trying to achieve or exceed budgeted sales goals, our division management team constantly seeks ways to operate within budgeted guidelines by maintaining effective controls. Included here is developing and forecasting accurate and aggressive long- and short-range financial objectives and monitoring it through daily, weekly, monthly, quarterly, and annual reviews of our performance.

General Functions

I am also expected to perform special projects as requested and maintain a high level of professional appearance, demeanor, ethics, and image of subordinates and myself. Part of our culture in this hotel concerns professional development of staff associates, and it is among my responsibilities to find ways to provide for this.

As you can see, the job of a hotel food and beverage director requires a high-energy person who loves working with people in a variety of dynamic situations. The ability to lead a group of employees in pursuit of operational goals is paramount. Students should actively seek experiences in their college career that provide opportunity to learn some of the skills mentioned in this article.

6.4   Best Practices in Food and Beverage Management

Judy A. Siguaw and Cathy A. Enz

One critical attribute of successful hotel food and beverage outlets is their ability to appropriately respond to the changing needs of the market while maintaining a profitable operation. Yet few hotel food and beverage outlets excel at this fundamental strategy. Instead, generic restaurants that provide undistinguished menu items and offer guests a poor value-for-money proposition frequently characterize hotel food service. Such hotel restaurants fail to provide menu choices, ambience, or service desired by the dining-out market (let alone their guests), and therefore they frequently operate at a loss. Indeed, some analysts have declared that hotel restaurants by their nature will lose money (Hanson, 1984).

Recently, as part of a large, comprehensive study on best practices in the United States lodging industry conducted by Cornell University's School of Hotel Administration (Dubé et al., 1999), we identified a group of best-practice food and beverage champions that had developed practices to successfully accomplish the strategic charge of profitably meeting customer needs. The champions selected via an intense screening process are the Boulders, the Breakers, Country Inns and Suites, Four Seasons and Regent Hotels and Resorts, the Greenbrier, Hyatt Arlington Hotel, the Pierre, Walt Disney World Resorts and Theme Parks, The Waldorf-Astoria, and Wyndham Hotels and Resorts (see Table 6.1). Through their best practices, this select group demonstrates the capability of executing on the strategic mandate of making money while responding to the needs of their target markets through revitalized food and beverage operations.

TABLE 6.1
Overview of food and beverage best-practice champions

F&B champions	Practice initiated, developed	Measure of success
The Boulders	Food forager to improve quality of restaurant offerings	Increased food quality, decreased food cost, decreased waitstaff turnover, and increased prices, profits, and wait-staff gratuities
The Breakers	Single-theme restaurant concepts	Increased revenues
Country Inns and Suites	Cobranding of hotel and brand-name restaurant	Increased customer satisfaction, reduced hotel capital cost (from not building a hotel restaurant), increased lunch and dinner business
Four Seasons and Regent Hotels and Resorts	Single dining venue with broad cuisine choices (and two dining rooms)	Boosted capture rate of hotel guests; increased local patronage, labor-cost savings
The Greenbrier	Establishing resort as a center for culinary excellence, including a culinary-apprentice program	Maintained occupancy and reputation, retained skilled kitchen staff, increased off-season business
Hyatt Arlington Hotel	Reconceptualization and redesign of dated dining room, sports bar, and lobby lounge	Doubled revenues and cover counts, received rave reviews
The Pierre	Independent consultant made responsible for food purchases (with preferred-vendor program)	Decreased food and kitchen labor costs, reduced number of vendors
The Waldorf-Astoria	Applying revenue-management practices in all F&B outlets (plus staff training)	Doubled cover counts, increased effectiveness of F&B marketing, improved customer satisfaction
Walt Disney World Resorts and Theme Parks	Restaurants designed to provide a "touchable" experience	Achieved high customer satisfaction and return rate
Wyndham Hotels and Resorts	Upgrade of organization's food and beverage culture	Achieved higher average checks, increased staff earnings and retention, increased total sales, wine sales, and profits

In the following pages we first present the several practices that have been used by our food and beverage champions to provide their outlets with a competitive advantage. We then examine the measures of success and report the advice our champions give others on how to prosper with hotel food and beverage (F&B) service.

THE BEST PRACTICES

The best practices adopted by our champions can be broadly categorized into three areas.

One group stresses providing a high-quality F&B product to their guests (comprising practices by the Boulders, Country Inns and Suites, Four Seasons and Regent Hotels and Resorts, the Greenbrier, and Wyndham Hotels and Resorts). A second group emphasizes the elements of restaurant concept and design in their best practices (namely, the Breakers Hotel, Hyatt Arlington Hotel, and Walt Disney World Resorts and Theme Parks). Finally, the Pierre's and the Waldorf-Astoria's best practices focused primarily on controlling costs and generating additional revenue (see Table 6.2).

TABLE 6.2
Food and beverage best-practices cases, descriptions, implementation, contact people

F&B champion, Title of case	Description of case	Method of Implementation	Contact person
The Boulders *Food Forager to Improve Quality in F&B*	Created position of food forager to obtain the best fresh products, allowing creativity in the kitchen.	Forager first focused on buying the highest-quality produce only within the state of Arizona, where the resort is located. Later, the forager broadened the search and expanded the number of items sought. Forager hot line keeps all F&B outlets apprised of incoming supplies. Menus are restructured around the products the forager finds.	Gray Ferguson, *food and beverage director* 602-488-9009 Fax: 602-595-4664
The Breakers *Annual Food and Beverage Staff Reorganization and Single-theme Restaurant Concepts*	Replaced formal-dining and casual-dining restaurants and bars with single-theme outlets to give the guest the choice of the cuisine desired rather that the choice dictated by guest attire.	Transformed old-fashioned formal dining room into a modern, Florentine restaurant; casual restaurant into a top-caliber steak house; main bar into an ocean-side restaurant; and a Victorian restaurant into a southern Italian pasta house; plus opened a French Riviera-style restaurant.	Joanne Schultz, *director of food and beverage* 561-659-8434 Fax: 561-659-8452
Country Inns and Suites *Successful Cobranding with Established Restaurant Concepts*	Developed cobranding strategy to locate Country Inns and Suites adjacent to (co-owned) T.G.I. Friday's or Italiani's.	Seeks an "A" location that provides visibility, convenience, high traffic count, and proximity to dense residential areas for the restaurant. Positions restaurant at forefront of property.	Paul Kirwin, *president* 612-212-1326 Fax: 612-212-1338
Four Seasons and Regent *Informal Dining Venue and Alternative Cuisine*	Uses only one F&B outlet with two dining rooms. Provides cuisine choices of Alternative Cuisine, home-style, and vegetarian options.	Single outlet allows for a focused approach for improving food quality and presentation, grasp of small details, and delivering of higher service levels due to small, qualified staff. Alternative Cuisine was developed in response to a need for healthier items, home-style cuisine was added for frequent travelers who were tired of traditional restaurant food, and vegetarian was added due to increased trend of vegetarianism among guests.	Alfons Konrad, *senior vice president, food and beverage* 416-441-4306 Fax: 416-441-4381
The Greenbrier *Programs Establishing the Resort as a Center for Culinary Excellence*	Instituting a formal culinary apprentice program, a culinary school for guests, conferences and seminars with food critics and writers, and a high school culinary-training program. Also publishes *The Greenbrier Cookbook* and sends newsletters to 600,000 guests.	Established relationships with principal culinary schools in the United States. Opened formal, three-year apprentice program to graduates of two-year culinary schools or individuals with equivalent experience. Successful applicants work in all areas of the hotel's kitchens and attend formal classes. Promises permanent employment to applicants from local high school.	Rod Stoner, *vice president of food and beverage* 304-536-1110 Fax: 304-536-7860

(continued on next page)

TABLE 6.2 (concluded)

F&B champion, Title of case	Description of case	Method of Implementation	Contact person
Hyatt Arlington Hotel *Redesigning and Revitalizing a Food and Beverage Outlet*	Dated dining room, sports bar, and lobby lounge were reconceptualized into Mediterranean-cuisine restaurant.	Comprehensive research and analysis indicated likely success of a fusion of contemporary and Mediterranean themes. Floor-to-ceiling windows replaced one side of building, and martini bar complemented redesigned restaurant.	George Vizer, *general manager* 703-525-1234 Fax: 703-875-3298
The Pierre *F&B Cost-Plus Purchasing Agreements*	Has given financial responsibility for food purchasing to an independent consultant.	The consultant and executive chef write specifications for food products; consultant negotiates contracts with a single vendor in each food category on a percentage markup basis. Consultant audits the vendors' books annually.	Franz Klampfer, *executive chef* 212-838-2000 Fax: 212-826-0319
The Waldorf-Astoria *Revenue Maximization for the Food and Beverage Department*	Instituted revenue management for all food and beverage outlets, scheduled staff more efficiently, and repositioned outlets to attract non-hotel markets.	Each unit developed a plan to increase revenue and profitability, with a focus on reducing labor costs. Matched staffing levels with expected volume of business. Trained line staff to ensure the highest level of service.	Christophe Le Chatton, *director of food and beverage* 212-355-3000, ext. 4804 Fax: 212-872-7272
Walt Disney World *Providing a "Touchable" Dining Experience*	A "touchable" dining experience is provided via the atmosphere and the food to transport guests to another setting, another country, or another culture while they dine.	Theme restaurants are designed to be as authentic as possible in the decor, menu, beverages, and service. Line-level employees are empowered to make decisions with respect to service recovery.	Dieter Hannig, *vice president of food and beverage* 407-566-5800 Fax: 407-560-9131
Wyndham *An Integrated Approach to Food and Beverage*	Created "Best of Class" program to upgrade the food and beverage culture.	Reengineered menus and recipes; reconceptualized restaurants; modified dining rooms and introduced exhibition kitchens; upgraded tabletops and uniforms, and china, glass, silver, and specialty merchandise; developed seasonal F&B festivals and promotions; promoted F&B products within the hotels; recruited culinary talent; obtained unique product from vendors; implemented wine-by-the-glass program; developed server-training program emphasizing product knowledge and upselling; implemented wait-staff incentive programs; and reinvented room service standard operating procedures.	Patrick Colombo, *vice president of food and beverage concepts* 214-863-1000 Fax: 214-863-1665

Note: The case titles correspond to the cases written on each champion in: Laurette Dubé, Cathy A. Enz, Leo M. Renaghan, and Judy A. Siguaw, *American Lodging Excellence: The Key to Best Practices in the U.S. Lodging Industry* (Washington, D.C.: American Express and the American Hotel Foundation, 1999).

FOCUS ON PRODUCT QUALITY

The problem for the Boulders was that the variety and quality of the produce it was obtaining were not up to the resort's high standards. As a result, the food and beverage department's culinary passion seemed to be declining along with the quality of the food ingredients. The resort's management responded by creating the position of food forager, who initially focused on buying high-quality produce locally (i.e., in Arizona). Later, though, the forager traveled farther afield and took on the additional responsibilities of purchasing spices, shellfish, cheeses, and meats. To keep the kitchen apprised of what items are coming, the forager uses a hot line to report expected delivery dates and expenditures. The Boulders' chefs then adjust menus based on the incoming items. Consequently, the food ingredients are of the highest quality, and the chefs have the chance to experiment with a continuously changing menu.

Also seeking to instill a passion for food and beverage, Wyndham Hotels and Resorts designed its "Best of Class" program, with the overall objective of making Wyndham a leader in food and beverage innovation, quality, and service. The Best of Class was a wide-ranging effort that involved both sides of the house. The chain

1. Reengineered menus and recipes.
2. Reconceptualized its restaurants.
3. Modified dining rooms and introduced display kitchens.
4. Upgraded tabletops, wait-staff uniforms, china, glass, silver, and specialty merchandising pieces.
5. Developed seasonal food festivals and beverage promotions.
6. Promoted F&B products within the hotels.
7. Recruited outstanding culinary talent.
8. Collaborated with food vendors to obtain distinctive products and with wine vendors to upgrade wine lists and conduct tastings.
9. Implemented a wine-by-the-glass program using premium varietals with high brand awareness.
10. Developed a server-training program that emphasizes product knowledge and upselling techniques.
11. Implemented incentive programs designed to motivate servers to become better educated about food and wines being served.
12. Reinvented room service procedures by providing training in proper service etiquette, modifying training videos and manuals, and upgrading equipment.
13. Revised in-house marketing materials, such as menus and in-room directories.

To deliver high-quality food and beverage products to its guests, Country Inns and Suites chose to develop a cobranding strategy with restaurant brands that are co-owned by Carlson but freestanding, primarily T.G.I. Friday's or Italiani's. This practice ensures the guest access to a high-quality, brand-name restaurant on-site, but it eliminates the capital cost of building a generic restaurant in the hotel. While the core concept of locating a limited-service hotel adjacent to a restaurant is not new, Carlson's approach to the strategy is innovative, since it owns all the brands (another brand that expressly pursued a strategy of locating next to restaurants in the 1980s was Days Inns). To implement this cobranding strategy, Carlson seeks a large, "A" location that will support the restaurant, which is built at the forefront of the property for visibility. Both the restaurant and hotel benefit from this arrangement.

The goal of Four Seasons hotels is to be rated as having one of a given city's top three restaurants. To achieve this goal the chain offers a single restaurant in its hotels—but that restaurant has two dining rooms, one more formal and one less formal. Thus, with a single F&B outlet the hotel can offer two dining rooms that differ in design, but that share the same menu, chefs, line cooks, and kitchens.

Compared to having multiple outlets, this approach allows its F&B staff members to provide greater attention to food quality and presentation, to focus on small details, and to deliver higher service levels via a small, highly qualified staff. In response to guests' stated desire for alternatives to a heavy, meat-based cuisine, Four Seasons has broadened its menu choices to include its trademark Alternative Cuisine, comprising a nutritionally balanced menu of alternative meals, vegetarian dishes, and home-style preparations. Alternative Cuisine items are low in fat, cholesterol, sodium, and calories to correspond with guests' greater interest in health and fitness. Similarly, vegetarian recipes have been added to the menu in response to an increased trend of vegetarianism among guests. Home-style recipes, on the other hand, are just what the name implies: they have been developed from the chefs' favorite family recipes. The latter cuisine choice suits travel-weary guests who wish for a home-cooked meal.

The Greenbrier has instituted several practices to establish itself as a center for culinary excellence. The resort had to address two major problems, both of which stemmed from its remote location. First, for a time the resort was having difficulty attracting and retaining experienced culinary personnel. To end a constant cycle of recruiting and training workers and to improve the food product being offered to guests, the Greenbrier established a three-year culinary-apprenticeship program. The resort recruits candidates from principal culinary schools in the United States to complete an apprenticeship in all areas of the kitchens, as well as attend classes. Because the program runs for three years, the apprenticeship has helped to stabilize the kitchen staff. Further stability comes from an agreement with the local high school by which the resort will provide permanent employment to interested students. The second problem is attracting guests during shoulder and off-season times. Continuing with its theme of culinary education, the Greenbrier established cooking classes for guests and promoted symposiums conducted by food critics and writers. The Greenbrier issues a quarterly newsletter to 600,000 guests and has published *The Greenbrier Cookbook* to further identify the resort as a culinary center—and to remain in contact with potential guests.

RESTAURANT DESIGN AND CONCEPTUALIZATION

The common thread of the following cases that feature restaurant redesign is that the existing restaurants were operated in a functionally competent fashion. They had lost their competitive spark, however (or stood in danger of doing so), because of changes in guests' preferences. In response, operators took a lead from freestanding restaurants and focused tightly on customers' current wishes for theme-based casual dining.

The Breakers recognized that the public has long had an aversion to hotel restaurants, which stems from the days when hotel restaurants tried to have some of every variety of food they thought a guest might desire—none of it particularly distinguished and all of it seemingly overpriced. In response to guests' negative feelings about hotel restaurants, many hotels have dropped food service entirely, but this option is not open to a five-star hotel or resort. Instead, the Breakers chose to create its own strong restaurant identities through single-theme outlets that replaced the resort's existing formal- and casual-dining restaurants and bars. The practice not only helped the Breakers change the public perception of hotel restaurants, but it allowed guests to choose their cuisine according to what they wanted to eat, rather than what they wanted to wear. Thus, the resort's old-fashioned formal dining room became a modern, Florentine-style gourmet restaurant. The owners converted the former casual dining room to a top-caliber steak house—with ambience to match. Perhaps most strikingly, the resort converted its main bar and lounge, which had virtually no business during the day, to a beautiful ocean-side seafood restaurant. The former Victorian restaurant became a southern-Italian-style pasta house, and the Beach Club was converted to a French Riviera–style restaurant. Thus, the resort now has five restaurants that feature their own distinctive decor and ambience, without a loss in food quality.

The food and beverage outlets of the Hyatt Arlington Hotel similarly had lost their customer appeal because of their dated concept and design. After the hotel undertook a comprehensive market-research study, the hotel's managers selected a restaurant theme that blends contemporary (postmodern) and Mediterranean concepts. In developing the new theme, the hotel replaced the restaurant's outer wall with floor-to-ceiling windows to transform the previously dark and unimaginative restaurant into a sun-drenched venue splashed with the Mediterranean's vivid colors. To complement the new restaurant, the hotel installed a quintessential martini bar.

Walt Disney World Resorts and Theme Parks (WDW) has long recognized the value of themes to a guest's experience—not only in its parks, but also in its many restaurants. Consequently, WDW set out to create a "touchable" food-service experience for the guest that combines design, decor, ambience, food, service, and entertainment in such a way as to stimulate all of the senses, not just the palate. The idea is to "offer a personal experience which is highly customized, memorable, and judged by our guests to be worth the price," remarked Dieter Hannig, vice-president of food and beverage.

With more than 500 theme food-and-beverage outlets, WDW's managers realized that a restaurant's design is crucial to providing the "touchable" experience for the guest. Each restaurant is designed to be as thematically authentic as possible so that all elements of the physical facility and operations combine to transport the guest to another setting, country, or culture. The dining adventure is intended to produce the feelings, tastes, sounds, and excitement the guest would experience at the actual locale being replicated. Access to the restaurants is designed to be easy and uncomplicated. Accordingly, many restaurants are freestanding so that guests do not have to walk into hotel lobbies or down corridors. Further, line-level employees are empowered to make decisions to improve service recovery and ensure a great dining experience for the guest.

CONTROLLING COSTS

Our last two champions focused on costs and revenues in the food and beverage arena. The Pierre focused on upgrading its restaurant's purchasing function—that is, setting specifications, selecting vendors, obtaining best prices, and monitoring receiving. However, the Pierre's management was concerned that controlling purchasing activities would divert the executive chef's attention from the kitchen's culinary creations. To allow the executive chef to focus on the menu, the hotel delegated financial responsibility for food purchasing to an independent consultant, who worked with the chefs to develop specifications for all food products. The consultant analyzes available foodstuffs and may recommend changing specifications if a less expensive item can be substituted without compromising quality or if off-site preparation would be equally good but less expensive than preparing the food item on-site. The consultant also trained kitchen employees to adhere to strict receiving standards. Most important to cost control, the consultant negotiated contracts with each vendor specifying that the vendor would earn a given percentage profit over its cost. (Some existing vendors may have blanched at this proposal, but most signed on to keep the hotel's business.) To ensure that costs are in line and that vendors are fulfilling their agreements, the consultant regularly audits inventory and cost lists from each vendor and annually audits the vendors' books to verify that the vendors are accurately stating the cost of each item.

The Waldorf-Astoria's management also believed that the revenue potential of the hotel's food service operations was not being achieved, but they looked beyond cost controls. Instead, the hotel took several steps to boost F&B revenue—instituting a revenue-management program, implementing cost-cutting measures, training chefs to schedule employees more efficiently, and repositioning F&B outlets to attract guests from outside the hotel. The hotel created a marketing position to coordinate the marketing efforts of all food and beverage units and to help implement revenue-maximization efforts. Service-recovery systems were improved. The hotel trained line employees on wines to improve their efforts in selling and serving wines. A new restaurant reservations system was introduced to improve dining room use, cut telephone use in restaurants, and improve communication with guests. Lastly, a dining-out program, which allowed servers and kitchen employees to dine in various Waldorf-Astoria restaurants, generated many ideas for improvement and created an increased awareness of food and service quality.

SUCCESS OF THE PRACTICES

The success of these practices can be gauged by various indices, depending on the practice. The food forager program at the Boulders, for instance, improved the quality of the food and lowered food costs. With new and interesting foodstuffs, the chefs have developed distinctive menus that allowed price increases—boosting average checks and profits. As a result of the increased average check, waitstaff gratuities are higher and employee turnover has been reduced. The resort also implemented menu meetings in which chefs explain their creations to servers. Chefs are

once again passionate about their creations, and the meetings have created a greater rapport between the front and back of the house.

Wyndham's "Best of Class" program also re-energized the chain's F&B culture—resulting in a 15 percent increase in total sales and a 40 percent increase in wine sales. Since costs were controlled as part of the program, the hotels enjoy a 55 percent profit flow-through on the newly generated revenue. As at the Boulders, Wyndham's higher average checks have increased staff earnings and improved retention. In addition, the promotion of high-quality food has upgraded the chain's overall image.

At the Breakers the new theme restaurants have increased F&B revenue by 70 percent over the last four years, with much of the growth being fueled by the substantial amount of local business attracted by the new outlets. Likewise, the Hyatt Arlington Hotel has doubled cover counts and revenues since its restaurant renovation, and the restaurant receives rave reviews.

One of many reasons that guests choose to stay at the Greenbrier is its excellent culinary reputation. Thus, its reputation as a center for culinary excellence plays an important role in maintaining guest room occupancy. The ability of Walt Disney World Resorts and Theme Parks restaurants to provide a "touchable" dining experience contributes significantly to WDW's profitability. Furthermore, both the number of return guests and percentage of satisfied customers are high—and several WDW restaurants have won awards in recent years (see "Walt Disney World's F&B Awards: A Sampling").

The Country Inns and Suites cobranding strategy has been a winning situation both for the hotels and for guests. For guests, having a popular brand-name restaurant adjacent to the hotel ensures that their dining needs will be satisfied. For the restaurant, the hotel guests account for 15 to 20 percent of its business. For the hotel, the proximity of a name-brand restaurant is an amenity that can encourage guests to book a room.

WALT DISNEY WORLD'S F&B AWARDS: A SAMPLING

Since 1989 Walt Disney World properties have earned more than 100 food and beverage awards. Listed below is a representative sample of those honors.

- "Award of Excellence" (1999), from *Wine Spectator* magazine, awarded to Victoria & Albert's.
- "Best Wine and Spirits Restaurant of the Year" (1999), from *Santé* magazine, awarded to California Grill.
- One of the "Top Ten Sports Bars in the Country" (1998), from *USA Today*, and one of the "Top Five Sports Bars in the Country" (1998), from *Men's Health*, both honors awarded to ESPN Club.
- "Best Kid's Menu" (1998, Readers' Choice Foodie Awards), from *Orlando Sentinel*, awarded to Chef Mickey's.

- Among the "Best New Restaurants" (1998), from *Esquire*, awarded to Citricos.
- "Best Cover" (1998), from *Restaurant Forum*, awarded to Flying Fish Cafe.
- "Restaurant Wine Award" (1995), from *Wine Enthusiast*, awarded to Artist Point.
- "Most Imaginative" (1993), from the National Restaurant Association, awarded to Grand Floridian Café.
- "America's Best Bar Menu" (1993), from *Cheers* magazine, awarded to Crew's Cup Lounge.
- "Top of the Table" (1991, first place), from *Restaurant Hospitality* magazine, one each awarded to Beaches and Cream Soda Shop and the Yacht Club Galley.

By using an independent consultant to negotiate with vendors and to monitor the F&B purchasing function, the Pierre was able to reduce food costs by approximately 5 percent and kitchen labor costs by 2 percent. In addition, the number of vendors used has decreased, resulting in greater efficiency for the hotel. Finally, the Waldorf-Astoria's revenue-maximization strategy improved cover counts by a staggering 100 percent, while increasing wine sales and guest satisfaction.

INSIGHTS

Our food and beverage champions offer the following advice and observations to managers seeking to implement similar programs:

1. The foundation for successful implementation is meeting challenges with enthusiasm and passion.
2. Some practices, such as food purchasing by an independent consultant, may not be warmly received by staff or vendors, but the commitment of upper management and a demonstration of benefits will help gain acceptance.
3. Those practices that require constant adaptation (like the food forager) will not work in a rigidly structured organization.
4. Cobranding strategies are suitable only when the hotels are partnered with restaurants that are targeting the same market segment.
5. Hotel F&B outlets' development must incorporate the guest's total experience (and focus on competing with freestanding restaurants).
6. Resources must be focused on a relentless commitment to food and beverage consistency, even when business is slow.

PROFITABLE AND VITAL

Contrary to much conventional wisdom, the experience of these F&B champions shows that hotel restaurants not only can turn a profit, but can contribute greatly to the hotel's overall competitive position. We note, however, that virtually all the F&B champions are operating in the upscale, deluxe, and resort segments of the lodging industry. While many hotel restaurants at all levels struggle to turn a profit, the actions of our champions indicate that focusing on guests' needs can radically reverse the downward trend of hotel restaurants. As Rod Stoner, vice president of food and beverage at the Greenbrier, pointed out, managers must stay abreast of industry trends, study the programs of other properties, and

seek distinctive ideas for adaptation to their own hotels. This overview of best practices in food and beverage champions provides a starting point for what Stoner suggests. We hope that those managers seeking to revitalize or maximize the revenue potentials of their F&B operations will carefully examine the practices discussed here and will continue their progress by also investigating the practices of other properties and other industries. As a result, forward-thinking managers will be able to identify those best practices that will serve as the catalyst for improving customer satisfaction and financial performance.

6.5   Strategic Alliances between Hotels and Restaurants

Robert W. Strate and Clinton L. Rappole

Over the years hotel restaurants have often been managed as a secondary function of the hotel—that is, as a costly amenity rather than a revenue center. In part because of the high cost structure of hotel restaurants, which means high prices relative to other restaurants, they developed among potential customers a reputation for being a poor value, offering indifferent service and inferior food. Today, however, many hotel companies are rethinking how to integrate food and beverage (F&B) services into lodging facilities. In the process of doing so, hotel owners and operators are asking at least four key questions about their property-level F&B service.

- What are the hotel customers' food and beverage needs and expectations?
- Which food and beverage concept best aligns with the positioning of the hotel?
- Would converting the hotel's restaurant to a brand-name restaurant concept improve the property's overall bottom line?
- Would turning to a brand-name F&B operation give the property a competitive edge?

Two results of owners' and operators' new focus on hotel food service are that (1) innovative hotel F&B concepts are being created, and (2) strategic alliances are being established between well-known brand-name hotel and restaurant companies (see the sidebar "Product Branding).

The primary focus of this article is to answer the four questions stated above and provide the basic decision-making framework for matching the correct F&B concept to the target market for which the hotel has been positioned. We will identify key criteria for establishing a seamless partnership between the hotel and the restaurant. The results of such a marriage should be an improved property image overall, enhanced customer value, increased revenues, and a competitive edge. The following four main topics will be addressed:

- The value of a brand-name partner.
- Existing hotel-and-restaurant alliances.
- A description of Bristol Hotel Company's alliance with Good Eats Grill (including critical-decision elements).
- Future trends.

PRODUCT BRANDING

Product branding refers to establishing a well-known name for a given product or service whereby the particular product or service and its attributes are highly recognizable and easily recalled by consumers. The basic concept behind such so-called branding is to establish a standard on which consumers may rely to predict value (e.g., price, quality, convenience). Within the hotel industry a multitiered branding strategy has evolved among lodging companies. The following table illustrates how some hotel brands have become associated with different tiers. Note that some companies have developed products for more than one tier.

Economy, Limited Service	Middle Market	Luxury, First Class	All Suites
• Motel 6	• Holiday Inn	• Four Seasons	• Marriott Suites
• Days Inn	• Ramada Inn	• Ritz-Carlton	• Embassy Suites
• La Quinta	• Sheraton	• Marriott Marquis	• Residence Inns
• Hampton Inn	• Hilton	• Beverly Hilton	• Homewood Suites
• Travelodge	• Courtyard by Marriott	• Hyatt	• Bristol Suites
• Sleep Inn	• Radisson	• Westin	• Clarion Suites
			• Guest Quarters

Source: Ron N. Nykiel, "Corporate Strategy within the Hospitality Industry," in *The Complete Travel Marketing Handbook,* ed. Andrew Vladimir (Lincolnwood, IL: NTC Business Books, 1988).

An example of the multiple-branding strategy can be illustrated by examining the different hotel brands of the Marriott Corporation. Marriott has developed Marriott Hotels, Marriott Resorts, Marriott Marquis, Courtyard by Marriott, Marriott Suites, Residence Inns, and Embassy Suites.

A somewhat similar branding strategy also exists in the restaurant industry, as shown in the following chart.

Quick Service	Casual, Family	Upscale	Theme
• McDonald's	• Red Lobster	• Ruth's Chris Steakhouse	• Planet Hollywood
• Taco Bell	• T.G.I. Friday's	• Trader Vic's	• Hard Rock Café
• Pizza Hut	• Damon's	• Del Frisco's	• Benihana
• Domino's	• Good Eats Grill	• Bice Ristorante	• Lettuce Entertain You
• KFC	• Chili's	• Palm Restaurant	• Front Row Sports Grille
• Church's	• Olive Garden	• NY Restaurant Group (Mrs. Parks)	• Country Kitchen

The Country Hospitality Partnership, a subsidiary of Carlson Hospitality Worldwide, is an example of a restaurant company with a multitier branding strategy. The Country Hospitality Partnership restaurants include Country Kitchen (252 restaurants), T.G.I. Friday's (365 restaurants), Italiani's (14 restaurants), and Front Row Sports Grille (3 restaurants). Additionally, Carlson provides a good example of a hotel company that owns and has vertically integrated both the hotel and the restaurant product into one corporation. Carlson Companies, Inc., owns both Radisson Hotels Worldwide and Country Hospitality Partnership. The T.G.I. Friday's concept is being integrated into many Radisson Hotels (see: Laura Koss-Feder, "Radisson Seeks Marketing Advantages," *Hotel & Motel Management*[1], pp. 3, 43; Ron Ruggles, "T.G.I. Friday's Cruises into Summer," *Nation's Restaurant News,* June 1996, pp. 14, 43; and Lawrence White, "Growth Meister," *Lodging,* September 1996, pp. 52–58).

The Marriott Corporation is another example of a hospitality company that owns and integrated its own restaurant brands into its hotels. The key point is that the brand is recognizable and this recognition equates to reliable value from the customer's perspective. This enhanced customer perception can be used by a firm to gain a competitive edge and, in turn, increase revenues and profits for the company.

ALLIANCES

Developing alliances between brand-name hotel and restaurant companies is not a new business strategy, but it does seem that this approach is currently being used more frequently than ever to help companies maximize their profit potential (*Lodging,* September 1996). There are at least five reasons for this. An alliance may

1. Create financial benefits.
2. Provide customers with greater value.
3. Improve a property's overall image.
4. Strengthen an operation's competitive position.
5. Create operational advantages.

One of the first branded restaurant concepts to operate in hotels was probably Trader Vic's, founded by Victor Bergen in 1937. By 1949 Western Hotels (which became Westin) integrated Trader Vic's into 13 hotel-based restaurants in nine countries (Withiam, 1995, "Trader Vic's," p. 14). Other chains also hosted the restaurants, and today, 60 years later, Trader Vic's still operates in such hotels as the Beverly Hilton, the Palmer House (Chicago), the Marriott Royal Garden Riverside (Bangkok), and the New Otani properties in Tokyo and Singapore. Ruth's Chris Steak Houses is another example of a popular restaurant brand operating successfully in unison with hotels, including properties operated by Hilton, Marriott, Holiday Inn, and Westin.

Despite the evidence of successful alliances between brand-name hotel and restaurant companies, most hotel companies manage their own food and beverage services, including those that also host Trader Vic's. In part that approach reflects the long industry tradition of offering travelers both food and lodging. The Marriott Corporation is a good example of a hotel company that has used this strategy of going it alone. John Randall, Marriott senior director of food and beverage concepts, states that it is Marriott's primary strategy to "completely manage our own F&B services to provide food, service, and quality consistency from property to property" (Hensdill, 1996).

The strategy of developing their own F&B concepts has not been successful for all hotel companies. This is evident from the frequent "reconcepting" found among hotel restaurants. A hotel might run a lounge one year, convert it into a brasserie the next year, and later decide to make it a grill. The end result is inconsistency in F&B service and quality, and therefore low sales and profits (Parseghian, 1996). Several factors may contribute to a general manager's believing that she or he can operate the hotel's restaurant services better than a branded restaurant company, not the least of which may be a sense of self-assurance. Some hotel general managers want to prove that they can provide a fine-dining experience whether or not a market actually exists. Others say it is because some hotel F&B operations continue to try to be all things to all people rather than providing a product that is affordable and matches customer expectations (Wolff, 1995, p. 24). Moreover, hotel restaurants in general have a high cost structure relative to the freestanding F&B operation down the street. Hotel restaurants have to contribute to the overall property's expenses while the restaurant next door has little capital expense and is probably just leasing square footage.

A current trend among hotels that have reevaluated their F&B operations is to replace the formal fine-dining, white-tablecloth concept with a more casual and relaxed dining experience (Allen, 1996; Liberson, 1996). Another trend indicates that more and more hotel companies are looking to establish strategic alliances with brand-name restaurant companies. Doing this has allowed hotel companies to focus on managing the hotel itself. Listed in Table 6.3 are some examples of strategic alliances between hotel and restaurant companies. These examples illustrate that some of the largest hotel companies have already established strategic alliances with major restaurant chains.

TABLE 6.3
Hotel and restaurant-company strategic alliances

Hotel Companies	Restaurant Companies
Holiday Inn Worldwide	Damon's, Denny's, Ruth's Chris Steakhouse, T.G.I. Friday's, Convenience Courts (Mrs. Fields, Little Caesars, Blimpies, Taco John's, Sara Lee)
Doubletree Hotel Corporation	New York Restaurant Group (Park Avenue Café, Mrs. Parks Café)
Marriott Hotels	Ruth's Chris Steak House, Studebakers, Benihana, Trader Vic's, Pizza Hut
Hilton Hotels	Trader Vic's, Benihana, Ruth's Chris Steakhouse, Damon's
Four Seasons	Bice Ristorante
Choice Hotels	Picks Food Courts, Pizza Hut
Promus Corporation	Grace Services, T.G.I. Friday's, Olive Garden, Pizza Hut
Radisson Hospitality Worldwide*	Carlson Hospitality* (T.G.I. Friday's, Country Kitchen), Damon's

*The relationship between Radisson Hospitality Worldwide and Carlson Hospitality is not an alliance per se but rather an example of a hotel company that owns and has vertically integrated both its lodging and food service products into one corporation.

Sources. See: "Restaurant Chains Partner with Hotels to Satisfy Different Needs, Tastes," *Lodging*, September 1995, pp. 1, 8–9; "Holiday Inn Offers Assorted Food Options with New Quick Food Concept," *Hotel Business*, June 1996, p. 9; "Holiday Inn Offers Convenience Court Concept," *Nation's Restaurant News*, May 1996, p. 208; Frank H. Andorka, "High Recognition Restaurants," *Hotel & Motel Management*, November 1995, pp. 43–44; Cherie Hensdill, "Partnerships in Dining," *Hotels*, February 1996, pp. 57–60; Judy Liberson, "A Working Marriage," *Lodging*, February 1996, pp. 63–66; and Madelin Wexler, "Partnerships That Pay Off," *Hotels*, May 1995, pp. 47–50.

BRISTOL AND GOOD EATS GRILL

To comprehend fully the rationale and advantages of a hotel's decision to turn to a brand-name restaurant for the hotel's food service, we analyzed the Bristol Hotel Company's decision to match two of their hotels with Good Eats Grill (Witham, 1995, "Trader Vic's," p. 13). Before creating the alliance with Good Eats Grill, the Bristol Hotel Company's primary F&B strategy was to use its own internally developed restaurant brands. This is a strategy that has worked well for Bristol—for example, eight outlets produced 32.4 percent F&B profit margins in 1995, and 20 out of 22 Bristol hotel-restaurants continue to use their own internally developed restaurant brands.

Despite the success of Bristol's own F&B operations, the firm decided to link two of its properties (Holiday Inns in Jackson, Mississippi, and Houston, Texas) with a franchised restaurant brand called Good Eats Grill—a concept developed by Gene Street, who also developed the Black-eyed Pea and Dixie House restaurant brands. We wondered why Bristol deviated from its successful formula, and so we decided to investigate why the Bristol Hotel Company elected to team with Good Eats Grill. We narrowed our focus and analysis even further by evaluating just the Houston property, using interviews of the principals involved.

We asked executives from both Bristol and Good Eats Grill 70 questions in all, conducted site visits, and found additional research information in various hospitality periodicals. Additionally, Mike Feldott, of HRC Consultants, L.C., was a key adviser on restaurant brands and operations for hotels.

Bristol Hotel Company

The Bristol Hotel Company is a 39-property chain with corporate headquarters in Dallas, Texas. In January 1995 Bristol acquired a Memphis-based hotel company, United Inns, Inc., that had 26 hotels based in six states. By the end of 1995 Bristol Hotel Company had grown from 8 to 38 properties with more than 10,000 rooms, which generated $192 million in total revenues.* The revenues predicted for 1996 are around $250 million. The following key indices summarize Bristol Hotel Company's performance in 1995:

- Average occupancy: 64.10%.
- Average daily room rate: $62.67.
- RevPAR: $40.20.
- Gross operating margin: 29.62%.
- Rooms margin: 71.61%.
- Food and beverage margin: 24.84%.

Bristol primarily uses an owner-operator strategy versus management contracts in managing its hotels. As of the time of our study it owned 36 of its properties (93 percent) and managed the other three properties. Bristol's primary focus was in the full-service segment, with 35 full-service properties (89 percent) and only four limited-service properties.

Its primary target market is the mid- to upper-level corporate traveler (the source of 90 percent of the company's revenues). It also does substantial group-meeting business. Bristol is anticipating that full-service hotels will play an important role in meeting the future lodging and business demand of those two market segments. John Beckert, the chief operating officer (COO) of Bristol, considers the "full-service segment as a segment that has been somewhat abandoned, but Bristol considers the segment to be 'solid' as far as de-

mand (anticipate 6 to 10 percent increase in demand) and a segment that allows for greater pricing power."

Bristol's overall strategy is to provide customers with a first-class-hotel experience—but without being stuffy—and extraordinary overall value (price and quality). While those goals are not unusual among hotel companies, Bristol has distinguished itself in several ways. First, it has an excellent track record established in part by achieving strong operating and financial results during the industry's recent recession. Second, it maintains a distinct corporate culture and management style that translates into low executive-management turnover. Third, its centralized management structure allows managers to focus on the quality of a guest's stay as the number one priority.

Throughout our discussion we will analyze Bristol's six operating strategies, listed in Table 6.4. However, our emphasis will be on understanding why Bristol Hotel Company aligns its F&B services within their hotels in a certain fashion and how it reaches the decision to do so one way instead of another.

Among its 39 hotels Bristol has 22 hotel restaurant outlets and uses three internally developed restaurant brands in 20 of those properties, as shown in Table 6.5. In addition to Bristol's own restaurant concepts and the two franchised Good Eats Grills previously mentioned, Bristol executives are considering leasing space to a branded restaurant in two of their limited-service properties.

Good Eats Grill

The Good Eats Grill Company is a privately held firm that currently has 17 restaurant outlets, of which 16 are located in Texas and another in Mississippi. Four of the seventeen restaurant outlets are franchised, while the others are owned and operated by the company founder, owner, and president, Gene Street. Bristol Hotel Company is the only ho-

---

*Many of the properties acquired in 1995 required renovation and many of those rooms were out of order, which negatively affected year-end 1995 financial numbers.

TABLE 6.4
Bristol Hotel Company operating strategies

Strategies	Implementation
Maintain a unique management culture	Entrepreneurial and team-oriented
Maintain control over hotel operations	Owner-operator focus
Assets in select geographic markets	28 properties located in Atlanta, Dallas, and Houston (fast-growing markets)
Direct sales and marketing	Focus on local market
Flexible use of brand names	*Operate under its own brand names:* Harvey Hotels, Bristol Suites, Harvey Suites *Operate under national franchise brands:* Holiday Inn, Marriott, Promus properties, Hospitality Franchise Systems brands
Emphasis on food and beverage services	Bristol's F&B profit margins (32 percent original eight and 25 percent overall) are above December 1994 national industry levels of 17.1 percent.

Source: Bristol Hotel Company 1995 Annual Report

TABLE 6.5
Bristol's Own Restaurant Brands

Brand	Concept
Scoops Diner (four units)	• Theme restaurant with a 1950s concept • Comfortable and casual
Remmington's (four units)	• Eclectic • More upscale than a Scoops • Nice hotel coffee shop
Bristol Bar and Grill (twelve units)	• Designed as a hotel restaurant • Flexible in handling fluctuations in sales volume • Self-serve • Friendly and fast

tel company that is currently allied with Good Eats Grill. In 1995 Good Eats Grill's annual revenues were $23 million. Good Eats Grill is a casual, family restaurant stressing food quality and low price. A Good Eats Grill can seat 150 to 200 diners, serves lunch and dinner, has a comfortable decor and casual atmosphere, and offers excellent food quality at an afford-able price. Good Eats Grill's best-selling entrées are its chicken-fried steak and vegetable plate. Table 6.6 summarizes the Good Eats Grill menu. The approximate square footage required for a Good Eats Grill is 4000 to 6500 square feet (includes both front and back of the house). The following key indices summarize Good Eats Grill's 1995 performance:

- Total revenues: $23 million.
- Food-revenue percentage: 94%.
- Beverage-revenue percentage: 6%.
- Overall F&B cost percentage: 28.5%.
- Food-cost percentage: 29%.
- Beverage-cost percentage: 22%.
- Average check: $8.12.
- Covers/year (approx.): 2.8 million.

At the time of this writing, Good Eats Grill was doing business with no other hotel company besides the Bristol Hotel Company. We wondered why, and asked key people within the Good Eats Grill management why they had agreed to team with Bristol Hotels. The key factors from the perspective of those managers were:

- The companies share similar proactive, team-oriented management styles.
- The firms' corporate cultures blend well.
- The projects were financially feasible.
- Bristol was looking for exactly the product that Good Eats Grill could deliver (i.e., customer value in terms of quality and price).
- Both companies wanted the deal to happen.

Good Eats Grill executives believe more hotel-and-restaurant alliances are imminent and such deals represent a trend that is here to stay. Good Eats Grill's management expects to do more restaurant-franchise deals with hotel companies as doing so offers a viable option for expanding quickly without intensive capital requirements.

Property Location

For our study we selected the Holiday Inn Intercontinental, a Bristol Hotel Company property located near the Houston Intercontinental Airport. From the outside, the Good Eats Grill appears as if it is a freestanding restaurant, but in reality the restaurant is as much a part of the hotel as the lobby is.

This particular Holiday Inn, a 400-room property opened in 1971, recently underwent $11.5 million in renovations (of which some $1.5 million was for the conversion of the previous restaurant into a Good Eats Grill). This hotel generates approximately $7.5 million in room revenues, operates at an 85 percent occupancy level, and has an average daily rate of $60 and RevPAR of $48. Restaurant revenues are targeted to be approximately $1.5 million; food profit, 25 percent; beverage profit, 55 to 60 percent; food cost, 28 to 29 percent; and beverage cost, 20 to 22 percent.

TABLE 6.6
Good Eats Grill menu

	Menu items	Price range	Comments
Appetizers	6	$1.99–$4.99	
Soups and salads	5	$2.19–$5.79	
Burgers and sandwiches	7	$5.29–$6.29	
Entrées	20	$5.99–$8.99	Steaks, pork chops, chicken, pasta, grilled fish Served with garden-fresh vegetables Add salad for 99 cents
Desserts	5	$2.49–$2.99	
Beverages (alcoholic and nonalcoholic)			Full service

Source: "Ride the Branding Wave," *Lodging*, September 1996, pp. 62–73.

Property Selection

During 1995, the year Bristol acquired the United Inns properties, Bristol Hotel Company executives evaluated all of their hotel-restaurant outlets and made decisions as to which restaurant concept best supported the targeted positioning of each individual hotel. Among Bristol's development strategies was a decision to use the Good Eats Grill concept in two of its properties. Just as we asked the Good Eats Grill executives "Why Bristol?", we asked Bristol executives "Why the decision to go with Good Eats Grill versus going with proven internally developed restaurant brands or renovating the existing restaurant?" The key element in Bristol's selection of Good Eats Grill for two new locations was in Bristol's overall assessment of which restaurant concept would be the best match for the repositioning strategies for those specific hotels.

At the Houston Holiday Inn Intercontinental, the existing restaurant, the Grand Cargo Café, was a typical hotel restaurant with a coffee-shop feel. The Grand Cargo Café had average food quality and service, low profit margins (5 percent), low sales volume, high employee turnover, little name recognition, and a below-average reputation among those customers familiar with the operation. In short, the Grand Cargo Café was a costly amenity for the hotel's previous owners, and Bristol executives quickly determined that a change was required.

Bristol first looked at the possibility of replacing the Grand Cargo Café with one of Bristol's own internally developed F&B concepts (i.e., Bristol Bar and Grill, Scoops Diner, or Remmington's). After some consideration it was determined that Bristol's own concepts did not adequately complement the property's repositioning strategy. The Bristol Bar and Grill is a quick-and-friendly self-serve concept that is primarily focused on serving hotel guests (i.e., banquet guests). Such a food-service arrangement would be inappropriate for the repositioned Holiday Inn Intercontinental, which has a large sales-volume potential

comprising both walk-in diners (85 percent of the lunch trade and 40 percent for dinner) and overnight guests (15 percent at lunch and 60 percent at dinner).

Another objective in replacing the Grand Cargo Café was to change dramatically the perceived atmosphere of the outlet from that of a coffee shop to a substantial restaurant. Bristol's Remmington's concept, also reminiscent of a coffee shop but more upscale than Grand Cargo Café in price and quality, was not considered sufficiently different to achieve that goal. Moreover, Remmington's did not completely match the "casual and comfortable" atmosphere desired to complement the overall hotel repositioning strategy.

Bristol's Scoops Diner concept offered a close match to Bristol's goal of providing the customer with good overall value in a casual and comfortable atmosphere. Scoop's 1950s-theme concept, however, was developed primarily for walk-in diners rather than a hotel's overnight and meeting guests. Like Remmington's, then, the Scoops concept did not exactly fit the needs of the property's new target markets.

While hotel guests were to be a prime customer base for the Intercontinental's restaurant, the property was seen to also offer great opportunity for walk-in business.* With that in mind, Bristol executives realized that the Scoops and Remmington's concepts did not have sufficient preexisting customer brand awareness in Houston to generate substantial walk-in traffic. In the final assessment, then, Bristol purchased the franchise rights to operate a Good Eats Grill in Houston (and at one other location).

---

*Here are some of the key site-specific characteristics of the Holiday Inn Intercontinental that indicated a freestanding restaurant could generate substantial walk-in business: (1) the physical layout of the property—parking, entrance, signs, and size—was considered excellent; (2) the property is located close to Houston International Airport on a major highway; and (3) there was limited restaurant competition in the area despite the potential for customers from local businesses and surrounding hotels (some of which are limited-service properties).

A Good Match

Bristol management considers Good Eats Grill to be a competitive concept that offers a quality product, a casual environment that customers enjoy, a respected and recognizable restaurant name in the Houston area, and proven sales volume. Another key factor mentioned by Bristol executives was that the two organizations "clicked," meaning that the corporate culture of each was well matched with the other. Both have an entrepreneurial base, both are flexible, and both have high-quality standards for a midlevel product at an affordable price. Table 6.7 compares the hotel, restaurant, and combined marketing strategies of the two companies.

Key Positioning Criteria

We found that a critical factor in the selection process of a hotel's F&B brand or concept is to determine the customer perception that you want to create at the property and then select a restaurant theme that complements the overall property's image. Bristol COO Beckert illustrated this by saying, "At Bristol we try to identify uniqueness in our F&B concepts, which then become selling points for the property. The restaurant then goes on a short list that our sales staff use to sell rooms."

The "right" match between the hotel and the restaurant can vary from property to property. At Bristol, all 39 properties were evaluated to determine which F&B concept best fit each property, and only two locations were selected for a Good Eats Grill franchise. As we will point out later, several key factors such as conversion costs and nearby competition must be taken into consideration prior to making the final decision.

Turn Up the Volume

Another element related to positioning is to determine the volume and customer-mix expected. For example, let's review Bristol's existing company-owned restaurant brands: Scoops, Remmington's, and Bristol Bar and Grill. Bristol management will locate a Scoops or a Remmington's in those properties that have above-average hotel volume, and where restaurant-customer volume comprises primarily walk-in diners who are not using the hotel's other services. A Bristol Bar and Grill concept is used when the F&B market is primarily hotel guests and banquet business. The Bristol Bar and Grill is targeted specifically to serve hotel patrons with a quick-serve breakfast, convenient lunch, and buffet-style dinner. The Good Eats Grill concept, on the other hand, generally operates as a freestanding res-

TABLE 6.7
Operating strategies

Hotel	Restaurant	Combined

• Primary market
    —Corporate business travelers
    —Mid- to upper-range travelers
• Secondary market
    —Family travelers
• Brand recognition
• First-class hotel, but not "stuffy"
• Physically competitive
	• Family-style restaurant
	• Excellent food quality
	    —Fresh
	• Value
	• Brand recognition
	• Casual, comfortable decor
		• Appeal to corporate and family travelers
		• Mid- to upper-market value
		• Casual and comfortable
		• Best overall value
		    —Price and quality

taurant, has a proven sales volume ($1.5 to 2 million per year), offers consumer value, and has a comfortable decor that's attractive to both walk-in diners and hotel guests.

During Bristol's examination of its hotel restaurants, it was determined that a Good Eats Grill should be used when (1) it is necessary to reposition the hotel; (2) a great restaurant-volume potential exists; (3) the physical layout and location of the property can sustain a freestanding restaurant; and (4) the market mix comprises both hotel guests and walk-in customers.

Why Houston?

Bristol's management felt that the Houston Holiday Inn Intercontinental needed repositioning and a recognized restaurant brand like Good Eats Grill was essential for any repositioning strategy to work. Good Eats Grill already had two successful freestanding restaurants in the Houston region. Additionally, Good Eats Grill maintained an ongoing investment in local advertising. By contrast, a Remmington's, a Scoops, or even the Grand Cargo Café did not have anywhere near the same level of local brand awareness and consumer acceptance.

The following list summarizes the key factors that Bristol's executives considered when selecting Houston as a location for a franchised Good Eats Grill.

- The property was being repositioned.
- Financial feasibility was evident.
- The property's existing hotel restaurants were producing low revenues.
- The physical layout of the property allowed for conversion.
- Parking, entrances, and signs would be relatively easy to provide.
- The local labor market could support the concept.
- The property was located in a high-traffic, commercial area near the airport.

- Since there was only one freestanding restaurant within a two-mile radius, the potential for non-hotel-guest business was great.

SELECTION PROCESS

A summary of the key advantages and disadvantages to consider when going with a franchised restaurant brand in your hotel are listed below (*Lodging,* 1995), while Figure 6.2 is a flow chart of the basic steps to take when evaluating and choosing which franchise restaurant company to use; also see the sidebar "Critical Elements to Consider."

Advantages include:

- Integral part of repositioning the hotel.
- Potentially increases revenues, occupancy, profits.
- Restaurant franchiser is continually assessing the menu, whereas a hotel's tendency is not to change the menu.
- Franchiser is knowledgeable about the restaurant business.

Disadvantages include:

- Franchise fee.
- Requires a certain level of volume to warrant utilizing a franchise brand.
- High initial investment.
- Brand can lose reputation and recognition, or quality levels could drop during the term of the franchise agreement.
- Room service and banquet service could still require a separate kitchen operation.

As previously noted, Bristol chose the Good Eats Grill concept over other restaurant companies because the Good Eats management was (1) flexible and (2) determined to minimize the bureaucracy to make the deal happen. In today's competitive market, business decisions must be made quickly and accurately or else the window of opportunity may be lost. In this particular example the basic deal was struck after two executive meetings (however, it did take the lawyers a little longer). The rest of the steps in the process caught up with the decisions that were made after those two executive meetings. Such a quick decision was possible because the two companies have similar proactive management styles, the project made financial sense for both companies, the corporate cultures blended well, and the decision makers went with their gut instinct.

FIGURE 6.2
Selection-process flow chart

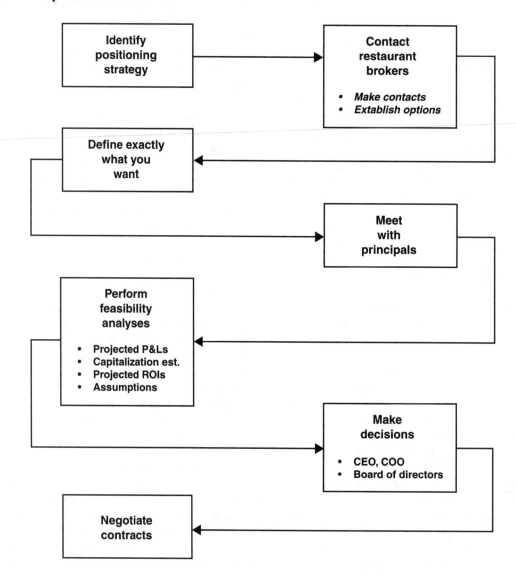

CRITICAL ELEMENTS TO CONSIDER

Summarized below are some of the critical elements to consider when assessing which restaurant-brand concepts will best match a particular hotel property.

1. Determine the desired hotel market position and customer perception you want to create for each property. This includes knowing all about the property's competition, environment, and customers, and involves creating a unique image for your property.
2. Make sure that you objectively assess the revenue and expense potential of each operational option when examining your financial trade-offs. Such options include running your hotel company's own brand, buying and operating a franchised brand, and leasing space to a brand-name restaurant company.
3. Select a restaurant company that has a corporate culture that mirrors your hotel's corporate culture and also shares the same basic operational goals.
4. Evaluate each property on a stand-alone basis using all available facts and data. Avoid making generalizations about what will work for all properties.
5. The key criteria in identifying which properties could benefit most from a brand-name franchise-restaurant concept are:
   1. Desired positioning of the hotel.
   2. Financial trade-offs and feasibility analyses.
   3. Competitive marketing analysis.
   4. Physical layout of the facility (parking, entrances, signs, location of kitchen).
   5. The site location.
   6. The local labor market.
6. The key criteria in selecting a particular restaurant company are:
   1. Similar business goals and corporate culture.
   2. Initial investment cost.
   3. The menu offered.
   4. Ongoing new-menu development.
   5. New recipes on a regular basis.
   6. Cooking specifications.
   7. Franchise fee.
   8. Restaurant decor.
   9. Training support.
   10. Management support.
   11. The ability to handle room service and banquets.
7. View the hotel's restaurant outlet as a selling point that can enhance rooms sales and as a profit center that can be held accountable for achieving established profit.

CONTRACT RELATIONSHIPS

There are four basic types of operational options that can be established between the hotel and the F&B outlet in a hotel. Those four options are (1) internally developed restaurant brand, (2) franchised restaurant brand, (3) straight lease, and (4) management contract. Bristol's first choice (used for 20 of its 22 restaurant outlets) is to use its own internally developed restaurant brands. Bristol believes it has a proven track record in managing F&B operations profitably (*Hotel Business*, 1996).

When Bristol introduced Good Eats Grill into two of its 22 hotels with food service, it showed a willingness to purchase a franchised brand provided Bristol could maintain full control of restaurant operations and products (as long as all franchise agreements were maintained). Currently Bristol is also assessing a leasing arrangement with yet another restaurant company for a couple of Bristol's Fairfield Inn properties. In those cases Bristol managers seem to be indicating that it would be more profitable for them to lease out square footage in the hotels versus operating the F&B outlet themselves.

Key Franchise Elements

Bristol has purchased the franchise rights for its two Good Eats Grill operations. The key elements of the franchise agreement are the menu, recipes, cooking specifications, franchise fee, restaurant decor, music package, training support, and negotiated special provisions (e.g., use of Good Eats Grill recipes for banquets). Basically, Bristol purchased a turnkey operation from Good Eats Grill. Moreover, Good Eats Grill provides pre- and postopening training support, new and updated menu development, and such regional management support as consulting, auditing, and troubleshooting.

In exchange for the franchise and its management services Good Eats Grill receives 3.5 percent of lunch and dinner revenues as a franchise fee.

MARKETING

We have already mentioned how the Bristol sales office uses the company's restaurants as a selling point to assist in booking rooms, meetings, and banquets. In addition there are three other marketing concerns that need to be considered: (1) the competition, (2) customer expectations, and (3) advertising.

Competition

The primary hotel competitors for Bristol's Houston Holiday Inn Intercontinental are a Marriott hotel (569 rooms), a Hyatt hotel (315 rooms), and a Sheraton hotel (450 rooms). As for nearby food service competition, Marriott uses internally developed restaurant brands (Allie's American Grill and CK's) along with a Pizza Hut kiosk, while the Hyatt and Sheraton offer typical hotel restaurants. Additionally, there are some limited-service hotel properties in the area that factor into the secondary-market competitive analysis.

The freestanding restaurant competition in the area is negligible. There is a Kettle Restaurant nearby, but it does not pose a strong business threat to Good Eats Grill as it has a different target market. There is a Bennigan's and T.G.I. Friday's within three miles of the Holiday Inn, but there is no other notable restaurant competition within a two-mile radius of the hotel. As it turns out, the Holiday Inn's Good Eats Grill is popular with Marriott's, Hyatt's, and Sheraton's hotel guests, and also with those hotel guests that are staying at the surrounding limited-service properties. It can be expected, then, that a guest who stays at a hotel other than the Holiday Inn yet eats at the Good Eats Grill may decide to stay at the Holiday Inn on return trips to Houston. The value of the strategic alliance between the hotel and the restaurant is that it establishes a unique identity for this property that sets it apart from its competition and provides a marketing edge.

Customer Expectations

A primary mission-statement goal of both companies is to exceed customer expectations. With the alliance of the Holiday Inn Intercontinental and Good Eats Grill, Bristol management believes the customer is pleasantly surprised with the overall product and services that the property provides. Even though the hotel and restaurant renovations were completed just recently, in July 1996, the perceived overall value of this property to the customer is already generating new corporate accounts. Bristol management believes the hotel repositioning strategy in combination with the addition of the Good Eats Grill is a major reason it is landing those new accounts.

Advertising

Bristol Hotel Company believes in a direct sales-and-marketing approach. The company therefore relies less on national promotion activities than many other firms. The Holiday Inn Intercontinental is no different in this regard. The hotel does some limited local advertising, but it relies primarily on a direct-sales approach along with making personal local contacts. Other than the signs around the property, there is no joint advertising or promotion done between the hotel and the restaurant. Good Eats Grill has four lighted signs on the property, and Bristol purchases no billboard ads for this property. There are two other Good Eats Grill restaurants located in Houston, and Good Eats Grill does do some radio promotion and rents billboards for those two restaurants.

OPERATIONS

As a franchisee Bristol maintains total operational control of the restaurant, but Good Eats Grill recipes must be followed exactly. Unlike other Bristol properties, the restaurant has its own general manager. Bristol determined quickly that this particular property needed to establish the restaurant as a priority, but did not want the hotel general manager to get distracted from managing the rest of the hotel. Bristol therefore elevated the restaurant-manager positions to that of restaurant general manager at this property. The restaurant GM reports to the hotel GM, and the result is that the property receives maximum management focus for all of its key operations.

Another distinguishing operational element at this property is the way room service and banquets are handled. The Good Eats Grill kitchen serves them. There is no separate kitchen or menu to handle room service. Bristol also uses the Good Eats Grill kitchen for banquets and has the final say in establishing banquet menus and costs. Moreover, Bristol has the option of using Good Eats Grill menu items and recipes in preparing the banquet meals (provided that the recipes are followed exactly).

FINANCE

We have shown how the correct match between a restaurant company and a hotel operator can help to reposition a hotel, increase occupancy, and increase F&B profit. We can investigate other potential financial gains by comparing a summary of the actual 1995 profit-loss statement of the Holiday Inn's original (pre-Bristol) food service concept (Grand Cargo Café) with a conservatively estimated profit-loss statement of the Good Eats Grill for 1997 (its first year of full operation; see Table 6.8).

A quick comparison of those profit-loss figures shows how establishing a strategic alliance between a hotel and restaurant can improve the overall profitability of the property. Other expenses such as franchise initiation fee ($40,000–$50,000), cost of renovation ($750,000), cost of signs ($5,000), and other miscellaneous marketing costs (grand opening, flyers), must also be factored into assessing the feasibility of converting or opening an operation prior to proceeding with a project like the one between Holiday Inn Intercontinental and Good Eats Grill.

Final Analysis

Throughout this case-study analysis we emphasized how important the repositioning strategy was in turning around the Houston Holiday Inn Intercontinental. A quick look at key property performance indicators shown in Table 6.9 demonstrates the success of that repositioning strategy.

Moreover, we focused primarily on only one part of the hotel's repositioning strategy, that is, its strategic alignment with a particular restaurant concept. Other factors also contributed to the property's improved performance, including new ownership and management, an influx of cash for renovations, and its new market position. Nevertheless, the alliance between Bristol and Good Eats Grill is seen

TABLE 6.8
Profit–loss comparison

Grand Cargo Café		Item description	Good Eats Grill	
Actual 1995	%		%	Projected 1997
831,519	70.5	Outlet revenues[1]	59.8	1,269,455
199,920	16.9	Banquet revenues	28.4	601,000
148,072	12.6	Other revenues[2]	11.8	251,430
1,179,511	100.0	Total revenues	100.0	2,121,885
405,354	34.4	Food cost	26.4	561,137
525,634	44.5	Payroll[3]	43.2	917,621
43,561	3.7	Other expenses	7.1	148,532
974,555	82.6	Total expenses	76.7	1,627,289
204,956		Profit in dollars		494,596
	17.4	Profit percentage	23.3	

[1]Outlet revenues include restaurant revenues and room service.
[2]Other revenues include banquet-room rental, house portion of the gratuity, and miscellaneous banquet fees.
[3]Including employee benefits and payroll taxes.

Source: Bristol Hotel Company.

TABLE 6.9
Key Property Performance Indicators

	1996	Projected 1997
Hotel occupancy	72%	85%
ADR	$49	$60
Food profit	5%	25%
Beverage profit	50%	60%

as key to the property's turnaround. The property's previous restaurant, the Grand Cargo Café, was being operated as a hotel amenity rather than as a profit center. To capitalize on the restaurant's potential, the Bristol management team recognized that a new restaurant concept was needed. After objectively evaluating their options, including their own F&B concepts, the team determined that a Good Eats Grill franchise matched Bristol's restaurant needs for this particular property.

The Bristol experience demonstrates the importance of evaluating each property on an individual basis rather than making generalizations about what will work for all hotel properties.

In conclusion, from our perspective there is no question that now and in the future we will see more hotel and restaurant companies establishing strategic alliances. It is no longer financially feasible for a hotel restaurant to be operated as just a support function to the hotel's lodging operations. The hotel restaurant must now be viewed as a selling point to generate increased room and restaurant revenues. The hotel restaurant must be managed as its own profit center where the goal is to maximize overall property profits. For the entire property to be profitable, the restaurant concept and the hotel's market position must complement each other. Put another way, in today's competitive business environment the hotel restaurant cannot be—and should not try to be—all things to all people. To achieve a competitive edge, hotel companies must consider operating a franchised restaurant brand or leasing space within the hotel to a restaurant company. Doing so may improve customer perception and value, and as a result increase the overall profitability of the property.

6.6 Menu Marketing

David V. Pavesic

The starting point for every new restaurant or food service facility whether it is freestanding or located within a hotel or resort is determining the type of food that is going to be served. This is communicated to the dining public through the menu—the one printed advertising piece that you are virtually guaranteed will be read by the customer. When a friend or family member suggests that we try out a new restaurant, one that we are not familiar with, the first thing out of our mouth is, "What kind of food do they serve?"

External advertising and promotion at least partially influenced us to try the new restaurant. It got us to come inside. Once there, the menu takes over. Its design will influence what a customer will order and how much they will end up spending. There are certain techniques we apply to the layout and design of the menu that will direct the customer's attention to certain parts of the menu and to specific items. It has been proven that the odds of a particular item being ordered increase significantly if the customer notices it. Think about it; if they never saw it, they could not consider it as one of their choices, could they.

Given the importance of the menu as a marketing, communication, and cost-control tool, it is surprising that so many restaurants spend so little time and effort in the design and printing of their menus. When we are seated at a table, the first thing we do is open the menu. Consider the importance of that menu in influencing what we will order. A properly designed menu is much more than a printed bill of fare. It is the restaurant's calling card. It is a critical tool for communicating the personality of the restaurant, as well as listing the food items and their prices. This is also true of hotel banquet menus that clients peruse when making their selection on what they will order for their association's lunch or dinner function.

More and more hotels and restaurants have come to understand the impact of proper menu design and pricing on resulting check averages. Successful chain operations like T.G.I. Fridays, Houlihan's, and Bennigan's all have spent many hours and dollars on menu design and production, with the goal of increasing check averages. They did so by laying out the menu in such a way that it would lead the customer from the specialty drinks on the cover to the appetizers on the first inside page, to the side orders, entrées, and desserts. Their menu formats have evolved from as many as 14 pages down to half that amount. The executives in charge of menu design determined that the old menu design might have deflected dinner sales by making it easier for customers to find and order an appetizer and never even get to the sections containing the entrées. A hotel banquet menu is no different, and it should be designed to feature the items that best reflect the capabilities and artistry of their culinary staff.

The "science" of menu design borrows heavily from the retailing industry and department store merchandise displays. If they can get the shopper to stop and look at an item displayed on a mannequin or counter, they increase the likelihood that it will be purchased. Again, if you never see it, you will not even consider buying it. A fairly recent article in the *Wall Street Journal* described menu designs that highlight the most profitable offerings. These are also the items that are touted by the servers when they practice "suggestive selling." While the customers' selection cannot be completely controlled, it can be directed and not left entirely to chance.

The menu should communicate a restaurant's personality to the public. I believe that the menu is the primary communication link between a restaurant and the customer. This is especially true in the moderate-priced table-service operations where the manager and chef are not known to the patrons, as is the case with most of the popular chain restaurants. The old saying "You can't judge a book by its cover" should not be true when it comes to restaurant menus. All aspects of the menu—its cover, the color, the size, the material used, and the design—should be selected to project an accurate image of what the restaurant reflects in terms of decor, service, formality, price range, and even the type of food served.

You can perform a little experiment to demonstrate my point. Have a friend or colleague collect menus from three restaurants unfamiliar to you. Describe the images that come to mind after looking at the menus. Describe the decor, the ambience, and degree of formality in service. Then visit each of the restaurants and rate the menu in terms of accurately communicating its personality. Were your expectations met, or did the menu lead you to expect something different?

The importance of menu design cannot be overstated. The menu will determine a large part of the success of a restaurant. Therefore, the menu planning and design process must be approached with seriousness and diligence. It needs to be given the attention and budget of a major capital investment decision. Unfortunately, this is often not the case. I have seen menus that were obviously an afterthought and grossly understated the elegance of the restaurant. Others were designed without any rhyme or reason and failed to emphasize the items the restaurant did best or wanted to feature.

If you agree with what has been said so far, you are likely asking, "How do you make your menu a better communication and marketing tool?" *Menu psychology* borrows from retail merchandising techniques and applies them to menu design. The menu is to a restaurant what a window or counter display is to a department store. You want your customers to see all things you have for sale in the hope that they will find something they like and ultimately make a purchase.

Now, any menu design or format will produce a predictable sales mix if used consistently without changes for an extended period of time. This is the main point of menu design; if *any* menu does this simply by default, think of how a menu designed to specifically emphasize the items you want to sell more (for whatever reason) could harness this phenomenon to work in your favor. Instead of leaving the selection process *entirely* to chance, you employ menu psychology techniques to *guide* the customer's attention to those items.

A properly designed menu can help any food service operation achieve its sales, cost, and profit goals. In fact, it can even help distribute the workload in the kitchen and speed up the order-filling process. It doesn't happen often by accident; it must be planned. There are certain practices that, when incorporated into the graphic design and layout of a menu, make items stand out. While these techniques cannot make an unpopular item popular or make fried giblets and noodles outsell southern fried chicken, they can help sell more orders than if they were randomly placed on the menu.

Menu psychology is most applicable to the printed menu, although there are techniques that can be employed with *verbal* menus; the discussion herein is limited to the printed menu. The techniques employed by a graphic designer when designing a menu include such elements as graphics, font style and size, menu size, number of folds or panels, ink and paper color contrast, and even the weight, texture, and finish of the paper or synthetic material on which the menu is printed.

Even the placement of an item on a page or where it falls in a list has an influence on its visibility. Actually, menu psychology is any technique employed to direct the reader's attention to a particular area of the menu or a specific menu item. In a study of the sales mix of a Bennigan's back in 1984, over 75 percent of the menu's sales mix were either appetizer or snack-type items. The menu had multiple pages and the entrées were listed on the last two pages. Apparently, customers didn't page through to the end, and it resulted in fewer entrées being sold.

When a customer picks up a menu and starts to read it, the natural tendency is to start at the upper left of the page. This is the way we have been taught to read, so it is automatic unless there is something than alters our "gaze motion." The eye can be drawn from a random gaze motion by the use of what I refer to as *eye magnets*. Eye magnets are nothing more than things that make an item stand out from the other items on the menu. Some of the best examples are graphic boxes that surround specific menu items; dot-matrix color screens used as backgrounds; larger or bolder type fonts; illustrations; and photographs. All of these techniques will draw the eye to a desired location.

Pricing the menu is also part of menu marketing. Prices must be competitive and reasonable. The pricing continuum ranges from the lowest price you can charge and still make a reasonable profit to the highest price the market will bear. Most popular restaurants price somewhere between those extremes. In a hotel, the main dining room where breakfast, lunch, and dinner are served is similar to a popular freestanding restaurant in terms of its pricing strategy within the hotel property. The challenge in menu pricing is to determine where to set the price on the continuum. Underpricing an item is as much of a problem as overpricing. The former sacrifices profits while the latter may provoke complaints and a decrease in demand.

This leaves the oft-pondered question, "What price should I charge?" Pricing can be either *market driven* or *demand driven*, and the approach one adopts will depend on the menu item and the operational concept. If a menu item is a commodity in an economic sense—that is, it is available just about everywhere and quality differences are nominal—a definite price point exists in the market and that price cannot be exceeded. An example of a menu commodity would be the ubiquitous hamburger. Every restaurant with a grill or broiler has one on the menu, and it is difficult to get more than $6.95 even if it is a gourmet hamburger. Other examples of commodities are your basic pepperoni pizza or chicken fingers. If there is nothing special or unique about the taste, preparation, or plate presentation, the price charged must fall in line with the prices charged by your competitors. This approach is also employed when introducing new menu items before any substantial demand for the menu item is present. Prices that are market driven tend to be on the moderate-to-low side of the pricing continuum.

The market-driven approach is taken by those seeking to appeal to the largest share of the market. Offering large portions and high-quality ingredients will win customers and compliments. This pricing strategy is employed in highly competitive markets. However, operations with the lowest prices need higher customer counts to make up for the low average check. They may not be optimizing their profit potential on each sale. With long waits each night for a table, it would seem that price increases would not result in lowering of demand.

On the other hand, demand-driven prices are on the high side of the pricing continuum and apply primarily to menu items that are offered only by you and one or two others in your market. Overall pricing can be demand driven when you have customers waiting in line every night to eat in your restaurant. You can be more aggressive in your pricing, but there is a caveat to that strategy. You will have to be on the leading edge in terms of food quality, portion sizes, and service, because the more a customer pays, the more critical they will be. Hotel room service menu pricing and banquet menus are both examples of demand-driven pricing. The same item ordered in the main restaurant is likely to be 40 percent less than the room service price. Specialty restaurants are similarly priced, and the profit margin in food and beverage is much higher in banquets than in the hotel restaurants. Classic hotel restaurants like Trader Vic's and Nicholai's Roof (Atlanta Hilton and Towers) are examples of demand-driven menu prices because they are destination restaurants with unique food and attentive service.

The specific menu item, the existing market conditions, the location of the restaurant, and the operational concept of the restaurant or food service will influence the pricing approach used. For example, take the pricing of a 3-pound Dungeness crab, served with fresh broccoli hollandaise; red bliss potatoes, sourdough bread, and Mesclun salad, compared to a quarter-pound hamburger, small French fries, and medium drink. The type of restaurant, its location, service style, competition, and ambience would all impact the price of either item. The same crab dinner would be priced differently

at a seafood restaurant in Atlanta than it would in a convention hotel in Seattle, Washington. Moreover, a quarter-pound hamburger from a Marriott Marquis coffee shop in New York City would not be priced the same as a similar-sized hamburger sold in a Marriott Courtyard in Valdosta, Georgia.

Any attempt to apply a standard markup indiscriminately to a given menu item is ineffective and dangerous because it lacks important qualitative factors that enter into the pricing decision. *Qualitative* considerations cannot easily be assigned *quantitative* values; they are subjective and require an "artistic touch." This tends to be intuitive and emotional, two elements that are difficult to program into a computer model.

Menu pricing philosophies are as disparate as political and theological beliefs and almost as controversial. Initially, only raw food costs were marked up when one was setting prices. Today many *indirect cost factors* influence the price charged and include such elements as labor, entertainment, location, time of year, special services and amenities, market standing, service commitment, desired check average, and even price elasticity. However, the financial requirements and profit goals of a business may not be compatible or realistic given the existing economic or market conditions.

The "cost" of the menu item has only a limited part in the pricing decision because the customer does not care about "your costs." All they are concerned with is how much they have to pay. If your prices are perceived as being too high relative to what the competition is charging or your portions too small, you negate any price value and the customer will go elsewhere and your sales and profit objectives will be adversely affected.

Pricing, therefore, is a far more complicated process than simply marking up cost. It cannot be reduced to a quantitative formula and still be effective. While such factors as food cost percentage and gross profit return are important residuals, the pricing process is more subjective and enigmatic than most people realize. It has been proven that it is the *buyer*, not the *seller*, that ultimately determines the market price. Therefore, the challenge to restaurant operators, whether freestanding or in fine hotels, is to be able to make a profit selling menu items at the price the customer is willing to pay.

6.7 Contemporary Hotel Catering

Patti J. Shock and John M. Stefanelli

Although on-premise catering is generally the second largest source of revenue for most hotels, following sleeping rooms, the on-premise catering area has been virtually ignored in the hotel school curriculum. The colleges that do offer a course in catering usually focus on hands-on classes consisting of planning, cooking, and serving a meal, which is good background, but is not the role of the hotel catering department.

Catering is often the highest visibility the hotel has on a local level. Catering can create an image for the hotel, both locally and nationally.

DEPARTMENT ORGANIZATION

In most hotels the director of catering reports to the director of food and beverage, with banquet managers and banquet setup managers reporting to catering. In other hotels you may find a director of catering and convention service reporting to the director of marketing, with the banquet positions reporting to food and beverage. In the latter arrangement, the convention service department usually handles food and beverage functions for groups with 20 or more sleeping rooms, with the catering department selling and servicing the local social and business markets. Convention service, then, does not sell; the room sales department handles that aspect. Convention service in most hotels, however, handles all of the non-food-related logistics, including room setup, audiovisual requirements, etc. In hotels where conventions are not an important market segment, convention service may not exist, in which case catering would handle all food and nonfood logistics.

The director of catering assigns and oversees all functions; oversees catering sales managers; oversees all marketing efforts; interacts with clients and catering managers; coordinates with the hotel sales director; and works with the chef to update and create menus.

Under the director of catering there may be an assistant catering director who helps with marketing, oversees catering sales managers, and services one or more accounts. There may be several catering sales managers, depending on the size of the hotel. Catering sales managers maintain client contacts and service accounts. Their role is to sell and service functions. They must seek and consult with clients; plan menus, themes, room setup, and decor; negotiate prices; and coordinate with inside departments and outside vendors. There are several excellent graphic roomsetup software packages available on the market.

The catering department may also employ catering sales representatives who are usually involved only with selling, leaving the servicing to others.

The banquet manager implements the director of catering's requests; oversees room captains; supervises functions in progress; staffs and schedules servers and bartenders; and coordinates all support departments. He or she is the operations director, as opposed to catering executives, who primarily sell and work with clients to plan events.

The assistant banquet manager reports to the banquet manager and supervises table settings and decor. There may be two (or more) assistants; for example, a hotel may have one for the day and one for the evening shift.

The banquet setup manager supervises the banquet setup crew; orders tables, chairs, portable bars, and other room equipment from storage; and supervises the teardown of the room after the event has concluded.

The scheduler, often referred to as the diary clerk, enters bookings in the master log (now usually computerized); oversees the timing of all functions and provides adequate turnover time between functions; is responsible for scheduling meeting rooms, reception areas, poolside areas, meal functions, beverage functions, other functions, and equipment requirements; keeps appropriate records to ensure against overbooking and double booking of space; and is responsible for communicating this information to relevant departments.

The maître d'hôtel is the floor manager. He or she is in charge of all service personnel and oversees all aspects of guest service during meal and beverage functions in the various function rooms on the floor.

The captain is the room manager and is in charge of service at meal functions in a specific room. Captains typically oversee all activity in the entire function room or, depending on the size of the room, in a portion of it. They also supervise the servers in their room or section of the room.

There are two types of servers—food servers and beverage servers. Food servers deliver food, alcoholic and nonalcoholic beverages, and utensils to the table; clear tables; and attend to guest needs. Beverage servers serve alcoholic beverages, usually at receptions. Servers are sometimes backed up by buspersons, whose primary responsibilities are to clear tables, restock side stands, and serve ice water, rolls, butter, and condiments.

The bartender concentrates on alcoholic beverage production and service. Bartenders are often assisted by bar backs, whose primary responsibility is to initially stock and replenish the bars with liquor, ice, glassware, and other necessary supplies.

Housemen (sometimes referred to as porters) set up function rooms with risers, hardware, tables, chairs, and other necessary equipment. They report to the banquet setup manager.

Attendants "refresh" meeting rooms during breaks by emptying ashtrays when smoking is permitted, refilling water pitchers, and removing trash. Some catered functions also require coat-check attendants or restroom sttendants.

The clerk (or secretary) handles routine correspondence, types contracts and banquet event orders (BEOs), handles and routes telephone messages, and distributes documents to relevant staff members and other hotel departments.

The engineering department provides necessary utilities service, such as air-conditioning/heating, setting up electrical panels for major exhibits, hanging banners, and setting up audiovisual displays.

Other miscellaneous positions include the following. A sommelier (or wine steward) is used only at fancy, upscale events. The cashier sells drink tickets to guests at cash bars. A ticket taker may be required to collect tickets from guests at the door to the function. Finally, most catering departments employ stewards to deliver the proper amount of china, glassware, and silver to function rooms.

Whatever the organizational structure, catering's favorable impact on hotel profitability is primarily due to the fact that catering has more control over the variable expenses than does the manager of a typical restaurant. In a restaurant, labor must be scheduled, heat or air-conditioning must be on, and food must be kept in inventory, whether or not any guests are present in the facility. In catering, a function must be booked before these items are scheduled or purchased. So there are more variable costs in catering, and more fixed costs in restaurant food service.

THE SALES AND SERVICE PROCESS

Selling is a vital part of catering (see Figure 6.3). To sell a catering event, potential markets must be identified and cultivated. Target markets must be established. Potential markets include association meetings (local

FIGURE 6.3
Steps in selling and servicing a catering event

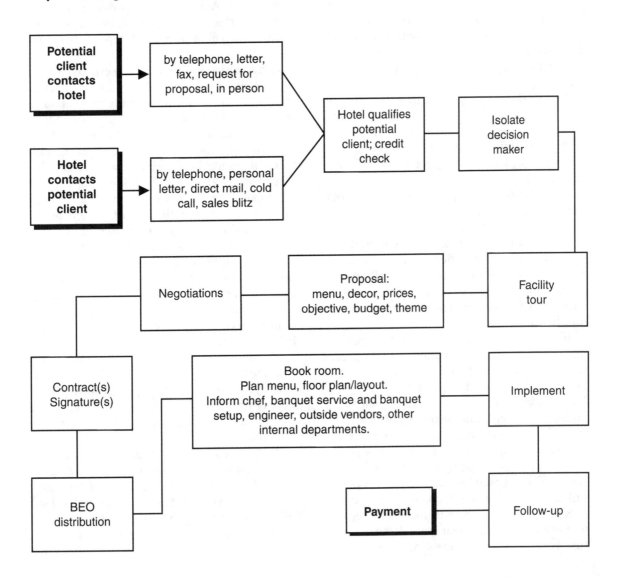

monthly meetings as well as the national annual conventions); corporate meetings, including training sessions and incentive banquets; weddings and anniversaries; bar mitzvahs; proms; garden clubs; holiday parties; reunions, both school and military; and fraternal organizations, such as Rotary and Lions. The list is endless.

A marketing plan should be developed that clearly defines the desirable target markets; defines the demand; describes competing caterers; sets financial goals; considers other potential income that catering can generate for the hotel; and describes standardized procedures that must be used to canvass for new clients, qualify leads, make sales calls, develop contracts, and provide required products and services.

The initial contact for a function can initiate from the client or the catering department. In many cases, the potential client makes the first inquiry. He or she may contact you by phone, letter, fax, or e-mail or in person.

If the contact is by phone, be sure the person answering the phone can answer questions, or that someone knowledgeable is always available. Too often a low-paid, untrained person in the office answers the phone, and this can hamper the selling effort. The phone should always be answered within three rings. Always secure the name and phone number of the caller.

If the initial contact is by letter, e-mail, or fax, try to answer with a phone call. Copies of the letter were most likely sent to several caterers, and it is best to be the first to respond. More information is often needed, such as the budget the client has for the event or the objective of the function. This initial contact also provides the opportunity to invite the potential client to the property for lunch and a tour. Every effort should be made to get the potential client into the hotel, on your home turf.

Sometimes a letter will include a request for proposal (RFP), which is a written prospectus from professional meeting planners. An RFP usually indicates that the potential client is very knowledgeable about catering and is usually a sophisticated negotiator.

If potential clients stop by in person without an appointment, have someone see them as soon as possible. Offer some light refreshments to keep them occupied until someone is available. Give an accurate estimate of how long they will have to wait. Have the receptionist obtain preliminary information, such as their desired date(s) and type of function, to get them involved in the planning process right away. Also, keep a binder handy for browsing that contains testimonial letters from happy clients and photos of previous events.

A group history file should be created whenever initial contact is made. The file should include all facets of the business relationship, from initial contact to final disposition. Standardized information includes name of contact, name of decision maker, titles, organization, types of events held, number of events held, when events are held, attendance figures, all correspondence, notes from phone conversations, contracts, credit history, potential for future business, and client preferences.

The manager responding to client inquiries must understand the hotel's capabilities. He or she especially needs a knowledge of food and beverage production and service. Planning a menu for a small group is quite different from a large group. For example, soufflé for 1000 would be quite impossible.

When planning a menu, the caterer must first know the occasion or reason for the event. The style of service also depends on the occasion. It would be inappropriate to have a deli sandwich buffet for an auspicious awards banquet.

With international events, protocol must be considered in everything from decor to dietary restrictions. The World of Culture Web site (http://www.webofculture.com/) provides good information on a variety of cultures.

Public space or function rooms must be forecast for space utilization, just as the hotel sales department forecasts sleeping rooms requirements.

Working well with inside departments is critical. Linens have to be requisitioned from the linen room; engineers must insure that the room temperature is appropriate; tables must be set up; and purchasing must order the correct amounts and types of food and beverages.

Outside vendors, such as decorators, audio-visual companies, florists, printers, and photographers may be needed by the client to ensure a successful event.

Performing well is the next step. Here the emphasis shifts from sales to service. Guests must be treated with care; service must be punctual; foods, presentations, cleanliness, and ambience must meet desired quality standards; professional attention must be paid to all details; the function host should be made to feel like a guest at the event, instead of a harassed and worried manager. Last-minute requests and crises must be handled quickly and efficiently. It is imperative to be flexible.

Follow-up is vital for repeat business. Standardized procedures should be developed for thank-you calls and individualized, personal thank-you letters. Completed events should be evaluated with staff and client input. Referral business should be solicited. Appropriate souvenir gifts may be presented. And outstanding accounts should be settled.

FUTURE ISSUES

Issues facing the catering department in the future include new alcohol restrictions; the demand for more menu alternatives, including low-fat, pesticide-free, generally safe, uncontaminated products; the competition from off-premise catering firms; waste disposal regulations and recycling; consumers becoming more value conscious; and service becoming a more important point of differentiation.

Subcontracting will become more common, especially for labor and food. Calling one company to provide servers is more efficient than having staff on the phone calling individual on-call workers. The independent labor contractor trains staff and does all of the payroll and paperwork.

Caterers can't afford to have all types of expertise on their staffs. To provide a Japanese theme, the caterer may subcontract a sushi restaurant. Or a local barbecue specialist, oyster roaster, or coffee service company can handle unique events. The hotel would add about 20 percent markup to the subcontractor's bill, and then add the cost of the rest of the meal prepared in-house.

In the past, menus rarely changed. Today, many menus are changed with the season. In the future it will be important to be able to distinguish between a fad and a trend. Fads, such as nouvelle cuisine, are short-lived. Trends, such as the demand for fresh foods and more nutritious food, are more permanent.

Probably the biggest challenge is the perception among guests that all caterers are exactly alike. Buyers may feel that there is always another caterer able to provide similar service. It is imperative for the successful caterer to differentiate their food and service from their competition. The price/value relationship will become more important as caterers attempt to rise above the competition.

There are a multitude of resources available on the Web, including, for example, a room calculator (http://www.mmaweb.com/meetings/Workshop/roomcalc.html), which will determine how many guests you can fit into a room in various configurations. Many caterers have their menus on-line, which are interesting to see. *Special Events Magazine* (http://www.specialevents.com/magazine/) and *Event Solutions* (http://www.event-solutions.com/) have timely articles that are archived on-line and are searchable. A large collection of useful catering Web links can be found at http://www.unlv.edu/Tourism/Catering_and_Special_Events.html.

6.8   Executive Director of Catering Sales–A Day in My Life

Rich Benninger

Each day I wake up saying, "Today is the day I will get everything done." It is my optimist side taking control before my realist side has a chance to ruin my day. Since I ply my trade at a 5,034-room hotel with over 380,000 square feet of banquet space, it is usually around 8 A.M. when my realist side kicks in. By this time I have been at work for an hour or more and start taking victories as soon as they come. The day is half over for the dedicated line cast members who started working at 4 A.M. so our thousands of guests could enjoy their morning breakfast. They are the backbone of catering. Their workday here will end in four more hours and many will go to a second job.

The day will not end for the catering director until a few things are completed. The director has just one job, sort of, and is the front person for the operation. Now, please allow me to take you on a journey through a typical day in the life of a catering director. But first I must make coffee. Nobody else in the office notices that 1 ounce of coffee left in a pot does not constitute "there's coffee in the pot."

Here is a listing of the things I did today.

BOOKING BUSINESS

Customers are the number one component to a successful catering operation. Without customers the grandest ballrooms, the most spectacular cuisine, and the best service are all moot points. So, every day you must work to fill the pipeline with customers. The rooms sales managers are really doing a great job. They are booking over quota and getting contracts with great food and beverage minimums. For just a moment, I fantasize that this will never end and life will always be good.

Oh no, we have just been asked why the week between Christmas and New Year's does not have any events. Transient room sales are strong but they do not use function space. It's up to catering sales to fill in the hole. My team tells me, had sales not already done so, they could easily fill space a week before or a week later but that holiday week is going to be tough to fill. I know this is true but the senior vice president does not care that something is tough. He wants to know what we are doing to get business. And by the way, not discount business. We start out looking for full-paying customers, and if that does not work we will look at discounting.

I am excited to meet a customer for a site visit at 7:30 A.M. I am the first property she is looking at for a 2500-guest reception and concert. I just talked to her yesterday for the very first time. All our meeting space is booked, but I'm in luck, we have space in our arena. I work with the arena for about an hour to get the space and brainstorm on things we can do to book this business. The arena operations guys are great to work with. They enjoy coming to the catering office for cappuccino. I smile when I think how cheap cappuccino is and how many favors it buys from operations cast members.

We spend an hour walking our customer through her event. The company sells very large industrial trucks, and when we tell her we can put a concrete mixer right in the middle of her reception she is all smiles. I make note to get the dimensions of the roll-up doors. We are going to be more expensive then the competition but we provide more value. We can make this a one-stop shopping experience. I make a note to call transportation companies and gather quotes. I know the other properties will not get involved in dealing with all of the outside vendors, and I use this as a selling advantage. I make a note to list this as a tentative piece of business worth $165,000 plus.

Next I make a hasty trip across the property to check on a breakfast we are doing on the stage of our production show. We are lucky to have an incentive house tour our property, and we have pulled out all the stops to let this VIP group know we value their business. I am pleased with the spectacular stage sets and the look of the breakfast. I laugh with the sales manager when he apologies for giving us only 36 hours' notice on the breakfast. I assure him the financial rewards of getting some large incentive bookings will more than make up for the short notice. I make a note to send each guest a thank-you note for taking the time to tour our property.

FINALIZING PROGRAMS

The only time a program is truly finalized is once the customers are gone and the final bill is paid. And then just the physical stuff is over. Conversations of the really good stuff and the sometimes bad stuff can go on for years. Repeat customers are usually the best ones to have, but they tend to remember that five years ago the potato salad did not have a spoon in it when the company president went to the buffet 15 minutes before it was scheduled to open. "Let's not let that happen this year."

You spend months working to get everything planned at least three weeks in advance. Then you give all the information to the operating departments two weeks out. For some groups this works really well, and once you work out the details they make only minor changes. Other groups are not quite so tidy in their planning.

Today I have a group arrive on-site, and we review their banquet event orders (BEOs). It would be easier to say we redo their BEOs. At 9:00 A.M. we start reviewing 45 meal function BEOs. By 2:15 P.M. we have made major changes to 42 of them. I wonder aloud if they would like to change the other three just for good measure. The chefs are circling the catering office like sharks. All the food ordering is on hold until the revised BEOs are signed

off on. While I'm working with the clients to "refinalize," the chefs and purchasing agents are on the phone undoing all the ordering they did days ago. Purveyors are all on standby to rush product to us. I am thankful we have excellent relationships with these wonderful people who will now pull off miracles to get us product over the weekend.

My assistant is ready to shoot someone. Making the changes once is enough of a challenge but now we are changing things for a second and third time in one day. I smile as I say, "Yes, I'm sure I can get you a completely new set of BEOs by 5:00 P.M." Just as I tell myself we must be done with changes, my contact calls and changes two of the remaining original three BEOs. I get no comfort from the fact that the one lone original BEO is for an event that does not happen until five days from now. I do, however, get great comfort from the knowledge that my clients will spend over $800,000 in the next eight days.

CREATING MENUS

I promise a major corporate client that I will write three custom menu options for their opening reception. I tell them I will do it on Saturday and I'll fax the menus so they have them for a Monday meeting. I promise myself I will not commit to doing any more projects on Saturday. It is going to be my catch-up day and I've been filling the day with new projects. I may have to work a few hours on Sunday to get on track for next week. The great thing about writing custom menus is every time I do one I add it to my hot menu file and just keep reusing it. I do make a notation of who I send each one to. I would hate to send someone the same *custom* menu twice.

In this world of ever more sophisticated customers the quest for new menus has taken on a life all its own. The unfortunate side of this sophisticated customer often comes with fond memories of a gourmet dinner for two at some exotic trendy restaurant. Other favorite sources of wonderful ideas are glossy cooking magazines and TV cooking shows. Now the simple task of any caterer is to figure out how to make these menus, designed to serve eight, work for hundreds or thousands. Of course, you are not alone in this situation. The culinary staff is right there with you. Please don't take it personally that many of them think you are crazy.

WORKING EVENTS

Luckily for my catering department we work at a property where we are cast in the role of being a salesperson. Another team of professionals handles operations. Still, I can't resist taking 10 minutes and going down to see how setup is going for a poolside reception. Somehow I spend 45 minutes at the pool, and now I'm going to have to rush to a precon meeting. The clients who spent the day making changes are very big customers, and the precon will be a big production. We have all our top executives coming by to say hello. I am anxious to see how the eight cheerleaders will do with the dance number they are performing in the center of the hollow square. I am very pleased to see the banquet and entertainment departments have everything in perfect order.

LEADING AN OFFICE

One of my catering managers comes into my office and asks to talk. In two days she will renew her wedding vows and she is very nervous. I go into "father mode" and we make a list of things she has to do. I laugh when I ask her why she is nervous about having a party for 30 people when every day she books parties for hundreds of guests. I try to ease her burden of preparing some of the food herself. I suggest she just brings in the bowls she wants to use and I'll have the kitchen fill them up with whatever she wants. I smile when she says, "No thank you, I make really good sal-

ads myself." I wonder, does that mean our salads are not really good?

Throughout the day my staff gives me encouragement while I am working to get all the changes made on my group. They all offer to help and I notice the number of things I am asked to look at is very low today. I am proud of my staff and make a note to have a special breakfast at our catering meeting next week. It has been almost two months since we started a new format for our catering meetings, and I must say they are much better and everyone seems happier at the meetings.

BUDGETS

Yesterday we had our review for next year's budget. I must start working on a really aggressive marketing plan to make the revenue number we are after. For today I'll just start by having a binder made so I feel like I'm making progress. I ask my assistant to run some reports so I can take them home and look at them. I know I'll never look at them while I'm home, but if I find spare time I'll have them, just in case.

MENTORING AND INDUSTRY INVOLVEMENT

I call two new interns from the university to confirm their Saturday appointments with me. I need to meet with them to determine their interests and what program we are going to follow for the eight months they will spend with us. I hope they will want to work on the marketing plan and be active in National Association of Catering Executives (NACE). I also have a protégé from the university, and it would be nice if all three can work together on projects. I feel pressure to provide these students with an overwhelmingly positive experience. Last year I was voted Outstanding Mentor of the Year and now I feel a higher level of expectation.

Unfortunately, I have to cancel my NACE board of directors meeting scheduled for today. I am the president of our chapter, and I have not had time to work on the things I need for the meeting. I do not want to waste the board's time. I make a note to call our NACE intern and schedule a meeting to see what tasks I can have her handle for the board. Involvement in NACE is rewarding, but it is like a part-time job. What was I thinking when we agreed to do a fund-raising dinner for 1000 in February? I'm sure it was the same thing I thought when I said I would love to teach an extension class at the university. It all seems so far away when I say yes. Somehow it all works out.

ENTERTAINING

It's 5:00 P.M. and I need to leave for a cocktail party at a sister property across the street. I am joining the vice president of sales and the executive director of convention services to entertain clients. We have a cocktail party and then a 7:30 P.M. dinner and a 10:00 P.M. show. The evening is wonderful. Our clients really enjoy the special attention we give them. When 10:00 P.M. comes I wonder if I'll stay awake at the show. My fears are unjustified. The comedian is so funny my sides hurt from laughing.

I think, what a great career. I get to have fun while I work. As the evening ends at 11:30 P.M. I confirm that I'll play golf in two weeks . . . just another sacrifice for my clients.

PERSONAL LIFE

My four golden retrievers are really happy to see me. I know they have had dinner and were well cared for while I was gone but I feed them again. It is the most wonderful thing I do each day. I take my suit off and get into sweats. It's time to go for a walk and tell them all about my day. They agree, making so many changes is just not right. We devise a plan to keep others from making my day so stressed. Then we talk about the three-day trip we are taking to Utah the day my in-house group ends. It will be our first motor home trip and we are all excited. It seems my golden retrievers are tired of camping in a tent. Additionally, I plan to spend time working on my on-line master's degree, and a motor home will be a good place to work. I try not to think too hard about my degree. It makes it hard to sleep when I think of working on my final project.

Now it's 12:30 A.M. and I need to get in bed. As I lie down I resolve that when I get up "it will be the day that I get everything done."

6.9   The Hotel Executive Chef

Gene Fritz

Today's hotel executive chefs are experiencing change and challenge as they enter the twenty-first century. Sheridan (1998) quotes Professor Clinton Rappole of the University of Houston's Hilton College of Hotel Management ". . . that hotels always considered dining as a costly amenity, not a revenue center; and that those days are clearly over and man-

agement is looking for food service to carry its full load of profitability." Based upon increased costs as a result of aggressive building and renovation of hotels during the late 1990s and an increase in mergers and new brand developments (Su, 2000), hotel restaurant operations are being analyzed, restructured, and eliminated as a simple guest amenity and cultivated as an expected profit center. These shifts in revenue emphasis have resulted in a whole new inventory of challenges for the hotel executive chef, and also include a balance of increased opportunities that will dramatically alter the chef's daily operational responsibilities.

Despite the challenges of this financial scrutiny on food and beverage operations, many hotel chains have taken this opportunity to reevaluate the role of the executive chef within their organizations. According to Patrick Quek, of the international hospitality consulting firm PKF Consulting, "hoteliers should take a hard look at the level and type of F&B service appropriate to the property, guest, and profits" (Marsan, 2000, "Changing the Unchanged").

The reader will find this chapter to be representative of current issues and changes that are taking place within the hotel food and beverage operation relative to the executive chef and the implications of Quek's remarks. We will be exploring the following topics:

1. Evolutionary history of the executive chef within the hotel restaurant operation.
2. The hotel chef as a resource to target new and enhance existing market segments.
3. Increased financial accountability.
4. Professional development and occupational responsibilities.
5. Reevaluation of internal and external relationships.

HISTORY

Historically, the status of a hotel chef has been one of great ego, independence, and little financial accountability, but there is evidence this is changing. Dean Fearing, chef at the Mansion on Turtle Creek, states, "The day of the glorified, ego-driven chef running a kitchen by yelling is over" (Sheridan, 1997). Traditionally, the hotel chef was responsible for managing culinary development and staffing issues, yet the twenty-first century has intro-

duced a new era—an era where the executive chef is now responsible for marketing the hotel's food and beverage operations and insuring that the restaurant contributes to the success of the overall hotel property, while operating at a profit. This new era is one where the hotel chef's strength is rooted in knowledge, understanding, and business savvy; hence formal education and training is common for today's hotel executive chef.

This new birthing of financial accountability didn't come without benefits to many hotel chefs within the upscale portion of the industry. Hotel chains are now capitalizing upon the same concepts that independent restaurants learned long ago. They are aggressively showcasing their chefs, who, in turn, tantalize the customers with special menus, chef tables located in the kitchen, and other merchandising ideas. They also seek to enhance profitability with gourmet cooking classes and demonstrations (Lee, 1999). Consumers are now drawn into the luxury hotel restaurants through means unheard of twenty years ago. The hotel executive chef is no longer sweating over the grill and reviewing the kitchen staff's daily *mise en place*, but is now serving as a form of direct entertainment to the hotel guests as a new addition to their job description. Chefs will now go to all extremes to enhance operational profitability through creativity, while experiencing a paradigm shift in what it means to be a hotel chef in the twenty-first century. Clifford Pleau, executive chef of the California Grill atop the Disney Contemporary Resort at Walt Disney World, states that he "intends to turn the restaurant into a location that is as exciting as a roller coaster [in order] to get guests to dine here" (Liberson, 1998).

Hotel chefs have carried a reputation of overextending labor and food cost because of their inability to meet the needs of each and every guest of the hotel. Diversification in the customer base has always justified diversification, and increased spending, in service provided from the chef and his or her staff.

According to Giulio Comacchio, vice president of F&B, the Americas of Bass Hotels and Resorts, "One of the mistakes that hotel chains make: they try to satisfy everybody in every aspect. . . . Take a look at independent restaurants. Why are they successful? They've created their own identity" (Marsan, 2000, "Changing the Unchanged"). The days of the hotel chef attempting to be all things to all people are over, and now the hotel executive chef evaluates all ventures in perspective to profitability and enhancing value to the overall guest experience.

The model in Figure 6.4 displays the historical progression and maturity of the hotel executive chefs' responsibilities. The underly-

Figure 6.4
Historical paradigms of the hotel executive chef

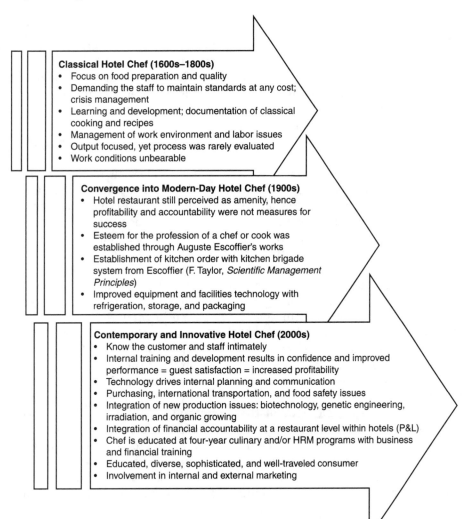

Classical Hotel Chef (1600s–1800s)
- Focus on food preparation and quality
- Demanding the staff to maintain standards at any cost; crisis management
- Learning and development; documentation of classical cooking and recipes
- Management of work environment and labor issues
- Output focused, yet process was rarely evaluated
- Work conditions unbearable

Convergence into Modern-Day Hotel Chef (1900s)
- Hotel restaurant still perceived as amenity, hence profitability and accountability were not measures for success
- Esteem for the profession of a chef or cook was established through Auguste Escoffier's works
- Establishment of kitchen order with kitchen brigade system from Escoffier (F. Taylor, *Scientific Management Principles*)
- Improved equipment and facilities technology with refrigeration, storage, and packaging

Contemporary and Innovative Hotel Chef (2000s)
- Know the customer and staff intimately
- Internal training and development results in confidence and improved performance = guest satisfaction = increased profitability
- Technology drives internal planning and communication
- Purchasing, international transportation, and food safety issues
- Integration of new production issues: biotechnology, genetic engineering, irradiation, and organic growing
- Integration of financial accountability at a restaurant level within hotels (P&L)
- Chef is educated at four-year culinary and/or HRM programs with business and financial training
- Educated, diverse, sophisticated, and well-traveled consumer
- Involvement in internal and external marketing

ing theme is a developing focus on consistent food preparation and improving of the work environment through technological advancements available to the restaurant industry. The contemporary hotel executive chef has increased responsibility in the areas of managing resources, financial accountability, and involvement in marketing. There is a shift from a primarily technical perspective, to an equality of responsibility related to the technical, managerial, and conceptual elements of hotel restaurant operations.

MARKETING

The executive chef is now acknowledged as the creative source for potential profitability related to hotel restaurant sales. Currently, the characteristic of creativity in a hotel chef is one that differentiates those who lead their restaurant(s) to financial success or failure. Indirect marketing that is relative to the executive chef is often common in hotel restaurants. Today's hotel executive chef often follows the marketing model of stand-alone restaurants for an organized marketing strategy. Today, the hotel executive chef often attempts to build confidence in their hotel patrons through the venue of establishing popularity with local diners. "In today's media-energized world, savvy hotel owners are continuing to exploit the reputations of celebrated chefs, not simply to energize food-and-beverage operations, but also to create national, and even worldwide, publicity for their lodging establishments" (Hayes, 1998).

David Nichols, general manager of the Seelbach Hotel, states that "the strategy of hiring or partnering with celebrity chefs amounts to a recognition that food and beverage continue to be among the most important ways to 'sell' a luxury hotel. . . . It's nothing more or less than a strategy to increase revenues" (Hayes, 1998). Other hotel companies have progressively economized and increased

the market share to midscale and budget-based properties, and the reputation of the turn-of-the-century hotel restaurant became less important.

The norm of the "best" chefs being found in hotels—as opposed to street restaurants—is slowly changing as luxury hotel chains see the necessity to have qualified and esteemed chefs in their restaurants in order to meet the needs of their expectant guests. Luxury hotels place great care in the process of selecting their executive chef. The individual chef must have the ability to add value to the hotel's restaurant operation by appealing not only to hotel guests, but also the patrons of local restaurants, through the offering of well-prepared food and excitement.

What follows are several recent examples of how a hotel chef might try to reach both local and guest-based clientele.

- Offering "high tea" during slow afternoon periods.
- Tours of local attractions, such as Pike Place Market in Seattle or the Farmers' Market in Los Angeles, and concluding the tour with a cooking demonstration and meal with the chef (Powell, 2000).
- Offering extended room service, and the option of catered events in hotel suites.
- Enhancing the "bath menu"—a special room service for guests enjoying a leisurely time in their rooms' tub—with chocolate-covered strawberries or truffles and champagne (Stephen, 2000).
- Offering the breakfast-all-day concept to guests around the clock to fill the gap between traditional restaurant service and the local all-night diner concept (Marsan, 2000, "Changing the Unchanged").
- Catering to in-suite meetings.
- Special multicourse meals offered through room service, which promotes in-room dining for guest convenience, comfort, and privacy.
- Conducting midafternoon cooking demonstrations and tastings to promote a specific

restaurant or regional cuisine available on the hotel property.

- Offering innovative special events and themed meal promotions linked with other local businesses (e.g., winemakers, brewmasters, and events with ethnic food themes).
- Building celebratory menu offerings with regional food.
- Partnering with popular local freestanding restaurants.

New marketing efforts often involve restaurant redesign and renovation and are often the responsibility of the executive chef. According to Joan Marsan, associate editor of *Hotels* magazine, "today's hottest hotel kitchens have personalities and philosophies as strong as the chefs inhabiting them" (Marsan, 2000, "Kitchen Philosophies"). Kitchen design and remodeling have taken on a new strategy with the result of opening the market to a consumer who likes to know what is happening in the "back of the house." The typical customer enjoys viewing the food preparation areas of a hotel kitchen, which is an opportune atmosphere for positive image building, if the chef manages their staff, and the kitchen remains immaculate in terms of food safety and sanitation. Many hotel executive chefs are taking an additional step beyond the popular "fish bowl" design, where the guest can view the kitchen staff through large display windows. Hotel chefs are now inviting the diner right into their kitchen to enjoy their meal at the "chef's table." Marsan goes on to say, "show kitchens, in particular, bring personality into the back room. The kitchens of the Mercer Kitchen, New York, and Aureole, Mandalay Bay Resort and Casino, Las Vegas embody their chefs' and designers' distinct culinary and aesthetic visions and host about 25 curious guests each evening. Combining architectural artistry, inbound customers and cookery can be tricky business, but chefs at both kitchens attest to the success of the mix" (Marsan, 2000, "Kitchen Philosophies").

Through creative marketing and an attempt to highlight hotel restaurants, chefs are also attempting to revitalize their room service programs. They are breaking away from the traditional perceptions of room service as the ugly stepchild of hotel F&B and are attempting to recreate it as a profit center for the hotel. Luxury-segment hotel chefs are now offering full-service menu options within the privacy of the guest's hotel suite. The chef is also offering menu options for guests who want to host a small gathering in their room. While at Jean Georges Restaurant, New York, "a trained chef and wait staff can be hired to come to a guest's suite or private residence to prepare and serve a four-course gourmet meal" (Hensdill, 1998). According to chef Michael Coaker, the chef must "keep the menu simple . . . have lots of dishes, but not necessarily lots of different ingredients" (Hensdill, 1998). The contemporary hotel executive chef is an individual who should have the creative ability, entrepreneurial spirit, and drive to draw locals and hotel guests alike into the hotel restaurant.

Celebrity Chefs in the Marketing Spotlight

Celebrity chefs such as Wolfgang Puck, Roy Yamaguchi, Jean-Louis Palladin, Emeril Lagasse, Daniel Boulud, and Alain Ducasse are known for recent integration of their signature concepts into hotel chains ranging from Las Vegas to New York. Celebrity chefs offer a new and unique marketing strategy to the hotel in which they are located. Signature concepts market to both the internal and external consumer, as these concepts carry a following unlike any other hotel and restaurant combination. According to Jane Coloccia of *Lodging F&B Magazine*, "In having a 'name' chef placed in the (hotel) restaurant, it gives a sense of credibility" (Coloccia, 1999).

The primary motivations for associating a well-known chef with a hotel restaurant are to gain better publicity, to penetrate two existing markets at the same time, and to ensure good restaurant reviews. Yet, one must remember that these concepts are hinged upon the star chef, who seldom makes an appearance, which inevitably leads to a random loss in quality and consistency due to the visionaries' most common absence. The originality and authenticity of these concepts, along with the stunning personalities of the entrepreneurial celebrity chefs, are a volatile combination for success in cities such as Las Vegas and New York.

FINANCIAL ACCOUNTABILITY

The position of hotel executive chef has been elevated in responsibility and accountability as the industry enters the twenty-first century. Opportunities for the chef to manage their kitchen and contribute to increased profitability were few and far between in the past. Now, however, hotel chefs are contributing to the financial success of the F&B segment of the hotel, which has resulted in an increase of 11.9 percent compound annual rate in profits between the years 1994 to 1999 (Mandelbaum, 2000).

As a result of this increased financial responsibility, today's hotel chefs are required to be more educated than ever before. In order to run a professional hotel kitchen with optimal financial efficiency and effectiveness, one must understand not only culinary artistry and food preparation, but how it relates to "the numbers." According to Professor Michael Redlin, of Cornell University's School of Hotel Administration, "a talented, world-class [hotel] chef has a vision of excellence . . . and he understands how to produce and deliver—from creating production stations that work, to spotting (culinary) talent, to knowing ingredients *and being a good business person*" (Sheridan, 1997).

Progressively, through the 1990s, there has been a growth in both hotel F&B revenues and profits at a national level. According to Mandelbaum (2000), increases in hotel food revenues can be attributed to upgraded restaurant outlets, increasing menu prices that follow a rise in room rates, an increase in higher-priced banquet activity, and increased volume from local patrons.

Organizational and Operational Restructuring

Executive chefs throughout the hotel industry are making dramatic changes to the way they organize and operate their restaurant kitchens. When these changes are coupled with those that take place at the corporate level, there is a direct impact upon the hotel executive chef.

Many budget, limited-service, and economy hotel chains have completely eliminated full-service restaurant operations, as they have historically not contributed to the profitability of the overall hotel property. Restaurant service at this level has often been substituted with a staff member who sets up a daily continental breakfast, with the addition of local restaurant take-out menus located in the guest rooms.

Midscale hotels have taken a slightly different perspective on their restaurant operations, which has often resulted in elimination of the executive chef position. Midscale hotels are often turning toward established regional freestanding restaurant chains as a source of providing food service for their guests—in effect outsourcing their F&B operations.

Full-service and luxury hotels are the market segment with the greatest potential for successful restaurant operations due to the expertise of the much-valued executive chef. Luxury chains are striving to establish an identity as a place where locals and hotel guests alike can enjoy a quality meal within a nice atmosphere. There are a number of different strategies for hotel chains to conduct when food service for the full-service hotel is under consideration.

- Management consulting is one option that involves hiring an outside entity to help develop a concept and then run the restaurant.
- Another option that hotel chains often consider is to pursue licensing agreements that allow a hotel to replicate a branded concept in exchange for a fee.
- The most popular method of reengineering the hotel restaurant is through leasing agreements, which are most often percentage based relative to profitability. Leased restaurants can be independent, functioning no differently than freestanding restaurants, or they can assume some or all of the hotel's food and beverage operations; including breakfast, room service, and catering (Taylor, 2000).
- The last method of upgrading and reorganizing that a hotel chain might consider, which directly affects the position of the executive chef, is the acquisition of a concept and celebrity chef as a package (discussed above). This strategy has proven to be quite lucrative in major markets such as Las Vegas and New York City. Through the media of cooking television shows and the writing and production of specialized cookbooks, personality-driven chefs and their hotels can reap the benefits of such exposure and the indirect marketing that goes with it. While entertaining thousands of people on stations like the television Food Network, a celebrity chef associated with a particular hotel can have a significant marketing effect. The chefs who carry the charisma and excitement on cooking shows across the nation have evolved into overnight successes as celebrity chefs.

According to Mark Shuda, corporate director of F&B development, Starwood Hotels, "whatever the arrangement, hotels realize that upgrading their food service usually up-grades their bottom line. . . . A hotel's food and beverage component affects how the establishment is perceived as a whole. . . . Good restaurants not only keep guests on the property, they are important assets when it comes to attracting bookings for rooms and special events" (Taylor, 2000). Luxury hotels have found what some might call the formula for success in the relationship between hotel restaurants and celebrity chefs. An advantage for the restaurant concept in a luxury property is less rent than the cost to operate a freestanding restaurant, and having a celebrity-chef concept located in a hotel offers the restaurant stability and continuity because of the consistent flow of guest from the hotel property. Another advantage is that in the transition of integrating a celebrity-chef concept into a hotel, the hotel sometimes supports start-up capital for improvements and renovations. Lastly, hotels also often support the celebrity-chef concept with their extensive advertising and marketing budgets, which results in the outcome of this perfect partnership, guests entering the doors of the hotel and restaurant simultaneously.

PROFESSIONAL DEVELOPMENT

The hotel executive chef must have an extensive background working within hotel restaurants in order to understand the vast range of responsibilities, challenges, and opportunities that occur in a given operating day. The chef's knowledge must be broader than the fundamentals of cooking and must encapsulate an understanding of marketing, accounting, finance, operations, purchasing, and the management of personnel. Hotel chefs, similar to independent restaurant chefs, are dealing with a multitude of management decisions in substitution to, and sometimes at the expense of, operational interaction. Chefs do have a required amount of involvement on the floor in order to lead their staff to consistency in food preparation and presentation, yet that involvement has been challenged by the many management and organizational decisions that need to be made by a hotel executive chef in a given day. Alessandro Stratta, executive chef of the Phoenician Hotel's Mary Elaine's Restaurant, in Phoenix, states that "he spends less time cooking than on organizational stuff, which makes the operation run smoothly" (Liberson, 1998). This depends, of course, on the size, complexity, and market segment as outlined in Figure 6.5.

Food safety, sanitation, and nutrition are a few areas in which hotel chefs must have superior ongoing training. Integration of proper safety and sanitation standards into a kitchen is mandatory, hence this is the responsibility of the hotel chef to continue formal training in these areas, and to then further disseminate that information throughout their staff in an effective manner. Nutrition is an issue in which the hotel chef needs to remain knowledgeable, as it is now integrated into cooking methodology and flavor dynamics throughout kitchen operations, and is simply something that the guest expects to be available on the menu. The hotel chef also needs to invest their time in professional development and continuing-education opportunities in order to understand the culinary world that surrounds them and to continue self-learning concerning cook-

FIGURE 6.5
Contemporary hotel segments F&B related to the executive chef

Upscale Hotel Restaurants—Dedicated Chef
- Metropolitan locations
- Celebrity/star chefs with promotions
- Consistent travel and local consumer
- Leasing F&B to high-end chains, street entrance

Midscale Hotel Restaurants—Dedicated Chef or Elimination of Position
- Dependent on location and consumer demographics
- Possibly rely on outsourcing restaurant or internal development of restaurant concept and roll-out at corporate level and rollout, with regional menu design
- Limited service venues, focus on rooms revenue and service
- Leasing to midscale familiar-brand chain restaurants

Economy Hotel Restaurants—Elimination of Chef Position
- Continental breakfasts built into room rate
- Often have independent chain restaurant concepts on property
- Relationships with local restaurants who have delivery programs, partnership
- Don't depend on restaurant profitability

ing related to ethnicity and culture at an international scale. Today's upscale hotel guest is considered to be educated, well traveled, and to have a sophisticated palate; hence the chef is required to spend extra time researching and learning about the issues that relate to their position as an ambassador of gastronomy to the hotel guest.

Some of the issues the hotel chef needs to understand and cultivate a professional opinion about consist of many (or all) of the following:

- Cooking equipment technology.
- Farming technology.
- Biotechnology and genetic engineering.
- Hybridization of crops.
- Animal husbandry.
- Food storage and the use of irradiation.
- Computer technology for inventory and food ordering.
- Web page and World Wide Web integration into operations.
- Understanding today's consumer behaviors.

This small list should demonstrate that the hotel chef is not only a person responsible for learning but is also committed to indirectly and directly educating their staff and customer through their opinions related to the above issues. To be a qualified and successful hotel chef, one must be a continual student of the surrounding environment and culture and have the ability to correlate that with what they prepare, how they prepare it, and whom they serve it to.

When considering education, the hotel chef has the opportunity to learn informally through professional development and continuing-education courses offered through various professional organizations. There are also formal opportunities through degrees in culinary arts and business/finance. This results in great opportunities for the hotel executive chef. The Culinary Institute of America and Johnson and Wales University—two of the top-rated culinary programs in the United States—have both integrated bachelor degree options into their curricula with an emphasis upon business and financial skills. Hotel chefs, and their staffs, are now graduating from either culinary or hospitality management programs with a foundation of culinary and financial knowledge that prepares them for success in the twenty-first-century hotel restaurant.

Successful hotel chefs must play two roles: as a student and as a teacher. In the latter case, they must be willing to educate and invest in those who surround them every day within the hotel kitchen. In the former instance, they must be prepared to continually upgrade and polish their skills to remain competitive not only on behalf of the hotel's guests, but also the new responsibilities of marketing, organization design, and financial accountability. A good illustration of the impact of these obligations is the sample job description in the sidebar "Hotel Executive Chef Job Description"—a job description typical of the duties an executive chef in a large hotel resort would be responsible for. This is by no means an exhaustive description of the responsibilities of a hotel executive chef.

HOTEL EXECUTIVE CHEF JOB DESCRIPTION

Job Overview
- Responsible for all aspects of managing the kitchen and kitchen personnel.
- Ensuring the quality preparation of all menu items and proper handling/storage of all food items in accordance with predetermined internal standards.
- Coordinates the purchase of all food and develops menus, while maintaining preapproved food costs and labor costs.

Reports To:

F&B vice president, general manager

Supervises:

Assistant executive chef, executive sous-chefs, room chefs, assistant room chefs, sous-chefs, cooks, master cooks, pantry workers, and kitchen helpers.

Work Environment

- Kitchen, service, and dining room areas.
- Job requires ability to work within the following environmental constraints:
  - Under variable temperature conditions.
  - Outdoors/indoors.
  - Around fumes and/or odor hazards.
  - Around chemicals.
  - Slippery floors.
  - General kitchen equipment.

Key Relationships

Internal

Staff in kitchen, stewarding, F&B, purchasing department, storeroom, engineering, sales, accounting, housekeeping, and executive committee members

External

Hotel guests/visitors, food vendors, equipment repair company personnel, health department inspectors

Standard Specifications

Requirements are representative of minimum levels of knowledge, skills, and/or abilities. To perform this job successfully, the incumbent will possess the abilities or aptitudes to perform each duty proficiently.

Qualifications

Essential

- High school diploma or equivalent vocational training certificate.
- Certification of culinary training or apprenticeship.
- Five years' experience in a similar position.
- Work all stations in kitchen.

- Food-handling certificate.
- Fluency in English, both verbal and nonverbal.
- Compute intermediate-level mathematical calculations.
- Provide legible communication.
- Knowledge of food cost controls and waste management.
- Work with all products and food ingredients.
- Operate, clean, and maintain all equipment required in job functions.
- Plan and develop menus and recipes.
- Expand and condense recipes.
- Ability to:
  - Perform job functions with attention to detail, speed, and accuracy.
  - Prioritize and organize.
  - Maintain calm demeanor, resolving problems using good judgment.
  - Follow directions thoroughly.
  - Understand guest's service needs.
  - Work cooperatively with fellow workers.
  - Work with minimal supervision.
  - Maintain confidentiality of guest information and pertinent hotel data.
  - Ascertain departmental training needs and provide such training.
  - Direct performance of staff and follow up with corrections when needed.

Desirable

- Culinary college degree.
- Driver's license.
- Fluency in a second language.
- Sanitation certification.
- Maintain good coordination.
- Certification in CPR.
- Input and access information in the property management system/computers.
- Previous guest relations training.
- Artistic talent.

Physical Abilities

Essential

- Exert physical effort in transporting up to 75 pounds.
- Endure various physical movements throughout the work areas for 7 hours during work shift.

- Reach 2 feet from shoulders.
- Satisfactorily communicate with guests, management, and co-workers to their understanding.

Marginal
- Inspect and/or detect odors to ensure product quality and safety.

Essential Job Functions
- Maintain complete knowledge of and comply with all departmental policies, service procedures, and standards.
- Maintain complete knowledge of correct maintenance and handling of equipment. Use equipment only as intended, and only after proper training has been demonstrated.
- Anticipate guests' needs, respond promptly, and acknowledge all guests, however busy and whatever time of day.
- Maintain positive guest relations at all times.
- Be familiar with all hotel services/features and local attractions/activities to respond to guest inquiries accurately.
- Resolve guest complaints within a reasonable period.
- Monitor and ensure cleanliness, sanitation, and organization of all kitchen work areas.
- Review the daily operational activities; such as:
  - House count.
  - Forecasted covers for each outlet.
  - Catering activity.
  - Purchases.
  - Meetings.
  - Appointments.
  - VIPs/special guests.
- Establish daily operational priorities and assign production and prep task to staff for execution.
- Review daily specials and offer feedback to sous-chefs and room chefs.
- Review banquet function sheets and make note of any changes; post function sheets for the next 7 days.
- Meet with executive sous-chef to review schedules, assignments, anticipated business levels, and changes.
- Communicate additions or changes to the assignments as they arise throughout the shift. Iden-

tify situations that compromise the department's standards and delegate these tasks for completion.
- Execute daily physical inventory of specified food items.
- Communicate needs with purchasing and storeroom personnel and ensure quality of products received.
- Meet with the executive steward to review equipment needs, banquet plate-up assistance, cleaning schedule and project status, and health, safety, and sanitation follow-up.
- Ensure that staff reports to work as scheduled and document any late or absent employees.
- Inspect grooming and attire of staff and rectify any deficiencies.
- Check and ensure that all opening duties are completed to standard.
- Ensure that each kitchen work area is stocked with specified tools, supplies, and equipment to meet the business demand.
- Ensure that recipe cards, production schedules, plating guides, and photographs are current and posted.
- Ensure that the entire staff prepares menu items following recipes and yield guides, and are in accordance with department standards.
- Maintain personnel appearance and hygiene in accordance with departmental policies.
- Monitor performance of staff and ensure all procedures are completed to the department standards; and rectify deficiencies with respective personnel.
- Work on line during service and assist whenever needed.
- Be aware of any shortages and make arrangements to increase inventory as needed.
- Ensure that F&B service staff are informed of sold-out items and amount of available menu specials throughout the meal period.
- Observe guest reactions and confer with service staff to ensure guest satisfaction.
- Conduct frequent walk-throughs of each kitchen area and direct respective personnel to correct any deficiencies. Ensure that quality and details are being maintained.
- Inspect the cleanliness of the line, floor, and all

kitchen stations and direct staff to rectify any deficiencies.

- Ensure that staff maintain and strictly abide by state sanitation/health regulations and hotel requirements.
- Maintain proper storage procedures as specified by health department and hotel requirements.
- Instruct staff in the correct usage and care of all machinery in the kitchen operation while stressing safety.
- Review and approve work orders for maintenance repairs and submit to engineering, while contacting engineering directly for urgent repairs.
- Develop new menu items, test and write recipes with the executive sous-chefs and room chefs.
- Assist catering department with developing special menus for functions while meeting with clients as requested.
- Supervise and direct the organization and preparation of food for the employee cafeteria.
- Review sales and food cost daily; and resolve any discrepancies with the controller.
- Minimize waste and maintain controls to attain forecasted food and labor costs.
- Ensure that excess items are utilized efficiently.
- Monitor and ensure that all closing duties are completed to standard before staff departure.
- Foster and promote a cooperative working climate, maximizing productivity and employee morale.
- Conduct annual performance appraisals on staff members and manage disciplinary problems through communication of hotel standards.
- Commend staff members when performance is satisfactory or exemplary.
- Conduct scheduled performance appraisals.
- Interview and hire new personnel according to hotel policies and standards.

- Prepare weekly work schedules for all kitchen personnel in accordance with staffing guidelines and forecasted labor costs.
- Adjust labor schedules throughout the week to match business demand.
- Prepare daily/weekly payroll reports.
- Document pertinent information in the logbook and follow up on items notated during other shifts.

Marginal Functions

- Plan and conduct monthly departmental meetings.
- Attend weekly staff meetings, F&B meetings, preconvention meetings, and BEO review meetings.
- Return business telephone calls.
- Answer correspondence.
- Research local farm products, new suppliers, and special markets.
- Attend gourmet shows and internal food and wine training.
- Perform at special events and off-premise functions.
- Schedule and conduct month-end inventories.
- Prepare menu analysis and recipe costing.

Note

A review of this description has excluded the marginal functions of the position that are incidental to the performance of fundamental job duties. All duties and requirements are essential job functions. This job description in no way states or implies that these are the only duties to be performed by the employee occupying this position. Employees will be required to perform any other job-related duties assigned by their supervisor. This document does not create an employment contract, implied or otherwise, other than an at-will employment relationship.

INTERNAL AND EXTERNAL RELATIONSHIPS

Internal and external relationships are extremely important for the hotel executive chef. There are four primary segments of relationships for the chef, which consist of staff, consumers, vendor/sales associates, and professional affiliations. According to the National Restaurant Association, "by 2010, restaurants can expect to generate sales of $577 billion and account for 53 percent of America's food dollar. But with unemployment at its lowest levels in decades, restaurants are among the hardest hit in today's extremely competitive labor market" (Misek, 2000). This has a direct correlation with the internal relationships between the executive chef and staff members.

The hotel executive chef is constantly torn between a focus on operations and the people whom they employ. Related to the proportion of the executive chef's time, operations often will win, with a result of increased employee dissatisfaction and a higher turnover rate. Relationships are critical to the success of the hotel restaurant. When the executive chef takes time to know and understand their staff, from the dishwasher to administrative clerk, the result will be success that is sure to have a positive impact on the bottom line. According to director of corporate communications at Brinker International, "Our studies show that there is a direct proportionate relationship between individual restaurant profitability and the tenure of its management.... Good managers who have been here for a while instill a team mentality in line staff and treat them well. In turn, the entire restaurant team functions in a way that is not only good for profitability, but good for employees" (Misek, 2000).

The chef has a tremendous amount of responsibility related to the training and supervision of their staff, which can sometimes consist of hundreds of employees. Figure 6.6 shows a sample organizational chart for a large hotel resort that exemplifies the multiple relationships a hotel executive chef must manage.

FIGURE 6.6
Hotel executive chef organization chart

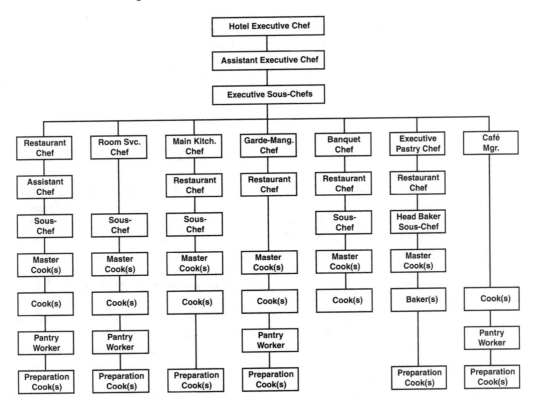

This organizational chart is by no means inclusive of all the positions available in a hotel food and beverage operation. The organizational chart increases or decreases in size with the size of the organization.

The demographics and guest preferences influencing hotel restaurants are quite broad. According to Joan Marsan, associate editor of *Hotels* magazine, "travelers will carry culinary influences across borders, fusing cooking methods and flavors and developing new techniques and dishes" (2000). Today's hotel restaurant patron is often well educated, well traveled, and has developed sophisticated expectations. As a result of hosting more of these sophisticated, internationally conscientious guests, hotel chefs are opting to offer more extravagant international dishes with a strong "value orientation." According to a segment study conducted by *Nations Restaurant News*, "hotels are finding the budget-conscious, value-oriented traveler now dominates the market, seeking the best buys in room quality and food service. While many new hotels offer only limited food service, older hotels are restructuring their food service mix to put emphasis on lower-cost food service and some chains are offering hotel owners the opportunity to bring in franchises to operate restaurants on their properties" (Ruggless, 1993). The hotel executive chef must participate in constant analyses of the restaurant guests' expectations in order to maintain a successful operation.

Vendor and sales associate relationships are extremely important for the hotel executive chef, as these relationships have a direct correlation to the receiving of quality food, beverage, and equipment items from the perspective vendor. The quality of these relationships has a direct link to the success of the restaurant, as the support and cooperation from sales associates and delivery personnel is a necessity. Receiving staples that are matched with the prearranged standards, and at the agreed price and quality level, is critical for the success of the hotel restaurant, as the quality of the raw product must be at the highest possible level in order for the staff to transform that item into a quality meal for the hotel restaurant patron.

Professional affiliations are important for the hotel chef, as this is an opportunity to collaborate with other industry professionals and to discuss issues related to hotel and restaurant operations. Three professional affiliations that aid in development, certification, and cultivation of learning and shared information consist of the American Culinary Federation (ACF), the National Restaurant Association (NRA), and the American Hotel and Motel Association (AH&MA). Another opportunity to learn for the hotel chef is to participate in continuing-education courses offered through institutions such as the Culinary Institute of America, such as those regularly offered at their Greystone facility in St. Helena, California. Attending continuing-education courses allows an opportunity for the chef to receive information formally through the class curriculum and instruction, and also informally through discussion with other professionals who are attending the course. As I said above, the position of executive chef is one of a student and teacher; hence professional development and relationships for the chef have a direct impact upon the learning and development of their staff, and to the overall guest experience.

CONCLUSION

The roles of hotel executive chefs have evolved into a position of great responsibility and challenge over the last century. The chef is no longer spending the majority of his or her time on the line prepping food or plating for banquets, but is more often playing the role of organizer, decision maker, opinion developer, and marketing and financial strategist for the hotel restaurant operation. The position of hotel executive chef has been eliminated at many budget and economy operations, and is often scarce at the midlevel hotel operation. The greatest amount of opportunity for the hotel executive chef exists within the upscale and luxury hotel segments.

As we enter the twenty-first century, the position of hotel chef can be seen as one of prestige, but at the same time one of accountability. We can also view the executive chef as one of the motivators that draw guests into the hotel restaurant from the local community and from other hotels. We can also view the chef as one who is critical to the success of the hotel's restaurant operations. The chef is an individual who is not only required to express artistry and creativity through their food preparation and presentation, but is now expected to have the knowledge and ability to express creativity through restaurant marketing, personnel management, accountability, and the ability to produce profits for the hotel.

6.10 Organization and Management for Hotel Beverage Operations

Valentino Luciani

BRIEF HISTORY OF BEVERAGES

A beverage, such as a glass of wine, a beer, or a cocktail, has the magic power of bringing people together. Beverages have always made some sort of impact on the evolution of humankind. Thanks to modern technology and more advanced carbon-dating techniques, archaeologists have now established with certainty that humans have been around for several hundred thousand years. A lot longer than it was estimated fifty years ago. In accepting the fact that alcohol is as old as we are, it would of great interest to discover what type of beverages were consumed by men and women over such a span of time. We can assume only that the earliest kind of beverages were fermented cider-type concoctions made from various kinds of fruit, or brews made from grain, seeds, and anything that nature had to offer. These drinks were perhaps enriched with spices, herbs, and probably more exotic flavoring agents, some of which have been forgotten or have been lost over the centuries.

What is known for certain is included in recorded history, and it is relatively recent when compared to the newly found life span of *Homo sapiens erectus*. In recent excavations, one of the first evidence of eating food and con-suming a beverage in a communal fashion is found in the Orkney Islands close to Denmark. It was a custom, then, to build dwellings all around a common dispenser where foods and drinks were prepared.

Egyptologists have recently published photos of wall paintings found in pharaohs' tombs. On these remarkably preserved works of art one can clearly see Egyptian workers harvesting and preparing for winemaking. Next to the tomb, wine jars were placed orderly. The Egyptian nobles believed that these types of beverages made the best companion for the pharaoh's eternal travel.

Greek and Roman historians report that wine and other alcoholic beverages played a vital role in their societies. The fun-loving Romans went as far as worshiping a beverage deity: Bacchus, the god of wine. Wine and brew shops, which are thought to be introduced approximately 6000 years ago, could be found at every street corner during the times of ancient Rome. In the United States the first person on record to own a tavern and sell alcoholic beverages to the tavern's patrons was Samuel Cole. His beverage business was already prospering by 1634.

Beer, which presently accounts for 51 percent of alcoholic beverage sales, carries a fine tradition in our country. According to the diary of the *Mayflower*'s captain, the ship was not scheduled to dock on Plymouth Rock but was made to stop there mainly because it had run out of beer.

Nonalcoholic beverages, such as coffee, tea, fruit juices, and, at a later date, carbonated beverages, have also made a considerable impact on our evolution and lifestyle. During the past five decades Coca-Cola has taken the world by storm. Of the hot beverages coffee and tea are the uncontested kings. In some of the smaller eastern countries the halting of tea production would mean the country's economic collapse.

OVERVIEW

The beverage industry grows in popularity every year. *Restaurants USA*, the official publication of the National Restaurant Association, reported in 1995 that total sales for bars and taverns neared the $11 billion mark. For the year 2005, total sales for bars and taverns are expected to exceed the threshold of $15 billion in sales. Hotels, restaurants, and resorts have for some time regarded the beverage sector as a profitable one. In a medium-to-large-size hotel a typical beverage department can produce a profit of over 50 percent of sales. In comparison, a food department would show, at best, a profit between 15 and 18 percent of sales. Beverage is also gradually gaining a larger share of sales. Hotel operators report that while two decades ago the sales ratio was 85 to 15 (85 percent food sales to 15 percent beverage sales), today the average is closer to 80 to 20.

Before World War II, in a small-to-medium-size hotel and restaurant operation, the person in charge of the beverage department was the restaurant manager. In many properties, a lead bartender or the wine steward was given the responsibility to run the department.

Today in a medium-to-large-size hotel operation, the beverage department has a distinct organization chart where the beverage manager is the person in charge of running and supervising all of the department activities. The organization chart is a diagram that shows the operation's working positions and how they interconnect. The beverage manager usually reports to the food and beverage director. In a very large hotel operation (over 2000 rooms), the F&B director reports to the vice president of food and beverage.

During the last decade some properties have adopted a different strategy where there is a separate food director and beverage director. In these properties the executive chef, who in most cases acts more as a food director than a bona fide chef, is placed in charge of the food department. He or she enjoys a higher degree of independence and reports directly to the general manager, vice president of operations, or in some instances directly to the hotel president. The same rationale applies to the beverage director.

Both of these directors are considered equal in the organization chart. They strive to work together effectively and to communicate on a daily basis. They are interdependent in many ways and aware of the need for communication, but also establish a sound working rapport with department heads of other hotel sectors. These include front desk supervisors, executive housekeepers, human resource directors, and so forth. Typical of this case, the food manager and the beverage manager, particularly, come together at the end of the month when the results of their efforts are included in the same profit and loss statement.

Although the above-mentioned larger properties find this organization chart modification to be beneficial to the operation, the majority of hotel properties still adopt the traditional hierarchy, thereby structuring the chain of command in the same fashion as it has been for the past six or seven decades. A typical example of a classic organization chart for a beverage operation in a large hotel is shown in Figure 6.7.

FIGURE 6.7
Organization chart of beverage department in a medium to large hotel

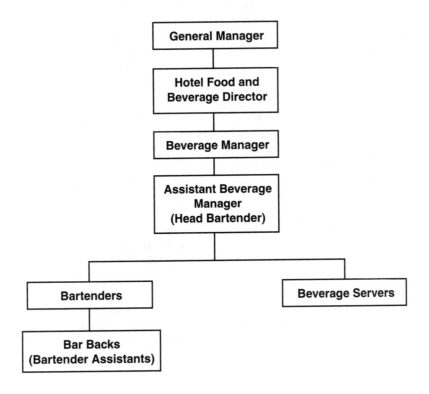

SHOPTALK AND THE ACTIVE MANAGER

The bar manager (or beverage director) is the person who "makes it all happen" in relation to all hotel beverages. Although specific responsibilities may vary from one hotel to another, the fundamental role of the manager is to make certain that the five basic functions of management are applied effectively. As in many other business sectors, these are planning, organizing, directing, staffing, and controlling. The wise and competent bar manager applies and adapts the fundamental principles of each of these functions to the specific needs of the operation. All five functions are a determining factor in meeting with the operation's ultimate objective: profitability.

It all begins with planning and continues in directing and organizing so that the staff on a daily basis diligently adheres to the established standards. This includes, for example, checking bartenders' opening and closing duties, standardizing drink recipes, verifying that the bar *par stock* (established amount of beverage product) is at the proper level, scheduling, forecasting, frequently communicating with other fellow managers, (in particular the catering manager and the executive steward), and so forth.

The competent bar manager always finds sufficient time to inspect the *underbars* (the working area behind and underneath the bar counter), the *jockey boxes* (the small compartment next to the ice bin), and the *speed racks* (where the inexpensive or "well" bottles and the more popular brand-name liquors are placed).

The above are also the areas where managers cannot place enough emphasis on how vital it is to the operation to have a continuous application of sanitary standards and utmost cleanliness. Glassware needs not only to be clean but sanitized, as well.

An important organizational and training function is the *sequencing* of beverage stock. This is the order in which spirits and cordials are placed on the shelves or speed rack. It also refers to the order by which the drinks are called to the bartender by the serving staff, and must always be the same. Supervising the beverage staff and ensuring that control methods are foolproof are crucial and demanding tasks; sequencing provides part of the structural mix that helps assure a consistency of product and service.

MARKETING AND MERCHANDISING

Many beverage managers consider smart marketing and effective merchandising as the keys to success. The marketing of the overall operation and the merchandising of the beverage product require time, experience, and commitment. To make the beverage operation attractive to different type of patrons and to convey a message of price/value in the service of beverages, bar managers and directors need to brainstorm on a daily basis. More trendy cocktails are being created daily. Light and refreshing blush wines and champagnes are introduced in the preparation of new drinks. Promotional programs and attractive entertainment are featured to keep lounges full and patrons made to desire to go back.

Conscientious beverage managers never rest on their laurels; they are always on the lookout for profitable ways to stay ahead of the competition. As the beverage sector grows and patrons' expectations increase, there are always new challenging tasks to deal with. The following is a list of managerial tasks that beverage managers are currently occupied with on an ongoing basis:

- Introducing control systems that are more effective in monitoring the operation, for example, upgrading forms for properly storing and issuing beverage products and for inventory purposes.
- Establishing ongoing training sessions.
- Evaluating beverage staff work performance.
- Checking city and county ordinances regarding the service of alcohol and reviewing state and federal laws on handling liquor responsibly.
- Preventing bartenders from committing fraud and from attempting illegal practices.
- Ensuring that proper sanitary standards are applied throughout the bar outlets, storage, and service areas.
- Making certain that everyone in the department adheres to proper safety standards.
- Writing, rewriting, and updating bar working manuals and handbooks according to needs.
- Evaluating the bar menu offerings and, whenever possible, substituting slow-selling liquor brands with more attractive and trendy ones.
- In particular, the manager needs to renew beverage product selection of specialty beers (e.g., by featuring microbrewed products), brandies, and cordials.
- A current trend is apparent in cordials or liqueurs. Beverage operators are finding that light, sweet, and pleasant-tasting cordials such as Godiva White Chocolate, Nocello, Grand Marnier, Frangelico, Drambuie, Bailey's Irish Cream, and so forth, are enjoying newfound popularity in any beverage operation's inventory. We are also seeing attractive new products such as Remy Red, and the fabulous premium tequilas and Polish vodkas introduced during the turn of the last century.

- Last but not least is the consistency and quality of the service provided to the bar and lounge patron.

HUMAN RESOURCES

Outstanding service is the result of a sound organization and diligent recruiting. Bartenders and beverage servers can be talented and willing, but if they are not provided with the necessary resources, combined with total management support, encouragement, and guidance, their efforts will be in vain. A situation may arise where the deciding factor in the delivery of fine and consistent quality service would not depend so much on personnel skills and attitude but mostly on the role played by management.

Service has become the backbone of the hospitality industry. According to Kotschevar and Luciani (1996), "with the new millennium passing by, customers' expectations are on the rise." An effective leader finds the proper ways and means to provide the employees with the tools they need to meet these expectations.

Progressive beverage managers now also use the empowerment concept. Empowering is a management decision by which an employee is given authority to take steps outside the spectrum of regular duties and make certain decisions that are normally management's domain. According to many new beverage managers, the "progressive coach" approach seems to bring along more positive results among beverage staffs. The old disciplinarian management style is increasingly out of place in today's beverage business world.

THE FUTURE OF BEVERAGE OPERATIONS

In medium to larger hotel properties, beverage managers, like all department managers, are required to prepare a business forecast based on historical data, hotel occupancy, and special-event bookings for the forecasting period. An accurate forecast helps the manager be prepared for clientele volume so that potential revenue can be maximized. It also helps greatly in effectively managing beverage stock, payroll, staff scheduling, and other expenses.

Many hotel executives agree that the first decade of the new century will be a significant one for the beverage industry. One peculiar prediction is that, although total hotel revenues are expected to grow considerably, the ratio of beverage sales as compared to room sales will remain the same or decrease slightly. Beverage, though, is expected to increase with respect to food revenue growth. Independent bar and lounge operators feel confident that, unless unpredictable events take place, the coming decade will be a challenging, but prosperous one.

Beverage distributing firms are also optimistic. They foresee a wider availability of beverage products not only for the hospitality industry but also in other areas such as convenience stores, supermarkets, and beverage-specific retail outlets. Beverages that are expected to substantially increase in sales volume are bottled waters, bottled specialty teas, single-malt Scotch whiskeys, cognacs, aged bourbons, premium tequilas, and grappas. There is a general consensus among vendors that beer sales are expected to remain static and that wine will experience a marginal but steady growth.

It is expected that federal and state liquor laws will remain substantially unchanged with minor exceptions. It also appears that the various states will maintain the basic structure of belonging either to "control" or "license" categories. Many beverage managers are concerned about government-imposed taxes on liquor and hope they will not be increased.

Beverage managers are also concerned about the continuing lowering of the blood-alcohol thresholds for driving under the influence (DUI) of alcohol and/or drugs. The lower the threshold—say 0.08—the more careful managers have to be in hiring, training, and supervising. This is an industrywide problem that presents managers with a variety of challenges. It is important to have policies under which the manager and operation work that will minimize the risk to the business and to the public, at the same time legally selling and serving beverages.

Education in beverage management is also expected to extend to new horizons. Sonoma State University will continue to offer a bachelor of science degree in wine management. Through a well-planned university extension program, the University of California, Davis, is expanding on specialized short courses associated with their degree programs in enology and viticulture. The William F. Harrah College of Hotel Administration at the University of Nevada, Las Vegas, will start a beverage management major commencing in the fall semester of 2001. Cornell University's School of Hotel Administration is considering expanding their professional development courses and adding courses on handling and serving alcoholic beverages with care.

AS I SEE IT

While reviewing the industry's projections for the future, it would be difficult to leave out hotel executives' most recent comments on labor issues and concerns. During the past decade it has been frequently reported that staffing or finding the right person that is best suitable for a particular job is becoming a tougher management function. Many managers agree that staffing responsibilities are requiring more time and effort than ever before. Part of this is attributed to labor trends. The general pool of steady and loyal workers is decreasing in size. In addition, the hospitality industry is experiencing unprecedented employee turnover. A major restaurant company has recently reported employee turnover of nearly 200 percent for hourly employees, 60 percent for clerical/secretarial staff, and 25 percent for managerial staff. The turnover ratio of bartenders and cocktail servers was reported to be almost the same as that of typical dining room staff such as food servers and buspersons (Lattin, 1998). One can imagine the frustration of a beverage manager who, after spending considerable effort, time, and company money in coaching and training a new bartender, then finds out the bartender is planning to quit the following week.

What can be done to deal effectively with this concern? Rewards as motivators have proven to provide some positive results. Other means of providing monetary incentives so that the operation can retain employees for a longer period of time may also be effective.

It is strongly recommended here that the very best measure that management can undertake for this purpose is to provide the employee with a comfortable working environment, promote teamwork and camaraderie, and foster healthy working relationships. In short, it is the challenge to the beverage manager to become the "employer of choice" for beverage professionals.

In general, the "beverage future" looks brighter than most other sectors of the hospitality industry. However, the managers and directors that truly will make a difference will be those who plan to take a more active participation and make things happen. The "aggressive" new manager always finds ways to establish a good rapport with community leaders and is tireless in devising and developing new means of attracting additional clientele. Whenever possible he or she makes the effort to attend beverage conventions and trade shows, uses the hotel Web site to reinforce marketing strategies, list bar special drinks, promotions, and happy hour times, and never rests on their laurels.

The modern beverage manager is no longer

just the "head bartender." This professional is responsible for millions of dollars of the hotel's assets and operates in a high-energy, fast-paced, and challenging environment. It's a lot of fun, though, and rewarding, too. It is a managerial position with a solid future.

6.11   Case Study: Food and Beverage Division

OUTSIDE THE BOX

The corporate food and beverage committee, through its executive director, has ordered each hotel in the SunRise Hospitality chain (11 medium-size, full-service hotels situated generally in the southeast, south, and southwest) to submit a plan to completely rethink one restaurant in each hotel. SunRise Hospitality specializes in catering to the upscale business traveler and, increasingly, the high-tech companies that are now moving to the south from California, the Seattle region, and the northeast. Their average room rates are consistently in the top 15 percent of all hotels in their market areas. Historically, though, this has been a fairly conservative and risk-averse hotel company.

The corporate office wants to change this and wants to involve each hotel in the decision process. The executive director of F&B wants to evaluate plans from each hotel's food and beverage director that reflect thinking "outside the box." Among the ideas that are floating around the company on the F&B directors' "grapevine" are the following:

- Feature menus that emphasize local or regional cuisine. The idea here is to utilize fresh ingredients and local meat, produce, and seafood and should feature the ethnic and cultural diversity of each hotel's local market area. One thrust of this plan is to make the hotel restaurant appeal to local clientele in addition to its guests.

- Outsourcing one restaurant to a well-established regional independent operator.
- Outsourcing one restaurant to a national chain.
- Hiring a celebrity chef to bring prestige and favorable publicity to the hotel.

These are only a few of the possibilities, and as food and beverage director, you have brought this plan to a meeting of your staff for purposes of general background discussion and ideas about how to proceed. Included in this meeting are the executive chef and chief steward; the manager and assistant manager of your (up to this point) formal French-service dining room; and the wine steward and director of purchasing.

After presentation of the corporate plan, you ask for ideas and comments. The chef, who is French, is absolutely devastated and seems to be treating the corporate directive as a personal insult. He walks out in a huff threatening to pack up his knives and recipes and go back to France. The restaurant manager is interested in the idea but says she has just spent the last five months hiring and training about one-half of her restaurant staff to learn tableside preparation and service of the French menu. She is worried that switching menus this fast may cause her operation to suffer, at least in the short term.

The wine steward considers this challenge a positive one because depending on what eventually is decided, he will have to choose a complementary wine list to enhance the new concept, but also a negative one because he could lose his job to an outsider.

The director of purchasing is intrigued by the possibilities of exploring new local markets if that is the ultimate direction. He, too, worries that some of the options may diminish his responsibilities.

Your job as director of food and beverage is to help each department head to come up with a plan that will satisfy their concerns while at the same time follow the dictates of corporate policy.

(Editor's note: Additional insights into the potential solutions to this case may be gained by reading "The Hotel Purchasing Function" by C. Lee Evans in Part VIII of this book.)

References

Allen, Robin Lee. 1996. "Hotel Chains 'Taking It to the Street' in Quests for Mainstream Dining Appeal." *Nation's Restaurant News* April 29: 30(17):124–128.

Bounds, W., and M. Higgins. 2000. "She's Stepping on My Spreadsheet! Hotel Bars, Once Serene Spots to Conduct Business, Turn Boisterous—and Profitable." *Wall Street Journal* January 21: B1, B4.

Coloccia, Jane. 1999. "Overcome: Getting the Restaurant on Your Property the Attention It Deserves." *Lodging F&B* May: 21–22.

Dubé, L., C. A. Enz, L. M. Renaghan, and J. A. Siguaw. 1999. *American Lodging Excellence: The Key to Best Practice in the U.S. Lodging Industry*. Ithaca, NY: Educational Institute of the American Hotel and Motel Association.

Hanson, Bjorn. 1984. "Hotel Foodservice: Where's the Profit." *Cornell Hotel and Restaurant Administration Quarterly* August: 25(2):92–96.

Hayes, Jack. 1998. "High-Profile Chefs Endow Top Hotels with Lucrative Luster." *Nation's Restaurant News* March: 45, 48, 50.

Hensdill, Cherie. 1996. "Partnerships in Dining." *Hotels* February: 30(2):57–60.

Hensdill, Cherie. 1998. "Redefining In-Room Dining: Hoteliers Demonstrate How a Good Restaurant, a Great Chef, and a Little Creative Management Can Boost Room Service Sales." *Hotels* July: 32(7):99–102.

"Holiday Inn Offers Assorted Food Options with New Quick Food Concept." 1996. *Hotel Business* June: 9.

Hubsch, Allen W. 1966. "Hotel Food and Beverage Management." *Cornell Hotel and Restaurant Administration Quarterly* 7(3): 9–11, 18–19.

Kotschevar, L., and V. Luciani. 1996. *Presenting Service*. Chicago: Educational Foundation of the National Restaurant Association.

Lattin, Gerald. 1998. *The Lodging and Food Service Industry,* 4th ed. East Lansing, MI: Educational Institute of the American Hotel and Motel Association.

Lee, D. T. 1999. "Young, But Seasoned, Hotel Chefs." *American Visions* January: 2.

Liberson, Judy. 1996. "The Global Dinner Plate." *Lodging* September: 22(1):85–88.

Liberson, Judy. 1998. "Top Toques: With Unique Talent and Flair, These Nine Chefs Add More Than Flavor to Hotel Restaurants," *Lodging* October:76–79.

Mandelbaum, Robert. 2000. "The Numbers Tell It All: The Changing Role of the Hotel F&B." *Lodging* November: 27, 28, 30.

Marsan, Joan. 2000. "Changing the Unchanged: The New Millennium Will Alter Virtually Untouched F&B Operations." *Hotels* January, p. 67, 70.

Marsan, Joan. 2000. "Kitchen Philosophies: Two Designers Envisioned Kitchens Attractive Enough to Draw in Guests. Chefs Find the Quarters Equally Enchanting." *Hotels* February: 73, 74, 76, 78.

Marsan, Joan. 2000. "Breakfast Designs." *Hotels* April: 85, 86, 88.

Misek, Marla. 2000. "In and Out: Restaurants Facing High Employee Turnover Must Innovate to Renovate." *Lodging* September: 19, 20, 22.

Parseghian, Pamela. 1996. "Branding Offers Hotels Opportunities to Increase Food

Sales." *Nation's Restaurant News* June 10: 30(23):96.

Pavesic, David V. 1998. *Restaurant Manager's Pocket Handbook Series: Menu Design.* New York: Lebhar-Friedman Books.

Pavesic, David V. 1998. *Restaurant Manager's Pocket Handbook Series: Menu Pricing.* New York: Lebhar-Friedman Books.

Powell, Laura. 2000. "Community Outreach: Strategies for Luring Locals and Eliminating the Off-Season." *Lodging* September: 24–24.

Ruggless, Ron. 1993. "The New Generation: Luxury Hotels Meet Value Dining." *Nation's Restaurant News* May: 51, 52, 54.

Ruggless, R. 1999. "Hotels Tap Mainstream Trends, Big-Name Chefs to Exploit Hot Economy." *Nation's Restaurant News* B3(26):160, 162, 165.

"Restaurant Chains Partner with Hotels to Satisfy Different Needs, Tastes." 1995. *Lodging*, September: 1, 8–9.

Restaurant Industry Forecast. 1999. "A Caring Culture: The Key to Management for the New Millennium." *Restaurants USA,* 18(11):F1–28.

"Ride the Branding Wave." 1996. *Lodging* September: 62–73.

Sheridan, Margaret. 1997. "Quantum Kitchens." *Restaurants and Institutions* November 1: 50, 51, 54, 56, 58, 60.

Sheridan, Margaret. 1998. "Room to Grow." *Restaurants and Institutions* November 1: 58, 59, 62, 64, 71, 73, 75.

Stephen, Beverly. 2000. "Front Burner: Soapy Sales." *Food Arts* November: 23.

Strate, Robert W., and Clinton L. Rappole. 1997. "Strategic Alliances between Hotels and Restaurants." *Cornell Hotel and Restaurant Administration Quarterly* June: 37(3):50–61.

Su, Keith. 2000. "Economic Trends and Influence on Hospitality Industry: The Case of U.S. Lodging Industry." *Hotel Online.* http://www.hotel-online.com/Neo/Trends/.

Taylor, Karen. 2000. "Celebrity Chefs: Fruitful Unions—Famous Chefs and Hotels Have Much to Offer Each Other." *Lodging* September: 28–33.

Wall Street Journal, October 25, 1999.

Withiam, Glenn. 1995. "Trader Vic's Wraps Up 60th Birthday Bash." *Cornell Hotel and Restaurant Administration Quarterly* April: 36(3):14.

Withiam, Glenn. 1995. "Harvey: Expansion and Conversion." *Cornell Hotel and Restaurant Administration Quarterly* August: 36(4):13.

Wolff, Carlo. 1995. "Hyatt Regency Columbus Blazes F&B Trails." *Lodging Hospitality* October: 51(9):24.

Suggested Readings

Books

Foster, Dennis L. 1992. *Food and Beverage: Operations, Methods, and Cost Controls.* Lake Forest, IL: Glencoe.

Shock, Patti J., and John M. Stefanelli. 1999. *Hotel Catering: A Handbook for Sales and Operations.* New York: John Wiley.

Articles

Withiam, Glenn. 1995. "Harvey: Expansion and Conversion." *Cornell Hotel and Restaurant Administration Quarterly* August: 36(4):13.

Source Notes

Chapter 6.2, "Hotel Food and Beverage Organization and Management," by Robert H. Bosselman.

Chapter 6.3, "As I See It: Hotel Director of Food and Beverage," by Dominic Provenzano.

Chapter 6.4, "Best Practices in Food and Beverage Management," by Judy A. Siguaw and Cathy A. Enz, is reprinted from the October 1999 issue of *The Cornell Hotel and Restaurant Administration Quarterly.* © Cornell University. Used by permission. All rights reserved.

7

Marketing and Associated Activities

7.1 Introduction

For most hotel companies, it was only during the 1980s that the word *marketing* was anything more than a euphemism for sales. Indeed, in the competitive landscape of the not too distant past, an aggressive and knowledgeable sales staff could accomplish most activities that related to putting guests in rooms. In the competitive environment of the present time, this has become impossible. Hotels companies that design and market a sophisticated inventory of hospitality services need a similarly sophisticated scheme for letting potential clientele know about their services.

For most hotel companies in the twenty-first century, true marketing has now evolved to reflect this sophistication. This also acknowledges increased sophistication on the part of guests and potential clientele. Business travelers, travel agents, and those meeting planners who represent and book group and convention business are well educated and informed consumers. To serve this clientele, hotels have had to develop marketing efforts

and product segmentation to first interest the market and, second, allow people representing that market to make intelligent choices from among competitors.

Marketing is thus an umbrella term that covers a number of strategic and tactical activities designed to tell the clientele the "story" of the hotel's services and encourage that clientele to make choices based on how one hotel's marketing message compares to alternatives. In any given hotel or hotel company, marketing includes: a range of sales activities; public relations; advertising in all media; design of symbols and images; and (increasingly) the departments of convention services, reservations, and perhaps catering.

It should also be noted that research plays a major role in designing marketing strategies and tactics. The articles and essays presented in this edition by Chekitan Dev and Michael Olsen, Eric Spangenberg and Bianca Grohmann, and Eric Orkin each have a research orientation at their core. Each is designed to assist managers in choosing and generating data that are useful to staying successfully competitive. It is important that managers understand the range within which this data may be interpreted and applied. Successful managers and high-quality organizations will always be seeking information and data that allows them to make accurate decisions and design effective marketing and/or managerial efforts.

These data can take a number of different forms, but for the most part deal with the various characteristics of the hotel's target market segment that affect their choice of hotels. Hotels will find mechanisms to accumulate the following sorts of data about their guests and potential guests:

- *Geographic*: what sorts of communities are represented; what parts of the country or world; how far do they travel?
- *Demographic*: age, sex, occupation, income, ethnicity, family, education.
- *Psychographic*: client's self image; social or peer group; lifestyle; personality traits.
- *Behavioristic*: is hotel choice a routine or special occasion; what does guest seek in terms of quality, service, economy; user status (nonuser, ex-user, potential user, regular user, first-time user); usage rate (light, medium, heavy); loyalty (none, medium, strong, absolute).

While many of the specific details or programs implied under the marketing umbrella may be farmed out to other agencies that specialize in advertising or public relations, the genesis of the hotel's strategic marketing plan has to be from within the hotel organization itself.

The articles contributed to this section by Fletch Waller and by Dev and Olsen also treat aspects of the strategic nature of marketing for the coming decade and attest to the new levels of sophistication that are becoming inherent in hotels' marketing activities. Waller's two contributions, when read together, provide a strong argument for broadening the defini-

tion of marketing to include all operational aspects of the hotel. He illustrates the relationship between marketing and operations as a "continuing process" without which hotels can probably not remain competitive.

Yield management, long a practice of the airline industry, has only recently started to find acceptance by hotel marketing and reservations systems. The article in this section by Orkin can be read in conjunction with that by Quain and LeBruto in Part IV for a comprehensive primer about yield management. Then, explore the various aspects of that practice from the viewpoint of a contemporaneous practitioner, Paul Chappelle. Chappelle lives the "theory" of yield and revenue management on a daily basis, and provides insights about how it all works in practice. Margaret Shaw's essay on hotel pricing should be read in context of the issues and suggestions raised by the contributions on yield management.

Nowhere, perhaps, does the concept of "word-of-mouth advertising" carry more potential weight than with the market of meeting planners. These hospitality professionals are the "gatekeepers" of millions of room-nights of hotel bookings annually. It is instructive that they base *their* hotel choices on internal and external information networks, peer advice, and informal word of mouth (Bloom, 1981; Lowe, 1984). It is for that reason that the recent article by Denney Rutherford and Terry Umbreit is included in this section.

Since this is such an important market to so many hotels, the collective views of the 52 meeting planners (MPs) these authors researched should be instructive to marketers and hotel managers as to what's important to this market segment. While much of the previous research about MPs focused on physical attributes of hotels (Bloom, 1981; Renaghan and Kay, 1987)—and by extension, the linkages to Lewis's advertising article (1990)—Rutherford and Umbreit specifically looked at the domains of behavioral interactions between MPs and hotel staff members. While on one level this article could be considered an operational piece, it is placed here to illustrate not only the importance of the other-than-physical needs of a major market, but to reinforce Waller's points about how a hotel's most effective and powerful marketing is *through* operations employees. Both of these concepts are reinforced by this research.

If marketing, as it has been said, is the *promise,* then it is the hotel's employees who *keep that promise.* This is particularly important with the above-referenced group market, represented in large part by meeting planners. In the Rutherford and Umbreit study, of the 316 critical incidents gleaned from 52 separate MP interviews, over 100 of those incidents, or 32 percent, had the convention services manager (CSM) as its central focus. It is the recognition of this central importance of the CSM in keeping the promise that many hotels include convention services as a functional component of the marketing department. These departments are staffed by professionals who design their activities specifically to make sure that the efforts and promises of the sales department and marketing messages are delivered to the group while it is on the premises of the hotel. Rhonda Montgomery and Denney Rutherford's profile of such managers provides graphic evidence of the importance of this position along with a detailed look at the responsibilities that are important for this professional to master in participating in the hosting of such an event.

Traditionally the function of public relations for any organization and particularly hotels was oriented toward the generation of favorable—usually free—publicity for the ho-

tel and the suppression or management of bad news. Louis Richmond proposes the different and expanded, but not necessarily contrary position that public relations activities can positively enhance the hotel's sales and marketing efforts. He discusses his experiences in the case of the Seattle Sheraton Hotel and Towers. Using that as an example, he argues that through creative cooperative efforts with local charity, cultural, and volunteer organizations, hotels can serve the activities of those groups' fund-raising efforts and simultaneously position themselves to show the arbiters of potential business how well the hotel can perform. His examples are instructive. Richmond, who is president of his own very successful public relations firm in Seattle, retains the Sheraton and other hospitality concerns as clients.

All in all, the strategies, tactics, activities, personnel, and concepts described by articles and essays in this section provide an overview that only hints at everything important to effective management of the marketing function. Marketing is perhaps the most-written-about topic in hospitality literature. Because there is such a diversity of opinion it can be argued that there is no one "right" way to market, nor is there any single piece of literature generally considered seminal to hotel marketing. The reader is urged to consider the references used by contributing authors, the suggested readings, and active perusal of recent hospitality journals to achieve greater understanding of this fascinating process and, by extension, its management.

7.2 Building Market Leadership: Marketing as Process

Fletch Waller

Over the last thirty years, change in the hotel business has been driven primarily by marketing issues and opportunities—new tools for acquiring customers, the ability to segment markets, brand consolidation and leverage,

distribution innovations, and globalization. Yes, new approaches to equity financing have provided wherewithal and reward for new hotel development; yes, new information technologies have improved operating productivity; but underlying all growth and change has been evolution in markets and in ways hotels relate to and capitalize upon them.

This section deals with "marketing." Not with the sales and marketing department, but marketing in its broadest sense. Definition? *Marketing is a process of creating and sustaining productive relationships with desirable customers.* The goal: *to produce such relationships more effectively than do your competitors.*

Let's examine these definitions and their implications.

- *Marketing is a process* . . . A process, a series of functions and actions approaching and dealing with opportunities. Marketing as used herein is not a job, but a way of proceeding to create and operate a hotel focused on customers and competitors, a way that incorporates all members of the hotel staff and its support.
- . . . *of creating* . . . The essence of marketing is creation: imagination, insight, willingness to change and evolve and, yes, discard.
- . . . *and sustaining* . . . Loyalty over time and repeat customers are the key to productivity and optimal contribution margins.
- . . . *productive relationships* . . . A relationship must be two-sided, with benefits for both partners in the relationship. In the case of customers, the benefits are wants and needs consistently fulfilled and full value received; in the case of staff, professional satisfaction and operating profits sufficient to fund improvements, provide attractive compensation, and provide returns on investors' or owners' capital.
- . . . *with desirable customers.* Not all customers are equally desirable; who we want are those willing to pay, growing in numbers, making multiple purchases, and that we are able to fully satisfy.

And the goal?

- . . . *to produce such relationships* . . . "production" implies inputs and outputs, and measurement of productivity.
- . . . *more effectively than do your competitors.* Marketing success is judged in relative terms, using competitors and like hotels as benchmarks. As a creative process, especially in a field like hospitality wherein innovations are easily copied and are unprotected, the benchmarks and goals are always moving targets. But besting the competition is the constant challenge.

The reader will find that I have authored two chapters for this section. The first—this one—explores marketing as a collaborative and integrating way of thinking about and addressing the hotel's opportunities. The other, Chapter 7.12, deals with current changes and productivity challenges in marketing, the need to bring under control the fast inflating costs of acquiring customers.

By the end of this chapter, it will become clear that successful marketing of a hotel requires the orchestration of a wide variety of talents and skills, of which "sales and marketing" personnel are only a part. Chain hotels approach the process one way; independents must do so another. But in either case, market success depends upon an effective integration of "marketing" and "operations" at the property level under the direction and leadership of a market-driven general manager.

It also will become clear that no hotel can afford to have on staff all the talents and skills necessary to create a coherent and integrated marketing process. Some hotels rely on franchise or management company staff support to bring to bear the requisite talents; others must engage outside service providers to get the job done. In either case, the management or orchestration of these talents requires an understanding and appreciation of how and when to bring such skills to bear. But few hotel managers developed in traditional career path progressions, that is, through rooms or food and beverage operations, are fully armed with such understanding. Today we need, and in the future we must have, marketers and leaders of hotels who have had benefit of a new, still-developing regimen of indoctrination, exposure, and training. Aspiring marketing directors will have to seek out opportunities to work with people skilled in analysis, research, use of databases, co-op promotions, inventory management, forecasting, and a host of other skills outside the traditional sales career progression. And aspiring general managers also must avail themselves of such exposure so as to be able to judge whether their marketing process is fully effective and productive.

THE MARKETING PROCESS

Every business has a marketing process, a way it "goes to market." It is the way they decide what they are going to do and offer, with whom they will compete, how they will attract the customers, and how they will satisfy and keep them. Most businesses, many hotels among them, do not think about their marketing process; they just do their thing by habit and by tradition. Other businesses make very concerted efforts to review and plan their "going to market." Before deciding to invest billions in developing and building a new jet airliner, for example, we would study and restudy each step of our marketing process with extraordinary care. Does a hotel need such care? Perhaps the scale is smaller, but considering our high fixed costs and the large leverage on profits from small changes in volume, yes—hotels also should take concerted and disciplined care of their marketing process.

A hotel is a 24/7 business, running without stop. Typically, because of the pressure just to keep up, we do what we've done in the past, repeating our marketing process by habit. This is risky, for customers and competitors are always changing. For a hotel to remain effective, it must review the marketing process in a formal way at least once a year to be sure that it is still effective or to revise it to fit changing customer and competitor patterns.

Peter Drucker (1974) says that the purpose of operating a business is to create a customer and keep him (or her). An investor in a hotel may have return on investment as their purpose, but for us operators, it is useful to conceive our purpose as being to create and keep customers. If we do this successfully, profits and capital returns flow. Our marketing process is our way of creating and keeping customers.

A hotel marketing process starts with *deciding what to be and what to offer to whom.* This is not just for new hotels in preopening; existing hotels need to adjust and fine-tune their offerings as market conditions change. Then, you must *set your price structure.* These first two steps establish your value proposition.

Next, you *create awareness and stimulate demand* among the people you hope to make your customers. Then you must *make the hotel available* to them, and close the sale, that is, *commit, confirm, and manage revenue.* Flexible rate management within your pricing structure and response to short-term swings in demand and supply are necessary to create customers and optimize revenue per available room.

Now we begin to transition into "operations," but no less a part of the marketing process. In fact, this is the critical part of the process. You must *prepare the hotel* to meet and fully satisfy the wants and expectation of these customers you have created. Then you have to work to *retain those customers* and turn them into repeat loyalists. Lastly, you need to *measure their satisfaction* and evaluate your performance.

Let's examine these steps.

FIGURE 7.1
The Hotel Marketing Process

DECIDING WHAT TO BE AND WHAT TO OFFER TO WHOM

↓

SETTING PRICES

↓

CREATING AWARENESS AND STIMULATING DEMAND

↓

MAKING THE HOTEL AVAILABLE

↓

CLOSING, CONFIRMING, & MANAGING REVENUE

↓

PREPARING TO DELIVER & DELIGHT

↓

RETAINING CUSTOMERS

↓

MEASURING SATISFACTION & EVALUATING PERFORMANCE

DECIDING WHAT TO BE AND WHAT TO OFFER TO WHOM

Even in an existing hotel, where the developer and architect may have decided already for you many of the things you are—high-rise or resort, in the business center or on the edge of town, large rooms and baths or smallish, one restaurant or several, wood or marble, with ballroom or not, and so on—the management team must still consciously examine what they intend to be and offer to whom. The type of customer originally in mind may not be available now in enough numbers to support your hotel. Perhaps a competitor has come in and taken away a piece of your market. Perhaps the business center has shifted to another part of the city. Perhaps new customers from Korea or California have replaced the original ones from Europe and the East Coast. Even though the owner has given you a basic envelope within which to operate, you still have options. There are many things you and your hotel team can control, many choices to be made on what to offer and to emphasize to various market groups. Are you the place to be seen or the place that guards privacy? Is it better for you to stress family style or crisp professional business style? Do you add services, like a Japanese breakfast, to meet the needs of one particular group? Do you put in meetings express and more small meeting spaces to tap the short-lead-time corporate meetings market? Do you drop some services the market no longer wants to support?

The answers to what to be and offer are found by studying your *marketing situation.* Your marketing situation is comprised of three parts: (1) your strengths and weaknesses, (2) the various kinds and numbers of customers available in your marketplace, and (3) the other hotels with whom you compete for these customers. Careful analysis gives you a picture of which segments you are best able to attract and serve. These become your *target markets*—your "to whoms"—and their needs and wants become your "what to be's."

The talents required to assess one's marketing situation, create a data model of the market's segments, calculate a feasible share of each, and select the targets on whom to focus are ability with data, ability to observe and infer, patience with detail, comfort with the hypothetical, and an analytic curiosity. Very often, this exercise is uncomfortably foreign to people with backgrounds in sales, catering, or conference and guest services.

SETTING PRICES

Having decided what to be and offer and to whom, the next most important decision is your price. Pricing is the critical decision because it determines whether or not your intended customers will purchase. Will they be satisfied with the value you offer and, thus, be willing to return? Will you will be financially healthy enough to maintain the hotel and reward its employees so that you can again satisfy the customers when they do return. Unfortunately, the wrong people often set prices, at the wrong time, and in the wrong way.

Price setting requires talents and skills of data gathering and analysis, accounting and building pro formas, interpreting and drawing inferences, and decision making. Only one person—the GM—can pull together the inputs of sales, control, operations, reservations, and the rest, and make this crucial judgment call. Setting prices is the one task the GM cannot delegate, for he or she will have to live with and be accountable for all that results from this critical decision.

CREATING AWARENESS AND STIMULATING DEMAND

Herein are the typical roles of the marketing department: using advertising, publicity, sales, and promotions to attract the target markets. But creating awareness is not only marketing's job. Everything the public sees and hears about the hotel—its name or brand, its signs, its restaurants, the public activities of its managers, its charitable support and festivals—all create a "meaning," a picture of what this hotel means and offers. It is important,

therefore, that every department understands the target markets and agrees on the idea, the meaning your hotel intends to have for each of the target customer groups. When all parts of the hotel are sending a coherent and consistent message of what the name or brand means and what underlying promise is being made, the hotel establishes a position in the mind of the prospects, ideally one that is attractively distinctive from competitors.

The range of communication options increases geometrically with proliferation of new ways of delivering television, new printed media, the Internet, and direct marketing. But the eyeballs are not growing apace, meaning the audience for any one medium is steadily shrinking, putting increasing demand on measures of productivity, care in allocating resources, and creativity to get through the clutter. And as audiences of prospects become increasingly expensive to reach through advertising, the tools of publicity, the Internet, and direct marketing will become increasingly the media of choice.

Promotions can powerfully stimulate demand. But too often, price promotions are resorted to as a last-minute attempt to save a weak demand period. Promotions should be planned, justified on a break-even basis, and used sparingly. And not all promotions need be price promotions; customers invest energy and time in transactions, too: value-added promotions that offer nonmonetary "savings" can be used to avoid habituating consumers to buy only on sale or to shop only on price. Well-forged alliances for copromotion can increase both productivity and absolute sales volume.

For most hotels, selling is the most comfortable area of creating awareness and stimulating demand. But sales efforts should be balanced with other parts of the marketing mix; many full-service hotels are over-resourced in group sales, underweighted in transient market efforts.

The skills and talents necessary in a comprehensive effort to create awareness and stimulate demand include

- *In communications*: An ability to write clearly; ability to select, engage, and manage professional creative talents; ability to evaluate and allocate resources between various options; comfort with and appreciation of the Internet and the Web.
- *In promotion*: Ability to analyze breakevens; creativity; anticipation; conceiving and selling partnerships and alliances.
- *In sales*: Initiative; being goal directed; listening with empathy and imagination; time management; self-confidence.
- *In sales management*: Coaching and counseling; quantitative skills (for setting booking goals and record keeping); priority setting, time management, and sense of urgency; leadership and problem solving; ability to manage incentive programs.

MAKING THE HOTEL AVAILABLE

Once your target markets are interested in buying, how do they reach you? Your hotel's reservations office, the central reservation system, airline global distribution systems, corporate sales offices, and your property sales office are all parts of a distribution network. Travel agents, corporate travel managers and secretaries, meeting planners, and travelers themselves reach out to your hotel through this network.

Travel industry distribution channels are in chaos. Increasingly, the Internet will become your key distribution channel, but in the meantime, one will have to manage two parallel systems, the traditional intermediaries—or channelers—network and the new, electronic media mix. Are the rooms you want to offer available in both systems, with helpful and up-to-date information? Making the hotel available is no longer a passive activity, but an active part of your marketing; that is, of creating customers and being able to keep them.

Channel management requires a comfort with and interest in technology and systems, and a knack for problem solving, anticipating, and risk taking (to cease past patterns and undertake new initiatives).

CLOSING, CONFIRMING, AND MANAGING REVENUE

How one commits space—a room, meeting space, ballroom, or even a restaurant table—and at what price you agree to sell your spaces and products determines the revenues and financial health of your hotel and determines your customer's expectation of value. Revenues must be managed to optimize financial returns and customer satisfaction, that is, the customer's willingness to return.

No one department controls the tools of revenue management. They are shared among salespeople, catering and banqueting managers, front desk agents, reservation agents, and so on. To manage properly requires frequent and open conversations between managers, good forecasting, skillful selling by customer contact people, and an appreciation of each week's goals and targets for the hotel. All the best advertising, selling, and promotion can be undone by poor forecasting, inflexible inventory policies, and conflicting approaches by different departments with whom the customer deals.

Through the same forecasting disciplines, hotel teams also manage their revenues to maximize the productivity of the hotel and assure its financial health. Revenue management tools and increasingly affordable yield systems can have a major effect on both financial health of the hotel and the guest's perception of value, a major component of their satisfaction. Revenue management requires attention to detail, analytic and forecasting skills, a tolerance for ambiguity, a comfort with change, and coaching, leading, and motivating (reservations agents).

PREPARING TO DELIVER AND DELIGHT

A marketer of a product can count on the factory quality-control system to deliver a consistent product for sale. When the sale is closed, the customer takes the product away and uses it. In a service business, however, our "product" is human behavior; our customer's use happens in our hotel. Because we are humans, both customers and employees, our interactions are never the same one time to the next. The jobs of the marketer are to help employees understand what the customer will want, need, and expect, and to sell employees on doing their job with enthusiasm.

A full-service hotel department that embodies this "preparing" idea as a function is conference services, the essential group-business broker between sales and operations. Conference services people can create loyal and repeat meeting planners; it takes empathy, attention to detail, willingness to work unusual hours, action orientation, internal relationship building, and persuasiveness.

Preparing the hotel to fully satisfy and regularly make customers happy is as much a marketing task as attracting the customer in the first place. What makes marketing hospitality services harder than marketing a product is that for every market segment there must be two marketing programs, one external to the customer, one internal to the employee.

RETAINING CUSTOMERS

The key to both financial health and market leadership is retaining a higher proportion of your customers than do any of your competitors. Retain more customers than do others, and over time your costs drop—because of efficiency, lower advertising and selling costs, better forecasting—and your occupancy and rates rise.

Retaining customers takes more than just doing the job well. Guests and customers must come to know they are valued. We need to build relationships—the glue that binds regardless of a new hotel opening in our market. Relationships are built on recognition and familiarity, on trust, and on appreciation. Thus guest and customer retention must be a

planned and creative activity that involves both sides of the relationship—the customer and the employees. It takes more than just smiling and trying hard. Among the talents and skills needed are analytic skills, curiosity, direct-marketing planning, and management of data retrieval and direct-marketing service providers.

MEASURING SATISFACTION AND EVALUATING PERFORMANCE

If the purpose of the business is, in part, *to keep customers*, does a financial statement of rate, occupancy, revenue, expense, and profit tell enough? No. We also need a scorecard of customer satisfaction, of how likely they are to return or tell another about your good hotel. That scorecard is the guest satisfaction survey. Accounting statements tell of your hotel's financial health; a guest satisfaction scorecard tells of your reputation's health. And it also helps you spot changes in expectations. Customers are not the same, one visit to the next. Experience with a new hotel, perhaps even in another city, may raise your customers' standards. One needs quantitative skills for tracking, analyzing, and reporting data, and the ability to manage the logistics of repetitive distribution, collection, and processing.

The information helps you figure out what you need *to be and offer next* in order to remain competitive and keep customers. Note, now, that we have come back to the first step of the marketing process.

THE CIRCULAR MARKETING PROCESS

In other words, the marketing process isn't the straight-line, step-by-step process as shown in Figure 7.1 above, but is, as shown in Figure 7.2, a continuous circle around which you must go again and again as your competition improves and as the customer segments in your market change. Only by reviewing and renewing their marketing process will a hotel get ahead and continue to be the leading hotel in its market. This model of the marketing process applies to the whole hotel, and also to any revenue or profit center within it. Use it as you would a checklist when thinking through improving the revenue and competitiveness of any operation.*

THE MEASURES OF MARKETING

The health of your marketing process should be measured in a longer time horizon than a month or quarter or fiscal year. And it should be measured by more than just profit and loss data. A healthy marketing process results in

- Rising room revenues per available room and rising food and beverage (F&B) revenues per available seat and catering space.
- Rising market share to a share index over 100, that is, a larger share of a competitive set's occupied rooms than your share of the set's available rooms, or your "fair share."
- Falling costs of acquiring customers, not on a percentage-of-revenue basis, but as dollars per unit of sale, for example, dollars per occupied room, dollars per cover, and so on. What is the "acquisition" cost? The total of your advertising and business promotion budget (more often now called the marketing and sales expense), plus com-

FIGURE 7.2
The Hotel Marketing Process

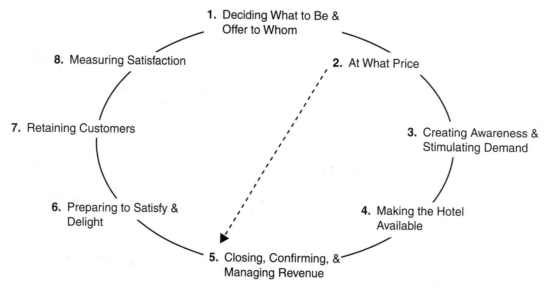

Copyright, FCW Consulting, 1996.

---

*For a PowerPoint file or copy of this diagram, e-mail waller@fletchconsults.com.

missions, reservation costs, franchise fees, and marketing fees. These costs in times of inflation may not actually decline, but at least should grow more slowly than do gross operating revenues. Unfortunately, as discussed in Part II, these costs actually have been ballooning, the fastest-growing cost category in the business.

- Rising customer satisfaction ratings.
- Increasing retention rates measured by the percentage of business from repeat customers.
- Growing top-of-mind awareness among your target customer segments and, if you can afford to measure it, preference by segment rising to number one among your competitive sets.

Management and owners should ask for an annual report card on the health of the marketing process—of the hotel, of a chain, of a franchise group.

MANAGEMENT OF THE PROPERTY'S MARKETING PROCESS

As should by now be clear, the marketing process is larger than any one individual's job. Further, no hotel can afford the myriad of talents and skills that must be orchestrated to create and sustain a healthy marketing process; a single hotel is just not large enough a business to afford having all those talents on staff.

Franchise companies and managed chains have the mass to employ a large proportion of those talents at headquarters, but even they must call upon outside services in design, database management, advertising, direct marketing, and so on. But the chains' ability to invest in new tools and hire diverse talents has led branded chains, both management companies and franchisers, to collect increas-

ing numbers of hotels under their umbrellas.* Another reason for this concentration of hotels under chain brands and flags is the reluctance of lenders to back independent projects; lenders have faith in both the higher profitability of chain-managed hotels and in the marketing power of brand systems. In the one case, such faith is justified by the numbers; in the second, however, the numbers belie the inherent attractive power of brands over independents. (See Chapter 7.12 for data on the decreasing ability of chains to outperform independents in occupancy.)

PROPERTY RESPONSIBILITY FOR ITS OWN MARKETING

To optimize performance, a property cannot abdicate its marketing to a chain or franchise group, nor passively rely on location and presence to bring customers to the door. Each property, whether flagged or independent, must be responsible for creating and managing a marketing process tailored to its particular marketing situation, that is, its available customers, its inherent strengths, weaknesses, and employees, and its competitors. Each marketing situation is unique, even among cookie-cutter chain properties. Each has its own location, competitor, and customer dynamics. Like politics, *all marketing is local marketing*.

So, given the wide range of talents and skills that must be orchestrated to create an effective marketing process, who is to lead it? Directors of sales and marketing cannot, for the process is much larger than the "marketing

---

*Chain percentage of U.S. luxury and upscale hotels has grown to 68.4 percent at year-end 1999 from 61.5 percent year-end 1995. In the midprice category, chain dominance has grown to 71.6 percent from 65.2 percent over that period. In the economy category, chain share has grown to 56.8 percent from 51.9 percent. *Source*: Smith Travel Research Standard Historical Trend.

department." Only the general manager can lead his or her marketing process; only he or she can integrate chain supports, operating departments, human resources (HR), the controller, and—yes, marketing and sales.

THE GM AS LEADER OF THE MARKETING PROCESS

General managers must come to see themselves as leader of their marketing process and be comfortable in that role. This does not mean becoming expert in all tools and disciplines; it does mean seeing the whole and appreciating when to bring in what talents, when to have what tools applied, and how to judge the effectiveness of the process. It means using the marketing process as an organizing concept for creating their management team and a unified viewpoint of mission and challenge.

Few GMs are trained to do this. Many come to appreciate that location and flag are not enough; many intuitively pick up a smattering of sales, distribution, advertising, and customer retention. But it is the rare GM who has hung these parts into a coherent whole and thought through the challenge of creating and leading their own marketing process. As marketing continues to develop more complex tools and as marketing productivity becomes a more pressing matter, owners, universities, and chains will have to address this issue of how to develop GM candidates

who are comfortable with and capable of leading a comprehensive marketing process.

THE MARKETING PROCESS MODEL AS A PROBLEM-SOLVING TOOL

One last word: This circular model of the marketing process has been presented here mainly in terms of rooms marketing. But the model can be applied to every revenue department—to food and beverage outlets, to catering, the health club, the business center, and even the laundry.* The model can be used for planning, for business reviews, for presentations to lenders and owners, for troubleshooting, and as a checklist when preparing proposals for new services or facilities.

Use the model, make it part of your management bag of tools, and get your team to see their role in terms of this holistic and never-ending marketing process. If you achieve that, you will have gone far to create a customer- and competitor-focused organization, one in which employees see themselves as operator/marketers, rather than just "in operations" or "in marketing" or "in HR." The few hotels that do achieve and nurture a well-tuned marketing process and whose employees see themselves as integral parts of it become leaders—in market share, in customer and employee loyalty, and in financial returns to owners.

---

*Given the incremental margins in guest laundry, few hotels ever examine how to assertively market laundry service in the room!

7.3 Marketing Challenges for the Next Decade

Chekitan S. Dev and Michael D. Olsen

The changes affecting (or afflicting) the travel industry are no secret. The industry faces broad-based globalization of its business, deregulation of industries and markets, privatization of state-owned assets, and revo-

lutionary technological advances. Those changes are affecting the industry in ways that are only now becoming apparent. If business operators are to succeed in such an uncertain environment, they need to anticipate those changes, analyze their impact, and, when possible, lead their firms into new opportunities as a result of this analysis.

Anticipating change and identifying new opportunities require industry leaders to discover the forces driving change, analyze how those changes will affect the industry, and define what firms can do to prosper in this dynamic setting. To complete such an analysis, one must obtain reliable information about forces shaping the future, find an appropriate framework to evaluate the effects of those forces, and determine appropriate courses of action. Such an analysis was the purpose of the marketing think tank described in this article.

The November 1998 think tank on marketing was sponsored by the International Hotel and Restaurant Association (IH&RA) in Manila, Philippines, in conjunction with the IH&RA's Annual World Congress and was co-sponsored by the Hospitality Sales and Marketing Association International (HSMAI). Over 30 marketing experts gathered for a two-day program to explore the changing role of marketing in the hospitality and travel industries. Participants were drawn both from within and outside the hospitality industry. The group included representatives from supplier companies to provide opportunities for cross-pollination of ideas and to stimulate creative thinking.

Assisting think-tank participants were two facilitators in addition to ourselves: Ewout Cassee, president of the board of directors of the Hotel School of The Hague, Netherlands, and Nicola Pogson, of the IH&RA.

In the following sections, we offer the rationale for the think tank, its objectives, and a description of the process, followed by the points arising from the discussions that took place.

WHY A MARKETING THINK TANK?

The methodology for the Manila think tank was tested at the Annual World Congress of the IH&RA in Mexico City in November 1996, with over 40 participants from several leading travel-industry organizations and firms. The need for a formal think tank was further validated by the more than 45 senior travel-industry executives participating at technology think tanks in Singapore and Nice (Olsen and Connolly, 2000, p. 35). The outcome of those pilot tests clearly identified the need for an in-depth look at the future of marketing in the travel industry.

THINK-TANK PROCESS

Thirty participants were invited based on recommendations from HSMAI, the IH&RA, and other contributing stakeholders. Drawn from a cross section of travel-industry segments and firms, the participants were engaged in work that required them to think about the future. The group included suppliers, consultants, analysts, academics, research-and-development specialists, government officials, and industry-association executives and leaders.

To define and describe the future of marketing in the travel industry, the 30 think-tank participants were given the following objectives:

1. Identify the major challenges facing travel marketers.
2. Determine the action steps to address each challenge.
3. Assess the priorities for the immediate future.

Using an interactive-workshop technique, the think tanks examined the major forces driving changes in organizations, industries, and government within the ensuing three to five years. Each participant had a chance to cast votes for those changes that she or he believed were most important.

THE FINDINGS: KEY CHALLENGES AND ACTION STEPS

We found that we could list the six challenges identified by the think tank by using the acronym MARKET. The challenges were as follows:

Manage distribution costs.
Analyze customers.
Rethink the business model.
Keep control of technology.
Evaluate Internet-based opportunities.
Track the next big thing.

KEY CHALLENGE #1: MANAGE DISTRIBUTION COSTS

Managing distribution costs has become a major concern among hospitality firms. Barry Sternlicht, the CEO of Starwood Hotels and Resorts, recently mentioned distribution cost as a key strategic priority. Airlines, for instance, rank distribution costs as their third-largest expense, after fuel and payroll, but also consider distribution costs to be the most controllable of the three. In the months before this think tank convened, at least five major airlines announced commission caps to travel agents, and hotel companies have considered taking similar action. Participants agreed that distribution costs will attract increased scrutiny for three reasons: the spiraling cost of distribution, pressure from financial markets to improve net income, and the opportunity afforded by the Internet to reduce distribution costs from as much as $30 per room to less than $1. Contrary to the think-tank participants' assumption, however, McKinsey and Company found that the Internet-based businesses had a higher cost of customer acquisition than did catalog firms, owing to the poor conversion of browsers to buyers on the Internet (Witham, 1999, p. 12).

Action Steps

Evaluate Distribution-Channel Effectiveness

Participants recommended examining each channel's costs (direct and indirect) and benefits (tactical and strategic). Companies should not just look at reducing travel-agent commissions, but must think about how they can get each channel to operate more effectively, how they can actually get more business, and how they can ensure that they obtain the right kind of business from each channel.

Consolidate the Distribution Function

The participants were concerned about the number of entities involved in booking business and the consequent potential for overlap and inefficiency. A hotel not only has a rooms reservation department, but its banquet department accepts reservations, and so do its restaurants, spas, and golf courses. In addition, every hotel handles its own reservations, but also receives reservations via the central reservation system, the Web site, and sales representatives, among others. Consolidating some or all of those offices seems inevitable. Some hotel companies are experimenting with accepting room reservations only at a central location. Participants see the following model for the future. The reservation function will be separated from the hotel. Salespeople at reservation departments will market the hotel and not just book reservations. Three factors that are driving hotels toward a model such as this one are saving costs by consolidation, increasing revenue via better conversion, and saving costs by locating to low-cost areas (since the marketing and reservations function can take place anywhere).

Understand the Customer's Desire for Direct Access to Inventory

The participants could not assess the extent to which customers want access to the hotel's inventory, so that they could book the "last room" directly. If customers do, in fact, want last-room capability, hotels may need to put selected inventory in customers' hands. That matter will require more investigation.

Simplify the Distribution Process

The consensus was that the distribution process is messy and getting messier, owing to the many channels and rates. The group's suggestion was to focus on finding ways to make it simple for the user, the individual supplier of the hotel involved, and for those using a given distribution channel.

KEY CHALLENGE #2: ANALYZE CUSTOMERS

The participants concluded that the industry doesn't understand as much as it needs to about its customers. While the industry captures considerable data on its customers, those data are rarely assembled to create useful knowledge about customers. Thus, hospitality marketers need to learn more about who customers are, why they buy, what they buy, and what motivates them to buy. Academe needs to conduct more studies on those topics.

Action Steps

Study Travel Patterns and Trends

Participants expressed considerable interest in knowing more about travel patterns and trends. The group believes that many studies are either ad hoc (with no systematic process) or done by companies that have a vested interest in the results. What's needed, the group concluded, is a clear assessment of travel patterns and trends and objective and unbiased studies of prospective travel patterns. Marketing studies need to go beyond telling us, for example, that last year 20 percent of people traveling did so in a combination of business and pleasure. That doesn't help us to make

proactive strategic decisions as much as knowing what is likely to happen three or four years ahead would.

Understand the Total Experience

The general manager of a major-brand hotel in an Asian capital city explained the difficulty his hotel faces in encouraging repeat guests: "The customer's repurchase doesn't just depend on his or her experience at just my hotel, but on the total experience. So, to the extent that it depends on the total experience, I need to co-opt other partners in the process of managing the total experience." Hoteliers need to recognize that the hotel stay is only part of the travel experience. Some entities are already attempting to influence travel purchases by offering destinationwide services. For example, a business hotel in a developing country uses its local contacts to facilitate a visiting executive's entire trip—helping with visa formalities, arranging business services and meetings with local officials and executives, providing information on current local events and cultural protocol, arranging customs and immigration clearance, setting up a seamless transfer of business messages to the hotel room (including Internet access), taking care of such local needs as gifts for local partners, and postdeparture follow-up and tying up loose ends.

Appoint "Solution" Managers

This action step derives from the concept that companies are really in the business of selling solutions rather than products and services. Participants talked about appointing "solution managers" as part of the business at both property and corporate levels. Some segments of the travel industry have begun to recognize the importance of this concept. For example, a series of advertisements by United Airlines in the *Wall Street Journal* declared, "For gate agents, read problem solvers." Hospitality operators need to implement this philosophy at all levels of the business. The opportunity here is to take isolated best-practice examples like those in use at Ritz-Carlton ("If you pick up the phone, you own the call") and Westin ('Service Express"), extend the idea to encompass all employees, and make it a standard operating procedure for all hotels.

Talk to Your Customers

This intuitively obvious action step often is not well implemented. Marketers need to establish a continuing dialogue with customers—before the purchase, during the stay, and after they return home. The participants urged hospitality operators to apply multiple methods for customer contact, and not rely only on such traditional methods as comment cards and surveys. Every customer-contact employee can have an ongoing conversation with customers as a way to understand their needs and responses to product offerings. What this means is that to create the ultimate customer-centric hotel, every customer-contact employee becomes a researcher, salesperson, and problem solver. Of course, employees must be trained to perform those functions. Where multiple languages are spoken, managers may have to provide all such employees with basic instruction in conversational English plus easy-to-identify devices such as flag pins identifying employees' languages.

KEY CHALLENGE #3: RETHINK THE BUSINESS MODEL

Participants urged new thinking about the contemporary hospitality-marketing model. The group generally agreed that the current business model is broken. Symptoms include declining satisfaction scores, diminishing brand loyalty, increasing commoditization of the product, disgruntled franchisees, disenfranchised local communities, increasing supplier control, underperforming technology investments, and high turnover of employees. A revised business model would take a balanced stakeholder approach by investing in value-adding products and services, building customer relationships, creating and developing knowledgeable workers, and giving back to the host community.

Action Steps

Define Value Drivers

Participants suggested examining whether the company's product and service offerings actually add value for its customers. Rather than simply add more services and call that better service, for instance, operators should ask, do the services we provide really add value? Customers may actually want fewer, carefully targeted services. This analysis will tell operators what they do that adds value for their customers.

Focus on Lifetime Value of the Customer

Participants stressed the need for businesses to incorporate in planning processes a measure of a customer's lifetime value. The keys are maximizing each customer's lifetime value and working to ensure customer retention, instead of focusing on individual transactions in isolation.

Invest in Lifelong-Learning Programs

Too many people who work for and with hospitality companies are not able to pursue a life of learning, for which many have a need or desire. As long as companies treat their employees as effectively exchangeable cost commodities rather than business partners, companies will be reluctant to invest in employees' lifelong professional development. In cases where companies do invest in their employees, lifelong-learning programs can help to ensure a group of effective employees who can themselves add to customer value. Participants suggested that marketing programs should offer employee educational incentives, recognize employee educational achievements, and actually pay for continuing education.

Incorporate Social Responsibility

Participants felt that companies can no longer pay lip service to social responsibility. Instead, socially responsible principles need to be incorporated clearly, precisely, and measurably into the business model. Whether it is planting trees, teaching in local schools, building houses, or providing surplus meals, participants concluded that social responsibility will become an increasingly necessary component of a winning marketing message. To make this work, this would entail tying measures of social responsibility to each employee's overall compensation plans, as some companies have begun to do.

KEY CHALLENGE #4: KEEP CONTROL OF TECHNOLOGY

Technology is a large and increasing expense for most corporations. At the same time, our participants noted that many managers feel technology is getting away from them. For example, none of the senior-level participants at the workshop professed to having a good handle on information technology's (IT) capabilities, how it works, how it benefits the company, and exactly what value it adds to the customer's experience.

Action Steps

Give Marketers Technical Training

The group said that marketers must learn to make effective use of technology. This means that marketers themselves must learn to use information technology, rather than rely on IT people for technical support.

IT Employees Should Report to the Marketing Department

The participants were well aware that this recommendation is controversial (especially for IT personnel). Indeed, one general manager remarked, "That's never going to happen on my watch." Nevertheless, the participants believe that IT has been underexploited for marketing functions. The group suggested that IT is headed down the same path as the reservations function, which formerly was part of the front-desk operation, but now is under the marketing umbrella. Reservations became part of marketing because its function was redefined to be revenue maximization rather than merely taking reservations.

Clearly Define Knowledge Needs and Transform Data to Knowledge

Participants concluded that at present there is too much emphasis on data and too little emphasis on knowledge. Thus, the consensus was to build a system based on what needs to come out of it rather than on what is going in. "Drowning in data, starved for knowledge" was a frequent refrain. Part of the problem, participants asserted, was that it was the "techies" who were defining the system based on technologically expedient solutions rather than usefulness to the user.

Along that line, participants agreed to refer to "knowledge-based" marketing instead of database marketing as a philosophical and practical shift from numbers of digits to useful information. Doing so would put the focus on developing technology-based marketing applications that were decision support systems rather than simply data generators. Examples might include merging yield-management and guest-history databases to create new and interesting ways to create offers for customers based on why they buy; what, where, and when they buy; who actually buys; how they buy; and how much they pay.

Broaden Technical Understanding to Include All Employees

Participants considered technology to be a modern Tower of Babel, where people are talking different languages, nobody's talking to each other, and we're all talking at cross-purposes. The marketers see IT as absorbing immense amounts of money, from which they're receiving too little of value. Thus, the participants see the IT department becoming the new whipping boy for some companies—with management viewing IT as disorganized, doing too little, asking for too many resources, and not being customer oriented.

KEY CHALLENGE #5: EVALUATE INTERNET OPPORTUNITIES

Even before the full, market-clearing effects of Priceline.com, eBay, and other Web sites became evident, the think-tank participants knew that the Internet would be important to future sales. The challenge is to make "e-commerce" work to the mutual best advantage of businesses and customers alike.

Action Steps

Study What Works

Participants worried that hospitality operations were throwing big money at the Internet without really understanding what works and what does not work. For example, while the Internet represents a potentially powerful and cost-effective business source, the group saw many unanswered issues. These included: how to expand Internet use without alienating existing channels of distribution; how to justify investment in Internet-related technology within the traditional return-on-investment framework; how to account for cannibalization of existing business as against new business; and how to prevent transaction costs from going up when customers use the Internet to look (i.e., to shop around) but still book through traditional channels.

Track Surfing and Consumption Habits

The group suggested tracking Web hits and consumption habits to determine what is re-

ally going on with the Internet and what the data are revealing about electronic commerce. The purpose here was to better understand who was visiting Web sites, where they were looking, how many were buying, what they were buying, how much they were paying, and when and whether they were coming back. The key to compiling this information, the participants believed, is balancing the marketer's need to know (by "tagging" surfers) with the consumers' desire to maintain control over their data and keep their actions private. Ideas on how to do this included creating, supporting, or funding independent entities that could provide this data to decision makers in a timely and accurate manner while keeping customer specifics confidential.

Identify Long-Term Business Opportunities

Taking the long-term view, participants considered the opportunities arising not only from the advent of the Internet, but also the increase in global travel and unprecedented levels of competition. They suggested that marketers need to know what role such diverse sites as Yahoo, Amazon.com, and Expedia will play in the future of hospitality marketing.

Log On to the "Dotcom" Generation

Participants noted the importance of connecting with cyber-savvy people under age 30. They felt that today's decision makers, strategists, strategic thinkers, and advisers generally could not relate to the needs of this customer group. Participants themselves did not have a sense of what members of the dotcom generation are looking for—or how they seek out their information. Certainly, because the Internet is a commonplace for young people, they use (or view) the Internet in ways that are different from the 40-plus baby boomers (not to mention 60-plus travelers).

KEY CHALLENGE #6: TRACK THE NEXT BIG THING

A number of participants thought that they had failed to foresee the potential of new media and felt surprised by the seemingly sudden popularity of the Internet. The participants speculated about what other technological marvels might be on the horizon. One possible next big thing (NBT) candidate was convergence of communication (telephone), information (computer), and entertainment (broadcasting and cable) and the implications of that convergence for hospitality marketing. Participants' general concern is to be more aware of the environment, so that they can proactively take advantage of any future developments rather than having them effectively drop from the sky.

Action Steps

Set Up a Research-and-Development Function

Evolving from operations analysts and revenue managers, a research-and-development (R&D) specialist is the next position required for key management support at the property and corporate level. Participants at both levels spoke of the need specifically to devote resources to continual research and development. The participants suggested, for instance, that managers regularly ask employees, customers, and suppliers whether there is a better way to do something. When someone offers a suggestion, the participants said that it is imperative that managers test those suggestions. Such environmental scanning has the potential for becoming a significant source of long-term competitive advantage.

Study Customers' Businesses

Granting that hospitality managers spend considerable time studying their own businesses, their competitors, and matters that relate to the hospitality business, participants identified an urgent need for hospitality managers to go a step further and study customers' businesses. They suggested studying the customers' customers, the customers' competitors, and the customers' suppliers. Such an analysis will give hospitality purveyors a fuller picture of how customers' businesses operate and how the hospitality industry can help them do a better job of succeeding in that business.

Maintain or Subscribe to a Data or Trend Bank

Marketers are hungry for knowledge and want to subscribe to services that provide useful knowledge. Thus, the participants suggested that marketers identify or develop data banks that can help managers keep pace with change in their businesses. Tying this to an earlier point about turning data into knowledge, an ideal solution might be one where a decision maker could support and contribute to a data bank that in turn allows the person to make queries about a specific opportunity or challenge and receive a customized response at a reasonable cost. The group also cited the importance of supporting the data-collection efforts of Horwath, Smith Travel Research, Pricewaterhouse Coopers, and PKF Consulting.

Support the Environmental-Scanning Function of Industry Associations

Participants saw the value of conducting more think tanks. Most participants said that being able to anticipate change was an important objective that could be reached in part with the assistance of professional associations.

PRIORITIES

By asking each participant to rank the action steps identified above, we were able to prioritize them on a two-dimensional Z matrix. Each participant was asked to vote on the top-three most-urgent action steps (need to be done immediately) and top-three most-important steps (will have the most impact). This matrix is interpreted in the fashion of the letter Z (see Figure 7.3). The top left-hand corner is Priority 1 (high urgency, high importance), followed at top right by Priority 2, and then at bottom left by Priority 3. We recorded no Priority 4 items, which would appear at bottom right.

AIMING FOR SUCCESS

Success in the future will belong to those who are able to identify strategic opportunities for survival and growth. The goal of any think tank is to raise awareness of key forces and probe deeply into their meaning and consequences. As a next step, the reader is encouraged to think through each of the key points presented in this report and is challenged to develop competitive strategies to address those points.

The results of this think tank should be considered more directional than definitive, for trends continue to develop rapidly around the Internet (as demonstrated by the merger of AOL and Time Warner, for instance). Moreover, the viewpoints represented here are those of the individuals who were able to attend the Manila congress. While we were careful to invite senior representatives from all the major industry segments and stakeholder groups, by no means did this group represent the entire industry.

We believe that creative, pioneering industry leaders will recognize the opportunities created by new marketing technologies and seek ways to adopt marketing strategies to develop competitive advantage. Marketers must shift their thinking toward developing a knowledge-intensive, interactive marketing environment.

FIGURE 7.3
Urgent–important (Z) matrix of marketing action steps

Participants were asked to vote on the top-three most-urgent action steps (need to be done immediately) and top-three most-important steps (will have the most impact). The top left-hand corner is Priority 1 (high urgency, high importance), followed at top right by Priority 2, and then at bottom left by Priority 3. No Priority 4 items were recorded.

7.4   Hotel Choice Decision Rules

Eric R. Spangenberg and Bianca Grohmann

Consumers' choices are influenced by the goals they attempt to achieve. Once a consumer has recognized a need, such as the need for accommodation when traveling for business or pleasure, they will engage in an information search to identify alternatives from which they can choose. Understanding how consumers evaluate competing alternatives in their purchase decision processes enables marketers in the hospitality industry to design advertising and promotional campaigns leading to a more favorable evaluation of their businesses in consumers' eyes. This is an important step in increasing the likelihood that consumers will choose their offering as opposed to that of their competitors. Given that there are several hotels at most travelers' destinations, how will they choose from among the alternatives? The answer to this question is found in research on consumers' attitudes and their relation to purchase intentions and purchase behavior. This chapter describes several methods by which consumers may make choices based on the evaluation of alternatives they have identified.

Attitude is the tendency to respond to a product or brand in a consistently favorable or unfavorable way. Attitudes are relatively stable, although they can change over time. What is important is that attitudes can be measured relatively easily by asking consumers to indicate to what extent they like or dislike a product or brand, or to what extent they consider it to be good or bad. It has been shown that attitudes predict behavioral intentions. For example, consumers often intend to choose a hotel brand they hold a positive attitude toward. However, behavioral intentions do not always translate into corresponding behavior. Although some consumers have preferences and therefore form intentions to stay at, say, Motel 6 properties when traveling across the country, they might end up choosing other forms of accommodation from time to time. Why would they act inconsistently with their intentions? Traveling with friends who have different attitudes and preferences, temporary price reductions of competitors, or the fact that a Motel 6 is not available in particular areas might be reasons for inconsistencies between behavioral intentions to stay at a Motel 6 and actual choice behavior.

Although attitudes may not always be congruent with behavioral intentions, and given that behavioral intentions do not always determine actual behavior, attitudes and behavioral intentions are ultimately very useful in predicting actual behavior. What is even more important for marketers is that by changing consumers' attitudes, the likelihood of them engaging in desired behaviors can be increased.

In order to change attitudes and subsequent behavior, it is necessary to understand consumer decision rules associated with attitudes. We therefore now introduce various decision rules likely to be implemented by different segments of consumers under varying market conditions.

DECISION RULES

Strategies consumers use to choose between various alternatives are called *decision rules*. Several factors influence what decision rule consumers will ultimately apply to a specific decision. In general, the more important and less frequent a purchase decision is, the more time and effort consumers are willing to expend making that decision. Choosing a resort property at which to spend a three-week vacation is a process consumers are not likely to engage in very often; they therefore are likely to be willing to evaluate alternatives more carefully and spend more time making a decision. On the other hand, for salespeople traveling frequently in their respective sales territories, hotel choice is more likely to be a routine process, where less consideration is given to various alternatives. Further, brand-loyal customers might choose to stay with the same hotel chain whenever possible, thereby avoiding a situation where they are forced to evaluate alternatives. In general, the stronger a consumer's motivation to search, and the greater the risk associated with product or brand choice, the more complex the decision rule that will be implemented.

Another important characteristic of consumer choice is the fact that (counter-attitudinally in some instances) consumers often do not try to optimize their choices. It usually requires considerably more time and effort to identify and evaluate alternatives if one desires an optimal choice. Very often, consumers will therefore choose a satisfactory alternative (as opposed to the best alternative possible) in order to save time and effort in the decision-making process. The use of some decision rules enables consumers to take shortcuts in making decisions in the face of apparently unlimited or overwhelming amounts of information available regarding all possible alternatives. In this context, these decision rules are referred to as heuristics, or more commonly, "rules of thumb." As such, decision rules save time and limit the complexities of information processing while still enabling consumers to make "reasonable" choices based on product and brand attributes that are most important to them at any given time. Brand attributes are simply characteristics of a brand. In the context of hotel choice, for instance, brand attributes comprise location, price, availability of a swimming pool or restaurant, etc.

Decision rules fall into two general categories: *compensatory* and *noncompensatory*. The following sections discuss how consumers make decisions using these rules.

Compensatory Decision Rules

The use of compensatory decision rules implies that consumers derive an overall evaluation of a product or brand. This means that products or brands performing poorly on one attribute can still make up (or compensate, hence the label *compensatory*) for their shortcomings by being evaluated positively on other attributes. For example, a hotel offering high-priced accommodations might not be perceived positively on the dimension of price by some consumers; however, they might be willing to spend more money knowing that they will receive better service or that the hotel is conveniently located. That is, service and location compensate for the perceived disadvantage of high price as compared to low-price competitors offering less extensive service or offering lodging in a less desirable location. The multiattribute attitude model described in the next section is perhaps the most popular compensatory decision rule.

Multiattribute Attitude Model
The multiattribute attitude model is also referred to as a *weighted additive model* or the *Fishbein linear compensatory model* (Fishbein and Ajzen, 1975). In this model, consumers not only assess the importance of the attributes of a product or brand, but also consider to what extent a given brand possesses these attributes. The evaluations of salient attributes and the beliefs that brands possess the salient attributes are included as weights in an equation determining overall brand attitude. The model is represented as

$$A_{\text{brand A}} = \sum_{i=1}^{n} e_i b_i$$

where

$A_{\text{brand A}}$ is the overall attitude toward hotel brand A,

e_i is the importance weight associated with attribute i (i.e., evaluation of i),

b_i is the extent to which the consumer believes brand A possesses attribute i (i.e., strength of belief that i is present in brand A), and

n is the number of salient attributes in consideration.

Operators or marketers typically measure importance weights and strengths of beliefs using a questionnaire format. First, consumers express how important each of the attributes being evaluated is in their decision. The importance of each attribute can be expressed by assigning numbers representing the weights to every attribute. An attribute that is not considered important for a particular choice decision, such as the availability of guest laundry, might be assigned a value of –3, whereas an attribute that is very salient, such as low price, might be assigned a value of +3. To demonstrate how this model works, we assume use of a 7-point scale on which –3 is the lowest importance rating possible, +3 is the highest, and a neutral importance rating would be 0.

Once the importance of the attributes has been determined, the consumer expresses to what extent he or she believes a brand possesses these attributes. (Again, for simplicity of demonstration, we assume that the belief strength regarding any of the attributes to be evaluated ranges between –3 [the brand does not possess this attribute to a great extent] and +3 [the brand possesses the attribute to a great extent].) For example, if a consumer believes that Hotel A is a relatively high-priced establishment, the consumer might assign a belief value of –2 to this hotel on the attribute "low price." This belief value indicates that Hotel A does not possess the attribute "low price" to a great extent. In other words, Hotel A performs poorly on the consumer's low-price criterion. The hotel offering the absolute lowest price, say Hotel B, could be assigned a value of +3 on the attribute "low price." This would indicate that the consumer strongly believes that Hotel B does indeed offer low prices.

The next step in the model is multiplication of attribute importance (e_i) and belief strength (b_i) for each of the salient attributes. If the consumer considered low price to be highly important ($e_{price} = +3$), and Hotel A received a belief score of $b_{price} = -2$, he or she will evaluate Hotel A on the attribute "low price" by multiplying importance and belief scores:

$$e_{price} \times b_{price} = (+3) \times (-2) = -6$$

The consumer's evaluation of Hotel B on the low-price attribute will be more favorable, namely

$$e_{price} \times b_{price} = (+3) \times (+3) = 9$$

The same procedure is followed for each salient attribute for all brands in a consideration set. Other attributes, for example, availability of room service, location near the airport, free breakfast, etc., are evaluated by multiplying $e_{attribute} \times b_{attribute}$ for each brand and attribute.

Finally, the products of $e_i \times b_i$ for each salient attribute are summed for each brand and the resulting scores represent the overall attitude a consumer has toward each brand. This weighted additive model is applied to all brands in the consumer's consideration set, and the brand associated with the highest overall attitude score is selected as the best alternative.

As an example, consider Consumer K who is looking for a hotel to stay at while traveling to see some of her relatives. She found four hotels (associated with four different brands) in the city she plans to visit. Table 7.1 shows the four salient attributes K considers, the importance of each attribute (e_i ranging from –3 to +3), and the beliefs (b_i ranging from –3 to +3) regarding the extent to which each of the brands possesses attribute i. (Note that there could be more or fewer salient attributes depending on the product or service in consideration and the attributes that are important to the perspective market segment [or individual].)

TABLE 7.1
Four Salient Attributes K Considers

Attribute	e_i	Hotel A b_{iA}	Hotel B b_{iB}	Hotel C b_{iC}	Hotel D b_{iD}
Convenient Location	+2	+3	+3	0	+2
Low Price	+3	+3	+1	−1	+2
Swimming Pool	−2	+1	+2	−1	−2
Free Breakfast	+1	−2	+1	+3	+3

To derive an overall evaluation of each of the hotel brands in this consumer's consideration set following the multiattribute attitude model, the marketer, based on survey information about consumer attitudes, computes the products of importance (e_i) and belief strength (b_i) for each attribute and then sums these products for each brand:

$$\text{Attitude}_{\text{Brand A}} = \sum_{i=1}^{n} e_i b_i =$$

$$(e_{\text{convenient location}}) \times (b_{\text{convenient location A}}) + (e_{\text{low price}}) \times$$
$$(b_{\text{low price A}}) + (e_{\text{swimming pool}}) \times (b_{\text{swimming pool A}}) +$$
$$(e_{\text{free breakfast}}) \times (b_{\text{free breakfast A}})$$

Note that the importance weights assigned to attributes remain constant across brands, while belief strength may differ from brand to brand (indeed, *should* differ unless brands are identical). The overall attitude toward hotels A, B, C, and D can therefore be calculated as follows:

$$A_{\text{Hotel A}} = (+2)(+3) + (+3)(+3) + (-2)(+1) + (+1)(-2) = 6 + 9 - 2 - 2 = 11$$

$$A_{\text{Hotel B}} = (+2)(+3) + (+3)(+1) + (-2)(+2) + (+1)(+1) = 6 + 3 - 4 + 1 = 6$$

$$A_{\text{Hotel C}} = (+2)(0) + (+3)(-1) + (-2)(-1) + (+1)(+3) = 0 - 3 + 2 + 3 = 2$$

$$A_{\text{Hotel D}} = (+2)(+2) + (+3)(+2) + (-2)(-2) + (+1)(+3) = 4 + 6 + 4 + 3 = 17$$

Hotel D scored highest in overall brand attitude (17) and is therefore the most likely to be chosen. Hotel C, on the other hand, scored lowest on overall brand attitude (2) and will probably not be selected. Note that the Fishbein linear compensatory model provides relative, not absolute, attitude scores. That is, an overall attitude value of +6 for Hotel B means little unless it is compared to the values for the competing brands.

Noncompensatory Decision Rules

Although many factors (e.g., high involvement, high physical, social, or economic risk) associated with a decision may lead consumers to use a compensatory decision rule, it is relatively complicated and often too time- and effort-consuming to engage in for many of our day-to-day decisions. As suggested above, you may use a compensatory decision rule for a big vacation or a decision about attending a university. However, you are unlikely to use such an elaborate rule when purchasing a beverage at a gas station, or when you need to find cheap lodging in the middle of a long drive to visit friends. Thus, many of our decisions are made using much simpler rules. Noncompensatory decision rules tend to simplify our decision making; they may lead to less than optimized results, but they are often employed when consumers seek a "satisfying" or "just good enough" decision.

When noncompensatory decision rules are used, a brand or product cannot compensate for weak performance on one attribute by performing well on other attributes, when compared to competing alternatives. For example, if consumers choose a hotel based on the criterion "low price," a hotel offering higher-priced accommodations with better service will not be considered. In this case, consumers do not trade off price and quality, but make their decision guided solely by the price of the offering.

The most commonly used noncompensatory decision rules are the *lexicographic decision rule*, the *elimination-by-aspects decision rule*, and the *conjunctive decision rule*. To demonstrate how noncompensatory decision rules work, the same measures of salient attribute evaluations and beliefs regarding brands possessing those attributes are collected in a questionnaire format as with the compensatory decision-making model. The information, however, is used in different ways described below. We therefore consider again the example of evaluations and beliefs regarding Hotels A, B, C, and D introduced in Table 7.1.

Lexicographic Decision Rule

When using a *lexicographic decision rule*, consumers rank the attributes to be considered in their brand choice according to their importance. Then, they select the brand evaluated most positively with regard to this attribute.

Consider the example given above: Four brands of hotels are evaluated on four attributes—namely, convenient location, low price, swimming pool, and availability of free breakfast. The importance of each of these attributes is given by e_i. Importance ratings are convenient location (+2), low price (+3), swimming pool (−2) and availability of free breakfast (+1). Low price is therefore the most important attribute in this case of hotel choice, followed by convenient location, availability of free breakfast, and swimming pool.

According to the lexicographic decision rule, low price is the attribute that determines the consumer's decision in this case. The consumer has reason to believe that Hotel A offers the

lowest prices ($b_{\text{low price A}} = +3$) as compared to the other hotels in the consideration set. Therefore, Hotel A will be chosen using the lexicographic decision rule with low price as the most important attribute.

Elimination by Aspects

When an *elimination-by-aspects* decision rule is used, attributes are again ranked according to their importance. Unlike choosing the hotel brand that performs best on the most important attribute as with the lexicographic rule, however, elimination by aspects involves the use of cutoff values. A cutoff value is a minimal performance score a brand must have to stay in the consumer's consideration set. A consumer will first look at the performance scores of brands regarding the most important attribute and eliminate all brands that do not exceed the predetermined cutoff value. In our example, low price is the most important attribute, with an importance rating of +3. Let us assume that the consumer's cutoff value is +2. That means that all of the hotel brands that have a score of at least +2 on the low-price attribute will be retained in the consideration set, while brands that do not meet this cutoff criterion will be dropped from the consumer's consideration set. For this example, only Hotel A ($b_{\text{low price A}} = +3$) and Hotel D ($b_{\text{low price D}} = +2$) meet the cutoff criterion (+2). Hotel B ($b_{\text{low price B}} = +1$) and Hotel C ($b_{\text{low price C}} = -1$) do not have low enough prices to be considered further.

The next step a consumer takes when implementing the elimination-by-aspects decision rule follows the same rule: The consumer now considers the performance of the remaining brands with respect to the attribute ranked second highest in importance. In our example, the consumer would now look at convenient location of Hotels A and D. Assuming that the cutoff value to be employed is +2, both brands will remain in the consumer's consideration set, since the scores for convenient location for Hotel A ($b_{\text{convenient location A}} = +3$) and Hotel D ($b_{\text{convenient location D}} = +2$) both meet this criterion. At this point, the consumer has not yet found the best offering according to the elimination-by-aspects rule. Consequently, the consumer would apply the same procedure to the attribute ranked third, that is, the availability of free breakfast. Assuming that the consumer would still use a cutoff criterion of +2, Hotel A ($b_{\text{free breakfast A}} = -2$) will be eliminated from the consideration set. Hotel D ($b_{\text{free breakfast D}} = +3$), on the other hand, exceeds the cutoff criterion. Hotel D is now the only brand left in the consumer's consideration set, and is therefore selected.

Note that the elimination-by-aspects decision rule leads to a different choice than the lexicographic decision rule. From a strategic standpoint, the fact that some consumers use an elimination-by-aspects decision rule should encourage hotels to improve their performance on several attributes that are important in consumer choice. It is not enough to merely offer low prices. Other aspects of the offering might also be important in consumers' hotel selections, and performance in these areas should be monitored and—if necessary—improved. You can see, however, that it is crucial to improve services that are valued by consumers, in other words, aspects of a hotel's offering that have high importance ratings. Shortcomings in aspects that are valued highly by consumers, such as cleanliness, employee friendliness, etc., cannot be compensated by strong performance in areas to which consumers attach no importance (e.g., internal cost-control systems).

Conjunctive Decision Rule

When a *conjunctive decision rule* is employed, consumers process information by brand, as opposed to attribute by attribute, as with the lexicographic and the elimination-by-aspects decision rules. With this rule, consumers establish a cutoff criterion that must be met by any of the brands in the consideration set on all salient attributes for brands to remain in consideration.

Let us assume that a consumer desires that the chosen hotel should have a score of at least +1 on all of the attributes that are considered important, namely convenient location, low price, availability of free breakfast, and swimming pool.

First, the consumer will evaluate the performance of Hotel A on each of these attributes. While Hotel A meets the cutoff criterion of +1 on convenient location, low price, and availability of a swimming pool, it falls short of the consumer's cutoff rule when it comes to free breakfast. Therefore, Hotel A will not be further considered.

The consumer will then turn to the evaluation of Hotel B. Hotel B meets the cutoff value of +1 on all of the salient attributes. As a result, Hotel B is a candidate for choice. The consumer's assessment of Hotel C and Hotel D will lead to the conclusion that both hotels have to be eliminated from choice, since both do not meet the cutoff criterion of +1 on all of the attributes. According to the conjunctive decision rule, Hotel B will be selected.

Note that ties can frequently occur using compensatory or noncompensatory decision rules; this usually results in consumers moving to a new rule in order to break the tie. For example, if compensatory values were equal for two properties (not shown in our examples above), a consumer might implement a lexicographic decision rule with convenient location as the most important attribute used to pick a hotel. Or, say the conjunctive cutoff value was −1 for all attributes, thus both Hotels B and C in our example would stay in consideration; a consumer may then use a lexicographic decision rule based on location, resulting in Hotel B being chosen as it is rated higher on this attribute than Hotel C.

MARKETING IMPLICATIONS

Once the importance consumers attach to salient attributes (e.g., the price of hotel accommodation, availability of room service) has been determined and consumers' beliefs regarding a hotel brand's offerings are known, hotels can use this information to improve their competitive positioning in the market. The goal of any strategy is therefore to increase positive attitude toward the hotel's offerings or to encourage the use of certain decision rules, thereby increasing the likelihood of consumer choice behavior.

As we have seen, when consumers use a compensatory decision rule, the overall attitude toward a hotel is determined by the sum of the products of the importance ratings and the beliefs regarding salient attributes associated with the offering. Consequently, consumers' overall attitude toward a property can be rendered more positive by strategies of increasing the importance of an attribute in consumers' decision making, or by changing consumers' beliefs about a hotel's offerings.

Stressing the attribute in advertising can influence the importance of an attribute in consumers' choices (e.g., less money spent on accommodations can be used to have more fun with the whole family by spending the savings on other activities). This strategy of changing attribute importance ratings is effective in attitude change and also relatively easy to pursue. It is, however, not a strategy recommended for changing consumers' attitudes when they are utilizing a compensatory model. The problem associated with this approach is that the importance ratings of attributes are constant across brands in a consideration set. The importance a consumer attaches to convenient location (+2) is the same in the evaluation of brands A, B, C, and D. If Hotel B was successful in increasing importance of convenient location with a segment of consumers, say to a rating of +3, it would increase consumers' overall attitude toward its brand. At the same time, however, consumers' overall evaluation of Hotel A would increase by the same amount as both brands do not differ as to consumers' beliefs with regard

to them being conveniently located (i.e., both have a belief rating of +3). In the end, Hotel B's attempt to increase consumers' overall attitude toward their hotel would also benefit some of their competitors.

Thus, a better strategy to improve compensatory decision-making consumers' overall attitudes toward a hotel's offerings is to improve consumers' brand-specific belief ratings. For example, Hotel D could strive to improve consumer belief that their hotel is conveniently located by providing consumers with directions for easy access, or by stressing its location in its advertisements. While consumer belief is then likely to increase, Hotel D's competitors will not benefit from its strategy, and Hotel D thereby improves its competitive position.

Assume now that Hotel C cannot do anything to increase consumers' belief that it is conveniently located. Maybe its location is indeed inconvenient. A strategy Hotel C could employ to increase consumers' overall attitude is to add a new salient attribute to the set of attributes consumers consider when making hotel choices. For example, Hotel C could provide free accommodations for children traveling with their parents. It is very likely that parents would consider this option important when choosing a hotel to stay. As long as other competitors do not offer this service, Hotel C enjoys some advantage in the choices made by its target market. It is essential that—when adding a new attribute—marketers consider the following. First, the attribute added needs to be important enough to the hotel's target market to be included in consumers' decision making. And second, the belief that a particular hotel possesses this attribute has to be stronger than the belief that any of its competitors offer this characteristic to a great extent. The strategy is likely to be successful when these conditions are met. This is often referred to as a strategy of *differentiation*, and is unlikely to be sustainable. That is, over time competitors identify what added attributes successfully attract consumers and copy these attributes, thereby creating consumer belief regarding their firms' offering. Thus, the firm that introduced the new salient attribute often loses its differential advantage over time.

Increasing the belief strength for attributes considered when making choices is not a strategy that will always lead to a higher overall evaluation of a hotel. For example, consumers may find it relatively unimportant whether the hotel offers a swimming pool or not. As you can see in the example, the importance rating for the availability of a swimming pool is -2. That is, consumers evaluate the availability of a swimming pool negatively, maybe because this implies for them (i.e., consumers in this market segment) that accommodations are more expensive, or that they will not make use of this service and therefore do not see a swimming pool increasing the value of their stay. In this case, stressing the fact that a particular hotel offers a swimming pool, thereby increasing the strength of consumers' beliefs, may actually adversely affect consumers' overall evaluation of the hotel. If you compare Hotels B and D, you will see that the strong belief that Hotel B offers a swimming pool ($b_{\text{swimming pool}} = +2$) negatively affects Hotel B's overall evaluation, since ($e_{\text{swimming pool}} \times b_{\text{swimming pool B}}) = (-2)(+2) = -4$. Hotel D, on the other hand, benefits from consumers not being aware of there being a swimming pool, such that ($e_{\text{swimming pool}} \times b_{\text{swimming pool D}}) = (-2)(-2) = +4$.

In general, it is crucial to find out what attributes targeted consumers feel are important in their decisions, or in other words, what attributes they value, and increase performance or perceived performance on these attributes. The resultant positive attitude toward the offering should then increase the likelihood of the hotel being chosen by consumers using a compensatory decision-making model. Alternatively, as a strategic move, particularly for special "niche" properties, marketers may want to encourage consumers to abandon the linear compensatory model. Niche market segments may exist, or can be

created through marketing communications; these target markets might be better served by properties focusing on one or more of the noncompensatory decision rules presented. For example, assume the segment of highly price-sensitive customers predominantly using a lexicographic decision rule with price as the most important attribute constitutes the primary target market for a low-budget hotel. In this case, customers can be best targeted by offering low prices without providing services not deemed necessary or important by this customer segment, such as the availability of a restaurant or swimming pool. The fact that some customer segments expect some minimal level of performance on several attributes (e.g., cleanliness, convenience, and low price) when they use an elimination-by-aspects or conjunctive decision rule implies, however, that focusing on good performance on one attribute might not be enough to target certain markets of travelers. A hotel would then benefit from an "at least acceptable" level of offerings, as well as from providing better service and facilities than competitors targeting the same market segment. Overall, knowing how consumers make decisions will help hotels to better design offerings appealing to their respective target market(s), thereby improving their competitive positions.

COMPREHENSIVE EXERCISE

Understanding of the decision-making rules discussed above will provide you with tools you can use to make strategy and marketing decisions to effectively target markets identified by the ways consumers make decisions using varying criteria when choosing hotel venues for different purposes. Further, as should become clear from the example used in the exercise, the compensatory decision rule in particular is a tool that can be effectively used from the consumer decision-making perspective when choosing a property for any number of professional or personal reasons.

Bob and Dave's, makers of trail mix and cereal bars, are in the process of planning their annual sales manager meeting for the northwest region in Portland, Oregon. The company has held these annual meetings for a number of years, and their headquarters staff knows very well what characteristics are important for choosing a hotel where the meeting is to be held. For example, corporate rates are very important as Bob and Dave's have a limited budget for meeting expenses. It is also important that conference rooms are available in various sizes and incorporate the latest technological equipment. On the other hand, it is not required that the hotel offer a good restaurant, since participants will go out at night to have dinner and visit downtown Portland. Other attributes considered in the choice of a conference venue are noted in Table 7.2.

Four hotels in the Portland area have submitted brochures and other information material to Bob and Dave's headquarters, making it easy to determine what services are offered at what prices. Bob and Dave's staff now has to make a decision as to which of the four hotels they should choose. Table 7.2 shows relevant attributes, evaluation ratings, and belief ratings to be taken into consideration in the decision-making process.

Practice Questions

Use the information provided in Table 7.2 to answer the following questions.

1. Calculate the overall brand attitudes for all of the brands using the Fishbein linear compensatory model.
2. According to the beliefs and evaluations shown in Table 7.2, which hotel is in the best competitive position? Which hotel is in the worst competitive position?
3. Describe three strategies that the hotel with the lowest overall attitude rating could use to improve consumer's attitudes.
4. What hotel would be chosen with a lexicographic decision rule, if Bob and Dave's consider corporate rates as most important? *A*
5. Which hotel would be chosen given the conjunctive decision rule with a cutoff value of 0? *D*
6. Given the lexicographic decision rule with friendly staff as the most important attribute, what should Hotel C do? What should Hotel B do? *improve belief*
7. List the salient attributes not included in the study that could be considered for conference hotels.

TABLE 7.2
Bob and Dave's Salient Attributes

Attribute	e_i	Hotel A b_{iA}	Hotel B b_{iB}	Hotel C b_{iC}	Hotel D $\checkmark$ b_{iD}
Corporate Rates	+3	+3	−1	+2	+2
Good Restaurant	−1	−2	+2	+1	0
Convenient Location	+2	+1	+2	+3	+2
Fitness Room	0	−2	+3	−1	+1
Conference Rooms	+3	+2	−1	+2	+3
Friendly Staff	+1	+1	+3	−1	+2
		20	−1	16	21

8. Using the elimination-by-aspects rule, which property would be chosen given a cutoff value of +2?

Answers to Practice Questions

1. The overall brand attitudes are calculated using the formula

$$\sum_{i=1}^{n} e_i b_i.$$

$$
\begin{aligned}
A_{\text{Hotel A}} &= (+3)(+3) + (-1)(-2) + (+2)(+1) + \\
&\quad (0)(-2) + (+3)(+2) + (+1)(+1) \\
&= 9 + 2 + 2 + 0 + 6 + 1 \\
&= 20
\end{aligned}
$$

$$
\begin{aligned}
A_{\text{Hotel B}} &= (+3)(-1) + (-1)(+2) + (+2)(+2) + \\
&\quad (0)(+3) + (+3)(-1) + (+1)(+3) \\
&= -3 - 2 + 4 + 0 - 3 + 3 \\
&= -1
\end{aligned}
$$

$$
\begin{aligned}
A_{\text{Hotel C}} &= (+3)(+2) + (-1)(+1) + (+2)(+3) + \\
&\quad (0)(-1) + (+3)(+2) + (+1)(-1) \\
&= 6 - 1 + 6 + 0 + 6 - 1 \\
&= 16
\end{aligned}
$$

$$
\begin{aligned}
A_{\text{Hotel D}} &= (+3)(+2) + (-1)(0) + (+2)(+2) + \\
&\quad (0)(+1) + (+3)(+3) + (+1)(+2) \\
&= 6 + 0 + 4 + 0 + 9 + 2 \\
&= 21
\end{aligned}
$$

2. If the Fishbein linear compensatory model is used, Hotel D is in the best competitive position, because its overall attitude rating (+21) is higher than that of its competitors'. Hotel B is in the worst competitive position, because its overall attitude rating (−1) is lower than its competitors'.

3. *Strategy 1*: Hotel B could attempt to change the perceived relevance of some of the attributes. Hotel B could stress the importance of a good restaurant and excellent fitness facilities for a conference hotel. The drawback of this strategy is that some of its competitors could benefit from it, too.

   Strategy 2: Hotel B could improve its performance on some of the attributes considered important by consumers in this target market, thereby increasing the strength of consumers' belief that it possesses these attributes. More specifically, Hotel B should offer corporate rates if financially feasible, and improve its conference facilities.

   Strategy 3: Hotel B could encourage consumers to consider other relevant attributes when choosing conference hotels. These attributes should be associated with a strong performance by Hotel B and a weaker performance on the part of other competitors. For example, Hotel B might introduce a shuttle service to the airport to make it even more convenient for conference participants to reach it, offer a coffee shop for short breaks and breakfast, and introduce secretarial services for meeting participants.

4. If a lexicographic decision rule is used, with corporate rates as the most important attribute, Hotel A would be chosen. It scores highest on this attribute ($b_{\text{corporate rate A}} = +3$).

5. Hotel D would be chosen, since it is the only one meeting the cutoff value of 0 on all the salient attributes.

6. Hotel C could change its hiring practices and attract friendlier employees, provide training for its employees, or consider a change in management style. Hotel B should maintain its high level of employee friendliness.

7. The following is a nonexhaustive list of additional attributes that might be salient for conference hotels: access to fax machines and Internet, secretarial services, coffee shop, convenience store or gift shop, cable TV, shuttle service, etc.

8. Using elimination by aspects (cutoff value = +2) we initially eliminate Hotel B and see that Hotels A, C, and D stay in consideration based on beliefs about those brands regarding the equally important attributes of corporate rates and conference rooms. The next most important attribute is convenient location, and we are left with Hotels C and D in consideration after eliminating Hotel A. Finally, we eliminate Hotel C and select Hotel D based on the friendly staff attribute.

7.5   Hotel Pricing

Margaret Shaw

Hotel practitioners have been making room-rate pricing decisions for centuries. From the small taverns and inns of Renaissance Europe to the 2000-room mega-fantasy resort hotels of the 1990s, some one has had the responsibility for making price decisions for travelers seeking lodging. The questions to be addressed include who are these travelers, what are their options, who are the price decision makers, and how do they go about it. As noted by Howard B. Meek (1938), a renowned and respected leader in the field of hospitality:

> The classical analysis explaining price in terms of supply and demand has passed through many examinations and revisions, but still stands in its essential idea as the most satisfactory, most generally acceptable explanation of the phenomena of price determination.

KEY ELEMENTS FOR PRICING DECISIONS

Meek's statement of over 60 years ago is correct. All pricing decisions are based on the economic principles of supply and demand. More specifically, demand relative to available supply on any given day determines the price in the marketplace. This basic tenet of economic theory holds true for the sale of a hotel guest room, as it does for the purchase of a loaf of bread, a life insurance policy, a college education.

The essential elements of price theory include demand, competition, and cost. As graphically shown in Figure 7.4, these parameters offer a framework from which hotel room rate-pricing decisions can be made. It offers a managerial perspective for pricing and is con-

FIGURE 7.4
Key elements of the pricing decision

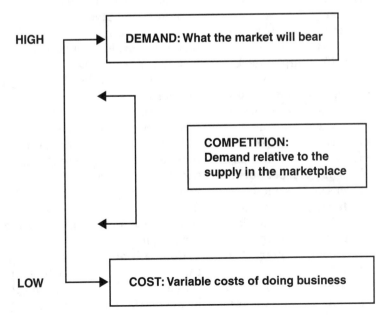

sistent with the economic theory of supply and demand. Supply, by definition, is made up of all the competitors in the marketplace and the costs they incur to conduct business. The model in Figure 7.4 adapts economic theory to management practice, that is, a management tool for effective and efficient hotel pricing decisions.

Demand

Demand determines the highest rate that can be charged, that is, "what the market will bear." Some business travelers to New York City are willing to pay a $300-plus daily room rate for first-class accommodations in midtown Manhattan. Some families will pay up to $5000 a week for a family vacation at a fantasy resort in the Hawaiian Islands. College students going downhill skiing for a weekend may put their "ceiling" at $10 per night.

A key point here is the purpose of purchase, or for our industry, the purpose of the trip. There are all kinds of travelers traveling for all kinds of reasons. "What the market will bear" will vary tremendously depending on the market. Thus, the particular target markets of a hotel need to be clearly defined when making a pricing decision for each target market.

Demand from any identified target market will fluctuate. Business travel tends to be heaviest in the fall and spring, and not surprisingly, hotel rates for this market peak during these time periods. Vacation travel of Canadians to Florida is particularly strong in the winter months. So are the rates they pay.

Education associations like to meet during the summer months, when school is out of session. This market is also fairly price sensitive. Thus, hotels targeting to business travelers in the fall, winter, and spring may target the education segment as a secondary market in the summer, at lower rates.

In short, demand determines the high end of a rate structure, depending on who the tar-

get market is and the price sensitivities of that market. Yet this is just a start. Competition in the marketplace, and the costs incurred by these suppliers, also have a major impact on final pricing decisions.

Competition

Competition can be viewed from both a direct and indirect perspective. Indirect competition refers to the broad range of alternatives available to travelers. Vacationers have the option of staying with friends and relatives, camping, or simply making day trips close to home. In other words, they have an option *not* to purchase a hotel room for overnight accommodations. The same holds true for business travelers. They, too, have the option of day trips only, or shortened trips of a 1–2 day duration. Indeed, the average night's stay for an individual business traveler is typically 1.3 nights. Faster jet travel, overnight couriers, fax machines, and the like have made the decision to even take a business trip in the first place a questioned business expense.

Direct competitors are those hotels who compete for similar target markets. Sheraton, Marriott, and Hyatt Hotels, for example, all compete on a national level for the upscale business traveler, including independent business travel, corporate business travel, and convention business travel. In many respects this market views these suppliers of hotel accommodations as close substitutes—or viable alternatives—when making a decision on where to book their room. Though the price of that room is only one of several factors in making the decision on where to stay, it is a salient and important factor. Suppliers who deviate from an acceptable relevant range will eventually lose potential customers to their competition.

Competition is a key element in putting a cap on or placing parameters for the relevant range of prices. When demand exceeds supply in the marketplace—known as peak demand periods—the relevant range is higher on the demand/competition/cost continuum. And conversely, when supply exceeds demand—known as off-peak periods or valley demand periods—the relevant range of prices is usually much lower. For example, in the Boston market first-class hotel convention rates can range from $150 to $200 during the September, October, May, and June peak periods. Yet, in the slower winter months, room rates offered to the convention market can fall much lower to the $100 to $125 range.

Experienced convention buyers are well aware of these price variations, or rather, the peak and valley fluctuations of the hotel business. Hotel price decision makers need to monitor the market closely, anticipate as best they can high and soft periods, and avoid the pitfalls of the "we don't discount" syndrome. This syndrome, especially when practiced in valley periods, can end up with lost business, missed budgets, and unhappy owners.

Discounting during off-peak periods in the hotel business is common. Different target markets have varying elasticities of demand, and thus, when supply exceeds demand, astute hotel management looks to the more elastic demand segments to fill their hotel rooms. Discounting recognizes that varying elasticities of demand do exist, and that the more elastic markets, such as educators, are willing to buy at discounted rates. Elastic markets, by definition, are the more price-sensitive demand segments who purchase greater quantities at lower prices. Discounted hotel room rates is a direct application of the economic principles of elasticity of demand.

Cost

There are essentially two kinds of costs for any business enterprise—fixed costs and variable costs. Fixed costs are the costs of *being* in business, that is, those costs that remain the same regardless of business volume (building and equipment, administrative salaries, and so

forth). The variable costs are the costs of *doing* business, that is, those costs that vary with business volume (materials, direct labor, and so forth). Though there are a number of semivariable and semifixed costs associated with running a business, the purpose here is to distinguish between the short-run costs of doing business and the long-run costs of being in business.

The short-run, or variable, costs for hotel guest rooms are largely housekeeping labor, bathroom amenities, laundry, and the like. It is essentially the cost of an occupied room. Variable costs in the hotel industry are relatively low, ranging from $20 to $75 per room per night depending on the service level of the hotel (budget, midtier, luxury), the location (metropolitan, suburban, resort), and the occupancy of the hotel (during high occupancy periods hotels often incur overtime labor costs). To give an example, variable costs for full-service hotels in metropolitan areas can range from $30 to $60 per occupied room per night.

In the short run, it is the variable costs that are relevant to the pricing decision. These daily costs of doing business need to be covered and thus are the minimum threshold for room-rate pricing decisions. Any revenue exceeding these costs contributes something to the fixed overhead, which is better than no contribution at all. It makes no sense (both intuitively and financially) to sell a room for $25 if the variable cost to sell that room is $30.

Most hoteliers recognize that profit margins can and will be lower in the off-peak periods. Contribution margins are simply lower during the slower periods, yet nonetheless contribute something to the fixed overhead costs of being in business. During peak demand periods contribution margins are greater and thus contribute significantly to these fixed costs of the hotel operation. It is in the long run, cutting across both peak and off-peak demand periods, that successful management realizes reasonable profits.

Profits vary across business cycles, as well. Contribution margins can be very low during a recession period, as the hotel industry experienced during the early 1990s. Even with deeply discounted room rates, special promotions, and aggressive selling, hotels worldwide faced a sharp falloff in demand. Business travel was down, and pleasure travel was almost nonexistent. Staying in business was a matter of survival, and not necessarily profitable. Economic stability has to occur before profitability can be realized. In the meantime, sell what you can at a price the customer is willing to pay, as long as the price meets or exceeds the basic costs of doing business at hand.

PRICING: A MARKETING DECISION

Marketing Objectives

Pricing is a marketing decision. And marketing's mandate is customer satisfaction. Indeed, charging the right price is clearly part of that mandate. Marketing is giving the target customers what they want, when they want it, where they want it, at a price they are willing and able to pay. The pricing decision needs to be made within the context of the consumer, and not in the confines of the accounting department. It is through customer satisfaction that long-run profit goals are realized.

Pricing is viewed in different ways by different constituencies. For example, liquidity issues are of concern to hotel owners. To hotel managers realities of the marketplace are of primary concern. Yet to the consumer, pricing is what they are willing and able to pay to rent a room for the night.

The customer doesn't care about liquidity issues, financial statements, or returns on investment. Nor does the customer care about market-share battles among suppliers in the marketplace. What the customer does care about is a hotel room for the night that is clean and secure—at a good-price value as perceived by the buyer.

Market Positioning

Customer perception is what positioning is all about. There is much truth to the adage "perception is reality." If the customer thinks the price is too high, it is, regardless of what the owners and managers think. The same holds true if a price is perceived to be too low. Price is a signal of quality. Too low a price can signal poor quality whether the quality is there or not.

Positioning enters the demand/competition/cost continuum as both a minimum and maximum threshold for the hotel room-rate pricing decision. If your rates are perceived to be too high (within a product class such as the midtier hotel market), the customers will go elsewhere. If your rates are perceived to be too low, no one will come. In either case profits will, of course, not be realized.

Positioning decisions, made by senior-level management, set the parameters for the relevant range of prices for a hotel. Actual price decisions, depending on the target market, will lie somewhere within that predetermined range. The term *rack rate* refers to the upper end of the range, often called *list price* in other industries. Deep discounts or special package rates are at the lower end of the range. If the rack rates are too high and/or discounts too low, the overall image or "positioning" of the hotel is in jeopardy.

A good example to demonstrate this point is the emergence of the weekend package. Now commonly referred to as the *weekend-package market*, weekend packages are, essentially, highly discounted rates directed to pleasure travelers and local residents to help boost weekend occupancies. Metropolitan hotels primarily cater to business travelers who are abundant during the week but absent on the weekends. Hotels needed a way to attract people during these softer periods at a price that would not fall below the variable costs. The strategy is to reach out to a more price-sensitive market with a lower price, but not so low as to compromise your position in the marketplace. Hotels are not willing to risk their image as perceived by their primary target market, which in this case is the weekday business traveler.

Thus, the concept of the weekend-package market was born. Local residents and/or pleasure travelers who cannot afford to stay at a hotel for $150 per night, can afford $90 per night when it is perceived as a good price-value. Just as importantly, the business traveler does not feel "squelched" or "ripped off" when he or she hears of these special weekend-package rates. In fact, a large portion of the weekend-package market is the business-person who is traveling for pleasure on the weekends. Hotel management realizes that individuals will surface in multiple target markets depending on the purpose of the trip. They also realize that the price sensitivities (or price elasticities) of these individuals will vary depending on the purpose of the trip, as well.

Yield Management

Yield management, or revenue management, grew in popularity in the late 1980s and into the 1990s and continues to be widely practiced today. Advanced computer technology has spurred its increased usage in hospitality management.

Yield management, in hotel vernacular, is a systematic (automated) approach to pricing decisions through guest room inventory management and respective prices allocated to each room in that inventory. Its primary objective is revenue maximization for any given day (or period). In other words, depending on forecasted demand for a future period, prices are adjusted to reflect that demand. It is essentially adjusting the price of available guest room inventory to reflect the realities of the marketplace. Forecasting is key to the successful implementation of a yield-management system.

Most hotels target multiple markets with varying degrees of price elasticity of demand.

Through automation, and the computer, hotel managers can capture the subtleties of market shifts (shifts in forecasted demand) and adjust the prices of the remaining rooms inventory to ensure that rooms *do not* go unsold. Conversely, when demand is higher than expected for the higher-rated rooms category, the number of available rooms in the discounted-rooms category is reduced.

For example, an initial forecast may show 100 rooms to be sold at a rack rate of $150, and 100 rooms to be sold at a discounted convention rate of $120. However, a revised forecast may show demand for the rack-rated rooms to be lower than expected. A yield-management system would automatically flag this revised forecast and reallocate 20 of the 100 rack-rated rooms to the discounted convention rooms inventory. In other words, the rack-rated rooms inventory would now be 80 rooms and the discounted convention rooms inventory would be 120 rooms. This is done to ensure maximum *revenues*, or the highest yield, for the given period. The primary assumption here is that the 20 rack-rated rooms would have gone unsold unless their price was reduced, or opened up to the discounted convention-rate market.

Again, the objective of yield management is revenue maximization. Getting the best price, relative to supply and demand conditions for a given period, is the goal. Advanced computer technology, that is, yield management, has enhanced hotel management's capability of achieving that goal. (Editor's note: For additional information on yield management and revenue management, see Chapter 4.5 by Quain and LeBruto, Chapter 7.6 by Orkin, and Chapter 7.7 by Chappelle.)

PRICING: A CUSTOMER DECISION

In summary, demand, competition, and cost all play an important role in the hotel room-rate pricing decision. Demand sets the ceiling and costs set the floor. Competition, or supply relative to demand, helps determine more precisely how high or how low a price will be. Positioning, or how you want to be perceived in the marketplace, sets the upper and lower limits of the price range to be offered. Some hotels may have wider ranges than others, depending on the desired position to be achieved.

Most importantly, pricing is a marketing decision. This is not to imply that only the marketing department makes pricing decisions. Pricing decisions are made every day in the reservation and front office departments. What it does mean is that the customer is the one who really makes the decision. And it is our job as marketing-minded hoteliers to find out just what it is that the customer really wants and what price they are willing and able to pay.

It is a tenet of marketing that the customer is always right. The hotel customer is always right, too.

7.6 Wishful Thinking and Rocket Science

Eric B. Orkin

One element of revenue management is to determine how much demand a hotel would enjoy in the absence of any constraints. Determining unconstrained demand is critical to the process of managing for optimum revenues. Revenue management means being selective about which reservation requests to take and which to turn away. The selection of criteria for accepting or denying any given request requires a reliable estimate of total, or unconstrained, demand. In this article I discuss the complexities of calculating unconstrained demand and outline how computer software can assist with the decision.

Unconstrained demand refers to the level of room-nights that guests would reserve in the absence of any limitations or constraints—whether those constraints are imposed intentionally by the hotel or whether they occur from a sold-out condition. Typical constraints include stay-pattern controls (e.g., requiring a minimum stay of three days), rate controls (e.g., close all rates below $92.50), and inventory limitations (e.g., deluxe rooms sold out). A day's total unconstrained demand is the sum of room-nights from guests wanting to arrive on that day plus room-nights generated by guests who would arrive earlier and stay through.

Simple intuition suggests that the most direct way to calculate unconstrained demand is to sum a property's realized demand (i.e., bookings) with its latent demand (i.e., denials). Denials are reservation requests that were turned down by the hotel because the desired accommodation or rates were not available for the stay requested.

Unfortunately, simply summing bookings and denials falters because recorded denials are almost always a poor estimate of latent demand. The complicating factor involves regrets, when a guest calls for a reservation but for some reason chooses not to book the room. The alternative to recording denials is to employ statistical methods for inferring latent demand. This is the province of computer algorithms.

One such algorithm is found in the application TopLine PROPHET, of which my firm is a purveyor. One of its users is Westin Hotels and Resorts. Tim Coleman, Westin's vice president of distribution, came up with the following apt and memorable analogy for how the inference is achieved. (Cross, 1997)

During the Gulf War the Allies launched Patriot missiles to intercept incoming Scud missiles when it was inferred from the path of an airborne Scud that it would probably land on friendly terrain. A successful Patriot "constrained" the incoming Scud—*kaboom!* Though the Scud exploded before landing, the Allies' confidence in their forecast of the intended target was unshaken.

The Allies' confidence was based on their historic knowledge of Scud performance plus the measurement of key parameters describing the missile currently on the scope. Shortly after a Scud's launch, its speed, trajectory, and other metrics were combined with the profile of typical Scud performance to provide an accurate forecast of the intended target.

TopLine PROPHET does essentially the same thing with regard to hotel demand. It uses historical demand for like days in the past (analogous to typical Scud performance) and realized demand-to-date for the day in question (analogous to the speed and trajectory of the Scud on the scope) to forecast how that day is likely to end up if no constraints are applied (analogous to forecasting the intended target if a Patriot is not launched).

Any constraint will depress the realized demand or, in Scud terms, change the trajectory. The difference between forecast demand in the absence of any constraint and the realized demand in the presence of that constraint is the statistically inferred level of denials.

Thus, revenue management is a great deal like rocket science (Cross, 1997).

THE DIFFICULTY WITH DENIALS

The routine recording of denials is an appealing method for determining latent demand, because it derives from real-world occurrences. Someone calls and asks for the government rate. The rate is closed, and so a denial is recorded—simple and straightforward, but unfortunately flawed.

A hidden problem with denials is the difficulty in distinguishing them from regrets. Denials occur when the guest's request cannot be met by the hotel because of a constraint, while regrets result when the hotel can accommodate the request but the guest declines to book. In practice, it is often impossible to categorize a particular call as one or the other. Making an accurate distinction is vital, however, because denials constitute latent demand while regrets do not. Latent demand is sales lost due to constraints imposed by the hotel, but there is nothing in the operational definition of a regret that says anything about the existence of a constraint. This means that regrets are not part of latent demand.

Many hotel companies track both regrets and denials, regarding them as an integral part of unconstrained demand. Some track regrets only, skipping denials. The rationale for the latter practice is that regrets can measure when the hotel did not make an acceptable offer to the caller. "Rates too high" is the most common reason an offer is deemed unacceptable. When a hotel experiences a day with substantial regrets but does not sell out, the implication is that lower rates should have been available—and, further, that some or all of those regrets represent latent demand just as much as do denials.

Two kinds of regrets exist, however, and that confounds one's ability to make projections. If a regret occurs because the overall rate structure of the hotel is too high, then a high level of regrets would tell management to shift the entire rate structure downward to meet the market. If, on the other hand, what occurred is the caller could not get to a low rate that exists but was restricted for the particular stay in question, it is not a regret, but a denial. A high level of denials without a sellout says nothing about a hotel's rate structure but quite a lot about the level of rate restrictions imposed. So-called regret tracking mixes the two types of regrets together, resulting in data resistant to meaningful conclusions.

BLURRY BOUNDARIES

The following two everyday instances exemplify the blurry boundary between denials and regrets.

Case One: Rate Shoppers   *regret → denial*

Penny Wise calls and asks for the lowest available rate. She is quoted $85 and declines to book. Is Penny a regret or a denial? If $85 is the low rate for the season, she is a regret. But suppose Penny responded, "Hey, I stayed with you last week for $65. What about that rate?" Now she is a denial because she was "constrained" out of booking when the hotel closed the $65 rate.

As in Penny's case, every regret is potentially a denial if a lesser rate is available but not quoted. The reason this situation is only a potential denial is because there is no way to know whether a caller would also have rejected the lowest available rate—a regret. While the distinction is blurry, the implication is not. Only when the lowest available rate is offered can one unerringly distinguish between a regret and a denial. All other situations are just guesses.

Case Two: Out-of-Market Callers   *denial → regret*

In a second example of the blurry boundary between denials and regrets, Sam Seenyor calls to request the 60-plus rate. It is closed, and Sam declines to book. Sam is recorded as a denial. Ben Binaround, remarkably like Sam in most every way, also requests the 60-plus rate. For his dates the rate is open, but when Ben hears the quote he bellows, "I had no idea your rates were so high. Good-bye." Ben is recorded as a regret. Ben's reaction raises the question: was Sam really ever a denial? Sam never actually heard the 60-plus rate quoted, so there is no way to know whether he was truly a denial and would

have bought if the rate were open, or was a regret like Ben.

SEEING DOUBLE

Denials have a disturbing propensity to be double- and triple-counted in the total demand equation. The following examples suggest that the problem surfaces in many ways.

Searching Multiple Room Types

Henry T. Aith requests a king room for dates when none is available. He declines the offer of an available queen room. The hotel records a denial. Doing so means that denials are associated with room-type availability, regardless of other availabilities in the hotel. Mac and Beth Dunsinane also request a king room (still unavailable) but accept the alternative offer of a queen. Should a "king denial" be recorded in the case of Mac and Beth? If yes, they are double-counted—once as a king denial and again as a queen booking. If no, then the real demand for the king has gone unrecorded.

Searching Multiple Dates

Tom Tempus's requested dates are unavailable, and a denial is recorded. Phil Fugit's dates are also unavailable, but he accepts the offer of alternate dates and books a room. Should Phil's original dates be recorded with a denial? If yes, Phil is double-counted: once as a denial and again as a booking. If no, the latent demand for the first dates goes unrecognized.

Searching Multiple Properties

Mortimer Mauss calls the toll-free number of a major chain and asks for a property near

Walt Disney World. The Corporate Reservations System (CRS) operator offers Mortie three properties before he picks one. Should anything be recorded to indicate the latent demand for the first two properties? If yes, Mortie is being triple-counted! Daphne Ducke calls to request the Main Gate Inn. She is quoted the only available rate—rack, at $195. Checking further, Daphne's agent finds a special rate of $105 at a nearby property, and she accepts that offer. Should the agent record a denial for the Main Gate Inn? If the Main Gate sometimes offers a $105 discount rate, Daphne certainly would have booked it, and she is a denial. If the Main Gate never offers such a

low rate, the case is less compelling, and she may be a regret. But even counting her as a bona fide denial is troubling, because Daphne ends up being part of realized demand for one hotel and latent demand for another. (See sidebar, "How the Software Estimates Demand.")

"Shopping" Calls

Glenn Trotter's request to use his travel-club card is turned down by a hotel's booking agent because the rate is closed. The agent records a denial. Not wanting to lose the sale, how-

---

HOW THE SOFTWARE ESTIMATES DEMAND

During the nightly demand-estimation process TopLine PROPHET records the level of actual reservations taken during the day and the inferred magnitude of unconstrained demand. This is done for all days in the future (within a reasonable horizon for the property).

For days without constraints, demand equals the number of reservations taken. Those future days for which one or more constraint was imposed at any time during the day are analyzed and the probable impact of the constraints (i.e., denials) is calculated based on the actual hors of the day that the constraints were in effect.

The system forecasts the number of reservations that the hotel is likely to take during the next 24-hour period for all future daysæbroken down by lengths of stay and by rate bands (in $1 increments). For example, one element of the forecast for October 12 might be the estimate that in the next 24 hours five reservations should be taken for arrival on October 12 with a two-day length of stay and a rate between $72 and $73. By forecasting at that fine level TopLine PROPHET is able to calculate the effect of closing out any particular

stay pattern or imposing a minimum-rate requirement.

This approach is responsive to the actual flow of reservations. If, for example, a special event on Saturday, October 12, is causing an unusually high percentage of two-day stays among guests arriving on Friday, October 11, TopLine PROPHET will note that trend and adjust the forecast accordingly. If the hotel were to impose a three-day minimum length of stay, on the other hand, the statistically inferred level of denials would reflect the trend already experienced.

The application's data-augmentation methodology uses what is actually happening to create a picture of what would be happening if the hotel had an infinite number of rooms to sell and no restrictions imposed. The difference between that picture and the actual reservations taken is the inferred level of denials. All this happens automatically and is not subject to any of the assumptions and uncertainties that plague the traditional approaches of denial recording. The result is a more accurate prediction of unconstrained demand as a critical input into the revenue optimization algorithm.—*E.B.O.*

ever, the agent does a great job and offers Glenn a promotional rate that is somewhat higher than the club rate, but that still represents a substantial discount. Glenn dutifully says he will check with his wife. Unknown to the original agent, Glenn calls back later and books the room at the promotional rate. Glenn has been double-counted—once as latent demand and again as realized demand. Shoppers often compound this effect even after booking! In hopes of finding that the travel-club rate has reopened, Glenn calls three more times before his arrival. Because the rate remains closed, with each call Glenn will further and erroneously increase the estimate of latent demand.

A ROSE FROM ANY OTHER SOURCE

Hotels receive reservations from such sources as walk-ins, the telephone, affiliated reservation centers, the global distribution systems (GDS), and the Internet. Almost all hotels that undertake denial tracking do so from one source only, and then use statistical tools to generalize those results to the other sources.

The critical assumption in this approach is that the source with denial tracking provides a representative sample of the others. The following three points (in italics) demonstrate one hotel's wishful thinking compared to its reality.

Wishful Thinking

Callers to the hotel are a reliable sample of all prospective guests. Instead of being a reliable sample, calls directly to the hotel disproportionately represent the local business community. They are biased toward short, midweek stays. Many are on a last-room-availability, fixed-rate contract. Most want king-bed rooms. *The hotel's agents quote rates just like CRO*

and travel agents. In reality, the process the hotel's agents use is entirely different from that of travel agents and central reservation office (CRO) operators. Hotel reservationists are trained in a top-down rate-quotation method. Faced with rate resistance, they may offer promotional rates. When a closed rate is requested, the agent offers an appropriate alternative. Neither the CRO nor travel agents take these steps.

CRO and travel agents sell the property just like the hotel's own agents. As with the above point, the CRO and travel agents have their own agenda and procedures. They often look at several properties at one time, tend toward an order-taking approach, and generally quote the least-expensive room type that fits the guest's request.

STATISTICAL SOLUTION

As a logical model, summing bookings and denials to derive unconstrained demand makes perfect sense, but the actual practice of denial tracking as a reliable measure of true latent demand is problematic. Statistical techniques are used in almost all fields of research to fill in missing data and can do so here. Computer simulations are used to test the effect of a crash on new-car design, for instance, and wind tunnels have been replaced by computers that infer the effects of particular design elements. These same types of technique can be used to infer the actual consequence of constraints on demand.

The techniques rest on two premises. First, for days without constraints, actual bookings are a perfect measure of unconstrained demand. Second, for days with constraints, demand lost due to constraints can be inferred from the nature of the constraint itself.

For example, a hotel is forecasting that 60 people will call today wishing to reserve rooms for arrival tomorrow. Thirty calls, or half of

TABLE 7.3
Two Scenarios of Inferred Demand

Scenario 1: Actual Bookings = 30 Minimum-stay length	Forecasted Demand	Actual Results	Inferred
2-Day or Longer	30	30	
1-Day	30	Closed	30
All Lengths	60		60
Scenario 2: Actual Bookings = 20 Minimum-stay length	**Forecasted Demand**	**Actual Results**	**Inferred**
2-Day or Longer	30	20	
1-Day	30	Closed	20
All Lengths	60		40

The effects of denials on the estimate of unconstrained demand are detailed in the text. In scenario 1, 60 people called, but only 30 could be accommodated due to a restriction on one-day stays, fulfilling the forecast with an estimated 30 denials. But if only 20 parties are accommodated after 60 calls, the forecast was off, and one could infer that some 40 guests were denied rooms due to the two-day minimum.

the requests, will be for one-day stays, but the hotel has closed that rate by requiring a two-day stay. Table 7.3 shows this situation as scenario 1. The results show that the forecast was accurate. By the end of the day 30 calls were for at least a two-day stay, while 30 callers were denied because they requested one night.

Based on the original forecast and the actual results attained, one can conclude that the total demand for the day was 60, or close to it (as calculated from the actual results of 30 room-nights times two nights). In other words, the level of denials due to the two-day minimum-stay requirement can be statistically inferred as equaling 30.

Suppose that two-day or longer stays had sold only 20 reservations, rather than the 30 originally forecast. The second part of Table 7.3 demonstrates the inference that might be made from this revised scenario, namely that demand for the day was closer to 40 room-nights (20 bookings times two).

These simplified scenarios demonstrate how results achieved by "like days" in the past,

and a day's own results-to-date, can be used to derive estimates of denials and unconstrained demand. Similar techniques for "unconstraining" demand are used to account for rate closures and sold-out inventory. Though the actual technology of deriving unconstrained demand is more complex than these examples, the principle should be clear.

TopLine PROPHET records in its database every type and degree of constraint, the time it was applied, and any changes over time. By doing so the system has the ability to "unconstrain" based on the demand-depressing effects of each particular constraint, as inferred from its degree and actual duration.

Hoteliers are comfortable with tracking denials because of their apparent direct link to market demand. Denial tracking is fraught with difficulties, however, as I have explained here. Inferring denials, on the other hand, may feel remote and theoretical, but is in fact firmly grounded in the reality of the market and the behavior of buyers and agents and in the hotel's revenue-management practices.

7.7   A Day in the Life of a Regional Revenue Manager

Paul Chappelle

As the sun rises so does the stack of reports on my desk. Every morning I am greeted with the accomplishments of the day, week, month, and year before. All in the form of paper-and-ink reports roughly 2 inches thick. Each report attempts to explain the basic numbers pertinent to the smooth function and revenue generation of a hotel.

The first meeting of the day is the revenue maximization meeting, or revmax for short. The meeting consists of the hotel's revenue manager, general manager, director of rooms, and the entire sales and catering staff. We discuss what happened the day and night before, and we evaluate any sales leads from the previous day. As a group, we decide what our approach is to each lead. We evaluate whether we will pursue the lead or refer it to a nearby hotel within the company. The revenue manager upholds any decisions made regarding the rate strategy for that day and for the next few days, which are set at that time. Any changes that need to be made are communicated throughout the day.

The next meeting of the day is the revenue management meeting. This meeting, facilitated by the revenue manager, happens once a week and is attended by the general manager, controller, director of sales and marketing, director of rooms, reservations manager, and most operations managers. In this meeting, similar to the daily revmax meeting with the sales team, we go over the numbers in much greater detail and for a much longer time period. We look at the number of room-nights and rates generated through the different revenue channels, trends both good and bad, upcoming marketing strategies, and the results of past marketing strategies, and we talk about anything and everything that may affect the number of room-nights and the rate the rooms are sold at the hotel for the past

year and as far out as one year. After the leadership team has identified our opportunities we discuss a plan for how we are going to exploit these opportunities and how we are going to measure whether what the team decided was an effective strategy. Each of these meetings is repeated in some form or another in person or over the phone for all of my hotels that I oversee.

RESPONSIBILITIES

The daily, weekly, monthly, and yearly forecasts are the most important responsibility of a revenue manager. I am responsible for forecasting the number of rooms and the rate at which the guest will pay for a given time period. I generate these forecasts based on many critical factors and some not so critical. History is always a good indicator of what the future will hold for hotels. The correlation between what happened last year on this day in this month to what happens today can be between 60 percent and 80 percent. What is going on in the area can have a huge impact on occupancy and rate of a hotel. Local events such as festivals, races, and tournaments can all impact the number if additional persons in the city are in need of hotel rooms. The competition can affect your hotel by running a special promotion that negatively impacts the hotel. On the other side of the coin, the competition can and will create a positive situation for the hotel when they have abysmal service or a ramshackle product. Other factors for consideration that contribute to creation of a forecast are: additions to the supply of hotel rooms in the area, weather, seasonality, pickup and departure patterns of conventions, the ever changing local and regional economies. However, when it comes down to it, a forecast is exactly that—it is a guess of what we think may happen or what we really want to happen.

Once the forecasts are completed they are used to project the amount of variable costs associated with running a hotel—things such as labor or how many housekeepers, front desk clerks, and hash slingers we are going to need for a given time period. Goals are set for sales and catering managers based on the forecast. The quarterly and annual forecasts are reported to the corporate offices for the purpose of forecasting the entire company's projected revenues and expenses. In turn, that information is then put out to the stockholders and others that hold a financial stake in the company.

Forecasts and tracking of how we did compared to the forecast take up 75 percent of my time. The other 25 percent of my time is spent spread amongst exploring new opportunities for revenue growth, maintenance of the various revenue channels into the hotel, managing the reservations department, acting as the liaison between the sales department and operations, and having fun.

Additional duties include exploring new revenue channels for the hotel. I have been known to visit the local competitor on a particularly busy day and offer a shuttle to our hotel and a "no line" guarantee. This, as the line behind the front desk stretches out the front door and half way to the street. I am responsible for the research of the demographics of the travelers coming to the area. Things like, why are they coming? Are they traveling because of business, conventions, leisure, or are they part of a contract piece of business? How often do they come? How long do they stay? How much do they spend when they come? Where are they coming from?

The most important thing that I do as a revenue manager is to insure that the different revenue channels are set up and functioning properly. These channels include the hotel brand's generic 1–800 vanity number and central reservations office, the convention and visitors bureau, the local hotel's reservation and front desk, the Internet, and the global distribution system (GDS). The most critical of these channels is the GDS. This is the systems that travel agents and the Internet uses to make reservations at my hotels. It contains information about rates and availability at a hotel. It has to be checked daily and routinely maintained. The scary thing about the GDS is that most hotels don't know that they have a problem until it is months down the road. As technology grows and more and more people stop calling and start booking through their travel agents and directly over the Internet, so does the need to understand the GDS and exactly how it affects the hotel. In the case of a competitor, when they initiated a cleanup of their GDS it resulted in several million dollars in additional revenue in 6 months.

Managing the reservations departments is the easy part of my job. The interaction with people is always easier than trying to interact with numbers and reports. The staff needs to be kept up-to-date on any changes in strategic goals of the hotel and any changes in marketing the different discount and frequent-stayer programs. I am responsible for insuring that the training of the reservations staff and anyone that takes reservations is consistent and up-to-date complete with on-going positive feedback.

It is key that a revenue manager be skilled in the art of diplomacy. As the liaison between the operations and sales departments it is sometimes necessary to mediate any challenges that may occur. Part of the diplomacy is understanding what each department's strategic goals are and how both departments depend on each other for their own survival. The easiest and simplest approach to serving as a liaison between the two departments is facilitating frequent, open, and honest communication between all parties.

Having fun is one of my key goals in working at a hotel and in a regional capacity. It is important to maintain a balanced approach to work in a hotel. It is very easy to get burned out trying to do too much. The nature of the hotel is that it is open 24 hours a day and 365 days a year. Anything that can happen to a person on any given day can happen at a hotel, as well.

7.8   Hotel Sales Organization and Operations

Margaret Shaw and Susan V. Morris

SALES AND MARKETING

Sales and marketing are related concepts, and each is an art and a science. Sales flow from marketing. Marketing, well stated by Lewis et al. (1995), "is communicating to and giving target market customers what they want, when they want it, where they want it, and at a price they are willing and able to pay." The primary focus of sales is on the communication aspect of marketing. It involves direct personal selling to potential customers that you and your organization have the right product, in the right place, at the right time, and at the right price—be it a hotel, a restaurant, a casino, or contract food services.

Marketing is getting and keeping a customer, a macro approach to managing a successful business. In a broad sense, marketing is the development and delivery of a successful product, that is, the development and delivery of a satisfied customer. Hotel sales comprises finding that customer and matching their specific needs with the right product offering, a micro or one-on-one approach to customer satisfaction. For example, a meeting planner from Texas Instruments (TI) is planning an annual sales meeting to be held in Dallas. From a macro perspective, this planner has selected the city and is searching for full-service lodging accommodations for 200 TI sales representatives for a five-day conference. From a micro perspective, he or she visits several hotel alternatives and meets with the hotel sales representatives to find the best "fit." Various aspects of the meeting being planned are discussed including dates, rates, guest room accommodations, function room requirements, food and beverage services, and so forth. It is the job of the hotel sales manager to learn the specific needs and wants of the planner and "create" the right product, place, time, and price for a successful conference.

A successful conference is what the planner is really buying, not bricks and mortar. Thus, successful selling is understanding the real needs of the buyer, communicating how your product and service can best respond to those needs, and then delivering it. In another context, McDonald's Golden Arches markets fun, simplicity, good service, and a good price. McDonald's sells friendly service, good value for price paid, convenient locations, and those delicious golden chicken nuggets on which many of us grew up. Ronald McDonald is an ancillary product, a public relations endeavour, which augments and supports the idea or concept of kids and why they are special.

Public relations, advertising, and special promotions often support the selling effort. Advertisements for the Ritz-Carlton Hotel Company are directed to their business traveler clientele. Such advertisements incorporate both the selling and marketing aspects of this upscale hotel chain. The company is simultaneously selling hotel rooms to busy business executives and marketing a hotel that "remembers your needs," and is hallmarked by the vision implicit in their slogan "ladies and gentlemen serving ladies and gentlemen." A travel agent, a corporate travel manager, or a secretary, however, may have handled the actual purchase of the hotel room. Thus, the Ritz-Carlton advertisements support the sale, but they do not actually make the sale happen.

SALES AND OPERATIONS

Sales is the critical link between marketing and operations. While hospitality professionals may espouse marketing, all too often it becomes ignored in the daily hustle and bustle of operations. It is the role of sales to help bridge this gap and find ways for the key customer-contact members of the hotel to keep the promise of marketing.

Selling starts by the professional sales managers prospecting, making contacts, establishing relationships with clients, uncovering their specific needs and wants. But it doesn't end there. Sales is also the host or hostess greeting restaurant patrons. Sales is the front desk clerk welcoming a guest at the local Holiday Inn or at the Waldorf-Astoria in New York City. Sales is the housekeeping staff delivering the extra set of towels requested by a guest. Sales is the sommelier in a gourmet restaurant recommending wines to complement an entrée choice. Sales is the front office cashier saying, "Thank you for staying with us. We hope you enjoyed your stay." It is amazing how a simple thank-you can express appreciation for a customer's patronage and bring them back.

All client-contact personnel of a hospitality organization perform personal selling either consciously or unconsciously. This includes staff who does not regularly have guest contact, such as the credit manager. One of the authors nearly lost a $100,000 annual account when a poorly trained credit manager called the client to collect a payment that had not yet been billed. A well-trained and motivated employee that understands how a hotel works is key to successful selling. This is accomplished through the hiring and training process, and although the many facets of human resources are beyond the scope of this chapter, its importance to guest satisfaction cannot be overstated.

In this particular context, however, the hotel's human resources department can perform services on behalf of the sales department by recruiting sales associates who understand the nature of the hotel industry and its place in the broader category of the services segment of business. Services are different from products and require specialized knowledge and training to be competitive.

Because hospitality is very much a part of the services industry, it is useful to understand how services differ from products. Those characteristics that are unique to the services industry product include perishability, simultaneity, heterogeneity, and intangibility.

Perishability refers to the short shelf life of the hospitality product. If it is not sold today, the potential revenue from the sales of that product is gone. A hotel room has a 24-hour shelf life. A restaurant seat has a two-hour shelf life. Manufactured goods have a much longer period of durability. If a television set is not sold today, it can be sold tomorrow or next week. The potential revenue from the sale of that product is not lost. But a Tuesday-night hotel room cannot be resold on Wednesday. Tuesday has come and gone. If the hotel guest room goes unsold Tuesday, the potential revenue lost from that vacant room cannot be recouped.

Simultaneity means that production and consumption occur at the same time. How can you produce a guest experience without the guest? Our customers, in a sense, are part of the assembly line. They need to be present for final production of the product offering. A vacant guest room produces nothing. Yes, the carpeting is installed, the bed is made, the bathroom plumbing works. But it all just exists until a guest arrives to use it. Simultaneous production and consumption is a unique challenge for successful operations in hospitality management. The guest needs to be present, because many of the facets of the service involve performances by hotel staff.

A related service characteristic in hospitality is *heterogeneity*. Heterogeneity refers to the variability of service delivery. Guest service agents have their moods. Customers have their moods. All have personalities of varying shapes and sizes. Hospitality is a very people-oriented business. Service personnel change from shift to shift, typically on an 8-hour schedule. Though operational manuals exist in most hospitality establishments, rarely are policies and procedures followed in an exact manner. Guests' "personalities," too, can change throughout their stay, and it may have nothing to do with how they were treated by service personnel. Dealing with heterogeneity in service operations is dealing with reality. Mistakes will happen. But more importantly, mistakes can be addressed. Often a simple apology can win back a customer regardless of who was at fault when a mistake happens.

Intangibility is a fourth major characteristic of service businesses. Some consider it the most important component to recognize. Intangibility refers to the highly intangible nature of the service product offering. Intangibility is a feeling; it is having a sense about something that one cannot fully articulate. The intangible nature of the service product cannot be prejudged. Consumers cannot really see, touch, smell, hear, or taste a service product prior to consumption. They can only anticipate. One can test-drive a car before an automobile purchase is made to see what it feels like to drive. But a hospitality customer cannot test-drive a hotel weekend package or a restaurant meal prior to consumption. The intangibility aspect of hospitality emphasizes that service delivery is critical to customer satisfaction. Most customers have an idea of what to expect. But, in the end, they are really not sure of what they are buying until the hospitality experience actually takes place. Finally, after the service has been consumed, the guest has only the memory of the performance.

The foregoing unique characteristics represent the foundational challenge to the hotel's sales staff: they must find a way promise performance and experience in such a way that the hotel's operations departments can deliver on the promise. If the essence of marketing is finding and keeping a customer, then the sales promise is fundamental to that effort. Operation's most important role is the keeping of that promise to the customer—having that customer walk away with a positive and memorable experience and want to return again.

MANAGEMENT OF THE SALES PROCESS

Sales management is effectively directing the personal selling efforts of a hospitality establishment. It involves managing the sales process from both an individual and team perspective. In other words, sales management addresses the logistics of sales solicitation and the development of sales account executives to enhance their sales productivity. Sales account executives need to manage their day-to-day activity, sales teams need to coordinate their efforts, and customers need to feel that they are working with a professional and well-managed organization.

There are several components to hospitality sales management. These include sales organization, sales account management, recruitment, training and development, goal setting, and performance appraisals. Sales organization refers to departmental and individual organizational issues and inventory management. The following section focuses on the sales organization aspect of hospitality sales management.

SALES ORGANIZATION

Sales organization can be viewed from three perspectives. These include departmental organization, individual planning of sales activity, and inventory management. A sales department needs to be organized, and sales managers within that organizational setup need to coordinate their efforts. Sales managers need to plan or organize their individual activities on a daily, weekly, and monthly basis. Allocating the sale of inventory to various customer segments needs to be managed, as well. These are important issues in hospitality sales management and following is a more detailed discussion of each.

Departmental Organization

Organizing a sales department means determining who is going to do what. Sales solicitation needs to take place, administrative tasks need to be completed, and managerial decisions need to be made on a regular basis.

In medium-to-large-size hospitality establishments, a director of sales and/or a director of marketing coordinates these efforts. In smaller operations, it is not unusual to have one individual responsible for all of the above. For most bed and breakfast operations in the United States and Canada and the small boutique hotels in Europe, for example, sales activities are typically handled by the owner and/or manager of the establishment.

Figure 7.5 is a sample sales organizational setup for a midsize urban hotel targeting business clientele. The sales managers in this example are organized by target market and by geographic territory. Sales manager 1 is responsible for corporate accounts located in the immediate downtown and surrounding area. Sales manager 2 is responsible for national corporate accounts. This refers to companies based in other areas that conduct business or

FIGURE 7.5
Organization of an urban hotel sales department

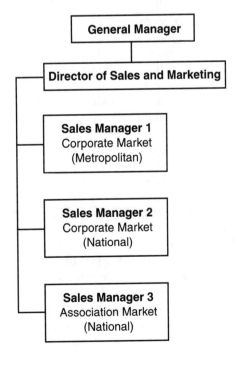

have the potential to conduct business at the hotel. Both of these sales managers solicit group and transient business from their account base.

Sales manager 3 targets meetings and convention business from national association accounts. This business may include executive board meetings, committee meetings, regional conferences, and annual conventions.

In this example, once group events have been booked they are turned over to the conference services department for service delivery. Both the sales managers and director of conference services report to the director of sales and marketing. The sales team meets weekly to discuss issues pertinent to achieving the department's sales objectives.

Weekly sales meetings are very much a part of a sales department's organizational structure, be it a sales force of two or twelve sales account executives. They are critical for effective communication within the department. At these meetings, each team member highlights his or her weekly activity with regard to new prospects uncovered, tentative bookings, verbal definites, cancellations, etc. (Verbal definites are bookings where a client has verbally committed their meeting or function to the facility but a signed contract is not yet in hand.) In other words, sales managers share with each other progress reports on various accounts they are currently working on. Thus, each team member gets an up-to-date informal report on the status of all current sales activity.

For example, one sales manager may be working on a tentative booking but considers it weak because of strong competition for this particular account. Call this Group A. Another sales manager may have a new prospect with similar space requirements interested in the same dates. Call this Group B. Assume, however, that the property has the capability of booking only Group A or Group B over the same dates because of space limitations. When these types of issues surface at sales meetings (which they frequently do), discussion will occur raising the following types of questions:

- What is the likelihood that either group will eventually book their business at the property?
- What is the estimated profitability and/or contribution margin for each group?
- Is either group a regular client?
- What is the likelihood of repeat business from either group? In other words, what is the long-term profitability for each?
- Can either group consider alternative dates? (A *very* important question.) What would incite them to move dates?
- Do convention history reports match their current space allocation requests?

These are just a sampling of questions that need to be raised and answered. It is a never-ending process in hospitality sales management to search for the best fit for both the buyer and seller.

CONCLUSION

The organization of sales management is the process of directing the personal selling efforts of a hospitality establishment. It involves effectively managing the sales process from both an individual and team perspective. Sales or account managers need to manage their day-to-day activity; sales teams need to coordinate their efforts. Sales account management involves developing, maintaining, and enhancing customer relationships. Sales managers develop expertise for specific market segments, industry segments, and/or customer accounts, and common traits among successful sales account executives include self-confidence, high energy, empathy, enthusiasm, and a sense of self-worth.

This chapter introduces the foundation for hospitality sales and marketing. First and foremost, sales flow from marketing. If management doesn't have a marketing mind-set, then sales efforts will be all for naught.

Marketing is giving the targeted customers what they want, when they want it, where they want it, at a price they are willing and able to pay. Sales is direct communication with potential customers letting them know we have what they want. In many respects, sales is the link between marketing and operations. Operations is essentially the delivery component of marketing and the final determination of a happy (or unhappy) customer.

Marketing begins, transcends, and ends with the consumer. Sales makes sure it happens.

7.9 Improving Interactions between Meeting Planners and Hotel Employees

Denney G. Rutherford and W. Terry Umbreit

INTRODUCTION

Service management and marketing researchers are beginning to make inroads in understanding the components of service quality. In particular, the focus on the *service encounter*, which is defined by Czepiel as the interactions that occur between participants in service exchanges (Czepiel, Solomon, and Surprenant, 1985), is helping organizations better manage their relationships with customers. Of no greater importance to hotels is their relationship and interactions with meeting planners (MPs), who represent a significant amount of business annually. Unfortunately, the management of this important relationship is difficult, as interactions take place during the entire service delivery process from early negotiations to the event evaluation. This process can last many months and take numerous contacts with a variety of hotel staff members.

Hotels can spend many months building trust and respect with meeting planners but can lose the confidence of these important individuals quickly as a result of poor service delivery, broken promises, and incidents of inappropriate behavior on the part of employees or their inability to respond to important requests during the event. If these incidents happen to a meeting planner on a regular basis, they can negatively impact significant blocks of business for many years to come.

Additionally, through negative word of mouth along the MP network, a hotel can easily acquire a reputation among MPs as being difficult or impossible to work with. Indeed, in two studies on marketing to MPs, recommendations by others and postevent reports accounted for three of the top five factors helping to influence the choice of a hotel as a meeting site (Bloom, 1981; Lowe, 1984). Certainly in today's highly competitive environment, hotels will succeed with this important client only if they meet or exceed expectations and manage positively the interactions taking place along the chain of activity comprising event management.

The vast majority of previous research on planners and hotels has focused on physical facilities, equipment, attributes, or amenities (see, for instance, Renaghan and Kay, 1987; Lowe, 1984; Wright, 1982; Hosansky, 1982; Finkel, 1980). Typically, these studies either ranked various factors or analyzed trade-offs between and among factors essential or important to a meeting's success or the selection of facilities. Employee and staff attitudes have been alluded to, but only in the most general anecdotal terms. These allusions take the form of references to staff or employee attitude, rudeness, and incompetence or similar observations that are difficult to quantify or inventory. One study of note should be mentioned. Stavro and Beggs (1986) surveyed the buying behavior of meeting planners and found that during site selection the most important factors were meeting room configuration and hotel location. Personnel were less important than site selection but reflected the greatest concern of the meeting planner once the meeting was in session.

According to Heskett (1990), investigations that center on causes of performance may well provide the most definitive insights into ways of improving such performance. Service firms that have studied important encounters between the server and the served have greatly improved the quality of their performance. For example, British Airways found the following four factors of critical importance to travelers as they moved through their travel experience: care and concern; spontaneity; problem solving; and recovery (Albrecht and Zemke, 1985). The care and concern and the problem-solving capabilities of airline employees were obvious to company airline executives; however, spontaneity and recovery were important surprises. Airline travelers were telling the company that they valued employees who were authorized to think on the spot and to use discretion in acting on their behalf. In the case of recovery, customers were interested in having airline employees who would make a special effort to correct a mistake and make it into a positive experience.

Of further significance is the work of Zeithaml, Parasuraman, and Berry (1990), who through extensive focus-group interviews produced an instrument for measuring customers' perceptions of service quality. The instrument contains the following five distinct dimensions: assurance, empathy, tangibles, reliability, and responsiveness. The most critical dimension was reliability, or the ability to perform the promised service dependably and accurately, followed by responsiveness, which is the willingness to help customers and provide prompt service. Their research has provided important knowledge on service performance gaps and how service firms can improve their service delivery to clients.

This article reports on a research project designed to identify the important dimensional aspects of the interactions taking place between MPs and hotel staff employees along the event management chain of activity. A collection of a substantial volume of incidents of effective and ineffective behaviors by hotel employees produced a profile that defines the major elements of the interaction process and the areas causing the biggest difficulties in a hotel's service delivery system. The result of this research should enable hotels to better understand the interaction process as well as how to more effectively manage their relationships with MPs.

METHODOLOGY

The authors used the critical incident technique (Flanagan, 1954) to collect direct observations of effective and ineffective hotel staff behaviors in hosting MP events. Over 316 incidents were gathered in the course of a three-year longitudinal study. MPs were contacted at national meetings and their base organizations in three major cities, with 52 consenting to provide narrative incidents of their experiences with hotel staff personnel.

Tape recordings of recitation of the incidents in a structured interview session (see "Applying the Critical Incident Technique") were gathered yielding an average of 6.07 incidents per MP. These in turn were edited to highlight the essential critical behavioral incidents in a format retaining as much original terminology provided by the MPs as possible.

These behavioral statements were then dimensionalized by a job-knowledgeable panel of meeting planner experts who reviewed each incident and placed them in piles according to descriptions of similar behaviors. These dimensions were then entitled and defined to form a base of critical behaviors for the researchers to analyze. Such a list of critical behaviors provides, according to Flanagan,

APPLYING THE CRITICAL INCIDENT TECHNIQUE

The critical incident technique used by the researchers in this study was developed by John C. Flanagan as a job analysis procedure to collect direct observations of human behavior. An incident, according to Flanagan, is any observable human activity that is sufficiently complete to permit inferences and predictions to be made about the person performing the act. To be critical, an incident must occur in a situation where the purpose or content of the act seems fairly clear to the observer and where its consequences are sufficiently definite to leave little doubt concerning its effects.

In applying the procedure, the researchers asked meeting planners, in a structured-interview format, to identify incidents of effective and ineffective performance on the part of hotel staff members during the entire event delivery process. Planners answered these questions about each incident: (1) What were the circumstances surrounding the incident? (2) What

did the individual do that was effective or ineffective? (3) What were the consequences of the incident? and (4) Did the hotel staff member have control over the situation?

Each interview was tape-recorded, and the researchers used a questionnaire to guide them in their solicitation of incidents. The researchers transcribed the 316 incidents and condensed them into short statements. In a work session a panel comprising three meeting planners was asked to place each of the incidents into a pile of incidents perceived to be similar in content. At the end of the exercise, the panelists labeled and defined each pile. In a discussion with the researchers, the panelists identified the dimensional aspects of interactions between planners and hotel staff members. Lastly, the researchers further defined the dimensions, and the panelists reviewed and revised the definitions.

"... a sound basis for making inferences as to requirements in terms of aptitudes, training, and other characteristics" (Flanagan, 1954).

These dimensions are reported in the following discussion as well as certain demographic and career data about the MPs.

Participants

Participants in this research project consisted of 52 meeting planners interviewed by the researchers over a three-year period. Meeting planners were interviewed during the 1989 Annual Conference of Meeting Planners International in Orlando. Planners were also contacted at their organizations in San Francisco, Seattle, and Chicago during 1990–1991. Of the total, 21 were corporate meeting planners (40.4 percent); 18 were association meeting planners (34.6 percent); 9 were independent

meeting planners (17.3 percent); and the remaining 4 were either government, incentive, or other types of meeting planners (7.7 percent).

Fifty-nine percent of the meeting planners were female and 41 percent were male. The mean years of experience as a meeting planner was 10.52. In terms of their education 32 reported themselves to be college graduates or possessing higher degrees, with 19 having some college education or an associate degree. One was a high school graduate.

Business degrees accounted for eight of the MPs' majors with only one reporting a hotel and restaurant administration (HRA) degree. The rest were literally from all across the academic board, ranging from anthropology to zoology. Seventy-six percent of the meeting planners were between the ages of 26 and 50, followed by 15.3 percent who were above 50.

Over 88 percent of the meeting planners

were employed in some other capacity prior to becoming a meeting planner. Their backgrounds varied considerably with hotel sales, marketing, trade show coordination, secretary, and hotel management accounting for 43.5 percent. The remaining majority came to meeting planning from over 20 different professional, clerical, military, and technical jobs.

Table 7.4 shows the length of time the collective planners in our study have been involved with meeting planner responsibilities compared to association and corporate planners in a biannual national study done by a trade magazine. On a percentage basis our group, which also included government, independent, and incentive MPs, appears to have been involved in planning activities over a longer period of their careers. Because many of our planners were asked either directly or by mail to participate, perhaps those with longer career tracks and more experience self-selected themselves and felt more comfortable relating the kinds of experiences important to the project.

The Hotel Staff Members

Hotel staff organizations have been in a state of continual evolution since Ellsworth Statler conceived the original "commercial" hotel around 1900. Prior to that, hotel organizations relied heavily on the European model that emphasized food and its service through a strong chef/maître d' arrangement. With the advent of more business travelers, the origin of convention and visitors bureaus, and the growth of conventions and trade shows, hotel organization charts have changed to reflect the character of the market the hotel sought. (Shaffer, 1986)

Nowhere has this change been more obvious than in the marketing area. Recently, in addition to the traditional functions of sales, advertising, and public relations, the hotels' marketing umbrella has been extended to include, in many instances, convention services, reservations, and in some cases, certain elements of catering staff activities.

These new organizational arrangements are reflected in the frequency with which the planners in this study mentioned various hotel staff members. Table 7.5 displays the hierarchy of staff members mentioned in the 316 critical incidents we collected. Also displayed here are similar results from a preliminary analysis of a portion of this data.

Preliminary data were reported at a national meeting in Las Vegas in February of 1991. These final data demonstrate a consis-

TABLE 7.4
Length of time with meeting planning responsibilities

Length of Time	Association[1] Planners	Corporate[1] Planners	1991 Critical Incident Technique Study[2]
Less than 2 years	8%	11%	2.9%
2 to less than 4 years	14	18	8.6
4 to less than 6 years	11	17	22.9
6 to less than 10 years	21	15	14.3
14 to less than 20 years	12	11	14.6
20 years or more	17	8	17.3

[1]Corporate and association planners surveyed by *Meetings & Conventions* magazine, "The Meetings Market, '87." Reed Travel Group, Secaucus, NJ.
[2]All planners, present study.

TABLE 7.5
Hotel staff members—frequency of mention

Cumulative Frequency	Relative Frequency	n^1	Staff Title	n^2	Relative Frequency	Cumulative Frequency
35.90%	35.90%	79	Convention services manager	101	32.00%	32.00%
59.08	23.18	51	Sales manager	83	26.30	58.30
68.62	9.54	21	Catering director, manager, or catering sales manager	32	10.10	68.40
73.16	4.54	10	Director of sales	17	5.38	73.78
77.70	4.54	10	Front desk clerk	14	4.43	78.21
81.79	4.09	9	Hotel general manager	11	3.48	82.01
85.42	3.63	8	Banquet staff (includes housemen and servers)	9	2.85	84.86
—	—	—	Director of food & beverage*	8	2.53	87.29
87.24	1.82	4	Banquet manager	6	1.90	89.29
89.51	2.27	5	Engineer/maintenance staff	6	1.90	91.19
		197	Subtotal of major players	287		
99.96**	10.45	23	All others (ranged from chef to golf pro to hotel board chairman)	29	9.18	100.37**
				316		

n^1 Preliminary Analysis
n^2 Final Results
*   Not separately tabulated in preliminary results.
** Does not equal 100 due to rounding.

tency of mention frequency from the preliminary ranking to the final. While mentions of convention services managers declined slightly, they still were the central figure in nearly one-third of all incidents. Among all mentions, convention services managers (CSM), sales managers (SM), catering staff, sales directors, and front office staff account for about 78 percent of all incidents from the preliminary to the final data.

The importance of the position of CSM is attested to by the clear lead in the number of times CSMs were involved in encounters with planners. Because CSMs were mentioned in 32 percent of the incidents, a strong case can be made that hotels are more widely recognizing the importance of having a staff member be assigned the task of guiding a planner's event through the hotel's organizational labyrinth from start to finish.

SMs were the second largest group of hotel staff involved in these incidents. Because many, if not most, events are initiated with the sales staff, planners often rely on these staff for much of their contact with the hotel. When coupled with the incidents that referred to the CSMs, nearly 60 percent of the encounters between planners and hotel staff involved these two groups.

While catering staff, sales directors, and front office people collectively accounted for another 20 percent of the incidents, with the remainder spread throughout the typical organization, the relative importance of the CSMs and SMs as an MP contact was dramatically borne out in one meeting anecdote. A meeting planner whose conference was about to open was dealing directly with the chairman of the board of the hotel company who was on-site because he had just fired the hotel's general manager and sales director with whom the planner had previously been working. The meeting planner was upset because he'd discovered the hotel parking lot was being repaved the very morning his event was to start. The planner's argument—that exhibitors were likely to find it difficult to unload in a freshly paved parking lot—was futile. He was no more successful in convincing the chairman that the fact of alternative parking was useless unless that news was posted on the reader board. Predictably, the meeting was a disaster.

This is not to suggest that all of our interactions resulted in similar disasters. Indeed, in about 50 percent of the incidents, behaviors of hotel staff were described as effective, with many described as ineffective but not necessarily a disaster.

CRITICAL ASPECTS OF HOTEL STAFF BEHAVIOR

After the piling and dimensionalizing procedure, in consultation with the job-knowledgeable experts, we labeled the incident dimensions and provided definitions and short explanatory or illustrative statements. These are abstracted in Table 7.6 and discussed along with pertinent examples below.

Communication

In the entire inventory of incidents none was more critical than the nexus of interaction between planners and hotel staff linked by various vectors of communication. Many planners described this in terms as simple as "staying in touch, being available." Others linked difficulties and significant successes to the relative ability of hotel staff to manage the communications process not only through effective use of modern equipment but through the understanding of channels of communication. Planners pointed out that the most effective staff not only knew the channels, but understood between and among whom they need to be established in order to be most effective.

Especially praiseworthy, according to planners, were the hotel staff who made deep pro-

TABLE 7.6
Dimensions of meeting planner/hotel staff interactions

Dimension	Definition	Illustrative Examples
1. Communications	Modes and techniques of communication among all participants. This includes internal and external communication among and between hotel staff, external service providers, and planners.	• Initiating an ongoing/periodic dialogue between planner and hotel representative from "x" time before event, up to and through event. • Effective use of phones, faxes, delivery services, and meetings necessary for communication both in and outside of the hotel for successful completion of event. • Assembling appropriate staff personnel to discuss, anticipate, and plan to meet specifications and details. • Establishing intrahotel communication channels among all departments and staff, which provides for continuity in event of staff changes.
2. Organization	Philosophy and resulting culture of the hotel that establishes an organization structure whose policies, procedures, and guidelines lead to the accomplishment of operational goals.	• Strong (or not always flexible) application of policies such as reservations, credit, and room guarantees. • Staffing limitations created by turnover, scheduling regulations, and duty assignments. • Existence of a profit orientation that leads to an attitude disruptive to service delivery.

(continued next page)

TABLE 7.6 (continued)

Dimension	Definition	Illustrative Examples
3. Execution	Performance of operational plans, strategies, and duties that enhance service delivery, including responsiveness to requests and instructions, and displaying appropriate follow-up.	• Agreed-upon meeting specifications not met nor implemented correctly. • Overselling the capacity of physical premises or staff capabilities in service delivery. • Performance behavior failures on part of hotel staff resulting in lack of cooperation. • Scheduling that places noncompatible events in same or adjacent meeting or public space in facility. • Develop "comprehensive" approach to convention management in facility.
4. Developing Relationships	Creation of an atmosphere of professionalism, ethical behavior, and the ensuing trust that leads to positive relationships between the hotel and planner.	• Meetings and interactions that take place outside of the formal processes and/or organizations that foster shared values, respect, and intergroup networking. • Negotiating positions having a direct effect on trust between the parties. • Adherence to generally accepted codes of ethics and industry standards reinforced by membership/participation in professional associations.
5. Initiative	Display of innovation and creativity in the service delivery process, often independently of outside influence and control.	• Suggestions by hotel staff members that exceeded expectations of clients in the areas of aesthetics, menus, and program execution. • Using knowledge of local contacts and networks to ensure success of meeting. • Displaying unusual willingness to take responsibility and exhibit recovery in discharging the hotel's obligations to clients.
6. Crisis Management	Ability to deal with and manage unanticipated events, emergency situations, and changing conditions that are not under the control of hotel.	• Managing a crisis created by an external event such as earthquake, flood, or other natural disasters. • Overcoming situations such as intergroup noise competition, overattendance, and service disruptions caused by building system failures. • Solving problems caused by renovation, remodeling, or construction projects (related also to dimension 2). • Installing plans/procedures for staff action in crisis situations, including training programs to ensure employee compliance.

fessional commitments to returning phone calls, faxes, and messages and acting upon them in an expedient manner.

Planners also went out of their way to point out that in executing successful events, one of the critical components is the preevent or precon meeting. Planners learned to judge a

hotel's capacity for successfully hosting events through their precon experiences. These experiences highlighted how well the hotel staffs were committed to an effective communications structure involving participation in all precon meetings by appropriate personnel from key hotel departments. Participation by key personnel was a signpost that the delivery of important meeting services on behalf of the hotel would be accomplished.

Communication is, however, a double-edged sword. Meeting planners reported numerous occasions where communications difficulties contributed to the hotel's poor performance. These communications failures could occur during the negotiation process, during the coordination of activities on-site, or during the act of delivery and execution of important services. In one case, the meeting planner sent a list of flame-retardant materials to the hotel for the city fire marshal's approval; however, when the planner's exhibit area was scheduled to open at the hotel, the fire marshal would not grant permission, because the hotel failed to forward the list to him for approval. In this particular instance, the hotel should have been serving as a communications conduit on behalf of the planner between the facility and an outside agency. Failure to do so can significantly set back an event schedule or disrupt it totally.

Several planners mentioned the great utility of communications planning. Specifically commended were hotels that provided charts and diagrams showing communications channels, home phone numbers, job titles, and relationships. In one memorable instance, the hotel even provided cellular phones to the planners and key hotel staff for the duration of the event. This created, in effect, the planner's own communications network.

Another insight provided by the MPs in this dimension of hotel staff/planner interaction was that the physical fact of communications media was one thing, but a thorough knowledge of the media and when to use it introduced a personnel/training-related aspect to this dimension that links it to other dimensions, particularly organization and execution. Some planners echoed stories that regularly appear in the meeting trade press (see, for example, Blair, 1988) that lament the historically high turnover among hotel staffs and directly attribute many communications failures to such turnover.

Organization

In reviewing the stories provided by MPs, it was clear that a big problem area in the interaction process was restrictive policies designed and implemented by certain hotels. Some hotels have policies that appear to be structured to allow them an "out." These situations were apparent when MPs discussed release dates for room blocks, booking date changes, flexibility in meal pricing, and extra service on short notice. The effect is an avenue through which to avoid responsibility and shift blame. This is a short-term expedient, at best yielding strategic disadvantage and lost business, especially through the MP grapevine (Bloom, 1981; Lowe, 1984).

Planners repeatedly revealed anecdotes and examples of employee behavior in which rigid policies negatively impacted the quality of their experience at hotels in a number of different contexts. For instance, meeting planners expressed difficulties with policies dealing with gratuities, such as the infamous "tax on tip or tip on tax" controversy. Room guarantees, reservations, cancellation policies, and "drop dead" room-rate levels consistently seemed to MPs to be "line in the sand" demarcations that may have served to drive business away from the hotel rather than welcome it.

MPs who had the best experiences in these contexts reported that during the negotiation process hotels were forthcoming about policies that would be enforced during the event and gave planners ample opportunity to tailor their activities in light of policy realities or to negotiate different circumstances. In one such case, a hotel permitted a meeting planner after the contract was signed to change menu selections to reflect more reasonable prices in order to keep the meeting cost within the association's budget.

One particularly sore point revolved around reservation policies that resulted in such problems as the displacement of important VIPs, as well as meeting staff. One would think MPs would receive the best possible treatment, but this was not the case, as revealed in many of the incidents. To illustrate, an MP informed a hotel in advance that she would be staying a full week in the property to supervise the scheduled meeting event. Upon arrival she was told the hotel was in an oversold situation. After much discussion she was given a room but informed the next morning that one of her members was walked to make room for her stay. It appeared to many planners that hotels hide behind policies when enforcing their positions, providing them an excuse for limiting service rather than going to the extra effort to find a mutually satisfying solution.

The problem of turnover among key hotel staff members is seen by MPs to be a pervasive and endemic one in the hotel world. When an event had a lead time or horizon in excess of two years, planners were almost unanimous in not expecting either a sales manager or convention service manager to be the same person as the one with whom they originally dealt. Respondents to a successful-meetings survey overwhelmingly supported this finding in 1988, where planners felt that many of their service problems with hotels stem from heavy personnel turnover (Tritsch, 1988).

Planners are increasingly viewing employee-scheduling policies of the hotel with skepticism and demanding a precon review of such policies in covering those circumstances where employee scheduling may negatively impact an event. On several weekend occasions MPs could not find help for completing meeting arrangements because appropriate hotel staff members were off duty or not on property. In another situation a meeting planner had to pay for extra bartender hours because the hotel was unionized and the contract required bartenders to work a minimum of four hours. In a similar case, a meeting planner was charged four hours for an electrician's time who merely turned on the slide projector switch.

In the policy area, meeting planners also mention encountering problems with outside contractors, such as audiovisual (AV), who want to charge them for additional equipment not used or services not rendered. Repeatedly, MPs had difficulties with outside AV contractors because of the aforementioned communication errors made by the hotel staff or the AV representative who was not on-site to correct mistakes or repair equipment. In these circumstances, planners were led to expect that hotels would make arrangements with contractors and see to schedules of those personnel who are critical to the execution of the event.

In other situations the hotel was not staffed sufficiently to handle problems or MPs had difficulty locating persons in authority to resolve issues dealing with meeting arrangements. These problems usually took place early in the morning or on weekends. Experienced planners in many of these cases had to fend for themselves making coffee, serving food, and setting up rooms.

Not all of these circumstances that started out negatively necessarily ended that way. Sometimes this is where hotel staffs really shone. In many of these cases hotel staff members performed not only above and beyond the call of duty but also above and beyond their places on the organization chart, with maintenance people making coffee and banquet setup staff serving breakfast. These are circumstances where the hotel scheduling and staffing limitations started out to create difficult hotel staff/MP interactions, but wound up being a net win for the hotel because of the willingness of other staff to recognize the situation where they could make a difference, step up to the challenge, and perform.

In spite of the courageous attempts of many hotel staff members to correct service problems, it is obvious to the researchers that some hotels are hampered by a profit orientation that impacts negatively on the attitude of their staff and the ability to meet the expectations of meeting planners during scheduled events. Unfortunately, some hotel organizations seem to have developed a culture and mode of operation that is inflexible and counterproductive to the delivery of anticipated service levels. We found many instances where hotels were more interested in negotiating a favorable position for themselves, reinforced by policies that protected their financial interests at the expense of service to the MPs' events. This particular difficulty became apparent in the next section, which deals with the dimension execution. Some hotels experienced considerable predicaments because of the way they approached their commitments to the service process.

Execution

This dimension of MP interactions with hotels can be viewed through the simple expedient of the concept that most of us learned when we were children: keeping our promises. In this dimension we focus on the hotel's ability to deliver meetings services negotiated and contracted for both from the physical asset standpoint and expectations of employee performance.

In a number of cases meeting planners reported problems with the physical condition of meeting rooms. The meeting rooms were of neither the appropriate size nor configuration; or the rooms themselves caused event interruption because of their proximity to other rooms where competing events were taking place. It was obvious from the volume of incidents in this area that hotels definitely face a gap in perception between what they agreed to in negotiations and were able to deliver in actuality.

In many cases hotels were either booking groups they couldn't handle or attempting to rearrange meeting room locations if additional more attractive business materialized after a contract was signed. This harkens back to the profit motivation referred to in the previous dimension and makes it clear to the aggrieved planner that his or her event was desirable only until a more profitable group came along.

An example of this was where one planner's group reception was relocated to the lobby of the hotel from a previously agreed-upon function room because another organization with a larger event wanted the promised space.

Overselling the capacity of the physical premises or the abilities of the staff to perform were highlighted in several instances. One planner said that she now requires that the convention services manager be present and a part of the negotiation processes (a tactic much discussed in the trade press; see, for instance, Bosker, 1988) because CSMs more than sales managers know the physical capabilities and limitations of the property. They know, for instance, if a certain seating configuration is impractical in some rooms because of sight lines impaired by columns. They also have a more realistic vision of what can and cannot be done given the physical limitations of individual buildings. Many planners pointed out that sometimes an SM, enthusiastic to book an event, "oversold" the building, saying, in effect, "Yes!! We can do that. We can handle that," promising, in effect, anything just to book the business, or, as one MP referred to it, "the book 'em and move 'em" mentality.

A final aspect of this dimension included the interpersonal behavior of hotel employees. While this was not an overwhelming issue, some planners, through their commentary, suggested that in some circumstances they were not treated properly or appropriately during negotiation. Less often, they reported difficulties when coming into contact with employees during on-site operations of their event. Several of these interpersonal problems were engendered through previously mentioned dimensions, such as overbooking, double-booking, or lost reservations, which could be directly traced to communications or policy failures. In these cases where employees became frustrated in their inability to resolve a situation, often they resorted to inappropriate interpersonal behavior in dealing with the MP clients. Because of this frustration, employees in difficult situations responded unprofessionally. These people were characterized by one planner as "the rudes and crudes."

Developing Relationships

MPs indicated that not all interactions always took place on premises or within a formal organization structure. Information sharing, networking, and informal relationship-building took place at social functions, meetings of professional groups where both planners and suppliers were members, and other business-related activities, such as chambers of commerce or business leagues.

Many times planners and suppliers found themselves involved in voluntary activities in their home communities. In many instances, these activities could serve as a basis for fostering relationships and atmospheres that positively affected both personal and interorganizational relationships.

MPs also reported incidents where positive or negative aspects of interactions could be traced to elements of the negotiation process. Planners relayed instances where negotiating positions of the parties had a direct effect on trust either positively or negatively in the ensuing business relationship. In one instance, a planner was negotiating the various aspects of bringing her event to a certain hotel, and the sales manager with whom she was negotiating seemed to purposely stall the negotiation process. The SM was never able to come to closure on even the most minor of points and left many aspects of the planner's event open to review by the director of sales or the general manager. These types of negotiation stances lead to tremendous frustration on the part of the MP and, in many instances, sabotages any possibility of developing a positive interactive working relationship between the planner and the hotel.

A legitimate question brought up by several planners was who trains hotel SMs and CSMs in negotiating and negotiation skills?

In cases where the planner was much more proficient in negotiation than the SM, the SM, to avoid getting "taken to the cleaners," simply kicked the decision-making process upstairs. Planners pointed out that it is difficult to foster any trust in this sort of atmosphere.

Contrary to recent debate and analysis in the trade press (Alderson, 1986) none of our planners alluded to anything terribly unethical in terms of inappropriate hotel staff behavior or the proffering of gifts that could be considered excessive. Being promised one thing and delivered another was deemed more an aspect of execution than ethics. The MPs were more likely to attribute such lapses to organizational difficulties (dimension 2), communications problems (dimension 1), or execution (dimension 3) than any particularly egregious ethical lapse.

They did suggest, however, that more professionalism would bring more industrywide recognition of hotel service standards. The planners pointed out that standards and codes of ethics are generally the result of highly committed professional organizations. It was suggested that membership and participation in professional associations can foster, develop, and support industry standards and codes of professionalism and ethics.

Initiative

This interaction dimension was a pleasant surprise to us. The dimension encompassed a pantheon of hotel staff/employee behaviors that brought smiles to the faces of the MPs and the researchers alike. MPs provided numerous examples of hotel staff members who displayed an unusual ability to respond to unique challenges occurring prior to or during the meeting or event. One aspect of this dimension mentioned frequently by meeting planners was the ability of a hotel staff to provide suggestions on improving menus and meeting room arrangements.

Beyond those, however, MPs were particularly pleased to point out the "above and be-yond the call of duty" type of behaviors that demonstrated the ability of hotel staffs to go the extra distance in the service of their events. In many cases these resulted in hotel staff suggestions that truly improved an event and went beyond mere profit-orientated "up-selling."

One planner with a very large midwestern telecommunications firm was working with a hotel in planning a series of 30 four-day meet-ings for executives of the communications firm over the course of a one-year period. Unbe-knownst to the MP and completely on their own initiative, the hotel SM and CSM con-tracted with a chocolatier in the Chicago area to provide miniature chocolate telephones to be placed on each attendee's pillow at turn-down each night during the course of these 30 meetings. This corporate planner and his meeting attendees were truly touched by this thoughtful gesture, and despite the fact that the planner knew he had probably paid for it in one way or another, the planner stated that for several years after this series of events the people in his organization who attended were still talking about those little chocolate tele-phones.

Attesting to the value of encouraging more than a two-year stint among SMs and CSMs at any single hotel were the number of inci-dents related by MPs that illustrated how hotel staff who had intimate knowledge of lo-cal contacts and networks could go a long way toward insuring the success of a meeting or event. In incident after incident, MPs reported that local artisans, specialty florists, entertain-ers, and craftspeople were suggested from the knowledge base of SMs and CSMs that truly enhanced the event. These hotel staff mem-bers became, in effect, knowledgeable "con-cierges" for their meeting events.

In another example, a hotel CSM arranged for rental cars for a group who participated in a lengthy training program and needed to get away from the hotel for short periods of time. Another hotel staff member used personal con-tacts outside the hotel to put together a won-derful floral arrangement for a banquet event. In still another situation, a CSM spent a con-siderable amount of time outside the hotel finding flags from foreign countries to deco-rate the hotel ballroom for an international dinner.

Hotel staff who showed unusual willingness to take responsibility in finding innovative and creative ways to respond to challenges also particularly impressed MPs. One MP who was on a very strict budget was seeking ways to arrange for helium-filled balloons to decorate final-night banquet tables. The only supplier in the area, to the knowledge of the CSM, who could respond on short notice would charge in excess of $1 per balloon. By happy serendip-ity, a maintenance manager was walking by at the time and said that he had several bottles of helium because he personally created bal-loon arrangements for kids' parties in his neighborhood. He volunteered that he would be happy to do the balloons for the MP's event for free.

While it's difficult for any of us or our em-ployees to "be creative" at the drop of the hat, planner networks are rife with anecdotes and examples of behavior similar to those we col-lected. Over the course of time astute plan-ners could identify people and organizations who have a reputation for positively exceed-ing expectations and, all things being equal, choose those venues for their events.

Crisis Management

Meeting planners pointed out during the inter-views that unusual environments, crises, or, in some cases, changing circumstances invari-ably occurred when meetings were in progress. Under such circumstances, hotels were judged based on how well they managed these crises created by external events, such as an earth-quake—truly an unanticipated event.

One planner who was executing an event on a site in a hotel in San Francisco in October of 1989 experienced what may have been the quintessential contingency plan for natural disasters. When the earthquake struck, the hotel hardly missed a beat. Flashlights were handed out to all of the planners' event members and other hotel guests. The kitchen staff went into action to put up complimentary (but cold) buffets, and all hotel employees generally contributed to an atmosphere of being in control in a circumstance that to many of the attendees was indeed quite frightening. As a direct result of contingency plans such as this hotel effected, the MP concluded this event on a positive note and walked away smiling from something that could have been much more serious than just a setup snafu.

One of the more troubling aspects of hosting an event in large hotels is that many of these regularly host multiple large events. Often events find themselves in competition for space, or adjacent events leak noise into the atmosphere of other groups. One MP related an event where she had, in fact, inquired in advance about a competing event in the adjacent section of the ballroom but was told that this was going to be a prayer meeting. It turned out that the prayer meeting attracted several hundred more of the prayerful than had been anticipated by the event's organizer. The prayer group organizer also failed to tell the CSM that their particular form of prayer involved extremely loud and unified attestation of their faith. The MP was very upset. The meeting was disrupted to the point of it being useless to continue, and the CSM was nowhere to be found.

Renovation or construction projects often interfered with meetings in progress or became service interruptions through inappropriate scheduling. Planners were consistent in their criticisms that hotel managements could have scheduled such activities and events more appropriately in light of their potential for disruption of activities in meeting areas and public rooms of the hotel. At the very least, MPs felt they should have been advised of the activity and offered an alternative.

It seems clear from these incidents relayed to us that as a regular part of negotiation and precon meetings, planners should inquire about competing events in adjacent rooms; hotel renovation projects; and the hotel's experience with weather disturbances, prayer meetings, and other "acts of God." It may also be important at this time for the planner to pin down the hotel on what their contingency plans are in the event of natural disasters.

Other, but more minor meeting disruptions could be traced to regular maintenance functions, such as window washing, heavy vacuuming, and even something as arcane as pool cleaning. ("The suction noise was very distracting!") Planners are learning to question hotels carefully about the potential for such distracting activities.

OBSERVATIONS, SUGGESTIONS

In our rich collection of incidents, the importance of communication, organization, execution, developing relationships, initiative, and crisis management became apparent to us as the key components to a hotel's ability to successfully deliver their required services to the meetings industry. Hotels that mastered these important fundamental aspects of service separated themselves from their competitors. More importantly, our assessment of the interactions between meeting planners and hotel staff members identified the areas of organization, execution, and professionalism as the most crucial to the success of event management. Improvement in these areas will greatly enhance the hotel industry's ability to serve this market segment in the current business environment.

Organizational Strategies

A number of problems brought out in the critical incidents can be traced to the current hotel organization structure. In many cases, hotels did not have in place the type of structure conducive to serving the needs of meeting planners. This difficulty was conspicuous in several areas. First, hotel sales staffs had a tendency to oversell the capabilities of the hotel or to overpromise the delivery of important services. There was a definite lack of communication between sales individuals and the hotel's operational staff in convention services, catering, or food and beverage. Some examples included the promise of a certain meeting room or suite, which was not available when the group checked in, or the hotel was in an overbooked situation and was not able to accommodate all group members. Not delivering on service promises is a sure way to drive important clients elsewhere. Better teamwork and coordination must be achieved to overcome this organizational flaw. We suggest several members of the hotel staff be assigned each major meeting group to enhance coordination and insure continuity of communication.

Second, it is critical that the organization and control of the meeting once underway should be assigned to one hotel staff member. No one is more important in this scenario than the convention services manager (CSM). In case after case it was the knowledge, training, and professionalism of this key staff member that made the difference between the success of a planner's event and difficulty or disaster. In those cases where the CSM had control of the hotel's processes and staff functions, planners generally had positive or outstanding experiences. This empowerment was exemplified by the planners in many ways, but one drew the analogy between the CSM and the bombardier in a World War II B-17. During the bombing run (execution of the event) the bombardier had complete control of the aircraft, giving orders to the captain and other crew (the GM and department staff) that contribute to the singular success of the mission (event). The point is, quite simply, that the person who is most responsible for the event should be endowed with the authority to marshal all of the organization resources to guar-antee success. Hotels need to reorganize to, in effect, give one staff member "ownership" of an MP's event.

The creation of the CSM position in the hotel has made a big difference in the delivery of services to meeting planners. Hotel organizations must take the next step and truly empower this individual to supervise all aspects of the meeting delivery process. One hotel, Chicago's Palmer House, exemplifies this concept by utilizing a redrawn organization chart highlighting this empowerment as part of a recent advertising campaign (Figure 7.6). A part of the Hilton chain, the Palmer House example is a bellwether of the rising importance of the CSM within the organizational milieu of hotel organizations.

Third, hotels must address the staff turnover problem at least in event-critical positions. On many occasions, contract misunderstandings, poor follow-up on important details, and service execution difficulties were caused by the departure of important hotel staff members, including sales representatives, convention services managers, catering managers, and food and beverage executives. This problem was reported by many MPs as a major impediment in their dealings with hotel organizations. More continuity and reliability among key staff members as identified in this study are crucial to a hotel's ability to establish credibility with MPs. We recommend hotels consider establishing these positions as careers in themselves and not stepping-stones to other executive responsibilities. Appropriate incentives should be developed to attract and retain these management individuals in hotel organizations. Performance should be evaluated and monitored on the basis of service quality delivered to meeting groups and not other company-defined goals that focus on short-term objectives.

Fourth, every attempt should be made by hotels to create a service culture. A commitment to service by top management is important for team building and the acceptance of service values by employees. A service vision

FIGURE 7.6
Palmer House advertisement exemplifies the concept of empowerment

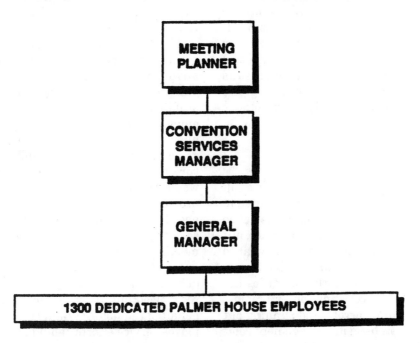

When you meet at The Palmer House we do more than rearrange the rooms.

We rearrange our organization. So that meeting planners have instant access to the hotel's top management.

Before, during, and even after an event, our staff of 1,300 dedicated employees provide outstanding service to meet your needs. Our entire organization is here to help chart your course to success.

In addition to our reputation for excellent service, The Palmer House offers: 38 meeting rooms in Chicago's most complete meeting facility, Conference Center 7; 36,000 square feet of exhibition space, and more.

Seventeen hundred guest rooms and suites are just an elevator ride away, as are five luxurious ballrooms, and one of the top hotel fitness centers in the country.

So give our Director of Sales a call and see just how well you'll fit in at The Palmer House.

The Palmer House.
A Hilton Hotel
A Pleasure to do Business With.

The Palmer House · 17 East Monroe Street · Chicago, IL 60603 · (312) 726-7500

© 1989 The Palmer House. Used with permission.

that replaces the profit orientation will encourage positive service attitudes among hotel staff members and enhance their willingness to provide the highest level of service possible. If hotels really want to be competitive in this market, they must be willing to change and adopt a more relevant philosophy that results in higher levels of satisfaction for group participants. Profit will inevitably follow.

Execution

Many of the negative critical incidents we collected across all dimensions clearly pointed to some aspect of execution failure. It was not so much an issue of employee incompetence, but more of ignorance or lack of knowing what to do. Examples of service failures such as meeting rooms not set up properly, amenities not placed in rooms, AV coordination errors, lost storage items, billing errors, and running out of food reflect a problem in management coordination, communication, and leadership. In these instances, the situation may have been avoided if appropriate monitoring or supervisory controls were used. We also found employees were prevented from correcting service errors or making adjustments because of hotel policies or regulations.

Because a number of the service failures resulted in critical and immediate problems for MPs, hotels could have recovered by positive employee responses. Our examination of the incidents revealed the employees were not adequately prepared to deal with emergencies because they did not have either personal control or knowledge of how to correct the problem. We suggest hotels more aggressively engage in training their guest-contact employees on how to deal with typical problems generated by group functions. Training sessions with key hotel staff members including CSMs and food and beverage managers should be held on a frequent basis to discuss corrective-action procedures and approaches to better serving MP needs. Continued use of precon meetings and other coordination

methods should be employed, as our study pointed out the advantages enjoyed by hotels that had key team members constantly in touch with MPs.

The overwhelming number of incidents we gathered that demonstrated initiative and creativity by hotel staff members in handling special requests and responding to crisis situations have convinced us of the value of empowerment. MPs were totally in agreement about the impact of positive employee responses that saved the day and resulted in future bookings in the same property. Hotels would be well served to empower employees, provide them with the authority, and encourage the independent decision-making necessary to respond to the unexpected needs of meeting groups. Employees who respond appropriately to both routine and emergency requests created by group functions should be recognized and rewarded for their efforts on behalf of the hotel. Examples of unusual employee service efforts should be announced in staff meetings and employee newsletters. The hotel must demonstrate that such initiative by employees is valued.

Professionalism Strategies

A national professional group, the Association for Convention Operations Management (ACOM), was formed in 1988 and has currently grown to over 650 members. Some hotel companies have formally recognized the importance of the CSM by establishing a corporate office or, in one case, a distinct management training track in convention services (Ghitelman, 1989).

Establishment of a national association such as ACOM is a positive step, for it is through such professional groups that members can access educational and training programs based on successful practical experience and research from their peers and other interested professionals. Networking, annual meetings, educational seminars, certification standards, and professional publications will contribute to positive professional development within the population of CSMs. It is also from associations such as these that industry standards and codes of ethics emerge (dimension 4). Planners will welcome the increased professionalism of CSMs and through their own network tend to direct their business to those organizations that successfully link professionalism with the aforementioned creativity (dimension 5).

Training, experience, and professionalism on the part of the CSM are not the only guarantors of successfully hosting a planner's event. In many instances during our collection of incidents, the critical link was often the sales manager. When an event experienced difficulty or disaster, planners often traced their problems to the sales manager who originally booked the event. Often these salespeople were new and inexperienced, being rotated through the sales department in a training component or became another number in the legendary turnover problem that planners see afflicting hotel sales departments (dimension 2). In the last instance, planners often cited frustration over being booked by one sales manager, only to find another one, invariably new, in charge as the event approached. The lack of personnel continuity from booking to execution often had negative effects on planners' events.

Increasingly, planners were insisting on the expedient of including the convention services manager as early in the sales process as possible, for it is the CSMs who have to deliver on the promises of the sales staff (dimension 3). In many cases related to us, planners indicated difficulties could have been avoided had sales managers been aware of the physical and/or organizational capabilities and limitations of the hotel that are the bread and butter of the CSM's job. Planners strongly endorsed the concept of cross-training sales managers in the convention services department or, failing that, inclusion of the CSM in the sales and booking negotiations as a control mechanism and reality check.

Recognizing that the sale of group business is a primary focus of an increasing number of hotel sales people, a companion organization to ACOM was recently established. The Association of Convention Marketing Executives (ACME) was founded to increase and formalize the professionalism of convention sales managers in hotels, convention and visitors bureaus, and convention centers. This organization is dedicated to the same sorts of professionalism activities as ACOM and should serve to prepare its membership to better understand, sell, and serve its group clientele.

Over and over, planners related incidents and analyzed hotel staff behavior as either effective or ineffective in ways linked to the concept of professionalism. Planners characterized this professionalism in various ways but kept returning to training, knowledge, control, and empowerment. In those cases where the hotel staff was trained, experienced, and knew what to expect from their clients, the chances for a successful event were greatly enhanced. When the hotel had made specific provisions to convey total authority for an event to a key staff member, there was almost never a negative outcome. In those happy circumstances where this key hotel staff member was also able to be creative and imaginative on behalf of the planner's group, the outcome usually bordered on the legendary in the planners' experience and recollection.

The most pervasive root causes of negative incidents were invariably traced to training and knowledge lapses, communication failures, or restrictive and overly rigid policies. Typically, these either singly or in some combination were judged by the planners to result in unprofessional behavior that contributed to difficulty in execution or failure of the event. Interestingly, many planners still thought the hotel had failed even if the meeting attendees didn't know something was amiss. They made the point that the planner *did* know, and the future potential of similar behaviors significantly colored the planners' purchase decisions regarding future events.

CONCLUSION

In Table 7.7, we outline a series of tactics for hotels to consider that are derived from the foregoing analysis and arranged according to the critical incident dimensions with which they are most closely associated. Some of the tactics apply across all dimensions, and their implementation can be seen as strengthening the entire structure of the hotel's staff and organization mix. Others are more appropriately specific to a single or couple of dimensions.

This research reports, analyzes, and comments upon six dimensions that seem to be unique in the "service interaction" literature. These dimensions begin to explain important aspects of the interchange that takes place between employees on behalf of the hotel organization and major clients representing literally millions of room-nights and other revenue.

If hotels are going to improve service to group markets, particularly in a tough economic atmosphere, they are well advised to understand the crucial variables that take place in the service exchange process. This article outlined the most complete inventory to date of the crux of the process. Hotels can use this knowledge and adaptations of the tactics explicit and implied to improve their service performance. They must, for MPs will use the same data from this analysis to judge the quality of their interactive relationships with hotels. MPs must respect the demands of the hotel staff, also. Otherwise, they will be confronted with a hotel sales staff similar tot he one described in the tongue-in-cheek sidebar, "Lament of a Super Sales Manager."

TABLE 7.7
Dimensions and tactics

Tactics	Communication	Organization	Execution	Developing Relationships	Initiative	Crisis Management
Develop a strategic plan for events	☎	↕	✌	♥	★	✔
Review policies that are restrictive		↕	✌			
Purchase and issue specialized communication equipment	☎		✌			✔
Reorganize to be "event friendly"	☎	↕	✌			
Cross-train convention services manager, sales mananger, and catering sales manager		↕	✌	♥		
Empower key staff		↕	✌		★	✔
Allow ownership of event	☎	↕	✌		★	✔
Encourage, pay for professional activities	☎			♥	★	
Limit turnover among key staff		↕	✌			
Train entire staff to be sensitive to groups	☎	↕	✌			
Learn about meeting planner job	☎		✌		★	
Provide training, familiarization for area meeting planners	☎	↕	✌			

IMPROVING INTERACTIONS BETWEEN MEETING PLANNERS AND HOTEL EMPLOYEES

*Lament of a Super Sales Manager**
—Anonymous

I am a hotel sales manager. I have unlimited resources at my disposal.

- I always keep at least ten guest rooms under my desk, and it is a policy here to automatically make reservations and tee times for your board of directors when you sign a contract.

- I can make any of my meeting rooms larger or smaller, depending on your needs.

- I will naturally remove any supporting pillars from your meeting space and will install windows in every room as needed.

- The "ocean view" is not scheduled to arrive until the second day of your program, and for this I sincerely apologize.

  - We will, however, move the hotel 2 feet to the left to accommodate your request by the end of your session today.

  - I can only throw myself on your mercy and grovel at your feet.

- I completely agree that it is inconceivable that we should have any other groups booked into this hotel during your program.

- The additional breakout rooms that you added this morning should be built no later than Wednesday.

- Naturally, it will be no problem to turn your general session for 800 people classroom style into a hollow square for 150 with rear-screen projection, simultaneous Japanese translation, and satellite hookup. I will do it personally during your 15-minute coffee break.

  - Unfortunately, due to space constraints and the fact that your final program bears no resemblance whatsoever to your contracted space, we will have to suspend your lunch buffet from the ceiling above your general session and then suck the gravity out of the ballroom. Engineering is dispatching a team right now.

- We have located the boxes that you sent last month (under your mother's maiden name) at the hotel down the street, and again, our apologies for not having found them sooner.

- In answer to your questions, it is, of course, understood that I am telepathically aware of all your speakers' requirements and will set up an overhead projector, LCD projector, dual slide projectors, two screens, a laser printer, podium and mike, two table mikes, six aisle mikes, a head table, *and* red and blue M&M's in each room at no charge just in case you need them.

- We will automatically adjust the temperature in every room every 15 minutes.

- Additionally, it goes without saying that the AV tech, an engineer, a babysitter, and myself will be underneath your head table during the duration of your event in case you need anything else.

It has been great working with you, and I can't wait to see you again upon your arrival at the hotel!!!

---

*This amusing anecdote has been floating around the Internet among hotel sales professionals during the latter part of 2000. It is included here as an illustration of the distance that can exist between meeting planners and hotel sales staffs' perceptions of the same expectations.

7.10 A Profile of Convention Services Professionals

Rhonda J. Montgomery and Denney G. Rutherford

A study of the relatively new position of convention services manager found that half are stable, professionally minded managers, while the rest may still be in search of a career.

Envision this situation: You're a hotel manager with 600 rooms allocated to a group of surgeons who are attending a convention to learn about new techniques for saving patients who have ingested Monopoly pieces. At the same time, one of your previously vacant function rooms is occupied by the Sisters of Salvation prayer meeting that was supposedly canceled but was instead miraculously called to order, even though the sisters' block of rooms was long ago released. In yet another function room, the Gotrocks' wedding reception has been prolonged due to the fact that Uncle Bob, the toastmaster, spent too much time toasting. The surgeons need the Gotrocks' reception room and the sisters seek shelter. To resolve this mess you turn to the only person in the hotel who can juggle and solve these problems (sometimes simultaneously)—the convention services manager (CSM).

That scenario is intentionally whimsical, but each day a hotel's convention services manager deals with real-life "traffic jams" as part of the effort to deliver top-notch service. CSMs have been variously described, defined, and profiled. In one writer's view, they "coordinate and service the convention. The CSM takes over after the sale has been made and begins to work out the fine details with the convention group. Any problems that arise during the convention will be directed to . . . [the CSM, who] . . . must work closely with all departments" (Astroff and Abbey, 1988, p. 125). As other writers explain it, CSMs "coordinate the activities of all departments to ensure maximum service to conventions and other groups once they are in the property" (Hoyle, Dorf, and Jones, 1989, p. 154). Regardless of the specific definition, CSMs are hotel professionals who "make meetings happen" (Myers, 1989, p. 77; Groome, 1992). Their importance to the meetings and convention market is best summed up in the words of internationally known meeting professional Barbara Nichols: "I know and you know that the services coordinator can make or break a meeting" (1986, p. 4). In this article, we discuss the rise of the CSM position and present the findings of the first known broad survey of these professionals.

RECENT VINTAGE

Although hotels have been hosting meetings for years, the CSM position did not crystallize until the 1980s, when hotels focused specifically on attracting the meeting business. Before the advent of the CSM, a corporate or association meeting planner might have to work with several members of the hotel staff to make the meeting work, or a particular employee, say, the catering manager, became the de facto CSM. Today, the CMS's office is the clearinghouse for meeting details, and the CMS's staff has final responsibility for a meeting's success.

The CSM has become the intermediary between the hotel's promises about an event and its execution of that event. David Dorf, of the Hospitality Sales Management Association International (HSMAI), wrote, "service is better because convention-service departments have improved. Once convention managers were either catering people or housemen who really were responsible only for setting up. Now you're starting to see convention services develop as a profession" (Hosansky et al., 1986, p. 55). As the profession of convention services management evolves, it becomes multidimensional, involving a complex array of relationships not only within the hotel, but increasingly in the community.

Today, virtually every major convention hotel has a CSM, and many smaller hotels, resorts, and other lodging and meeting locations such as conference centers have at least one individual who holds that title. As reliance on the conventions and meetings market grows, we expect hotels to devote increasing resources to convention services. In a typical large convention-oriented hotel, there is a director of convention services with a staff of several convention service managers. We envision such a department developing in many more hotels.

That the job of CSM has become organizationally formalized in hotels and recognized broadly across the entire conventions and meetings industry further serves to point out the importance of this position in the hotel organization. A typical job description for a convention services manager can be seen in a text by Hoyle et al. on managing conventions (1989, pp. 156–157). It should be noted that in the Hoyle group's sample job description (adapted in "Sample Job Description: Convention Services Manager"), the typical CSM discharges his or her duties under four general categories: administrative responsibilities involving group business; working relationships with the sales and marketing department; the various interdepartmental relations within the hotel organization structure; and specific responsibilities for serving clients.

Writer Holly Hughes described how a CSM's responsibilities play out in the typical day after she followed a CSM at the Chicago

---

SAMPLE JOB DESCRIPTION: CONVENTION-SERVICES MANAGER

The convention services manager (CSM) is responsible for representing the property to convention and corporate meeting officials and their guests once the booking has been made, including continuous coordination with all operating departments.

As the liaison between the property and the meeting group, the CSM's responsibilities include ensuring that schedules are maintained and that services are rendered properly, and facilitating the booking of future business.

Administrative Responsibilities

1. Develop objectives, goals, and policies relating to group business.
2. Develop administrative and daily review procedures.
3. Maintain records and filing systems.
4. Maintain and manage an inventory of equipment and supplies.
5. Work with outside audiovisual companies.
6. Work with the convention bureau and with counterparts in other properties.

Working Relations with Sales and Marketing Department

1. Work with the director of marketing and the sales marketing staff to develop and implement programs.
2. Coordinate directly with the account executive responsible for each booking.

Interdepartmental Relations

1. Work with the rooms division manager.
2. Work with the catering manager.
3. Work with the food and beverage manager.
4. Work with the housekeeping department.
5. Work with the maintenance and engineering departments.
6. Work with the security departments.
7. Work with the accounting department.
8. Coordinate the activities of all departments involved in serving the meeting.
9. Prepare and distribute detailed information to all department heads in advance of each convention or meeting.

(continued next page)

SAMPLE JOB DESCRIPTION: CONVENTION-SERVICES MANAGER (continued)

Customer-Service Responsibilities

1. Take over each account after confirmation of booking, contact the group's meeting planner, and establish a schedule.
2. Meet with association executives, corporate meeting planners and other convention officials to finalize plans.
3. Maintain a checklist of services available from the property and local firms.
4. Inform meeting officials of safety and legal restrictions and regulations.
5. Ensure that all departments are following the outlined plans.
6. Update operating departments of any changes, additions, or deletions.
7. Work with the meeting planner to prepare daily, detailed service requirements and distribute those to departments.
8. Schedule a preconvention briefing session.
9. Greet meeting officials upon arrival and show them the meeting-area setup.

10. Check daily on each function room, exhibit area, and registration area.
11. Ensure that an event's schedule is posted daily on reader boards and in elevators, and is distributed as daily events sheet to all departments; and ensure that function and directional signs are in place.
12. Maintain close communication with the customer.
13. Contact convention officials at the program's end, discuss plans for future events, and invite them to return.
14. Prepare a detailed critique at the end of the convention.
15. Schedule a postconvention briefing between the convention officials and property department heads.

Adapted from: Leonard H. Hoyle, David C. Dorf, and Thomas J. A. Jones, *Managing Conventions and Group Business,* East Lansing, MI: The Educational Institute of the American Hotel and Motel Association, 1989, pp. 156–157.

Marriott Downtown during a major convention and watched the CSM juggling details for other upcoming and current events in the hotel (Hughes, 1984). The piece she wrote provides a behind-the-scenes look at the sorts of details and interactions that the CSM encountered while delivering on the hotel's promises to the organizers of that convention.

Typically, CSMs have the authority and responsibility for determining strategy and tactical details of a meeting or convention during the time it is in the hotel. Once the group is in-house, the CSM usually has authority equal to that of the general manager as far as decision making for that group is concerned. It is clear that a CSM must be detail oriented and tolerant of a high degree of organizational stress over long periods of time. As Nichols noted, "the hallmarks of a CSM are long hours and the need to adapt to varying personalities and degrees of competence" (Nichols, 1985, p. 132).

The CSM's specific duties begin when the files and contracts compiled by the sales and catering departments come to the CSM's desk. Even though the events covered by those contracts may be many months away, most convention services managers view it as essential that they become familiar with the contract and the group's specific needs so that planning mistakes or incorrect estimates of the hotel's capabilities might be caught at the earliest possible stage. The convention services manager will typically write a letter of introduction and greeting to the meeting or convention planner that states how to contact the CSM and lets the planner know how preparations are proceeding.

At this early stage the CSM will apprise the group's meeting planner of any potential problems that may have been inadvertently incorporated in the contract, perhaps reopening negotiations on certain items. Because of the CSM's familiarity with the hotel's facilities and how those facilities can be best configured and used for group events, the CSM may be deeply involved in planning the final details of catered events that were arranged by the catering sales staff (Myers, 1989, p. 96). Once the event begins, the CSM should oversee the entire process. He or she will work closely with the meeting planner and other key event figures, including trade show managers, exposition service contractors, and, of course, every hotel department that plays a role in the event (Hosansky, 1986, p. 55).

PROFESSIONAL APPROACH

The CSM position has become a recognized part of many hotels' professional management structure (Myers, 1989, p. 84). A CSM needs in-depth knowledge of multiple market segments; a good grasp of convention- and meeting-related services available in the local market area; and broad and deep knowledge of the management, organization, and staff involved in every hotel department. The CSM can be a member of the hotel's executive committee, as is the case with the director of convention services at the Waldorf-Astoria Hotel and at many other hotels (Ghitelman, 1989). Many of the major hotel chains (e.g., Marriott) have standardized the position of convention services director chainwide.

A further indicator of the CSM's professional status is the development of an international association to advance the goals of that profession. Currently, with close to 650 members, the Association for Convention Operations Management (ACOM) has been operating as a resource and voice for CSMs since its infancy in 1989. According to William Just, by 1989 the association had listed 4000 hotels in the United States and Canada with an identifiable convention services management func-

tion. Furthermore, by that time Hilton, Hyatt, Marriott, and Sheraton had all established corporate directors of convention services. Marriott Hotels was actively recruiting CSMs and had established a management-training track for people to become convention services managers and directors at that firm's hotels.

Two-thirds of ACOM's membership comprises hotel convention services managers, and the remaining members are event and client-services managers from convention centers and convention and visitors bureaus. The broad emergence of the CSM position across the many types and categories of hotels and meeting facilities seems to underscore the importance with which this function is being viewed by hotel management (Myers, 1989, p. 77–78).

Meeting planners appreciate being able to depend on CSMs. In a study of the interactions of association and corporate meeting planners with hotel staff, Rutherford and Umbreit found that meeting planners most frequently dealt with CSMs (32 percent of over 300 incidents studied). Moreover, CSMs were often the key to an event's success, owing to the CSM's thorough knowledge of the hotel's capabilities and its limitations (Rutherford and Umbreit, 1993, pp. 71, 75, 77). The meeting planners surveyed generally felt they could count on CSMs to be practical about what the hotel could deliver, while sales managers, in their eagerness to meet goals, sometimes oversold the facility's capabilities.

Such trust and confidence is predicated in large part on stability of employment. Therein lies one of the implicit problems of the relationship between meeting planners and CSMs. Many meeting planners consider turnover of hotel employees to be a major impediment to the successful planning and execution of their events. Consequently, they highly value hotels and CSMs that treat convention services as a true profession and not a stepping-stone to other career options.

The demand for stability and continuity among CSMs presents a dilemma. Retaining a CSM for many years provides good service but can make the CSM feel "dead-ended." On the other hand, if CSMs are constantly moving from property to property, the continuity required by meeting planners is interrupted. How does a hotel continue to offer challenging and professional growth to CSMs while keeping them in a position with no real prospect of promotion? The question becomes even more troubling in the wake of the reorganization (also known as reengineering or reconfiguration) experienced by most hotel corporations and individual properties.

UNDER PRESSURE

Although convention services management is still a relatively young profession, CSMs have not had as easy a time in the 1990s, compared to the halcyon days of the 1980s. According to one writer, "the high-profile focus and support [of the 1980s] has waned. And what's more, it appears as if these managers are more overloaded than ever" (Migdal, 1993, p. 1). Commented one CSM in a 1993 article, "We just aren't held in as high esteem as we once were" (Migdal, 1993, p. 38). Such a lack of support will trouble meeting planners who consider the CSM to be the critical interface between the hotel and the planner's event.

STUDYING CSMs

With all that has been written about convention services managers, we could find only anecdotal information about who they are, where they came from, and how they view their position. Consequently, we designed a study to assess the current state of the CSM profession. Our objectives in this study were (1) to discover how today's convention services managers view their profession; (2) to determine where the position stands in the organization, how much authority the CSM has regarding processes and personnel, and at

what stage CSMs are brought into the event; (3) to ascertain demographic data; and (4) to provide an overview of the career paths taken by most CSMs.

The sample consisted of all members of the Association for Convention Operations Management (ACOM) employed by hotels, plus other convention services managers from selected hotel organizations. Our questionnaire was divided into three parts, as follows: the Riegel career commitment index (Riegel, 1983); questions regarding the placement of the position within the hotel organizational structure and items asking for opinions about the organization; and questions seeking basic demographic and career-progression information.

We mailed questionnaires twice to the sample of 466 and received 260 usable surveys (a response rate of 56 percent). Individuals participating in the study were promised anonymity and were offered a report of the raw data if they returned a postcard included in the package. The substantial number of returned cards (nearly 75 percent of the sample) indicated a good cross section of hotels in terms of size, geographic distribution, and market segment.

Data were subjected to a chi-square or t-test, depending on the type of data generated. The large response rate suggests that we might draw conclusions about the CSM population as a whole with a relatively high degree of confidence. In the remainder of this article, we present their reported personal and professional characteristics, job- and organization-related factors, and level of career commitment.

WHO THEY ARE

With a mean age near 35 years, the participating CSMs were highly educated and somewhat evenly divided in terms of gender (see Table 7.8). Eighty-nine percent of the respondents reported having attended at least some college. Nearly half the sample (125) held bachelor's degrees. Those degrees came in 43 different disciplines, ranging literally from anthropology to zoology. A total of 51 respondents had hospitality degrees (41 percent of those holding bachelor's degrees), and an additional 21 held general business degrees.

The responses suggest that convention services is not necessarily the exclusive province of hospitality-degree holders, or even college graduates. Instead, we suggest that anyone who has the requisite grasp of detail coupled with organizational and social skills can be a successful convention services manager.

About half of the surveyed CSMs reported that they were members of the ACOM professional organization, but only 20 respondents, or less than 10 percent, had achieved any other

professional certification (i.e., the Certified Meeting Professional [CMP] designation conferred by the Convention Liaison Council).

Respondents reported a workweek averaging 60 to 70 hours, a statistic that is certainly not unusual in the hospitality business. For this effort, these CSMs were averaging close to $40,000 a year in annual salary. (It should be noted that this represents base annual salary paid by the hotel; we decided not to ask questions about the distribution of gratuities because such "side money" is not universal.)

At first glance, it might appear that these CSMs are demonstrating remarkable job stability. They reported an average of nearly six years as a CSM and slightly over four years at their present hotel, but considering their

TABLE 7.8
Personal and professional characteristics of CSMs

Age

Range:	21 to 69
Average:	35.4

Gender

Male	123
Female	137

Education

High school or equivalent	29
Some college but without a bachelor's degree (including 17 with associate's degrees)	29
Bachelor's degree	125
Postgraduate study, degree, or other	31

Note: Totals may not equal 260 due to nonresponses.

Experience, professional data

Years as CSM	range: 1 to 22	average: 5.9
Years at present hotel	range: 1 to 22	average: 4.0
ACOM membership		109 (52 percent)
Professional certification		20 CMPs
		(Certified Meeting Professionals)

Hours worked each week

range: 35 to 81+	average: 60 to 70

Salary

range: $5,000* to $80,000	average: $39,176

*This is an unexpectedly low figure for which we received no explanation.

mean age, most of these managers could have nearly 15 years in the hotel business.

To gain a clear picture of their professional backgrounds, we asked respondents to provide us with an outline of their career track. If they had not always been a CSM, we asked them to list in chronological order their four most recent positions (and in what industries). The industries in which those jobs were held were distilled into the three categories of "hotels," "unrelated to hotels," and "hospitality (outside hotels)," as displayed in Figure 7.7. If those positions were in the hotel industry, the respondent was assigned to one of six categories, as shown in Figure 7.8.

The overall picture drawn from the demographic data is one of a group of professionals who are committed hotel employees and who have come to the CSM role either from catering or convention services. The CSMs responding to this study had specific and pertinent job experience in the hospitality industry that allowed them to become professionals in convention services. The demographic data create the impression that hotel companies accord the CSM's job the respect and importance given it by the hotels' meeting-planner guests. However, the findings from the questionnaire's career commitment index belie the depth of commitment.

FIGURE 7.7
Career paths by industry

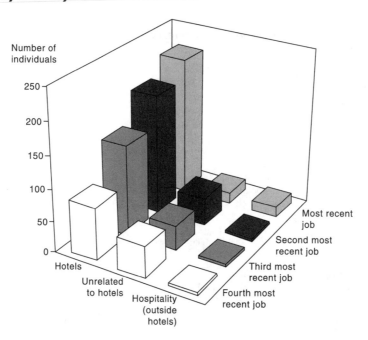

Industry	Fourth most recent job	Third most recent job	Second most recent job	Most recent job
Hotels	82	141	187	217
Unrelated to hotels	49	38	45	17
Hospitality (outside hotels)	4	3	4	14

FIGURE 7.8
Career paths by hotel department

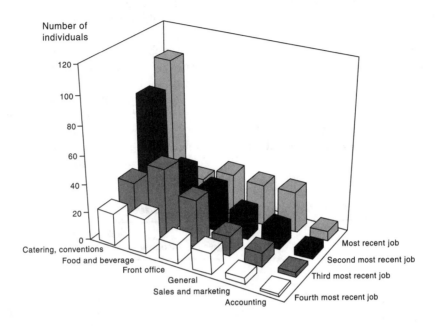

Hotel departments	Fourth most recent job	Third most recent job	Second most recent job	Most recent job
Catering, conventions	22	34	84	102
Food and beverage	25	49	38	21
Front office	14	33	29	30
General	15	14	18	28
Sales and marketing	5	9	14	29
Accounting	1	2	4	7

TENUOUS COMMITMENT

For this study, career commitment refers to the degree of personal attachment people associate with specific professional or vocational fields. It is characterized by the degree of satisfaction individuals derive from their chosen work and by the strength of their belief that the chosen vocation fulfills expectations that arise from their work values.

Riegel's career commitment index (CCI) is designed to assess the following factors:

1. The extent to which individuals are willing to act on behalf of their chosen vocation.
2. The extent to which people devote or are willing to devote time and energy to improve their status within career fields.
3. The extent to which people value this career over others they might have pursued.

4. The strength of conviction that this vocation provides intrinsic satisfaction.
5. The strength of the individual's desire to remain in the field.

The CCI has been used in a variety of settings and is considered to be a reliable instrument. Consisting of 17 Likert-type items scored from 1 to 5, the index has a minimum score of 17 (low commitment) and a maximum score of 85 (high commitment). In practice, however, scores most typically range between 42 and 68.

The CSMs' scores on the CCI suggested a moderate to high level of commitment to the career field of convention services. The mean score was 63.75. A Cronbach's alpha test (Cronbach, 1951), to measure internal consistency, returned a relatively high value of 0.7202, indicating that the results of the CCI are reflecting a consistent measure of respondents' attitudes. The CCI statements and their associated average scores are presented in Table 7.9.

TABLE 7.9
Career Commitment Index—statements of industry attitudes

	Strongly Disagree 1	Disagree 2	Neither Agree nor Disagree 3	Agree 4	Strongly Agree 5
1. I talk up convention services to my friends because it is great to be part of this industry				3.865	
2. I would not consider an offer to work in any other field		2.488			
3. Sometimes I am embarrassed to tell people that I work as a convention services manager	1.483 (Reverse: 4.664)				
4. I would just as willingly work in some other line of work as long as the characteristics of jobs available were appealing to me				3.609 (Reverse: 3.934)	
5. The nature of convention services work inspires me to contribute my very best in job performance				4.377	
6. I am very loyal to the field of convention services				4.081	
7. If another field of work offered similar advancement and compensation opportunities, I would be interested in pursuing my career in that field				3.612 (Reverse: 3.899)	
8. I am extremely happy that I chose a career as a convention services manager over others that I have considered at one time or another				3.869	
9. There is not much for me to gain by staying in convention services		2.354 (Reverse: 4.000)			
10. I see my future as being tied to the future of convention services			3.248		
11. For me, the career I have chosen in this field is the best possible career choice I could have made			3.400		
12. Deciding to work as a convention services manager was a mistake on my part.	1.550 (Reverse: 4.488)				
13. I see myself as advancing rapidly in salary and position in this field		2.745			
14. I regularly read trade publications that are written about convention services			3.481		
15. I subscribe to two or more industry trade publications			3.151		
16. Work in this field is challenging and interesting				4.296	
17. I will not be in convention services in 10 years			3.375 (Reverse: 3.907)		

Note: Items 3, 4, 7, 9, 12, and 17 are reverse-scored in analysis. Score reversal is used to test strength of disagreement with negative or career-move items.

The scores of the CSMs in this study ranged from a low of 48 to a high of 82. Fifty percent of the CSMs scored 63 or higher, suggesting those at least half have a moderate to strong level of career commitment. (The mean of 63.75 represents about 75 percent of the 85 available points on the index.) For the other half of the sample, which had scores under 63, there is little to indicate a deep and abiding career commitment. The numbers suggest a division in the CSM ranks, with a substantial portion viewing convention services less as a career and more as a step in a career progression, and indicate that long-term commitment is not particularly high.

We divided the population into the quartiles, cross-tabulating those groups with other variables from the questionnaire to see whether organizational, operational, demographic, or professional data could give us any further insights into the level and depth of career commitment. (A chi-square test was used to determine significance of those cross-tabs.) Table 7.10 shows variables for which there was a significant difference between those in the top quartile of career commitment and those in the three lower quartiles.

The CSMs who have risen to the title of director of convention services appeared to have a higher level of commitment than those with such other titles as convention services manager, conference services manager, or convention services specialist. We believe that individuals' titles influence their assessment of career success. Those with the title of director were also more likely to have higher salaries and to be ACOM members. We found that one of the most important things influencing career commitment in this population is the value placed on convention services by the hotel and the hotel's parent company. Those reporting the highest levels of career commitment were located in hotels and hotel companies that placed a high value on convention services. The respondent's gender had no influence on career commitment.

Education (represented by bachelor's degrees), ACOM membership, and salary level had about equivalent significance for higher levels of career commitment. Members of ACOM, however, had substantially higher salaries than nonmembers.

A useful aspect of the CCI is that its items can be subdivided into two related scales: a career-viability measure (using items 2, 3, 4, 7, 9, 12, 13, and 17), and a job-satisfaction measure (using items 1, 5, 6, 8, 10, 11, 14, 15, and 16). The career-viability scale provides an index of how strongly positive the respondents feel about their careers and their ability to move up or on, as well as indicating their confidence in their own skills. A high index score suggests career strength but not necessarily in convention services. A low score may indicate someone who is predisposed to either a career change or an industry change. The job-satisfaction measure provides an indicator of how comfortable the responding CSMs felt about their jobs, their performance, and the intrinsic value they derive from their jobs.

We created those two measures and partitioned them at their midpoints to create two new dependent variables with two levels each. These were then tested against organizational and demographic data to gain additional insights into how the CSMs view their careers and the satisfaction that they have in their current positions.

As shown in Table 7.11, the chief difference between those with a high career-viability index and those with a low career-viability index was their view of the value with which convention services is held by the hotel. The fact that those with high career-viability scores differed so sharply from the low-score group suggests a likelihood that those with high career-viability will probably remain in convention services, even if they are inclined to move around within the industry. A cross-tabulation of the value placed on convention services in the hotel and the level of career commitment further established the value of the hotel's commitment to convention services. These data again showed the extremely high career commitment among CSMs in hotels where convention services were deemed valuable by

TABLE 7.10

Career commitment by various demographic measures

Variable	Probability
Director of convention services (versus other titles)	.026
To whom do you report	.180
CSM valued by hotel	.000
CSM valued by hotel company	.000
Gender of respondent	.352
Bachelor's degree	.057
ACOM membership*	.059
Salary level	.059

*Members of ACOM (Association for Convention Operations Management) had significantly ($p < .001$) higher salaries than nonmembers.

Convention-services managers who scored in the top quartile on career commitment were compared with the other (bottom) three-quarters of the CSMs on the variables listed above. Low probability numbers ($p < .05$) indicate variables for which the differences were significant. So, for example, having the title "director of convention services" was significantly related to the CSM's career commitment, while, on the other hand, a respondent's gender had no effect whatsoever on career commitment.

management and ownership ($p < .000$). Moreover, hotels that place a high value on convention services also appear to attract not only the most satisfied CSMs but also those with the highest potential for career viability ($p < .000$).

On the other hand, those with high job-satisfaction scores differed significantly in their professional attitudes from those with low job-satisfaction scores. While such a finding is not particularly surprising, the extent of that difference is profound, as shown by the numbers in this study. For over half of the measures suggested by previous research, trade literature, and professional publications that were used as a basis for this survey of professional attitudes, those with high job satisfaction clearly felt much more strongly about the role the CSM should have in hosting and producing events. The data supplied by this sample of CSMs strongly suggest that the entire population of CSMs who are job-satisfied are also strongly committed career professionals.

These results are consistent with similar tests performed on personal and demographic data, as can be seen in Table 7.12. While there are few significant differences based on career viability, with the possible exception of age, those with high job-satisfaction indices differed significantly in every measure from those with low job satisfaction. Those with high job satisfaction were slightly older, had been CSMs longer, and had been at their present hotels longer. They also reported significantly more hours of work per week. Although we have no indication regarding whether those long hours were voluntary or expected, CSMs we contacted generally agreed that the idea of expecting any arbitrary fixed number of work hours per week was inconsistent with the nature of the job.

While number of hours worked per week is always important and interesting to people first entering a profession, it appears to be less of an influence on people's career satisfaction after they have been in the profession for a while. To further test this idea, we partitioned the hours worked per week into five categories and cross-tabbed those categories with the

TABLE 7.11
t-tests of career viability and job satisfaction and various professional attitudes

Item:	Low career viability (n =108)	High career viability (n =152)	Probability	Low job satisfaction (n =127)	High job satisfaction (n =133)	Probability
Amount of authority during events (scale, 1–10)	7.8333	7.9803	.555	7.7323	8.0977	.136
Amount of authority prior to events (scale, 1–10)	6.7870	7.1842	.142	6.6535	7.3684	.007
Number of months before events CSM becomes involved	10.2979	9.5147	.333	9.2264	10.3548	.156
CSM should be detail oriented	4.8148	4.8618	.321	4.7953	4.8872	.148
CSM should see the big picture	4.7130	4.7171	.948	4.6535	4.7744	.051
CSM should be both detail oriented and see the big picture	4.7963	4.7697	.627	4.7402	4.8195	.140
CSM makes meetings happen	4.5000	4.6184	.141	4.4409	4.6917	.001
CSM–planner relationship important	4.7593	4.8158	.302	4.7402	4.8421	.058
CSM needs total authority over events	4.5278	4.5329	.956	4.4803	4.5789	.275
CSM should be involved in event negotiation process	3.3889	3.3841	.971	3.4762	3.3008	.176
✓ Convention services highly valued at this hotel	3.6481	3.9934	.007	3.5794	4.1053	.000
✓ Convention services highly valued by this company	3.1308	3.6490	.000	3.1111	3.7424	.000
CSMs need to understand other industry members	4.2222	4.2649	.605	4.0873	4.3985	.000

Note: Numbers reported are group means.

This table compares factors that might affect career viability and job satisfaction. Factors with a low probability score ($p < .05$) have a statistically significant effect. Other factors, which apparently do not have any effect, are presented as benchmarks for future studies. Items are scored on a scale of 1 (low) to 5 (high), unless otherwise stated.

TABLE 7.12
t-tests of career viability and job satisfaction and various personal and demographic data

Item:	Low career viability (n = 108)	High career viability (n = 152)	Probability	Low job satisfaction (n = 127)	High job satisfaction (n = 133)	Probability
Age (range: 21 to 69)	34.3	36.3	.048	33.3	37.4	.000
Years as CSM (range: 1 to 22)	5.47	6.23	.170	4.79	7.01	.000
Years CSM at present hotel (range: 1 to 22)	3.94	4.14	.650	3.50	4.60	.010
Hours worked per week	57.08	59.55	.246	54.99	61.83	.001
Base annual salary (range: $5,000 to $80,000)	$38,814	$39,425	.711	$36,628	$41,812	.001

Note: Numbers reported are group means, except as noted.

job-satisfaction measures. With that calculation, respondents with high job satisfaction were still significantly more likely ($p < .000$) to work longer hours, bolstering the old industry cliché that "40 hours a week gets you a paycheck; more than that gets you a career." There was also a significant difference in the size of salaries reported by those with high job satisfaction—an annual average difference of over $5,000—which might possibly establish a connection between income level and job satisfaction.

Finally, those with high job satisfaction were significantly more likely to be ACOM members ($p < .001$). This is consistent with measures of success in other careers where those active in any profession are, generally speaking, those who are also active in their professional organizations. Professional organizations provide ongoing education, an opportunity to work with one's colleagues, and the chance to contribute to the profession through volunteer activities. The opportunity to learn and apply the newest strategies and tactics to make oneself more valuable to an employer is also a benefit.

WHAT ABOUT THE FUTURE?

Since this study is apparently the first of its kind, we have no definitive set of data with which to compare these results. We therefore offer the results as a baseline for future study. The results indicate that CSMs should be oriented not only to details but also to the big picture, and that they do, indeed, "make meetings happen." Moreover, to fulfill their important relationship with meeting planners, CSMs need close to total authority over their events.

Like many other hospitality positions, the CSM job is characterized by long hours; at least, that is true for the hotel professionals who are most committed and best rewarded. At least half of the CSMs are working at developing the position as a profession, as evidenced by their commitment to their career and the value they place on membership in their professional association, ACOM. The connection between ACOM membership and longer work hours, higher satisfaction, and greater income and career stability cannot be ignored. While it is not possible to suggest a causal relationship, it is certainly instructive that members of the CSM professional organization are more highly satisfied and compensated.

The other half of this population remains in somewhat of a state of limbo, at least as far as this study goes. Without further data, we do not know for sure whether they will leave the industry or simply bounce from hotel to hotel, with many of them doing a mediocre job along the way. It is that very prospect that meeting planners dread, because CSM turnover creates the likelihood of dropped details between the time the event is planned and the time it is executed.

Our data lead us to believe those hotels that highly value convention services will be winners in the economic arena for a greater share of the conventions and meetings market. They will gain business from meeting planners who want to work with high-quality CSM professionals who are committed to their organization and profession because of the commitment demonstrated by their employers. In contrast, a hotel that does not highly value convention services will find itself stuck with less-than-satisfied CSMs who view this as a temporary post and who will not be able to enhance their hotel's position in the meetings and conventions market. Both effective and ineffective hotels are soon identified by the meeting planners' grapevine. With the growing importance of conventions and meetings business, hotel managers should examine the results of this research and look to providing support for their CSMs.

Areas for future research on convention services certainly include future changes in the organizational arrangement of the convention services function, the autonomy with which it operates, and the extent to which hotels value CSMs' contributions (Nebel, Rutherford, and Schaffer, 1994). Additional paths of research and inquiry would include changes over time in demographic data and other personal characteristics and the way in which convention services managers exhibit further professionalism, including the potential and the future for professional certification through ACOM.

Finally, since this can be viewed as a baseline study of convention services, some future iteration of the career commitment index should be conducted to determine whether an increased level of professionalism has had any discernible effect on what appears to be a group that is split down the middle in terms of its commitment to a convention services career.

7.11   Putting the Public in Public Relations: The Case of the Seattle Sheraton Hotel and Towers

Louis B. Richmond

The powerful world of nonprofit organizations can make or break a hotel. A very strong statement when you consider our public relations firm, Richmond Public Relations, represents the Seattle Sheraton Hotel and Towers, a hotel that has potential revenues of $80 million to $100 million a year in rooms, food, and beverage and employs more than 600 people. Although the fortune of large convention hotels usually rests on the approval of large associations, meeting planners, Mobil and AAA awards, and a myriad of corporate decisions, nonprofit organizations definitely play a role in a hotel's financial success. The time and effort that hotels allot to public relations and nonprofits can profoundly influence destination decisions of meeting planners and major associations.

DONATIONS, DONATIONS

Every day the Sheraton receives three to four letters from local organizations soliciting donations of cash, rooms, and meals for benefits, auctions, and raffles. These seemingly simple requests add up to approximately 1000 requests every year. All of these organizations have nonprofit status and are doing valuable work in the community. They range from the symphony, opera, and ballet to large hospitals and universities. The smallest of preschools and local grassroots citizen activist organizations are also regular solicitors. Each of these organizations has a mission and purpose, which, if realized, could make the community a better place in which to live. Since mostly every request is valid, how does the hotel or public relations firm go about deciding which organizations to support? Each decision must be based on a benefit to the hotel.

Let me give an example of how working with the community has, indeed, benefited the hotel. One such request was a handwritten note from an elementary school student requesting a complimentary room for her school raffle. We were promised in the letter that the hotel would be mentioned in the raffle and given as much publicity as possible. This school was located 20 miles from the hotel in a small town that, on the surface, did not seem it could provide a lot of return benefit to the hotel. Due to the sincerity of the request, we decided to donate a room package. About four months after the donation was made, our firm received a call from someone who worked for a very large company in Seattle wanting to make room reservations. He called me rather than the hotel because he wanted me to know that he was booking the Sheraton because of its donation to his child's school. Since we were the only hotel to donate a room to his child's school auction, he felt an obligation to have his guests stay at the Sheraton. Therefore, his company was moving from another hotel to ours because of a donation that in actuality cost about $35. The potential revenue from his account was valued in the thousands of dollars. Additionally, his company is a member in trade associations that hold numerous regional and national conventions that can also influence business to the Sheraton.

Other benefits linked to this donation were that the Sheraton's name was seen in print on more than 1000 raffle tickets, and people who attended the drawing were made aware of the Sheraton's contribution. The return on investment from this one donation was enormous in direct revenue alone, but also generated an excellent amount of goodwill in the local community. All of this revenue and potential revenue was due to one small donation!

ASSOCIATIONS, NATIONAL MEETINGS

When large associations decide that Seattle will be the host city for their national conferences, the individual hotels bid on being the host hotel. The host hotel is in a very favorable situation concerning room rate and food and beverage functions. A well-thought-out public relations program can play a very important role in having an association decide which hotel to use. Working with the sales staff, the public relations firm can obtain as much information about the association as possible and decide how they can then influence the association to use the Sheraton.

A major southwest association was in the process of deciding which hotel to use for their Seattle conference. With research, we found that this particular organization supported a major national charity that was also supported by the Sheraton. We contacted the director of the local charity organization, who, in turn, phoned his counterpart in the southwestern city. He was informed of the Sheraton's sponsorship of his nonprofit and that one of his large corporate sponsors was looking for a hotel to use in Seattle. The director of the southwestern nonprofit called his contact in the corporation and apparently did a good job of convincing him to use the Sheraton.

Whether or not the decision was made directly because of this call or the combination of other sales efforts, most of the sales and marketing staff concurred that the hotel's support of the local nonprofit organization was instrumental in securing a major piece of association business. We have found that the nonprofit world will go all out to help corporations that help them. In addition, nonprofit organizations can effectively utilize this win-win model of partnership between business and nonprofits to solicit help from other companies and businesses.

SOCIAL EVENTS AND FUND-RAISERS

The social catering business is fiercely competitive. Nonprofit organizations are always seeking the lowest possible rates and prices, but because of their standing in the community, they sponsor very important events at hotels. The more prestigious the organization, the higher the ticket price and the more potential that the attendees can generate revenue for the hotel in the future by booking rooms for other events. Most members of the boards of directors of nonprofit organizations are leaders in the community and business world. Their recommendation can go a long way toward securing a very favorable image for the hotel in the local market.

In dealing with social catering events for nonprofit groups, we always inform organizations that the hotel staff will work closely with them to insure the success of their event. However, the nonprofit needs to clearly understand that the hotel is a *for-profit* business. We have to "strike a deal" that is good for the organization and, at the same time, good for the hotel. The organization is helped to understand that the more profitable the hotel, the more support can be provided for the nonprofit organization. If the hotel does not make a profit, there is no way that the hotel can continue offering its support. By offering the organization special services rather than lowering the price to

the point that the hotel will not make any profit, we ultimately help the organization raise even more money for their event. We have come up with many creative contributions to nonprofit organizations that not only increase their potential for raising money, but also favorably highlight the services of the hotel.

One of the hotel's most popular donations to nonprofit organization auctions is a series of cooking classes for ten people that includes a kitchen tour and lunch. This item, usually set at a minimum bid of $500 to $700, enables a group of people to combine their financial resources for a potentially higher bid. The cooking classes, also, enable the hotel to highlight one of its chefs and give people a back-of-the-house view of the kitchen. We have been able to track the success of these cooking classes and have found that almost every one of the participants has booked reservations in the hotel restaurants. What is given away, as donation, comes back many times over in increased business and greatly enhances the perception of the hotel's goodwill in the community.

Another innovative donation has been a tour with the hotel's curator of the corporate art collection. The Sheraton, well known for its art collection, employs a professional curator. Most of the major social service organizations or nonprofit organizations have always shown an interest in the arts, and this type of donation stands out from the overnight accommodations that are typically offered by other hotels.

The hotel's limousine can also play a part in the donation program. The use of the limousine has always added a prestigious quality to a gift and has been able to raise more money for the organization while costing the hotel only a minimal labor and operating cost.

By making a major donation to social catering fund-raisers that are booked in the hotel, it helps insure that the event will be rebooked the following year (assuming that the food and service are high quality). The ability to predict annual bookings provides savings in sales staff time and marketing efforts.

When major social catering events are held in other hotels, the Sheraton also made significant donations to show organizations that it is interested in supporting their cause no matter where their event is held. Of course, the hotel remains interested in having the group book their event at the Sheraton next season. However, our agency always encourages the Sheraton to purchase a table when events are hosted in another hotel, for several reasons: to show support for the organization; to let the staff see how the event is managed at another facility; and to compare quality of service and food.

HOLIDAY CARD PROGRAM

Another significant community contribution we make is our annual holiday card. Each year we select a different organization to be the beneficiary of this program. We print the Sheraton corporate holiday card and then provide the organization with an extra 10,000 cards for its own fund-raising campaign. These cards are printed at no charge to the organization as long as they provide us with original artwork. The organization that is chosen is always selected so that there is a return to the hotel. The organization chosen in 1987 had previously held a major event at another hotel. We informed them that if they switched to the Sheraton, they would be the beneficiaries of the 1988 holiday card campaign.

CONTROL

The hotel has certain prerequisites in making donations to nonprofit organizations.

1. The organization must be a 501(c)3 organization recognized by the Internal Revenue Service.

2. A request must be received in writing on the organization's stationery.
3. The organization must return to the hotel written notification of the donation through a raffle advertisement, program book, or announcement.
4. The donation must be in a "live" and not a "silent" auction whenever possible.
5. All responses are filed, and when a request for next year's gift arrives, we check to see if we received the recognition that we required.

Different levels of donations are awarded based on the event and the amount of recognition received. There have been times when gift certificates to the dessert buffet have been donated and in other instances a dinner for 100 people in Fullers, the Sheraton's award-winning restaurant.

Our commitment to the community is based on the belief that each member of the community organizations we support can act as a public relations spokesperson for the hotel. When businesses help organizations, their members and volunteers usually develop a loyalty to the giver. Our goal is to infiltrate the community aggressively as a good corporate citizen. At the same time, we want the community to know that we need their business. The more business that they give to us, the more help that we can return to the community.

CLASSIFICATION OF ORGANIZATIONS

The nonprofit world can be divided into six general areas, as set out below. For each classification, some major examples of the many possible representative organizations are listed.

Cultural Organizations

Most of these organizations have a large and prestigious board of directors. There is a tremendous amount of potential room business and catering functions from the organizations and their board members.

- Symphony orchestras, opera companies, ballet companies, chamber music organizations, and presenting organizations, as well as campus cultural organizations.
- Art museums, museums of history and industry, science museums, and craft and folk art museums.
- Major, alternative, and community theater companies.

Health Organizations

- Hospitals.
- Medical schools.
- Research centers.

Educational Organizations

- Alumni associations.
- University and college fund-raising campaigns.
- High school and PTA organizations.
- Preschool and private school fund-raisers.

Religious Organizations

- Churches.
- Synagogues.
- Religious schools and camps.
- Adult religious community organizations.

Social Service Agencies

- United Way.
- Community charity groups.
- Neighborhood grassroots organizations.
- Charities such as Easter Seals and March of Dimes.
- Food banks.
- Cystic Fibrosis Foundation.

- Juvenile Diabetes Foundation.
- Boy Scouts of America.

Social and Fraternal Organizations

- Rotary.
- Kiwanis.
- Elks.
- Shriners.

MARKETING APPROACHES

Before you approach an organization, you need to have a plan that puts you on the offensive rather than the defensive. Many times hotels are put in the position of having to respond to people asking for money rather than actually going to the organization to tell them that they are there to help them. The more creative you can be, the easier it will be for the organization to work with you. Your plan should include researching the following items.

- The members of the board of directors and their company affiliations.
- The needs of the organization.
- Their budget—easy to do since they are a tax-exempt organization.
- Past catering functions—where they were held, prices, and number of attendees.
- Housing needs of the organization and how you can help.

Read newspapers about the organization and totally familiarize yourself with their goals. Make sure you meet with a major staff member and a board member. To have a meeting with just a member of the staff or a member of the board simply means you will have another meeting to review what you discussed at the last meeting. The most important overall consideration is to understand the nonprofit organization's needs and to work together with their representatives for a win-win solution.

Make sure you work out before the event how the hotel will be credited and recognized. Recognition of the hotel's contribution is often assumed, forgotten, or left to chance. There are many ways that the hotel can be recognized. A complimentary ad in a season's program or newsletter will go a long way in justifying your investment. If you are trying to attract the organization, it must have an audience that is part of your marketing mix. Calculate what it would cost to advertise in their program book throughout the season. Bargain with the organization so that you receive a complimentary ad for the amount of donation that you are making. Other possible returns for your donation include:

- Having the organization give the hotel complimentary tickets that can be used by the staff for entertaining clients. This strategy can be very effective if certain concerts are sold out and your hotel is in possession of the only tickets.
- Asking the organization to give you access to their mailing list. This strategy can be crucial in trying to publicize a new weekend program or the opening of a new food and beverage outlet.
- Requesting the organization to commit to a two-year contract. This strategy not only makes it easier for the organization to plan ahead, but helps the hotel in projecting revenues.
- Donating meeting rooms to the organization for seminars and retreats if food and beverages are ordered. Most organizations have to pay for meeting facilities.

One of the most important aspects of any donation is the follow-up. Make sure you are aware of the news that is created by the organization you are helping and make them feel that they are part of your organization. If major events take place, have the hotel's general manager send a congratulatory letter. If someone is having a birthday, have your pastry chef send over a birthday cake. If you can help them in publicizing their events in your newsletter, work with them and inform them that you are giving them complimentary publicity. Work together all the time so that each organization receives something from each other, if possible, on a fairly regular basis.

Case Study

Our firm approached the board of directors of the Seattle Symphony in hopes that they would move a major luncheon to the Sheraton. We told them that we would be happy to offer complimentary room accommodations for their conductor and his wife during the duration of the symphony season if they would help influence their women's organization to use the Sheraton for their luncheon. By hosting the conductor and his wife in the best available room, we not only built up a good relationship with the conductor, but showed the board of directors that we were very interested in supporting the symphony.

By proactively informing the board of directors that the Sheraton was committed to the symphony, we, at the same time, helped them understand our need for their board members' business so that we could continue our support for them. Donating to significant cultural institutions is often a sound business decision because most members who serve on boards of large cultural organizations are often the community's business leaders. They know the wisdom of a sound decision, and, indeed, continue to offer ongoing support to the Sheraton. As a result of the Sheraton donating a room to the conductor and his wife, the symphony moved the luncheon to the hotel. The hotel maintains a very strong relationship with the conductor, and the symphony continues to use the Sheraton for their room, food, and beverage business. A classic example of a win-win situation, the symphony supporters, their board of directors, and their musicians act as public relations spokespeople for the Sheraton. In many ways, the results of this strategy have ensured several hundred people working on our behalf.

Press and Media

It is important to remember that the people in the press are also part of the community. Ultimately, donations to nonprofits will touch many press and media people in personal ways by helping their local organizations, such as schools, hospitals, and social service and cultural organizations. They will be especially interested in publicizing events with personal impact. It is also important to realize that hotels with many events create a "buzz" that generates more local press activity. Organizations like to be involved in active and exciting hotels. If a certain number of events are in one hotel and twice that amount are in another hotel, the more active hotel is bound to have more requests for events.

Cosponsorship

Another effective way to maximize public relations in the area of nonprofit donations or charities is to cosponsor events with radio stations or newspapers. The exposure that can be provided through this medium not only places your property with other responsible companies but helps spread the word of your company's involvement automatically through the media.

Take advantage of your local and regional radio stations to develop joint promotions. Work with the promotion director to find out how the hotel can help the station's favorite charity. Donate the ballroom or smaller meeting rooms for dances, parties, etc., with a guarantee of having a no-host bar. The radio station acts as a free advertising service to draw people to the event. It is in their best interest for their advertisers to draw large audiences. Have the nonprofit organization receive an admission charge to the event so that it is up to the nonprofit organization to also try to draw a large audience. By working with the radio station and the charity, the hotel not only maximizes its exposure, but also increases its potential revenue.

Regional Organizations

Identify major nonprofit organizations in feeder markets and work with them in their major fund-raising events. This will help increase weekend business and act as a reinforcer to advertising that is placed in those markets. The impact of these regional organizations can be just as strong as your local organizations. If your property has a strong regional weekend market, this program can be a very effective way to increase room business.

Identify corporations that have branches in feeder cities with ties to major nonprofit organizations. Any time that your property can get its name across to the public in a major feeder market, you reinforce advertising dollars or actually save advertising dollars. Remember, the return on investment, if carefully monitored, can be very significant.

CONCLUSION

The more times your hotel property is written and talked about, the more people automatically identify your property with positive community activity. It is eventually in the best interest of a community to ensure the business success of your hotel when it knows that you will help its favorite charities or organizations. In order to work with the community, you must educate the community to work for and with you. The best recommendation is the recommendation made by the public, and only when public relations truly works with the public can the property benefit. By putting the public in public relations, the public speaks for you and your property and results in profits through public relations.

7.12   Building Market Leadership: Improving Productivity of the Marketing Process

Fletch Waller

In Chapter 7.2, "Building Market Leadership: Marketing as Process," we explored marketing as *a process for creating and sustaining productive relationships with desirable customers*. We conceived the process as an eight-step continuous cycle of planning, actions, and assessments—one that embraces all employees in the hotel (see Figure 7.2 in Chapter 7.2).

When a hotel is led by a general manager (GM) who sees herself or himself as leader of their marketing process, when that process is thoughtfully conceived and well executed, when all employees see themselves as joint operator/marketers, that hotel becomes customer-centered, very competitive, and a leader in its markets.

Such a hotel might be said to have an *effective* marketing process, as measured by rising market share, revenues, customer satisfaction, and repeat rates. One of the characteristics of a healthy marketing process is the ability to change and adapt—to new technologies, new customer tastes and needs, new competitive innovations.

But in addition to effectiveness, a healthy marketing process also must be *productive*; that is, it must provide an attractive return for the dollar and effort invested. Productivity is best measured by the cost of acquiring a customer, not only as a percent of sales, but also as dollars per *unit* of sale, for example, dollars per occupied room, dollars per group contract, dollars per cover. If marketing efforts are a cause of customer decisions to purchase, an effect, then, of marketing productivity is the cost of stimulating that purchase decision, as well as the value of that decision.

Over the decade of the 1990s, rising costs of acquiring customers in U.S. hotels have been masked by strong increases in the average daily rate (ADR). In 1995, costs of acquiring a customer (franchise and marketing fees, commissions, reservation costs, and property marketing and sales expenses) in full-service hotels averaged 15.3 percent of ADR.* By 1999, it had risen to 15.6 percent; that three-tenths of a point increase over four years hardly alarms people. But consider, of the expenses that make up "costs of acquiring customers," only commissions vary directly with rate; most of the expenses are purchases—of ads, brochures, sales calls, Web sites, global distribution system (GDS) delivery services, telephone time—and personnel compensation and benefits. Sure, these expenses grow over time but not as a function of the rate at which a room is sold. If marketing was truly productive (and retained customers are less expensive to keep than replacement customers), we should have been seeing costs per unit dropping.

But in actuality, full-service hotels have seen acquisition costs per occupied room balloon 30.4 percent in just four years, to $16.94 from $12.99 per room-night! In higher-rated full-service hotels, acquisition costs rose to $21.47 from $15.86, a 35 percent increase. Resorts suffered a 25 percent increase, to $22.64 from $18.07 just four years earlier. Marketing productivity must be addressed.

So, this second part of "Building Market Leadership" deals with the challenge of increasing unit productivity and slowing, if not reducing, the costs of acquiring customers. Three expense categories make up the cost of acquiring customers, and we shall address each in turn:

---

*This and the other data in this discussion come from PKF Consulting's annual *Trends in the Hotel Industry*, 1991–2000.

- In rooms department, commissions and reservations costs.
- Franchise and central marketing fees.
- In the property marketing and sales department, property marketing costs.

COMMISSIONS AND RESERVATIONS COSTS

The major driver of these increasing costs of acquiring customers has been commission and reservation expenses. During the 1990s, commissions and reservations costs grew faster than any other expense line item in U.S. hotels. In upscale full-service hotels, this expense on a per-available-room (PAR) basis was up 187 percent, 1999 versus 1995, and up 84 percent just since 1995. Rising far faster than room rates, full-service hotels' distribution costs more than doubled, from $648 per occupied room in 1993 to over $1445 per occupied

room five years later.* All categories of U.S. hotels suffered similarly insupportable increases.

Commission Business Increases

What accounts for this rise? Change in *channels of distribution*, the fastest-changing part of the hotel and travel industries. Figure 7.9 shows the traditional distribution channels.

In the 1980s and early 1990s, expansion of global distribution systems (GDS) into an electronic information and booking network available to travel agencies worldwide, coupled with improved capabilities and marketing of chains' central reservations systems, plus corporate contracting with travel agents all created a huge rise in the proportion of commissionable room-nights in urban hotels, from typically under 10 percent of volume in 1980 to 40 percent or more today. Travel agency managers,

FIGURE 7.9
Traditional distribution channels

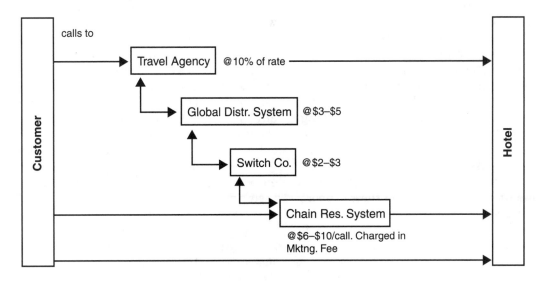

---

*Source: PKF Consulting's *Trends in the Hotel Industry*, 1994 and 1999.

trying to control costs, insisted their agents book airlines and hotels via the GDS rather than by phone. This shift not only laid on the hotel the 10 percent commission, but also a cascade of associated fees for GDS, the switch, and central reservations support. None of these distribution channel changes generated new, primary demand; they simply funneled demand more effectively (and expensively) into the hotels that were wired and alert. But its also brought about cancerous growth in distribution and marketing costs per occupied room.

Leisure travel placed through agencies did not grow commensurately. Resort commissionable volume from individuals stayed around 10 percent or so, since vacationers more often than not want to call and talk with the property directly.

In group meetings, conversely, downsizing corporations more and more turned to meeting-arrangement service providers, who in turn seek commissions from the resort or hotel for group meetings. One of my clients found in 1998 that over a quarter of their group business was commissionable, up from negligible amount five years earlier. So even in resorts, with their mix of leisure and meeting business, distribution costs per occupied room doubled in the five-year period 1993–1998.*

Today, with agencies reeling under airline commission caps and many going out of business, with business travel agencies charging clients a fee for services, and with surviving independent agencies shifting focus to leisure and cruise suppliers—which so far have not capped commissions—traditional brick-and-mortar agencies are in chaos. It's time hotels reassess their sales efforts and their support of travel agencies. Who will be the first to reduce or cap the traditional 10 percent commission rate?

*Source: PKF Consulting's *Trends in the Hotel Industry*, 1994 and 1999. Resort distribution costs per occupied room: 1993, $852; 1998, $1634.

Yet more change is coming—from, of course, the Internet. Already, many airlines have opened up sites for direct bookings from consumers and businesses, and subtly—so as not to overly anger travel agents and invite vengeful boycotts—are offering reduced fares that in effect share the commission saving with consumers. In the spring of 2001, a consortium of airlines will launch an owned-and-operated site, Orbitz, that will sell directly to consumers, bypassing both travel agents, GDS systems, and the new on-line-only agencies like Expedia and Travelocity. In cruises, Carnival has followed suit with a direct-booking site (plus testing its own retail outlets in malls.) This is the "disintermediation" that gurus write about with respect to the Internet: taking the intermediary GDS provider and travel agent out of the connection between the traveler and his or her hotel/car renter/airline/cruise line. In response, nearly every week there is announcement of GDS and major switch companies investing in, launching, or acquiring on-line travel services.

Figure 7.10 shows how the new distribution channel may evolve and offer better value for both hotel and consumer. The travel agent will be increasingly squeezed, however, and will have to demonstrate the value of their fees for services to both consumer and hotel.

Many hotels are still using one type of intermediary—one or more electronic booking services—rather than letting the consumer directly access their automated inventory and reservation control data. This step saves some of the transaction costs. It will be only a matter of time, however, before hotels allow and encourage direct, no-commission access to their systems.

In short, our distribution channels are in chaos. But let's take heart from an ancient Far Eastern insight. The Chinese character for *chaos* is a combination of two other ideograms: *danger* and *opportunity*. Lower costs, easier access to information, and better values for the traveler will eventually result from this channel chaos. In the interim, hotel market-

FIGURE 7.10
Evolving Internet distribution channels

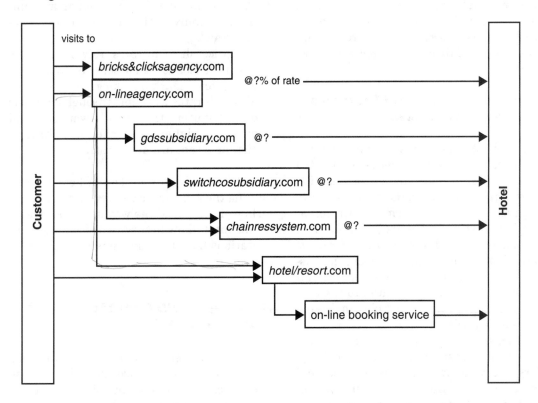

ers are challenged, and it's only going to get more challenging. (Imagine a future in which the prospective guest at your front desk is checking via their Palm Pilot what your competitor across the street is offering!) The danger is to those who cling to their habitual "tour and travel" sales and marketing efforts; they will be eclipsed by those who embrace the opportunity to promote the new channels and make it easier and less costly for consumers to buy. Another opportunity is for the independent hotel or resort, heretofore closed out of GDS systems, to get on-line visibility with their own Web site, links to related destination and services sites, and an on-line booking procedure, all at significantly lower costs.

For the foreseeable future, both the traditional and Internet-based distribution systems will coexist and will have to be managed. But this also raises a new question: what channels do you want to encourage, and what ones discourage? Conventional wisdom in recent years has been to make one's inventory and rates available in as many channels as possible so as to capture the last drop of demand for arrival on a given day from anywhere in the world. Given their sharply differing costs, however, and the difficulty of managing coordinated presence in these new and overlapping channels, the time may be coming for a new strategy. One possibility is to starve undesirable channels with limited information and access while being fully open and transparent to others. Another approach might be to price differentially among channels to reflect their different costs; a large Hawaiian resort group is already doing that, and explaining to consumers what comparative options and costs are. Whatever, the rising costs of commissions and intermediary and reservations system fees cannot be suffered much longer. The distribution chaos must be addressed proactively so that hotels are not simply at the whim of these technologically savvy intermediaries.

Reservation Systems and Personnel Become More Expensive

The second part of commission and reservation cost increases are expensive automated reservation systems, incentive compensation for reservation agents, and the personnel costs of a higher level of management in reservations. These cost increases are justifiable and desirable, for as yield management, forecasting, and channel management become increasingly complex, the reservations department/function (RD/F) is being elevated to the central and proactive role it must play in driving revenue into hotels.

So, how should hotels rein in commission and reservation costs? Before doing anything, understand your own commission, fee, and reservation costs. Do a careful analysis of where the costs are coming from and for what segments of business. Have your costs ballooned over the last five years? Are there any single sources that have grown inordinately? From how many channels are you getting business and in what mix?

There may be some cautious policy moves that can be taken without undue risk.

- Bid all group business on a net-price basis; the better agencies are moving toward fee-for-service business models.
- Offer lower prices to consumers visiting one's Web site either through e-mail reservations requests or booking services and warn Internet users that booking through an on-line agency that delivers immediate confirmation will entail somewhat higher costs. Give the consumer options and explanations.

More extreme steps for the bold to ponder:

- Cap commissions at some dollar amount, perhaps equivalent to 10 percent of a two-day stay.
- Net-price all room rates; rely on agencies to collect fees for their services from their clients or to mark up your rates.
- Make all rates available through channels of distribution that have lower fees, and only the higher rate schedules through channels that are most costly.

But be ready to take lots of heat for pioneering these moves. However, know that the airlines have paved the way and those travel agents most likely to survive as fee-for-service operations have already adjusted to this new era.

FRANCHISE AND CENTRAL MARKETING FEES

Franchise and central marketing fees are tied to revenues, so as rates rise, the dollar expense rises also. These often run 8.5 percent to 10 percent of sales or more, plus per-transaction program-participation costs. Typically, there is little opportunity to negotiate these fees down, though some programs whose costs are borne by the property on a transaction basis—for example, airline mile credits—can be opted out of. But the overriding question is whether you need that flag or not.

Chains Are Losing Leverage

Conventional wisdom has it that a flagged or chain-branded property will enjoy higher occupancy than its unbranded and independent competitor because of the chain's reservation system, brand awareness, central sales offices, frequent-stay programs, and so on. But that conventional wisdom is increasingly obsolete. Over the decade, chains have been losing their

TABLE 7.13
Chain occupancy advantage

	Chain Occupancy % minus Independent Occupancy %	
Price Category	*1994*	*1999*
Luxury	+3.3 OP*	+ 2.1 OP
Upscale	+5.5 OP	+4.7 OP
Midprice	+6.1 OP	(–0.6) OP
Economy	+7.4 OP	(–0.9) OP
Budget	+6.8 OP	– 0 – OP

*Occupancy percentage points.

demand leverage. For what reasons is unclear, but the data, shown in Table 7.13, are incontrovertible. These data come from Smith Travel Research (2000) and represent several thousand hotels in each category. The supposition that lenders have traditionally made—that a chain flag assures superior occupancy and higher profits—is questionable, at least as far as demand leverage and occupancy go.* The graph in Figure 7.11 shows the year-by-year patterns.

One can only speculate on the forces bringing about this leveling of occupancy performance: brands proliferating too fast for customer impression to keep up; independents being found on the Web, and being seen and found in GDS systems by virtue of using contract reservation suppliers; travelers becoming more price and deal conscious; weakening power of frequency award programs; whatever. We can only speculate at this point. But the meaning is clear: one cannot passively rely upon national brand recognition. You have to mind your own process and build your own recognition, whether flagged or not.

For a new property, or one that can cancel or escape from management agreement or franchise contract (by virtue of reorganization or sale, perhaps, or just renewal time), careful analysis of the costs and benefits of continuing are a must; offsetting this, of course, are the added self-marketing responsibilities and costs of replacing what might be of value in the chain relationship. Our point, here, is not to trash flags nor to encourage defections; rather, the point is not to assume a flag is necessary, and to analyze the independent option very thoughtfully.

For a property committed to a flag relationship, the issues are to analyze costs and returns of every "benefit" and program; to opt out of those that are discretionary (like some frequent-flyer mileage programs, sales events, or national ad overlay programs) and do not carry their weight; and to demand production increases from those in which participation is mandated.

For starters:

- Don't promote airline miles; those to whom they matter will ask for them, and giving away $15 per stay to those who already have more miles than they know what to do with is foolish.
- Avoid double-dipping if possible (one major

*Smith Travel Research's HOST Data Services reports show that the average chain still delivers a higher gross operating profit (GOP)percentage than the average independent in the same price category.

FIGURE 7.11
Chain occupancy advantage graph

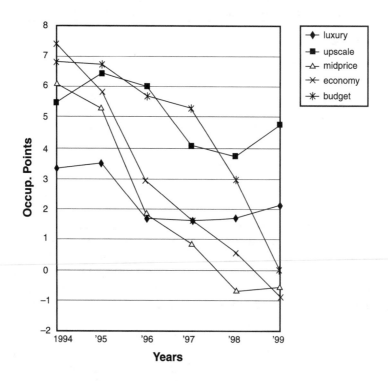

chain promotes double-dipping, i.e., giving both air miles and frequent-stay program credits.)

- Examine very critically sales events and trade show participation; if you are saddled with a flag and central sales process, use them. Be demanding of production, and wary of your sales team's eagerness to travel and participate in New York or Washington or other fun places. More often than not, the central sales staff doesn't want all the member property people cluttering up the booth anyway.

PROPERTY MARKETING COSTS

On-property marketing and sales expenses, formerly called advertising and business promotion, are a rich area for productivity in-

creases and often outright cost reductions. Over the years, these have held steady as a percentage of revenue, masking their rise in terms of dollars per available and per occupied room. What we are talking of is basically

- Communicating—that is, running ads or direct mail, producing collateral, or generating publicity.
- Promoting, to stimulate short-term sales increases.
- Selling.

These activities are unit based, not rate based. By that is meant that ads are run, mailing pieces sent, customers called on in units, irrespective of the price of the room being offered. There is no reason why such marketing costs should keep pace with ADR increases.

Let's examine these activities for where one might search for savings and increased productivity.

Communicating

Hotels typically rely on a mix of three kinds of communications: advertising, collateral, and publicity. Advertising—material produced by the advertiser and placed in purchased space or time slots controlled and distributed by a medium—is only getting more expensive per set of eyes or ears reached, whether in print, like newspaper or magazine or directories; in broadcast, like radio or TV; in billboards; in bus cards, airport posters, or whatever. Collateral is material one produces and distributes oneself, such as brochures, rack cards, in-room notices, and elevator posters. Collateral costs have actually decreased as digital design and printing has taken hold. Direct mail is a bit of a hybrid; you control the time and place, but may have to buy lists of recipients that may or may not precisely target the desired audience. Publicity is under control of another; one can only hope it carries the right message to the right audience at the right time.

Increasingly, hotels are leaving *advertising* to the chains for brand support and are migrating to collateral and direct mail. Why? Because advertising is a big-boys game; it is expensive, risky, difficult, and hard to measure. Moreover, mass media are becoming increasingly fragmented, and audiences for any one medium shrinking. Advertising works when an unbroken chain of links is successfully forged: it must be placed in front of the right audience . . . *and* at the time when that audience might be receptive . . . *and* be noticed, that is, break through the ho-hum barrier . . . *and* say something relevant to their interests or needs . . . *and* change their beliefs, or provide the promise, . . . that you can deliver upon. Reach (i.e., exposure to cover a significant percentage of the intended audience) and fre-

quency (i.e., repetition so as to set the idea and hit a responsive chord) make effective advertising expensive.

Advertising is an art and a profession; amateurs rarely get their money's worth. Directors of marketing (DOMs) who proudly show me advertising done on the cheap—copy written by the director of F&B or marketing, layouts pasted up by an art shop or by the local paper, commercials recorded by the local station—these DOMs are invariably bragging about money wasted. But to advertise via professionals is expensive and difficult. Moreover, hotels are unattractive clients to an ad agency. We require a lot of production effort, and there is little continuing media to place (which is where agencies earn their compensation), so a hotel is a high-cost, low-return client.

Thus, more and more, hotels are shifting away from media advertising to the more controllable and targeted *direct mail*, especially direct mail to prior guests and people identifiably like them. Direct mail offers several advantages over media advertising.

- It can be executed in very small, affordable scales. A set of Houston hotels traded guest lists for a cross-promotion for leisure weekenders. Each spent about $700 for a small, targeted mailing, and generated several thousand dollars' worth of demand. Ads cannot be scaled down in the same way.
- Audience waste is minimized. Guest histories and household-level mailing lists allow precisely tailored audiences that can only be approximated by other media.
- It can be tracked and measured more precisely than can general advertising.
- A campaign can be executed with shorter lead time than can all but newspaper advertising.

This is not to say that it is any less demanding in creating layout and copy. Creating direct mail requires as much skill and professionalism as does media advertising. Don't "save money" by doing it yourself. Your mail piece has to get through the junk mail defensive screen, trigger interest, and hit a responsive chord. But if you are talking to former guests or people whom you know are your kind of customers, you have a better chance of hitting their hot buttons.

Mailing lists are the key. Once, mailing lists were based upon where people lived. The idea was that birds of a feather flock together. But for hotel purposes, that isn't good enough. One neighboring household may vacation in summers; another may take golf vacations in February; across the street, the Jones go skiing during spring break; the Smiths down the block sail in the Virgin Islands. If we're selling a ski resort, or a charter boat service, or a sunny golf resort, it doesn't matter that these families have similar education, income, and professional patterns. We want to talk only to our prospect—our skier or our golfer or our sailor.

More and more, it is possible to profile one's guest histories and buy people whose interests, whose proven past behavior qualifies them as prospects. Develop your guest database from folio information so that you know who buys what. Purchase lists built of household preference and behavior patterns, not mere demographic segmentation. Such lists are more expensive by a multiple of five or more, but the response potential is even more enriched.

Publicity

Practitioners prefer the term *public relations*. Buy publicity, not public relations; buy a very targeted effort to provide a specific editor or broadcaster with material they can use to register an idea that reinforces your name or brand meaning and stimulates interest in your offer or promise. Seek publicity that stimulates action.

Publicity is hard to control. One can send out a release or announcement, but that is no guarantee that the message will run. But it's worth the effort and uncertainty, because third-party publicity that is on target, from a commentator or travel writer or restaurant reviewer, is much more powerful at changing peoples' beliefs than is either advertising or collateral or direct mail. By "on target" we don't mean mentions that the opera gala was held in your hotel, or pictures of a celebrity being greeted on arrival by a smiling GM. We mean a marketing message that reinforces the meaning of your name, the promise of what your hotel does, the enticement being offered. Publicity should be no less objective-oriented than any paid form of communications.

If a hotel successfully increases its publicity presence and third-party endorsements, and decreases its advertising thereby, it will have substantially cut its communications costs and increased communication effectiveness.

Positioning

We've said a lot about the marketing staff not writing copy or designing direct mail campaigns without professional help. What, then, is the role of the marketing department staff? It is to define the positioning the communication is to deliver. Positioning, as used here,* is not something you do to your product; rather, it is something you do in the mind of your prospect. It is getting them to hold an idea, a belief about you relative to your competitors, that will lead them to act in the way you want them to. The job of the marketing director is to give their communications support services a clearly defined positioning objective to which they then can apply their professional execution skills. A simple positioning-statement format works wonderfully well. It answers five questions:

1. Who are the prospects, in terms of what they value, find of interest, want, and need?
2. What do they now know or believe about our hotel (or restaurant or health club)?
3. What do we want them to come to believe . . .

---

*With thanks to Al Reis and Jack Trout, *Positioning: The Battle for Your Mind* (New York: McGraw-Hill, 1981).

4. . . . so that they will do what? (Communications should be aimed at actions, not just images or beliefs.)
5. What reasons can we offer for their adopting and holding this new belief?

A hypothetical example of a positioning statement is shown in the sidebar "Positioning Worksheet." When a client has carefully described and defined the positioning in this way, the odds of crafting an effective communications campaign are greatly increased. And it doesn't take much effort. Above all, don't delegate the positioning statement to your agency or copywriter. It is the client who must be accountable for setting objectives and guiding the creative and media support team; it is their responsibility to deliver the execution that in their professional opinion most productively will achieve the objectives. When they propose the creative execution, these same questions can be used as the test format to review and approve their recommendation.

POSITIONING WORKSHEET

(Assume for an upscale Hong Kong hotel)
Market Segment: Southeast Asian budget-conscious business travelers.
1. *Who is the prospect; how do we identify and reach them?*
   These are small-business operators and entrepreneurs, somewhat new to traveling to major trade centers, conscious of being seen as worldly but also concerned about expense. They are 35 to 44 years old, mainly males. They read their local business press and national airline magazines.
2. What do they now believe, if anything, about our hotel?
   That like most chains in the central business district, we cater to Japanese, European, and North American travelers and charge very high prices.
3. What must they come to believe so that they will act as we want them to?
   That the Shangri-La is the city's business center where influential people meet and do business, including entrepreneurs and leaders from home. It's good to be seen there, and it's worth it if you know how to get the deal and take advantage of its special services.
4. What do we want them to do?
   Try our hotel and learn that the benefits of staying here are worth a premium.

5. Support for holding this new belief:
   A. The "first-time-stayer" package, with its special price and guest services guide to doing business in the city.
   B. Our national enrollment clubs, which provide a 15 percent discount from the corporate rate and a quarterly newsletter about trade news between our country and each club chapter's nation.
   C. Voice mail to assure no language problems in messages; native language guest services and business center staffs.
   D. National breakfast-table seating for those who would like to meet fellow countrymen over breakfast.
   E. Breakfast specialties from all Southeast Asian nations.
   F. Home newspapers available for room delivery upon request.

The Basic Promise upon which the Hotel Must Deliver

That the businessperson will leave having been welcomed, valued, and given full value for the price paid.

The Internet

The Internet's World Wide Web of communications has brought a new, exciting, but also ambiguous dimension to creating awareness of a hotel or resort, stimulating demand for it, and channeling that demand to it. A Web site can be your ad and your catalog of services and facilities; it, in turn, can appear in a catalog or a directory of similar properties; it can be linked in a chain of partnerships and alliances with travel companies, media companies, suppliers, whatever; it also can be an advertising medium on which space may be bought. Little wonder that traditional hotel marketing and sales teams find it beguiling but bewildering. In Chapter 7.2, the first part of "Building Market Leadership," we briefly addressed the Internet as a channel of distribution in step four of the marketing process, *making the hotel available*. Now, we will devote a bit more time to the Internet, here in communications.

Leisure travelers, business travelers, and meeting arrangers are all turning to the Web, but each for somewhat different uses. Leisure travelers are using the Web extensively to study options and find e-mail or toll-free numbers to follow up with inquiries. B&B operators report that over 50 percent of their new customers are learning about them via the Web. In focus groups I have been doing, more than 70 percent of weekend getaway and planned vacation takers report turning to the Web for options.

Business travel arrangers are using the Web to check rates and availability, and to book. This is growing fast in the airline ticket and rental car portions of their trip logistics and can be expected to grow in hotels as confidence in the security and efficiency of the Internet grows. The Web gives independent hotels a chance to present their story alongside the branded chain properties, somewhat leveling the playing field with those who research destinations on the Internet. So an independent's Web presentation should highlight the nonchain distinctiveness, if possible.

Meeting planners gather information via the Web, but also are speeding communication, asking for proposals, even auctioning off their meeting via e-mail and meeting management Web sites.

The point is, your Web site must be driven by and suited to your selection of target market segments and the wants, needs, and motives of each. Don't do it on the cheap with some computer-literate employee that is at hand; don't let some "artsy-techie" Web designer develop an "award-winning" state-of-the-art site. Your design must be functional in the *audience's* terms: simple to find, simple to use, and quick to get to, into, and out of.

- Use a designer who thinks about the consumer's use rather than about wowing the consumer.
- Use one who can both design the site and advise on and manage the process of making it visible and accessible, that is, of marketing the site itself, so that the right consumer prospects will find it.
- Brief the designer thoroughly on your market segments and what might impel them to search for and open your site.
- As you assess the proposed design and its utility, apply the positioning discipline to every part of the site.

Having a Web site is, of course, not enough. You must manage to make it visible and accessible. Maintaining high-visibility ranking in search engines is a constant struggle and takes continual auditing and knowledgeable management; good design houses can provide that at modest annual cost. Banner ads are highly suspect; no one yet knows what impact and recall they generate. Best are links to other sites and subjects that your prospects are likely to visit. Alliances and partnerships are the best way to improve the odds that consumers will find their way to your site.

Integration and Coherency

One last—and I think—obvious point on communications: all communications to the same market segment should be coherent and consistent in terms of what the name or brand means and what underlying promise is being made to that segment. Ads, direct mail, collateral, the Web site, signs, and in-house displays and posters should be sending the same message so that the cumulative effect is an image, a belief about your hotel relative to your competitors. Nothing so weakens a positioning as does projecting inconsistent images, feelings, and promises in your communications.

Promoting

The term *promotion* is often used in a general sense, but here we are talking narrowly about making an offer specific in time and place to entice a customer to buy in a way they would not otherwise:

- To buy more than normal.
- To buy sooner than they normally would.
- To buy something they normally would not.

Hotels often turn to promotions when business is soft, and usually think in terms of reducing price. But price promotion is dangerous; all too often, the hotel is merely lowering price to customers they would have gotten anyway. And any damn fool can cut price, and competitors will match the offer right away. The challenge is to limit the offer to prospects you would not have gotten, to generate *incremental customers or purchases*, while maintaining rate and contribution margins on your base business, and keeping your competitors in the dark.

One way to do this is to limit distribution of the offer to populations rich in non-customers. Cooperative promotions between travel partners, for example, a rental car company or airline, offer such opportunities. A new airport hotel we opened made a special introductory offer through a rental car partner's list of frequent renters from that airport, an offer not made in general media and, hence, of which our competitors were unaware. The coupon was good for a specific time period and offered the partner's frequency-program credit as well as a "trial" price. That hotel leaped out of the blocks, exceeding pro forma handily the first six months after opening.

Restaurant promotions can be made to work to generate extra covers. Offer a free meal for a party of four to your regular luncheon two-top customers; next time in, a number will come with four instead of a partner.

Breakeven

All promotions and advertising campaigns must be held up to a breakeven test. This means that given the cost of what you intend to do—run an ad, offer a special deal, mail a brochure—it must generate enough responses to contribute margins at least sufficient to pay back your expenses, or it isn't worth doing. The *reasonable-person breakeven test* is the simplest management tool to apply to proposals for creating awareness and, especially, for stimulating demand through a promotion. *It should always be applied before authorizing expenditures on a marketing campaign.*

An Example

Say your director of marketing proposes to mail a piece promoting a special Valentine's Day package. The art costs $200 and the folded self-mailer can be produced and mailed to your local mailing list for $0.38 each. A list of 1500 names is in hand, from guest histories and prior mail work. You offer standard weekend February rates, $95, but throw in another $14 worth of breakfast buffet and an $8 bottle of champagne. Your variable cost per occupied room is $13. How many incremental room-nights do you need to break even? Would a reasonable person think that such a mail offer would produce that given the historic level of business? Last Valentine's Day, your reservations manager tells you, your 180-room hotel had occupancy of 64 percent, but that was a Thursday; this year, Valentine's Day falls on Friday. Last year, occupancy on the Friday after Valentine's Day was 38 percent.

The analysis:

Costs of Promotion

Art	$200
Mailing	$570
Total costs	$770

- Standard room margin = $95 − $13 variable cost per occupied room = $82.
- Less champagne and breakfast @ $22 = $60.
- Incremental room-nights needed to break even = $770/$60 = 12.8 or 13 room-nights.

The reasonable-person test:
- 13 room-nights is what percent increase over the 38 percent occupancy we might expect anyway?

13/(180 rooms × 0.38 occupancy) = 19%

- Is it likely that a mailing offer could boost volume by nearly one-fifth? Perhaps so.
- Is it likely that 13 people would respond out of 1500 mailed the offer, or less than 1 percent? Very likely so.

But the F&B director objects to giving away champagne and a buffet. "People will be looking for a Valentine's Day deal. Why not just reduce our rate to $75 to be sure we capture them? We'll get the breakfast revenues, have good occupancy, and sell some champagne anyway." And, he persuades the GM, "we'll save all that cost of mailing and giveaways. Our rooms profit is 86 percent; that leaves plenty of room for a hot deal."

The analysis:
Lost margins on reduced room rate:

- Standard room margins = $95 − $13 variable cost per occupied room = $82 (or 86 percent of $95).
- New margin = $75 − $13 = $62 (or 83 percent of $75).
- Lost margins = base volume × margin reduction.

- Base volume = 180 rooms × 38 percent expected occupancy if we do nothing = 68 room-nights × $20 = $1360.

The reasonable-person test:
- Incremental room-nights needed to break even = $1360/$62 = 22 room-nights.
- Is it reasonable to think a $75 room rate with no advertising would generate a 32 percent jump in volume? Possible, but not likely.

So, the "cost-saving" proposal is really the more expensive. It gives away more money and requires half again as many extra room-nights to break even, with no advertising support. Which approach should the reasonable GM take?

This example embodies several ideas.

1. Contribution margins are dollars, not percent; it's amazing how often managers act as if the rooms profit percentage applies no matter what the price discount.
2. Costs include opportunity lost, that is, the price reduction you are giving to customers you would have gotten anyway.
3. The reasonable-person breakeven test can illuminate issues in proposals and bring differing viewpoints into useful discussions of probabilities. It doesn't prove one approach is wiser than another, but it gives managers a chance to make rational judgments about what path to follow, or when to search for a more attractive alternative.
4. Above all, don't run breakevens on revenues; use margins contributed by an extra unit of volume—a room-night or cover or health club membership or whatever.

Selling

The major marketing expenditure in most hotels is for direct sales personnel. Traditionally, this is what hotels have relied upon for their "marketing" efforts. It is up through the sales ranks that most directors of sales and marketing have been developed. Sales calls are the most powerful tool for creating awareness and stimulating demand—but also the most expensive. Salespeople are aimed, therefore, not a sources of one or two room-nights but at corporate travel arrangers, tour operators, and meeting planners—sources of perhaps scores, even hundreds of room-nights. For the most part, U.S. full-service hotels understand sales, and many provide good training and support systems. For limited-service hotels with limited group business, however, a sales force is often regarded as unaffordable; their challenge is how they, too, can avail themselves of salesmanship wisely and productively. Rather than focus here on selling skills, we will explore how to increase sales productivity and use salespeople effectively.

The definition and goal of marketing—creating and sustaining productive relationships with desirable customers better than do your competitors—is perfectly applicable to group sales. The keys to success are *productive* relationships and *desirable* customers. Targeting salespeople is the job of the director of sales and is key to sales productivity.

A former client of mine, operator of a 295-room resort, convinced himself that he should keep adding salespeople to his staff. So long as a salesperson booked sufficient meetings business to generate department contribution margins, after variable costs, in excess of the salesperson's salary, benefits, and expenses, he reasoned, the resort was ahead. Over time, as the sales staff ballooned to seven people, group business soared to over three-quarters of the hotel's volume. When new competitors opened and the economy softened, rate cutting became epidemic. The resort not only lost groups, but having abandoned its former individual guests, could not replace the group business with vacationers and did not know how to win them back; both occupancy and revenues slumped. This was a case of not balancing marketing tools to the market segments one set out to target.

Many full-service hotels and resorts have too large a sales force and allocate too much of their marketing resources to sales. How does one establish the size of a sales force? You have to think about units of work—customer calls, files, contracts.

Go back to step one of the marketing process, *deciding what to be and what to offer to whom*. Look at the average size of the groups your hotel handles. Calculate from the room-night target for the meetings and tour operators the number of contracts needed to deliver that volume of business. For example, if your meetings goal is 25,000 room-nights, and your typical group books around 60 room-nights, you need to confirm some 416 contracts for each foreseeable year, call it 450 to be safe. How many can a salesperson close in 50 weeks? Three a week? You need three salespeople. Four a week? Two. There is no rule of thumb; what is feasible production is a function of how well known your hotel is, how many competitors you face for those groups, how much repeat business comes to you—in other words, a function of your competitive situation. But invariably, this simple exercise challenges the GM and the director of marketing or sales because they always presuppose and are comfortable with a larger staff. So then the question arises: what can we do to increase each salesperson's rate of close?

This is classic process improvement. Think of what a group salesperson does: prospects among known and past clients; makes cold calls; responds to inquiries; staffs exhibits and attends industry conferences; follows up on leads; hosts planners on inspection visits; submits proposals; negotiates dates, spaces, and rates; suggests meeting events and banquets; submits and closes contracts; updates client files; turns meeting over to conference service or banqueting management; briefs staff on upcoming meeting and arrivals; greets planner when meeting begins; checks folio when meeting is over; thanks planner for their business; suggests or tries to book next meeting. But how much of this should the *salesperson* do? What so often impedes output and reduces productivity is valuable sales talent doing things that other, less-expensive help can do. Let's review the list:

- *Prospects among known and past clients*: No, use less-expensive teleprospecting clerical workers.
- *Makes cold calls*: No! Engage a lead-generation service that does customized list calling; put them on retainer plus flat fee per accepted, qualified lead.
- *Responds to inquiries*: Screen with administrative assistant; follow up with salesperson for live prospect.
- *Staffs exhibits and attends industry conferences*: Only when key, target market segment planners and arrangers are in attendance. Minimize "looks good on résumé" shows and "fun to travel" trips. For all but big convention hotels and national conference resorts, group leads are generated in your home market.
- *Follows up on leads*: When the lead is qualified, yes.
- *Hosts planners on inspection visits*: In concert with conference services person to show the planners with whom they might work if they book. The salesperson should spend only as much time as needed to move planner to proposal and negotiation stages.
- *Submits proposals*: Yes.
- *Negotiates dates, spaces, and rates*: Yes.
- *Suggests meeting events and banquets*: Yes.
- *Submits and closes contracts*: Yes.
- *Updates client files*: No, leave to administrative or clerical personnel.
- *Turns meeting over to conference service or banqueting management*: As soon as possible after closing.
- *Briefs staff on upcoming meeting and arrivals*: No, conference services should do this.
- *Greets planner when meeting begins*: Yes.
- *Checks folio when meeting is over*: No. (Accounting should do this.)

- *Thanks planner for their business and assesses satisfaction*: Through or in concert with conference services.
- *Suggests or tries to book next meeting*: No, conference services either rebooks or develops lead, which is turned over to salesperson for contact when planner indicates.

In other words, using sales talent for administrative routines is to be avoided. Get a support system in place and let salespeople sell. And give them the tools: a computer with e-mail; ACT or some other customer management software; and word processing set up with standard forms and letters easily customized.

The second key to salesperson productivity is focus on important customers and prospects. Each year ask salespeople to rate their customers. This need not be an intensely researched project; just make intuitive judgments. Rate them on two 10-point scales: How much value does a customer represent, and how wedded to your hotel are they? Next, array the customers on a grid of importance and loyalty, as shown in Figure 7.12. Then toss out the files in the lower left quadrant. This frees the salesperson to focus on the family jewels in the upper right *and* to mount customer-development campaigns for one or two of those in the lower right. These "developables" are your future growth, your future family jewels.

Compensation of salespeople need not be complicated. First principle: tie compensation to goals set in terms of what you want them to do. Second: provide them near-term reward and reinforcement; not postponed rewards. Third: build teamwork so that one salesperson supports and encourages another. Fourth: separate performance bonus from overall job appraisal.

Let's talk about group salespeople. You want them to book groups. You may have need for future bookings, beyond the end of the calendar year. First principle: set goals in terms of

FIGURE 7.12
Focus of sales staff

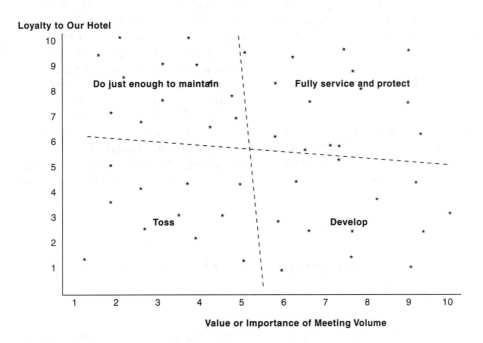

booked room-nights, not realized annual revenues. Current group revenues may have been determined long ago, even by other salespeople no longer on staff; keep the reward tied to one's own, recent performance. Second principle: set quarterly booking goals and pay bonuses quarterly rather than delaying reward to year-end. Third principle: reward individual booking performance but add a kicker or multiplier if the whole sales force makes its total goal. (Don't pay on commission; that is poison for teamwork.)

Setting a booking goal is not simple, but is necessary to an incentive system that is viewed as fair and equitable. One starts with the monthly room-night volume desired from group segments, then works back to how much lead time is typical for that segment (e.g., small corporate groups 30 to 45 days; conventions, 18 to 30 months; etc.) and how much shrinkage one expects (corporate groups, 5 percent;

associations, 15–20 percent; social and reunion groups, even more.) Next, ask the sales teams to set their booking goals by segment by quarter, and assign to each salesperson his or her share based on segment and customers assigned. Having salespeople participate in their own goal setting increases morale, appreciation, and motivation (and decreases bitching about unrealistic and unfair goals later on.)

We have been talking in terms of group sales forces. But don't forget that salesmanship should be applied throughout the hotel. Reservation agents should be salespeople, not order takers and information givers. Train them in selling skills, set average rate goals, run monthly contests, and give them bonus programs, too. Front desk clerical staff should have upselling goals; every customer moved into a higher-rated room than reserved and confirmed earns a cash payout—daily or weekly, if possible. Wait staff should be given courses in suggestive selling, and a regular series of short-term selling campaigns—for desserts, wines, whatever—with bonuses to reinforce good salesmanship skills. Every guest-contact person is a potential salesperson!

MARKETING PRODUCTIVITY MEASURES

As should by now be evident, the costs of acquiring customers should be tracked and measured in dollar terms, not just as percentages of sales in various parts of the profit-and-loss operating statement. A hotel controller might well gather the different parts of the acquisition expense, from rooms, administration and general (A&G) expenses, marketing, and so on, and present it monthly as a goad to looking critically at how we generate unit sales. This would stimulate review and reflection, for the biggest source of cost creep is our habit of repeating what we did last year, in spite of the turmoil of new competitors, new market sources, new channels of distribution. Bringing a productivity discipline to an effective marketing process assures a hotel team of both market leadership and financial health.

7.13   Mini Case: Revamping the Marketing Research Department

You're the new director of marketing research for the Mississippi Region Affiliated Resorts (MRAS), located along the length of the Mississippi River from Minneapolis to Memphis. This "branded distribution company" of 38 independently owned and operated hotels has become a major player in its regional competitive marketplace. As part of the company's strategic plan, however, it has been determined that the structure of the market is changing, and the general future direction of the hotels will be toward more sales and service to the conventions and meetings market that has become increasingly important because of the central location of the chain.

To become more competitive in this burgeoning market, the company has undertaken and encouraged an ambitious remodeling program among its members that has upgraded the furnishings, fixtures, and equipment of the hotels. The hotels are also committing to a minimum of the following capital investments:

- 60,000-square-foot ballroom.

- 30,000 square feet of meeting and breakout rooms.
- 15,000-square-foot registration and prefunction areas.

With these upgraded facilities, the company feels it can compete effectively for the lucrative conventions and meetings market with the "hard-flagged" chains.

This strategy and capital investment requires a consequential change in research paradigms. As the director of marketing research, you've been requested by the company president to propose a completely revamped research department that will reflect this new strategy and be designed to help the independent member hotels market their new facilities most effectively.

Propose a model marketing research department for your firm that will produce the sorts of data that other hotels in the chain can use to help them compete with the national chains. Include in your proposal what new sorts of data would be most useful, where those may be found, and how they might be specifically useful to reflect the new mission.

References

Albrecht, Karl, and Ron Zemke. 1985. *Service America! Doing Business in the New Economy.* Homewood, IL: Dow Jones-Irwin.

Alderson, Jeremy W. 1986. "When Does a Gift Become a Bribe?" *Meetings and Conventions* February:30–36.

Astroff, Milton T., and James R. Abbey. 1988. *Convention Sales and Service,* 2d ed. Cranbury, NJ: Waterbury Press, p. 125.

Blair, Adam. 1988. "Hotels' Revolving Door Sabotages Planners' Best Efforts." *Meeting News* September:1.

Bloom, Heidi. 1981. "Marketing to Meeting Planners: What Works." *Cornell Hotel and Restaurant Administration Quarterly* 22(2):45–50.

Bosker, Julie. 1988. "Meet with Convention Services Managers Up Front to Avoid Meeting Mishaps." *Meeting News* April.

Cronbach, L. J. 1951. "Coefficient Alpha and the Internal Structure of Tests." *Psychometrika* 16:297–334.

Cross, Robert G. 1997. "Launching the Revenue Rocket: How Revenue Management Can Work for Your Business." *Cornell Hotel and Restaurant Administration Quarterly* April: 38(2):32–43.

Czepiel, John A., Michael R. Solomon, and Carol F. Surprenant (eds.). 1985. *The Service Encounter: Managing Employee/Customer Interaction in Service Businesses.* Lexington, MA: Lexington Books.

Drucker, Peter F. 1954. *The Practice of Management.* New York: Harper and Row.

Finkel, Coleman. 1980. "The Total Immersion Meeting Environment." *Training and Development Journal* September:32–39.

Fishbein, Martin, and Icek Ajzen. 1975. *Belief, Attitude, Intention, and Behavior: An Introduction to Theory and Research.* Reading, MA: Addison-Wesley.

Flanagan, John C. 1954. "The Critical Incident Technique." *Psychological Journal* 51(4):327–357.

Ghitelman, David. 1989. "Conventions Services Managers Get Respect." *Meetings and Conventions* May:109–117.

Groome, James J. 1992. "Today's Convention-Services Managers: What Their Job Is and What It Isn't." *Meeting Manager* June:75–80.

Heskett, James L. 1990. "Rethinking Strategy for Service Management." In *Service Management Effectiveness,* D. E. Bowen, R. B. Chase, T. G. Cummings and Associates, San Francisco, CA: Jossey-Bass Publishers.

Hosansky, Mel. 1982. "The $27.8 Billion Meetings Industry." *Meetings and Conventions* December:28.

Hosansky, Mel, et al. 1986. "The Evolution of an Industry." *Meetings and Conventions* June:55.

Hoyle, Leonard H., David C. Dorf, and Thomas J. A. Jones. 1989. *Managing Conventions and Group Business.* East Lansing, MI: Educational Institute of the American Hotel and Motel Association, p. 154.

Hughes, Holly. 1984. "Maximizing the Meeting Environment." *Successful Meetings* September:31–34, 38.

Lewis, R. C. 1990. "Are You Listening to Customers—Or to Competitors?" *Hotel & Motel Management* November 2:55.

Lewis, R. C., R. E. Chambers, and H. E. Chacko. 1995. *Marketing Leadership in Hospitality: Foundations and Practices,* 2d ed. New York: Van Nostrand Reinhold, p. 3.

Lowe, James E. 1984. "A Study of the Meeting Planner Market." Master of Professional Studies thesis, Cornell University.

Migdal, Dave. 1993. "Convention Service Managers: An Embattled Profession." *Meetings and Conventions* September:1, 37.

Meek, Howard B. 1938. *A Theory of Hotel Room Rates.* Ithaca, NY: Cornell University, p. 2.

Myers, Elissa Matulis. 1989. "Making Meetings Happen." *Association Management* September:77.

Nebel, Eddystone, III, Denney Rutherford, and Jeffrey Schaffer. 1994. "Reengineering the Hotel Organization." *Cornell Hotel and Restaurant Administration Quarterly* October: 25(5):88–95.

McNulty, Mary Ann. 1992. "Glory Days Are Gone for Convention Service Managers and Meetings Suffer." *Meeting News* November: 16(11):1.

Nichols, Barbara (ed.). 1989. *Professional Meeting Management*. 2d ed. Birmingham, AL: Professional Convention Management Association, p. 132.

Nichols, Barbara. 1986. "President's Message." *Convene* 1(3):4.

Olsen, Michael D., and Daniel J. Connolly. 2000. "Experience-Based Travel: How Technology Is Changing the Hospitality Industry." *Cornell Hotel and Restaurant Administration Quarterly* 41(1):30–40.

Renaghan, Leo M., and Michael Z. Kay. 1987. "What Meeting Planners Want: The Conjoint Analysis Approach." *Cornell Hotel and Restaurant Administration Quarterly* 28(2):67–76.

Riegel, Carl D. 1983. "Career Choice, Work Values, and Career Commitment of Food Service and Housing Administration Students at the Pennsylvania State University: A Social Learning Perspective." Ph.D. dissertation, Pennsylvania State University.

Rutherford, Denney G., and W. T. Umbreit. 1993. "Improving Interactions between Meeting Planners and Hotel Employees." *Cornell Hotel and Restaurant Administration Quarterly* February: 34(1):71, 75, 77.

Shaffer, Jeff. 1986. "Structure and Strategy: Two Sides of Success." *Cornell Hotel and Restaurant Administration Quarterly* 26(4):76–81.

Smith Travel Research. 2000. *Smith Travel Research Standard Historical TREND Reports*, 1994 to 2000. (September).

Stavro, Lisa, and Thomas J. Beggs. 1986. "Buyer Behavior and the Meeting Planner: An Exploratory Study." In *The Practice of Hospitality Management II,* Robert C. Lewis et al. (eds.). Westport, CT: AVI Publishing Company.

Tritsch, Catherine. 1988. "Thumbs Up, Thumbs Down: Planners Rate Suppliers." *Successful Meetings* 37(1):24–27.

Withiam, Glenn. 1999. "The Internet 1: Is Anyone Making Any Money Here?" *Cornell Hotel and Restaurant Administration Quarterly* December: 40(6):12.

Wright, Rudy. 1982. "Adjusting Acoustics to the Meeting." *Meetings and Conventions* July.

Zeithaml, Valarie A., A. Parasuraman, and Leonard L. Berry. 1990. *Delivering Quality Service*. New York: The Free Press.

Suggested Readings

Books

Astroff, Milton T., and James R. Abbey. 1998. *Convention Sales and Service,* 5th ed. Cranbury, NJ: Waterbury Press.

Ismail, Ahmed. 1999. *Catering Sales and Convention Services*. Albany, NY: Delmar Publishers.

Ismail, Ahmed. 1999. *Hotel Sales and Operations*. Albany, NY: Delmar Publishers.

Kotler, Philip, John T. Bowen, and James C. Makens. 1996. *Marketing for Hospitality and Tourism*. Upper Saddle River, NJ: Prentice Hall, Inc.

Kudrle, Albert E., and Melvin Sandler. 1995. *Public Relations for Hospitality Managers: Communicating for Greater Profits*. New York: John Wiley and Sons, Inc.

Lewis, Robert C. 1989. *Cases in Hospitality Marketing and Management*. New York: John Wiley and Sons.

Lovelock, Christopher. 2001. *Services Marketing: People, Technology, Strategy,* 4th ed. Upper Saddle River, NJ: Prentice Hall, Inc.

Lovelock, Christopher, and Lauren Wright. 1999. *Principles of Service Marketing and Management*. Upper Saddle River, NJ: Prentice Hall, Inc.

Shaw, Margaret, and Susan V. Morris. 2000. *Hospitality Sales: A Marketing Approach*. New York: John Wiley and Sons, Inc.

Articles

Cunningham, Mark W., and Chekitan S. Dev. 1992. "Strategic Marketing: A Lodging 'End Run.'" *Cornell Hotel and Restaurant Administration Quarterly* 33(4):36–43.

Jarvis, Lance P., and Edward J. Mayo. 1986. "Winning the Market-Share Game." *Cornell Hotel and Restaurant Administration Quarterly* 27(3):73–79.

Levitt, Theodore. 1981. "Marketing Intangible Products and Product Intangibles." *Cornell Hotel and Restaurant Administration Quarterly* August:37–44.

Lieberman, Warren H. 1993. "Debunking the Myths of Yield Management." *Cornell Hotel and Restaurant Administration Quarterly* 34(1):34–41.

McCleary, Ken. 1993. "Marketing Management." In *VNR's Encyclopedia of Hospitality and Tourism,* Mahmood Kahn, Michael Olsen, and Turgut Var (eds.), New York: Van Nostrand Reinhold.

Morgan, Michael S. 1991. "Travelers' Choice: The Effects of Advertising and Prior Stay." *Cornell Hotel and Restaurant Administration Quarterly* 32(4):41–49.

Nordling, Christopher W., and Sharon K. Wheeler. 1992. "Building a Market-Segment Model to Improve Profits." *Cornell Hotel and Restaurant Administration Quarterly* 33(3):29–36.

Source Notes

Chapter 7.2, "Building Market Leadership: Marketing as Process," by Fletch Waller.

Chapter 7.3, "Marketing Challenges for the Next Decade," by Chekitan S. Dev and Michael D. Olsen, is reprinted from the February 2000 issue of *The Cornell Hotel and Restaurant Administration Quarterly.* © Cornell University. Used by permission. All rights reserved.

Chapter 7.4, "Hotel Choice Decision Rules," by Eric R. Spangenberg and Bianca Grohmann.

Chapter 7.5, "Hotel Pricing," by Margaret Shaw.

Chapter 7.6, "Wishful Thinking and Rocket Science," by Eric B. Orkin, is reprinted from the August 1998 issue of *The Cornell Hotel and Restaurant Administration Quarterly.* © Cornell University. Used by permission. All rights reserved.

Chapter 7.7, "A Day in the Life of a Regional Revenue Manager," by Paul Chappelle.

Chapter 7.8, "Hotel Sales Organization and Operations," by Margaret Shaw and Susan V. Morris, adapted from *Hospitality Sales: A Marketing Approach*, by Margaret Shaw and Susan V. Morris, Copyright © 2000 by John Wiley and Sons, Inc. Reprinted by permission of John Wiley and Sons, Inc.

Chapter 7.9, "Improving Interactions between Meeting Planners and Hotel Employees," by Denney G. Rutherford and W. Terry Umbreit.

Chapter 7.10, "A Profile of Convention-Services Professionals," by Rhonda J. Montgomery and Denney G. Rutherford, is reprinted from the December 1994 issue of *The Cornell Hotel and Restaurant Administration Quarterly.* © Cornell University. Used by permission. All rights reserved.

Chapter 7.11, "Putting the Public in Public Relations: The Case of the Seattle Sheraton Hotel and Towers," by Louis B. Richmond.

Chapter 7.12, "Building Market Leadership: Improving Productivity of the Marketing Process," by Fletch Waller.

8

Financial Control and Information Management

8.1   Introduction

A new configuration for this edition of this textbook is the following section on financial control and information management. At the suggestion of reviewers and textbook users articles have been chosen to illustrate the relationships among and between the various activities that contribute to the hotel's profitability and operational success through various procedures and policies and different departmental activities designed to discharge the managerial responsibility for operational control.

As a department, financial management in a hotel is far more important to the success in management of that hotel than the few readings included here would suggest. In most major hotel firms the chief financial officer/executive, or controller, as this manager is more often called, ranks among the top two or three decision makers in the hotel's hierarchy. The importance of this job can be established by the observation that many traditional hotel departments have been re-organized so that major portions of their functions are now responsible to the controller's office. The prime example of this is in the front office, where in the past the front office manager supervised the activities of the night audit staff, cashiers, and other front desk clerks. Increasingly, hotel firms are transferring the responsibility for night audits and cashiers to the accounting office, with the ultimate responsibility for these information gathering and controlling functions resting with the hotel controller.

It should also be noted that an increasingly important department in hotels is the one responsible for the swiftly changing world of information management, or information technology (IT). In many instances IT is now also the responsibility of the hotel controller. This recognizes the training and the ability of hotel controllers to provide for the structured accumulation, storage, and reporting of data in forms that are most useful to the operating departments and other executives of the hotel.

In his lead article on the hotel chief financial executive, longtime contributor to this series of books Professor Ray Schmidgall, Hilton Professor with the School of Hospitality Business at Michigan State University, reviews the updated research on the hotel controller and compares these over time. Through this review, it is possible to get a good view of the job and responsibilities of this key hotel executive. Schmidgall finds some interesting differences in the groups studied over a period of years and provides a wider window for viewing the hotel controller as a career path in management of a modern hotel operation. In the past students had been merely instructed in the process of accounting and auditing and for the most part have been unaware of the sort of career that can result from a flair for both management, leadership, and "number crunching."

In Schmidgall's companion piece with Agnes DeFranco, the critical practices of budgeting and forecasting are examined. While this is only a sampler of the critical duties of the hotel's financial function and its leadership, in today's business environment, the accuracy of forecasting and budgeting may indeed be the difference between profit and loss.

If the Schmidgall and DeFranco pieces represent the academic side of examination of the hotel's financial leadership, Mike Draeger is the chief financial executive who lives the theory on a daily basis. After a significant career component with Four Seasons Hotels and Resorts, Draeger now serves as hotel controller at the Cal-Neva Lodge and Casino, which straddles the California-Nevada border at Lake Tahoe. An interesting assignment; half of the hotel has to be managed under California law, and half (the casino half) under Nevada law. Join Mike for a look at the chief financial executive's job in his "As I See It" essay.

No discussion of financial and operational control in a hotel would be complete without some attention paid to the extremely important function of purchasing.

In the past when the bulk of a hotel's purchasing revolved around food and beverage items, the executive chef, chief steward, and other department managers usually developed their own sources for goods and services and needed to effectively and efficiently run their department. In the modern context, however, with the vast and diversified needs of various hotel operating and staff departments, this practice is no longer advisable. Neither is it a very good idea from a control standpoint. Most hotel companies have adopted a policy of establishing a professional purchasing function. If this is not a whole department, it is at least one highly experienced individual.

In his essay on hotel purchasing as a control function and profit generator, updated for this edition, Carl Riegel argues a strong case for the proposition that effective attention to proper purchasing can contribute more and more easily to the bottom line than the generation of additional sales.

The purchasing director or manager will typically be a person who knows a great deal about departmental operations in every phase of the hotel. He or she will be able to discuss and analyze intelligently the needs of various department managers. This individual will also be one who is expert in the markets where hotels purchase goods and products essential to accomplishing their department's and hotel's missions. The purchasing director will be familiar with variety, quality standards, style, and methods of packaging. Such arcane technical details as chemical composition, fabric and furnishing lifetimes, and other details too numerous to mention here will also be the responsibility of the purchasing manager.

Lee Evans, who previously has held corporate executive positions in purchasing with Station Casinos, Westin Hotels and Resorts, and at the hotel level, has provided the reader with real-world insights into the duties, responsibilities, and interactions of the hotel purchasing director. His essay provides rich detail and examples as to how a hotel's purchasing director fulfills the conceptual context outlined by Riegel. Evans is currently vice president of Level Source, Inc., a new company that provides aggregate purchasing services for independent and small chain hotel operators.

Few people in this day and age would disagree that the management of data and information in all its forms is critical to business success. As recently as the year the last edition of the book was published—1995—the Internet and World Wide Web were still pretty much off the "radar screens" of most businesses. Well . . . Now it would seem that the pace of technology and the means and necessity to manage huge volumes of information are as common as any other aspect of business in the twenty-first century.

That's why I am a little hesitant to include too many readings here about IT and information management; it will be old news in a couple of years. The article by Judy Siguaw and Cathy Enz, from the previously mentioned national study on hotel "best practices" can be seen as "framing" what the best thinkers in the business are doing currently. Because these operators are doing the "best," they can be considered as representing the structure of where this exciting aspect of lodging leadership is headed.

The success of any hotel firm in the modern era will depend on how well they manage, control, and utilize the information that is available to them. This is true not only for their current operations, but as managers develop other, newer—unheard-of now—sources of information in the lodging business environment, it has to be managed like any other asset or product component. That is why the article by Robert Griffin is included here. Data warehousing, in his words, represents a "central information storehouse designed to answer business questions." This usually involves a companywide database system designed to provide information to all corporate components. In a way, information has become a commodity, and data warehouses are designed to most efficiently manage this new commodity.

Because this area is so volatile and developments in IT are happening so swiftly, it is probably best for the student to develop broad, general outlines of what is possible than, in the context of this textbook, to focus specifically on the details of current technology. As we've seen, progress in even our desktop computers has been so rapid that any current writing will probably be outdated by the time this book reaches print.

The articles included in this section are designed to help the reader gain knowledge about and appreciation for the range and realm of activities, largely behind the scenes, that contribute to the financial and operational health of the hotel. These are activities that are often overlooked by those of us who focus our attention on the more public aspects of hotel management but are, nonetheless, critical to any hotel's success.

8.2   The Lodging Chief Financial Executive

Raymond S. Schmidgall

Chief financial executives of lodging operations have been given various titles including controller, chief accounting officer, vice president of accounting, chief financial officer, etc. The most common title, at the property level, is controller. Who are these people? What are their skills? What responsibilities do they have? Answers to these questions and many others are provided in this chapter.

The lodging financial executive historically was viewed as a mere bookkeeper, that is, the preparer of financial statements. Research shows that the lodging controller has evolved into a full-fledged member of the management team of a lodging property.

Considerable research has been conducted over the past 20 years of the membership of the Hospitality Financial and Technology Professionals (HFTP), formerly known as the International Association of Hospitality Accountants. The results of this research is the major basis for this chapter. The HFTP was founded in 1953 for the purpose of advancing the accounting profession. Its chief publication, *The Bottomline*, is published eight times annually (bimonthly and two special editions). The HFTP currently has over 4300 members in over 50 countries. The HFTP in 1981 established the Certified Hospitality Accountant Executive (CHAE). Since that time more than 840 hospitality accountants have earned their CHAE. In 1994, the HFTP established the Certified Hospitality Technology Professional (CHTP), and in the past six years over 100 technology professionals have earned their CHTP. These two certifications bring immediate recognition to these professionals in the hospitality industry.

PAST RESEARCH

Over the past 20 years several studies have been made of HFTP members. One of the first studies was conducted by Geller and Schmidgall in 1984. They surveyed 1000 HFTP members, and 311 lodging financial executives completed questionnaires covering education, skills, authority, responsibilities, salaries, and involvement with committees of their properties.

This study was replicated in 1990 by Geller, Ilvento, and Schmidgall. This questionnaire was mailed to 750 members of the HFTP associated with the lodging industry.

DeVeau and DeVeau surveyed the 291 CHAEs in 1988. Their survey covered the usual demographics of age, gender, title, compensation, and education. They also covered marital status, hours worked, and community/ industry participation. This study included all CHAEs, not simply those in the lodging segment of the hospitality industry.

Tse surveyed the HFTP membership in 1989, covering three specific areas as follows:

- Demographic information such as age, gender, and educational level.
- Professional activities such as position title, years in profession, and buying authority.
- Information about the respondents' companies.

Her survey was not limited to members associated with the lodging industry, though hotels and resorts employed over 65 percent (648) of the respondents.

Damitio and Schmidgall updated Tse's 1989 study in 1995. Three hundred members associated with the lodging industry responded.

PROFILE OF THE LODGING FINANCIAL EXECUTIVE

The demographic information of lodging financial executives will include age, gender, education, certification, experience, and compensation.

Age

Three of these studies report the age distribution of respondents to their studies. DeVeau and DeVeau's respondents averaged 40 years, and the largest group of respondents (57 percent) was between 30 and 39 years of age. Tse reported that 25 percent of her respondents were 31–35 years of age and that two-thirds were in the 26–45 age groups. She did not report an average age; however, based on her reporting of salary by age it appears that the average age was approximately 38. Damitio and Schmidgall reported an average age of 37, with 72 percent of the respondents between the ages of 30 and 46. Thus, the trend suggests a slight reduction of the average age as the HFTP membership expanded from 1988 through 1995. This trend can be expected to continue as HFTP's membership continues to grow.

Gender

The three studies covering age also included gender of respondents. DeVeau and DeVeau reported 20 percent of their respondents were female, while Tse reported 25.7 percent and Damitio and Schmidgall reported 28.7 percent. This trend of an increasing percentage of females is expected to continue as a majority of students in both accounting and hospitality programs at colleges and universities across the United States are female.

Education

All five studies surveyed lodging financial executives in regards to their levels of education as shown in Table 8.1. The most common degree in all studies is the four-year college degree. DeVeau and DeVeau reported 68 percent of their respondents have the bachelor's, while Tse reported a low of 55 percent. The DeVeau study was limited to CHAEs, while the Tse study covered members of HFTP from

all hospitality segments. DeVeau and DeVeau reported only 8 percent had earned master's degrees, while later studies reveal master's recipients in double digits and increasing to 14 percent in the most recent study by Damitio and Schmidgall. Graduate degrees can be expected to grow in numbers as we enter the twenty-first century.

Three studies included the major of the college graduates. Both studies by Geller et al. report 55 percent to 56 percent have degrees in accounting, while DeVeau and DeVeau report only 37 percent. Another interesting statistic is the increasing percentage of financial executives with degrees in hospitality education. Geller and his coresearchers in their 1990 study suggest a dramatic increase to 17 percent from only 8 percent in 1983 may be either because students graduating from hospitality programs are choosing to work in accounting or because lodging companies are beginning to recognize the value of the hospitality education for accounting positions.

Certification

The DeVeau and DeVeau study focused on HFTP members holding the CHAE. In addition,

TABLE 8.1
Level of Education

	Level of Education					Major of College Grads	
	High School	Associate's	Bachelor's	Master's	Other	Accounting	Hospitality
Geller and Schmidgall	10%	11%	61%	11%	2%	56%	8%
DeVeau and DeVeau	12%[1]	11%	68%	8%	1%	37%	7%
Tse	22%[2]	9%	55%	13%	1%	—	—
Geller et al.	7%	15%	58%	13%	6%[3]	55%	17%
Damitio and Schmidgall	15%[4]	11%	58%	14%	2%	—	—

[1]The DeVeaus reported 12 percent as "none" but did not include high school as a level. Presumably these CHAEs have at least a high school diploma.

[2]Tse reported 18 percent as having some college but less than an associate's degree. This 18 percent is combined with the 4 percent with high school diploma to equal the 22 percent reported above.

[3]Geller et al. states that in most cases "other" represents multiple degrees, such as two master's degrees.

[4]Damitio and Schmidgall combined 3 percent with high school diplomas with 12 percent of those with some college.

they reported the highest percentage of CPAs. The other studies suggest an increasing percentage of lodging financial executives earning the CHAE from 8 percent in the Geller and Schmidgall study in 1983 to 20 percent in the Damitio and Schmidgall study conducted in 1995. In addition, the total certifications have increased from 21 percent in 1983 to 52 percent in 1995, as shown in Table 8.2. By any measure, this is a dramatic increase. This increase clearly supports Schmidgall and Kasavana's conclusion in 2000 regarding certifications:

> . . . initials after one's name suggest excellence, failure to have earned the initials may well lead one's peers and supervisors to question not only one's knowledge but also abilities.

Most likely, lodging financial executives will continue to earn various certifications in the future as proof of their excellence.

Experience

Several studies provide limited insight into the professional work of the lodging financial ex-

ecutive. DeVeau and DeVeau reported that 53 percent of the CHAEs have between 10 and 15 years of work experience and that the average is 16 years.

Tse reported that a plurality (24 percent) of lodging controllers had 11 to 15 years of work experience. Geller et al. reported a median average of 10 to 12 years of hospitality accounting experience, while the median from the Damitio and Schmidgall study was 11 to 15 years. Across these four studies, the average years of experience (generally hospitality related) is around 10 to 15. The average years added to an expected age of 21 or so at graduation with a bachelor's degree suggests that most lodging financial executives have spent most of their professional years working in the hospitality industry, since the average for the most recent study was 37.

Compensation

A major element of each study is the compensation of hospitality financial executives. Of course, over time the average pay is expected to increase. Table 8.3 provides insight to the

TABLE 8.2
Certifications of Lodging Financial Executives

	CHAE	CPA	Other	Total
Geller and Schmidgall	8%	13%	—	21%
DeVeau and DeVeau	100%	22%	18%	140%
Tse	14%	15%	12%	41%
Geller et al.	17%	14%	12%	43%
Damitio and Schmidgall	20%	12%	20%	52%

TABLE 8.3
Compensation

	Median Salary	Bonus
Geller and Schmidgall	$30,000–$34,999	9%–12% (median)
DeVeau and DeVeau	$49,900 (mean)	44% received benefit packages including a bonus
Tse	$30,000–$40,000	$2,000–$5,000 (median)
Geller et al.	$40,000–$49,999	11%–20% (median)
Damitio and Schmidgall	$45,001–$50,000	$6,100 (mean)

increasing compensation. The Geller and Schmidgall study conducted in 1983 revealed a median salary of $30,000 to $34,999 and a median bonus of 9 percent to 12 percent of the controller's salaries. Using this information the average annual bonus approximated $3,400. The 1995 study by Damitio and Schmidgall reported the median salary between $45,001 and $50,000 and the average bonus of $6,100. At the beginning of the twenty-first century it appears lodging financial executives' median salaries are most likely to be greater than $50,000, since the last study was conducted five years previously.

SKILLS AND KNOWLEDGE

What skills and knowledge should the lodging financial executive have and how have these changed over time? Geller and Schmidgall studied the technical skills and knowledge of lodging financial executives in 1983, and Geller et al. studied them again in 1990. Table 8.4 reflects the results of these studies. The 1990 study included more skills, and the report covering their study provided results by type of controller. As expected, the percentage of respondents revealed technology knowledge (computers) increased, and most likely a study conducted "today" would result in a 100 percent response. Other areas, which more than 90 percent of respondents indicated were required skills and knowledge, included cash management and internal controls.

A study by Cichy and Schmidgall in 1996 focused on leadership of lodging financial executives. Financial executives not only must know the "numbers" but must lead since they supervise several employees. The Damitio and Schmidgall 1995 study revealed that the number of employees supervised by these financial executives varied from one to more than 30. Just over one-third (34 percent) manage two to five employees, while nearly another third (31 percent) manage six to ten people.

Another one out of five (22 percent) manage 11 to 30 people, and 6 percent manage over 30 individuals. They found that lodging financial executives are expected to have skills and knowledge beyond the technical skills covered in the two Geller studies. Their study of lodging financial executives covered seven keys to leadership (see Table 8.5) and 17 secrets of leadership (see Table 8.6).

Lodging financial executives strongly agreed that four of the seven listed keys to leadership were important to their own leadership style. The most important key was "trust your subordinates" followed by "develop a vision." Consistent with all other surveys of U.S. chief executive officers and presidents in lodging and food service, "be an expert" was dead last. Leaders from all segments clearly realize that being an expert is not the most essential aspect of leadership. Nevertheless, "be an expert" received a score of 4.0, indicating that respondents believe that having relevant expertise is not unimportant, either. Rather, the survey results indicate that these leaders believe that it is more important for them to surround themselves with the necessary expertise than to have the expertise themselves.

Of the 17 secrets of leadership, respondents strongly agreed or agreed that leaders in their organizations must have 14 of them. At the top of the list were dependability, credibility, responsibility, and accountability. At the bottom of the list was physical stamina, with a score of 4.4. (A score above 4.0 indicates inherent importance; in this case, the low score for physical stamina is merely an indication of its relative unimportance when compared to the other secrets of leadership presented to the survey participants.)

Responsibility and Authority

Four of five of the studies focused on authority. Table 8.7 reveals the results of the two studies (1983 and 1990) conducted by Geller

TABLE 8.4
Technical skills and knowledge

Skills, Knowledge	Corporate	Division or Area	Hotel	Other	Total	1983 Study
Taxes	89%	77%	74%	69%	75%	60%
Computers	92	96	99	95	97	70
Personnel	81	82	84	77	82	78
Cash management	100	89	94	81	91	89
Capital budgeting	87	89	87	77	85	80
Statistics	68	81	85	71	88	82
Auditing	87	96	87	72	84	†
Internal controls	92	100	100	94	97	†
FASB* rulings	28	23	14	18	18	n/a
Risk management	55	35	36	26	36	n/a

*Financial Accounting Standards Board.
†In 1983, "auditing" and "internal control" were presented as a single item. Ninety-five percent of the respondents in 1983 indicated they possessed skills in those areas.

TABLE 8.5
Keys to leadership

	Mean Level of Importance*
Trust your subordinates	5.4
Develop a vision	5.3
Simplify	5.2
Keep your cool	5.1
Encourage risk	4.8
Invite dissent	4.5
Be an expert	4.0

*The scale is from 1, "very unimportant," to 6, "very important."

TABLE 8.6
Secrets of leadership

	Mean Level of Agreement*
In our organization/company, leaders must possess . . .	
Dependability	5.6
Credibility	5.5
Responsibility	5.5
Accountability	5.5
Self-confidence	5.3
Decisiveness	5.3
Emotional stamina	5.2
Loyalty	5.2
Desire	5.2
Stewardship	5.1
Courage	5.1
Empathy	5.1
Tenacity	5.0
Anticipation	5.0
Timing	4.9
Competitiveness	4.8
Physical stamina	4.4

*The scale is from 1, "strongly disagree," to 6, "strongly agree."

and others. The 1990 study divides the responses by type of controller. The vast majority (over 75 percent) of lodging financial executives have authority to sign checks, approve purchases, and extend credit. Tse found that only 56 percent of hospitality financial executives have authority to approve purchase decisions. Damitio and Schmidgall reported 56 percent were authorized to make purchasing decisions without the approval of others. They indicated controllers were most involved with technology purchases (90 percent) and to lesser degrees, guest supplies (29 percent), furnishings and equipment (44 percent), security/maintenance systems (43 percent) and fire/safety/energy conservation systems (30 percent).

The expansion of authority based on the two Geller studies is the greatest for investing funds (from 2 percent to 46 percent) and to set or changes prices (from 21 percent to 41 percent).

Both the Tse and Damitio and Schmidgall studies covered hiring and firing authority. Tse found that more than 80 percent of the respondents have the authority to hire and fire either in their own department or in their companies. The percentage increased to 90 percent when only accounting personnel were involved. The 1995 study by Damitio and Schmidgall revealed 76 percent have authority to hire and fire within their own department while 7 percent have no authority to hire or fire.

Only the two Geller studies (1983 and 1990) covered responsibility, and the comparative results are shown in Figure 8.8. Again the 1990 study provided in-depth detail by type of controller and included additional areas not covered by the 1983 study.

More than 90 percent of the respondents indicated that they have responsibility for such standard accounting functions as general accounting, receivables, and payables. Other major areas of responsibility shared by most controllers (75 percent or more) include payroll, night and income audits, computers in accounting, and cash management.

There are some indications that controllers are becoming increasingly involved with the operational aspects of their hotels. More than 50 percent of the respondents indicated that their responsibilities included purchasing, receiving, food and beverage controls, and storage (inventory). The number of respondents responsible for the storage function increased 18 percentage points from 1983 to 1990, going from 34 percent to more than 52 percent, and a purchasing function was claimed by 60 percent of the respondents in 1990, which is ten points greater than in 1983. Responsibility for hotel security, the least commonly

TABLE 8.7
Extent of authority over specific functions

| Functions | Type of Controller | | | | | 1983 Study |
	Division or Corporate	Area	Hotel	Other	Total	
Invest funds	70%	46%	48%	30%	46%	2%
Sign checks	79	85	88	59	79	87
Extend credit	66	85	92	63	80	85
Set or change prices	26	62	48	28	41	21
Borrow funds	36	27	20	10	20	19
Approve purchases	83	89	94	69	86	82

TABLE 8.8
Controllers' responsibilities

| Responsibilities | Type of Controller | | | | | |
	Division or Corporate	Area	Hotel	Other	Total	1983 Study
Hotel security	15%	27%	25%	18%	22%	9%
Receivables	89	89	100	73	91	95
Payables	89	92	99	77	92	93
General accounting	89	92	98	80	92	91
Payroll	85	89	95	68	87	89
Night auditors	60	85	94	60	80	83
Income auditors	57	81	89	60	77	79
Cashiers	43	65	77	47	64	63
Food controls	47	77	78	44	65	53
Computers: Accounting	83	89	95	73	88	*
Computers: Front office and reservations	49	77	65	44	58	*
Purchasing	32	62	77	40	60	50
Receiving	28	54	66	36	52	50
Storage (inventory)	23	58	66	39	52	34
Tax returns	70	58	61	54	61	n/a
Risk management	51	39	37	24	36	n/a
Cash management	85	81	86	51	77	n/a
Beverage controls	49	77	81	42	67	n/a
Investments	75	39	40	27	42	n/a
Internal auditors	47	62	46	31	44	n/a

* In 1983, a single question asked controllers about their computer-system (EDP) responsibilities. Fifty-two percent of the respondents in 1983 had some responsibility for EDP.

shared function among the controllers, more than doubled in the last six years, growing from 9 percent in 1983 to almost 22 percent in the 1990 study.

The controllers' role in electronic data processing (EDP) and computer-system management grew by leaps and bounds during the 1980s. In 1990, 88 percent of the respondents indicated responsibility for the computer systems used for accounting functions.

Additionally, 58 percent indicated responsibility for front-office and reservations-system computers—systems clearly not under the umbrella of traditional accounting functions. In the 1983 study, respondents were asked just one question about responsibility for EDP, and 52percent of the controllers indicated that they

had some responsibility for EDP. It's clear that over the years computer-oriented responsibilities have escalated sharply, and it can be expected to continue into the twenty-first century.

Committee Involvement

Just how involved have lodging financial executives been on committees of their lodging businesses? Both of the studies conducted by Geller and others reported over 80 percent of the respondents were members of the executive committee, while the Tse study showed only 71 percent (see Table 8.9). The difference may be because the Tse study covered all hospitality segments employing HFTP members while the Geller studies were restricted to the lodging industry. In addition, the involvement of financial executives from 1983 to 1990 increased significantly on both the compensation and strategic planning committees. The 1990 study by Geller and others also included involvement in training and risk management committees and a majority (66 percent and 72 percent) of lodging financial executives revealed involvement.

A 1998 study by Woods and others surveyed general managers of large hotels (500 rooms or more). In this study 81 percent of the respondents reported either the VP of finance or controller of their hotels were members of the executive committees of their hotels.

CONCLUSION

Considerable research has been conducted over the past 20 years on lodging financial executives. These studies indicate the most common title is controller and the average age is the late thirties. Males are still dominant though females are increasingly assuming the top financial position with lodging operations.

The majority of these leaders have bachelor's degrees and majored in accounting. An increasing number of lodging financial executives are certified and have 10 to 15 years of hospitality accounting experience.

The skill set of financial executives include both technical and leadership skills. The technical skill set includes technology, cash management, internal controls, and statistics. The most important leadership skills are trusting subordinates, developing a vision, dependability, credibility, responsibility, and accountability.

Financial executives commonly have authority to sign checks, extend credit, and approve purchases. To a lesser extent, they invest funds, may set or change prices, and borrow funds.

Their responsibilities are wide-ranging from managing receivables, payables, payroll, general accounting, night and income auditors, cash, computers in accounting, and to a lesser extent being responsible for hotel security, risk management, investments, and internal auditors.

Finally, financial executives commonly serve on the executive, compensation, strategic planning, training, and risk management committees of their hotels.

TABLE 8.9
Committee involvement

	Executive	Compensation	Strategic Planning
Geller and Schmidgall (1983)	82%	23%	41%
Tse (1988)	71	—	—
Geller et al. (1990)	86	75	94

8.3 Budgeting and Forecasting: Current Practice in the Lodging Industry

Raymond S. Schmidgall and Agnes Lee DeFranco

Financial forecasts and budgets can strengthen management's control of hotel operating expenses and help determine the profitability of the property (Chamberlain, 1991, pp. 89–90; DeMyer and Wang-Kline, 1990, p. 64; and Karch, 1992, pp. 21–22). Specifically, forecasts give owners a projected level of sales, while budgets alert owners and operators alike to significant expenditures that are on the horizon or predictable shortfalls in revenues. Used together, forecasts and budgets can provide a benchmark for sales-incentive programs, executive-compensation bonuses, incentive-based management fees, and capital expenditures (Temling and Quek, 1993).

A major difference between forecasting and budgeting is that budgeting is normally viewed as a process that covers a longer period of time than forecasting. Budgeting often results in a formal, long-range plan, normally expressed in terms of dollars over time—for example, the predicted revenues and expenses of a hotel for 24 months (Schmidgall, 1997, pp. 369–372, 411–413). On the other hand, forecasts are generally prepared by hoteliers to establish staffing levels and may cover a period of just seven to ten days (Schmidgall, 1989, pp. 101–102, 104–105). Long-range budgeting, therefore, is a form of strategic planning. It may entail several years' financial projections, a coordinated management policy, and a control-and-correction mechanism that allows actual results to be compared to estimates and followed by corrective steps, if necessary (Coltman, 1994).

THE CURRENT STUDY

Our study serves the following purposes:

- To determine the purposes, methods, and procedures in performing an operations budget.
- To determine how an operations budget is used in budgetary control.
- To determine the techniques used in forecasting revenues in the various operating departments in lodging properties.

Limitation

Our study used a random-sampling technique to select 600 samples that yielded 171 re-

sponses (almost 30 percent of the sample). As a result, there may be respondents who belong to the same national chain and thus represent the same set of corporate operating procedures. In addition, with the full-service and luxury segments of the hotel industry constituting more than 90 percent of our responses, the results are likely more applicable to those two groups than to limited-service hotels. Thus, although more than one-quarter of the hotel executives solicited by this study responded, it may not be useful to generalize the study's results (particularly beyond full-service hotels).

The Instrument

We designed a four-part questionnaire with the assistance of a number of lodging controllers and by modifying a survey previously used in 1995 (Borchgrevink and Schmidgall, 1995). We also employed a pilot study in which other lodging controllers offered comments and allowed us to fine-tune the final survey. Part I of the questionnaire included six questions that collected demographic data about the respondents and their lodging operations. Parts II and III consisted of 14 questions regarding the procedures and methods used to develop an operations budget, and about how the budget is used for financial control. Finally, the last part of the questionnaire asked respondents to provide information regarding their various operating departments' forecasting techniques.

Sampling

As mentioned, a simple random-sampling technique was used to select our study's population. Six hundred financial executives who are associated with lodging operations were chosen from the 1997 membership list of the association of Hospitality Financial and Technology Professionals (formerly the International Association of Hospitality Accountants).

Data Collection and Analysis

We first sent the survey in October 1997 to each of the 600 executives, requesting them to participate in our study. To ensure a good response rate, we sent a second copy of the survey to everyone in January 1998, as a reminder. Data received were analyzed using the software package SPSS for Windows.

RESULTS AND DISCUSSION

Of the 600 executives who received our survey, 171 responded, yielding a 28.5 percent response rate. The majority of the respondents held the title of hotel controller (147, or 86 percent), while the others reported such titles as assistant controller, regional controller, corporate controller, VP-controller, executive VP-CFO, and director of accounting. Respondents were mainly associated with full-service hotels (72 percent). Together with those from the luxury segment (21 percent), those executives constitute well over 90 percent of the responses. As for affiliation, the majority (62 percent) were part of a national chain, and 29 percent reported working for independent lodging properties. International chains ac-

counted for another 7 percent, while 2 percent of the responses came from franchisees. Most of the properties reported having more than 250 rooms (71 percent) and enjoyed 1996 annual gross revenues of at least $10 million (also 71 percent). Figures 8.1 and 8.2 show the details of the lodging-property size.

Preparing the Budget

The operations budget is an integral part of the financial operation of a lodging property, and virtually all of the respondents reported that they prepared an operations budget for the year; only three reported not preparing a budget. Moreover, almost 60 percent indicated that they set a tentative financial goal prior to developing the operations budget. The majority of those (64 percent) related that tentative financial goals were based on either sales (33 percent) or net-income (31 percent) levels. (In this case, sales equals revenues, while net income refers to the financial statement's bottom line.) Other financial executives' financial goals were based on gross operating profit, net operating profit, EBITDA, debt-service coverage, occupancy percentage, RevPAR, or some combinations of those.

FIGURE 8.1
Lodging-property size, by number of rooms

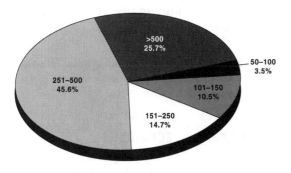

Profile of properties represented in this study.

FIGURE 8.2
Lodging-property size, by annual gross revenues (1996)

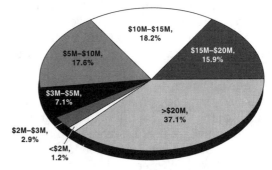

Figures in U.S. dollars (millions). Profile of properties represented in this study.

We presented five possible reasons why an operations budget might be prepared, and we also offered the fill-in-the-blank answer "other." When asked to give one major reason why a budget was prepared, 45 percent selected the option that stated "It is used as a standard by which the lodging operation is managed." Another 28 percent chose the answer "It is a planning tool." About 15 percent of the respondents gave more than one reason, and their responses almost always noted a budget's value as a standard of comparison or as a planning tool.

More than 90 percent of the respondents reported that a cooperative effort among hotel departments was used to prepare the operations budget. Nevertheless, 73 percent reported that the controller was the one who held the main responsibility for preparing the operations budget using the input provided by other department heads and the general manager.

Only five respondents indicated that the controller prepares the budget with little input from others. Thus, in more than three-quarters of the hotels surveyed, the controller was primarily in charge of budget preparation. In another 5 percent, the lodging units' controllers and general managers jointly prepared it, and in 12 percent of the hotels, the general manager coordinated the budget-preparation process with the various department heads. Other responses indicated that budget-preparation responsibility fell to an executive committee, department heads, the general manager (with input from the owner), or a budget team (for example, a team might comprise the general manager, owner, and controller).

While all but three of our 171 respondents confirmed that they prepared an operations budget for the year, less than half prepared a long-range budget (i.e., for more than a year at a time). Of those who prepared long-range budgets, more than three-quarters used a five-year time span for future planning.

Making Adjustments

Only one in four of the respondents revised their budget at any point during the operating year, with the most common frequency of change being monthly (40 percent). Other responses to this question included "as needed" (21 percent), "quarterly" (16 percent), "semi-annually" (12 percent), "bimonthly" (3 percent), and some combination of the above (4 percent).

BUDGETARY CONTROL

The majority of the respondents who used budgets declared that the operations budget was used for budgetary control, with 90 percent reporting that budgets were prepared for all of the hotel's operations, versus just for selected departments. Next, we asked what level of variance between the budget (original or revised) and actual performance is permitted before corrective action is taken. The results for this question are summarized in Table 8.10. About a third of the respondents try to hold food, beverage, and labor costs within the range of 1 to 2 percent of the budgeted amounts. One-fifth of the respondents hold "other" budget items within a range of 2 to 3 percent. (The median of the responses for food and beverage costs was about 2 percent, with the medians for labor and "other" costs at about 3 percent.) Compared to responses to a similar question in a 1996 study, it appears that hotels today are slightly more tolerant in food and beverage cost variances and slightly less tolerant in allowing labor and other operating costs to deviate from the budget (Schmidgall, Borchgrevink, and Zahl-Begnum, 1996).

FORECASTING TECHNIQUES

The last part of our questionnaire outlined in a grid presentation seven forecasting tech-

TABLE 8.10
Cost tolerances between budget and actual costs

	Food cost	Beverage cost	Labor cost	"Other" operating costs
Less than 1%	11.5	14.3	8.2	8.2
1% to 1.9%	33.8	33.3	26.5	16.3
2% to 2.9%	29.0	23.1	25.9	21.1
3% to 3.9%	10.1	13.6	16.3	14.3
4% to 4.9%	6.1	4.1	12.2	17.0
5% to 5.9%	6.8	8.2	6.8	17.0
More than 5.9%	2.7	3.4	4.1	6.1
Median	2.2%	2.1%	2.6%	3.3%
*Median, 1996 Study**	*1.9%*	*1.9%*	*2.8%*	*3.7%*

*R. S. Schmidgall and C. P. Borchgrevink, 1996.

TABLE 8.11
Various departments' forecasting techniques

Techniques	Rooms	Room Service	Restaurant	Banquet	Beverage
Prior year's budgeted dollar amounts multiplied by 1 + X%	10%	8%	9%	10%	10%
Number of guests by expected spending per guest	7%	28%	46%	25%	41%
Expected units sold by expected average price per unit	73%	27%	27%	26%	21%
Change in advance bookings from prior year	27%	6%	4%	22%	5%
Last year's actual revenues	16%	18%	16%	19%	16%
Last year's actual revenues adjusted subjectively	20%	24%	25%	33%	29%
Average of several past years' revenues multiplied by 1 + X%	5%	6%	5%	6%	6%

Source: R. S. Schmidgall and C. P. Borchgrevink, 1996.

niques, ranging from simple to complex (i.e., smoothing-constant method), and five principal hotel revenue-generating departments. We also allowed space so that respondents could write in other techniques. Respondents were then asked to reveal the methods they used for forecasting department revenues (see Table 8.11).

From this exercise, we find that some hoteliers used more than one technique for each department and that the methods used var-

ied among departments. More than 40 percent of the restaurant and beverage departments, for example, appear to favor the use of "number of guests by expected spending per guest." While the chief technique applied to the rooms department was "expected units to be sold multiplied by the expected average price per unit" (reported by 73 percent of respondents), the banquet department was the high user of "last year's actual revenues adjusted subjectively" (33 percent).

LITERATURE REVIEW

Accurate budgets are considered essential to profitable hotel operation. Yet obtaining reliable data is a problem. Smith and Lesure state that perhaps the greatest problem with forecasting and budgeting is the number of widely varying forecasts that are regularly published side by side, without question or support, and in some cases making all predictions vague.[1] Moreover, business prejections and financial trends are often published without any explanation of the underlying assumptions. Smith and Lesure contend that perhaps the way to construct reliable forecasts and budgets is to build a statistically reliable industrywide database that can be regularly updated with and compared to new economic and financial information. Those numbers can then be used to develop a short-term outlook for the industry as a whole or various geographic and market segments.

Hoteliers' desire and need for accurate budgeting and reliable data are not new. In 1989 hoteliers reported being generally satisfied with their forecasting accuracy, and yet they desired improvement.[2] Just one year earlier Lasky noted that budgeting was one of the factors hoteliers ignored when opening a hotel. Thus, he wrote, he was personally involved in rescuing 130 hotels and motels from bankruptcy due to this oversight.[3]

Besides the budget's role as the business plan for owners and operators, Temling and Quek discuss the importance of hotels' budgets to lenders.[4] The budget is important to this group since it can indicate a lodging company's potential for success. It also lets the officers of financial institutions know about the financial health of the business.

As the lodging industry's competitiveness increases, so does the interest in budgeting practices, as indicated by studies that appear biennially, on average. In 1995, 122 U.S. lodging properties were asked about their budgeting practices.[5] The areas of investigation included: budget-development processes, budget-reforecasting procedures, and budgetary-control methods.

To further investigate the budgeting process, 140 U.S. lodging controllers were asked in 1997 about their use of forecasting and budgeting at the department level.[6] That study reported that controllers rated "proper staffing" as the main benefit of preparing forecasts and "strategic planning" as the main benefit of budgeting. That study's results also showed that a hotel's size (as measured by the number of rooms) did not significantly influence the perception of the usefulness or the practices of forecasting and budgeting.

Some years earlier Records and Glennie provided insights to the Boca Raton Resort and Club's budgeting and business-forecasting processess.[7] Forecasting business volume and scheduling the required labor to serve its customer are crucial steps in maintaining an operation's quality. Thus, using a relatively simple computer network and basic software, the Boca Raton Resort and Club ensured it could control budgets, forecasts, and labor schedules.

[1] R. A. Smith and J. D. Lesure, "Don't Shoot The Messenger— Forecasting Lodging Performance," *Cornell Hotel and Restaurant Administration Quarterly*, Vol. 37, No. 1 (February 1996), pp. 80–88.

[2] R. S. Schmidgall and J. D. Ninemeier, "Budgeting Practices in Lodging and Food Service Chains: An Analysis and Comparison," *International Journal of Hospitality Management*, Vol. 8, No. 1 (1989), pp. 35–41.

[3] M. Lasky, "An Rx for Hotel Health," *Lodging Hospitality*, Vol. 44, No. 6 (May 1988), pp. 75–77.

[4] W. P. Temling and P. Quek, "Budget Time," *Lodging Magazine*, Vol. 19, No. 3 (November 1993), pp. 21–22.

[5] C. P. Borchgrevink and R. S. Schmidgall, "Budgeting Practices of U.S. Lodging Firms," *Bottomline*, Vol. 10, No. 5 (August–September 1995), pp. 13–17.

[6] A. L. DeFranco, "The Importance and Use of Financial Forecasting and Budgeting at the Departmental Level in the Hotel Industry as Perceived by Hotel Controllers," *Hospitality Research Journal*, Vol. 20, No. 3 (February 1997), pp. 99–110.

[7] H. A. Records and M. F. Glennie, "Service Management and Quality Assurance: A Systems Approach," *Cornell Hotel and Restaurant Administration Quarterly*, Vol. 32, No. 1 (May 1991), pp. 26–35.

THE EFFECTS OF AFFILIATION, SALES, AND PROFITABILITY

To see whether a property's (1) affiliation, (2) size in terms of sales, and (3) profitability have any effect on its budgeting practices, we used the chi-square statistic. The properties' budgeting practices were reflected in the answers to eight questions that asked about the procedures and methods used to develop operations budgets and how those operations budgets were used in budgetary control.

We first classified the responses according to the properties' affiliation. A chi-square was then calculated by cross-tabulating the affiliation on one hand and the eight questions on the other. Next, the same procedure was used to classify the responses according to sales level, and then by profitability. If an effect has a probability value (p-value) or a significance level of less than 0.05, it is significant. That means, in general, the effect happens due to chance less than 5 percent of the time. As seen in Table 8.12, two of the practices were affected by property affiliation, one was affected by sales, and one was affected by profitability (see those data marked with an asterisk).

When the chi-square test was performed based on annual sales, a significant difference ($p < 0.05$) was found in the preparation of long-range operating budgets (Table 8.13). That is, the higher the sales level a property enjoyed, the greater the likelihood that the property prepared a long-range operations budget.

Our second set of cross-tabulations determined whether differences occur between branded lodging operations and independent properties (Table 8.12). We noted two statistical differences, namely (1) the major reason for having an operations budget and (2) whether a tentative financial goal was set in advance.

First, it appears that national-chain hotels cited different reasons for having an operations budget than did the independent properties, as shown in Table 8.14.

TABLE 8.12
Property characteristics correlated with budgetary practices

Budgetary practices	Selected Property Characteristics		
	Chain versus independent operation	Size (sales)	Profitability
Major reason for having an operations budget	0.009*	0.015*	0.017*
Tentative financial goal set in advance	0.018*	0.562	0.156
Base for the tentative financial goal	0.116	0.292	0.202
Long-range operating budgets prepared	0.062	0.008*	0.067
Revision of operating budget	0.252	0.914	0.675
Monitoring food costs	0.440	0.516	0.398
Monitoring beverage costs	0.535	0.342	0.447
Monitoring labor costs	0.447	0.299	0.416

*Significance level is less than 0.05.

TABLE 8.13
The effect of annual sales on long-range planning

Annual sales	Percentage of respondents who prepared long-range operations budgets
Less than $5 M	28%
$5 M to $10 M	28%
$10 M to $15 M	37%
$15 M to $20 M	48%
Over $20 M	74%

Figures in US dollars (millions).

Hoteliers affiliated with national chains tend to have more than a single reason for creating an operations budget. In addition, it appears that national chains prepare the budget to be used for comparison purposes more often than do the independents, and that the independents prefer to use the operating budget as a planning tool (compared to the national chains).

Second, 65 percent of the chain properties responding to our questionnaire established tentative financial goals prior to developing their operations budgets compared to only 45 percent of the independent properties. This difference is most likely due to pressure from chains' corporate offices on individual properties to deliver the required "profit" to meet the chains' overall financial objective.

The last step of our research was to test for differences according to profitability. The profitability of each respondent was determined by dividing the net income reported by each hotel by its total sales. Respondents were then divided into four categories according to their profitability: less than 11 percent, 11 to 20 percent, 21 to 30 percent, and over 30 percent. (Table 8.15). The greater the respondent's profit margin, the more likely that more than a single reason was cited for having an operations budget.

TABLE 8.14
The effect of affiliation on budget usefulness

| Affiliation | Major reason for having an operations budget | | |
	Planning tool	Use as a standard	More than one reason
Chain property	26%	53%	22%
Independent property	48%	48%	5%

Note: Totals may not add to 100 due to rounding.

TABLE 8.15
The effect of profit margin on budget usefulness

| Affiliation | Major reason for having an operations budget | | |
	Planning tool	Use as a standard	More than one reason
< 11%	45%	52%	4%
11% to 20%	46%	46%	9%
21% to 30%	36%	44%	20%
> 30%	10%	60%	30%

Note: Totals may not add to 100 due to rounding.

CONCLUSION AND FUTURE RESEARCH

Operations budgeting is an important part of U.S. hotels' financial planning. The majority of hoteliers set tentative financial goals prior to preparing their operations budgets. The goal for the majority of hoteliers is based on either sales or net income. Most hoteliers indicated that the major reason they used budgets at all was as a standard for comparison to actual performance figures. The second most common use was as a planning tool. At the majority of hotels, a cooperative effort among departments was used to produce the budget. In a clear majority of those hotels, the financial executives coordinated this process. Less than half of all respondents prepared long-term operations budgets, and less than a quarter of all respondents indicated that their budgets were revised during the year.

All but two of the 171 respondents indicated that their operations budgets were used for control purposes. For all departments, the mean of the allowable deviation between the budget and actual performance ranged near 2 to 3 percent. That range is slightly tighter and smaller than the range measured in a similar study in 1996 (Schmidgall, Borchgrevink, and Zahl-Begnum).

Respondents' revenue-forecasting techniques varied by department within individual hotels. A number of respondents reported they used multiple techniques for a single department. The most commonly used technique was "expected units sold by expected average price per unit." Other techniques that were used by more than 20 percent of the respondents included "number of guests by expected spending per guest" and "last year's actual revenues adjusted subjectively."

Our research uncovered several points that deserve attention. First, virtually all hotels use an operations budget and yet less than half of the hotels budget beyond one year at a time. Future researchers might explore the reasons why more hoteliers don't prepare long-range operations budgets. Second, few hoteliers revise their budget during the year (only about one in four). Budgeting is not an exact science, so regular adjustments should be expected and planned. Third, for most hotels, the largest single cost is labor. Yet our research shows that hotels' food and beverage costs appear to be more closely controlled than are labor costs.

Future research could also focus on specific control techniques to monitor hotels' costs and to determine whether more-profitable hotels use different techniques than less-profitable hotels. Finally, further study could examine closely the forecasting techniques actually used by the operating departments. For example, in our study, the technique "last year's actual revenues adjusted subjectively" was rated high, and future research could explore exactly what "subjective" adjustments are being used.

8.4   As I See It: The Hotel Controller

Michael J. Draeger

Usually, the controller is the manager with total responsibility of the accounting department. This executive is credited with having his hand on the purse strings, his eye on the bottom line, and the ear of the general manager, all the while continuing to count the beans. In fulfilling this role, the controller must know the hotel operations and be familiar with what goes on in each department. As is the same with all other managerial roles, the controller must have many skills, which are used daily.

Obviously, the controller is an administrator. He or she will supervise the accounting functions, including payroll, payables, receivables, purchasing, and auditing. The controller will want to know that procedures are being followed and deadlines are being met. He will question what is happening in each hotel department. Is all the money getting to the bank, and is there enough to pay all the vendors and staff? That large group function in the ballroom is being extended 30-day credit; have their references been checked? Are purchase orders on file in the receiving department? Do the actual payroll tax deposits equal what is reported on the IRS form? Accounting affects almost every aspect of the hotel operation, and the controller is the one looked to when it comes to the proper functioning and conduct of this department.

The controller is an adviser, meaning he provides information and recommendations to every department in the hotel. Regarding giving information, accounting generates more reports than any other department in the hotel. Daily reports to management reporting on sales, labor. and purchases are a must in any business, with comparisons to budgets and/or last year. The financial statements including a balance sheet and income statement are produced periodically in accounting. The controller is expected to be prepared to discuss these types of reports with managers and owners, making some sense of all the numbers and percentages. A hotel will have any of a number of meetings where the controller will discuss the financial results. At these meetings, the controller will be a part of recommendations and suggestions to improve operations in areas the reports might point out. Often a morning operations meeting will find the controller pointing out that labor costs are creeping higher than appropriate given current levels of business, or the monthly manager's meeting will start with the controller giving an overview of last month's financial results and the hotel's standing, year to date. When the owners visit the hotel, there usually is a meeting to discuss the financial results and what is being done to ensure that profit expectations are being met. The controller might

even be asked to sit in on a specific department's staff meeting as they brainstorm ways to reduce their departmental costs. As others digest the accounting information, the controller needs to advise and counsel on its significance.

The controller is also a technician. He or she must have a foundation in the debits and credits of accounting. Regardless of whether the accounting department is staffed with one person or two dozen, the controller is prepared to jump in and do the work. A tight labor market and staff turnover often necessitate that the controller assist in any function. There are always balance sheet accounts to reconcile, budget variances to explain, or journal entries to post in getting through the processes that it takes to keep an accounting department functioning. A good bookkeeper or accountant is primarily a good technician in accounting aspects, and a good controller will not lose sight of this ability as he develops in his career.

Additionally, the controller is an educator. All managers have a responsibility to instruct and train others, and the controller is no exception. Obviously the accounting staff need to be proficient in their duties to perform their jobs, and the controller needs to ensure this is happening. However, to the majority of the hotel, what accounting does and how they do it can be quite a mystery. Controllers need to demystify what accounting does. Managers with an understanding of accounting and its abilities find they have more tools to work with in the operation of their departments. Often a controller can lay the foundation for a manager's financial understanding by sitting down with a new manager and explaining an income statement for that manager's department. More managers seem to respect and understand their accounting departments after they have been involved in just one year's budget process. The controller can be building "public relations" for accounting by using opportunities to develop others' financial awareness and expertise.

Finally, controllers should be mentors. They need to be involved in the development of people. An accounting staff should experience new challenges to keep them interested. Cross training in other accounting or hotel positions can give staff new understanding in areas not previously known. This aids staff in developing within their careers and additionally helps within the department when staff is short. Besides the accounting staff, the controller should be on the lookout for promising managers that show potential. Managers enjoy having a few minutes of the controller's time, over coffee or lunch or even just sitting in the office, to talk about their objectives and goals. Often the controller can facilitate a manager's accomplishments by being a friend and having awareness for the manager's developmental needs.

Mentoring and educating can benefit the controller in many ways, maybe most interestingly, his or her personal advancement and compensation. Several hotel companies have begun to evaluate and pay bonuses in the back-of-the-house departments for criteria previously reserved for more service-oriented or revenue-producing departments. As a controller of an accounting department, I am measured by the service my department provides to the hotel operation—our internal customers. Accounting becomes a support department, and the rest of the hotel are its "customers." In this way, accounting now offers products and services, and works to have satisfied customers. The manager and even staff can establish quantifiable objectives focused

on the department's "product." These become the criteria for performance evaluations, bonuses, and other incentives and rewards.

Current emphasis in accounting might now include:

- Working professionally with all other departments.
- Meeting deadlines and issuing timely reports.
- Achieving superior results on internal and external audits.
- Training operational managers in the financial aspects of their departments.
- Stocking storeroom levels at appropriate par levels.
- Keeping the accounting offices neat, orderly, and presentable.
- Being willing to answer questions and assist with problems.

With this type of product and service attitude, there is no limit to what a department might now do for its customers.

It is not easy to generalize the controller's job into a daily routine. However, there are skills and traits to this position, which are continually required or called upon. Just as with all other aspects of the hotel, the scenery is always changing, guests are coming and going. Each day brings new challenges and opportunities, and the controller, as part of this, needs to show many facets of the hospitality industry.

8.5   Hotel Purchasing as a Key Business Activity

Carl D. Riegel

The term *purchasing* means different things to different people. This is probably because it is an extremely complex activity that can affect everything from the perceived quality of the guest experience to the bottom line of large hospitality organizations. In many respects, the hospitality industry can be termed *pur-*

chasing-intensive. This is because, compared to many other industries, the sheer quantity of goods and services bought by hospitality firms is staggering. Purchases can range from swizzle sticks and maraschino cherries to complex property-management systems or original artwork for display in hotel lobbies. In the hospitality industry the purchasing function is concerned primarily with *processes* and *systems*, which can ultimately affect business functions ranging from operational efficiency to competitive position. Some of these business functions include:

- Product research and development.
- Determining needs.
- Specification development.
- Vendor selection and development.
- Price negotiation.
- Order and delivery management.
- Developing receiving systems.
- Storage and inventory management.
- Procuring capital goods.

While this list is not exhaustive, you can see that purchasing is a complex activity, which involves a great deal more than ensuring that lodging organizations have an adequate supply of goods and services. Let's take a look at how purchasing affects the important areas of operations, control, and profitability.

OPERATIONS

The support of hospitality operations is probably the most basic contribution of purchasing. Purchasing contributes to hospitality operations by insuring that goods and services are purchased in the proper quantity at the proper quality, by making sure that deliveries are on time, and by managing storage in such a way that raw materials are fully utilized. The purchasing department or managers charged with purchasing responsibility make this happen by working with operations managers to determine department needs, by selecting reliable vendors. and by developing systems to assure a smooth throughput of raw goods through the operation—from the receiving dock to the storeroom, to the food and beverage facilities, to housekeeping, or to whatever operating department requires these

products. In this age of multibrand lodging firms and chain restaurants many tasks such as vendor selection, specification writing, and product research and development are accomplished at corporate levels. However, determining need, selecting local vendors for items such as produce, developing storage and receiving systems, placing orders, and scheduling deliveries are most often a property-level task.

CONTROL

Purchasing exerts a significant influence on both quality and cost control. The quality of capital goods such as furniture, fixtures, and equipment (FF&E) affects both the image and the efficiency of an operation. Through product research and selection, purchasing managers assure that the proper FF&E items are available when they are needed. Similarly, the quality of food and beverage material is a key ingredient in the ultimate quality of finished goods. Managers charged with purchasing responsibility do a lot for food and beverage control by ensuring that purchased food and beverage items measure up to the quality specifications and by doing research to determine the necessary quality and cost specifications for new items.

Purchasing also exerts a major influence on cost control. Since the cost of materials, including food, beverage, and supplies, often runs between 35 and 50 percent in food and beverage operations, the ability of purchasers to save money through prudent and systematic buying is substantial. Hospitality organizations cannot be competitive unless they can deliver products and services to guests at a quality and a price that the guest feels is acceptable. When competition is based on price, as it often is, being able to purchase goods for resale at a lesser price than competitors goes a long way in enhancing competitive position. Take, for example, a chain restaurant organization that is able to purchase seafood on a national contract basis or through a purchasing cooperative. This reduces their portion costs by, say, 50 cents as compared to their competitors. A reduction of 50 cents in cost may mean that the restaurant has the ability to sell that item for as much as $1.25 less than their competitor. This improves their position vis-à-vis their competitors. Summarily, being able to source and purchase higher-quality or trendier food items will also further their competitive position.

PROFIT

Purchasing influences profit in two very important ways. First, every dollar saved through prudent and judicious purchasing goes directly to the bottom line; and second, the effective use of assets ultimately affects a firm's return on investment (ROI).

Let's explore the relationship between savings in purchasing and bottom-line results. This typical situation illustrates the profit-making potential of wise purchasing. Assume that the Guest Comfort Hotels and Resorts has a sales volume of approximately $267,000,000 of which 30 percent, or approximately $80,000,000 is contributed by food and beverage sales. Material costs for food and beverage run about 40 percent on average, and profit margins average around 10 percent pretax, or about $8,000,000. If management were astute and were able to increase sales by $20,000,000 (25 percent) this would represent a $2,000,000 increase on the bottom line (0.10 x $20,000,000 = $2,000,000). However, if purchasing were able to decrease the cost of sales to 35 percent, a 5 percent decrease, the $2,000,000 saved would go directly to the bottom line and, therefore, equal as much on the bottom line as a 25 percent increase in sales! The following simple formula can be used to determine the sales equivalent of cost-reduction savings in purchasing:

$$x = y \div z$$

Where

x = the additional sales volume required to produce a before-tax profit equal to that produced by a purchasing cost reduction.
y = the reduction (expressed in dollars) in purchasing cost.
z = the firm's pretax profit margin expressed as a decimal.

In the preceding example, the equation would look like this:

$$x = \$2,000,000 \div 0.10$$
$$x = \$20,000,000$$

Thus, it would require a $20,000,000 sales increase to equal the effect of a $2,000,000 cost reduction on the bottom line. While a 5 percent reduction in purchasing costs would be difficult, it is not impossible. Similarly, a 25 percent increase in sales would not be impossible, but it would be a lot more difficult than achieving a 5 percent reduction in costs. The effect of purchasing on return on assets (ROA) is similar, if less dramatic.

To assess an organization's overall performance, it is essential to consider the rate of return produced by all capital invested in the operation. This is called return on investment, or ROI. While profit margin on sales is important, it is only half of the ROI equation. The effective use of the organization's resources is equally important, and the formula for ROA (a commonly used way of calculating return on investment) illustrates why. In accounting terms ROA is equal to the profit margin times the asset turnover rate. In mathematical terms this would be expressed as

ROA = Operating Income (or Profit) ÷ Total Assets

or

ROA = (Operating Income ÷ Sales) × (Sales ÷ Total Assets)

As you can see, one half of the equation is devoted to how well managers use assets in relationship to total sales, and the other is devoted to how well managers control costs in relationship to sales.

Let's use the following example to illustrate. A hospitality organization has made a profit of $1 million on $10 million in sales, and its total assets are equal to $9 million. If we plug this into the equation listed above for ROA, the equation would look like this:

$$($1,000,000 \div $10,000,000) \times$$
$$($10,000,000 \div $9,000,000)$$
$$= 0.11 \text{ or } 11\% \text{ ROA}$$

Purchasing can influence both the profit side through cost reduction and the asset side through total asset reduction. Let's say that through judicious purchasing and inventory management we were able to increase operating income to $1.2 million and to decrease the asset base to $7 million. Let's calculate the effect on ROA:

$$($1,200,000 \div $10,000,000) \times$$
$$($10,000,000 \div $7,000,000)$$
$$= 0.17 \text{ or } 17\% \text{ ROA}$$

The influence of purchasing on ROA is obvious.

CONCLUSION

Hopefully, this short article will help you to see that purchasing is a broad-based and key business activity. On the one hand, it is a support activity that ensures that operations run smoothly and efficiently, but on the other hand, purchasing is a lot more than product research and ordering. It has a direct relationship with quality control and cost control, and because of that it also directly influences profit as expressed in the bottom line and in return on investment.

8.6   The Hotel Purchasing Function

C. Lee Evans

The hotel purchasing function did not change very much from 1970 to 1990. Up until the late 1980s various tax advantages/benefits were the primary reason for the construction of U.S. hotels. Providing a substantial return on investment was not expected or required.

In our current economy, expectations on hotel profitability have changed. Profitability is now required, along with maintaining the established level of quality. This has brought about a new level of interest on the purchasing function and greater importance placed on cost savings.

The financial aspects of the hotel business have changed in the past 7 years. It has enjoyed the longest boom in revenues and profitability ever over the past 40 years.

Today, hotel managers realize that true cost savings generated in the purchasing department are dollars that drop directly to the bottom line without any associated incremental cost. It is not difficult to generate arbitrary savings; the true challenge is to create cost efficiency utilizing a standard specification.

Purchasing for the hotel requires much more than obtaining three bids and circling the lowest price. The true definition of purchasing should be *purchasing the right product, at the right price, at the right time.*

The statement sounds extremely simple, but when it is applied to the 1000 to 2000 items a hotel purchases, it presents a great challenge for the purchasing manager. The hotel purchasing function supports virtually every department within the property, whether purchasing chemicals for housekeeping or stewarding, office supplies for marketing, computer supplies for accounting, or food and beverage products for the restaurant outlets.

The purchasing manager usually reports to the hotel controller or the hotel's financial control division. I am convinced that this will change in the future. There is a need for a more operational approach to managing the purchasing function. We need to build a team that is committed to the common goal of servicing our customers. The reporting structure will begin to shift to operations, with the purchasing manager directly reporting to the general manager or to the executive assistant/operations manager in larger properties. This would help to promote the philosophy of team building and would support and service customers directly rather than being viewed as a support department to other departments within the hotel.

With the increasing importance of the purchasing function, the utopian mission of the purchasing manager is to procure products and services cost effectively that will meet or exceed the customer's expectation. It is necessary to continually evaluate product specifications to incorporate new products and technology.

The purchasing function is changing for several reasons. In the past 5 to 7 years hotel companies have undergone tremendous consolidation. With this consolidation has come economies of scale for support areas, which include marketing, accounting, purchasing, and reservation systems. Many of the hotel companies today have centralized the purchasing function to some extent. They negotiate purchasing agreements with producers and processors and distribute products and supplies through predetermined distribution channels.

PURCHASING ORGANIZATION

The purchasing department can be organized into three basic areas:

- *Administrative:* This area would consist of pricing, vendor selection, and the purchase of nonstocked items. Nonstocked items are products purchased for immediate use or held in storage in other departments throughout the hotel.
- *Receiving:* There are two categories of receiving: (1) hotel goods that are placed in storage in the purchasing area or items that are immediately issued to the requesting department or guest/group; and (2) items that have been shipped to a registered guest or expected guest/group.
- *Issuing:* Product issuing falls into two categories: (1) consumable food and beverage supplies consisting of all food items and liquor, beer, wine, and mixes to be held in the purchasing department storerooms; and (2) items consisting of office supplies, printed forms, and linen. This is just a small listing of items, depending on the physical layout of the hotel areas.

The staffing and segregation of duties varies from hotel to hotel depending upon the property size and physical layout of the back-of-the-house areas. A partial organization chart is shown in Figure 8.3. See sidebar, "Samples of Job Descriptions."

INTERDEPARTMENTAL RELATIONSHIPS

It is essential that the purchasing manager develop close working relationships with key managers within the hotel. These relationships should build and demonstrate trust, confidence in judgment, and integrity. Key managers would include the following:

- Corporate purchasing function.
- Hotel general manager.
- Executive assistant/operations manager.
- Director of food and beverage.
- Executive chef.
- Director of housekeeping.

FIGURE 8.3
Partial hotel organization chart

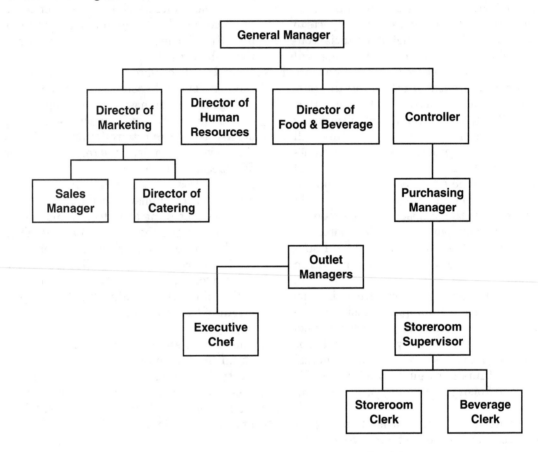

SAMPLE JOB DESCRIPTIONS

Purchasing Manager

POSITION TITLE: Purchasing manager

DIVISION/DEPARTMENT: Administrative and general

REPORTS TO (TITLE): Controller

DIRECTLY SUPERVISES: Storeroom supervisor, beverage clerk, storeroom clerk

NO. OF EMPLOYEES SUPERVISED: 3

BASIC FUNCTION OF POSITION: To support the hotel department with dependable sources of materials and services; to buy competitively; to control inventories; to develop and train personnel; to implement planning to avoid emergencies; and to implement and supervise all procedures and staff in the purchasing department.

EDUCATION AND EXPERIENCE OR SKILLS NORMALLY NEEDED: College helpful but not required. Previous buying experience a must. Food and beverage buying necessary. Accounting background needed. Extraordinary organizational skills required. Must display excellent management skills and a great deal of diplomacy.

TYPE OF GUIDANCE REQUIRED TO DIRECT THE ACTIVITIES OF THE POSITION AND MAGNITUDE OF INDEPENDENT DECISION-MAKING RESPONSIBILITY: Must have the ability to function independently within the parameters established by the controller and other upper management in the hotel. Has the authority to hire and terminate.

FUNCTIONS:

20%: Develop and monitor policies, procedures, and performance objectives for the purchasing team.

30%: Solicit competitive price quotation.

40%: Supervision of purchasing staff.

10%: Miscellaneous duties (O-G = ongoing):

O-G: Review par stock levels.

O-G: Schedule storeroom hours.

O-G: Develop employees for supervision position.

O-G: Maintain high levels of employee motivation.

O-G: Insure proper handling of receiving, storing, and issuing.

O-G: Assure accurate and timely preparation of daily records for purchases and issues for food and beverage forms.

O-G: Visit surveyors and stay abreast of market trends.

Storeroom Supervisor

POSITION TITLE: Storeroom supervisor

DIVISION/DEPARTMENT: Purchasing

REPORTS TO (TITLE): Purchasing manager

DIRECTLY SUPERVISES: Beverage clerk, storeroom clerk

NO. OF EMPLOYEES SUPERVISED: 2

BASIC FUNCTION OF POSITION: To supervise the storeroom staff and resolve day-to-day problems in food and beverage storerooms. To assist in the procurement of all consumable food and beverage items assuring that they are of the right quality and right quantity. To maintain minimum investment and reduce unnecessary expenditures to maintain high

sanitation standards and enforce all hotel policies relating to the food and beverage storerooms.

EDUCATION AND EXPERIENCE OR SKILLS NORMALLY NEEDED: College degree helpful but not required. One to two years' prior food and beverage background required. Must be able to read, write, and speak English fluently. Must have good organizational skills.

TYPE OF GUIDANCE REQUIRED TO DIRECT THE ACTIVITIES OF THE POSITION AND MAGNITUDE OF INDEPENDENT DECISION-MAKING RESPONSIBILITY: Must have the ability to act as administrator of the purchasing department in the absence of the purchasing manager. Must have the ability to function independently within the parameters established by the purchasing manager. Has the authority to hire and terminate.

FUNCTIONS:

50%: Supervise food and beverage clerks and provide assistance when necessary.

5%: Prepare daily food order.

5%: Prepare semiweekly food order.

5%: Maintain perpetual inventory (liquor, beer, wine).

2%: Assist purchasing manager in placing orders.

5%: Prepare weekly food bid sheet.

5%: Prepare monthly food bid sheet.

2%: Maintain accurate food and beverage vendor files.

2%: Assist in monthly inventory.

2%: Prepare monthly Food Dead Stock list (raw materials for which there is no finished product) for chef.

2%: Prepare monthly Beverage Dead Stock list for director of food and beverage.

10%: Assign miscellaneous duties (O-G = ongoing):

O-G: Product quality inspection.

O-G: Communication with the chef.

O-G: Keep abreast of industry trends and information.

O-G: Maintain accurate and organized filing system.

(continued on next page)

SAMPLE JOB DESCRIPTIONS (continued)

Storeroom Clerk/Beverage Clerk

POSITION TITLE: Storeroom clerk/beverage clerk

DIVISION/DEPARTMENT: Purchasing

REPORTS TO (TITLE): Storeroom supervisor

DIRECTLY SUPERVISES: None

NO. OF EMPLOYEES SUPERVISED: None

BASIC FUNCTION OF POSITION: To receive, store, issue, rotate, and secure merchandise as outlined in the storeroom procedures. To accurately record transactions and to follow written policies and procedures relating to purchasing and the food and beverage storerooms.

EDUCATION AND EXPERIENCE OR SKILLS NORMALLY NEEDED: Prior experience in food and beverage consumable receiving. Prior storeroom experience in issuing stock, and inventory control. Must have math aptitude and be detail oriented.

TYPE OF GUIDANCE REQUIRED TO DIRECT THE ACTIVITIES OF THE POSITION AND MAGNITUDE OF INDEPENDENT DECISION-MAKING RESPONSIBILITY: Must have the ability to function independently within the parameters established by the purchasing manager and storeroom supervisor.

FUNCTIONS:

25%: Responsible for the second thorough inspection of the product as it is being stored and rotated; assure proper stock storage location on shelving units.

10%: Maintain high standards of sanitation and inventory organization.

10%: Participate in monthly inventory.

40%: Insure completion of paperwork in a timely manner:

A Form (daily record of purchases and issues of food).

B Form (daily record of purchases and issues of beverage).

Issue recap food.

Issue recap beverage.

Perpetual inventory, beverage.

Perpetual inventory, paper.

Food stock levels.

Beverage stock levels.

15%: Miscellaneous:

To complete projects in a timely manner.

Interaction between the purchasing manager and all other departments occurs on a regular basis. Verbal interaction, either by telephone or in person, is the most frequent. With the technological implementation of the Internet and e-mail, the communication process has become more efficient. Communication can be done quickly with large numbers of people.

Most day-to-day interaction by the purchasing manager would involve some of the following key managers and issues:

- *General manager/executive assistant manager:* Issues relating to quality changes and all discussions regarding capital expenditures (defined as equipment or renovation purchases exceeding $2000).
- *Director of food and beverage:* Unresolved food purchasing issues and information related to wine, liquor, and beer purchases.
- *Executive chef:* Issues relating to food purchases. This area requires close communications regarding vendor performance, various food markets, quality, and availability information.
- *Director of housekeeping:* Coordination and purchase of linens, paper goods (toilet paper, facial tissue, paper towels), uniforms, and laundry and cleaning chemicals.

A good purchasing manager bases purchasing decisions on the same criteria for all business decisions—data. There is no way possible to be an expert on every product available. This is where purchase specifications come into play. Written specifications must be developed for all key products. These products should also be tested periodically to verify that they meet or exceed specifications. Examples of testing could be a monthly butcher yield test on specific meat cuts, or yearly test of terry linen by an independent laboratory.

PURCHASING SOURCES

There are many sources of information for identifying producers, processors, and manufacturers. Technical data is also available. Suppliers are the best source of information. The listings in the sidebar "Purchasing Sources" are a small example of material available to the purchasing manager.

THE PURCHASING MANAGER'S DAY

7:00 A.M. Inspect the quality of food and beverage consumables as they are delivered to the hotel. This includes rejecting incorrect or inferior products and then contacting the appropriate vendor(s) to rectify issues or determine another source, if necessary. The average daily purchase cost could vary from a low of $3,000 to a high of $50,000 depending on the size of the property and level of business.

9:00–11:00 A.M. Attend daily meeting with catering department, chef, stewarding, and banquet departments to review upcoming banquet business. Included would be a review of the room setup for each scheduled function, menus, and, most important, the guaranteed attendance numbers.

12:00 Noon. All food and beverage purchases have been received and issued. Inventory is now taken on all items in storage to determine the next day's needs. After reviewing the current levels and calculating banquet business requirements, the vendors are selected. Orders are now placed with all suppliers. The number of suppliers could range from 1 to 25.

The rest of the afternoon is spent working on nonconsumable food and beverage purchases, obtaining bids, and following up on outstanding purchase orders overdue for delivery.

The average workweek for the purchasing manager is 50 to 60 hours and may include

---

PURCHASING SOURCES

The Meat Buyers Guide (1988)
by National Association of Meat Purveyors
8365-B Greensboro Drive
McLean, VA 22102
(703) 827-5754

Fresh Produce Manual (1989)
by the Produce Marketing Association
P.O. Box 6036
Newark, DE 19714–6036

The Food Professional's Guide
by Irena Chalmers
American Showcase, Inc., New York

Quantity Food Purchasing (2d ed.)
Lendal H. Kotschevar
John Wiley and Sons, Inc., New York

The Encyclopedia of Fish Cookery
by A. J. McClane
Holt, Rinehart, and Winston, New York

The Advanced Seafood Handbook
Seafood Business Magazine
P.O. Box 908
Rockland, Maine 04841

The Packer 1990
Produce Availability & Merchandising Guide
Vance Publishing
7950 College Blvd.
Overland Park, Kansas 66210

weekends. For the most part, normal business hours are usually 7:00 A.M. to 6:00 P.M., Monday through Friday, and 7:00 A.M. to noon on Saturdays.

CORPORATE DIRECTION AND INTERACTION

Corporate direction and control varies with each hotel company. As a rule, many hotel companies that manage rather than franchise their properties are more involved in setting policies and procedures. The minimum standards of the purchasing manager will vary by hotel company.

The corporate purchasing function is still viewed with some skepticism, although not as much as in the past. Today, purchasing is non-profit and established to benefit managed properties. The idea is to do more with less and applies to the corporate level as well as to the individual properties. The most efficient method of purchasing systemwide is targeting where dollars are spent and creating the most cost-efficient way to purchase high-volume expense items. Corporate hotel purchasing offices are currently working to accomplish this goal. Examples of items that could be considered for systemwide agreements between corporate and property purchasing offices are uniforms, flatware, paper goods, laundry sup-

plies, and various food products; these, too, will vary by company.

CONCLUSION

Hotel purchasing must focus on and utilize resources in the most efficient manner today. In the past, a heavy-handed approach was used to resolve issues with suppliers. As we move toward building partnerships with key vendors today, a teamwork approach provides an environment to build upon the strengths of both the hotel and the vendor. This is now called *supply-chain management.*

Another key component in business today is communication, both internal within the hotel and external with suppliers. One of our national suppliers has the capability to link their customer service for placing orders with our domestic properties through a mainframe computer network linked to each property by PCs. Our hotels can place orders directly with the supplier through the network system and receive immediate confirmation from the supplier. This nationwide system allows both our properties and the corporate office to access pricing, availability, and consumption.

To be able to succeed in the future, we must resist the confines of our traditional paradigms. We must continually examine the ways we conduct business and strive for new and innovative approaches.

8.7   Best Practices in Information Technology

Judy A. Siguaw and Cathy A. Enz

"The successful companies of the next decade will be the ones that use digital tools to reinvent the way they work. These companies will make decisions quickly, act efficiently, and directly touch their customers in positive ways" (Gates and Hemingway, 1999).

As Bill Gates notes in the quote displayed above, the companies that effectively use in-

formation technology (IT) will be the ones that best improve customer service, whether those customers are external (e.g., guests) or internal (e.g., employees, stockholders). Certainly this holds true for the lodging-industry champions who were nominated by peer organizations and managers for their efforts in information technology (Dubé et al., 1999). The hotel companies designated specifically as information-technology champions are listed in Table 8.16. All of these companies have worked to develop or improve technological systems that influence the guest experience.

In this paper we provide a detailed account of the information-technology practices of individual best-practices champions and identify the outcomes of each practice. We also present the advice and suggestions that these champions provided for those managers seeking to implement their own technological practices.

TABLE 8.16
Overview of IT best-practice champions

IT champions	Practice initiated, developed	Measure of success
The Balsams Grand Resort Hotel	Comprehensive guest-history program	High occupancy rates from return guests and word-of-mouth recommendations
The Barbizon Hotel and Empire Hotel New York	Software eliminates logbooks and standardizes record keeping	Increased repeat-guest rate and the quality of service and productivity; eliminated paperwork; and increased ability to analyze trouble spots
Candlewood Hotel Company	Implemented system of recording and storing accounting and construction records electronically	Increased productivity and reduced labor costs; improved response time to vendors, guests, and employees; and decreased storage costs
Carlson Hospitality Worldwide	Industry's most efficient and productive reservation system	Highest contributor at the lowest cost
Cendant Corporation	Computerized system integrates all hotel MIS functions into one system	Increased franchisees' ADR and corporate profits; and increased ability to serve guests
Courtyard by Marriott	Intranet system replaced manuals and other printed information	Increased productivity; reduced labor costs; and eliminated production and distribution costs of standard operating-procedure pages and binders
Fairmont Copley Plaza Hotel	Property-management system used to improve concierge performance	Increased guest satisfaction and loyalty
Hotel Nikko at Beverly Hills	Portable phone system installed throughout hotel; used by guests and employees	Increased telephone use and revenues and increased customer satisfaction
IMPAC Hotel Group	Lobby-based kiosk touch-screen guest-tracking system	Improved maintenance and productivity and improved overall quality and image of property
Inter-Continental Hotels and Resorts	Global strategic-marketing database	More-effective targeted mailings; increased ability to measure advertising effectiveness; increased guest loyalty-program participation; and altered decision making of senior management
Kimpton Group Hotels and Restaurants *and* Outrigger Hotels and Resorts	Private-label reservation system	Increased ADR and profits; reduced labor costs; and increased attention to guests

(continued on next page)

TABLE 8.16 (continued)

IT champions	Practice initiated, developed	Measure of success
Marriott International	Information technology aligned with corporate strategy; and revenue-management systems for revenue enhancement	Increased operational efficiency; reduced costs; and eliminated guesswork. Increased revenues; improved profile of guests; and identified weak-occupancy periods
Omni Hotels	Integrated property- and revenue-management system	Increased revenues; increased service levels to guests; and reduced overbookings
Promus Hotels	Computerized, integrated payroll-and-benefit accounting system	Reduction in errors in selection of benefits and increased speed of response and productivity
Radisson Worldwide	Reward program for travel agents	Increased travel-agent participation and profitability
Ritz-Carlton Chicago	"Compcierge" position to handle guests' computer-related problems	Increased customer satisfaction and increased morale among concierge, business center, and MIS personnel

THE BEST PRACTICES

Interestingly, the vast majority of our best-practice champions focused primarily on using innovative technology to improve the efficiency of internal operations. The indirect effect on customer service and guest satisfaction was a secondary goal (and, in some cases, a happy accident). Those champions are the Barbizon Hotel and Empire Hotel New York, Candlewood Hotel Company, Carlson Hospitality Worldwide, Cendant Corporation, Courtyard by Marriott, Inter-Continental Hotels and Resorts, Kimpton Group Hotels and Restaurants and Outrigger Hotels and Resorts, Marriott International, Omni Hotels, and Promus Hotel Corporation.

The main goal of four other champions was to use technology specifically to improve service to the external guest. In those cases the secondary objective was indirectly to improve operations and financial measures. Those champions are the Balsams Grand Resort Hotel, Fairmont Copley Plaza Hotel, Hotel Nikko at Beverly Hills, and the Ritz-Carlton Chicago.

Two of the best practices equally benefited both operations and guests. The champions

with these "balanced" practices were IMPAC Hotel Group and Radisson Worldwide. Table 8.17 provides a summary of each best practice, the method of implementation, and the name of a contact person. The text below elaborates on the descriptions in Tables 8.16 and 8.17.

IMPROVING OPERATIONS EFFICIENCY

The companies and properties listed in this section used information technology to enhance substantially some aspect of hotel operations. In some cases guest services also improved as a result of implementing the IT best practice, and that was an added benefit (but not the primary goal).

HotelExpert

Managers at the Barbizon Hotel and Empire Hotel New York were dissatisfied with the traditional logbooks that are used to register guests' comments, requests, and complaints. The entries were often indecipherable, and there was no way to know whether a request

TABLE 8.17
IT best-practices cases, descriptions, implementation, contact people

IT Champion, Title of case	Description of case	Method of Implementation	Contact person
The Balsams Grand Resort Hotel *A Guest History System*	Created a comprehensive guest-history program that tracks each guest's preferred room, room layout, dining room, server, food and beverage items, housekeeper, and activities.	Each time an individual telephones or stays at the property, requisite information is entered into the guest-history database system. If the caller is a previous guest, that person's file is pulled up and the data reviewed and updated. The system is fully integrated with operations.	Steve Barba, *president* (603) 255-3400 Fax: (603) 255-4221
The Barbizon Hotel and Empire Hotel New York *Standardized Record Keeping for Operations and Guest Calls*	Developed HotelExpert software to eliminate logbooks and to standardize record keeping.	Software allows employees to activate calls from anywhere in the hotel. The system automatically assigns tasks and can activate employees' pagers. Computerized form is used to order items in advance and to schedule internal projects and preventive-maintenance assignments. Provides on-screen reports and graphs.	Pamela Graber, *general manager* (212) 838-5700 Fax: (212) 753-0360
Candlewood Hotel Company *Electronic Record Management*	Implemented an electronic system of recording and storing ("imaging") virtually all accounting and construction records, thus eliminating the need to file and store hard copies of documents.	Worked with software providers to find a system that would be easy to use. As part of the document-processing procedure, the document is scanned into the system and retrieval is easily accomplished via the file-index program.	Lisa Penn, *records-management coordinator* (316) 630-5500 Fax: (316) 630-5588
Carlson Hospitality Worldwide *Worldwide Reservation System*	Created the most extensive, efficient, and productive reservation system existing today.	Built from scratch its own reservation system that is designed to provide more-specific information on each property and more capabilities than the airlines' inflexible CRS mainframe systems were providing, while retaining the ability to connect with the CRSs. Developed seamless interface to GDS years before other companies.	Scott Heintzeman, *vice president of knowledge technology* (612) 449-3333 Fax: (612) 449-1126
Cendant Corporation *Integration of All Hotel MIS Functions*	Computerized system developed to integrate all hotel MIS functions into one system, so that all 6000 franchised hotels can use the information contained in Cendant's huge database.	The activities of property management, central reservations, Internet communications, and direct marketing are integrated into one system. operates 9 A.M. to 6 P.M., Mondays through Fridays.	Scott Anderson, *executive vice president–sales and marketing* (973) 496-8655 Fax: (973) 496-8445

(continued on next page)

TABLE 8.17 (continued)

IT Champion, *Title of case*	**Description of case**	**Method of Implementation**	**Contact person**
Courtyard by Marriott *Intranet Information Sharing*	Developed intranet information resource that organizes information into a single, easy-to-use property resource, using computer and electronic technology to replace manuals and other printed information.	Twenty regional technology leaders train Courtyard managers and key people on its intranet system, which provides brand standards, answers operating questions, assists users in expediting routine tasks, and provides timely and accurate information to solve hotel problems. A minimum of two computer stations are available in each hotel to allow immediate access to the system.	Kelly Vytlacil, *brand executive* (301) 380-8482 Fax: (301) 380-1333
Fairmont Copley Plaza Hotel *Using a Property Management System to Improve Concierge Desk Excellence*	The property-management system supports concierge services with a database that places guest information at the concierges' fingertips, thus freeing them for more direct guest contact.	The PMS records each guest's preferences and reminds the concierge of guests who need special attention. It also contains area restaurant schedules and attributes, and is capable of printing directions for guests.	David Jamieson, *director of concierge services* (617) 267-5300 Fax: (617) 267-7668
Hotel Nikko at Beverly Hills *Portable Telephone System throughout Hotel*	Installed a portable telephone system throughout the hotel. Phones can be used for any outgoing or incoming calls, but work only within the confines of the hotel.	A portable system was chosen over a cellular one because of its greater reliability. It was installed at night to minimize inconvenience to guests.	Bradford Rice, *front-office manager* or Max Malek, *systems manager* (310) 247-0400 Fax: (310) 247-0315
IMPAC Hotel Group *A Lobby Kiosk Touch-Screen Guest-Tracking System*	Each lobby contains a kiosk with a touch-screen monitor on which guests can respond to a survey about their stay. Data are downloaded and made available to the property manager the next morning.	System was developed in-house in conjunction with a third-party software company. Kiosks were placed in each property and now incorporate a work station connected to a mainframe computer in Atlanta via T1 phone lines.	Nancy Wolff, *chief information officer* (404) 365-3830 Fax: (404) 364-0088
Inter-Continental Hotels and Resorts *Building a Global Marketing Database*	Created global strategic-marketing database containing detailed and extensive guest histories and consumption patterns for guest stays worldwide.	Jointly developed by the rooms department and the information-technology department to meet the marketing department's needs. After developing the technology, standards and training were implemented to ensure standardized coding worldwide. Data is regularly e-mailed from all worldwide locations for uploading.	Annette Kissinger, *director of rooms and database marketing* (203) 351-8240 Fax: (203) 351-8222

(continued on next page)

TABLE 8.17 (continued)

IT Champion, *Title of case*	Description of case	Method of Implementation	Contact person
Kimpton Group Hotels and Restaurants *and* Outrigger Hotels and Resorts *Private-Label Reservation System to Encourage Upselling*	Private-label reservation system has cross-selling capability that serves to contribute to improved occupancies and rates. System provides different quotes for specific dates and includes an on-line incentive to encourage upselling the customer.	When a reservation agent selects a hotel and room type for a specific date, the system provides three initial quotes, each showing an on-line incentive-point value. The system also provides data for any rate and room-type combination available, so the agent can sell the customer without having to enter multiple requests.	Dean Di Lullo, *director of reservations* (415) 955-5433 Fax: (415) 296-8031 or Ken Taylor, *vice president, information systems* (808) 921-6701 Fax: (808) 921-6715
Marriott International *Aligning Information Technology with Corporate Strategy*	Developed process to ensure that future systems and technologies support the corporate business strategy. The alignment is guided by a plan for a series of projects that must be executed to deliver the appropriate capabilities.	The plan covers three phases: baseline assessment, strategy development, and plan formulation. Each phase examines the use of information technology throughout the organization.	Barry L. Shuler, *senior vice president, information resources strategy and planning* (301) 380-6586 Fax: (301) 380-3801
Marriott International *Revenue Management Systems for Revenue Enhancement*	Developed revenue-management system that isolates the different market segments that use Marriott properties and provides a comprehensive understanding of those segments' reservations behavior, price sensitivity, and stay patterns.	Current system evolved from earlier yield-management systems. Fully integrated with the reservation system, the revenue-management system creates arrival-demand forecasts and provides inventory restriction recommendations. It also provides overbooking recommendations for each property.	David Babich, *vice president, revenue management* (301) 380-1517 Fax: (301) 380-5728
Omni Hotels *Integrated Property-Management and Revenue-Management System*	Integrated a companywide property-management system in its reservation system to produce a fully integrated, highly efficient reservations system that includes revenue management capabilities.	The development team collected information from all critical property managers to determine what was needed in the system. Based on these data, a third party developed a user-friendly Windows NT–based program, which expedited training on the new system.	Dennis Hulsing, *senior vice president for sales and marketing* (972) 871-5624 Fax: (972) 871-5667
Promus Hotels *On-Line Integrated Payroll-Benefit Accounting System*	Developed a computerized, integrated payroll-and-benefit accounting system that is accessible on-line. Using a customized Windows program, the system displays the various benefit options available to an employee. After employee selections are made, the choices are automatically forwarded to corporate headquarters.	The system was developed by the technology department with input provided by human-resources managers, general managers, and the corporate human-resources department. Memos, manuals, instructions, and technological support were provided to the hotels as the system was implemented. The system replaced manuals and forms.	Kelly Jenkins, *vice president of corporate compensation* (901) 374-5510 Fax: (901) 374-5509

(continued on next page)

TABLE 8.17 (continued)

IT Champion, Title of case	Description of case	Method of Implementation	Contact person
Radisson Worldwide *Reward Program for Travel Agents*	Developed "Look to Book" program, which rewards travel agents with points that can be redeemed for travel or gifts based on the number of reservations they book on-line with Radisson.	The goal was to develop a seamless, paperless loyalty-point program for travel agents that would instantly recognize and reward each travel agent's Radisson booking. After technical and programming work were completed, a training and support system was developed to instruct agents on its benefits and how to participate.	Brian Stage, *president* (612) 449-3443 Fax: (612) 449-3401
Ritz-Carlton Chicago *"Compcierge" Position to Handle Guests' Computer-Related Problems*	Created new "compcierge" staff position within the MIS department to serve guests who are experiencing computer-technology difficulties and to provide computer equipment on a loaner basis.	MIS personnel handle guests' computer-related problems as an added service to guests. Additional hardware and software were purchased to meet guests' needs, and requests for new software are reviewed immediately to determine feasibility. The compcierge service is located at the concierge desk, found in front of the hotel's business center, and operates 9 A.M. to 6 P.M., Mondays through Fridays.	Tom Kelly, *general manager* (312) 573-5001 Fax: (312) 266-9498

Note: The case titles correspond to the cases written on each champion in: Laurette Dubé, Cathy A. Enz, Leo M. Renaghan, and Judy A. Siguaw, *American Lodging Excellence: The Key to Best Practices in the U.S. Lodging Industry* (Washington, D.C.: American Express and the American Hotel Foundation, 1999).

had been fulfilled or, if it had, how much time it had required. To eliminate the logbooks and to standardize record keeping for all operations activity and guest calls, a central database was developed with one computerized form. Now known as HotelExpert, the specialized software allows employees to activate calls from virtually anywhere in the hotel via telephone or PCs connected to the local area network. The system automatically assigns tasks to the proper employee or manager and can also activate pagers, thereby ensuring that calls go to the right employees. (Tasks that are transmitted to pagers are followed within 15 minutes by a "reminder" page.) If a task goes uncompleted, the system notifies the manager on duty. In addition, to order items in advance, such as cribs and wake-up calls, all departments use a single computerized form. The primary users of this system are the housekeeping and maintenance departments. Lastly, the software provides on-screen reports and graphs so that previously hard-to-retrieve data can be easily analyzed.

Measuring Success

The use of HotelExpert at the Barbizon and Empire Hotels has enabled those properties to offer an efficient, high level of service, and it has improved overall physical-plant operations. In turn, those improvements have resulted in a 30 percent increase in repeat-guest patronage. Moreover, the software system has enabled the two hotels to save a total of

$750,000 over a three-year period through increased productivity and decreased paperwork, and the ability to analyze trouble spots.

Record Keeping

Candlewood Hotel Company found that its accounting personnel were spending valuable hours searching hundreds of boxes and file cabinets to find needed documents. This document search impeded responses to vendors, customers, and employees—resulting in less efficiency for everyone. In response to this problem, an electronic system of recording and storing virtually all documents was implemented. Only those records that contain original signatures (e.g., contracts, leases, deeds) are retained as hard copies, although they are also included in the electronic system for information-retrieval purposes. Development of the system involved a time-consuming process of researching software developers and vendors. Once selected and installed, however, the system itself has been easy to use and has added only one extra step to Candlewood's normal document-processing procedure—that of scanning the document into the system.

Measuring Success
Candlewood estimates that its electronic record-management system will save approximately $90,000 per year through employees' enhanced productivity and the decreased need for storage space. In addition, vendors, guests (especially group master accounts), and all employees benefit from the reduced time required to research and solve a problem or answer a question. Lower operating costs have also translated into lower room rates for guests.

Reaching beyond the CRS

Over a decade ago Carlson Hospitality Worldwide was the last of the major hotel compa-nies to develop an on-line, computerized reservations system (CRS). At that time Carlson decided against following the path other lodging firms had taken, namely, that of adapting existing airline reservations systems. Instead Carlson developed its system from scratch. The system was designed to provide more-specific information on each property and included more capabilities than what the airline CRSs were capable of providing, while still being able to communicate with the airlines' systems. Carlson also developed seamless connections to global distribution system (GDS) technology long before other hotel companies pursued those benefits. Since that time Carlson has continued to upgrade its system, and based on contribution and cost data, Carlson believes its system is the most extensive, efficient, and productive reservations system in existence today.

Measuring Success
Compared to the industry as a whole, Carlson's worldwide reservations system makes the most money at the lowest cost (in terms of cost as a percentage of revenue). Specifically, Carlson's reservations system's cost is 2 percent of revenue produced, whereas its five peers' reservations systems' average cost is 2.7 percent of revenue, and the 21 industry leaders' average cost is 3.4 percent of revenue. Furthermore, in a 1997 independent (proprietary) study, Carlson's reservations system was ranked number one in occupancy contribution; data from that study were provided us by Scott Heintzeman of the Carlson Companies.

MIS Uniformity

Cendant Corporation has linked all 6000 of its franchised hotels' management information system (MIS) functions into one system that is tied to Cendant's huge database. The goals of this undertaking are to give each owner and manager more control of each property, to make each hotel more efficient and profitable, to improve communications, and to improve local marketing efforts. Called Power Up, the system consists of four main functions: property management, central reservations, Internet communications, and direct marketing. For example, in the area of property management, Power Up permits the user to perform:

1. Inventory management and central reservations with a seamless interface.
2. Yield management.
3. On-line credit-card processing.
4. Workforce assignments.
5. Room-maintenance management.

Moreover, the system allows operational connectivity to Cendant's other computer systems and allows the hotel to stay in touch with its corporate brand-support team, other franchises, and the rest of the world. Power Up also gives individual hotels access to data that they can use to conduct targeted direct marketing. Franchisees receive extensive training on the Power Up system. While there is no fee to the property for the basic system, after the first year an annual service contract fee is charged.

Measuring Success
Cendant's integration of its hotel MIS functions into one system resulted in an average ADR increase of $8 at Cendant properties using the system (which in turn increases the percentage-of-sales revenues collected by the company). The system benefits guests in that the enhanced database facilitates providing them with VIP treatment.

Intranet Communication

Courtyard by Marriott expanded so rapidly that its ability to train and develop managers was stretched to the limit. A communication tool was needed that would be fast, easily disseminated, and user friendly. Courtyard managers determined that an intranet system would be best for this purpose. Outside vendors were hired to assist in designing a system that would allow information to be readily accessible and would require no more than four clicks to gain entry to any topic or subtopic. The result is a system called the Source that uses computers and electronic technology to replace manuals and other printed information. It organizes information into a single, easy-to-use property resource. The Source includes brand system standards, international sales and marketing, incentive marketing, STAR (acronym for *Skills to Achieve Results*) training modules, accounting, new-hire processing, and a manager's guide to benefits. At least two computer workstations are located in each hotel to allow accessibility to the Source. Updating and changing information is easy and eliminates the need to print and mail hard copies to individual properties. Moreover, the system ensures that all new information is received at the property level in a timely fashion (versus the uncertainty associated with ground-transportation delivery services such as the U.S. Postal Service and private couriers). The program design also includes a section called "What's New" that flags and highlights the latest information.

Measuring Success
The intranet system used by Courtyard by Marriott has virtually eliminated paperwork-preparation and hard-copy-distribution costs and improved staff efficiency, training, and morale. For example, the system has saved a minimum of one hour each time a new employee is hired. Since Courtyard hotels hired some 6600 new workers in just the first nine months of 1998, that intranet savings allowed more than 6600 employee work-hours to be expended on other projects. Because the system contains up-to-date operating information and is easily accessible, the need for midlevel supervisors has been reduced, thereby saving even more time and money. Guests are indi-

rect beneficiaries of hotel standards that are consistent, efficient, and timely.

Global 2000

Inter-Continental Hotels and Resorts recognized that it lacked the capability to answer some basic marketing questions about its guests and corporate clients. To overcome that limitation it created a centralized system to collect and store (for easy retrieval) guest data about length of stay, travel patterns, and services used. Global 2000 is a strategic-marketing database that is designed to interact with a wide range of reservation and property-management systems worldwide. Implementation of the system required numerous steps. After defining and developing the technology, Inter-Continental determined standards and training processes by taking into account the international nature of the data. Next, a standardized format was created to accommodate different office systems and to summarize revenue information into different source categories. Third, the use of and format for distributing the data were determined. Fourth, the company addressed direct-marketing applications and developed a user-friendly method for data retrieval. To build the database, data are collected from more than 100 hotels (out of 160 within the chain). Those properties represent 90 percent of Inter-Continental's worldwide rooms revenue. Data are gathered from all customers staying at participating hotels, and not just frequent travelers or loyalty-program members. Moreover, data are obtained at checkout rather than at the time of reservation to capture guests' complete consumption behavior.

Measuring Success
The cost of Inter-Continental's targeted mailings has been reduced, and because the mailings are more focused, they have generated more sales (compared to previous mail-marketing efforts). Participation in the guest-loy-alty program has been increased by targeting previously unenrolled frequent travelers with special promotions and reduced membership fees. The cost-effectiveness of the firm's advertising campaigns can now be tracked by noting the sources of new-customer acquisition. In another vein, Global 2000's data patterns aid managers in finding creative solutions to operational issues, while the database provides an added incentive for business partners to join the company. To further measure success, a new series of management and benchmarking reports was developed based on the data for individual hotels, regional sales offices, and Inter-Continental's marketing departments.

In-House Cross-Selling

Kimpton Group Hotels and Restaurants wanted to ensure its position as market leader in boutique hotels, and wanted to encourage greater cross-selling among its properties. Kimpton's managers turned to Outrigger Hotels and Resorts, which had been developing a private-label central-reservation-system application for several years (in conjunction with OPUS 2 Revenue Technologies and Enterprise Hospitality Solutions). Kimpton used customer focus groups to determine how the system should be configured to meet its needs. The system was designed so that when a central-reservation agent selects a property and accommodation combination for a hotel for a particular date, the system provides the agent with three initial quotes. Each quote has an on-line incentive-point value assigned to it. This incentive induces the agent to try to sell the most attractive accommodations to earn as many incentive points as possible. Further, the system provides a listing of all rate and room-type combinations available to the general public, so the reservation agent has the opportunity to keep selling to the customer without having to enter multiple requests. The reservation program also encourages cross-selling by allowing the agent to search for a rate category or special package across all Kimpton Group hotels with one search.

Measuring Success

The Kimpton Group's private-label reservation system has improved profits by allowing an 8 to 11 percent increase in ADR with no apparent loss in occupancy. (One way it does this is by ensuring availability for customers who are willing to pay the highest rates.) Centralization of the reservation system has allowed each property to reduce its reservation staff from an average of four or four-and-a-half reservationists to just one-and-a-half (on average). Moreover, it has reduced the number of abandoned phone calls from previous highs of 8 to 10 percent to fewer than 2 percent, and is providing a 90 percent service level (meaning that 90 percent of all calls are answered within the first 20 seconds). Additionally, front office employees can now be more attentive to guests because they are no longer handling reservation calls. Finally, the system provides meeting planners, travel agents, and individuals with the ability to book any Kimpton Group hotel with a single phone call.

Supporting the Corporate Vision

Marriott International has developed a strategy and planning process to align its information systems, resources, and technology with the strategy of its operating business. This approach to information technology permits Marriott to assess how well current applications and technology systems support the business and how to improve this support in anticipation of future needs. The information-resources division developed a three-step process to provide both the vision for future systems and technologies and a set of plans to guide execution of current information-based projects.

The three-step process includes (1) baseline assessment, (2) strategy development, and (3) plan formulation. The strengths and weaknesses of the current information-resources organization and the systems and technology it provides is assessed in the first stage. A baseline is established using facilitated workshops with senior managers to evaluate current application systems and using benchmarks to compare Marriott with other companies. From this assessment, a list of "quick hits" or short-term projects is developed that immediately can improve information-resources support for business operations. For example, several different user help desks from various brands and departments were consolidated into one help desk for all Marriott end users. In the strategy-development phase, information-resources managers work with senior managers from the business (e.g., marketing, food and beverage, sales, rooms operations) to envision and document future business processes and the hotel-of-the-future from a systems-and-technology perspective.

The third phase, plan formulation, involves creating a framework for taking information resources from the current state identified in the baseline-assessment phase to the strategic vision defined in the strategy-development phase. This final phase describes priorities, timing, staffing requirements and sourcing strategies, costs and benefits, required training, and other projects needed to implement as much of the technology plan as possible within a three-year time horizon.

Measuring Success

Marriott International's information resources, strategy, and planning process supports its business strategy. The identification and execution of so-called quick-hit actions discovered during the baseline-assessment phase have yielded increases in operational efficiency and reductions in costs. The framework for annual review and updating of the technology plan and strategy allows the information-resources department to remain aligned with

Marriott's business strategy and to stay abreast of important systems and technology trends.

Revenue Management

Marriott International has also developed a revenue-management system that isolates the different market segments (e.g., leisure travelers, business travelers) that use the spectrum of Marriott properties and provides a comprehensive understanding of those segments' reservations behavior, price sensitivity, and stay patterns. This information enables Marriott to optimize room revenue by increasing room sales. The system uses proprietary software and is fully integrated with Marriott's reservation program. It creates arrival (demand) forecasts and provides sophisticated inventory-restriction recommendations. The revenue-management program offers the same inventory and rate information to all distribution outlets, so guests find no variation among channels. It also produces overbooking recommendations for each property by factoring in cancellations, early departures, and stay-overs. Finally, the system helps managers to maximize revenue on each room sold by adjusting rates according to demand and provides Marriott with the ability to cross-sell its properties on a referral basis to any of its guests by allowing sales agents to access occupancy and room-rate information on any Marriott property.

Measuring Success
Marriott International's revenue-management system has increased revenues by 1 to 3 percent, which translates into hundreds of millions of dollars. Individual properties receive better guest-profile information for marketing purposes and learn about potentially weak occupancy periods in time to initiate targeted sales efforts. Customers benefit from more-effective inventory control and pricing,

and through better management of demand patterns in the following ways: customers are more likely to find a room when they need it, and those who are price sensitive can be accommodated on certain days when they might otherwise have been turned away.

OmniCHARM

Omni Hotels introduced a companywide property-management system into its CRS to yield a fully integrated, highly efficient reservations system that includes a state-of-the-art revenue-management system. This system, known as OmniCHARM, employs user-friendly PC-based software that is said to be less complicated than the revenue-management systems currently in use by the rest of the industry. Each night all Omni Hotels properties feed their reservations data into OmniCHARM via the central-reservation-information system. OmniCHARM then formulates length-of-stay restrictions to help Omni Hotels maximize room availability and revenue by determining selling strategies for each property regarding rates, length-of-stay restrictions, and the necessary adjustments on weekends versus weekdays. Projections can be made as far into the future as desired.

Measuring Success
The OmniCHARM system has resulted in revenue increases of 3 to 7 percent. Guest-service levels are also increasing as a result of the CRS center's database because Omni's managers can stay current on what their customers want and expect. In addition, Omni has significantly reduced hotel overbooking.

No More Paperwork

At Promus Hotel Corporation, the traditional paper forms used for employee-benefits selection were difficult for employees to follow, and so they made many mistakes. Additionally, it often took a long time for the forms to arrive at corporate headquarters and for the information to be entered into the company system. Moreover, Promus's rapid growth signaled a need for a more efficient payroll-and-benefit system, at a reasonable cost. Promus therefore developed a computerized, integrated payroll-and-benefit accounting system that is accessible on-line. Paperless and seamless, the customized system displays on a computer screen the various benefit options available to an employee. After the employee makes her selections, those choices are automatically transmitted to corporate headquarters where they become part of the payroll-information system.

Measuring Success

Promus' on-line integrated payroll-and-benefit accounting system results in virtually no errors in employees' selection of benefits, which saves time in recording and administering those employee choices. Moreover, human-resources employees can now devote their efforts to other pressing employee issues (rather than spending time correcting administrative mistakes).

IMPROVING GUEST SERVICE

The companies and properties listed in this section used information technology to improve guest services, offer distinctive service, or respond to the expressed needs of customers.

Guest-History Program

Due to its remote location in the White Mountains of northern New Hampshire, managers at the Balsams Grand Resort Hotel have long recognized that the resort needs a high ratio of return guests if it is to be successful. To entice guests back to the Balsams year after

year, management chose to institute a guest-history program that would allow as much customization for each guest as possible. The program developed was one of the first attempts at using artificial intelligence in a real-time mode for multiusers. The resort collects data on every guest and on every individual who makes an inquiry about the hotel and places those data into that individual's file. The type of information collected includes the dates of the guest's previous visits, the room type and number (and any special requests for room layout), and the rate paid; the guest's housekeeper and server team; and the guest's preferences regarding dining rooms, food and beverage selections, special activities, and tee times or ski runs. Virtually any special request or stated preference can be recorded in the system. The system is fully integrated into the resort's operations, which allows the guest's every need to be anticipated and fulfilled.

Measuring Success

The detailed guest-history database at the Balsams has generated high occupancy rates for the hotel. In fact, some 85 percent of the resort's business is from either repeat guests or first-time visitors who are there based on the recommendation of a former guest.

The Concierge's Helper

Managers at Boston's Fairmont Copley Plaza Hotel wanted to provide the most consistent guest service possible. A study indicated, however, that the concierge desk was overloaded with routine tasks, in part because a business center was located there. The Fidelio property-management system was therefore adopted to support the hotel's concierge services. The system allowed the director of concierge services to build a guest-history database that allows the concierge to expedite guest services and otherwise improve overall service levels. This allows the concierge to fulfill all guest needs. For example, the PMS records each guest's stated preferences regarding a daily newspaper, breakfast, and wake-up call, and whether the guest uses the overnight laundry service. The system identifies those guests who need special attention and allows guests' dining choices to be prioritized. The PMS also contains details about every street in Boston, including how far it is from the hotel and the best way to get there.

Measuring Success

Fairmont Copley Plaza Hotel's use of a property-management system to support its concierge services has pushed the concierge's guest-satisfaction index consistently close to 90 percent. Moreover, the program has encouraged loyalty among a core group of guests who frequently stay at the hotel.

Telephones to Go

At the Hotel Nikko in Beverly Hills, guests' comments repeatedly indicated that many guests desired a third phone line so that they could handle multiple data and voice functions simultaneously. A feasibility study, however, indicated that the cost of installing a third wire to each guest room would be prohibitive. Instead, the hotel's managers installed a portable phone system. (Portable service was selected over cellular because of the reputed greater reliability of portable systems.) The system was installed in a relatively short time and with a minimum of inconvenience to guests. The portable phones are available in all guest rooms and meeting rooms and are issued to selected hotel employees, including housekeepers, bell staff, and workers from the convention-services, maintenance, security, food and beverage, and front-desk departments. The phones have the same features as any other phone, including long-distance-call capability, but they operate only within the confines of the hotel. Extra phones are available upon request and, for billing purposes, are easily programmed to relate to a specific

guest room or to a group's master account. Guests pay $9.95 per day for use of each portable phone.

Measuring Success

Nikko's portable telephone system has been popular with guests. It gives them the ability to place and receive calls from any location within the hotel. As a result, the system has increased guest telephone use by 6.5 percent and telephone revenues by $2 per room-night sold.

High-Tech Concierge

The Ritz-Carlton Chicago found that its concierge and business-center personnel were increasingly being asked computer-related questions for which they did not have answers. In some cases the concierge simply did not have the technological expertise necessary to assist guests, and in other cases the software requested by guests was not available in the business center. The hotel's managers determined that the hotel's MIS department was capable of handling most of the guests' computer-related problems and questions, so a new staff position, the "compcierge," was created within the MIS department. The hotel also purchased additional hardware and software to maintain the desired level of guest service. The compcierge serves guests who are experiencing technological difficulties and loans computer equipment at no extra charge. The compcierge is stationed alongside the concierge desk, near the hotel's business center, from 9:00 A.M. to 6:00 P.M., Monday through Friday.

Measuring Success

The Ritz-Carlton Chicago's compcierge position has been well received by guests. Guest requests for computer assistance have increased from two to five per day, and morale among the concierge, business center, and MIS personnel has increased.

IMPROVING BOTH GUEST SERVICE AND OPERATIONS

The two companies listed below used information technology to solve guest-service problems, knowing that the solution would benefit the overall operation of their hotels at the same time.

Guest Feedback

IMPAC Hotel Group was dissatisfied with its guest-feedback program, which primarily consisted of in-room guest-survey cards. Besides the obvious limitations of such surveys, too much time was elapsing between when the data were collected and when they were compiled and shared with managers. Consequently, the information became essentially a historic review and was not useful for immediate action. IMPAC worked with a software graphics-design company to develop a system that would allow rapid reporting and response to guest feedback. The result is a kiosk containing a touch-screen monitor in the lobby of each IMPAC property. Using the touch screen, guests can answer a series of questions regarding their stay. The guest-tracking questions are designed to solicit comments and allow the guest to rate all hotel departments. The data are downloaded each night and distributed daily to the property's general manager and the corporate office. Data are available at any time during the day, providing the opportunity to immediately address any problems. Additionally, each month the kiosk is rolled into a more-private location and guests are invited to participate in an "associate satisfaction survey." This survey allows guests to provide extensive, confidential comments regarding the performance of the hotel's employees and its operations. Those data are also distributed to managers and executives at the end of the day.

Measuring Success

IMPAC's kiosk-based touch-screen guest-tracking system has improved hotel mainte-nance, employee productivity, and the overall quality and image of IMPAC properties. Guests favor the computerized system, as it gives them greater confidence that the information they provide will be used (compared to completing cards that are left in the room or mailed to some obscure address). Moreover, guest service has improved and response time has been dramatically reduced. Indeed, in some cases the hotel can initiate changes based on guest feedback before the guest has checked out of the hotel. The data have also been useful in the preparation of capital budgets by enabling managers to pinpoint and justify capital-expenditure requests based on the needs and observations reported by guests.

Look to Book

Radisson Worldwide, which is firmly committed to maintaining good working relationships with the travel industry, sought to develop a competitive advantage by strengthening its ties with travel agents. As a result it developed its Look to Book program. This travel-agent award program requires no paperwork and no manual processing, and it works on all GDSs worldwide. Best of all, it allows Radisson instantly to recognize and reward each travel-agent booking. The program was designed to communicate with travel agents within three to seven seconds of a booking and includes a "bank" that securely manages the rapid deposit and withdrawal of Look to Book points. Using the Look to Book program, a travel agent can earn points redeemable for hotel stays, travel, and gifts each time the agent reserves a Radisson room on-line. After every transaction, an electronic notice is immediately sent to the individual, showing the number of points that have just been earned, as well as giving the status of the agent's total current redeemable points and the earned points pending from reservations not yet consumed. Radisson also created a seamless interface between its host systems and agents'

GDSs, which allows for rate integrity. That interface also allows travel agents to bypass the GDS database and view full-text room descriptions directly from Radisson's own database. (That innovation is now an industry standard.)

Measuring Success

Radisson's Look to Book program has enticed more than half of the world's travel agents to participate in the program. Agents like the fact that they can individually earn and redeem Look to Book points. As a result the program has been profitable and adds value to the hotels that come into the Radisson system. Radisson does about $1 billion in worldwide travel-agency business annually.

INSIGHTS FROM CHAMPIONS

The IT best-practice champions, for the most part, believe that using technology to enhance marketing efforts is a necessity in today's competitive environment. These champions believe that the capital required for the technology was negligible when compared to the benefits accrued. Because the support of senior management is crucial when proposing new technology, however, managers and others who propose such changes must be prepared to "show incremental profit and revenue," according to Inter-Continental's Annette Kissinger.

Second, when designing or greatly modifying the organization's technology, ensure that the marketing and operations departments are involved in the project. As Courtyard's Kelly Vytlacil suggests, "Spend the time to research the needs of the field personnel," to which he adds, "design the information around how users want to see it, rather than how content owners want to present it." In other words, design the system to be user friendly.

Third, our champions repeatedly noted the importance of ensuring that all personnel are informed about and trained in all operational aspects of any new technology prior to fully implementing the system. Consequently, managers should consider slowly rolling out the new technology to keep from overwhelming the training staff and to allow time for employees to adapt to the changes.

Fourth, use technology to eliminate paperwork and reduce response time to guest requests. In general, new technology should improve employee productivity and morale. Such has been the experience of many of the best-practice champions profiled here, including the Barbizon Hotel and Empire Hotel New York, Candlewood Hotel Company, and Courtyard by Marriott.

Fifth, take the time to extensively research third-party system and software providers to find the most cost-effective vendor. That is not always an easy task, yet as Candlewood's Lisa Penn noted, "The cost, time, and effort are well worth it."

Sixth, consider the use of only network architecture instead of personal computers when designing a system. IMPAC Hotel Group, Courtyard by Marriott, and the Barbizon Hotel all found network systems to be faster and more economical than individual PC-based workstations.

Seventh, recognize that technology is a long-term investment and design the system to accept future changes. Finally, the technology should not detract from personal service to the guest, but instead should enhance it.

STREAMLINING FOR PROFITABILITY

We believe that the ability to harness technology to improve the efficiency of hotel operations and service to guests will be the key to future success in the hotel industry. The IT best-practice champions mentioned here have shown us how they used information technology to develop specific competitive advantages and generate increased revenues in the process.

For the most part, the best practices related to information technology involved streamlining operations by reducing paperwork, speeding information dissemination, and increasing employee productivity—thereby increasing profitability. Other practices entailed collecting more detailed data on guests or providing more data to reservations agents, both for the purpose of increasing sales. Few practices, though, emphasized using information technology for the sole purpose of upgrading guest services. While a focus on improving hotel operations through

information technology is crucial and commendable, the paucity of IT practices designed strictly for the guest is surprising, since such practices could easily result in enhanced revenues as well as more-satisfied guests. This gap in applying information technology to guest services may indicate there is much room for innovators to use technology to substantially improve the guest's lodging experience and thereby position the hotel organization as the preferred choice of the consumer.

8.8   Data Warehousing

Robert K. Griffin

The ability to collect, store, and process large amounts of data can provide hospitality companies with strategic competitive advantages. It can help managers make more effective decisions and fewer ineffective decisions. American Airlines, for example, analyzes hundreds of gigabytes (GB) of data every day to support its yield-management activities. American Airlines CEO Robert Crandall estimates that these activities deliver the company an additional $500 million per year in revenue (Smith, Leimkuhler, and Darrow, 1992, p. 31). Even small companies find their need for large amounts of data has increased with their need for more and better information. Trend analysis, for example, requires a great deal of historical data no matter what size the company.

The latest concept for information handling is data warehousing. In a data warehouse a group or company develops a central information storehouse designed to answer business questions. The concept goes back to the mid-1980s and is generally credited to Bill Inmon of Prism Solutions (Teraske, 1997).

A data warehouse is a corporatewide database-management system that allows a company to manipulate large volumes of data in ways that are useful to the company: establishing sources, cleansing, organizing, summarizing, describing, and storing large amounts of data to be transformed, analyzed, and reported (see Figure 8.4). By contrast, a data mart is a smaller, more limited version of a data warehouse that is established for one group of users or for one subject area and is available to a relatively small number of persons (see Figure 8.5). In this article I discuss the development and application of data warehouses and data marts.

Data warehouses and data marts are differentiated from traditional database systems by more than just their size, although size is a factor. While traditional database systems are capable of accumulating large amounts of data, their limits are soon exceeded when they are connected with operating systems, such as hotel reservation systems, that continuously feed the database. Traditional database systems also tend to break down when the quantity and intensity of queries expand to support intense analysis. In addition, traditional databases have the following problems: They do not always store data in the appropriate formats for analysis; they do not offer the most effective analytical tools; their data may not be freshened often enough; and their data are sometimes inaccurate or incomplete. Data-warehousing technology provides solu-

Figure 8.4
Conceptual diagram of data warehouse

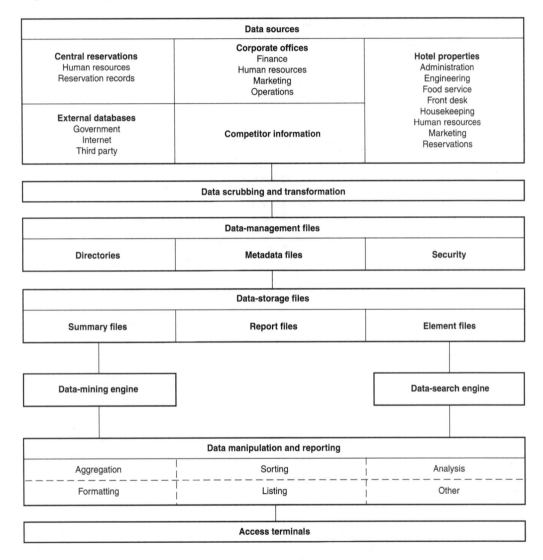

tions for these shortcomings of traditional database systems.

DATA WAREHOUSES VERSUS DATA MARTS

Data warehouses are built to serve the information needs of an entire organization, while data marts serve the information needs of a discrete group. The two perform many of the same functions, but data warehouses contain much more data because the data warehouse is a central depository for all of the business's information. Data warehouses reduce redundancy of data storage among different departments while at the same time allowing many users to perform a wide variety of analyses. When a data warehouse is available through either an intranet or the Internet, it may be called a *web warehouse*.

Figure 8.5
Conceptual diagram of data mart for guest information

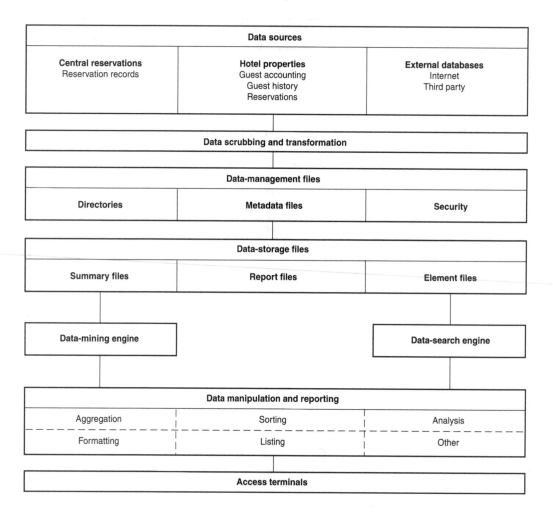

Companies do not always prefer data warehouses to data marts, because data warehouses are expensive to build and maintain. O'Sullivan found that the initial outlay for warehouses is often over $3 million (1996). Nevertheless, when the project is successful, it is well worth the investment. International Data Corporation, for example, examined 62 companies with successful data-warehouse applications and found that the average ROI was 401 percent and that the mean payback period was 2.31 years (Robinson, 1996, p. S13).

However, this finding may be skewed by the fact that respondents are unlikely to discuss unsuccessful projects, because the personnel who were responsible for a failed project often do not want to discuss such a failure or are at risk for their jobs.

While a typical data warehouse is around 300 GB (Cafasso, 1996), large companies such as AT&T, Bank of America, BellSouth, Blue Cross–Blue Shield, Chase Manhattan, Kmart, MasterCard, MCI, Tandy, Target Stores, Union Pacific, UPS, U.S. Customs, and Wal-Mart own data warehouses in excess of one terabyte (TB), or 1000 GB. This means their systems routinely collect, store, and manipulate the equivalent of more than one billion documents the size of an average business letter (Foley, 1996, p. 34).

Data warehouses can be designed to limit the user's access to a specific amount and type of data. This may be done for security reasons or to make the database more manageable. Such a limited application of a data warehouse—when it is tailored to one group of users or for one subject area—is referred to as a *virtual data mart*, a true data warehouse that functions as a data mart for those users (see Figure 8.6). This approach actually increases the processing demands on the data warehouse because it must do everything a warehouse does, plus partition data and run multiple interfaces. An alternative approach, which reduces the load on the warehouse, is to download selected data to a separate server in the form of a data mart (see Figure 8.7). This alternative combines the central power of a data warehouse with the simplicity and security of a data mart.

Figure 8.6
Data warehouse with four virtual data marts

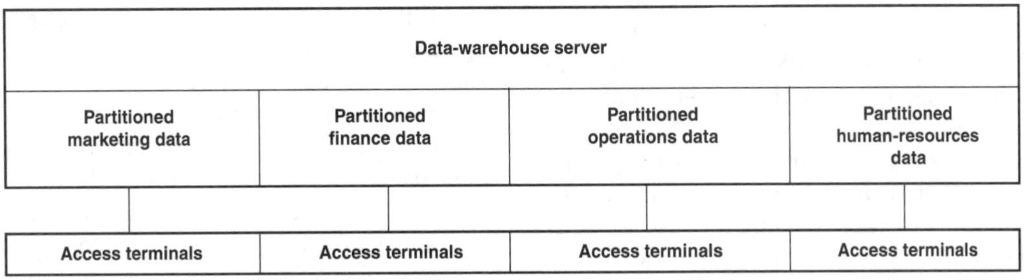

Figure 8.7
Data warehouse supporting physical data marts

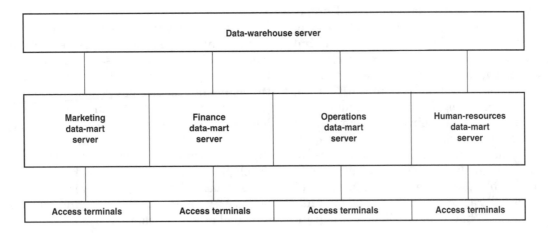

DATA MARTS

Data marts are developed to serve a small group of users, usually in a single subject area. A data mart might focus, for instance, on guest information. Such a system would be used to analyze repeat business, guest loyalty, frequent-guest programs, guest demographics, guest use of amenities, guest complaints, and guest satisfaction.

Beside increased security and greater manageability, data marts are much less expensive to build than data warehouses. Since they hold less data, they require less powerful engines, less expensive hardware, and fewer resources to develop and maintain. Data marts can be built for around $300,000, which is about one-tenth the cost of a data warehouse. (Moreover, failure may be less critical to the job security of those involved.) Data marts usually require from three to six months to develop compared to one to two years for data warehouses.

Many experts recommend beginning with a data mart, thereby enabling the company to learn about data-warehousing technology with lower risk. While data marts are a good product to start with, the long-term objective of most companies that embrace this technology is to develop a central data warehouse. An additional problem with this approach is that a data warehouse is more than a "grown-up" data mart.

The success of one data mart will propel people's desire and interest to build additional data marts. If marketers, for example, find that their guest-information data mart is valuable, they will want to develop new and more comprehensive systems. People in finance, human resources, operations, and administration may each want their own data marts, as well. Having multiple data marts, however, leads to the very problems data warehousing is supposed to solve. A congeries of data marts is also problematic because certain types of analysis will require data that reside in multiple marts. While it is possible to integrate multiple data marts into one large system, the cost of this approach would likely exceed the cost of creating a data warehouse in the first place. Maintenance is difficult, moreover, and the systems will likely be error-prone. In addition, the systems may well be overburdened by performing analysis that cuts across multiple marts. The situation would be even worse if data formats, software, and hardware are not standardized. For these reasons, companies that start small should think big.

DATA WAREHOUSING BY LODGING FIRMS

My literature review indicated that data-warehouse systems have been developed by airline, car rental, and restaurant companies, but I found little on data warehouses among lodging corporations (Halper, 1996). To determine whether lodging companies were involved with this technology, I contacted the MIS departments of the 12 largest lodging corporations, based on a listing found on the AH&MA Web site. I restricted my sample to only the largest corporations because the cost of data-warehouse systems prohibits their use by small companies and because my purpose was to learn about the technology and its application, rather than to survey its use.

Metamidwife

I was fascinated to discover that my study occurred at the birth of these systems in the lodging industry. As a consequence, applications and approaches were as varied as were the companies themselves. When I found companies that were involved with data warehousing, I asked the project managers whether they were building a warehouse or a mart, how long they had been working on the project, where development was at this time, the system's focus, what technology they were using, their philosophy, their future plans, and whether they had any practical tips.

The next section of this chapter gives the results of my study, as summarized in Table 8.18, which provides a list that compares the use and focus among the companies contacted. Only 7 of the 12 large hotel corporations that I contacted are involved in data warehousing, and only two of those have developed warehouses (as opposed to marts). Five of the seven companies involved with large-scale data management focused their systems on marketing or guest data. One had a general focus and one had a finance focus. Development time for warehouses ranged from 18 to 24 months, and development time for marts ranged from 3 to 18 months. Two of the seven systems had not been rolled out at the time of my study, while data in four of the systems were available to unit managers at the property level.

Company A

Company A is part of a diversified corporation that owns and franchises economy and midlevel properties. Its warehouse was developed to serve both its lodging and nonlodging businesses. This was possible because its businesses are hospitality related and customer focused, and because data are stored in their simplest elements.

The principal advantage of storing data in their most elementary form is that the database architecture will remain relatively stable. Don Haderle, of IBM, said that "when first building a data warehouse you should expect to remodel your database structures from three to six times" (Foley, 1996, p. 34). Remodeling the database architecture means that all of the data are removed, the database is restructured, and all the data are put back in—an expensive and time-consuming process. Company A took two years to develop its warehouse, and because the data were stored in their simplest elements, the architecture never had to be changed. The principal disadvantage to storing data in their simplest elements is that the relationships between data must be stored logically, rather than in some random or chronological order, which demands more processing up front and during analysis.

TABLE 8.18
Lodging data-warehouse applications

Company	Type of properties	Storage type	Focus	Months in development	Months in use	Unit access
A	Multiple brands	Warehouse	Marketing	24+	1	Yes
B	Midlevel	Warehouse	General	18+	36+	No
C	Midlevel	None				
D	Multiple brands	None				
E	Multiple brands	Mart	Guest	3	0	Yes
F	Upscale	Mart*	Guest	6	24	No
G	Upscale	Mart	Marketing	18	12	Yes
H	Multiple brands	Mart	Marketing	6	3	No
I	Upscale	None				
J	Economy	None				
K	Upscale	None				
L	Upscale	Mart	Finance	18	0	Yes

* Flat-file database using limited data-mart technology.

According to Company A's project manager, the warehouse has a distinct marketing focus. The data warehouse is used to feed data marts that are spread out geographically. Summary data are developed and held at the mart level, rather than at the warehouse. The warehouse uses an Informix engine and has grown to 750 GB in size.

Company B

Company B owns and franchises midlevel properties. It has been involved with data-warehousing technology longer than any other company surveyed. About 500 GB in size, its data warehouse has a general focus. At the time of my study, it was not available to unit-level managers, who had to submit requests to corporate analysts, but plans are in the works to make the system directly accessible. The warehouse supports a few specialized data marts.

Given that Company B has been using its warehouse for more than three years, I asked the project manager if he felt it had earned more than it had cost. He stated that he felt its benefits had certainly outweighed its costs, but added that many of the benefits were hard to quantify and that investments are continuous, as is its development.

Company E

Company E owns and franchises midlevel and upscale properties. It had just begun to develop a data mart that will focus on guest information. The data mart will replace a system that was storing reservation and guest-history data and was expected to be in service in about nine months after my study. The project manager would like to link the mart to each property, but differences among unit-level guest-accounting systems must be eliminated before that is possible. When asked about future plans, he stated that the company will take a wait-and-see approach. He also mentioned that about 60 percent of his budget was allocated for manipulating data (finding sources, gaining access, loading, and cleansing).

Company F

Company F owns and manages upscale properties. This company uses a large flat file (a form of database) to store its guest-related data. The project manager feels that this is sufficient for its intended use of analyzing frequent-guest programs. On its own, this does not qualify as a data mart, but the firm employs data-warehousing tools to manipulate data (gain access, load, cleanse, and transport) for the central database. The project manager felt that this combination provides his company with the most benefit for the expense.

Company G

Company G is part of a diversified corporation that owns and manages upscale properties. Unlike Company A, it is developing its data warehouse independent of the other businesses owned by the parent corporation. This may be because the other businesses are not hospitality related.

The data mart took 18 months to develop and has been in use for 12 months. Like Company F's database, Company G's data mart focuses on frequent-guest programs, but its scope is much broader, addressing all of the marketing and sales data. Unit-level managers have access to reports produced by the system, but cannot run any analysis tools. The project manager stated that the system has paid for itself and that the next step will be to develop a comprehensive data warehouse.

Company H

Company H owns and franchises midlevel and upscale properties. The company just merged with another hotel company that has traditionally not invested much money in technology. The project manager pointed out that both companies are successful. Company H's data mart is relatively small, at only 130 GB. It is designed to support marketing functions and has no summary tables or external linkages. It uses an Informix engine and has been in use for only a few months.

Company L

Company L owns and manages upscale properties. Its data mart had been under development for 12 months at the time of my study and was expected to roll out six months after the study. A project of the finance department, this mart will focus on financial information. The project manager feels that because of the way that projects such as these are approved, it would be likely that other

data marts would be developed, rather than a comprehensive data warehouse. If his mart is successful and other marts are developed, he hopes that they will be designed so they can be networked.

Others

Companies C, D, I, J, and K did not have data warehouses. Company D was considering the development of a data warehouse.

DEVELOPING DATA WAREHOUSES AND DATA MARTS

Proper executive sponsorship is required to begin the project. Without a champion at the top of the organization, the project probably will not be funded to completion and be properly maintained. One of the project managers

FIGURE 8.8
Networked data marts

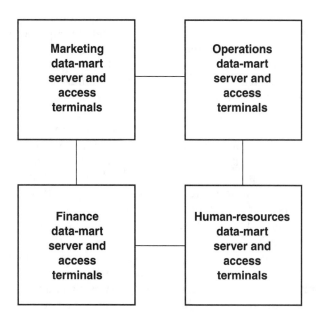

in my study mentioned that at first no one wanted to claim ownership, and without a sponsor the project would have failed. He also noted that once people began to use the warehouse, they began to claim it. Cafasso believes it is important to determine who owns the data and who is responsible for the data warehouse from the beginning (Cafasso, 1996, p. 15).

Next, the company must organize a team that has the proper technical knowledge. Several of the lodging project managers felt that it was not necessary to include business experts (that is, end users) on the development team, but that business users had to be consulted. All of the project managers stressed that meeting the business users' needs must drive the entire project. Several of those interviewed explained that determining user needs was difficult, since users do not always know what they need until they engage the system. Users also develop new needs as data are added, as their analytical skills improve, and as the business environment changes. Earl Hadden, an independent consultant, suggests that data-warehouse operators should develop new business benefits every 90 to 120 days (Strehlo, 1996).

Careful planning is required to determine user needs, prevent oversights, and stay focused on objectives. Since system use is the measure of success, it is imperative to take a participative approach, involving all of the stakeholders from design through implementation.

The two project managers who developed data warehouses claimed they were going gray over the ensuing politics. They found it difficult and time consuming to get people to agree on how data should be represented, described, or even owned. One project manager stated that *standardization* quickly became a four-letter word in his group. As part of the process, decisions must be made on data modeling, database architecture, data maps, data-analysis tools, tool integration, deployment, and implementation.

The development team must select software vendors in the early planning stages. Kight

suggests that the vendor who sells the primary database engine should be treated like a partner (1996, p. 91). Thus, one must find a vendor who not only provides a product that will do the job, but who is reliable, compatible, and willing to be part of the process from beginning to end.

The organization must also manage the system's maintenance and growth. A survey of managers at small and large warehouse sites by the Data Warehousing Institute reported that three months after launch the average system had 19 users, but 24 months after launch the typical system had 255 users (Cafasso, 1996, p. 17). If a system is allowed to grow too fast, its response can become so slow that users will abandon it. Likewise, if users obtain bad information, they will cease to use the system, causing its demise. Thus, the system requires constant maintenance to ensure that data are accurate and complete.

DATA-WAREHOUSING COMPONENTS

Data-warehousing applications require specialized hardware and software. Figures 8.4 and 8.5 provide conceptual diagrams of how these components are associated. The hardware must be capable of quickly processing large data sets. The equipment should be scalable—able to grow as data volume expands. Data-warehousing hardware should also be able to support software developed by mainstream warehouse vendors, so that the company has as much hardware and software independence as possible. This will help reduce the chances that user needs will grow beyond the system's capabilities. At this time, small, data-mart-type applications (up to 500 GB) can use a symmetric multiprocessor, but larger projects need massive parallel processors.

The important software elements involve processing the data: extraction, capture, transport, scrubbing or cleansing, design, definition, transformation, mapping, query, analysis, mining, reporting, delivery, communications, access, and security. Other software issues include management, engine, directory, metadata (data about the data), system performance, system monitoring, and system backup and restoration. Most of these elements are common to standard database systems, but some are associated only with data warehousing, namely, extraction, capturing, transporting, scrubbing, metadata, transformation, mapping, and data mining. But even standard database elements must be redesigned to operate with the large warehouse data sets.

SELECTED DATA-WAREHOUSING ACTIVITIES

Before data are stored in the warehouse, they must be prepared—source identified, extracted, cleansed, sorted, broken down, and (sometimes) rebuilt. Most project managers indicated that their data sources were existing information systems. One project manager explained that his data mart was linked to all of the property-level information systems, which allowed him to push or pull data at will. He also explained that when property-level managers used their local systems for corporate-level data, they were not even aware that they were drawing from the data mart.

Whether data are supplied from existing information systems or other sources, they must be checked for accuracy and completeness. Software tools can assist in this process, but systems should be designed to help ensure accuracy at the source. According to Perry Youngs, of Sara Lee Meats, people who supply data to the system should benefit from the system so they have an incentive to keep it up to date (Marion and DePompa, 1997). Scrubbing or cleansing software may be used to remove replicated or inconsistent data and to perform sampling. The importance of quality data cannot be overemphasized, because once a user runs into trouble because of bad data,

he or she may never use the system again.

Data may be transformed before it is stored, while it is stored, and after it is stored, depending on the nature of the data and the nature of the request. According to Allen Paller, of the Data Warehouse Institute, 70 to 80 percent of time and money spent on data warehouses are spent on data transformation (Robinson, 1996, p. S15). Transformation is a major activity, because it converts raw data into information. The cost of data transformation should decrease as the tools become more sophisticated.

Summary tables (summarized data) are an important form of transformed data because they speed up the system's response times. Appropriate summary tables can be developed only when the patterns of user demands are monitored and analyzed. Monitoring software can help do this. Typical upgrades in hardware processing speeds do not increase performance as effectively as does the use of summary tables, which can drop response times from minutes to seconds. Robinson suggested that at least half of the data in a mart should be in the form of summary tables (1996, p. S15).

Users also need descriptions and maps of stored data. They otherwise may not even be aware that the data for which they are searching are available. Metadata and data-mapping software fulfill these functions. Metadata act like a card catalog by providing descriptions, definitions, statistics, and locations of the data. Mapping software tells the user where to find the data.

A new breed of data-analysis tools, known as *data-mining software*, can search for patterns in large databases. What that software finds often becomes the basis for a new set of questions that may not have even crossed the user's mind. Data-mining software has been used, for instance, to locate unpaid accounts, reveal unique customer traits, and identify success factors.

A new type of query tool called *on-line analytical processing*, or OLAP, supports multipart questions and multidimensional analysis. Traditional data-analysis tools, such as multivariate analysis, linear programming, and forecasting tools, have also been designed to work with data warehouses.

LODGING APPLICATIONS

The potential applications for this technology in the lodging industry are many. Most of the hotel corporations in my survey were using their warehouses and marts to support market analysis. These companies were identifying and targeting new customers, evaluating and fine-tuning loyalty programs, performing sales analysis, and conducting trends analysis. One hotel company was using its data mart to support financial analysis.

Additionally, data warehouses and data marts can be used by hotels to develop concepts for new facilities, target new sites, identify potential franchisees, manage retirement funds, analyze productivity, investigate equipment failures, locate new labor markets, and track employee performance in relation to guest satisfaction. The most beneficial applications may be realized when data warehouses are seamlessly integrated into systems for decision support, property management, and financial, human resources, marketing, and executive information. This will have the effect of increasing the analytical power of all of these systems and provide access to all of the employees who might benefit.

NEWLY ADOPTED

My survey revealed that the lodging industry is just beginning to adopt data-warehousing technology. The number of hotel corporations that can afford a data warehouse is limited for the moment because of the high cost. Data marts offer a lower-cost alternative to data warehouses and an opportunity to become familiar with the technology. When multiple data marts are built they should be designed so that they could later be integrated in a data warehouse. A warehouse that supports multiple data marts is preferred over the development of multiple data marts to create an enterprisewide system. The application should start small; sponsorship should be established; the design should be user-driven; and growth and maintenance must be managed.

References

Borchgrevink, C. P., and R. S. Schmidgall. 1995. "Budgeting Practices of U.S. Lodging Firms." *Bottomline* August–September: 10(5):13–17.

Cafasso, R. 1996. "Data Minefields." *PC Week* March: 17.

Chamberlain, D. 1991. "A Written Budget Is a Valuable Tool for Tracking Your Meeting Dollars." *Successful Meetings* May:40(6):89–90.

Cichy, Ronald F., and Raymond S. Schmidgall. 1996. "Leadership Qualities of Financial Executives in the U.S. Lodging Industry." *Cornell Hotel and Restaurant Administration Quarterly* April:56–62.

Coltman, M. M. 1994. *Hospitality Management Accounting,* 5th ed. New York: Van Nostrand Reinhold.

Damitio, James W., and Raymond S. Schmidgall. 1996. "A Profile of the Lodging Financial Executive." *Bottomline* September:9–11.

DeMyer, J. P., and D. Wang-Kline. 1990. "What's on the Books? A Practical Guide to Forecasting and Budgeting." *Hotel & Resort Industry* January:13(1):64.

DeVeau, Patricia M., and Linsley T. DeVeau. 1988. "A Profile of the CHAE: Gaining Strength in Numbers." *Bottomline* October/November:18–19.

Dubé, Laurette, Cathy A. Enz, Leo M. Renaghan, and Judy Siguaw. 1999. "Best Practices in the U.S. Lodging Industry— Overview, Methods, and Champions." *Cornell Hotel and Restaurant Administration Quarterly* August:40(4):14–27.

Foley, J. 1996. "Towering Terabytes." *Information Week* September:34.

Gates, Bill, with Collins Hemingway. 1999. *Business @ the Speed of Thought: Using a Digital Nervous System.* New York: Warner Books, p. xxii.

Geller, A. Neal, Charles L. Ilvento, and Raymond S. Schmidgall. 1990. "The Hotel Controller Revisited." *Cornell Hotel and Restaurant Administration Quarterly* November:91–97.

Geller, A. Neal, and Raymond S. Schmidgall. 1984. "The Hotel Controller: More than a Bookkeeper." *Cornell Hotel and Restaurant Administration Quarterly* 25(2):16–22.

Halper, M. 1996. "Welcome to 21st-Century Data." *Forbes* April:49–53.

Karch, R. 1992. "Streamlining Your Hotel Cost." *Hotel & Resort Industry* November:15(11):88–90.

Kight, B. 1996. "The Smart Way to Build a Data Warehouse." *Datamation* October:42(16):91.

Marion, L., and B. DePompa. 1997. "Warehouse Uptime." *Software* March:55–57.

O'Sullivan, O. 1996. "Data Warehousing—Without the Warehouse." *ABA Banking Journal* December:88(18):30–34.

Robinson, T. 1996. "It All Starts with Good, Clean Data." *Sentry Market Research*, p. S15.

Schmidgall, R. S. 1989. "While Forecasts Hit Targets, GMs Still Seek Better Guns." *Lodging* November:15(3):101–102, 104–105.

Schmidgall, R. S. 1997. *Hospitality Industry Managerial Accounting,* 4th ed. East Lansing, MI: The Educational Institute of the American Hotel and Motel Association, pp. 369–372, 411–413.

Schmidgall, R. S., C. P. Borchgrevink, and O. H. Zahl-Begnum. 1996. "Operations Budgeting Practices of Lodging Firms in the United States and Scandinavia." *International Journal of Hospitality Management* 15(2):189–203.

Schmidgall, Raymond S., and Michael Kasavana. 2000. "Certifications by HFTP." *Bottomline* April/May:20–22.

Smith, B. C., J. F. Leimkuhler, and R. M. Darrow. 1992. "Yield Management at American Airlines." *Interfaces* January–February:22(1):8–31.

Strehlo, K. 1996. "Data Warehousing: Avoid Planned Obsolescence." *Datamation* January:42(2):32–33.

Temling, W. P., and P. Quek. 1993. "Budget Time." *Lodging,* November:19(3):21–22.

Teresko, J. 1996. "Data Warehouses: Build Them for Decision-Making Power." *Industry Week* March 18: 245(6):43–46.

Tse, Eliza C. 1989. "A Profile of the IAHA Member." *Bottomline* October/November:12–18.

Woods, Robert H., Denney G. Rutherford, Raymond S. Schmidgall, and Michael Sciarini. 1998. "Hotel General Managers." *Cornell Hotel and Restaurant Administration Quarterly* December:38–44.

Suggested Readings

Articles
Damitio, James W., and Raymond S. Schmidgall. 1990. "Internal Auditing Practices of Major Lodging Chains." *Hospitality Research Journal* 14(2):255–268.

Source Notes
Chapter 8.2, "The Lodging Chief Financial Executive," by Raymond S. Schmidgall.

Chapter 8.3, "Budgeting and Forecasting: Current Practice in the Lodging Industry," by Raymond S. Schmidgall and Agnes Lee DeFranco, is reprinted from the December 1998 issue of *The Cornell Hotel and Restaurant Administration Quarterly.* © Cornell University. Used by permission. All rights reserved.

Chapter 8.4, "As I See It: The Hotel Controller," by Mike Draeger.

Chapter 8.5, "Hotel Purchasing as a Key Business Activity," by Carl D. Riegel.

Chapter 8.6, "The Hotel Purchasing Function," by C. Lee Evans.

Chapter 8.7, "Best Practices in Information Technology," by Judy A. Siguaw and Cathy A. Enz, is reprinted from the October 1999 issue of *The Cornell Hotel and Restaurant Administration Quarterly*. © Cornell University. Used by permission. All rights reserved.

Chapter 8.8, "Data Warehousing," by Robert K. Griffin, is reprinted from the August 1998 issue of *The Cornell Hotel and Restaurant Administration Quarterly*. © Cornell University. Used by permission. All rights reserved.

9

Human Resources Policy Management

9.1 Introduction

This section on human resources is a different creature than it has been in previous editions of this book. It used to be called "The Management and Processes of Human Resources," and included more of the how-to type of articles. I have changed my view of this and believe that rather than provide articles that focus on specific technical aspects of human resources management, the reader will be better served by contemplating some broader, more strategic policy considerations.

Part of this shift in focus grew out of the recent consortium of researchers who were asked by the Educational Institute of the American Hotel and Motel Association to provide the industry with insights about how to better prepare for the challenges of the twenty-first century. Interdisciplinary teams of researchers representing educators from ten of the top hospitality programs in the country attacked a number of problem issues.

Several of those researchers present either partial results of their projects or custom essays that grew out of their activities in the consortium.

Among observers and participants in the hotel management scene are those who have compared human resources, formerly personnel management, to the weather: everyone talks about it, but few people have done anything about it. This is a dilemma that faces a good many managements. If a human resources (HR) department is to be effective in dealing with the people they recruit, hire, and train, they need a strategic view of the future and strategies to achieve that view.

It has been said that we should be very interested in the future, for that is where we are going to spend the rest of our lives. It has also been said that "predicting is difficult, especially about the future" (Yogi Berra, quoted in Woods, 1999). That is the premise of the lead

457

article in this section, by Bob Woods, who at the time this article was written was the director of the Center for the Study of Lodging Operations at Purdue University. He bases his "predictions" on two premises: Human resources will become much more important in this millennium, or it will disappear as a component of hospitality organizations. His discussion of these two possible "futures" is compelling and troubling. It is highly recommended for those who aspire to this component of the hospitality professions.

Perhaps the most insidious and pervasive human resource challenge the above-mentioned research consortium tried to address was that of turnover. For whatever reasons employees leave hotels companies (and there are a lot), whenever it happens, it is expensive—not only to the hotel, but also to the employee. Several of the projects had turnover and finding and keeping great employees as a subtext to their primary research activities. That is why Carl Riegel's presentation of a conceptual model of turnover is an important inclusion here. It is an update of research he and two colleagues did among food service employees, but the conceptual model holds equally well for hotel employees. It is included here because in many ways each strategic concept of legal environment, teamwork, and mentoring addressed by other authors here contributes in its own way to reduce and control turnover.

In a series of guest lectures in my class at Washington State University, Jim Treadway, formerly president of Westin Hotels and Resorts–North America and currently president and CEO of MTM Management LLC, has outlined how he sees the job of hotel general manager (GM). Among the components of his job description is *to keep the owners out of jail,* and by that he means that the GM has to manage the business in such a way it does not get in legal trouble and avoids all possible risk of liability. Sue Murrmann and Cherylynn Becker's essay on the legal environment dis-

cusses the realms of risk facing hotels and, specifically, their human resources departments. Increasingly, also, hotels are finding themselves at legal risk on the basis of hiring the "high-risk employee." The chapter "De Facto Security Standards: Operators at Risk," in Part V, by Rutherford and McConnell pays some attention to the concept of "negligent hiring" and can also be read in a human resources context. Many of the issues central to the risks they analyze happened as a result of the acts or behavior on the part of hotel employees.

Two other consortium researchers, M. Chris Paxson of Washington State University and Melenie Lankau, then of Cornell's School of Hotel Administration and now at the University of Georgia, contribute essays based on their research on how the concepts of teamwork and mentoring can provide pathways for human resource managers at hotel properties to deal effectively with turnover and legal challenges. From a strategic and practical standpoint, these are ideas whose time may have come in the twenty-first century and as such are highly recommended.

There is no lack of research and commentary in hospitality publications, both academic and trade, that deal with issues of human resources. As pointed out in the paragraphs above, many of the articles and essays presented in this book could be and should be looked at with an eye toward what the implications are for the management of human resources in a hotel. Perhaps, second only to marketing, human resources is among the most written-about topics in not only the academic, but the trade press. The reader is encouraged to find those publications that offer solid, practical, objective, and legally valid advice in determining the reader's individual model of how a human resources philosophy and its resultant practices should be designed. A good place to start is the list of suggested readings and the references at the end of the chapter.

9.2 Predicting Is Difficult, Especially about the Future: Human Resources in the New Millennium

Robert H. Woods

INTRODUCTION

The title of this chapter is a quote from the baseball player, coach, manager, and American philosopher Yogi Berra. I agree with Yogi; predicting the future is difficult.

After reading about and considering the future of human resources (HR) in the hospitality industry for several months, I have come to the conclusion that HR is at a crossroads and has two likely futures:

- HR will evolve and adapt and become much more important to organizations.
- HR as we have known it will disappear and be replaced by a combination of outsourcing and technology.

By definition, a paradox is something that cannot be controlled or understood in any conventional, systematic, or rational way. There are many paradoxes in management. Human resources management is a paradox in the sense that we have never truly mastered it. This appears to me to be even more likely in the future than in the past.

It is important to remember that either or both of the two HR futures might occur, of course. They might even occur at the same time (but not likely in the same organizations). There is even evidence to suggest that some organizations have chosen which future to take. For example, some organizations already have downsized HR. There are also examples of the opposite, however. In fact, in some organizations it appears that HR is already becoming increasingly important and may, even and at last, become a stepping-stone to the CEO's chair.

Which path HR takes will likely depend on the culture of the organization. There likely is no one best way for HR. Instead there will be "best ways" for each company, ones that fit their culture.

I believe it is important first to begin this discussion about the future of HR by discussing the differences between leaders and managers. I promise to be brief with this.

I have written in previous research that I believed that which path an organization takes may depend on the *leadership* exerted within the organization. I have put *leadership* in italics to call attention to the term. I believe that leaders lead, managers manage. There is a real difference in my mind. Good leaders manage paradoxes and dilemmas well using weapons such as an understanding of ambiguity, a tolerance for change, and the ability to realize that opposites may exist simultaneously. I believe that managers, in contrast, primarily attempt to control events. I favor the leadership approach.

Managers limit themselves by their own rational thinking. To many people, rationally, things must be good or bad, old or new, yes or no, true or false—but not both. This is not necessarily true. In reality, opposites are often very closely related and may even coexist. Opposites may even enhance one another. An example is found in pleasure and pain. Scratching an itch is pleasure, but when one scratches too much, then it becomes all pain. In his 1996 book, Farson pointed this out and offered the following example, which illustrates why opposite realities may exist simultaneously: A healthy organization needs full and accurate information transferal. True. But it is also true that diplomacy and tact are needed in the same organization and that these two may require "distortions" of the truth both because workers need to believe that their leaders are confident, fair, and in control and because no leader needs to know all of the little problems his or her organization faces. Knowing these would surely bog the leader down indefinitely.

Some managers tend to want to control information, that is, to know every little detail that goes on. Some leaders do this, too, of course. I believe that this approach actually inhibits productivity. I also believe that a manager who realizes that the "reciprocity rule" (I will like you if you like me) is more valuable than attempting to control behaviors is close to becoming a leader.

To put it another way, managers too often believe that their job is to mold people, like an artist would mold clay. Farson (1996) notes how wrong this approach is. Leaders make impressions on people, they do not mold them. Making an impression is more like falling into a bed of clay and leaving an image than it is molding. Leaders who understand this tend also to be trusting, caring, courageous, and passionate—while those who do not understand it tend to be controllers and would-be molders. Carl Rogers, who I think is one of America's foremost psychologists and philosophers of human behavior, noted how this works when he described the role of a therapist. According to Rogers, therapists lose control over their patients when they first believe that, based on their understanding of what has transpired so far, they can accurately "handle," or predict, what that patient might do (Farson, 1996, p. 30). Fortunately, neither therapists nor managers ever know everything there is to know.

My final preprediction comments have to do with the *invisible obvious*. I also learned about this from Farson. The invisible obvious is what makes predicting so hard. To predict, you rely on a keen knowledge of the present. Unfortunately, much of the present is not completely obvious to most of us. Those of us who have studied culture to any extent would all immediately agree with this concept.

Think about the best place to hide something. Sometimes it is in the most obvious lo-cation, right? We do not see things that are obvious. That is why Herman Kahn and Anthony Wiener, two of the best futurists of their age, missed so much when they predicted what America would be like in the year 2000. Writing in 1967 Kahn and Wiener accurately predicted some fascinating things. For instance, they predicted that Japan would become an economic power. If you are old enough to remember 1967 well, then you will realize that virtually everybody thought of Japan as that little country that made cheap small objects, transistor radios and things like that. We certainly did not think of Japan the way we do now, as a country that exerts enormous economic leverage (even after the recent economic decline in the Far East). Kahn and Wiener (1967) also predicted the development of both the resurgence of religion and the growth of the exercise industry. These, too, were major predictions. However, Kahn and Wiener missed on many predictions—all examples of the invisible obvious. They failed to predict the ecology movement, the women's movement, the focus on pollution—all issues that had already begun when they were writing. Because these issues had already begun, they were too obvious. The cultural values, tunnel vision, selective perception, and a deference to the judgment of others that Kahn and Wiener were subject to (as we all are to some extent) prevented them from seeing the invisible obvious. Why? Because each of these obscure the invisible obvious.

I have tried to observe what is going on today, as well as predict what will happen in the future. Of course, I, too, am subject to the same limitations that caused Kahn and Wiener to fail; in fact, those limitations probably affect me to a much greater extent since their life's work was predicting and mine is not. Time will tell whether or not I have been successful.

In the pages that follow I first briefly discuss some events that may cause HR to change. It seems to be a requirement to mention factors that are affecting change, before discussing their long-term impact. Naturally, I will miss a lot of these. Then I discuss what I consider the "high road," that is, HR evolving into a powerful force within organizations. The decision to discuss this potential future first is based on my hope that it comes true. The second future, a diminished and/or disappearing HR, will be addressed next. At the end I discuss my hopes for hospitality and for HR.

WHY WILL HR BE ANY DIFFERENT IN THE FUTURE?

This is a good question. It may not be much different. Certainly, there are several very strong demographic and social trends that could dramatically affect HR in the future. However, many, which have occurred in the past, have not had much effect. At any rate, the factors that might influence HR in the future include the numbers of available workers (at last the baby boomers are going to actually retire and leave large voids). By 2010 for the first time ever the number of job replacements needed will exceed the number of new positions to be filled. By 2020 the U.S. economy will require 144.7 million workers.

The continued feminization of the workforce will also likely affect the future of HR. The percentage of workers who are female has risen for the past four decades and will continue to rise. Several scholars have noted that work is becoming increasing "female" in the sense that it requires more brains and less brawn. The number of female managers will most assuredly increase dramatically. It will not take many more females to outnumber males in hospitality management positions, of course. Today, the ratio of male to female managers in the lodging industry is about 51.5 to 48.5 (Woods, 1999). While many female managers occupy positions that have not historically been rungs on the ladder to top management (sales, catering managers, personnel, and so on), this, too, will likely change. This may be particularly true in hospitality where nearly 75 percent of the workforce overall are female. This increase in the number of female managers will not be bad news, of course. While the overall increase in female workers, especially those of childbearing ages, may mean companies will have to address such issues as flexible hours, telecommuting, and family leave more rigorously, the fact that we will have more female managers dealing with such issues may help us. Most studies comparing male and female managerial tactics continue to show that females are better at such things as team building, motivation, and fostering an open environment (all likely descriptions of work in the future) (Finigan, 1999).

The workforce will also continue to diversify, but perhaps not as dramatically as most people think. Today Caucasians occupy 76 percent of the total jobs in the United States. By 2020 they will still occupy 68 percent of the jobs. Most of growth in the nonwhite workforce will come from Asians and Hispanics, which will become 6 percent and 14 percent of the workforce, respectively. Blacks will remain at about 11 percent. More importantly, many more Americans will fall behind in basic math, science, and language skills. How many depends on the nation's response to the education crisis we face. For these Americans, the future will be nontechnological and their real wages will be less than they are today.

By 2020 approximately 83 percent of Americans will work in the service industries. And they are increasingly likely to change jobs more often because of shifting opportunities and competitive pressures. The average job tenure for American male workers is today about 4.0 years. For females, it's about 3.5 years. These are not the figures for hospitality workers, of course, where turnover results in much less tenure, perhaps an average of as low as slightly over 1.5 years. Turnover in the lodging industry among workers was estimated at 52 percent in 1997, the first time a national study of turnover was undertaken (Woods, Sciarini, and Heck, 1998).

The role that immigrants play in the future will likely greatly increase in importance. Immigrants may very well provide the mainstay of the hospitality workforce of the future. The annual average immigration to the United States in 1991–1995 was 900,000 per year. However, this number can and will likely change to accommodate labor needs. In any case, immigration will likely become the chief cause of American population growth in decades to come.

The final major influence on the American workforce will be its graying. Workers will likely work longer, and U.S. companies are very likely to have many older workers than before. This will put greater pressure than ever before on hospitality companies to learn to address the needs (health, physical, and otherwise) of our senior employees. Some companies have already realized this and are successfully employing thousands of older workers. Those others that have yet to dip into this market may be forced to in the very near future.

It is within the context of these and many other demographic and social changes that HR leaders must work in the future.

ALTERNATIVE FUTURE #1: HR AS ORGANIZATIONAL LEADER

HR has always been a cost center, an overhead that produced little return on investments. It has always emphasized people over process and operations over strategy (Burke, 1997). In one of the more thought-provoking books I have read recently, Ulrich et al. (1997) propose that HR should be managed more like a business. I agree completely with Ulrich and have adopted ideas liberally from this wonderful book, and many of the citations in the first part of the chapter are drawn from the Ulrich book.

Little has changed in HR over the past 40 or so years. To see the proof in that pudding consider the table of contents presented below from a best-selling HR textbook.

- Employee motivation, personal vs. organizational goals.
- Organizational careers.
- Job fatigue, pathological organizational behavior.
- The changing role of the supervisor.
- Sharing decisions with subordinates.
- Sharing management authority with unions, customers, suppliers, and external organizations.
- Job and institutional consequences of technological change.
- Cross-cultural comparisons.
- The need for organizational social responsibility.

The book from which this table of contents was taken was written over 40 years ago (Dubin, 1961), and the *HR* in the title of the book stood for *Human Relations,* not *Human Resources!*

There have been some additions to HR topics over the years, to be sure. Today HR books will likely discuss cost containment, health care, mergers and acquisitions, downsizing, and other issues ,whereas those of the 1950s did not. Overall, however, the topics (and some of the treatments) have remained virtually the same.

When Ulrich wrote that HR needed to be managed more like a business he meant that the days of the textbook topics such as those discussed above were over. Other scholars have agreed. For instance, Alvares (1997) described a future HR that must be more strategic in nature, one that is focused on the development of human capital. Alvares describes this as evolving HR into a "customer-centric" business, in which the managers and employees of the organization as well as competitors, networks, and even clients themselves are the customers. In his view, Alvares sees HR as a much more "externally oriented" function—not one that is simply put to the task of preparing the workers within the organization. To accomplish these goals HR will have to focus less on managing the records of current personnel and focus more on the strategic management of the entire organizational process.

C. K. Prahalad, one of the foremost strategic thinkers of our time, recently addressed a conference of HR professionals. In his address Prahalad noted that the main problem with HR is that it has no coherent theory base from which to operate. According to Prahalad, because of this the field has wandered and adopted areas no other function was interested in. He explained this using the example of finance. Finance works off of the theory based on the assumption that investors invest in order to profit. Surely this is true. Unlike finance, however, HR does not have a theory based on the core competency of the organization. Instead, it has always been viewed as a support unit for other functions that were more focused.

In response to Prahalad's challenge, Christensen (1997) developed a coherent theory base for HR. In the model that Christensen developed, HR evolves from somewhere (competencies) into core capabilities, business vision, strategies, priorities, and goals and eventually into working the external business environment. Unlike the support-based HR of old (or of today), which focuses on the development of people required by others, this model projects HR as a leading force that can help an organization to identify and attain its strategies and objectives.

Hewitt (1997) has noted that in many organizations there is a strategic vacuum that is created by three forces. First is the gap between strategic rhetoric and reality. These are the managers who talk the talk but do not always walk the talk. Second is the paradox of today's managers, the best-prepared, best-read managers to ever walk the earth. Although they may be the most strategically literate of all time, a great deal of evidence indicates that they are not strategically competent. They still make short-term decisions. The third force is the lack of any systematic link between strategic planning apparatus and long-term, superior performance. While not all would agree with Hewitt that there is little evidence that strategic planning actually leads to increased performance, there are many who believe this is true and even some who have suggested that there is a negative relationship between the two (Hewitt, 1997, p. 40).

To be successful in re-forming itself into a business, HR must focus on deliverables, of course. This accountability for its actions is something new for HR. In the past, HR has not been challenged to produce results that actually bring resources into the organization.

One of the ways that HR can focus on deliverables is to ally itself with top management as a partner in bringing about change and development (Lombardo and Eichinger, 1997). In effect, HR can become the initiator, the innovator, and the designer of change instead of the function called upon to carry out others' bidding. Lombardo and Eichinger have suggested that this can take place in part through first proactively identifying the competencies managers and employees will need in the future and then by developing these in each individual. By working to close the gap between needed skills and current competencies, HR can serve a strategic purpose in the organization, one that Lombardo and Eichinger (1997, p. 73) call "competency futurists."

In this future, HR will likely be judged on whether it enhances corporate competitive advantages by adding real measurable value. Other departments already adhere to this credo. Kaplan and Norton (1992) have provided a model (the balanced scorecard) that could assist HR in identifying how to remold itself into a profit center. Using the balanced scorecard with the finance department, for example, would yield such comparisons of the department's effect on long- and short-term profits, earnings per share, equity appreciation, return on assets, and so on. Using the balanced-scorecard approach for HR instead of measuring such things as the number of people trained (a common measure in the past but one that is overhead based) HR would measure new sales, customer satisfaction, speed of delivery, productivity ratios, and the delivery of "right" behaviors (Kaplan and Norton, 1992, p. 71). In this way, HR could add to value through helping to build the core competency of an organization through workforce enhancement (Schneier and Beatty, 1995).

As a "business" HR should be responsible for the care and feeding of the organizational strategy (Schneier and Beatty, 1995). By being responsible not only for helping to project the future strategy but also for melding the processes, people, and cultures that will attain it, HR can become *the* integral part of an organization.

We know from prior research that organization and management can make a difference in the bottom line of an organization (Collins and Porras, 1994). What HR needs to do now in order to attain its business status is learn how to overcome the obstacles to change, whether they are the capabilities of employees or the views of top management, and learn how to fuel a culture that will be profitable. As Huselid (1995) noted, HR needs to add the "performance enhancers" that will lead to profit.

HR is positioned to take leadership. As Knicely (1997) noted, HR is already at the heart of many of the "organization speak" issues today, for example, acquisitions, merger mania, benchmarking, core competencies, family-friendly practices, empowerment, and culture change. Globalization, health care costs, ISO and QS 9000, knowledge work, intellectual capital, learning organizations, new contracts with employees, quality and continuous improvement, professional and career management, reorganization and restructuring, seamless organizations, visions and values, workforce demographics—all are common HR topic areas. To utilize these to make HR more important, Knicely believes that HR leaders must be able to demonstrate seven skills:

1. See around corners to find opportunities and threats.

2. Venture out to utilize external market practices.
3. Captivate the MTV generation—with its high thirst for knowledge and its demand for empowerment and ownership of ideas.
4. Practice brutal optimism, by defining the reality of the organization.
5. Steal (and share) shamelessly the ideas of others (benchmark).
6. Balance the scorecard, as Kaplan and Norton have suggested.
7. Model the 3 Cs—the credibility to lead, the competence to upgrade, and the courage to take risks and to promote change.

Kochan (1997) echoes the same message by noting that HR leaders should be addressing seven priorities today:

1. Helping organizations reinvent/redesign themselves to compete more effectively.
2. Reinventing the HR function to be more customer focused and cost justified.
3. Attracting and developing the next generation of leaders and workers.
4. Contributing to the continuous cost containment/management effort.
5. Working to become an effective "business partner" with their line customers.
6. Rejecting fads and quick fixes.
7. Addressing the diversity challenge.

Each of these activities will help the organization to overcome the inward focus that so often devours its resources.

Finding the right people to manage these challenges will be difficult. The skills they need are not the same old ones HR managers of the past held and protected. In describing a conversation with a CEO looking for a new HR leader, Johnson (1997) reported the following comments.

I don't want a typical HR type. I don't think I even want someone from HR. I want this person to be the brightest, smartest, bravest, most strategic, and highest potential individual on this management team. That's probably not going to be someone from HR.

This may not be someone from HR as we describe it today. As Ulrich et al. (1997) noted, the terms that best describe what the HR leader of tomorrow needs include such words as *player, pioneer, motivator, innovator,* and *architect.* While this may already be the case in some organizations, for comparison, choose four or five terms to describe the current HR managers that you know today. My guess is that these terms are not often used.

Too often we expect to find simple solutions to HR problems in organizations, but this has rarely been the case in the past and is not likely to be the case in the future. More likely, we will find the types of problems that prompted Churchill (1938) to describe Russia as "a riddle, wrapped in a mystery, inside an enigma." Fitz-Enz (1997) may have had these in mind when he identified the eight best human-asset management practices an HR leader needs.

- *Values:* A constant focus on values and adding to them.
- *Commitment:* Dedication to a long-term core strategy.
- *Culture:* Proactive application of the culture and systems of the organization.
- *Communication:* An extraordinary concern for two-way communication with all stakeholders.
- *Partnering:* Using people within and outside the organization as needed.
- *Collaboration:* Fostering a high level of cooperation between all departments.
- *Risk and innovation:* The willingness, ability, and know-how to shut down the current operation and reinvent it.
- *Competitive passion:* A constant search for improvement.

Too often today, organizations have forgotten that their employees are *human.* While the term *human capital* has become popular in recent years, many employers have yet to grasp its true meaning. Employees are unlikely to work for one organization throughout their careers as they once did. This creates a paradox for HR leaders: How to create a sense of caring and involvement among "short-timers" that career employees, the type that once thought "we all are in this together," once had. Helping people make sense out of what they are currently doing and convincing them to "be on the bandwagon"—even though they may seldom know which bandwagon they are actually on at the time—is the job of HR.

Business has chosen to take the current HR approach, of course. When business decided to break the psychological contracts organizations had long had with workers, the ones that led employees to believe that they were in it for life, things changed dramatically. Our employees today are all "temporary," in the sense that they are all employed "at will" and they "know" they will not work for the same company for long. In describing the situation, Drucker (1995) noted that most managers still believe the old nineteenth-century adage that "employees need us more than we need them." This, of course, is not true. Instead, organizations have to be willing and able to "market membership in much the same way that they market products." Drucker has even referred to today's employees as *volunteers*, a useful term in many organizations.

In this first of two possible futures for HR, the emphasis is on HR changing from a functional, overhead- and cost-centered department hidden in the shadows of the organization to one of the real leaders of change. This shift from administrative to strategic, from functional to business, will not be easy. However, it is taking place in many organizations today already, and if we look down the positive road of HR's future, it is easy to imagine it happening again and again. Recent studies of the road that GMs took in the lodging industry show, once again, that the way to the top seldom passes through HR (Woods, Rutherford, et al., 1998). When, and if, the changeover to HR as a business happens, we will know it because top-level managers in organizations, the CEOs and presidents who were once GMs, will start moving up through HR instead of through finance, food and beverage, and the front office.

ALTERNATIVE FUTURE #2: HR WILL DISAPPEAR AND BE REPLACED BY OUTSOURCING AND TECHNOLOGY

Workers are accepting more responsibility for their own careers today. While HR is the department that traditionally teaches this skill, by doing so it may be working itself out of a job.

Throughout much of its past, the HR department has been seen as the enforcer and regulator of employees. This has created a cadre of specialists, many devoted to making sure that employees follow the rules—controllers, if you want to think of them as that. As employees take more responsibility for their own careers, and as organizations become more flexible and temporary through network-

ing with others, the "policeman" role that HR has played becomes less important. As a portent of what may become the future of HR, a recent study conducted by the American Management Association (AMA) of 592 executive and managers *outside* of HR noted that only 16 percent of them believed that HR delivered value to their organization. The other 84 percent still saw HR as a non-revenue-producing overhead department (Condodina, 1997). Even more telling is that less than one-third of those surveyed gave HR performance marks that indicate even a mediocre performance (see Table 9.1).

What this study indicates is that HR may be taking care of the nuts and bolts of their responsibilities, but little more. As one participant in the study noted, "trends show a gap in what companies need skill-wise and what the pool of applicants and employees possess. Where strategic initiative is needed most—in recruitment and training—it is lowest." Eric Greenberg, the director of management studies at AMA, noted further that the problem is exacerbated by the availability of trained workforce. Said Greenberg, "When you can't

TABLE 9.1
How effective is the performance of your human resources department in each of the following areas?

| | Effective | | | | Ineffective |
	5	4	3	2	1
Administration	20%	44%	27%	6%	1%
Counseling, coaching, disciplinary actions	17	37	30	11	3
Employee training	9	23	37	22	7
Legal compliance	2	43	22	6	2
Recruitment	13	31	34	14	6
Strategic partner with line management	13	30	30	19	6

Source: Condodina, J. 1997. "Echoes from the Line: HR Lacks Strategic Initiative." *HR Focus* 74(7):21.

buy talent, and you can't rent talent, you have to work with what you have got . . . and HR isn't helping to solve this problem."

A second study, this time of HR departments, found that 60 percent of the costs in HR were associated with administration (record keeping, compliance, paper shuffling, etc.), 30 percent were associated with recruitment, training, counseling, and performance management, and only 10 percent were associated with strategic planning (Wilkerson, 1997). The reality is that expert systems can replace much of the administrative costs that fall into that 60 percent category.

A downsized and less important HR department likely is being gradually replaced by outsourcing. Another AMA study conducted in 1996 showed that 77 percent of the participants were then outsourcing some part of former HR functions. We can assume that the percentage is more today. While recruitment and training likely remain stalwarts in the HR department, one wonders how long this will be true unless HR begins to develop leaders and becomes more of a strategic asset.

In 1996 Thomas Stewart, senior editor of *Fortune* and author of the best-selling book, *Intellectual Capital,* offered his proposal for HR. It was succinct. "Why not blow the sucker up?" To confirm what he meant by this, Stewart (1996) went on to say, "I don't mean improve it. I mean abolish it. Deep-six it. Rub it out; eliminate, toss, obliterate, nuke it, force it to walk the plank, turn it into road kill." Obviously, Stewart believes that HR has outlived its purpose. And remember, Stewart believes that intellectual capital is an organization's most important asset!

The charges against HR, and the bases for Stewart's attacks, are fairly widespread, from top to bottom in organizations and from one company to the next. They include:

- HR has no vision. Despite the endless strategic statements HR has helped to draft, what they actually do strategically that helps attain the mission remains fuzzy. Too

often their work is fuzzy and nonmeasurable.

- HR is the enemy. Too often CEOs think that HR sticks up for the workers without taking the big picture into consideration. On the other hand, ask the worker and she or he will say that HR people are just mouthpieces for the company line and the executioners in an endless wave of downsizing and reengineering that dominated the headlines of the 1990s.

- HR is inefficient. Too often managers claim that HR cannot send out timely information about performance, and workers say that HR cannot file insurance claims quickly. In addition, HR has been accused of not capturing employees' attitudes in real time (today), of not databasing job postings on a timely basis, and so on.

- HR is out of touch. A common criticism is that HR does not understand the business because it's not a business (Brown, 1997).

To some, the future of HR is linked inexorably with the development of technology. "Virtual HR" will be a strange place, a place where all services will be available instantaneously, on demand, and at the place most convenient to the employee. Imagine kiosks where employees and managers can access their files and search for work within, and perhaps outside of, the organization. This process is already under way, in one fashion or another, and in many organizations employees can access their own HR files immediately. As this becomes more prevalent, the need for HR becomes less important.

MY HOPE FOR THE FUTURE

Hospitality has long been a "pass-through" industry. Many of its workers have been simply passing through on their way to other careers. For years the industry has endorsed, and even praised, this policy. Even today, as hospitality companies fall far short in many areas of both needed and desirable employees, leaders in the industry continue to praise this "passing-through" mentality. Recent McDonald's advertisements show kids working there with tag lines such as "Joe, future engineer," or "Jill, future doctor." In all of these ads there is not one that identifies a current employee as a future hospitality manager.

Hospitality could easily become the employer of choice. Right now it is more the employer of necessity for many workers, young and old. Nearly three-fourths of the minimum-wage employees in the United States work in the hospitality industry, and its leaders continue to fight to hold down the minimum wage whenever possible. Why is beyond me. If you ask, you will learn that hospitality leaders are afraid of what they call wage inflation; that is, increased minimum wages will result in increased wages for those up the ladder who already make a little more. I believe that this is self-defeating. There are few cities in the United States where companies can actually pay the minimum wage anyway. Yes, there is a federal minimum wage, and there is also a "real" minimum wage. The latter is the amount that businesses must pay to actually compete for employees in their markets.

The average weekly pay of a full-time hospitality employee today is $371. That comes out to approximately $19,000 per year. Is it any wonder that people trying to survive and raise families choose hospitality as a last resort?

Hospitality has a lot to offer if we would simply forget attempting to keep wages so low. In addition, savings in turnover costs could easily offset increases in wages. As we know from prior research the average cost of losing an hourly worker in hospitality is approximately $2500 to $3000. Much of this comes in the form of soft dollars, such things as lower productivity. Instead of wasting that money, why not put it to work for our companies. An organization with 50 percent turnover (and that's pretty good) and 200 employees loses 100 employees per year. That costs somewhere

around $300,000 annually in lost revenues and real costs. Why not put that money to work by paying more, managing better, addressing the HR issues of employees, and keeping them an extra year or two—or more. What, exactly, is wrong with hospitality employees who have worked for the same company for 15 to 20 years? If we think we want the turnover to ensure that we have young, attractive employees working for us, we can forget it. That is not part of the future today anyway; demographic changes are working against that option.

My hope is that hospitality will wake up (some have already, of course) and begin genuinely thinking about and working on the issues that cause us to have such poor employee relations. We should not only teach employees reading, writing, and math, but also teach them how to manage their own careers. What do we have to fear here? They are likely to leave their employer soon anyway. Perhaps some mentoring and education would encourage them to stay longer. The same is true with basic benefits such as health care, education reimbursement, and the like. Instead of leading in these areas, hospitality is falling far behind.

I can envision a hospitality company that provides health care to all its workers, day care to young families, transportation to and from work, mentoring, career planning, social gatherings for young people to meet and mate, learning opportunities and classes of all kinds, succession planning (even for line workers), better pay than a worker can get anywhere else in town, and an opportunity to succeed in life. This company I envision also engages in the HR practices outlined in the first half of this chapter. It actively engages in creating a workforce to attain its desired strategic future. It helps build the bottom line through encouraging employees to do better each day and through turnover reduction. It is, in fact, a "customer-centric" business wherein its customers are its employees. It emphasizes accountability and deliverables; it keeps a scorecard for each employee to help them see how they are doing; it opens its books for employees to understand the role they play in the big picture; and it rewards hard work and innovation.

Unfortunately, I can also see many, many hospitality companies following the second path—the path wherein HR is primarily record keeping and legal compliance. In these companies I foresee an entirely different future, one beset with constant employee shortages, legal problems, diminishing revenues and returns, and eventual bankruptcy. I just do not understand why everyone does not see it.

I challenge hospitality leaders to take the lead, to show the courage to create HR departments where people are important. To change from what things could be (as opposed to what they are). I challenge these leaders to imagine their own children as their employees. I do not mean the young kids in upscale restaurants, clubs, and hotel who are using hospitality as a pass-through to something better. I mean imagine your own children as those employees who have no other alternatives. Perhaps then you will begin to realize the importance of human resources management.

9.3   The Causes and Consequences of Turnover in the Hospitality Industry

Carl D. Riegel

Turnover is and has been a pervasive problem for the hospitality industry. There is substantial anecdotal evidence to suggest that turnover rates can reach as high as 200 or 300 percent in rank-and-file positions, and management turnover, at least at the operations level, can approach 100 percent in some organizations. While the importance of turnover as a problem for our industry was somewhat obscured by the recession of the early and mid-1990s, it has been moved to the forefront with the advent of unprecedented full employment.

A low unemployment rate presents a three-pronged challenge for the industry. First, the number of workers in traditional target markets for hospitality is decreasing. This is likely to remain this way for some years to come. Second, unless the industry can present opportunities for meaningful advancement in pay and responsibility, it will continue to attract, in large measure, a transient workforce. That is, employees will view working in the industry as something to do while they prepare to do something else or while they wait

for "something better" to come along. Unfortunately, at the time of this writing, "something better" can easily be found by talented people who are not happy working in the industry. Finally, despite unprecedented efforts to change its image, the industry is frequently perceived as the "employer of last resort" rather than the much-touted "employer of choice." Although this perception is probably not deserved, it acts to make the current labor shortage much worse for the hospitality industry than for many other fields of employment.

For service industries like hospitality, turnover is a serious problem. It makes an existing workforce shortage worse, and it can also be argued that in some cases turnover is a symptom of an insidious organizational "disease." More important than this, however, is that recent research has established a strong link between employee satisfaction and overall profitability. In this article we will examine the concept of turnover in detail—what it is and why we should care. Next, we will examine what many believe to be the causes of turnover, and we will then turn our attention to emerging areas of concern about the real costs of employee turnover. Finally we will examine what some researchers believe will help stem excessive turnover.

WHAT IS TURNOVER AND WHY SHOULD WE BE CONCERNED?

In general, turnover refers to either voluntary or involuntary separation from organizations (Bluedorn, 1982). Involuntary separations (firings) can be a problem if they occur frequently, but the focus of this article will be primarily on voluntary separation from organizations—that is, the process by which people quit their jobs.

Historically, hospitality organizations have perceived turnover in two different ways. First, many companies are concerned that turnover costs the organization money, and because of that, unacceptable levels should be avoided. Turnover costs money for a variety of reasons, including:

1. The actual costs related to separation.
2. The cost of replacing employees, such as advertising, interviewing costs, and moving expenses.
3. Learning-curve inefficiencies by new employees.
4. Costs associated with the temporary disruption of the work force.
5. Nonquantifiable costs due to diminished image, customer loyalties to previous employees, and so forth.

Second, some hospitality firms take the view that turnover is *not necessarily undesirable,* because performance and longevity have an inverse-U-shaped relationship (see Figure 9.1). As Figure 9.1 suggests, performance increases over the short to intermediate term, but decreases or stagnates over the long term. That is, the longer employees stay, the less likely they are to demonstrate increases in performance. More importantly, the longer they stay, the more they will *cost* in raises and increased benefits. Firms adopting this tenure/performance position will be concerned primarily with the distribution of tenure

FIGURE 9.1
Tenure/performance philosophy

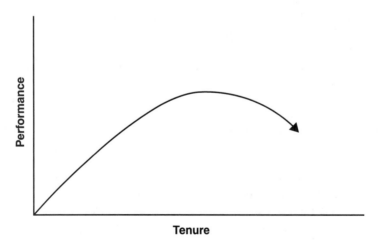

Source: Adapted from Staw.

throughout the organization and more likely will concentrate on appropriate rates of turnover rather than reduced rates of turnover. For many firms holding this philosophy, turnover control strategies may be viewed as not worth the effort when pay raises are combined with anticipated future performance.

The problem with both of these philosophies, as we shall see later in this article, is that they are limited. They view turnover as an *event* or *phenomenon* rather than a process. Thus, it is the event that managers need to control either by adapting to it or by controlling it rather than the process. A more expansive and probably a more effective approach would not focus on the turnover event per se. Rather it would come from a *process* perspective that views turnover as but one outcome of a sequential chain of events. Before we discuss this *phenomenon versus process* notion, it would be useful to turn our attention to the causes of turnover.

THE CAUSES OF TURNOVER

Many researchers (March and Simon, 1958; Porter and Steers, 1973; Price, 1977; McFillen, Riegel, and Enz, 1986) believe that turnover occurs as a result of a complex series of factors that influence employee attitudes and eventually affect employee behavior. Models sometimes oversimplify the processes they represent; however, a model is useful to provide a reasonable approximation of reality and is, therefore, useful in assisting our understanding and predicting outcomes.

The model shown in Figure 9.2 uses *intent to leave* as a measure for actual departure. Intent to leave is a surrogate or stand-in measure; however, it has been well substantiated in previous research as a proxy for actual departure. As the model suggests, intent to remain and/or leave an organization is a function of two interrelated factors: the level of job satisfaction and the degree of an employee's commitment to the organization. These factors in

combination with personality traits of the employee and specific job events influence the employee's level of job satisfaction. If the level of job satisfaction is high, then the employee's commitment to the organization tends to be strong and he or she will hold positive job attitudes and can be expected to stay on the job. On the other hand, if the level of job satisfaction is low, commitment decreases, job attitudes decline, and the employee, *if given the opportunity,* will leave the organization. This gives rise to new areas of concern.

NEW AREAS OF CONCERN

We previously explored two of the traditional philosophies that describe how hospitality organizations view turnover. While these philosophies point out reasons for organizations to control or reduce turnover, they offer a limited perspective of the potential damage excessive turnover can have. As we discussed earlier, a more comprehensive model would view turnover not as an isolated event, but as a process. This process views turnover as a series of related events, and *each* of these events can have negative consequences for employees as well as for organizations. A closer look at Figure 9.2 demonstrates this. According to the diagram, turnover results from negative attitudes toward the organization and will occur *only if* an employee has the *ability to leave.* This means that he or she must have other job options, not need to work, or not care to work. If employees have limited or unacceptable options and *do not* have the ability to leave the organization, they may adopt other "withdrawal" behaviors such as complaining, absenteeism, poor performance, or unacceptable customer-service behavior. This implies that turnover is only one choice of a variety of withdrawal behaviors available to disaffected employees, and disaffected employees can act out these behaviors either as an individual act or as a set of behaviors. Furthermore, the individual choice of withdrawal behavior de-

FIGURE 9.2
Model of turnover

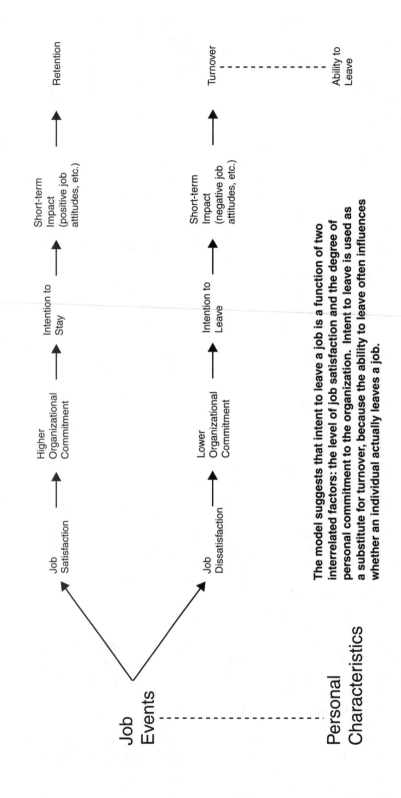

The model suggests that intent to leave a job is a function of two interrelated factors: the level of job satisfaction and the degree of personal commitment to the organization. Intent to leave is used as a substitute for turnover, because the ability to leave often influences whether an individual actually leaves a job.

Source: Adapted from McFillin, Riegel, and Enz, 1986.

pends upon a variety of other factors, such as their degree of unhappiness, their perception of self-worth, and, most importantly, their ability to find acceptable alternative employment.

Given this view of turnover, companies with high rates of turnover will likely experience a variety of negative outcomes. One way to categorize these outcomes is to look at how they affect individual employees as well as how they impact the organization both in the short and long term. Figure 9.3 indicates that both organizations and individual employees suffer from the effects of high rates of turnover, including attendance problems, decreased cooperation, decreased work performance, and even sabotage. In the longer term, however, the effects are more systemic and potentially more devastating. For example, high rates of turnover can worsen existing turnover rates, contribute to system problems such as poor customer relations, and even eventually limit a firm's ability to develop and implement strategy. The potential dollar cost of this is incalculable but potentially enormous. A question of major importance for firms with high turnover rates is not only *who leaves* but also *who stays.* In some cases, it may be that employees who stay with an organization are not necessarily the ones that the organization would want to keep, and those who do leave are not necessarily the ones that the organization would want to see go. In some cases outstanding employees find the organizational environment so dissatisfying that they will opt to separate from the company, and those who remain will be those who can adapt to a dysfunctional environment or those who have no choice but to stay.

In addition to these effects there is evidence that excessive turnover rates can have a substantial and negative impact on profitability. Recently, a great deal of discussion has centered on customer loyalty and the importance of avoiding customer defections. Simply put, the argument goes something like this: It costs a great deal to *create* new customers. The costs associated with advertising, promotion, and other marketing-related items are staggering. Thus it is wiser to try to retain existing guests than to create new ones. Furthermore, the longer a customer stays with a company the more they are worth. Generally, they buy more, buy more frequently, and are less price sensitive. In fact, one management writer (Reichheld, 1996) has suggested that decreasing customer defections by as little as five points—say from 10 percent to 15 percent per year—can *double* profits. With respect to the monetary value of customer or guest loyalty, several researchers (Haskett et al., 1994) have suggested a strong relationship between employee satisfaction, customer loyalty, and profitability. They call this concept the service-profit chain. As Figure 9.4 illustrates, employee retention is a key driver in creating customer retention and is therefore a critical factor in determining profitability.

These new concerns about turnover discussed in this section strongly indicate that the conventional thinking about turnover may capture but a small portion of its devastating effects. Now, let's take a look at ways of reducing turnover.

WHAT CAN BE DONE?

A study of turnover in the hospitality industry (McFillen, Riegel, and Enz, 1986) found that hospitality employees in one organization ranked these reasons as the most likely causes for high turnover rates:

1. Treatment by superiors.
2. Amount of work hours.
3. Job pressure.
4. Scheduling.
5. Training.
6. Fringe benefit packages.
7. Better opportunities elsewhere.
8. Physical demands of the job.

An effective strategy in the short term would be for managers to focus on these rea-

FIGURE 9.3
Effects of turnover on hospitality organizations

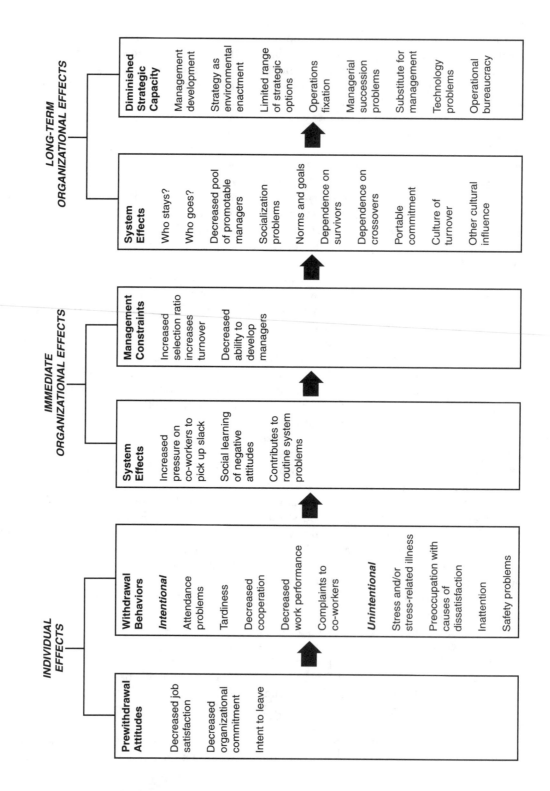

sons, in other words, work on fair treatment of employees, create fair and reasonable schedules, and so forth. However, these strategies do not necessarily address the causes of excessive turnover and are likely to have limited effectiveness and to be short-lived. A longer-term solution would take into account the causes of worker dissatisfaction and attempt to deal with these in a comprehensive and continuous manner.

Frederick Herzberg (1976) suggests that dissatisfaction occurs as a result of a lack of what he calls *hygiene factors* and that satisfaction occurs as a result of what he calls *motivators*. And while there is not necessarily any linkage in the organizational behavior litera-

ture between job satisfaction and job performance, there is a substantial body of theory to suggest that satisfied employees adopt prosocial and, therefore, committed behaviors toward the organization. Herzberg says that hygiene factors that can cause dissatisfaction among employees include things such as salary, working conditions, fringe benefits, job security, and so forth. While paying a fair salary or providing job security will decrease dissatisfaction, they will not necessarily create satisfaction in employees. Motivators or satisfiers recognized by Herzberg include achievement, recognition, challenging work, responsibility, advancement, and so forth. These factors, if provided for by the organiza-

FIGURE 9.4
The service-profit chain

Increased Profitability & Growth

Customer Loyalty

Customer Satisfaction

Perceived Service Value

Employee Retention & Productivity

Employee Satisfaction

Internal Work Quality

Source: Adapted from Heskett et al., 1994.

tion, will create satisfaction and therefore commitment. Thus, hospitality managers who are concerned about turnover as an insidious disease process need to not only take care of the extrinsic job factors, such as job security and salary, they also need to pay a great deal of attention to providing opportunities for advancement, challenging work, and so forth.

In addition to attending to environmental factors in the organization, paying attention to the selection of employees in the first place will go a long way in quelling dissatisfaction and, therefore, in diminishing turnover. An axiom in the human resource field is that the goal of selection is *not* to hire the best-qualified employee, but rather to hire the best employee for the particular job—the point being that it is important to match prospective employees to the organization and the job. Similarly, efforts to select employees who will be successful in a particular job as well as successful in the organizational culture will enhance the likelihood of their retention. Selection is an important human resource

function that is worthy of substantial effort and care.

CONCLUSION

Turnover has been a problem of long-standing significance for the hospitality industry. The effects of high turnover rates on hospitality businesses are substantially greater than many existing philosophies suggest, and dealing with turnover as an isolated event fails to acknowledge its causes and, therefore, is likely to have limited impact as a turnover control strategy. Comprehensive approaches that attempt, on the one hand, to eliminate sources of dissatisfaction and, on the other hand, to promote employee satisfaction and retention have the potential to strengthen commitment and, therefore, encourage a wide variety of prosocial behaviors that will strengthen organizational effectiveness, eliminate withdrawal behaviors of which turnover is one, and ultimately contribute to guest loyalty and profitability.

9.4   Current Issues in Hospitality Employment Law

Suzanne K. Murrmann and Cherylynn Becker

Fairness in the workplace is a significant issue affecting the productivity, loyalty, and commitment employees have to their organizations. The treatment that an employee receives from his or her supervisor will affect the worker's motivation to provide excellent service to customers, ultimately affecting the bottom-line profits of the organization. Many factors influence workplace justice. These include the voluntary human resource management policies that organizations have put into place to provide fair and equal employee treatment. In addition, there exist a significant number of federal and state laws and regulations that protect employees from

various forms of discrimination, provide employees with certain rights, and specify actions that employers must take when hiring and managing their workforce. Such laws may vary in their wording and coverage from state to state. However, they generally mirror law at the federal level. These laws, which significantly affect the human resource function in hospitality organizations, fall under four general categories:

- Those governing equal employment, equal opportunity, and nondiscrimination.
- Those governing compensation and working hours.

- Those governing the health and safety of workers.
- Those governing labor relations and collective bargaining (Jackson and Schuler, 2000).

The judicial process is a dynamic one. Continual changes occur in laws and regulations due to amendments to existing laws and enactment of new laws, as well as interpretations made by courts and regulatory agencies. It is mandatory for managers to keep up-to-date with the status of laws that affect their HR activities. Even with appropriate legal counsel, day-to-day activities of supervisors and managers are often the point where organizations run into legal problems. Therefore, it is necessary that managers be aware of their legal obligations.

Since space does not permit a full discussion of all relevant employment laws, the following text will concentrate on federal laws that have seen significant changes in the last decade as well as those that are forecasted to change significantly in the next several years (Flynn, 2000; Goldberg, 1998). They include sexual harassment and employer liability under Title VII of the Civil Rights Act, the Americans with Disabilities Act, the Family and Medical Leave Act, and the Immigration Reform and Control Act. A discussion of these laws and implications for hospitality managers follows.

SEXUAL HARASSMENT

In general, sexual harassment is defined as unwelcome sexual conduct in the workplace that is a term or condition of employment. Complaints of sexual harassment fall under two different categories: quid pro quo and hostile work environment. Quid pro quo harassment is said to occur when submission to or rejection of unwelcome sexual conduct by an individual is used as a basis for employment decisions affecting an employee. In other words, when a supervisor demands sexual fa-

vors from his or her subordinate and either promises an employment benefit such as a raise or promotion, or threatens the employee with loss of such benefits, quid pro quo harassment exists. Such activities may be subtle or overt, and the employee must show that he or she belongs to a protected group, was subject to unwelcome harassment that was based on his or her gender, and that acceptance or refusal resulted or could result in tangible changes to the working conditions.

While quid pro quo harassment implies an exchange of sexual favors for work benefits, hostile work environment harassment refers to the overall working environment in which employees function. Hostile work environment harassment is conduct that unreasonably interferes with the ability of an employee to perform his or her job properly or creates an intimidating, hostile, or offensive working environment. This may be so even if it does not lead to tangible or economic job consequences. As in quid pro quo harassment, the activities or conduct in question are unwelcome by the employee and are based on gender. The employee must also show that they are sufficiently pervasive and severe as to have caused an abusive working environment and that the employer is liable for these activities. Typical examples of this type of harassment include unwelcome physical touching; whistling, leering, improper gestures, or offensive remarks; unwelcome comments about appearance, sexual jokes, and the use of sexually explicit derogatory or otherwise offensive language.

Sexual harassment in the workplace continues to be an important discrimination issue, particularly with recent Supreme Court rulings (Goldberg, 1998). Two of particular note, *Burlington Industries v. Ellerth* and *Faragher v. Boca Raton*,[1] have significantly shaped the obligations of hospitality manag-

---

[1]*Burlington Industries v. Ellerth*: 524 U.S. 742; 118 S. Crt. 2257 (1998); *Faragher v. Boca Raton*; 524 U.S. 775, 118 S. Ct. 2275 (1998).

ers. In them, the Court clearly articulated the liability of employers for the actions of their harassing supervisors. First, in cases on which an employee has suffered tangible, detrimental employment actions, such as demotion, termination, or loss of benefits, the employer is strictly liable regardless of fault. Strict liability is premised on the fact the supervisors are acting for the employer (company) and regardless of whether or not the employer can show that it has an antidiscrimination policy, final responsibility rests with the company. In cases, however, where the employee has suffered no loss of tangible job benefits, the employer can avoid liability by showing that reasonable care was taken to prevent and promptly correct any sexual harassing behavior. Documentation that the harassed employee subsequently failed to take advantage of any preventative or corrective opportunities provided by the employer will further minimize likelihood of employer liability for harassment charges.

For hospitality managers to protect themselves against charges of sexual harassment, they need to focus on three major areas: (1) implementation and dissemination of antiharassment and complaint policies, (2) training of personnel, and (3) complaint investigation.

Though the Court has not specifically ruled that companies must have policies specifically targeted to sexual harassment, many human resource management professionals feel that employers can more easily demonstrate their "reasonable duty of care" by developing separate antiharassment policies. Such a policy would explicitly define sexual harassment, both in terms of quid pro quo and hostile environment harassment, and give specific examples of inappropriate conduct. Though seemingly obvious, the policy would also unambiguously prohibit such conduct. It should also indicate protection for employees from retaliation for reporting harassment. Numerous studies have shown that employees are often afraid to report inappropriate activities because of the fear of retaliation by their su-

pervisors. Managers should develop and include in their policy multiple avenues for filing harassment complaints. One such avenue would be to start with the employee's immediate supervisor; however, an additional route would be to bypass the supervisor and complain to an individual outside of the supervisor's direct chain of command. Assurance of prompt and thorough investigations and privacy are equally important components of an antiharassment policy.

As necessary as a well-developed and written policy is, it is also important that the policy be disseminated in such a way that all personnel in the hospitality organization are aware that the policy exists. Merely including it in an employee handbook may not be sufficient. Antiharassment policies should be posted in locations visited by employees on a regular basis, and discussed with new employees. This is especially important in an industry where a significant part of the labor pool is composed of employees who do not read and speak English as their primary language. The company should also attempt to keep some written acknowledgment of the fact that employees understand the policy.

Periodic training on sexual harassment is essential for the prevention of misconduct in the workplace and the defense of the employer against liability in court. The purpose of such training is to make supervisors and employees aware of conduct that constitutes harassment and provide them with mechanisms for effectively dealing with such conduct. Training needs to be tailored to the individual workplace and take into account the diversity of the workforce. However, there are a number of key components to training in this area. Though all employees should attend training, separate sessions should be held for supervisors and managers to instruct them on their obligations to subordinates and their responsibilities for investigating harassment complaints. The language and the customs of employees should always be taken into account when developing training materials, particularly when such activities as role-playing are used. Training in the hospitality industry should take into account the interaction of employees with third parties such as customers and outside vendors. Managers must be aware that the employer has an additional duty of care in the area of customer harassment of employees, and should be trained to delicately but effectively deal with such situations. Finally, care must be taken to select an appropriate resource for carrying out training. This may be an in-house trainer, or an outside individual or firm. In any case, the individual selected should have recognized expertise in the area of sexual harassment.

The final area of concern for managers is prompt investigation of harassment complaints. The employer who fails to document fair investigation of employee complaints will more than likely be found liable for harassment. All complaints should be investigated as swiftly as possible, by an unbiased investigator who is sensitive to the privacy concerns of the complainant. If, during the course of the investigation, there is sufficient reason to believe that the complainant and the accused need to be separated, the complainant should not be assigned to a less comparable job. Such action could be seen as retaliation for filing a complaint. Relevant material and information should be obtained, in private, from the accused and additional witnesses. Based on this, immediate and appropriate corrective action should be taken by doing whatever is necessary to end the harassment, and make the employee whole by restoring lost employment benefits or opportunities, and prevent the misconduct from recurring. If appropriate, disciplinary action should be taken against the offending supervisor or employee, ranging from reprimand to discharge. Generally, the corrective action should reflect the severity of the conduct. Document the findings and subsequent steps taken, if any, and place this documentation in a confidential investigation file. Equal Employment Opportunity Commission (EEOC) policy guidance on sexual harassment suggests that follow-up inquires be made to ensure that harassment has not resumed and that the employee has not suffered retaliation. Finally, use what was learned from these investigations to streamline or customize future training and policy restatements in this area to more closely align with specific company needs.

AMERICANS WITH DISABILITIES ACT

The Americans with Disabilities Act of 1990 (ADA) prohibits an employer from discriminating against a qualified individual with a disability in regard to job application procedures, hiring, advancement, discharge, compensation, training, and other "terms, conditions, and privileges of employment." The act has undergone almost a decade of interpretation by the courts that continue to refine and define its coverage and the responsibilities of hospitality managers. As noted by many professionals in human resource management, these rulings at times leave as many unresolved questions as they answer concerning employer responsibilities.

Under the ADA, a qualified individual is defined as "an individual with a disability who, with or without reasonable accommodation, can perform the essential function of the employment position that such individual holds or desires."[2] There are two questions that the manager must ask when determining whether an individual is qualified. First, does the individual satisfy the prerequisites for the position, such as the appropriate educational background, employment experience, skills, or licenses? And second, can he or she perform the "essential functions" of the position with or without reasonable accommodation? The former is answered by comparing the qualifications of the individual to job-related requirements and production standards traditional

---

[2]42 U.S.C. §1211(8).

to the industry, for example, number of rooms cleaned per day. When identifying requirements, employers should use those that they have used for other employees in the position and not those selected to intentionally exclude the disabled. The latter question may be answered by defining the fundamental job duties of a position, in a well constructed, written job description. Factors suggested for identifying essential functions include the amount of time spent performing the function, the number of employees available to perform the task, the work experience of past incumbents and present employees in the position, and the consequence of not performing the function. For instance, several courts have found attendance to be an essential function of the job because the inability to maintain regular attendance creates an undue hardship upon an employer.[3]

A disability is defined under the ADA as (1) "a physical or mental impairment that substantially limits one or more of the major life activities of such individual," (2) "a record of such an impairment," or (3) "being regarded as having such an impairment."[4] Impairments may include physiological disorders or conditions, cosmetic disfigurements, and anatomical loss affecting one or more major body systems. Before 1998, it was generally accepted that for an impairment to be covered under the definition of a disability, it needed to be a permanent condition that, if uncorrected, substantially limited a major life activity such as walking, seeing, hearing, speaking, etc. Several Supreme Court rulings have limited this definition, stating that "an individual's corrections, medications, and even subconscious mechanisms for coping with an impairment are to be considered when assessing whether that individual is disabled" and covered under the ADA (Sherwyn, Eigen, and Klausner, 2000). These rulings, though limiting the definition of a disability in one respect, in no way clear up the issue of what is considered a disability, nor may it actually limit the number of individuals claiming discrimination if managers continue to perceive individuals impaired even with corrective devices.

Traditional human resource functions and employment decisions can be considered discriminatory under the ADA. These include such activities as recruiting, advertising, and the processing of applications for employment, hiring, updating, promotion, termination, compensation, job assignment, and the like. In other words, the ADA mirrors to a great extent the rights of protected groups under Title VII of the Civil Rights Act. Hospitality managers should be aware of a number of issues unique to disability law. An employer risks violating the ADA by asking about medical conditions and disabilities in a preemployment situation. Questions at this point should be job related with inquiry limited to the applicant's ability to perform the essential functions of the job as described in the written job description. Preemployment medical examinations and tests, with the exception of testing for illegal drug use, would also be seen as discriminatory in the hospitality industry. The ADA also prohibits disparate treatment discrimination, that is, limiting and segregating employees in a way that affects their opportunities because of a disability. A hospitality employer that demonstrated a pattern of hiring disabled job applicants for back-of-the-house, noncustomer-contact positions, though such applicants could demonstrate the ability to perform effectively in customer-contact positions, would be demonstrating potentially discriminatory behavior. The use of employment tests or other selection criteria, which are not job related, to screen out disabled applicants is prohibited under the ADA. For example, if an employer requires an interview that is job related and consistent with business necessity as part of the application process, it would not be possible to reject a hear-

---

[3]*Tyndall v. National Education Centers*, 31 F.3rd 209 (4th Cir. 1994); *Earl v. Mervyns Inc.*, No. 99-4264 (11th Cir. 2000)

[4]42 U.S.C. §12102(2).

ing-impaired applicant solely because he could not be interviewed.[5] Finally, failure to reasonably accommodate disabilities, either those of job applicants or employees, constitutes discrimination under the ADA.

Accommodation for individuals with disabilities is at the core of the ADA. By law reasonable accommodation mandates employers to make accommodation for qualified individuals who can perform the essential functions of a job unless this causes significant difficulty or expense, that is, undue hardship.[6] Accommodations can be modifications or adjustments (1) in the job application or testing process that allows a qualified applicant with a disability to be considered for a position equally with other applicants; (2) in the workplace or in the manner or method in which the job is performed that allows the employee for perform the job; or (3) that enable the disabled employee to enjoy the benefits and privileges of the job equally to those without disabilities. Types of accommodations may include but are not necessarily limited to the following:

1. Modifications of existing facilities (ramps and entrances, bathroom facilities, workstations, etc.).
2. Job restructuring.
3. Modified work schedules.
4. Reassignment to vacant positions.
5. Acquisition and modification of equipment or devices.
6. Adjustment or modification of examinations or training materials.
7. Provision of qualified readers and interpreters (for preemployment activities, etc.).

---

[5]29 CFR Part 1630, Appendix § 1630.15(a).
[6]Undue hardship is assessed by reviewing the nature and cost of the accommodations needed; the financial resources of the employer; the size of the company and the number of its facilities; the financial resources of the facility itself; and the effect of the accommodation on the expenses or operations of the facility, on other employees' ability to do their jobs, and on the facility's ability to conduct business (ADA Sec. 101[10], 42 U.S.C. 12111[10]; EEOC Sec. 1630.2[p].)

The EEOC has issued guidelines for employers to follow for compliance. Hospitality managers should follow these procedures. Using an interactive process outlined by these guidelines should increase the likelihood of employees viewing a manager as reasonable and concerned about their needs.

1. Notify employees and job applicants of the employer's obligation under the ADA to make reasonable accommodations.
2. Employers should wait for a request for a reasonable accommodation by a qualified individual with a disability.
3. Analyze the particular job to determine its purpose and essential functions. Communicate to the employee your understanding of the essential functions of the job and the abilities needed to perform them.
4. Consult with the disabled individual to ascertain the precise job-related limitations imposed by the disability and how those limitations can be overcome.
5. With the disabled individual's assistance, identify potential accommodations and assess the effectiveness of each in enabling the individual to perform the essential functions of the job.
6. Consider the disabled individual's accommodation preferences and select and implement the accommodation most appropriate for both the employee and employer. This is a final decision that should be made by the manager.

Given the relatively young age of the ADA, it is anticipated that interpretation of even the most basic areas of the law, for example, the definition of a disability, will continue to evolve. There are, however, certain steps that many feel to be appropriate for managers to take (Sovereign, 1999). Facilities should be made as accessible as possible. This is particularly true of the hospitality industry given its public-accommodation requirement. Since the concept of reasonable accommodation is based on a clear understanding of the essential functions of the job, well-written job descriptions become extremely important in managing liability associated with the ADA. With the exception of drug testing, all preemployment medical inquiries and examinations should be eliminated. Always attempt to accommodate a qualified disabled individual. A case of undue hardship can be made after accommodation is researched. And finally, in organizations that are large enough to support service staff, an individual should be designated as the ADA resource for other managers and used when accommodations are requested.

FAMILY AND MEDICAL LEAVE ACT OF 1993

All hospitality employers with 50 or more employees are covered by the Family and Medical Leave Act of 1993 (FMLA). The FMLA was passed in an attempt to balance the demands of the workplace with the family and medical needs of employees. Employers both in and outside of the hospitality industry expressed grave concerns over the impact of the law on workplace productivity and employer compliance. Many of these fears proved to be unfounded; many, however, were not. Compliance with the law has proved to be cumbersome, given its technical record-keeping nature. Since the enactment of this act, the U.S. Department of Labor (DOL), which oversees the FMLA, has seen thousands of complaints filed and has changed the guidelines and directives to comply with dozens of court rulings.

The FMLA allows employees up to 12 weeks of unpaid leave during any 12-month period to deal with family and medical issues. Companies that employ 50 or more people (within a 75-mile radius), including part-time and temporary workers, during each of 20 or more calendar workweeks in a year are covered. In order for an employee to be eligible for leave he or she must have worked at least 1250 hours for the employer. An eligible employee

may take unpaid leave for the following reasons:

- The birth of a child.
- The placement of a child with the employee for adoption or foster care.
- A serious health condition of a spouse, child, or parent.
- The employee's own serious health condition.

The DOL regulations define a "serious health condition" as any illness, injury, impairment, or physical or mental condition that involves:

- Any period of incapacity or treatment involving inpatient care in a hospital, hospice, or residential mental care facility.
- Any period of incapacity requiring absences from work, school, or other regular daily activities of more than three calendar days that also involves continuing treatment by a health care provider. (Continuing treatment means either treatment two or more times by a health care provider or one treatment that results in a regimen of continuing treatment. A "regimen of continuing treatment" includes only those treatments that cannot be initiated without a visit to a health care provider, such as taking prescription drugs. It does not include taking over-the-counter medication; nor does it include therapy such as bed rest, drinking fluids, and exercise.)
- Continuing treatment by a health care provider for any period of incapacity due to pregnancy or for prenatal care, or for a chronic or long-term health condition that is incurable or so serious that, if not treated, would likely result in a period of incapacity of more than three calendar days.

As a general rule, ailments such as the common cold, the flu, earaches, upset stomach, minor ulcers, headaches other than migraine, routine dental or orthodontia problems, and periodontal diseases are not serious health conditions unless complications arise.

Employers covered by the FMLA must post notice of the act and their obligations, as well as provide additional information to employees concerning their entitlements and obligations through standard mechanisms such as employee handbooks and manuals. An employee requesting leave is required to give 30 days' notice to his or her employer, if possible. If such notice is not possible, the employee must provide "such notice as is practical" so that the employer has an opportunity to plan for the employee absence. As little as 1 to 2 days' notice (or less) may be sufficient in emergency situations. Employers may require a medical certification, such as a doctor's statement, from a health care provider to support leave requests. Additional opinions concerning the employee's condition and periodic reports from the employee on leave regarding his or her status and intent to return may also be required. During the time of the leave the employer must continue existing health care benefits.

Leave can be taken intermittently or on a schedule that reduces the typical number of hours per workday or workweek when medically necessary. Incremental leave may be taken in increments as short as one hour.

Under the FMLA the employer is obligated to place the employee, once returned from leave, in the same position that he or she left. If this is not possible, the employee must be placed in a position equivalent in pay, benefits, and other terms and conditions of employment. Based on rulings to date, *equivalent* appears to be construed as *identical* by the Labor Department.

There are a number of significant compliance issues that cause difficulty for human resource professionals and employment law attorneys. Due to their technical nature they will not be discuss here. However, several issues are worthy of note since they affect hospitality managers and supervisors in general.

While attendance has been successfully defended by several employers under the ADA as an essential function of the job, FMLA-leave absences cannot be used in discipline and termination decisions. Therefore, it is particularly important in intermittent-leave situations to record the reasons for absences. Supervisors should be encouraged to document "verbatim reasons" for absences. This information would allow a manager to conduct a "FMLA audit" of employees who may be undergoing disciplinary action for excessive absenteeism.

Though the act does allow for managers to require medical certification from employers for leave purposes, as well as second opinions, overuse of such information could open up liability under the ADA (Shea, 2000). Managers must be wary of asking for more medical information than is necessary for the purposes of granting FMLA leave. Medical certification is a useful tool to employ if there is doubt about the existence or extent of an employee's health condition. However, it is not necessary as long as the absence has been noted as FMLA leave.

A "serious" health condition under the FMLA may include many "minor" illnesses and conditions of short duration. Absences of less than three days may also be considered legitimate reasons for leave. This is due to the interpretation of the FMLA specific wording. Indeed, many experts in the area agree that regulations have gone beyond the intent of the legislation in terms of interpreting what a serious illness should be, and managers need to be aware that, at this point, a liberal interpretation needs to be placed on this definition.

IMMIGRATION REFORM AND CONTROL ACT OF 1986

In 1986, Congress enacted the Immigration Reform and Control Act (IRCA) in response to significant increases in undocumented immigration and vocal concerns from unhappy voters. This law was an attempt to control undocumented immigration in a number of ways, including the imposition of sanctions on employers for knowingly hiring undocumented immigrants. In addition, the law provided for amnesty for undocumented immigrants who could demonstrate a record of continuous residence in the United States for a designated period of time. These regulations, along with increased support for border patrol activities, were thought to significantly eliminate the attractiveness of U.S. jobs for undocumented workers, thereby protecting jobs and wages for legal workers in the United States.

Critics of the IRCA argued that it would encourage employers to engage in greater discrimination against U.S. citizens and legal aliens based on their appearance and cultural background, and safeguards against such discrimination were included in its content. However, several studies to date have shown that even with these safeguards in place, there exists a pattern of discriminating against individuals based on their physical appearance or accent (Phillips and Massey, 1999). Such discrimination includes the denial of jobs, as well as paying lower wages to undocumented workers. This decrease in pay, below legal minimum, is thought to take place to compensate for the risk involved in being sanctioned under the IRCA.

The IRCA requires employers to verify the employment eligibility of all employees hired by and working for the organization and to complete and maintain eligibility paperwork. This paperwork, commonly referred to as I-9 forms, must be maintained on all employees, U.S. citizens as well as aliens authorized to work in the country. The Immigration and Naturalization Service (INS) is charged with enforcing the IRCA. However, any number of other federal agencies, including the EEOC, the Justice Department, and the Department of Labor, may request to review the eligibility documentation records of a company. Employers must verify an employee's or applicant's identity and eligibility to work by requesting proof of both within three days of hire. Documents, which can be used to verify identity, include such items as a state driver's license,

state or school ID card, or a voter's registration card. Eligibility to work may be established using a number of documents, including a social security card, birth certificate issued by U.S. state, county, or municipal authority, or an unexpired INS employment authorization. There are also documents such as a U.S. passport that establish both identity and work eligibility. A complete list of all appropriate documents is provided on the back page of the I-9 form.

As mentioned earlier, the IRCA contains antidiscrimination provisions, which are in addition to and do not change discrimination under Title VII of the Civil Rights Act. The IRCA bans discrimination against legal aliens or those intending to become U.S. citizens. An alien has employment rights equal to a U.S. citizen, unless citizenship is a bona fide occupational qualification. If an alien is authorized to work in the United States, an employer cannot give preference to a U.S. citizen who is less qualified.

Employers have several responsibilities under the law.

1. Employers cannot request more or different documents than are required under the provisions of the law. Though it is oftentimes easier for managers to require specific, approved documentation such as a driver's license or social security card, they must accept any qualified document from the I-9 list if it appears to be valid.

2. Employers cannot knowingly use, attempt to use, possess, obtain, accept, or receive any forged, counterfeit, altered, or falsely made documents. It is often extremely difficult to identify counterfeit documents. However, managers should closely scrutinize the documentation of all applicants for obvious falsification, for example, multiple individuals with the same or similar social security numbers.

3. Employers cannot backdate or otherwise falsely make I-9 forms appear as if they are or have been in compliance with the IRCA.

Eligibility verification should be performed by individuals responsible for hiring on an ongoing basis. Paperwork should be kept up-to-date.

4. Employers must have new employees complete section 1 of the employment verification I-9 at the time of the hire by filling in the correct information, signing, and dating the form.

5. Employers are responsible for reviewing and ensuring that the employees fully and properly complete section 1 of the employment verification I-9. Applicants who do not fully complete this section should not be hired.

6. Employers must examine the original document(s) (the only exception is a certified copy of a birth certificate) presented by the employee and then fully complete section 2 of the employment verification I-9.

7. Employers must keep the employment verification I-9 for three years after the date employment begins or one year after the person's employment is terminated, whichever is later.

In order to avoid penalties under the IRCA, hospitality managers should use the following checklist:

- Verify the employment status of every person hired.
- Employ only U.S. citizens and aliens authorized to work in the United States.
- Verify employees' status within three days of their being hired to work.
- Inform each new job applicant, either verbally or in writing, that you hire only U.S. citizens and aliens lawfully authorized to work in the United States and that you will require all new employees to complete the designated verification form I-9.
- Examine documentation presented by new employees, record the information on the I-9, and sign. Retain these documents for three years.
- Do not ask for proof of citizenship or authorization to work before having made the decision to hire the applicant.
- Do not refuse to offer employment to anyone on the basis of foreign accent or appearance.
- Do not discharge present employees based on foreign appearance or language.

The above discussion of these key issues only scratches the surface of the legal challenges facing hotel HR managers. When you consider that the 535 members of Congress and the members of 50 state legislatures are constantly proposing laws that result in regulation, it is easy to see why HR managers can face some daunting tasks in assisting the organization and its managers in staying out of legal trouble.

9.5 Employee Work Teams in Hospitality

M. Chris Paxson

In the previous edition of this book, the editor noted that human resources management in the hospitality industry "is a bit like the weather: Everyone complains about it, but no one does anything about it" (Rutherford, 1995). The best-managed firms dedicate significant resources to finding better ways to hire, train, and retain employees. Other firms use human resources—that is, cut jobs—to counterbalance budgets during economic downturns.

Sustained low unemployment rates and demographic shifts have raised the human resource consciousness of the industry. Much has changed, but much remains to be done. Let's begin by examining the traditional roles and functions of human resources. Later in the chapter we will discuss how team approaches have changed operations and human resource management.

HUMAN RESOURCE MANAGEMENT IN TRADITIONAL HOTELS

The traditional functions performed by human resource professionals in mid- to large-sized companies in the hospitality industry are:

- Recruiting and selection.
- Compensation and benefits management.
- Training and development.
- Performance appraisal.
- Labor relations.
- Employee relations.

Today's human resource managers monitor the legal environment, deal with issues related to safety and health including communicable disease, and increasingly handle problems that their predecessors rarely faced. In this era of labor shortages, managers in general, and especially human resource managers, work constantly to reduce absenteeism and unwarranted turnover. More and more frequently, human resource managers deal with day care, transportation to and from work, helping employees develop basic work-related skills such as personal hygiene and punctuality, and assisting with family conflict. One human resource manager (at a midsize, airport property with a prominent hotel chain) explained how she had become involved with the family of a young employee, working to find a way to help him stay in school. She knew that if he stayed in school, he was likely to continue working. She also knew that finishing high school would increase this young man's chances of becoming a valued employee and building a career. This depth of involvement with employees' private lives was rare in the recent past.

Small companies may or may not have a human resource specialist on staff to deal with today's human resource issues. Operations managers take on human resource tasks like recruitment and selection as added duties.

Another truth about the human resource function is that human resource managers, whether with large or small organizations, share responsibility for human resource activities with line managers. Contrary to popular belief, the human resources department in traditional firms does not hire and fire employees. Rather, the role of the human resources department is to design and monitor major components of the hiring process. The same can be said for other responsibilities. Human resource managers assist line managers to perform their human resource responsibilities. That is, they serve as internal consultants.

In traditional organizations, the role of the human resource manager runs the gamut of activity from consulting and forms processing to working closely with operations managers to develop business strategies focused on increasing profit. The traditional human resource manager's effectiveness often depends on the individual's ability to form effective working relationships with other department managers (Nebel, 1991). As recently as the late 1980s, hotel managers assigned human resource management the lowest value of all hotel functions. Operations and marketing aspects were rated highest (Umbreit and Eder, 1987).

HUMAN RESOURCE MANAGEMENT IN TEAM ENVIRONMENTS

In team-based organizations, human resource and line managers work together more closely than in traditionally managed firms. The degree of interdependence varies, however, partly because there are many different types of team environments. Another reason for the variation is that much of what is being done with teams in hospitality is experimental. In general, relationships between human resource professionals and all employees are closer in team-based organizations than in traditionally managed firms. We found that in hotels with self-directed work teams, for example, human resource managers partnered with top managers, middle managers, and line employees to continuously identify and solve problems and build the team. One general manager of a five-star U. S. hotel said it best. He was forced by the self-directed team environment to accept that not all great ideas and decisions come from the general manager. His role changed from decision maker to facilitator. In team-based organizations, human resource professionals are business partners. Only a handful of hotel properties in the United States use self-directed work teams. Nevertheless, team approaches to management play a larger role in the hospitality industry than ever before. In the process, the role of human resource management has grown and become more central to the functioning of the organization than ever before.

Given that the role of the human resource professional differs in traditional and team-based organizations, you may be asking yourself several questions:

1. To what extent are teams used in the hospitality industry?
2. What types of teams are there?
3. How do team approaches to management differ from other approaches?
4. How can teams be helpful? What are their limitations?
5. Are teams worth the effort?
6. How do I decide whether a team approach will work at my company?
7. How would I go about implementing teams?

These questions are the focus of this reading. We hope that what you learn helps put teams into their proper perspective as one of many management tools available to aspiring hospitality managers.

This reading attempts to answer the questions, providing an introduction to the topic of work teams for aspiring hospitality managers. It describes team types, how winning teams behave, and why they fail. Finally, we provide some advice from research studies and interviews with practicing hospitality managers about successfully launching and sustaining teams.

The movement toward teams is still in its infancy, and it is obvious that the full potential of teams has yet to be explored. We hope that this chapter will add to your knowledge and understanding of what works and what does not where teams in the hospitality industry are concerned.

A BRIEF HISTORY OF TEAMS IN THE UNITED STATES

The word *team* is everywhere. There are sport and medical teams, news and legal defense teams. People who work together often call themselves a team regardless of the nature of the work. Their jobs may be done independently, yet the unit may think of itself as a team. Actually, teams are a kind of formal work group. That is, they are clearly defined and structured. For example, committees are a type of formal group.

The popularity of teams mushroomed in the 1980s. Currently, bookseller Amazon.com lists no less than 233 books about teams. Most praise the business worthiness of teams or team building in modern organizations. Americans may have latched on to the concept because in the late 1970s and again in the 1980s the Japanese and Europeans used teams to improve productivity, customer satisfaction, and return on investment. At a time when Japan and Europe boomed, the U.S. economy was faltering. Inflation raged. Company downsizing produced massive unemployment, and business travel dwindled to a trickle, devastating hospitality industry revenues. Experiments with work teams in the United States started out of desperation.

The origin of teams is associated with a

management model that the researcher Edward Lawler calls high involvement, high participation. (Recardo et al., 1996) This idea originated in the coal mines of England during the early 1950s. According to this theory, productivity improves when workers are highly involved and participate in every aspect of the work they do. Thus, teams were born.

The popularity of teams peaked and then faded in the 1970s, reemerging in the 1980s. Just-in-time (JIT) production techniques revolutionized the factory floor, first in Japan and then in the United States in the late 1970s. JIT management reduced inventories to a minimum by arranging for parts and components to be delivered to the production facility "just in time" to be used. JIT is based on the management philosophy that products should be manufactured only when customers need them and only in the quantities customers require in order to minimize the amounts of raw materials and finished-good inventories that manufacturers keep on hand (Certo, 2000). The focus shifted from company needs to customer needs with the idea of reducing cost.

W. Edwards Deming (followed by Joseph M. Juran and Philip Crosby) took this idea further. Deming, a pioneering statistician, lecturer, author, and consultant, emphasized a systems and leadership approach to management. He taught that quality is achieved by studying and constantly improving processes and systems so that the final product or service delights the customer. In other words, understanding customer needs and how customers use services is the critical element for achieving high quality. For example, if you are asked to clean off a table, knowing how to do it depends upon whether the table is used for eating, cooking, or surgery.

Deming (1993) also called attention to employee needs. He emphasized the positive effects of involving employees in decision making, productivity improvement, and customer satisfaction. Where once there may have been barriers, rivalries, and distrust, the organization must foster teamwork and partnerships with the workforce and unions. The partnership is not a gimmick or "old wine in new bottles." The focus is on the common struggle for the customers, not separate struggles for power.

Despite considerable media attention, for the last 40 years high-involvement, high-participation approaches to management have been largely a curiosity, not a mainstream management practice. And impressive results credited to work teams in manufacturing at companies such as Kellogg, General Electric, and Lincoln Electric have not materialized in the service sector. The verdict is still out about service team effectiveness. With only a short track record, very little is known about what it takes to create and maintain effective teams in the service sector.

A HISTORY OF TEAMS IN THE HOSPITALITY INDUSTRY

Restaurant industry entrepreneur, executive, hospitality educator, and consultant Donald I. Smith says that successful restaurants have always taken a team approach to their work (see the sidebar "Donald I. Smith: Teams in Restaurants). After all, it would be difficult to welcome and seat guests, prepare food, serve it, and then get ready for the next customers if workers did their jobs totally independently. Imagine the following unlikely (and unsuccessful) scenario: cold plates of food waiting for customers as they are seated; customers eating what the chefs felt like cooking; the manager dispatching a server to buy paper plates because the dishwasher runs the machine only once a day. There's no simple formula for developing a great restaurant. Great food, good location, a pretty space, a unique identity are important. But it takes a team of well-trained, committed employees and a willful, demanding, caring coach to achieve greatness. One might call this velvet-gloved command and control.

DONALD I. SMITH: TEAMS IN RESTAURANTS

What role do teams play in restaurants?

There's no one simple answer to that question. A restaurant is the sum of its parts, and every part is distinct and important. Like the conductor leading eccentric and temperamental musicians, the great restaurateur combines and balances the elements into a cohesive "orchestrated" whole.

Donald I. Smith, legendary restaurateur, industry executive, hospitality educator, and consultant, built the fifth largest restaurant in the Chicago area—35 miles from the city. Chateau Louise was the talk of the town in the 1950s and 1960s. Chateau Louise, with a continental theme, was a celebration restaurant, *the* place to go for birthdays, anniversaries, and other special occasions.

Don talks about the willfulness of the owner in running a popular, profitable restaurant. There's an attitude or personality that's a product of the owner's vision and a confident sense of how-we-do-it-here that infuses the business. The kitchen and wait staff feel it; it gets passed on to the customers. It's a kind of institutionalized "specialness."

Like great coaches, great owner-managers work hard, work smart, are committed to their jobs, and expect the same from those who work for them. They are winners, who "work your butt off" in exchange for teaching employees their jobs and caring to help them reach personal goals. Successful managers also care enough to enforce the rules. Gradually, employees become proficient. Mutual trust and respect develop, so that outstanding employees become valued partners. They make decisions on their own and really run the restaurant, but always under the watchful eye of the owner. "The coach makes the difference" is Don Smith's motto.

How does this view of teams compare to your experience? How does it compare to the ideas about teams presented in this reading?

Hotels and restaurants have a notorious command-and-control history. Pot-throwing chefs and imperious general managers stereotyped in popular movies were reality in European kitchens a generation ago. Even today many hotels and restaurants operate with a command-and-control style, where employees are simply warm bodies that can be replaced.

Tough economic times for U.S. hotels in the early 1980s brought on by recession drove companies to look for ways to be profitable. Human resource executives at Marriott proposed team approaches to management as a way to improve productivity and reduce costs at a time when news of Japan's great success with teams was making headlines. Marriott, eager to grow and foreseeing chronic labor shortages because of lower birthrates and lower U. S. immigration targets, decided to implement teams in all of its hotels. Unfortunately, in a clash of the old and new approaches, the transition to teams was itself transformed into a drive to reduce the size of the management force at Marriott. Management levels were reduced and positions cut. The corporate director of human resources for Marriott believes that disguising downsizing as team development destroyed all possibility of implementing teams at Marriott. Trust was shattered to the extent that the word *team* is not used today at Marriott to describe current experiments with teams.

Fifteen years after the company's failed efforts, teams have resurfaced at Marriott. The LINKS project teaches elements of teamwork companywide, but does not use the word *team* in its curriculum or promotional materials. And selected Courtyard by Marriott and Fairfield Inn properties currently are experimenting with teams.

In one North Carolina city, the Courtyard

by Marriott and the Fairfield Inn have the same general manager. But it wasn't always that way. Both hotels opened with the conventional structure: a general manager and an assistant general manager. However, the Courtyard by Marriott was managed any way but conventionally. The Courtyard by Marriott's general manager improved productivity and saved labor cost by means of several bold experiments that satisfied employees and radically changed how work was organized at the hotel. First, housekeepers, whose work peaked early in the morning and late in the day, were offered the opportunity during slow periods to work in the property's limited-service breakfast bar, replenishing supplies, busing tables, and cleaning up. This doesn't sound very revolutionary, but in the past housekeepers were rarely cross-trained. Employers hired full-time or part-time workers to do the job. As it became more difficult to hire and retain housekeepers and other hourly employees, employers have been forced to create more attractive, interesting jobs. Enriched jobs reduce turnover and may improve productivity at a minimum by redirecting labor where it is most needed.

In another bold experiment, a longtime housekeeper was promoted to executive housekeeper at the property. Later, this employee was promoted again to serve as both executive housekeeper and assistant general manager. Promoting a housekeeper to executive housekeeper is unheard-of in the lodging industry. The benefits of this creative approach were significant. Combining management duties in housekeeping and as assistant to the general manager saved labor cost. In addition, the employee was being developed. She was highly motivated by the general manager's confidence in her. There was a chance that she would manage a property of her own someday. Another unanticipated benefit was that the experiments inspired and motivated other employees at the hotel. Turnover plummeted from more than 200 percent annually to 25 percent.

However, not everyone at Marriott was happy. The Fairfield Inn general manager working next door to the Courtyard property was asked by corporate executives to work with his neighboring general manager to implement team-based programs. First, the general manager resisted. Later, he flatly told his Courtyard antagonist that he would not cooperate with her. Finally, he issued an ultimatum to the corporate offices: either the Courtyard general manager had to go or he would quit. The complaining manager was fired.

The Courtyard general manager was asked to lead both hotels. Her loyal executive housekeeper/assistant general manager oversaw day-to-day operations at the Courtyard, while the general manager devoted more time to analyzing the processes and problems at the Fairfield Inn. Marriott hoped to disseminate the Courtyard property's laborsaving practices throughout the system.

Despite the successes, this case study highlights one of the disadvantages of team approaches to management. Managers often become disoriented by, resist, and even resent the loss of power and control characteristic of high-involvement, high-participation approaches to management.

DEFINING TEAMS

The experiments with teams at the on North Carolina city Courtyard and Fairfield Inns illustrate several important features of teams. First, work groups may call themselves teams even though they are not. In many organizations co-workers are called teammates and are collectively called a team. But in many cases individuals are neither teammates nor do they work as a team.

So why do they call themselves a team? From what we can tell, the everyday use of the word *team* implies that members work together in harmony and with a spirit of cooperation. This means, by simple definition, that most of the groups called teams are not really performing as teams. In our definition as observed at the North Carolina Courtyard and Fairfield Inns, teams have specific characteristics. We define a team as

> a unified, interdependent, cohesive group of people working together to achieve common goals (Recardo et al.,1996).

Each worker may have a specialized function, for example, checking guests in and out, busing tables, or supervising the work of housekeepers. In a team each worker also needs the resources and support of others and must be willing to give up individual autonomy to the degree necessary to accomplish the hotel's objectives.

A successful team will have the following characteristics:

1. *Definable membership.* This means that the roles, responsibilities, and limits of the decision-making authority of each member must be clearly defined. Each team member also must clearly understand what he or she is expected to deliver or produce as part of their job. Team members must mutually agree about the results that the team is expected to achieve, specific projects and plans, and how the team will be accountable to the hotel and one another. There are two kinds of accountability for the team to address: accountability within the team itself and accountability to those outside the team. Asking "Who does what around here?" helps prevent conflict. Clarifying values and beliefs improves how teams make decisions. Planning defines team action.
2. *Stable membership.* Teams must have a core of members who will be with the team throughout its life. This core provides continuity.
3. *Common goals.* Team members must understand the goals and objectives that they were brought together to achieve. Team sponsors and managers play a pivotal role in defining goals and objectives and communicating them to team members. Of equal importance, the team members must think that the goals are worthwhile so they will do all that is needed to achieve them.
4. *A sense of belonging.* Team members must feel that they belong to the team and are full contributing members. This can be facilitated through ongoing discussions of team members' perceptions, ideas, and concerns.
5. *Interdependence.* A team is a team only if there is a great degree of interdependence. That is, one team member's performance must depend on the inputs and outputs of the other team members.
6. *Interaction.* Team members must interact with each other to be considered a team. Experience suggests that the most successful teams usually occupy the same physical space. Close proximity helps solidify and bond team members together.
7. *Common rewards.* Having common performance measures and reward systems is essential to a team's long-term success. Most organizations reward workers for individual, but not team effort. This single factor is one of the most important underlying differences between real teams and groups that call themselves teams. There is no team if members are in direct competition for rewards with one another. Team members, on the other hand, work cooperatively and should be compensated for the skills and knowledge they bring to the team, how well they work together as a team, and what the team accomplishes together.

BENEFITS

Some common benefits of teams are:

- *Better solutions.* A group of individuals brought together to solve a business problem is much more likely to come up with a better solution than an individual working alone is. The collective brain power of a team frequently outmatches the single brain power of an individual. In a team it is more likely that an individual will be willing to say that an idea is bad and needs to reconsidered.

- *More motivated workers.* Most managers are not trained, rewarded, or reinforced for making the workplace a sociologically and psychologically healthy experience and therefore misunderstand the importance of these things in forging a good team. Employees who work in teams typically report that they have received more support than they would have in a nonteam environment. In a well-run team the social interaction of team members is a positive and rejuvenating force. Workers we interviewed at the Fayetteville Courtyard by Marriott hotel said that the experience was one of their best, most productive, and most creative.
- *Increased knowledge.* Teams provide all members with connections that can lead to new opportunities and new work experience that would be less likely to occur in a traditional work environment. People are exposed to other jobs and ideas that make them more valuable in their own jobs.
- *Better use of resources.* In today's increasingly competitive environment, waste reduction is an important competitive advantage. Teams often are a cost-effective way of reducing resource costs through sharing human as well as material and financial resources. One general manager leads both the Fayetteville Courtyard and Fairfield Inn hotels. Housekeepers clean rooms and work in the Courtyard property's small restaurant. Both hotels experience considerable cost savings because of these innovations.
- *Increased productivity.* Teams go through a life cycle. Early in the process, team failures are very frequent. It is not unusual for some types of teams, such as self-directed teams or those that cross departments, to have failure rates as high as 60 percent. But

once through that cycle, initial productivity gains of 40 percent to 100 percent are not uncommon. Sustained productivity gains of 15 percent to 30 percent are common. In organizations with a long history of implementing teams, success rates are much higher, and consequently, productivity increases come more rapidly and with fewer failures.

CHALLENGES

Teams are not a cure-all. When used appropriately, they can provide startling results. However, they are not risk free. Some of the more common problems associated with implementing teams include:

- *Loss of control.* Most Americans have grown up in this century without experience working in a communal or team environment. Furthermore, the compensation system in almost all corporations is based on rewarding the individual and not the team. Teams make many people feel as though they have lost some control or freedom over their work lives, whereas employees who have worked on factory floors or in the back office are much more likely to be at home in teams. Managers and supervisors may be threatened by teams as was the general manager of one Fairfield Inn because they have to give up some of their traditional power and control to advance the team.
- *Forced consensus.* In a team environment, individuals may not always get what they want. All of us have identified and oftentimes offered what we think is the perfect solution to a problem. With teams we may find that we are the only one who thinks this is the perfect solution. In order for teams to work, a consensus among different opinions must be worked out and acted upon as a team. More time must be invested in decision making.

- *Difficulty managing multiple relationships.* In a team composed of ten members, the effort to manage relationships is complex. This is especially true when the team is a task force or a cross-functional team because managers from other departments have their own agendas.
- *Changing roles and responsibilities.* These change significantly when teams are implemented, and change is uncomfortable. Employees gain more power to influence work and must assume more responsibilities and be more proactive than in the past. Employees also tend to be held more accountable because they, not their bosses, are responsible for what is produced, the services delivered, or other outputs. Managers become leaders instead of drill sergeants—coaches instead of controllers. To many employees and managers, this shift of roles is disorienting, especially if they have not received enough training to take on the new responsibilities.
- *Cost.* Initially, teams are expensive to implement. Training costs increase and productivity is lost. Sometimes old systems must be operated along with new structures during the transition period. Human resource systems, such as compensation and performance management systems, may have to be redesigned. Employee turnover may increase, especially in the early stages of the transition to teams.

So far, we have described teams as if they represent a single, uniform idea. Teams are characterized by:

- Definable, stable membership.
- Common goals.
- Interdependence.
- A sense of belonging.

Members must work on projects together and share the rewards and other consequences of their efforts. However, not all teams are the same. Mention *team* to a sports fan, and he or she is likely to refer to a favorite sports franchise or a daughter's or son's local soccer league team. *Team* means something else, however, within the organizational setting. Our tendency to categorize may lead us to think of teams in one way, our own way, and not pay attention to the differences among them.

TEAM TYPES

Four types of teams are most prevalent in today's organizations:

1. Problem-solving teams.
2. Task forces.
3. Cross-functional teams.
4. Self-directed (self-managed) teams.

Simple problem-solving teams allow people to share information and best practices. These teams make decisions about the day-to-day tasks that they perform, work processes they use, and problems they deal with in their functional area. Five to twelve members typically are appointed to the team (they usually are not volunteers) to resolve problems within their work unit over a fixed period of time, usually less than one year. Simple problem-solving or functional teams tend to be reactive rather than self-managed and focus on predefined problems rather than "big picture" issues. Simple problem-solving teams are fairly easy to implement because they do not require adjustments of the organization's compensation plan, structure, or employee selection practices. Many of the major lodging companies in the United States use problem-solving teams. For example, a problem-solving team composed of front office representatives at a Marriott property worked to increase the efficiency of group check-ins.

Special-purpose teams evolved in the United States during the middle 1980s from problem-solving work teams. There are many types of special-purpose teams. Some of the most common are task forces, cross-functional work teams, and self-directed work teams.

Task forces usually are made up of team members who have highly specialized skills. Members are brought together from different functional areas (i.e., departments such as the front office, security, catering, stewarding, or housekeeping) to solve complicated problems that require special expertise and knowledge. One five-star lodging company, for example, brought together employees from diverse functional areas, including housekeepers, food and beverage directors, kitchen stewards, sales managers, and front office guest-service representatives to identify processes that needed to be improved for its most frequent, highest revenue-producing guests. These guests accounted for nearly 80 percent of all revenues at the hotel. The task force identified several key processes, including check-in/checkout and the handling of fax messages, that were critical to satisfying frequent guests. Task forces typically do research and make recommendations but do not implement solutions.

Cross-functional teams also are made up of team members brought together from different functional areas to investigate problems or processes, recommend solutions, and solve complicated problems. Unlike a task force, a cross-functional team implements its recommendations. Historically, these teams are made up of highly skilled specialists. In the hotels that we studied, cross-functional teams included food and beverage or rooms division directors and several department managers. Typically, these teams also included one or two representatives from the hotel's hourly staff.

One cross-functional team at a five-star hotel property in the United States studied the problem of fax message delivery errors. Team members determined that 20 percent of guests at the hotel generated 75 percent of the property's annual revenue. Team members also knew that frequent guests, who were usually business travelers, considered fax errors to be a serious problem. The team's solution was to install fax machines in selected guest rooms.

The team's careful analysis of the problem saved money and satisfied a key group of customers. Fax machines were not installed in every room, because the team's investigations indicated that this level of service was critical only for frequent guests. The expense was justified, given the anticipated revenue payoff. Installing fax machines in all guest rooms would have been wasteful and costly.

As organizations adopt a higher involvement strategy for solving the organization's problems, cross-functional teams tend to include members from every part and level of the organization. Some organizations have tried to establish permanent cross-functional teams, but the results so far have been discouraging (McDermott et al., 1998). The problems seem to be universal to cross-functional teams, but are correctable. They include such things as turnover or borrowing team members for other projects, a poorly developed notion of needs, deliverables, and due dates, unclear team member roles and responsibilities, no clear chain of command, and lack of top management support.

Self-directed work teams (SDWTs) or self-managed work teams (SMWTs) manage themselves. More than any other type of team, SDWTs evolve over time. They may come to control human resource decisions, such as hiring, firing, compensation, and scheduling vacations. They often have financial and budgetary control, work directly with customers, plan work schedules, and generally have the authority to improve work processes and procedures.

Self-directed work teams are by far the most difficult type of team to implement. They require that a culture de-emphasize status. Jobs are redesigned, unit boundaries and supervisory reporting relationships change, so that workers' roles must be redefined and in some cases employees need to be retrained. Self-directed work environments require a participatory management style. Employees also must want to accept new responsibilities (such as scheduling work shifts or handling recruitment and selection) that were previously handled by managers or support staff members. In a sense, SDWTs are cross-functional teams in which members are cross-trained and take the participatory management style to its extreme.

No matter how you look at it, implementing SDWTs means more work. The goal is to get more output with less input. With the right rewards and incentives, employees are typically willing to invest in the SDWT approach, but their investment must be rewarded appropriately. Organizations should have in place a compensation system that rewards flexibility and team output.

Think back to the example about the North Carolina Courtyard by Marriott described earlier in the reading. What type of team environment did the hotel have?

It operated somewhat like a SDWT, didn't it? How the general manager managed the hotel and organized the work evolved over time. Status was de-emphasized. Recall that the general manager promoted a skilled and talented housekeeper first to executive housekeeper and then to assistant general manager. Housekeepers were cross-trained to work in the dining facility during off-peak hours. These are characteristic of SDWTs.

At the same time, employees did not hire, fire, or make other human resource decisions on their own, although they participated in these decisions. Employees also did not have fiscal or financial control of operations. Did this hotel operate like a SDWT?

One explanation for the differences between the Courtyard by Marriott team and the ideal SDWT may be related to the change process. All teams go through a life cycle (see Figure 9.5), gradually progressing from one stage to another. The stages of team development are planning, team formation, development, independence, and self-direction. Each stage requires different kinds of preparation, leadership, team activities, and training (Recardo et al., 1996).

During the planning stage, top managers and the team sponsor, usually the property general manager, draft the mission, identify critical success factors, objectives, deliverables, milestones, due dates, and activities the team will have to complete in order to be successful. During this stage, management decides the feasibility of using teams. The leadership style of top managers during the planning stage should be directive. That is, managers should do the following:

- Organize and direct team activities.
- Establish expectations.
- Perform traditional supervisory roles.

During the formation stage, the sponsor and team members meet to present the organiza-

FIGURE 9.5
Stages of team development

	Stage 1 Team Formation		Stage 3 Independence	
Planning Stage		Stage 2 Development		Stage 4 Self-direction

Increasing Involvement and Participation

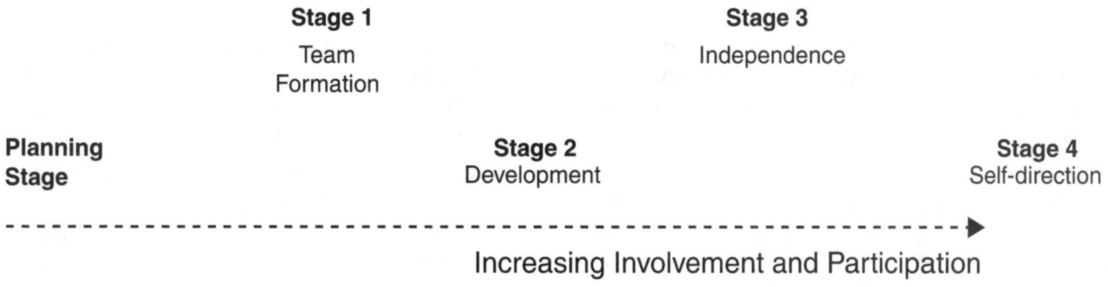

tional mission to the team. There are many purposes for meeting, only one of which is team building. Other purposes are to:

- Identify and agree about key deliverables and due dates.
- Clarify roles, responsibilities, and spans of authority.
- Identify what and how many financial, human, and material resources will be needed.

As the team is formed or built, the team leader must be somewhat directive, nudging the team to begin to take more responsibility for actions, and ultimately, survival of the firm. There will be complaints about the team-building process from some team members; they will complain that they could be getting some "real work" done in the kitchen or front office. Pay attention to those who feel this way and express their feelings so vocally. They could be telling you that they don't want to participate on the team. A judgment must be made as to whether the risk of disruption is less important than the potential loss of this person's participation on the team.

During the development stage, the team works on the business issues of importance to the firm and begins to grow into a solidified work unit. In successful teams, managers begin to be less directive, working more as facilitators. Simple problem-solving and self-directed work teams need training at this stage about the fundamentals of working together effectively. All kinds of teams need training about project management, 360-degree feedback and assessment, coaching, and improved technical skills. Teams also needs to be introduced to financial reporting, business planning, and budget-based decision making. Recent college graduates may be asked to teach some of these skills to fellow employees.

During the independence stage, team members begin to become a committed, cohesive work group and become less dependent on the team manager. The primary goals for this

stage of team development are for the team to take on more responsibility for ensuring that the team aligns its performance with the firm's goals and objectives, increases contact with customers, and continues to improve work processes. The team also will begin to go beyond team boundaries, establishing contacts with other teams and perhaps making some financial decisions.

Team members build their skills moving toward running the team with minimal supervision. In terms of training simple problem-solving teams, task forces, and cross-functional teams, little additional training is needed and, for that matter, would not be cost effective. But self-directed teams need much more training such as advanced project management and personnel policies and procedures including hiring, firing, performance appraisal and feedback, compensation, and vacation scheduling.

During the self-direction stage, team members use business goals that they may have helped develop to develop a business plan, assign roles and responsibilities, do what is needed to accomplish the business goals, monitor and align the team's performance with the organization's overall plan, and make all human resource decisions.

Team members share leadership, sometimes on a rotating basis. The team manager or general manager controls the team's boundaries. Training should continue to focus on business, organizational, and technical knowledge. Essentially, any training or conference opportunity that you would consider for a line manager is potential training for self-directed work team members.

The progression from planning to self-direction sounds very much like Donald I. Smith's approach to management at his Chateau Louise restaurant outside of Chicago in the 1950s and 1960s. First, he was directive and set expectations. Only later did he come to value some workers as employee partners, granting them varying degrees of self-direction in their work. Employees first had to demonstrate that they could be trusted to do the work. Once trust was firm, initiative could be granted.

It is important to remember that any successful organization must continuously monitor tasks and relationships. Missed milestones and due dates, lack of monitoring and performance review contribute to business failure. Improvisation is possible once systems and structure are in place and everyone knows and performs work roles well. New managers sometimes become impatient with the process of learning the business. They would prefer to be given the freedom to improvise immediately. It is critical to your career success to understand that the freedom of self-direction comes from loyal service, hard work, patience, and learning. These foster trust and then freedom under enlightened leadership.

NO PURE TYPES

Another truth about teams is that there really are no pure types. The Courtyard by Marriott example seemed to fit the model of a self-directed work team. Yet, it did not have all the characteristics of a SDWT. Rather than identifying four distinct types of teams, they should be viewed as a continuum like the one in Figure 9.6.

On the left side of this continuum, teams tend to be reactive, focus on narrower issues that tend to be centered on their team, and produce modest results. Further to the right along the continuum, teams tend to be more proactive, address broader, often strategic, is-

sues, and focus on employee self-management instead of simple problem solving. Four points along this continuum have been established arbitrarily, representing four commonly used types of teams. This does not mean that there are only four different types of teams that can be used by organizations. Actually, there are many different types of teams.

Most teams active in American companies today are functional teams. Members are brought together by a leader, who runs most meetings and sets (or at least approves) most agenda items and decisions. The leadership skills required for this kind of team management are quite conventional. The leader works to:

- Maintain control.
- Focus and direct team members' activities.
- Assume responsibility for decisions.
- Set and enforce work and quality standards.
- Distribute rewards and address poor performance according to individual member, not group, performance.
- Motivate team members.

This set of leadership skills is well suited for many business situations and purposes, at least for reaching an organization's short-term goals. It may fail, however, to serve organizations well in the long run. With teams, traditional approaches to management exercise the leadership skills of the manager but do little to encourage independent thinking, innovation, and accountability among team members (Skopec and Smith, 1997).

FIGURE 9.6
Continuum of team types

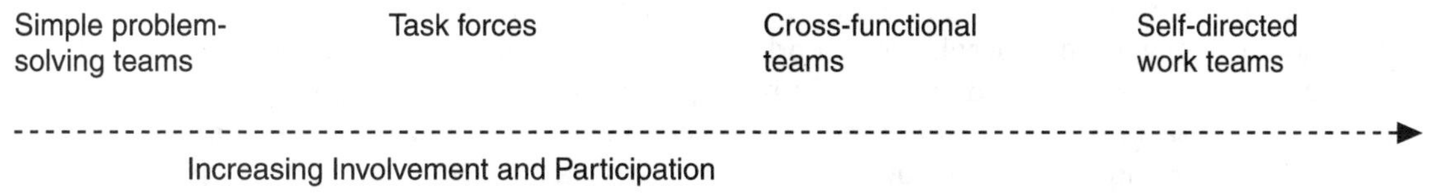

Simple problem-solving teams	Task forces	Cross-functional teams	Self-directed work teams

Increasing Involvement and Participation

IMPLEMENTING TEAMS

If an organization decides to implement teams, what is needed for them to be successful? Research and management practice offer several key lessons about implementing teams:

Teams and the Environment

Teams are not right in every environment, for every type of work, or for every employee. News of management trends such as teams travels quickly to the farthest reaches of the business community. Over the last two decades, senior managers at major corporations in the United States and beyond have been bombarded with published accounts of dramatic performance improvements credited to the introduction of teams into the workplace. We are drawn to these dramatic successes. This causes us to overlook what doesn't work: roughly 50 percent of all teams fail to provide viable solutions or perform as expected and are abandoned. The cure-all notion of teams has been oversold in the literature.

If there is one thing that has been learned, it's that a team is not a motor that continues to whirl along smoothly as long as someone supplies the fuel. A team is made up of individuals in a dynamic relationship, both with team members and with their work environment.

Teams and Management Leadership

There is a common misconception that managers who have an authoritarian leadership style have little concern for people, while those who practice participative leadership are more caring about those who work with and for them. An authoritarian leader is someone who uses his or her power to control, command, enforce obedience, and make decisions. Participative leadership, on the other hand, involves both leader and follower in the process of joint decision making (Nebel, 1991). Every-

one in the group has a chance to have a say. When the general manager of a property asks the executive committee to jointly decide a rooms-pricing policy for the next year and when servers vote on the criteria that will determine who gets specific tables in the dining area, participative leadership and decision making is being practiced. Taken to the extreme, all key decisions can be made on the basis of group consensus under a participative decision-making approach.

It is not necessarily true that authoritarian leaders are less concerned about people than participative leaders. Parents are perfect examples of benevolent autocrats who lovingly force their children to do their homework, eat lettuce, and get to sleep by 9 P.M. On the other hand, it's also possible for a participative leader to have little real concern for his or her followers. Concern for followers usually is considered to be another, separate leadership dimension. It is unclear what forms and amount of participation in management decision making and teams work best.

Teams and Productivity

Another common misconception about management is that happy employees are more productive. In other words, a satisfying or pleasant work environment is commonly believed to cause employees to work harder or better. This is not true for individuals and also does not seem to be true for teams (Spreitzer et al., 1999).

Langfred and Shanley (1998) found that member cohesiveness, that is, the degree to which members identify themselves with the group, was enough to ensure good performance of work groups at a family service agency. The more strongly members identified with their work group, the better the group's performance. However, only a small part of these groups' performance depended on cooperation. Employees worked mostly on their own.

Where members depend on one another to get most of their work done, such as in the military units Langfred and Shanley also studied, group performance declined even though unit cohesiveness was high. These groups also happened to have low commitment to getting work done (i.e., weak task norms). This greatly affected group performance, making it decline.

To take a hospitality example, a team approach to cleaning rooms failed at one company, when housekeepers refused to change how they did the job. They preferred working alone. Only when managers at another property changed the process so that housekeepers were rewarded for increased speed and reduced errors as a team did housekeepers change their approach to the work and improve overall work performance. The lesson here is that managers cannot implement teams simply by announcing that the hotel or department will adopt such an approach. The right processes, support, and incentives must be in place for teams to succeed.

An example to which you might relate as a student is project teams for college or university courses. The independent efforts of group or team members can "cover" for the poor performance of weakly committed members in such groups, because only a small part of the work often depends on cooperation. Most of the work can be done independently by one or a few members.

One other surprising fact is that quality work life (commonly called QWL and considered to be an indicator of employee well-being), customer satisfaction, and team productivity also seem to be unrelated. In other words, employee satisfaction does not increase work productivity nor does it result in happy customers. Recent research suggests that the three factors operate independently (Spreitzer et al., 1999). This finding has important implications for managers, which are explained in the last section of the reading.

Teams and Employee Motivation

The design of the work affects employee QWL. It is a well-established management principle (Hackman and Oldham, 1980) that workers feel more satisfied with their work and with the organization and feel greater trust and commitment if their jobs are motivating. Performing a complete task or an identifiable part of a complete task and working on one's own (i.e., autonomy) were found to be particularly important in one study of service-industry teams (Spreitzer et al., 1999). Employees are likely to be more committed to their hotel jobs when they can see the results of their work, that is, how what they do affects the customer. It's also important for workers to have freedom to schedule the work and decide how to get it done.

Skill variety is another component of work design that is closely related to commitment and motivation. Skill variety is the degree to which the job provides a variety of different work activities or requires that employees use a number of skills and talents to get work done. Researchers have found that when skill variety is high, employees are internally motivated, satisfied with their jobs, and perform well. However, skill variety seems to have both positive and negative effects where teams are concerned. Spreitzer, Cohen, and Ledford (1999) found that when skill variety was high, employee teams rated their quality work life (QWL) high. However, more tasks meant more learning time and higher training costs. Thus, introducing more variety into the design of the team's work resulted in trade-offs between team performance and team member QWL.

According to the Hackman-Oldham job-enrichment theory (Hackman and Oldham, 1980) of motivation, jobs that make it possible for employees to make decisions, get feedback about how well they are doing, and use a wide variety of skills make work meaningful. Current research suggests that this may not be true for at least some types of teams.

Teams and Employee Involvement

Interestingly, employee involvement also is not always an advantage with teams. In one study,

Spreitzer, Cohen, and Ledford (1999) found that self-managed teams, which had the power to make decisions, received training and information, and were rewarded based on performance, were more effective. In this study, employee involvement was the only team success factor that was related to QWL, customer satisfaction, and team performance—strong support for the value of employee involvement.

Uhl-Bien and Graen (1998) found that self-management could both help and hinder teams. Functional and cross-functional teams with more power to self-manage reported higher general satisfaction with their jobs. On the other hand, self-managing activities affected productivity differently depending on the type of team. Self-management increased the effectiveness of functional teams but not cross-functional ones for professionals working in a service context (e.g., a government regulatory agency). Thus, individual self-management may be effective for increasing job satisfaction throughout team-based organizations, regardless of team type. But self-management may interfere with a team's effectiveness.

How can we explain such contradictory findings? Some self-managing activities must be given up to have an effective cross-functional team. Cross-functional teams typically are brought together for a short period of time to investigate and solve problems. Perhaps cross-functional team members do not work together long enough to develop the levels of commitment and trust characteristic of self-managing teams. Another explanation might be that the role of the independent, self-managing professional and the team member role conflict to produce the mixed results.

Another consideration is the role of professionalism and gender in the two studies. Spreitzer et al. (1999) studied service agents with a religiously affiliated insurance provider, most of whom were female. Uhl-Bien and Graen (1998) worked with mostly male employees of a government regulatory agency. It would be important to measure team member characteristics, such as gender, and aspects of professionalism, including competitiveness, elitism, focus on one's discipline, reluctance to share knowledge, etc., to understand the forms of self-managing behavior that work best with each type of team.

Team Characteristics

The characteristics of the team also are related to team effectiveness. Teams that perform well have clear norms for the behavior of members (that is, they formally and informally enforce rules about how the team works together and about getting work done), coordinate their efforts well, and constantly improve work methods and the group. It is especially important to bring together people with needed knowledge and skills. Another key factor is team membership. It must be stable enough to develop norms that support effective performance (Spreitzer et al., 1999). The high turnover characteristic of the hospitality industry would likely interfere with the successful implementation of teams. Interestingly, Ritz-Carlton, a hotel company that has experimented extensively with teams, enjoys lower rates of employee turnover than companies in other segments of the industry.

Team Leadership

Leadership is important in ways that seem to contradict popular beliefs about its influence. Leadership has been defined in a variety of ways as consideration, insistence on hard work, visibility, and encouragement of criticism, rehearsal, goal-setting, high expectations, and self-evaluation.

Leadership was a liability in one study, because upper-level managers believed that if leaders spent a lot of time with workers, then the team must be performing poorly. In other words, upper-level executives subscribed to the classic management belief that if a manager had to intervene, the team must be failing. Leadership was related to low manager ratings of team effectiveness and poor customer-service ratings.

At the same time, leadership and employee QWL were positively related. Employees were more satisfied if they felt that they were treated with respect and consideration and set high goals for productivity, and if managers were highly visible to them and interacted frequently with the team (Spreitzer et al., 1999). It is important to note that 84 percent of the employees at this organization were female. Is it possible that female and male employees respond differently to leadership? Research shows that employees respond differently to male and female leaders, but to our knowledge, no study has investigated the role of gender in team leadership or how leadership affects member performance.

IMPLICATIONS FOR MANAGERS

Team Benefits and Complications

Findings from research and management practice suggest that the promise of teams has been oversold in the literature about teams. We have shown that trade-offs among benefits and complications are common, and the dimensions of team effectiveness do not necessarily relate to one another.

Teams and Organizational Factors

Organization-level factors are important for team success. Several studies have found that higher-level managers determine the climate for employee involvement (Spreitzer et al., 1999; Tesluk et al., 1994). This, in turn, affects beliefs and practices at both the team and individual levels. Thus, top manager support is a necessary ingredient for team success. This means real support, including release time to work with team members to solve problems

and develop the team, team-based rewards, and as-needed training.

Teams and Customer Satisfaction

Studies of bank tellers by Schneider and Bowen (1993) found a significant relationship between employee QWL and customer satisfaction. Other studies found no significant relationship between these factors (Spreitzer et al., 1999, with insurance company professionals; Sutton and Rafaeli, 1988, with convenience store employees). Customers did not care whether employees were friendly or displayed positive emotions. They cared only whether the employees could solve their problems quickly with few costs.

The mixed pattern of results suggests (and reminds us) that customers want different things. Some may want a close relationship with employees; others desire efficiency above all else. It is important to ask about and understand the customer's needs in order to make the best use of teams.

Teams and Employee Involvement

The most important ingredient for successful self-directed (self-managed) work teams in service companies is employee involvement (EI). The role of EI may be more important in service companies, because the work involves nonroutine information processing. Customer contacts are unique events that require flexible decision making. Whether a conference sales representative is working with a customer to plan a convention or a front desk representative is checking in a guest, information needs to be analyzed and judgments must be made. Knowledgeable, informed, and motivated employees are in the best position to exercise good judgment. Organizations can create the conditions for employees to exercise good judgment by providing team members with performance feedback, training in interpersonal and technical skills, the power to influence decisions, and rewards linked to performance. These are the key ingredients of a high-involvement organization. When work is of a more routine nature, as in many manufacturing contexts, employee involvement may not be as critical for the success of teams. It is interesting to note that the kitchen staff and housekeepers at one Ritz-Carlton property were not organized as self-directed teams like the rest of the property's employees. Perhaps these areas lend themselves less readily to the team model because of the more routine nature of the work. This important issue needs to be investigated.

An EI context for teams in service organizations may also be important for another reason. Providing service to customers is less tangible than producing a product. Thus, the interactions that occur between employees and customers help to shape perceptions of service quality. The degree to which a conference sales representative understands the customer's needs influences the customer's views about service quality at that property. Boundaries between the internal workings of a hotel and service delivery are more permeable than for organizations that produce tangible products, such as automobiles, clothing, or laundry detergent. Because of this permeability of boundaries between the organization and its customers, an EI context can shape service quality more directly.

Teams and Supervisors

Managers and executives also need to reconsider the role of the supervisor in team environments. Despite all the attention given to coaching behaviors in the literature about work teams, research evidence suggests that coaching may be overrated. One hotel general manager told us that he subscribed to the management-by-walking-around philosophy until employees told him and in other ways signaled their displeasure with the approach.

He learned that experienced employees wanted the freedom to do their jobs as they saw fit with minimal supervision. This observation is echoed in the research literature. Leaders' coaching behavior did not positively influence team performance.

Nevertheless, there may be another important role for leaders of work teams: a design role focused on facilitating the three success factors described earlier in the reading. Leaders can help to create a team with sufficient knowledge and skills, stable membership, and norms that support team performance. Leaders also can make sure that work is designed properly for teams. Team members will feel ownership and be motivated to perform well if they have responsibility for providing a whole service, or at the very least, an identifiable part of that service. Team leaders can also ensure that members have collective goals for which they are mutually accountable. Finally, team leaders can make sure that employee involvement is designed so that it supports effective teamwork. More specifically, the leader has a key role in making adequate training and resources available to team members. The leader needs to make sure that the systems are in place for performance feedback. The team leader also needs to work with upper-level managers and human resource representatives to create a team-based reward system based on achieving organizational goals. Thus, rather than managing the day-to-day work of the team, the more effective role for the team leader may be in the area of work design.

Creating Successful Teams

Because quality work life, customer satisfaction, and team effectiveness operate independently of one another, managers need to work on all three simultaneously in order to create successful work teams. A more realistic alternative might be to target a specific dimension of effectiveness and then focus on success factors that are related to that dimension. For example, if absenteeism increasingly becomes a problem among front office customer-service representatives, time would be better spent on helping teams develop norms to support self-regulation than getting the team involved in redesigning tasks or supervising employees more closely. Managers cannot assume that working on any dimension related to team effectiveness will produce the desired outcome.

Teams and Quality Work Life

Finally, many managers, including human resource managers, value employee quality work life (QWL) because they believe that by improving working conditions for employees, they will improve team effectiveness. The lack of a relationship between QWL and team performance suggests that QWL is not a means to an end (that is, performance), as implied in the literature about managing service employees. Instead, employee QWL is an end in itself. Thus, managers cannot justify investing in employee QWL for the sake of performance results alone. They must decide to invest in QWL because they think it is the right thing to do to manage the human resources of the organization. This creates a moral challenge for companies. This moral challenge contrasts with the trend in hospitality organizations to favor the needs of the owner and customer-related dimensions of company effectiveness while de-emphasizing the employee dimension. In the face of unprecedented corporate downsizing, mergers, and cost cutting, unless organizations see a direct and immediate link to performance, we question whether many companies will make the investment needed to enhance the QWL of their employees.

BEYOND THE LAUNCH PAD

Many questions remain. Are teams simply a fad or do they have staying power? Can they be implemented successfully in all segments of the hospitality? After all, the focus in this reading has been mostly on teams in the lodging industry. How are they being used in food service, the airline industry, clubs, etc.? Are the factors that make teams successful in these environments different from what works in lodging? Do teams work in the economy sector of the lodging industry? The questions demand that we "look beyond the launch pad."

9.6   Mentoring to Boost Employee Productivity and Retention in Hotel Organizations

Melenie J. Lankau

A recent report on turnover in full-service, deluxe, and luxury hotels conducted by the Educational Institute of the American Hotel and Motel Association and KPMG Peat Marwick reported annual turnover rates of 158 percent for line-level employees, 136 percent for supervisors, and 129 percent for managers (Educational Institute, 1998). Retaining committed and motivated employees has become not only an important human resources issue but also a bottom-line strategic issue for the hospitality industry. High turnover rates affect operational costs, as well as the delivery of consistent quality service to guests. Among the causes of turnover that have been cited in many hotel organizations are: lack of training, lack of career growth, and lack of employee voice and recognition. One of the human resource strategies that has been suggested to retain employees is organizational mentoring.

Mentoring has been widely recognized as a working relationship that contributes to adult and personal growth and an important phenomenon in organizations. An organizational mentor is someone who helps a less experienced employee navigate in his or her world of work. A mentor supports, guides, and counsels the employee as he or she accomplishes the task of becoming proficient in his or her role in the organization (Kram, 1985). Two types of mentoring relationships exist in the workplace: informal and formal. Informal mentorships arise spontaneously without organizational intervention, between organizational members who share similar vocational interests. Formal mentoring relationships, on the other hand, are facilitated by the organization through a structured program to meet specific objectives. Participation in mentoring can range from a traditional hierarchical one-on-one relationship to a group-based coaching circle (see Table 9.2). Whatever the form, mentoring provides important benefits for the protégé (recipient of mentoring), the mentor, and the organization. Companies that can foster successful mentoring relationships will have a competitive advantage in retaining well-trained, skilled, and motivated employees. This reading will provide an overview of mentoring in the workplace, including research on mentoring in hospitality organizations, highlight key indicators of successful formal mentoring programs, and present alternative forms of mentoring.

MENTORING AT WORK

Mentoring is not a new concept. Many credit the Greek poet Homer for the term *mentor*. Centuries ago, Homer wrote of Odysseus and how he entrusted his son's education to someone named Mentor who became counselor, guide, tutor, coach, and sponsor for his son, Telemachus (see Homer's *The Odyssey*). Mentoring garnered attention by organizational researchers in the late 1970s. In 1978, *Harvard Business Review* published interviews with top executives who stated that everyone who succeeds has had a mentor or

TABLE 9.2
Mentoring in Organizations

Form	Description
Traditional or Hierarchical Mentor	One-on-one relationship between an older (8–15 years), more experienced adult and younger, inexperienced adult. Mentor is typically two levels higher in organization. Mentor offers vocational support, psychosocial support, and role modeling.
Supervisory Mentor	Direct supervisor serves as mentor to subordinate. In addition to supervisory responsibilities, mentor commits to develop protégé's managerial talents.
Cross-Functional Mentor	Mentor is at least one level higher than protégé and holds a position in a different functional area within the organization. Objective is to expose protégé to duties and responsibilities of a position in a different function in the hotel.
Peer Mentor	Mentor can be older or younger, in the same or a different department in the organization, but at the same hierarchical level. Relationship is characterized by mutual advising, information sharing, and support.
Team-Source Mentor	Team leader or member serves as a coach to other participants on the team. Assists in the development of team member skills and sharing knowledge about organization.
Coaching Circles	Top-level manager or executive assigned to a committee of protégés. Meet together periodically to discuss career strategies, answer questions, and socialize new employees to organizational values.
External Mentor	Member of hotel organization serves as mentor to a high school or college student for an internship experience. Purpose is to provide real-world exposure and training to the student and hopefully attract him or her to work in the industry after school.

mentors. That same year, a book entitled *The Seasons of a Man's Life* was published in which the authors interviewed 40 men and found that the mentor relationship was cited as one of the most important developmental relationships a man had in the early stages of his career (Levinson et al., 1978).

The men interviewed reported that mentors served as counselors providing moral guidance and advice, teachers providing instruction to enhance skills and knowledge, sponsors providing opportunities and challenges to facilitate advancement, guides providing information on the values and norms of the organization, and role models.

The following year, Roche (1979) conducted a survey study of executives to examine the prevalence of mentoring relationships in business and whether having a mentor added measurably to the success and satisfaction of people at work. The study found that two-thirds of the executives reported having had a mentor. Those who had mentors earned more money at a younger age, were better educated, and more likely to follow a career plan than those executives who had not had a mentor. Mentored executives were also more likely to engage in mentoring than nonmentored executives. Mentored executives also reported higher levels of satisfaction from their career and work than executives who had not been mentored. These initial inquiries into mentoring ignited substantial interest from researchers. Twenty years later, the study of mentoring has flourished and much has been learned about mentor and protégé characteristics, the mentoring process, and outcomes from the mentoring relationship.

MENTOR AND PROTÉGÉ CHARACTERISTICS

Mentors have been characterized as generally older than their protégés by 8 to 15 years (typically in their forties or midlife); in high enough position to have access to resources and influence on other people in the organization; and

possessing a high degree of self-confidence and interest in the career development of individuals (Kram, 1985; Levinson et al., 1978). Protégés, on the other hand, are younger individuals usually in the establishment or advancement stages of their careers who have high needs for power and achievement, and aspirations of moving up the corporate ladder (Fagenson, 1992).

STAGES OF THE MENTOR-PROTÉGÉ RELATIONSHIP

Initiation

In the initiation phase, two individuals first meet and get to know one another either through a direct reporting relationship, or if the mentor is not the immediate supervisor, some type of event that facilitates interaction between the two parties such as a committee or work team meeting. This phase lasts 6 to 12 months and is characterized as a courtship. The mentor perceives the protégé to be someone with potential, coachable, and enjoyable to work with. The protégé perceives the mentor as knowledgeable and interested in his or her career (Kram, 1985).

In informal mentorships, the mentor or protégé can initiate relationships. Mentors tend to select protégés based on past performance and perceived similarity with respect to personality, work ethic, and career direction. In addition, they have a general liking for the individuals they choose to mentor. Protégés can also initiate a mentoring relationship. Individuals who believe their success is attributable to their own efforts (internal locus of control) and display emotional stability were found to be more likely to initiate and receive mentoring (Turban and Dougherty, 1994).

No differences have been found between males and females in initiating mentoring relationships or willingness to mentor. However, many women perceive that there are more barriers to obtaining a mentor due to difficulties associated with a male mentor. Cross-gender dyads can create tension, anxiety, and confusion for both the mentor and protégé due to concerns about intimacy of the relationship, stereotypical roles for each person, and fear of public scrutiny of the relationship (Ragins, 1989). In addition, there is a lack of females in hierarchical positions or in male-dominated occupations to provide mentoring to female protégés.

Cultivation

The second phase of the relationship, which is termed the cultivation phase, lasts from two to five years and is where expectations that were formed in the initiation phase are tested against what actually occurs in the mentoring relationship. Two broad categories of mentoring functions are provided during this stage: vocational, or career, support and psychosocial support. Vocational support establishes the protégé as an independent and successful professional. The mentor accomplishes this by providing job-related functions such as sponsorship, which involves actively nominating the protégé for desired lateral and upward career promotions; exposure and visibility, which involves assigning the protégé tasks that allow him or her to interact with important people in the organization; coaching, which adds to the protégé's knowledge and skill base for how to do the job and how to get along in the organization; protection of the protégé, which means intervening in situations where conflict, controversy, or potentially damaging effects could impact the protégé; and the assignment of challenging tasks and projects so that protégé learns important technical and managerial skills (Kram, 1985).

Psychosocial support enhances the protégé's sense of competence, identity, and effectiveness in his or her role. The mentor accomplishes this by serving as a role model of desired behaviors and a person that the protégé can identify with in terms of work attitudes and values; counseling the individual when anxieties and fears arise about problems and relationships that are work and nonwork related; and providing confirmation and friendship (Kram, 1985).

Research has investigated the individual and situational variables that influence the type of mentoring functions provided to protégés. Mentoring functions have been shown to be affected by race, gender, age, frequency of interaction between mentor and protégé, the number of subordinates of the mentor, and whether the mentorship was formally assigned. Burke and McKeen (1994) found that female-female mentoring dyads report higher amounts of psychosocial support than male-male dyads or cross-gender dyads. In regards to racial differences, Thomas (1993) found that the individuals' strategies for dealing with the issue of race affected the types of functions provided to protégés. If the mentor and protégé followed the same strategy, whether it was denial and suppression of race issues or direct engagement (discussing issues openly), the senior person offered psychosocial support and friendship along with career support. If the mentor and protégé differed in their preferred strategy for dealing with race issues, then the mentor provided only career support. In addition, older mentors, mentors with fewer subordinates, and mentors that frequently interact with their protégé were found to provide more career and psychosocial functions (Burke, McKeen, and McKenna, 1993).

Protégés in an informal mentorship reported receiving more career-related support than formally assigned protégés and nonprotégés (Chao, Walz and Gardner, 1992). Fagenson and Amendola (1993) found that formally assigned mentors may provide less friendship and psychosocial support functions than informal mentors.

Separation

The third phase of the mentoring relationship is the separation stage, where the protégé has learned all that is required to fulfill his or her role as a manager or senior member in the organization. The protégé becomes independent of the mentor and is no longer considered a protégé. This separation can cause anxiety for both the protégé and the mentor since the protégé will have doubts whether he or she is ready to assume the responsibility of his or her promotion or senior position and the mentor will have to adapt to the separation. The relationship can undergo the separation phase for functional reasons such as the protégé being promoted, mentor being promoted, or mentor or protégé leaving the department or organization. Separations can also occur for dysfunctional reasons, which refer to one of the individuals in the relationship terminating the relationship because of negative experiences such as the mentor being jealous, dependent, or overly demanding of the protégé (Ragins and Scandura, 1994).

Redefinition

The final phase of the mentoring relationship is redefinition of the relationship, and this is where the former mentor and protégé now become friends/peers. Their roles are redefined and there is more of a mutuality to the relationship rather than the one-way helping, guiding, and coaching that characterizes the mentoring relationship.

OUTCOMES OF THE MENTORING RELATIONSHIP

Outcomes for Protégé

Mentoring relationships may have positive or negative outcomes for the mentor, the protégé, and the organization. Positive career and attitudinal outcomes for the protégé (compared to nonprotégés) include:

- Higher performance and productivity ratings.
- Higher promotion rates and salaries.
- Greater job and career satisfaction.
- More knowledge of business; increased awareness of organization.
- Greater organizational policy influence.
- Greater access to important people.
- Greater recognition.
- Higher career opportunities.
- Increased career and organizational commitment.
- Higher intention to stay with the organization.

Additionally, studies have examined whether there are differential outcomes for male versus female protégés, and for protégés involved in formal mentoring programs versus protégés that were in mentoring relationships that developed informally. Studies have shown that male and female protégés do not report any differences in experienced outcomes of a mentoring relationship. However, the gender of the mentor may make a difference. One study revealed that protégés being mentored by female mentors reported higher job satisfaction and lower levels of role ambiguity than protégés mentored by males (Baugh et al., 1994). In regards to formal versus informal protégés, Chao, Walz, and Gardner (1992) found no differences between formally and informally assigned protégés on three outcome measures—organizational socialization, intrinsic job satisfaction, and salary.

While much of the work in the mentoring literature supports the notion that mentoring has positive effects on the career development and work experience of junior members of organizations, a few researchers and practitioners have suggested that there is the potential for negative outcomes for the protégé involved in a mentoring relationship. Negative outcomes can damage the protégé's career and work attitudes by lowering self-esteem and increasing frustration. Negative outcomes result when the mentor assigns busywork, overloads the protégé, serves as a negative role model (exhibiting behaviors the protégé does not want to emulate), blocks the progress of the protégé, prematurely ends the relationship or the relationship ends for dysfunctional reasons, or the mentor ceases to achieve and be successful in the organization (Ragins and Scandura, 1994). In addition, the protégé may neglect core job duties, have unrealistic expectations about promotion, and may become the object of jealousy or gossip in a highly visible mentoring relationship (Murray and Owen, 1991).

Outcomes for Mentor

In addition to outcomes experienced by the protégé in a mentoring relationship, the mentor may also experience positive and negative outcomes due to his or her involvement in a developmental relationship. The mentor receives internal satisfaction from passing on wisdom and skill to protégés, pride from the development of protégés as independent professionals, and recognition from the organization for a successful protégé. More recently, it has been suggested that mentors may obtain technical information and feedback from their protégés (Kram and Hall, 1996). The costs of becoming a mentor, however, may outweigh the benefits, due to the time and energy involved, visibility of the relationship especially if the mentor chooses a poorly performing protégé, and the possibility of being backstabbed by protégés (Halatin and Knotts, 1982).

Outcomes for Organization

There can be positive and negative outcomes of the mentoring relationship that impact the organization. The organization can benefit from positive developmental relationships since the they provide a forum for socialization, nurture good talent, pass on central values and practices for the effective functioning of the organization, and transmit corporate culture to junior members (Wilson and Elman, 1990). Additional benefits include increased productivity of individuals involved, improved recruitment efforts (promoting mentoring in organization to applicants), cost-effectiveness over off-site training methods (e.g., seminars, lectures, etc.), and improved succession planning and management development (Murray and Owen, 1991).

The organization can also suffer negative outcomes when attention is drawn away from the organization and to the mentor-protégé relationship, especially in cross-gender relationships where there are problems with sexual assumptions about close relationships between men and women (Bowen, 1986) and cross-race/cross-gender relationships where societal taboos still exist (Thomas, 1989). Another negative outcome of mentoring relationships for an organization is the issue of fairness. Resentment from individuals who do not have mentors or feel that they cannot obtain mentors due to the old-boy network or discrimination may negatively impact work performance and employee attendance.

MENTORING IN THE HOSPITALITY INDUSTRY

Despite practitioner articles that herald the benefits of mentoring and offer anecdotal evidence for the importance of mentoring, few studies have specifically addressed mentoring in the hospitality industry. An initial study in 1984 by Denney Rutherford examined whether mentoring relationships exist within hotel organizations. The study surveyed front office managers, directors of housekeeping, food and beverage managers, and general managers and found that 40 percent reported having a mentor. However, contrary to previous research at that time, significant differences were not found in indices of job satisfaction between respondents who had mentors and those who reported not having mentors.

A follow-up study was conducted the next year with general managers to explore the form and dynamics of the mentoring relationships. The mentoring functions reported by general managers in this study closely resembled findings from the general business literature. Mentors provided the general managers with confidence, career counseling, political advice, and technical expertise. Rutherford and Wiegenstein (1985) examined indicators of career movement, success, and satisfaction. Although differences were not statistically significant, a general pattern emerged where mentored managers reported greater success and satisfaction with their job and careers than mentorless managers. The study concluded that mentoring positively impacted the careers of hotel general managers.

In these previous studies, the overwhelming majority of the sample was male. A recent study, however, confirmed the importance of mentoring for females in the hospitality industry. Interviews with 21 women association executives revealed that a mentor was an important influence in their early career stages. Female executives indicated that mentors helped them attain their first association position and even assisted in negotiating salary. Mentors also provided them with career-oriented advice, task-oriented coaching, and access to networks and information (Coffey and Anderson, 1998). As stated earlier though, mentors for women may not be accessible inside the organization. Hence, outside associations such as the Network of Executive Women in Hospitality play a critical role in providing mentors for aspiring female hospitality leaders (see the sidebar "Network of Executive Women in Hospitality).

Most of the research on mentoring in hotel organizations has focused on the manager or executive level of employees. One recent study explored the role of mentoring in front-line hotel employees' work lives and assessed the extent to which mentoring contributed to a more positive work experience. Approximately 457 front-line employees (nonsupervisory

---

NETWORK OF EXECUTIVE WOMEN IN HOSPITALITY

The Network of Executive Women in Hospitality (NEWH) is a nonprofit organization dedicated to promoting a high standard of achievement for women in hospitality and related fields. It was founded in 1984 in Los Angeles by a group of women who shared a common bond in their work. Their hope was that women who had established careers in the hospitality field at that time could lend their support and share their experiences with younger women just entering the field. In addition to offering networking opportunities for members, NEWH has the following goals:

1. Increase awareness of the hospitality industry as a career option.
2. Encourage students to pursue careers in hospitality.
3. Provide financial support and recognition to young women entering the hospitality industry.

NEWH has 14 chapters nationwide, three in formation, as well as a growing international membership. NEWH has awarded more than $750,000 in scholarships to young women pursuing careers in the hospitality industry. For more information on NEWH, log on to their Web site at http://www.newh.org.

level) from three different first-class hotel properties were surveyed. The results from the study indicated that having a mentor positively influenced the level of effort that individuals put forth for the organization, the pride they feel about working for the hotel, the level of inspiration for job performance, their emotions about working for the hotel, congruence of personal and organizational values, and concerns about the future of the hotel. In addition, having a mentor also seemed to make a difference in employees' decisions about whether to remain working in the organization or find employment elsewhere. Mentored employees were also more satisfied with how their performance was evaluated than nonmentored employees (Lankau and Chung, 1998).

In sum, mentoring has been shown in general business and hospitality organizations to have important consequences for the protégé, mentor, and organization. These effects translate to higher individual performance, retention, sustained quality service, and bottom-line costs savings for organizations. The rapid growth of the lodging industry coupled with the low unemployment rate strain the industry's ability to develop the customer service and management skills needed in today's competitive environment. To capitalize on the benefits of mentoring, organizations can facilitate the development of mentoring relationships through a formal program.

FORMAL MENTORING PROGRAMS

More hospitality organizations are realizing the need for mentoring in their organizations due to several economic and environmental trends:

- *Mergers and acquisitions:* When hotel companies merge or acquire other companies, employees may be faced with uncertainties regarding roles and responsibilities. Mentors can provide important information re-

garding changes in organizational structure, goals, values, policies, and practices.
- *Changing demographics of workforce:* Mentoring programs may be needed to provide targeted coaching and support to help women and minorities move into management positions.
- *Labor and skill shortage:* Mentoring can be used to cross-train employees in several functional areas so that labor can be more efficiently utilized. Mentors can also be used for specific skill development such as tutoring employees in English and providing support during ESL (English as a second language) training. In addition, managers need to provide coaching for job duties that involve constant updating of customer-service quality improvements. External mentoring is currently used to attract high school students to enter the industry through youth mentoring and school-to-work initiatives such as the Hospitality Business Alliance (to learn more about the Alliance, log on to http://www.h-b-a.org).
- *Changes in work design and technology:* A mentoring program can support the dissemination of knowledge with respect to new methods of accomplishing work and changes in technology associated with operations.

Mentoring programs requires careful planning, commitment, and support. Organizations that have experienced failures with attempts to institute a formal mentoring program often overlooked important organizational obstacles (Murray and Owen, 1991). Some important factors general managers and human resource managers should discuss when considering a formal mentoring program include:

1. What is the objective of the program? That is, what are the needs of the organization (management development, specific skills training, socialization, create opportunities for minorities, etc.)?

2. Do the organizational culture and reward structures support the mentoring process? In other words, is developing others valued by the organization? Are mentoring behaviors such as coaching, providing feedback, and supporting others included in the performance expectations and appraisal of supervisors and managers? Are these behaviors rewarded? People will engage in activities if they find them rewarding. For some individuals, the reward is gratification from helping others succeed. For others, it may be necessary to provide financial or public rewards such as bonuses, recognition in the company newsletter, or others symbols of appreciation.

3. What are the criteria and selection procedures for mentors and protégés? How will the organization determine who gets to participate in the program? Will it be voluntary? Will protégés have to be nominated? Will there be some kind of eligibility requirement such as experience, past performance, and/or position?

4. What is the strategy for the mentor-protégé matching process? Will it be based on compatibility of interests, background characteristics, or more formal assessment procedures of strengths and weaknesses?

5. How will training be handled? Should mandatory orientations be held for mentors and protégés? What additional training sessions need to be provided to prepare protégés and mentors for their roles?

6. Who is going to coordinate the program? What will be the scope of responsibilities of this position? Will it be a self-standing job in the human resources department or added to the director's job description?

7. How structured will the program be? Will the organization mandate a requirement on meeting times, relationship duration, and stated performance goals and outcomes for the relationship? How will they document this?

8. How and when will the formal mentoring program be evaluated?

Research on formal mentoring programs suggests several keys to effectiveness (Murray and Owen, 1991). The first and foremost is voluntary participation. Formal mentoring relationships tend not to have the same level of intimacy as informal relationships due to the possible lack of chemistry or attraction that naturally occurs in spontaneous relationships. However, participants in a formal program are more likely to have a positive experience if they feel a sense of control or ownership over the process by volunteering rather than being mandated by superiors. Second, it is important to identify a pool of mentors at the highest possible levels (ideally two levels above the protégé). While supervisors can make excellent mentors, potential problems could arise in the relationship due to competitiveness or jealousy from the supervisor who may be preparing the protégé to assume his or her job or due to lack of requisite skills for mentoring (such as career planning). Successful mentoring programs allow flexible time periods for the relationship duration that are adjusted to the developmental needs of the protégés in the program.

Organizations may have a limited pool of potential mentors and may be tempted to assign several protégés to one mentor. Experts caution against this practice for new mentors, especially if the objective of the program is management development, which would require more time than socializing new employees to the organizational culture. Another key element of successful formal mentoring programs is the inclusion of a "no-fault" exit agreement. If mentors and/or protégés realize the formal assignment isn't working, they should be allowed to terminate the relationship and get reassigned if possible.

Another important key to effective implementation of a formal mentoring program is to integrate the program with other human resources development programs and policies. The mentoring program should be coordinated to support a system of other training practices that are linked toward internal staff development in order to reduce redundancy and maximize the use of resources. Accordingly, clear policies on standards and practices of the mentoring program should be congruent with the broader set of policies created and communicated by the HR department.

Lastly, successful implementation is dependent on continuous program evaluation. Depending on the objectives of the program, desired results should be explicitly articulated so that they can be measured. Effectiveness can be measured in many different ways. Improvements in job performance of the protégé, job-related attitudes for mentor and protégé, promotion rates of protégés, absenteeism and turnover rates, and perceptions of the quality of the relationship are a few examples.

Formal mentoring programs represent a proactive human resources strategy to develop and retain a productive workforce for hospitality organizations. However, organizations may be limited in their capacity to implement a program successfully due to limited resources or availability of top-level managers. There are other vehicles that organizations can utilize to foster learning and skill development among organizational members.

ALTERNATIVE FORMS OF MENTORING

Peer Relationships

Peer relationships offer unique advantages to individuals, being both more accessible and more enduring than most mentoring alliances. In an organizational environment of increasing turbulence, peers can empathize with the challenges of making sense of what is occurring within an organization and provide a unique form of support.

Kram and Isabella (1985) reported findings from interviews with 25 peer pairs that resulted in identification of developmental benefits that are provided by peer relationships that are quite similar to conventional mentoring relationships, such as information sharing, career strategizing, job-related feedback, confirmation, emotional support, and personal feedback. An individual may have an information peer where the primary exchange is information sharing; a collegial peer where the relationship also includes career strategizing, job-related feedback, and friendship; and lastly, a special peer that involves many more personal aspects to the relationship, such as emotional support, confirmation, and personal feedback. Their study of peer relationships suggest that these types of relationships may offer unique developmental opportunities due to the mutuality of a two-way exchange of guidance and support, and the fact that the absence of a hierarchical relationship may make it easier to establish closer communication and collaboration.

A more recent study found that peer mentors provided more psychosocial functions than vocational functions. The researchers suggest peer mentors are able to provide guidance about day-to-day operations more so than a traditional mentor who may not be available to supervise daily tasks (Allen et al., 1995).

Work Teams

Another forum for mentoring in an organization is the work team. The accomplishment of organizational objectives through teams can influence the development of positive relationships at work. Furthermore, team members may serve as an additional node in an employee's competence network contributing to his or her individual learning. Leaders of teams should build coaching relationships with their members, helping them to develop mastery of the procedures, standards, and operating norms of the team. Team leaders can help members share expertise and learn from one another, show them how to work interdependently, and coach members in performance strategies (Hackman and Walton, 1986). Team members can also learn from one another's skills and talents. People who participate in teams should try to actively learn two or three new things from others in the group, putting themselves in a learning mode (Savage, 1990). Graen and Uhl-Bien (1991) note that developing interpersonal relationships inside one's team is an important process that contributes both to the individual's success as a team player and to his or her career strategy.

CONCLUSION

The competitive advantage for companies today lies within the competence levels of their employees and their ability to adapt to changing circumstances. In this era of mergers and acquisitions, rapid technological change, increasing customer expectations, and labor shortages, mentoring represents an important strategy to address the continuous learning demands of employees in hospitality organizations. Hospitality leaders in the twenty-first century must embrace their role as coaches and mentors to create a foundation of well-trained, skilled, and motivated staff.

References

Allen, T. D., S. E. McManus, J. E. Russell, and A. Reiniger. 1995. "An Examination of the Impact of Peer Mentoring on Socialization and Stress." Paper presented at the Southern Management Association meeting, Orlando, FL.

Alvares, K. N. 1997. "The Business of Human Resources." In *Tomorrow's HR Management,* D. Ulrich, M. R. Losey, and G. Lake (eds.), New York: John Wiley and Sons, Inc., pp. 7–17.

Baugh, S. G., M. J. Lankau, and T. A. Scandura. 1994. "An Investigation into the Effects of Protégé and Mentor Gender on Responses to Mentoring." Paper presented at the Southern Management Association meeting, New Orleans, LA.

Bluedorn, Allen C. 1982. "The Theories of Turnover: Causes, Effects, and Meaning." In *Research in the Sociology of Organizations,* vol. 1, S. E. Bacharach and E. J. Lawler (eds.),. Greenwich, CT: JAI Press, pp. 75–128.

Bowen, D. 1986. "The Role of Identification in Mentoring Female Protégés." *Group and Organization Studies* 11:61–74.

Brown, T., 1997. "My Fair HR Professional." *HR Focus* 74(6):3.

Burke, R. J., and C. A. McKeen. 1994. "Gender Effects in Mentoring Relationships." Unpublished paper, York University.

Burke, R. J., C. A. McKeen, and C. McKenna. 1993. "Correlates of Mentoring in Organizations: The Mentor's Perspective." *Psychological Reports* 72:883–896.

Burke, W. W. 1997. "What Human Resource Practitioners Need to Know for the Twenty-first Century." In *Tomorrow's HR Management,* D. Ulrich, M. R. Losey, and G. Lake (eds.), New York: John Wiley and Sons, Inc., pp. 96–110.

Certo, S. C. 2000. *Modern Management,* 8th ed. Upper Saddle River, NJ: Prentice Hall.

Chao, G. T., P. M. Walz, and P. D. Gardner. 1992. "Formal and Informal Mentorships: A Comparison of Mentoring Functions and Contrast with Nonmentored Counterparts." *Personnel Psychology* 45:1–16.

Christensen, R. N. 1997. "Where Is Human Resources." In *Tomorrow's HR Management,* D. Ulrich, M. R. Losey, and G. Lake (eds.), New York: John Wiley and Sons, Inc., pp. 18–24.

Churchill, W. 1938. Russia as a riddle, wrapped in a mystery, inside an enigma. 1938 radio broadcast. As noted in J. C. Collins and J. I. Porras. 1994. *Built to Last: Successful Habits of Visionary Companies,* 1st ed. New York: HarperBusiness, p. 217.

Coffey, B. S., and S. E. Anderson. 1998. "Career Issues for Women Association Executives: Mentors, Pay Equity, and Boards of

Directors." *Cornell Hotel and Restaurant Administration Quarterly* 39(4):34–39.

Collins, J. C., and J. I. Porras. 1994. *Built to Last.* New York: Harper-Collins.

Condodina, J. 1997. "Echoes from the Line: HR Lacks Strategic Initiative." *HR Focus* 74(7):21.

Deming, W. E. 1993. *The New Economics for Industry, Government, Education.* Cambridge, MA: MIT Center for Advanced Engineering Study.

Drucker, P. 1995. *Managing in a Time of Great Change.* New York: Truman Talley Books/Dutton.

Dubin, R. 1961. *Human Relations in Administration,* 2d ed. Englewood Cliffs, NJ: Prentice Hall.

Educational Institute, American Hotel and Motel Association. 1998. *U.S. Full-Service, Deluxe, and Luxury Hotel Benchmarking Study,* Technical Report.

Fagenson, E. A. 1992. "Mentoring—Who Needs It? A Comparison of Protégés' and Nonprotégés' Needs for Power, Achievement, Affiliation, and Autonomy." *Journal of Vocational Behavior* 41:48–60.

Fagenson, E. A. and K. Amendola. 1993. "TQM—Total Quality Mentoring: Factors Influencing Mentoring Functions Provided and Received." Best paper proceedings of the Academy of Management, pp. 58–62.

Farson, R. 1996. *Management of the Absurd: Paradoxes in Leadership.* New York: Simon and Schuster.

Finigan, K. 1999. "The HR Advantage: Planning for Year Requires Awareness of Long-Term Trends." *Capital District Business Review* January 18: 25(41):1–4.

Fitz-Enz, J. 1997. "The Truth about Best Practices: What They Are and How to Apply Them." In *Tomorrow's HR Management,* D. Ulrich, M. R. Losey, and G. Lake (eds.), New York: John Wiley and Sons, Inc., pp. 217–226.

Flynn, G. 2000. "Predictions about the Future of Employment Law." *Workforce* 79(1):78–80.

Goldberg, A. C. 1998. "Top Employment Law Issues for 1999." *HR Focus* 75(12):1–3.

Graen, G. B., and M. Uhl-Bien. 1991. "Leadership-Making Applies Equally Well to Sponsors, Competence Networks, and Teammates." *Journal of Management Systems* 3:75–80.

Hackman, J. R., and G. Oldham. 1980. *Work Redesign.* Reading, MA: Addison-Wesley.

Hackman, J. R. and R. E. Walton. 1986. "Leading Groups in Organizations." In *Designing Effective Work Groups,* P. S. Goodman (ed.), San Francisco: Jossey-Bass Publishers.

Halatin, T. J., and R. E. Knotts. 1982. "Becoming a Mentor: Are the Risks Worth the Rewards?" *Supervisory Management* 27:27–29.

Herzberg, Frederick. 1976. *The Managerial Choice: To Be Efficient and To Be Human.* Homewood, IL: Dow Jones-Irwin.

Haskett, J. L., T. O. Jones, G. W. Loveman, W. E. Sasser, and L. A. Schlessinger. 1994. "Putting the Service-Profit Chain to Work." *Harvard Business Review* March–April.

Hewitt, G. 1997. "Corporate Strategy and Human Resources: New Mind-Sets for New Games." In *Tomorrow's HR Management,* D. Ulrich, M. R. Losey, and G. Lake (eds.), New York: John Wiley and Sons, Inc., pp. 39–47.

Huselid, M. A. 1995. "The Impact of Human Resource Management Practices on Turnover, Productivity, and Corporate Financial Planning." *Academy of Management Journal* 38:635–672.

Jackson, S. E., and R. S. Schuler. 2000. *Managing Human Resources: A Partnership Perspective.* Cincinnati, OH: South-Western College Publishing.

Johnson, H. E. 1997. "Don't Send Me One of Those Typical Human Resource People: A True Life Adventure." In *Tomorrow's HR Management,* D. Ulrich, M. R. Losey, and G. Lake (eds.), New York: John Wiley and Sons, Inc., pp. 130–136.

Kahn. H., and A. J. Wiener. 1967. *The Year 2000: A Framework for Speculation on the*

Next Thirty-three Years. New York: Macmillan.

Kaplan, R. S., and D. P. Norton. 1992. "The Balanced Scorecard—Measures that Drive Performance." *Harvard Business Review* July/August:71–79.

Knicely, H. V. 1997. "The Future of Human Resources: Superhuman Resource Leadership in the Twenty-first Century." In *Tomorrow's HR Management,* D. Ulrich, M. R. Losey, and G. Lake (eds.), New York: John Wiley and Sons, Inc., pp. 111–118.

Kochan, T. A. 1997. "Rebalancing the Role of Human Resources." In *Tomorrow's HR Management,* D. Ulrich, M. R. Losey, and G. Lake (eds.), New York: John Wiley and Sons, Inc., pp. 119–129.

Kram, K. E. 1985. *Mentoring at Work: Developmental Relationships in Organizational Life*. Glenview, IL: Scott, Foresman, and Company.

Kram, K. E., and D. T. Hall. 1996. "Mentoring in a Context of Diversity and Turbulence." In *Managing Diversity: Human Resource Strategies for Transforming the Workplace*, E. Kossek and S. Lobel (eds.), Cambridge, MA: Blackwell Business.

Kram, K. E., and L. A. Isabella. 1985. "Mentoring Alternatives: The Role of Peer Relationships in Career Development." *Academy of Management Journal* 28:110–132.

Langfred, C., and M. Shanley. 1998. "The Importance of Organization Context, II: An Empirical Test of Work Group Cohesiveness and Effectivesness in Two Governmental Bureaucracies." *Public Administration Quarterly* 21(4):465-485.

Lankau, M. J., and B. G. Chung. 1998. "Mentoring for Line-Level Employees." *Cornell Hotel and Restaurant Administration Quarterly* 39(6):14–20.

Levinson, D. J., C. Darrow, E. Klein, M. Levinson, and B. McKee. 1978. *The Seasons of a Man's Life*. New York: Alfred A. Knopf.

Lombardo, M. M., and R. W. Eichinger. 1997. "Human Resources' Role in Building Competitive Edge Leaders." In *Tomorrow's HR Management,* D. Ulrich, M. R. Losey, and G. Lake (eds.), New York: John Wiley and Sons, Inc., pp. 57–66.

March, J. G., and H. Simon. 1958. *Organizations*. New York: John Wiley.

McDermott, L. C., N. Brawley, and W. W. Waite. 1998. *World-Class Teams: Working across Borders*. New York: John Wiley and Sons.

McFillen, J. M., C. D. Riegel, and C. A. Enz. 1986. "Why Restaurant Managers Quit and How to Keep Them." *Cornell Hotel and Restaurant Administration Quarterly* November:37–43.

Murray, M., and M. A. Owen. 1991. *Beyond the Myths and Magic of Mentoring: How to Facilitate an Effective Mentoring Program*. San Francisco: Jossey-Bass.

Nebel, E. C., III. 1991. *Managing Hotels Effectively: Lessons from Outstanding General Managers*. New York: Van Nostrand Reinhold.

Phillips, J. A., and D. S. Massey. 1999. "The New Labor Market: Immigrants and Wages after IRCA." *Demography* 36(2):233–246.

Porter, L. W., and R. W. Steers. 1973. "Organizational Work and Personal Factors in Employee Turnover and Absenteeism." *Psychological Bulletin* 80:151–176.

Price, J. L. 1977. *The Study of Turnover*. Ames, IA: Iowa State University Press.

Ragins, B. R. 1989. "Barriers to Mentoring: The Female Manager's Dilemma." *Human Relations* 42:1–22.

Ragins, B. R., and T. A. Scandura. 1994. "Separation and Redefinition of Mentoring Relationships: A Test and Expansion of Mentorship Theory." Paper presented at the National Academy of Management meeting, Dallas, TX.

Recardo, R. J., D. Wade, C. A. Mention, III, and J. A. Jolly. 1996. *Teams: Who Needs Them and Why?* Houston: Gulf Publishing Company.

Reichheld, F. F. 1996. "Learning from Customer Defections." *Harvard Business Review* March–April.

Roche, G. R. 1979. "Much Ado about Mentors." *Harvard Business Review* 59:14–18.

Rutherford, D. G. 1984. "Mentoring Hospitality Managers." *Cornell Hotel and Restaurant Administration Quarterly* 25:16–19.

Rutherford, D. G. (ed.). 1995. *Hotel Management and Operations,* 2d ed. New York: Van Nostrand Reinhold.

Rutherford, D. G., and J. Wiegenstein. 1985. "The Mentoring Process in Hotel Managers' Careers." *Cornell Hotel and Restaurant Administration Quarterly* 25(4):16–23.

Savage, C. M. 1990. *Fifth Generation Management: Integrating Enterprises through Human Networking.* Bedford, MA: Digital Press.

Schneier, C. E., and R. W. Beatty. 1994. "Making Culture Change Happen." In *The Change Management Handbook: A Road Map to Corporate Transformation,* Lance A. Berger and Martin J. Sikora, with Dorothy R. Berger (eds.), Burr Ridge, IL: Irwin Professional Publishing.

Schneider, B., and D. E. Bowen. 1993. "The Service Organization: Human Resources Management Is Crucial." *Organization Dynamics* 21(4):39-52.

Shea, R. E. 2000. "The Dirty Dozen." *HR Magazine* 45(1):52–56.

Sherwyn, D., Z. J. Eigen, and A. A. Klausner. 2000. "Interpreting the ADA and Civil Rights Law: Five Supreme Court Rulings." *Cornell Hotel and Restaurant Administration Quarterly* 41(1):85–93.

Skopec, E., and D. M. Smith. 1997. *How to Use Team Building to Foster Innovation throughout Your Organization.* Lincolnwood, IL: Contemporary Books.

Sovereign, K. L. 1999. *Personnel Law,* 4th ed. Upper Saddle River, NJ: Prentice Hall.

Spreitzer, G. M., S. G. Cohen, and G. E. Ledford, Jr. 1999. "Developing Effective Self-Managing Work Teams in Service Organizations." *Group and Organization Management* 24(3):340–366.

Stewart, T. 1996. "Taking on the Last Bureaucracy." *Fortune* January 15: 133(1):105–108.

Sutton, R. I., and A. Rafaeli. 1988. "Untangling the Relationship between Displayed Emotions and Organizational Sales: The Case of Convenience Stores." *Academy of Management Journal* 31(3):461–487.

Tesluk, P. E., R. J. Vance, and J. E. Mathieu. 1994. "Examining Employee Involvement in the Context of Participative Work Environments: A Multilevel Approach." In *Organizational, Group, and Individual Determinants of Employee Involvement Program Success,* R. J. Vance (Chair). Symposium conducted at the meeting of the National Academy of Management, Dallas, TX, August.

Thomas, D. 1993. "Racial Dynamics in Cross-Race Developmental Relationships." *Administrative Science Quarterly* 38:169–194.

Thomas, D. A. 1989. "Mentoring and Irrationality: The Role of Racial Taboos." *Human Resource Management* 28:279–290.

Turban, D. B., and T. W. Dougherty. 1994. "Role of Protégé Personality in Receipt of Mentoring and Career Success." *Academy of Management Journal* 37:688–702.

Uhl-Bien, M., and G. B. Graen. 1998. "Individual Self-Management: Analysis of Professionals' Self-Managing Activities in Functional and Cross-Functional Work Teams." *Academy of Management Journal* 41(3):340–350.

Ulrich, D., M. R. Losey, and G. Lake (eds.). 1997. *Tomorrow's HR Management.* New York: John Wiley and Sons, Inc.

Umbreit, W. T., and R. Eder. 1987. "Linking Hotel Manager Behaviors to Outcome Measures of Effectiveness." *International Journal of Hospitality Management* 6(3): 139–147.

Wilkerson, J. L. 1997. "The Future Is Virtual HR." *HR Focus* 74(3):15.

Wilson, J. A., and N. S. Elman. 1990. "Organizational Benefits of Mentoring." *Academy of Management Executive* 4:88–94.

Woods, R. H. 1999. "Managerial Diversity in the Lodging Industry." Unpublished study funded by the American Hotel Foundation.

Woods, R. H., D. G. Rutherford, R. S. Schmidgall, and M. P. Sciarini. 1998. "Hotel General Managers: Focused on the Core Business." *Cornell Hotel and Restaurant Administration Quarterly* 39(6):38–44.

Woods, R. H., M. P. Sciarini, and W. Heck. 1998. "Turnover and Diversity in the Lodging Industry." Washington, DC: American Hotel Foundation.

Suggested Readings

Books

Jerris, L. A. 1999. *Human Resources Management for Hospitality*. Upper Saddle River, NJ: Prentice Hall.

Tanke, Mary L. 2001. *Human Resources Management for the Hospitality Industry,* 2d ed. Albany, NY: Delmar Thomson Learning.

Woods, Robert H. 1992. *Managing Hospitality Human Resources.* East Lansing, MI: Educational Institute of American Hotel and Motel Association.

Source Notes

Chapter 9.2, "Predicting Is Difficult, Especially about the Future: Human Resources in the New Millennium," by Robert H. Woods. Reprinted from the *International Journal of Hospitality Management*, Volume 18, Robert H. Woods, "Predicting Is Difficult, Especially about the Future: Human Resources in the New Millennium," Pages 443–456, Copyright 1999, with permission from Elsevier Science.

Chapter 9.3, "The Causes and Consequences of Turnover in the Hospitality Industry," by Carl D. Riegel.

Chapter 9.4, "Current Issues in Hospitality Employment Law," by Suzanne K. Murrmann and Cherylynn Becker.

Chapter 9.5, "Employee Work Teams in Hospitality," by M. Chris Paxson.

Chapter 9.6, "Mentoring to Boost Employee Productivity and Retention in Hotel Organizations," by Melenie J. Lankau.

Index